# Carlos Montezuma, M.D.

# Carlos Montezuma, M.D.

## A YAVAPAI AMERICAN HERO

The Life and Times of an American Indian, 1866–1923

## Leon Speroff, M.D.

Professor of Obstetrics and Gynecology
Oregon Health & Science University
Portland, Oregon

arnica
PUBLISHING, INC.
Portland, Oregon

Library of Congress Cataloging-in-Publication Data

Speroff, Leon, 1935-
  Carlos Montezuma, M.D., a Yavapai American hero : the life and times of an American Indian, 1866-1923 / Leon Speroff.
      p. cm.
Includes bibliographical references and index.
  ISBN 0-9726535-4-6
1. Montezuma, Carlos, 1866-1923. 2. Indian physicians--United States--Biography. I. Title.

R696.M66S66 2003
610'.92--dc21

2003005571

Cover design by Aimee Genter
Text design by Becky Slemmons

620 SW Main, Suite 345
Portland, OR 97205
arnicapublishing.com

*Arnica books are available at special discounts when purchased in bulk for premiums and sales promotions, as well
as for fund-raising or educational use. Special editions or book excerpts can also be created for specification.
For details, contact the Sales Director at the address above.*

# Dedication

On a cool Fall evening in 1975, I boarded an airplane in Minneapolis for a flight to New York City. I had spent the day making an educational film on hypertension in pregnancy. The project was supported by the Pfizer Pharmaceutical Company, and assisting was Leon Summit, the medical editor of Pfizer's monthly medical periodical. I sat on the aisle in first class (courtesy of Pfizer) and Summit sat next to the window. Sitting across the aisle was Leon Chesley, famous for his research on hypertension in pregnancy. I said to Leon Summit: "Surely this deserves a line in Guiness's Book of World Records, the most Leons in aviation history sitting in the same first class row."

As we flew through the night, Leon Summit told me Carlos Montezuma stories. In the 1960s, he was in Chicago researching an article on the great Chicago fire, and he kept encountering Carlos Montezuma in old newspapers. Intrigued, he set out to learn more and eventually with the help of the Chicago Historical Society obtained and saved from being lost a significant collection of Montezuma material. His intention was to write a biography.

As we approached New York, Summit asked: "You have been so quiet. Have I been boring you?" "Are you kidding?," I replied, "I'm trying to memorize these stories so that I can share them with my family." By now I knew his politics (having discussed the Spanish Civil War), and I said to him: "This collection you have really doesn't belong to you. This man was a genuinely noteworthy Indian and American. The collection belongs to the public, the people." Summit smiled and replied: "Of course it does, and I have already made arrangements to make it available after I write the biography."

In 1978, my mother and father rode a Greyhound bus from Ohio to Oregon to pay us a visit. Leaving my mother with my wife, my father and I set out for a three-day camping trip. As we made the five-hour drive down the interstate highway to southern Oregon and the redwood forest, I told my father Carlos Montezuma stories. When I finished, there was total silence in the car. I turned to my father, a tough hardworking man, and was astonished to see him staring out the window with tears rolling down his cheeks. "Dad, what's wrong?" In a quivering, emotional voice, he said: "That was a wonderful story." At that very moment a resolution stirred within me to do something with the Carlos Montezuma stories. But of course, Leon Summit had first dibs.

As the years went by I diligently and carefully watched for the appearance of Summit's biography. Finally in 1996, I called Leon Summit, then living on Long Island. After re-establishing our connection. I asked: "Where is that biography?" He answered: "I've been too busy earning a living, sending my children to college." Growing more anxious, I waited only two years to call again, and I was saddened to learn that Leon Summit had passed away, never even getting around to starting the biography. My resolution became firm; my heart was in this project.

In 2000, I called Leon Summit's son, Paul, a lawyer in Boston. I reminded him of what his father said about making his collection available. Paul said: "You're right. He did say that. I had forgotten." I arranged for Roger Bruns, the Deputy Executive Director of the National Historical Publications and Records Commission of the National Archives and Records Administration, to get together with Paul Summit, and in 2001, Leon Summit's Montezuma collection was microfilmed, making it publicly available, exactly like Leon Summit intended.

For many years, every night just before sleep, my mind filled with Carlos Montezuma. I have taken countless imaginary journeys to his home, his haunts, his historical collections. I have composed sentences and paragraphs, revised titles and headings. Running miles and miles on a machine in my local gym, I have planned, organized, and composed my campaign and mission to tell the story of Carlos Montezuma. He and the main characters in his story have been my companions for so long I am sad to bring the process to an end, but joyful to see the words that represent the distillation of so much mental energy and passion. It seems right to me to dedicate this book to Leon Summit (1914–1998), the man who kept the dream alive of telling the Carlos Montezuma story. Of course my version is not the same as his would have been, but I choose to believe that he would have liked it.

I also want to dedicate this book to Tim Goldfarb. When Tim moved into our rural neighborhood I knew he was the CEO of our hospital (University Hospital in Portland, Oregon), but I was amazed to learn that not only is Tim part Jewish, he is part Pawnee with Yavapai relatives by marriage, sharing a heritage with Carlos Montezuma. He was with me when I first visited Fort McDowell and introduced me to his cousin, Robin Russell, who at that time was vice-president of the Yavapai Tribal Council. Tim is a great friend and has been an enthusiastic supporter and faithful reader.

John Larner deserves part of this dedication. "Jack," now a retired professor of history, made the job of field research easier for scholars by producing the microfilm collections of the Carlos Montezuma Papers and the Papers of the Society of American Indians. In many letters and telephone conversations I could always count on Jack to provide words of encouragement, a revealing insight, or a colorful anecdote. He has been an enjoyable and valuable companion on this journey—thanks, Jack.

It gives me great pleasure to make this dedication to the men who helped me bring the story of Carlos Montezuma to this book: Leon Summit, Tim Goldfarb, and Jack Larner.

# Contents

A biography tells a person's story, but it should also bring to the reader an understanding of the person. Although there is an archival blizzard of Montezuma details, everything is *not* available; too much is unknown. And so our understanding cannot be complete, our view of the man must be at least slightly wrong. A lesser man would remain obscured, but Montezuma was a substantial man, a man of import and impact. The force of the man comes through, and by viewing him through the history that surrounded him, we are able to know Carlos Montezuma, M.D.

# Maps

## CHAPTER ONE

# Captured by Pima Warriors

PIMA WARRIORS ATTACKED the Yavapai camp in October 1871, early in the morning, long before dawn.

There was little opposition because the Yavapai (YAH-vah-pie) warriors were not in camp. The Yavapai were in constant rivalry and conflict with the Pima and Maricopa, and unfortunately for the Yavapai, the U.S. Army enlisted Indians from these tribes to serve as scouts. In the year of the attack, U.S. soldiers with Pima and Maricopa scouts were pursuing Yavapai who were hiding in the mountains of Arizona. The Yavapai had agreed to join other bands in going to Camp Grant (south of the Gila River at the confluence of the Aravaipa and San Pedro Rivers) to make a treaty.[1] Hearing of this, the Pima resolved to make a raid on a nearby camp of about 150 Yavapai.[2] The Pima learned the location of the Yavapai by successfully following a Yavapai raiding party back to their camp. The next day, the Yavapai warriors left camp for the peace conference, and early the next morning the raid occurred. Using guns and arrows, as well as knives, stones, and tomahawks, most of the old men, women, and children were killed. The camp was burned and looted, and thirteen children were taken captive. A Pima calendar stick documented the attack on the Yavapai camp and the capture of Wassaja.[3] However, either the recording or the interpretation was inaccurate, indicating that the attack took place in 1873–1874.

Wassaja (Was-SAH-jah), which means signaling or beckoning, was five or six years old that October in 1871 when he was camped in an area called Iron Mountain, east of the Superstition Mountains (fifty miles east of Phoenix). Years later, Wassaja, now Carlos Montezuma, remembered it as shaded with many trees of pine, cedar, and juniper.[4] He was with his father, Co-lu-ye-vah (Broad Back), his mother, Thil-ge-ya (Stone Bead), along with his two sisters (one older and one younger) and his baby brother.[5] Wassaja and his sisters, Ho-lac-cah (Sore Nose) and Co-wow-sa-puch-a (Hair Hanging Down Her Back) were captured and carried back into the Pima valley. Some of the Yavapai escaped, including Wassaja's mother, and made their way to the San Carlos villages. Wassaja's father, on the day of the attack, was returning with the Yavapai warriors from the peace conference. The baby brother survived only a few weeks after the Pima raid. Wassaja's mother's sister also escaped with her infant. She was later to become Susie Dickens, the mother of George (the infant she carried that night), Charles, and Richard Dickens, Montezuma's cousins whom we will meet later in our story.[6]

In my fright I ran for my life. As I was running along I overtook my two sisters, the older one carrying the younger on her back. I passed them, and continued on my way until I stumbled and fell. There was a bush nearby and I crept into it, and looked around to see if I could discover anyone. I noticed, only a short distance away, a tall man approaching. I drew back my head, and held my breath, but he got hold of me. I gave one of my loudest yells, and pleaded for my life. He took me back over the same ground that I had covered in running from the house. I saw something lying in front of the house. I took it for my mother. Never having seen a dead person, I closed my eyes until I was commanded to stand. I was crying all this time. I heard a familiar cry beside me. I opened my eyes, and to my surprise, next to me was one of my playmates. I looked farther on and there was another and another. There were thirteen of us standing in a row.

My attention turned next to the fire which was in front and all around us, blazing away among the treetops. I thought that this big fire was for us. I imagined I could hear my flesh sizzle. A little on one side, I saw a body with just enough life to give forth a few terrible groans, and a little further on, in the midst of a blazing fire, was a sight which I shall never forget. It was a dear mother with her babe. She was wounded and had been thrown into the fire. The babe was held to her breast by one of her arms, while the other was extended, and her hand was clenched. The child, suffering from the heat, cried, "Oh, mother, mother!" until silenced in death, while the brave mother would reply, "Child, be still. Child, be still!" She also died in great agony.[7]

The Yavapai traveled by foot, a method made difficult by the extremely rugged landscape. Criss-crossed with narrow gullies produced by heavy rains and flash floods, the land is not flat anywhere. The terrain is full of rocks, desert dirt, shrubs, and cacti, with small, narrow valleys containing cottonwood trees, obvious sites of some water. It is very quiet country; on a summer day the heat is intensified by the stillness. Despite the difficult terrain, the Pima traveled by horseback to raid the Yavapai village. It is not a landscape in which a horse can

*Approach to Iron Mountain*

gallop. By necessity and by desire, the Pima raiding party led by Chief Azul approached with great stealth to achieve their total surprise, traveling only about five miles per day and making the final approach to the top of Iron Mountain by foot (the story was told to Montezuma by Chief Azul many years later).[8]

People who grow up in this land find it special. Those not in harmony with its subtleties find it monotonous and desolate; those who love it find it peaceful. Where one sees an absence of multiple colors, another sees soothing shades of brown, green, mauve, and ochre. Like most Indians the Yavapai have a sacramental attitude towards nature. Robin Russell, former vice-president of the Yavapai tribal council, told me: "You don't want to walk around when the snakes are out. But when you see the first one, throw a rock over its head, tell it to get out of here, and you'll never see another."

*Saguaro*

The Yavapai people had been living in this land for hundreds of years, along with the cacti. There are four kinds of cacti, saguaro, cholla, prickly pear, and barrel, saguaro being the most prevalent. The largest cactus in the United States, saguaro is usually two and one-half feet thick and thirty feet high at maturity, but it can grow to fifty feet.[9] Acquiring maturity, however, is a slow process. It takes fifteen years to achieve the first foot of growth, seventy-five to one hundred years to establish the first branching arms, and 150 to 200 years to reach the end of its lifespan. After a rainstorm, the saguaro can soak up to 200 gallons of water, reaching a weight of nine tons. Some of the saguaro presently in the Iron Mountain area were there the day Wassaja was captured.

## THE YAVAPAI PEOPLE BEFORE 1875

The family of Wassaja belonged to the Kwovokopaya (also Kwevikopaya or Kewevkopaya), the southeastern group of Yavapai that now calls Fort McDowell home. The Yavapai people were nomads, roaming the land on foot searching for food in Central Arizona from the Gila River near Florence, to the San Francisco mountain peaks in the north near Flagstaff. The total population never exceeded more than a few thousand, occupying a large area of about 20,000 square miles.[10] The name Yavapai is from *enyaéva* (sun) and *pai* (people), meaning people of the sun.[11] The Yavapai belong to the linguistic Yuman family, native people who occupied the southwestern portion of the United States and lower California, including much of the valley of the Colorado River and the lower valley of the Gila River.[12] Although the languages of the Walapai, Havasupai, Mohave, Quechan, Cocopah, Maricopa, Halchidhoma, Kamiah, Diegueno, and Yuma were similar, only the Yavapai, Walapai and Havasupai could understand each other. The total Yavapai population was scattered in three main geographical and separate political groups—southeastern, northeastern, and western.

According to Yavapai legend, the people came out of Ahagaskiaywa (Montezuma Well), a lake with no bottom.[13] Years ago, there was no water, and people were living there. A chief angered his daughter by touching her when she was asleep. Enraged, she caused the chief to become mortally ill, and she called for a flood. The chief, knowing he was to die, instructed

## Location of Arizona Indian Tribes

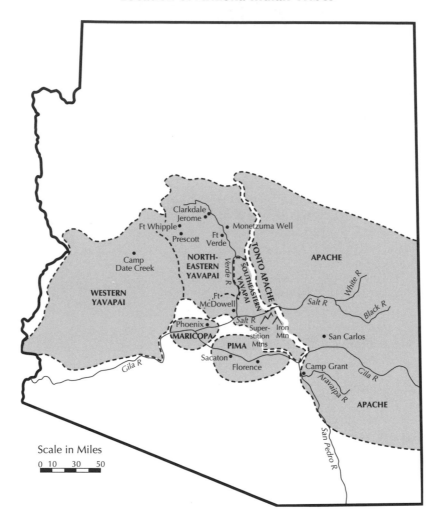

his people to bury him so that something would grow from his heart. Indeed, a corn stalk grew, and it was this stalk the people climbed to emerge from the flooded lake. A second flood left only one survivor, a girl who became "First Woman" and the Yavapai people came from her and from Father Sky. Montezuma Well, a limestone sink near Fort Verde, is said to be the place of origin for the Yavapai and the Tonto Apache (who obviously have a similar legend).[14]

Prior to 1100, the central Arizona area was occupied by the Hohokam, who developed irrigation systems to maintain farming along the Salt and Gila Rivers.[15] These original settlers were pushed north, south, and east into defensive pueblos by the movement of nomadic tribes. The Hohokam disappeared as a culture, replaced by the Pima and Papago, believed to be the descendants of the Hohokam. The Pima continued to farm around the Gila River, irrigating the land with canals.

The Yavapai were one of the first bands of Indians to move into the Arizona area. The Maricopa moved from the Colorado River Valley and encountered the Yavapai; they called them *Nyidwra*, which means old, because they had been living in this area for such a long time.[16] When the Spaniards first met the Southeastern Yavapai, they called them *Yabibai* or *Niojoras*, the *Niojoras* being derived from the Maricopa *Nyidwra*.[17] The Southeastern Yavapai people, therefore, came to the Arizona land before the Apache and the Navajo, who moved into Arizona after the middle of the sixteenth century and did not reach the area of the Southeastern Yavapai until after 1750.[18] The Spaniards easily differentiated these friendly people from the Apache whom they named *Tonto*, meaning unruly or crazy. The Apache were aggressive and troublesome for Whites, but they developed their raiding behavior in order to survive in a time of competition for land and food.[19]

The Yavapai were often erroneously classified as Apache (a problem that was to vex Wassaja later in his life as Carlos Montezuma).[20] How this began is a mystery lost in history. Perhaps the first American Whites noted that the language was similar to Mohave (another Yuman family tribe often confused with Apache), and in addition, the Yavapai often cooperated and intermarried with the Tonto and San Carlos Apache, hence their designation after 1860 as the Mohave Apache and Tonto Apache.[21] Perhaps it was a generic classification of all Indians in that area, especially by military ethnohistorians casting them as opponents to be battled. The Apache, consisting of numerous tribes and clans, are of Athapascan heritage, sharing linguistic similarities with the Navajo.[22] The name Apache is thought to come from *ápachu*, the Zuñi name for the Navajo that means enemy. Another possibility is that the name derived from the Yavapai word for people has been written as *apatieh*, *axwaatcha*, or *apadje*.[23] The Apache called themselves *Inde*, people, and lived and fought differently than the Yavapai.

The tribes living in the Territory of Arizona (established in 1863) included the Pima, Maricopa, Papago, Mohave, Moqui, Oriva, Pueblo, Yuma, Yavapai, Hualapai, Navajo, Hopi, and different bands of Apache. The Southeastern Yavapai (Kwovokopaya), Wassaja's tribe, lived in the area of the Verde River Valley and the Mazatzal, Four Peaks, and Superstition Mountains. There were two main bands. The northerly band, the Wikedjasapa, lived mainly in the Mazatzal Mountains and just south of the Salt River, and the southerly band, the Walkamepa, extended into the Pinal Mountains.[24]

THE ACCURATE DESCRIPTIONS of the Yavapai and their life in the 1870s come from three sources. The memoirs of a remarkable man, William H. Corbusier, who in 1873–1875 served as a military surgeon in the Arizona Territory, portrayed mainly the Northeastern and Western Yavapai, the Wipukyipaya and the Tolkepaya.[25] The Southeastern Yavapai, the Kwovokopaya (Wassaja's tribe), were presented by E. W. Gifford in great detail in 1932 in the University of California Publications in American Archaeology.[26] Gifford's descriptions were derived from fifteen days of discussion with Wassaja's cousin Michael Burns, when Burns was seventy years old in 1929–1930. Albert H. Schroeder published a detailed study of all three groups of Yavapai, first in 1959 and again in 1974, work performed for the Indian Claims Commission (Chapter 13).[27]

**Appearance.** The Yavapai are dark-skinned people with coarse hair that is black and straight.[28] The women wore their hair loose and shoulder length, with bangs to their eyebrows. The men cut their hair only when mourning a dead member of the tribe. The men tied their hair with a piece of cloth, inserting a stick or bone about eight inches long, used for scratching or combing. A beard was never seen; the few coarse facial hairs were plucked out.

Yavapai men averaged five-feet-eight and one-half inches in height and 158 pounds in weight.[29] Yavapai eyes are dark brown, under prominent eyebrows and low, narrow foreheads. Noses are broad and flat, and sometimes the men pierced the nasal septum and inserted a bead or a string of beads. The ears of the males had openings in the lobes, made shortly after birth with a piece of wood hardened in fire, to hold pieces of material or long strings of beads. The teeth were small and closely set, often yellow, decayed, and worn down by constant use to provide traction when working hides. The women practiced tattooing, but not the men, using charcoal pricked into the skin with cactus thorns or needles. A married woman was marked by seven narrow lines running from the lower lips down the chin; the outermost lines were distinguished by points at the bottom ends or by being zigzag rather than straight. Younger women often put a tattoo of a child on their forearms for luck in becoming a mother. Some put two or three lines running around the forearm.

A paint was used by both sexes for ornament, and for protection from the sun in the summer and against the cold in winter.[30] Red was commonly used, obtained from red clay, dried to a powder and mixed with saliva, then baked into small cakes. After baking, a string was inserted through a hole in each cake, used to tie the cake to their clothing. For use, it was mixed with saliva and rubbed over the skin, making designs with the fingers. Galena and burnt mescal were also used for facial designs (war paint).

**Clothing.** In the summer, women wore strips of bark hung over a belt or a kilt made of fringed buckskins, one in front over a belt and one in back. In winter, a third buckskin was placed over the chest suspended from the neck by strings on which rabbit bones were placed for ornamentation. The men dressed in the summer in a coat of red clay, a pair of moccasins, and a strip of buckskin or cloth passed between the legs, held up by passing it over a belt in front and back. The end in the back was traditionally long, almost reaching the ground. When buckskin was used with hair on it, it looked like a tail. In the winter, the men wore a Navajo blanket or an animal skin wrapped around the shoulders; sometimes trousers without seats and a jacket were made from deerskin. Yavapai moccasins worn by the men were unique in reaching nearly to the knees. Each was made of half a buckskin folded in three parts and attached to soles of cowhide. The Yavapai traded their expertly tanned animal hides for Navajo and Hopi blankets. There is no known record of hostilities between the Yavapai and their neighbors, the Navajo and the Hopi.

The skins were prepared by the men. After soaking in water, the hide was placed against a smooth stone or tree and the hair scraped off. It took an entire day for one man to scrape the hair off the hide of an adult deer.[31] After drying, it was rolled for storage. For use, the skin was soaked again and dressed with a preparation made from partly cooked animal brains, then worked in the sun by hand, pulling until dry and soft. Each man did his own tailoring, using sharpened bones and stones. The making of baskets and pottery was women's work. Pottery was created from clay made formable by adding water and boiled cactus. Using one-inch rolls one at a time, the pots were smoothed and formed by hands inside and out. After drying, the pots were burned in an open fire.

The men, never the women, often wore prized feathers, wearing two or three tail or wing feathers from an eagle, hawk, or wild turkey, tied to a lock of hair on the top of the head. The men wore bracelets on their left forearms, two to four inches wide, made of deerskin, ornamented with paint, beads, or brass buttons. These bracelets were functional, for protection from the insult of the bowstring.

Beads were used as currency, usually small white beads, worn as many strands around the neck, and the women also wore them around the wrists. Amulets included quartz crystals to bring good luck and rattlesnake fangs to ward off harm. Almost everyone carried a small mirror in a buckskin pocket, to be used when applying paint and ornaments.

**Housing.** The Yavapai often lived in caves or rock shelters. In the absence of a cave, the Yavapai lived in a *u-wah* or *oo-wah* (similar to the Apache *wick-ee-up*), a circular brush hut, about five feet high, six to eight feet in diameter.[32] A space was excavated about one and one-half feet deep with sticks and hands, banking the earth around the circumference. Bushes or tree branches were stuck around the edges, bent over and fastened to form a round top. In winter, grass was added as a thatched roof. Only one side had an opening, determined by the prevailing wind to allow the egress of smoke. The fire was just inside the opening. Beds were made over broken ground covered with dry grass. The Yavapai disposed of their dead by cremation, and if death occurred within an *oo-wah*, the entire hut and its contents were burned along with the body.[33]

**Food.** The Yavapai in the 1800s lived off wild animals (except for fish), wild plants (acorns, pinon nuts, walnuts, prickly pears, fruit of the saguaro, and seeds from the jajoba, paloverde, and bursage), and some farming.[34] They lived in small groups, moving from place to place according to the readiness of foods, but returning to the same areas year after year.[35] By the 1800s, many families had drifted back to the hills around the Verde River Valley. Gardens were watered by irrigation ditches dug with makeshift tools. Crops included corn, squash, beans, melons, and gourds for containers. Hunting and gathering, however, continued to be the main form of sustenance until the Yavapai were confined to reservations.

During the nomad years, mescal served as food year around. Mescal is the century plant (*Agave parryi*) of the agave family, found in the dry, rocky slopes of the higher country. Plants were selected at least eighteen inches high and cut close to the ground.[36] The ends of the leaves were trimmed to form a large ball of leaves and base, like a cabbage. A fire pit was built three to ten feet in diameter and two to four feet deep. Stones were added when the fire was large. The mescal was thrown on the hot stones, then covered with grass and earth. Forty-eight hours later, the pit was opened and each woman removed her plants, identified by individual marks. The plants were shrunken and brown from the fire. The fleshy part of the plant became a sweet, juicy pulp (like sugar cane). For future use, pieces were hammered and spread on sticks to dry, then rolled for carrying. These became hard and tough and required

*Agave parryi (Mescal)*
*Next to a Manzanita Bush*

soaking in water before eating. Mescal water, made by dissolving the pulp in water, was a favorite beverage and also used to treat the sick, although it acted mainly as a laxative. The flower stalk of a mature mescal can reach fifteen feet in height, and was eaten raw or roasted in an open fire. The Southeastern Yavapai did not make alcoholic drinks.[37]

**Weapons.** The Maricopa and the Pima, living to the southwest across a stretch of uninhabited country, were regarded as enemies, and raids were common.[38] The Yavapai made arrows from the branches of the mataki bush growing along riverbanks.[39] These arrows, about two to three feet long, were attached to arrowheads made from obsidian, fastened with muscle sinew from a deer. Deer muscle was cut from the back in strips and dried. Chewed in the mouth to make it soft, it was wrapped around the arrowheads and feathers when wet; when dried, it shrunk and made a firm seal. Three feathers were used, either eagle or hawk feathers. The bow, called an *apu*, was made from the wood of the wild mulberry tree. Stripped wood was buried in the ground and heated by a fire over it. This heated wood could then be bent and held in place by the bowstring made of deer sinew. A bow would reach from the ground to a man's chest. Arrow poison was applied as a paste made from a rotten mixture of the liver of a deer, spiders, tarantulas, and a rattlesnake head.

Other weapons included spears and clubs. Men and women carried a war club from their belts, a *pa ave*. This hammer used to hit people was made from ironwood, one of the heaviest and hardest woods in the world, from trees found in desert washes. The club was made from a forked branch cut into a T-shape. Heating and grinding produced a club about two feet long. Wet deer hide was wrapped around the club, and sewed together with deer sinew. At the end, a hide handle was attached to hang it from the wrist or belt. The *sumkova* was a war shield made from buffalo hide, and later in history from cowhide. The hair was left on, sticking out and making it effective for deflecting arrows. Two hides were cut in a circle, stretched over a wood frame and allowed to dry to become hard. The two hides were sewed together with the wood frame still inside. A hole in the middle allowed the attachment of a handle.

**Social Organization.** Most men had only one wife, but occasionally had two if the man were a successful hunter or fighter (Wassaja's father had two wives). Girls married at age fourteen or fifteen. Boys were treated with great respect and often were consulted for advice. As was the custom among many Indian tribes, names often changed, being descriptive of notable acts or a particular physical or mental characteristic. Each family usually had its own medicine man, an individual picked in late teen years because of some unusual behavior denoting communication with the spirits. Disease and injuries were attributed to evil spirits. The medicine men used charms and singing (often lasting all night or several days) to summon familiar spirits. Each medicine man had his own familiar spirit. They also practiced multiple superficial cuts and bleeding to relieve a site of pain. Sweat lodges are still constructed and used in the old way.

The basic unit of economic, social, and military organization was the band, mostly families related by marriage.[40] Most of the bands were named for a trait, or a geographical feature or location. These were loose confederations for the purpose of defense, aggression, or social occasions. The leader was a warrior who had proved himself in battle. With defeat, the band turned to a new leader. This leadership was exerted mainly in military activities, not in daily life. Although cooperation between bands occurred, such as sharing food areas and raids, overall leadership and organization were never attained. Itinerant quests for food prevented tribal unity and caused wide dispersion of the small bands.

## CORBUSIER: AN ARMY DOCTOR

William H. Corbusier was an army doctor. The army doctors on the western frontier were more than medical men.[41] They were required to pass a very rigorous and competitive examination that included Latin, Greek, French, German, arithmetic, algebra, trigonometry, calculus, geography, history, literature, mineralogy, botany, physics, and finally all of medicine. These doctors represented the best of American physicians and surgeons at that time (although they were limited by the lack of available medical knowledge). The U.S. Army also hired contract physicians to fulfill its needs, and these doctors, too, had usually passed the comprehensive examinations. They kept daily records of departures, arrivals, weather conditions, illnesses, births, deaths; they were expected to serve in the field, carrying a weapon that was to be used only in an emergency. A physician in the Regular Army was commissioned as an Assistant Surgeon, the equivalent military rank of First Lieutenant or Captain. The rank of Surgeon included Majors, Lieutenant Colonels, and Colonels. Only the Surgeon General of the army was given the rank of General. Contract physicians were designated as Acting Assistant Surgeons and remained in that rank.

William H. Corbusier was an army doctor of such high moral integrity and courage, and endowed with such humanitarian concern, that military men, civilians, and especially Indians came to trust and respect him. Corbusier loved and understood Indians, providing a strong motivation for him to work for their welfare. He and his wife learned to speak several Indian languages. By 1874, he was invited to participate in Indian ceremonies. Fanny Corbusier and Dr. Corbusier had five sons who were brought up on a succession of fifteen Army posts in the midst of Indian warfare. Only years later did his sons learn of the accomplishments and bravery of their father. His memoirs, *Verde to San Carlos. Recollections of a Famous Army Surgeon and His Observant Family on the Western Frontier 1869–1886*, published in 1968, were being written by father and son (William T. Corbusier), when Corbusier died in 1930 at the age of eighty-six.[42]

Corbusier served in the Civil War as a surgeon, although he did not receive his medical degree from Bellevue Hospital Medical College in New York City until after the war, in 1867. During his service in the West, in addition to the Yavapai, he was involved with the Oglala Sioux under Red Cloud, the Shoshone and Bannock, Geronimo and the Apache, and the Buffalo Soldiers' Tenth Cavalry. In conjunction with the expedition to the Philippines (1898–1900), Corbusier helped organize the Red Cross and developed the "dog tag" as a method of identification for soldiers. In the Philippines, he was in charge of the first trained female nurses to serve abroad with the army.

Corbusier knew Michael Burns, Wassaja's cousin, very well. Burns learned English as a frequent guest in the Corbusier home in the Verde Valley (Burns was later to attend the Carlisle Indian School).[43] Forty-six years later, in 1921, Corbusier visited Fort McDowell and was presented with an autobiographical manuscript written by Burns entitled *The Indian Side of the Question*. The Corbusiers, father and son, worked on this manuscript, but were unable to find a publisher. The original manuscript can be found today in the Sharlot Hall Museum in Prescott and a copy in the Department of Archives and Manuscripts of the Arizona State University. An edited version was published in 1998, *Hoomothya's Long Journey, 1865–1897*.[44]

Mike Burns (*Hoo-moo-thy-ah*, Little Wet Nose) was named after Captain James Burns, who captured him about two weeks before the Skeleton Cave Massacre.[45] Burns was about the same age as Wassaja, maybe five years older. All of Burns' relatives were killed in the Battle of the Caves, or the Skeleton Cave Massacre. In 1869, several hundred Indians (Tonto and

Yavapai) came to Camp McDowell to make peace and a treaty. Burns and his family were with this group. Camped across the Verde River at Camp McDowell, the Indians were told that the soldiers had sent for Pima and Maricopa scouts. Remembering a similar episode some years earlier when the Pima killed those in camp, the Indians left—the old people and children during the day and the warriors that night after stealing some horses. This band (about 225 Indians, but only fifty warriors) was led by Del-che, a Yavapai chief. In December 1872, a large force was gathered to go on a campaign against Del-che.

SKELETON CAVE WAS a major hiding place, situated 200 feet below a canyon rim that is 1,000 feet above the Salt River. The cave was reached by a slippery, rocky, and dangerous trail that rose from the canyon floor and increasingly narrowed until it was only two feet wide. The small canyon (the Salt River Canyon) is now flooded by Canyon Lake. On December 28,1872, a Yavapai scout showed a military party of about sixty men to the cave.[46] Mike Burns accompanied the soldiers, in the care of his captor, Captain Burns. Many of the Indians left prior to the fight, including Del-che, who assured those remaining that no one could find them. The cave was situated above a smooth rock wall, ten feet high, making it a formidable assault. Requests for surrender were refused; indeed, the response was a battle chant. A fusillade of bullets was largely aimed at the inner faces and the roof of the cave, causing death by ricochet. Safety in front of the cave at a rock rampart was obliterated by gunfire and rocks from a party at the top led by Captain Burns. After several hours, the cave was silent. No attempt was made to bury the dead, the bones were retrieved by Montezuma in 1920 (Chapter 11). In the official report, seventy-six Indians were killed (some say it was in the hundreds), thirty-five were still living but most would die, and eighteen women and children were captured and taken to Camp McDowell; many if not all of Burns' relatives died here. These were enormous numbers. We are accustomed to the wholesale slaughter of modern warfare, but when Indian bands fought other Indian bands, death counts usually amounted to less than five, and often no one died.[47]

In spring, 1873, about 1,000 Yavapai and 500 Tonto Apache were collected and taken to the Rio Verde Reservation, located on the Verde River near Clarkdale (the present site of Cottonwood); some were sent to San Carlos.[48] Dr. Corbusier arrived at the Rio Verde Reservation on September 12, 1873. At that time, there were a few tents, one unfinished adobe house, and the Indians in their brush and grass huts. The Indian agent and his employees were all prostrate with fever in this mosquito infested area. The Indians were in poor condition, having been pursued by troops, leaving little time to gather food. The troopers numbered only fifteen, and most of their time was spent going after the Indians who left, to bring them back.

In 1874, under the supervision of Julius W. Mason, the commanding officer at Fort Verde, who was also a professional engineer, the Indians constructed a dam and a four-mile ditch for irrigation.[49] Corbusier, Second Lieutenant Walter S. Schuyler, and Lieutenant George O. Eaton helped the Indians raise crops of corn, potatoes, melons, and pumpkins.

Corbusier earned the name of *Pi-ka thak-vo-ka*, Brings Back the Dead.[50] Being told that medicine men could bring a dead man to life, he chloroformed a rat, threw it on the ground and declared it dead. After a short time, he picked up the tail and swung it around until it revived.

This early successful farming came to an end with an episode in history called by the Yavapai their own Trail of Tears, similar to experiences of other tribes when they were forcibly removed to reservations of the government's choosing.

## REMOVALS AND RESERVATIONS

The confinement of American Indians on reservations and the resulting impact on Indian lifestyles were to have an enormous effect on Montezuma's political and social beliefs. An understanding of Montezuma's reactions requires an appreciation for the historical events of the time.

Treaty making with the Indians was an American colonial policy based on the previous English, French, and Dutch experience in which the sovereignty of Indian tribes was recognized. However, treaties with Indians were nothing more than the legalization of gains made by conquest, not true bilateral agreements. Law is based on justice between individuals, groups, and nations—and a treaty is a promise of justice. Throughout recorded history, this principle has been repeatedly proclaimed in all societies. By its very nature, a treaty cannot and should not be unilaterally abrogated, but the Indian treaties were a long history of repeated disregard of agreements by the government. As the nineteenth century progressed, treaties increasingly became instruments of government Indian policy, and the principle was established that the Federal Government would regulate Indian affairs.

Because frontier interactions between Whites and Indians were often violent, Indian responsibility was first under the secretary of war and the War Department. In 1824, the secretary of war created the Office of Indian Affairs within the War Department, and soon this came to be called the Bureau of Indian Affairs. In 1849, the Bureau of Indian Affairs with its commissioner of Indian affairs was transferred to the Department of the Interior, where it remains today.

Many Indian tribes in the nineteenth century were forced by successive losses of land to move repeatedly. For example, the Fox (the Mesquakie, "red earth people," were called the Fox by the French) migrated from the Atlantic Coast around the St. Lawrence River and lived, in 1600, in Michigan. They united with the Sauk, or Sac Indians, either is correct. Saginaw, in Michigan, means "place of the Sauk." In the late 1600s, they moved to the area of Green Bay, Wisconsin. Both groups moved to Illinois, ceded their land in Illinois and accepted land in Missouri, ceded their land in Missouri and accepted land in Iowa, ceded their land in Iowa and accepted land in Kansas. Today the Sac and Fox Nation, about 2,200 members derived from those who sold their land in Kansas, is located in Oklahoma, left with only 1,000 acres after allotment (Chapter 3). Some of the Fox returned to Iowa where they bought land in 1859 and now have about 5,000 acres (the Sac and Fox of the Mississippi in Iowa—about 1,100 members), and there is also a small Sac and Fox reservation, the Sac and Fox of Missouri, about 400 members, in Reserve, Kansas.

The story of the Cherokee Nation stands as testimony to Indian resiliency.[51] By the 1820s, the Cherokee were a strong and cohesive nation in the southeast, successfully adapting Anglo forms of government and social organization, but at the same time maintaining their history and traditions. This development took place despite constant White pressure resulting in the loss of land. In 1802, Georgia had ceded land in the Mississippi Territory in exchange for a government agreement to eliminate Indian land in Georgia. Repeated cessions by the Cherokee produced a tighter and tighter compression into the southeast. The first Cherokee to move west of the Mississippi took place in 1817 when about 2,000 members of the Nation exchanged their eastern land for land on the Arkansas River (later, they were forced to move again). By 1836, more than 6,000 Cherokee lived west of the Mississippi River, but the majority remained in the East, and with effective leadership, created a democratic political structure and judicial system. The Cherokee bartered with missionaries, granting permission for evangelizing only in return for the establishment of schools. Soon, the young men and women of the Cherokee were relatively well educated.

During this time period, Sequoyah developed the Cherokee alphabet. Sequoyah was a Cherokee Indian who lived from 1760 to 1843, a total of eighty-three years. As a young man, he had a considerable reputation as a fighter and scout with the U.S. Army. During his military career, he suffered an injury to his legs. The limitation of his mobility forced him to turn inward. He became an accomplished painter and silversmith, and the only man known in history to have developed an entire alphabet single-handedly. In 1809, at the age of thirty-four, he began, and twelve years later living west of the Mississippi, in 1821, he had perfected eighty-six symbols to represent all of the sounds in the Cherokee language. At first he made up his own symbols, then because he recognized it would be easier to use a printing press, he adapted letters from English, Greek, and Hebrew found in books borrowed from missionaries. In the beginning, his friends and relatives made fun of him, but in four years, by 1825, the majority of the Cherokee adults were literate in their own language, motivated partly to be able to write from the Indian Territory to those still at home in the East. The Cherokee taught this language in all of their schools and published books and a newspaper, the *Cherokee Phoenix*. In Washington, D.C., the Hall of Statues exhibits two statues from each state, representing significant citizens of the state. The State of Oklahoma selected Sequoyah to be one of its two representatives because of his contributions to the early development of Oklahoma. In 1847, the Austrian botanist, Stephen Endlicher, was so moved by Sequoyah's achievements, that when writing about the great redwood trees, he gave them the botanical name, Sequoia.

SOUTHERN AND WESTERN LEGISLATORS PASSED by one vote the Indian Removal Act on May 28, 1830, despite vigorous opposition from eastern members of Congress. The act provided for treaty negotiations to move eastern tribes across the Mississippi River.[52]

The Cherokee were the most influential Indian nation in the Southeast. But in 1829, gold was discovered in the Cherokee country. The Cherokee Nation questioned the right of the State of Georgia to remove them from their land, and it was their case in 1831, challenging the Indian Removal Act of 1830, that resulted in the landmark decision written by Chief Justice John Marshall that established Indian tribes as dependent domestic nations (not foreign nations), and a second decision in 1832 established the right to self government.[53] The Supreme Court affirmed the principle that cession of lands would require a voluntary agreement with the Federal Government. This political right of the Indians was eventually abolished in 1871, when Congress brought to an end the making of treaties with Indian tribes, an incredible period of activity that produced over 370 treaties.[54] The treaty system came to be viewed as incompatible with the Protestant movement toward individualism (Chapter 3). The philosophy of assimilation that dominated Indian policy in the late 1800s and early 1900s had as its objective the elimination of tribal organization and Indian culture.

With the support of President Andrew Jackson, a powerful campaign was successful in producing a treaty in 1835 with the Cherokee (The Treaty of New Echota) that agreed to removal. Despite the fact that only a minority of the Cherokee leaders had signed the treaty, the Cherokee Nation, like all the other tribes in the Southeast, was ordered to move to the Indian Territory (Oklahoma without the panhandle). In 1838, General Winfield Scott and 7,000 troops collected the Cherokee into thirty-one forts built for this purpose and began the process of removal. The first Indians to be moved suffered greatly, and subsequently the Cherokee were allowed to supervise the migration of small groups that lived off the land and traveled over several routes over many months, some by water and some by land. Out of about 16,000 migrating Cherokee, 4,000 died during the removal, now known as "The Trail of Tears," although the direct translation of the Cherokee is "The Trail Where They Cried."[55] Those who were able to hide in the mountains combined with those who accepted U.S. citizenship and land in an 1819 treaty (the Oconaluftee Cherokee) to form the Eastern Band of the Cherokee Indians that remained in North Carolina. Another 4,000 Cherokee died of disease and starvation after reaching Indian Territory.[56] The descendants of those who survived the removal now constitute the Cherokee Nation in Oklahoma, with about 165,000 members in 2003.

Over 100,000 American Indians were moved west of the Mississippi River in the first half of the nineteenth century.[57] Removal to the West did not solve the problem of White pressure; it only postponed it. But in contrast to the 200 years the conflict took in the East, the rapid growth of the White population and the rise of the United States to become the sole military power combined to limit the White-Indian duel in the West to forty to fifty years. During the 1850s, over sixty treaties were created with Indian tribes in which the United States acquired over 170 million acres of land.

## American Indian History

| Removal and Reservations | Assimilation and Allotment | Reorganization | Termination | Restoration and Recognition |
|---|---|---|---|---|
| 1880 | 1934 | 1954 | 1970 | |

A large number of tribes from all sections of the country east of the Mississippi River, more than thirty, were packed into the Indian Territory, most enduring their own Trail of Tears in harsh weather with insufficient food and supplies. The astounding total number of 60,000 Indians included the Delaware, the Ottawa, the Shawnee, the Pawnee and Potawatomi, the

Sauk and Fox, and the Miami and Kickapoo. The Indian Territory became home between 1831 and 1848 for the Creek, Cherokee, Choctaw, Chickasaw, and Seminole—the so-called Five Civilized Tribes. These southeastern tribes were primarily agricultural and had adapted many of the White ways (dress, housing, and social organization), and therefore they were viewed by White society in the early 1800s as more "civilized" in contrast to western tribes. After removal to the Indian Territory, this adaptation with borrowed features from White society continued; however, tribal languages and culture were maintained. A school system was re-established and literacy rates (in English as well) were high. These achievements were recognized by allowing the allotment process with the Five Civilized Tribes according to the Dawes Act of 1887 only with the consent of the tribes. Because of Creek and Cherokee opposition to allotment, the Curtis Act was passed in 1898, and upheld by the Supreme Court, which dissolved the governments of any tribes that rejected allotment.[58] After 1898, the Five Civilized Tribes joined all other Indians as a people without political independence.

THE REMOVAL OF TRIBES to reservations was part of the general policy dedicated to the denial of Indian self-determination, culminating in the policy of assimilation and allotment (Chapter 3). This program was a formulation stemming from a dominant way of life, exemplified by the Protestant ideals and concepts of work, family, and religion, directed to the replacement of tribal communal land management, tribal governments, and tribal religions.

Life was not exactly the same on every reservation, but certain basic characteristics can be described. Only the Pueblo with their well-organized towns and the Navajo whose large reservation remote from Whites allowed them to retain political and economical autonomy escaped the general pattern that began in the 1880s and persisted through the 1920s. The reservation agent maintained authority by controlling the availability of food and supplies, and by organizing and commanding the Indian police to enforce his regulations. The agents were assisted by doctors, clerks, field matrons, farmers, and teachers. The agents (about sixty in number) became increasingly powerful and the reservation communities became small dictatorships as all decisions were made unilaterally without consultation or participation of the Indians. To be sure, there were some honest and kind agents, but in general, the reservations were ruled, not governed.[59] John Collier, commissioner of Indian affairs under Franklin D. Roosevelt, wrote in his memoir published in 1963: "Indian Service personnel in the field were expected to be absolutist toward the Indians. Not only were Indians subjected to quasi-military rule within the Indian Bureau ...but also Indians were shut out from all other Federal agencies of helpfulness, and from state and local agencies."[60] The tribal organization by bands slowly decayed, and no Indian system of organization and government was substituted. Tribal functions such as feasts and dances were not permitted. The result was a life marked by community apathy, dependence on government officials, and stirred by factional strife underneath an imposed order.[61] This situation was intensified by insufficient appropriations from Congress leading to insufficient rations and supplies, making living conditions marginal at best.

President Grant tried to improve the quality of the Indian agents by calling for nominees from religious denominations. It was an attractive, praiseworthy idea that proved difficult to implement and led to unproductive competition among the various denominations. It was almost impossible to recruit capable individuals who were willing to serve in remote areas for insufficient pay (about $1,500 per year). The agent did receive family quarters, a team for transportation, and the services of a clerk and the agency physician. Those that were moved to serve were often well intentioned, but almost always totally ignorant of Indian culture. This system "provided instructors in agriculture who had never farmed, clerks who couldn't write, and teachers too dissolute or incompetent to hold positions in other schools."[62] This policy soon waned, defeated by the lack of sustained interest on the part of the churches as well as interdenominational rivalry, and by 1882, the appointments were once again products of political spoils at about the same time that military conflicts drew to an end. After 1892, a short-lived attempt was made (not without civilian protest) to improve the quality of agents by detailing army officers to the position. After 1900, many reservations were under the supervision of the school superintendents (157 of them by 1912), appointed under the civil service rules, and the quality did improve.[63]

There was a rapid turnover among Indian agents. This was partly due to the low pay and difficult living conditions, but mainly because the positions were the political rewards provided by elected politicians, and every new election brought new appointments. However, there was no shortage of applicants because of the many opportunities for rapid financial gain if ordinary scruples could be put aside.[64] There was repeated failure to see dishonor when a profit was to be made. For example, Indian agents profited from arrangements with lumbermen and ranchers to harvest Indian timber and graze cattle on Indian grasslands, sold cheap goods at higher prices, and benefited from contracts for the transportation of goods from eastern markets. In their use of government funds, which amounted to many thousands of dollars, the agents often collaborated with White traders, who not infrequently were relatives of the agents.[65] The more remote the reservation, the better, because then there was little chance of supervision or detection of irregularities. By 1880, the secretary of the interior supervised a corps of inspectors and the commissioner of Indian affairs had his special agents—individuals who were charged with investigations and the exposure of reservation affairs.

As the Sioux were compressed into their reservations, the agents set out to develop a cattle industry. By the 1890s, the Sioux reservations were checker-boarded with White ranches. Adopting this lifestyle, the Sioux families became scattered and abandoned the old tradition of camps. The Sioux cattle herds thrived and increased in size. At the beginning of World War I, cattle prices were very high. The Sioux were induced to sell their cattle and lease their lands to White cattlemen. After the war, when prices fell, the Sioux were without their herds of cattle, and were now landlords for White men who could not meet their lease payments. By the 1930s, the Sioux were in desperate economic shape, having sold their cattle, their land, and even their horses.

## YAVAPAI HISTORY AFTER WHITE CONTACT:
## CONFLICT AND CONFINEMENT

The United States obtained Arizona after the Mexican War and the Treaty of Guadalupe Hidalgo in 1848. The land was surveyed in the 1850s, and established as a Territory in 1863. Prior to 1860, the Yavapai had very rare contact with either the Spanish or Anglo-Americans.[66]

By 1864, the U. S. Army was building forts to protect settlers against the Indians and to preserve federal land against Confederate intrusion. Camp McDowell was established on the Verde River in 1865. After 1865, the White population grew rapidly, and the total Yavapai population decreased to less than 1,000, mainly a consequence of malnutrition and disease.[67] A nomadic and hunting culture is fragile; the constant search for food does not allow for a secure life. Such a way of life was especially susceptible to outside pressures and change. By the early 1870s, the Yavapai Indians were being confined to small reservations and forced to change from a lifestyle of hunting and gathering with a small component of agriculture to a dependence upon irrigation agriculture. At the time of Wassaja's capture, the Yavapai Indians were in poor condition, desperate for food.[68]

## Fort McDowell Yavapai History

In 1861, Joseph Walker led prospectors into northern Arizona. Having no luck around the San Francisco Peaks, they wintered in Santa Fe. There Walker met General James Carleton, military commander of New Mexico. Both men were excited by rumors of gold. Carleton directed Walker to an area near present day Prescott, and in May 1863, the Walker Party hit the first of several lodes that started a gold rush.[69]

In 1863, five mining districts were created in Yavapai land in the Prescott area. Carleton established Fort Whipple as a military post for the protection of settlers and miners. Fort Whipple became the town of Prescott, and the capital of the Arizona Territory was moved from Tucson to Prescott. The Weaver Mining District was named after Paulino Weaver—mountain man, Indian scout, explorer, and a member of the Ewing Young-Kit Carson trapping party on the Salt and Verde Rivers in 1828–1831. During the early days of the Arizona gold rush, Weaver taught the Yavapai a password, "Paulino Tobacco."[70] When Indians used that password, settlers knew that the Indian was friendly. This didn't last long, and Weaver himself was attacked by Yavapai in 1867; wounded, he made it to Fort Lincoln (later Fort Verde), but died, causing genuine grief among the Yavapai. His tombstone reads: "His greatest achievement was as peacemaker between races."[71]

King Woolsey, a member of the Walker party, was the first to mine along Lynx Creek, which is in the heart of Yavapai country. He established a ranch on the Agua Fria River. P. K. Safford, the territorial governor, identified Woolsey as a resource for aid and refuge for settlers during Indian conflicts. Woolsey led 100 men in 1860 on a violent expedition, featuring Sugarfoot Jack. Sugarfoot Jack threw Indian babies into burning wickiups, and pursued a policy of violent total extermination. Jack Swilling was another member of the Walker Party who tried to protect his mining interests by exterminating Indians. He was a former Confederate officer, and in 1867, organized the Swilling Irrigation Company to restore ancient Indian canals using the Salt River, eventually leading to the city of Phoenix.

In January 1864, Yavapai and Pinal Mountain Apache were invited to a "peace feast." The food was poisoned, and thirty-six died (although at least one source claimed the poisoning never happened[72]). Called the Pinole Massacre or Incident at Bloody Tanks, it was a scheme carried out by the citizens of Prescott.[73] Charles Poston, the Arizona Territory's first Superintendent of Indian Affairs, defended this episode, arguing that it was live or die for either side. This event strengthened the Yavapai resolution to oppose the White men. In February, one month after the massacre, the Yavapai chief Qua-shac-a-ma warned Indian Agent Bennett that any more encroachment on Yavapai land would not be tolerated. In March, the Yavapai began attacking ranches and raiding stock, partly driven by the threat of starvation because of loss of land.

In September 1864, Captain John Moss negotiated a treaty with the Yavapai, aimed at keeping trails and roads safe. During 1864, the effort to isolate the Indians on reservations began. The army would first build a fort, and then entice the Indians to live around the fort with promises of food, supplies, and housing. Initially, the Yavapai went to Camp Date Creek and Camp McDowell, but promises were not kept, abuse was common, and smallpox was a scourge.

The first Territorial Legislature met in Prescott on September 26, 1864. King Woolsey at age thirty-two was appointed chairman of Militia and Indian Affairs. This session appropriated $1,487 to fund expeditions against Apache, led by Woolsey. Yavapai and Apache were now considered to be the same. In a gesture of peace, twenty-seven Northeastern Yavapai agreed to work on the Fort Mohave Toll Road in May 1865, under the protection of the Superintendent of Indian Affairs, G. W. Leihy. All were attacked and killed by Fort Whipple soldiers.[74] Four months later, the Yavapai joined the Mohave and Yuma tribes in a war against Piute and Chemehuevi Indians who were serving as army scouts.

Chief Echa-waw-cha-comma (Hitting the Enemy) met with the soldiers to talk peace on April 13, 1866, near Grapevine Springs in Skull Valley. Fort Whipple troops killed thirty Indians and wounded forty in an ambush.[75] Skull Valley is a name from a later time when the Yavapai found many bones and skulls in that area. That summer, 100 Yavapai attacked at Grapevine Springs, but were repelled. Nevertheless, the Yavapai took control of the surrounding country, and began to charge a toll for use of the roads. In September, Superintendent Leihy and his clerk were killed by the Yavapai at Bell Canyon near Prescott.

In 1867, a military camp and reservation were established along Date Creek, initially called Camp McPherson (named after General J. B. McPherson, killed in Atlanta during the Civil War), later renamed Camp Date Creek. This camp was situated in a strategic location, surrounded by settlers along the creeks, miners in the mountains, and near a main road from La Paz to Prescott. Two months later, troops from this camp pursued a Yavapai party that had attacked a wagon train. Captain Williams and his troops surprised and attacked the Yavapai in Hell's Canyon, followed by a series of battles throughout the summer and fall.

By the close of 1867, the White population of Yavapai County was 2,337, out of a total of 7,136 in all of Arizona. The army was led by General Gregg, a seasoned combat veteran but inexperienced in Indian affairs. Gregg declared all Indians as hostile, and revoked all passes and permits for travel. Conflict increased in intensity. By summer, 1868, the military had completed forty-six expeditions against the Yavapai and Apache in that fiscal year, reporting 114 Indians dead and thirty-five wounded.[76] Nevertheless the Indians appeared to be superior. In May 1869, 100 Indians attacked a military wagon train within sight of Fort Verde.

The winter of 1869–1870 was a high point of Indian raids, marked by decreasing numbers of troops and supplies. The Indians were skilled in their type of warfare, using ruses and ambushes, and if events or circumstances were not advantageous, they dispersed widely in all directions to make pursuit difficult. At the end of 1870, reinforcements arrived as well as a new commander, General O. C. Ord. Ord made it clear what the policy would be: destruction of all hostile Indians—the extermination policy.

General George Crook assumed duty in Arizona in 1871. His General Order #10 proclaimed that all Indians not on reservations by February 15, 1872, were to be considered hostile. The Rio Verde Reservation was established in the upper Verde River Valley in 1871. Raids and killings continued. But on December 28, 1872, the Skeleton Cave Massacre broke the Yavapai resistance. White accounts in newspapers and magazines labeled this as a victorious battle with Apache, but according to Yavapai accounts, the inhabitants of the cave were all Yavapai who were not fighting, but hiding and living there. All the Indian men were killed; not one soldier was injured.

## Yavapai Trail of Tears

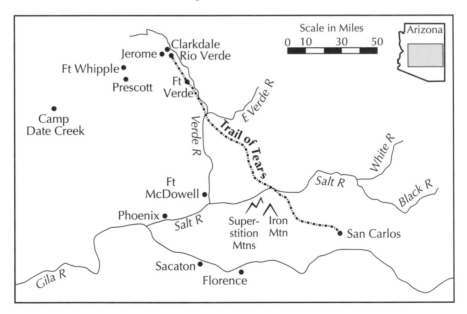

### THE YAVAPAI TRAIL OF TEARS

The Yavapai had their own Trail of Tears. They were accompanied by Corbusier, and his account is believed to be the most accurate.[77]

In the summer of 1873, Camp Date Creek was abandoned, and about 1,100 Indians were moved to the Rio Verde Reservation, sixteen miles from Fort Verde. Soon, the Indians at Rio Verde totalled about 2,000, including about 900 Southeastern Yavapai,[78] and they were successfully planting their irrigated land. In February 1875, they were anticipating enlarging their acreage. Promised seeds and equipment, however, had not arrived, although similar supplies had arrived at Fort Verde and San Carlos. Second Lieutenant Schuyler and Corbusier, as well as the Indians, were suspicious of the agent and other Whites. General Crook must have heard of unrest, for he arranged for fifteen more troopers, bringing the total to thirty. Actually, the government, under pressure from those seeking Indian land and water as well as contractors who supplied Indian rations, had been considering the consolidation of the Indians in Arizona for some time. When a new agent, John P. Clum, brought order to the San Carlos Reservation with the inauguration of a force of Indian policemen, the process was ready to begin.[79]

Runners from the San Carlos Reservation arrived telling of preparations at San Carlos to receive more Indians. Now the Indians were very disturbed, besieging Corbusier and his wife for help. The Tonto were gearing up for warfare. On February 21, Assistant to the Commissioner, Special Agent L. Edwin Dudley arrived with several assistants and with orders from Washington to move the Indians immediately to San Carlos. The night was filled with excitement and anxiety. Dudley announced his plans, despite it being winter, to take the Indians across the mountains on foot instead of around by wagons and horses because it was shorter and quicker. The chiefs refused to come to conference, until Corbusier persuaded them to assemble.

About 600 Indians appeared before Dudley's tent, many armed and ready for action. A short distance away stood Schuyler and his thirty troopers and about forty enlisted Indian scouts. Dudley came out of his tent, threw a buffalo robe on a step, sat down, and leaned on one elbow as he talked. His speech was thick; Corbusier heard one Indian say: "He is drunk." He read portions of his orders "to take them to a much better place where they could be together among their friends." Then he abruptly rose and went back into his tent, assumed by all, to have another drink.

When he emerged again, an ominous silence settled over the crowd. Two rifles were cocked; Corbusier moved over and leaned against the two Indians who then lowered their hammers. This time Dudley repeated his statements in an incoherent fashion.

A spokesman for the chiefs said they would not go where their enemies would outnumber them. He spoke of this land as theirs from ancient times, of the promise made that the country along the river and ten miles on each side was theirs by agreement. He asked the commissioner why he called the Indians brothers. He asked the commissioner to not drink any more whiskey until the next day so that he could know what is being said. Many others spoke in an emotional and masterful way. With a wave of his hand, Dudley returned to his tent. The Indians crowded Corbusier, asking for his help, but he said they must obey orders from Grant, even though he felt he had forsaken them in their hour of need.

*William H. Corbusier—1875*

The next day Dudley appeared in better shape. Corbusier and Schuyler again made a plea that the Indians be taken around the mountains. Dudley replied: "They are used to the mountains, they're Indians. Let them walk. It is the shortest way."

On February 27, 1875, 1,500 Yavapai and Tonto Apache Indians started from the Rio Verde Agency, all on foot, to walk for six weeks 180 miles by rough trails over the mountains and across streams, through the Verde River Valley along Tonto Creek to the Salt River, then through Globe to the San Carlos Reservation. Only two months later, an executive order eliminated the Rio Verde Agency, restoring the land to public domain.[80]

Corbusier had no orders to accompany the Indians; indeed, he had been told to proceed to Fort Verde and await orders. But that morning, about a dozen chiefs appeared at Corbusier's tent to "escort" him. Upon being told he could not accompany them, they squatted in protest. Because Corbusier was an agency employee as well as an army officer, he was subject to the agent's orders, who in turn had been ordered by Dudley to say that a doctor was not needed on the trip. The Indians, obviously knowing Corbusier was their strongest advocate, refused to budge. Assistant Commissioner Dudley promised to make a decision about Corbusier when they reached Fort Verde, a promise reluctantly accepted by the Indians. Corbusier and his family stood and watched the procession leave, in long and silent lines, carrying all their belongings. One old man placed his aged wife in a large basket, her feet hanging out, and carried her on his back, a band from his head attached to the basket. He refused help, except at stream crossings—and he carried her the entire way.[81]

Fort Verde was sixteen miles down river and the easiest part of the journey. They reached Fort Verde on the third day, now accompanied by a herd of cattle. Corbusier was not found here, and the Indians refused to go on. Schuyler, however, had contacted General Crook, and when Corbusier reached Fort Verde he found orders to accompany the cavalry escort.

Keep in mind this band included young and old, healthy and sick, all clothed inadequately for winter. They were accompanied by Lieutenant George O. Eaton, who had relieved Schuyler, with fifteen troopers of Troop K, Fifth Cavalry. Al Sieber, Chief of the Indian Scouts, joined them at this point as well. Harry Hawes, the chief packer, and his four muleskinners, had fifteen to twenty mules for the march. In the early days of the trip, troubles centered around keeping the cattle together and getting along with the Tonto. Al Sieber directed the Tonto to lead the march—a position that made them comfortable with their enemies behind them.

As the line crossed the Verde River, it started to snow. They made four miles that day and camped in the snow. The next morning two of Dudley's assistants deserted and were never heard from again. All the old superstitions were active. The medicine men repeatedly attempted to avoid evil spots. Each chief had a different favorite trail. An organized march was impossible.

By March 10 the flour and meat supply was exhausted, and now the party faced the prospect of crossing the Salt River. The first difficult crossing was Strawberry Creek, swollen chest deep with storm water. Sieber and Eaton wished to delay the crossing, but Dudley urged them on. The soldiers rode back and forth carrying the old people, children, and babies. Tumbling rocks and debris in the rapid water caused multiple injuries and broken bones. As the water flow decreased, the crossing became easier, but two more difficult crossings followed. The Indians were now eating thistle and agave. Although there was plenty of game available, the Indians were not allowed to hunt.

After ten days, old animosities finally led to an outbreak of fighting with the Tonto. After making camp on the east branch of the Verde River near Bloody Basin, the Yuma Apache

(Western Yavapai) and the Mohave Apache (Eastern Yavapai) began yelling, their women crying out, "kill the Tonto." About fifty warriors rushed a mesa upon which the Tonto were camped, dropped to knees and bellies, and began to fire their guns. Dudley called for assistance from Eaton, and the troopers rushed the fight. As soon as the cavalrymen reached the mesa, the firing stopped. Al Sieber, Chief of the Indian Scouts, was instrumental in calming things down. Eaton advanced to the Yavapai leader, took his gun, and the Yavapai were driven back down the hill. Corbusier found twenty-five to thirty wounded Indians and four dead. These were buried, and these were the four skulls Corbusier sent to the Armed Forces Institute of Pathology when on the way back to Fort Verde he dug up the bodies, a direct response to a directive of 1862 by William Alexander Hammond, the first Surgeon General of the army, to collect and forward anatomical specimens.

Following this fight, Sieber took the point, followed by several scouts, then the Tonto. Next came the pack train with soldiers as a buffer in front of the Yavapai. Ahead was the hardest segment of the trip, a long hard climb, requiring single file, leading the horses (carrying the children), along the east slope of the Mazatzal Range, through the Mazatzal Wilderness, eastward into the Tonto Basin, along Tonto Creek to reach the Apache Trail near the present Roosevelt Dam. A total of twenty-five new babies arrived at San Carlos; Corbusier suspected that others were stillborn, some froze to death, and others were abandoned because nearly every day saw the birth of one or more babies.

After crossing the Salt River, the Yavapai again were in war paint. A bullet was fired, prompting Dudley to call out that he would go ahead and send back food. At the second camp, flour and beef awaited and better spirits returned. The San Carlos agent met the expedition thirty-five miles from San Carlos. The 1,361 surviving Indians straggled into San Carlos, located on the banks of the Gila River, a site now covered by the San Carlos Lake created by Coolidge Dam. San Carlos Reservation was later moved up the San Carlos River.

Several days later, Corbusier departed to return to Fort Verde. The Indians begged him to stay, and he later remembered well the wailing of women and children. In 1921, when Corbusier returned to the area he met some of the Yavapai who were children on the trip. He was dismayed to find that little had changed, their conditions were not different than that in 1875, still living in *oo-wahs*, sleeping on the ground. However, many had learned English and some had schooling. They reported that the missionaries had done little for them, so they had organized their own religious services, taking place on the weekend, combining Christianity with ancient beliefs and rites. Corbusier attended one such service, and one of the older men said: "Me John Brown." Corbusier forty-six years earlier had used the old tune *John Brown Had a Little Indian* to teach English. Soon the entire crowd was singing and dancing variations of the song. They wanted to know who was John Brown. Corbusier delighted them by replying that the only John Brown I knew was a Yavapai.

SEVERAL THOUSAND INDIANS, mainly Apache, were placed on the San Carlos Reservation in the 1870s. They were prohibited from hunting or gathering food in the surrounding mountains. A daily roll was taken in conjunction with the provision of rations.

The rationing system and the control it provided were maintained for over thirty years, until farming was re-established.

At San Carlos, the Yavapai lived in an area called Mineral Strip located in the southern part of the reservation; separated by the Gila River, the Tonto lived in the northern part. These were mountain and river people forced to live on hot, desert land that required irrigation. By 1882, treatment by the agent, J. C. Tiffany, had reached an intolerable level. Children were being systematically sent away to boarding schools. Several outbreaks led to battles and killing causing General Crook to be recalled to Arizona.[82] Riding a mule named Apache on an inspection tour, he heard and saw the sad state of affairs. He immediately expelled all those supported by Tiffany in their exploitation of the Indians. Two months later, Tiffany was also expelled from the reservation as a federal grand jury concluded the Indian reservation had been mismanaged, and the outbreaks and episodes were a consequence of Tiffany's behavior.

Geronimo and 120 of his Chiricahua followers fled the San Carlos Reservation in May 1885. Crook promised that any Indians who helped as scouts to recapture Geronimo could return to their land; thus about 100 Yavapai and Tonto Indians volunteered.[83] Whether Crook meant that the Yavapai as a people could return to their land is not clear, but that was the Yavapai interpretation that has persisted in their traditional history. A year after Geronimo's capture, the Yavapai and Apache were given permission to return to their homeland. Immediately a campaign of protest began by the Verde Valley settlers (approximately 300 families). Thus the Yavapai and Apache were not allowed to return. From December 1885 on, one of the Yavapai at San Carlos was Montezuma's cousin, Mike Burns. Descendants of the people who traveled the Yavapai Trail of Tears are still living today on the San Carlos Reservation.

Fort McDowell was abandoned in 1890. For about ten years, the Yavapai repeatedly requested permission to return to their land. In 1900, the Yavapai simply walked away from the San Carlos Reservation, leaving everything, including a few Yavapai who had married Apache. They actually received permission to do so, largely because the portion of the San Carlos Reservation where they lived, the Mineral Strip, was being mined by non-Indians for coal, and there was considerable pressure to have the Indians leave.[84] They returned to the Verde River Valley and the rest of the story occupies a good portion of this book. Many Yavapai (about 200 of the 500 that remained after years of epidemics and starvation) settled in the area around the old fort, and in 1903 the Fort McDowell Reservation was established by an executive order from President Theodore Roosevelt.

Today the Tolkopaya (also Tolkepaya), or Western Yavapai, are known as the Yavapai-Prescott Tribe (158 members in 2003). In 1935, seventy-five acres from the old Fort Whipple Military Reserve were transferred to them, along with two cows per family. With growth of the herd, the government later granted more land, making a total of 1,395 acres adjacent to Prescott.

The Wipukyipaya, people of the red rocks, (the Northeastern Yavapai or the Yavepe), and the Dilzhée (Tonto Apache) live at Fort Verde, fifty miles south of Flagstaff, as the Yavapai-Apache Nation, 1,250 tribal members in 2003 on 653 acres with a farming cooperative and a casino. Fort Verde was established in 1916.

The Kwovokopaya (also Kwevikopaya or Kewevkopaya), Southeastern Yavapai, were granted a reservation in 1903 at the old Fort McDowell military post, the largest of the Yavapai and Apache's three reservations, near the confluence of the Salt and Verde Rivers, abutting affluent Scottsdale and Fountain Hills. In 2003, tribal enrollment in the Fort McDowell Yavapai Nation was about 1,000 with 600 living on the reservation. The boundaries of the reservation were established by a survey in 1876—24,680 acres, ten miles along the Verde River, about four miles in width, including both sides of the river.

THESE WERE THE PEOPLE of Wassaja's early boyhood. They were the people to whom he returned in the last twenty-three years of his life as Carlos Montezuma.

## CHAPTER TWO

# Purchased by Gentile, Buffalo Bill, Ghost Dancers and Wounded Knee Creek

WASSAJA WAS PURCHASED by Carlo Gentile for thirty silver dollars.

The Pima Indian warriors who captured Wassaja and his two sisters took them by horseback (the first horse Wassaja had ever seen) on a two-day trip over the desert to Blackwater Camp, twenty-five miles north of Sacaton.[1] After living there for about a week, frightened and tormented by his captors, Wassaja was taken by three warriors on a journey (it was to be as far as Mexico if necessary) in an effort to sell or trade him for goods. At that time in the Arizona Territory, it was a common practice to sell captured women and children as slaves, to other tribes, to Mexicans, and even to White settlers.[2] Their first stop was Adamsville; the only remnant today is an overgrown old cemetery about two miles west of Florence, Arizona.

In Wassaja's story as told by Montezuma in later years, the Pima had already refused an offer of a horse.[3]

> I was taken from horseback, led to the store room and treated with cakes and candies. I took to them like a little pig. While waiting there I looked up on the wall, and whom should I see but another boy. He gazed at me constantly, and seemed to imitate me in everything. I moved, he moved; I grinned, the boy grinned; I swung my feet, he did the same. By this time I began to get my spunk up, and to look round for something to get even with that lad. I stepped to one side, he disappeared. All I could see now was the counter. It was a long time before I found that this was a looking-glass, and the boy who had provoked me was myself. …The white people tried to trade off the horse for me, but my captors thought I was worth more.[4]

Carlo Gentile (Jen-TILL-ee) purchased Wassaja for nearly all the money he had, thirty silver dollars.[5] Gentile himself, when interviewed in 1875 by a reporter for the *Chicago Tribune*, told a different version, claiming that he encountered the returning Pima warriors and persuaded them to sell Wassaja.[6] Supporting this version is Montezuma's claim in that same 1875 newspaper interview that Gentile was the first White man he ever saw.[7] Nevertheless, Montezuma later consistently placed his purchase in Adamsville.[8]

> I was amazed to see so many buildings. We rode on into the heart of the town, where we halted, tied our horses, went into a house and into a large square room. The first thing that attracted my attention was a suspicious looking object in the center composed of a large box with a neck-like projection pointing toward me (a camera on a stand). I thought this was a gun, so I moved away from that place.

## Arizona Territory

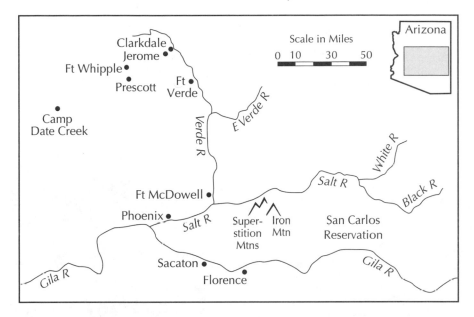

My other Indian friends were talking to one of the white men, while I was entertained by another. He showed me pictures on the wall. When I saw them I thought that holes were made through the walls and I was looking at the landscape through these, and that men's faces were placed in the walls.

While I was interested in the pictures, the three warriors stepped out of the room. Presently I looked round, and saw only the two white men. I made a rush for the door. It was locked. I beat against the wall, and struggled in the men's grasp. A new captivity faced me with more terror, because I was still attached to the Indians in so far that they were of my own race. After struggling awhile I fell backward from fatigue and fear. The door was unlocked. I took courage and made a rush out of the house. I looked down the road. I could see no trace of the Indians. Once more the fear of death seized me.

I was taken back into another room, and placed before a table on which were knives and forks and food. I did not want to eat, on account of being so thirsty. In my own language I asked for water. The people stood about me to catch the meaning of my words. "Water! Water!" I said, but they could not understand my want. An old squaw was brought in to interpret. She could not understand either, but she suggested water, and a pitcher full of water was handed to me. I took it with a shadow of a smile as if to say, "Thank you," and drank. Next I grabbed the meat, but dropped it on account of the taste of onion in which it was boiled.

A tureen of beans then attracted my attention. I nibbled these for awhile, to test them. They were good. I dipped my hands into them alternately and carried them in this way to my mouth. Before I had finished I was covered with them from head to waist. It was hard to tell whether "Injun" ate beans or beans ate "Injun."

The Indians who captured me belonged to the Pima Nation, and were friendly to the whites. The whites encouraged the tribe to make raids upon the Apaches, by giving them something for their captives. Today the mention of an Apache to three of four tribes along the Gila and Salt rivers makes them shudder, for the Apaches are very great enemies to them.

It was Mr. C. Gentile, an Italian gentleman, who had passed most of his life away from Italy, who bought me from these Indians. He paid thirty dollars for me. On the morning following my purchase, Mr. Gentile took me to the well to be washed. This was done in a tub, and this was my first step toward civilization.[9]

*Adamsville—1871*

Wassaja's father was reunited with his wife at the San Carlos Agency. Several months later, Wassaja's parents were told that he had been sighted at Camp Date Creek, but an effort to persuade him to escape had failed. Montezuma, at age nine recalled, "We had hard times sometimes and did not get enough to eat. They did not treat me kindly either and used to beat me and drive me out of the tent. A squaw told me that my father was there [San Carlos] and told me to run away. I told her that I would not—that I had nice things to eat now."[10] Wassaja's capture took place at a time when conflict with Whites had disrupted the Yavapai lifestyle, and acquiring adequate nutrition was a constant and formidable challenge.

A pass to leave the San Carlos Reservation was denied the parents, but, in an attempt to reach Wassaja, his mother left anyway. It was in a March 15, 1901, letter from Michael Burns, that Wassaja, now Carlos Montezuma, was told that his mother left camp without permission.[11] Discovering her absence, Apache Indian scouts were sent after her. Refusing to turn around, she was killed by a single shot near the Tonto Basin.[12] Wassaja's father lived at the San Carlos Reservation for four more years before dying in one of the epidemics. Another cousin, Seward C. Mott (Captain of the Indian police on the San Carlos Reservation) told Montezuma a different version of his mother's death, in an earlier letter in June 1898. Mott reported that Montezuma's mother and her aunt left the reservation without permission after his father's death, but she was indeed shot and killed by the Indian scouts.[13]

## CARLO GENTILE, AN ITALIAN PHOTOGRAPHER

Carlo Gentile was born in 1835, in Naples, Italy, into a wealthy, educated family from the foothills of Mount Vesuvius.[14] Gentile (often spelled Gentilé to emphasize the Italian pronunciation), taught by private tutors, became a young man sophisticated in the arts. When he left Italy with his father's inheritance, he never returned, traveling to Australia, the West Indies, South America, California, and eventually to Vancouver Island in British Columbia where he spent several years photographing Indians and people, and scenes in local mining towns.

Soon after arriving in Victoria, British Columbia, in September 1862, Gentile opened an imported and fancy goods store on Fort Street, under the Occidental Billiard Saloon. In the *Daily British Colonist*, he advertised trimmed straw bonnets and hats, evening dresses, ladies' underclothing, two rosewood pianos, musical boxes, violins, photographic albums, stereoscopic slides, and books lent to read. About a year later, he advertised the opening of his new photographic gallery annexed to his Fancy Goods Store, emphasizing portraits of children. Portraits soon became an important source of income for Gentile at the substantial sum at that time of twenty-five cents per person.

Indians from many tribes came to Victoria to trade and sell goods and services. Gentile established a good reputation among these Indians, and became the first British Columbia photographer to specialize in Indian portraits, using two techniques, one in the native state (perhaps with an eye toward marketing his pictures in Europe) and the other with the Indians sitting in non-Indian dress for formal portraits. His Majesty, King Freezy I, and His Royal Spouse, the Queen of the Songhish, visited the city on February 1, 1864, and sat for their portraits with Gentile. "Their majesties appeared to be highly delighted with their counterparts, although in neither case could the words of the poet be applied with justice,

*The Queen and King of the Songhish—1864*

'Love and Beauty still that visage grace.' Before taking his departure the wily but uxorious old King requested the artist to potlatch his better half four bits, which was immediately done, and the chickamen having been safely ensconced in the folds of the Royal robes (three point blankets) their majesties stalked off with a dignity becoming of their exalted station."[15] Unfortunately, King Freezy, after imbibing excessively, drowned with the capsizing of his canoe in the Victoria harbor.

Gentile himself was a gold prospector and even triggered a minor gold rush in the Alberni district.[16] He was very successful, both professionally and personally, and was recognized by society and politicians. It is surprising, therefore, to find an advertisement in the *Daily British Colonist* from March 16, 1865, listing his photographic gallery for sale. Nevertheless, he remained in business and active, making trips to photograph rough interior mining areas such as the Cariboo District and the Thompson River region. These photos drew praise and many of them can be seen in the National Archives of Canada in Ottawa and in the British Columbia Archives in Victoria.

By the age of thirty-one, Gentile, along with his wife, was friends with Governor William Pickering of the Washington Territory. Gentile and his wife were noted guests at Governor Kennedy's ball in British Columbia in honor of Queen Victoria's forty-seventh birthday. In August 1866, Gentile hired another photographer, Noah Shakespeare, to manage his business as he planned to visit Europe to present his photographs of the Pacific Northwest. 1866 recorded two events that led to our story: Wassaja was born south of the Four Peaks Mountains area of Arizona and Carlo Gentile set sail from Victoria on a steamer bound for Europe. At the very first stop in Olympia, Washington, Gentile discovered that the box containing his entire collection of photographs was missing, and he canceled his trip to Europe.

A month later, Thomas Allsop, who held Gentile's power-of-attorney, placed an advertisement in both the *Daily British Colonist* and the *Victoria Chronicle* stating: "LOST, SUPPOSED TO HAVE BEEN LEFT ON board the Eliza Anderson or Josie McNear, on or about the 13th of September last, a SQUARE DEAL BOX without lock, containing Photographic and Stereoscopic views of places in British Columbia and Puget Sound, cartes de vistite and other articles. Any one furnishing such information as shall lead to the recovery of the same, will be suitably rewarded."[17] Gentile obviously could not remember the name of his steamer!

Gentile never returned to Victoria, selling his gallery to Shakespeare in 1868. He went to San Francisco where in 1867 he again established a business in photography. What happened to his wife? Her disappearance is one of the mysteries in our story.

During his time in California, Gentile spent time in the Sierra gold fields, especially at Gold Run, eight miles north of Colfax near Lake Tahoe. Here he met John Ross Browne, a popular writer of the West. Browne aroused Gentile's interest with his stories of the Apache in Arizona, and late in 1867 or early in 1868, Gentile went to Arizona, which at that time, was in the midst of conflict with the Indians.[18] In fall 1868, Gentile was in the Verde River Valley, and the November 14, 1868, weekly *Arizona Miner* announced his arrival and the establishment of a studio in Prescott. He was only there a short time, however, and in January 1869, he returned to California, with a new gallery in Santa Barbara.

The lure of Indians, and perhaps of gold, was strong, and a year later Gentile returned to Arizona. In 1871, he was living in Florence and joined a party of about 300 miners aroused by the tales of a man in Prescott, Tom Miner, who sought a rich gold strike Miner had abandoned because of conflicts with hostile Indians. The party, called the Mogollon Mining and Exploration Company, led by Governor A.P.K. Safford, set out in August 1871.[19] This expedition was involved in several fights with Indian war parties, but by October, Gentile was back in Florence, ready for his fateful encounter with Wassaja and his Pima captors.

## WASSAJA AND GENTILE

Gentile was a cultured, kind, and very gentle man. Most incorrectly believed him to be a bachelor. He was also an adventurer, a risk taker, and a restless traveler.[20] Montezuma remembered that he "had no idea what would become of me. I was sure of a cruel death or be made to work as a slave forever and ever."[21]

*Carlo Gentile—Unknown Date*

*Savage Son*, the novel written by Owen Arnold and published in 1951,[22] presents a Christian missionary-slanted account of Montezuma's life, portraying every stereotypic image that characterized the Christian religious confrontation with Native Americans. Nevertheless, it is tempting to believe the stories of Gentile and Montezuma about these first days in the Florence area as recounted in the novel. The research for this novel, according to the Preface, was by Will C. Barnes, and the notes, records, and partial manuscript were obtained by the author from Barnes' widow. This material was collected by Barnes from Montezuma's widow, and subsequently placed as the Will C. Barnes Collection with the Arizona Historical Foundation in the Arizona State University Library.[23] Comparing the novel with historical documents, it is apparent that much of the story was the work of the author's imagination. A skeptical attitude toward the novel is further encouraged by the stereotypic Christianized attitude of the book. For example, the novel emphasizes the good father and son relationship between Montezuma and Gentile, saying it was better than that with Wassaja's parents because a savage father could not have been as devoted about the responsibility as a Christian. A romanticized biography of Montezuma written by the wife of the novel's author fares no better, with many historical inaccuracies and sentimental portrayals from a White point of view.[24]

Gentile learned that two girls captured by the Pima Indians had been given in exchange for two cows to Charles G. Mason, living on a ranch on the Gila River, near Adamsville. Gentile and Wassaja visited the ranch, and the two girls, in colored dresses and sunbonnets, recognized Wassaja as their brother.[25] A picture of all three survives in the National Anthropological Archives of the Smithsonian Institution, all three neatly dressed, holding hands and looking sad. This was the last Wassaja was to see of his sisters. After the death of Charles Mason, the woman who lived with Mason, Helen Grijalva, took them to Mexico.[26] One, now named Marianna, married a Mexican named Manuel Ruiz and was living in Globe, Arizona with her five children when Montezuma made contact by mail twenty-three years

*Wassaja and Sisters—1871*

later, in 1895.[27] Montezuma, by that time the school physician at the Carlisle Indian Industrial School in Pennsylvania, arranged for the two older boys, Juan and Manuel, to attend Carlisle. They were returned to Arizona in 1901; Montezuma's sister had died and Manuel Ruiz, their father, needed their help at home.[28] In addition, the school physician recommended that Juan be sent home because he had "tuberculor disease of the lymphatic glands of the neck and face."[29]

"La Capilla del Gila" was the first Church of the Assumption in Florence and also the first Catholic church in Central Arizona. Built by Father André Echallier in 1870, it was brand new when Carlo Gentile and Wassaja knocked on the door in November 1871. The building is standing today next to the newer church built in 1911.

On November 17, 1871, Father Echallier in La Capilla del Gila baptized Wassaja in a Catholic ceremony. Gentile named him Carlos after himself, adding an "s" for the Spanish version, and Montezuma, either because of the Montezuma ruins near Adamsville,[30] or because he was familiar with the legend of Montezuma Well, or because Montezuma, the great Aztec ruler, was an important mythological figure for the Indians of the Southwest. Wassaja was born in the same area as his capture, south of the Four Peaks, the southern extent of the Mazatzal Mountains, fifty-six miles due east of Phoenix.

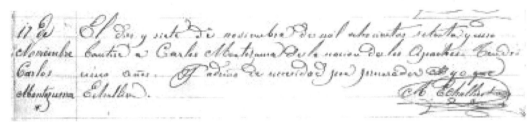

*Church of the Assumption Register* [31]

Although the exact date of his birth is not known, March 27, 1866 was chosen for the date of record on his baptismal entry written in Spanish in the Church of the Assumption Register.[32] His gravestone incorrectly indicates 1869.

Traveling to the Grand Canyon was no longer hazardous. The Walapai Indians, a Yuman-speaking tribe in northwestern Arizona, had been defeated by the army and interned at Camp Beale Springs, with some at Camp McDowell and some at Camp Date Creek. In November 1871, Gentile packed up and left with Montezuma for the Grand Canyon.

*La Capilla del Gila*

Gentile and Montezuma joined a party of explorers traveling in wagons.[33] At the Walapai camp, Montezuma was surprised and pleased to find people speaking his own language. It was at this camp that Montezuma was urged to escape to join his parents, but he declined, remembering at a later date that he was worried about replacing his three meals a day. They traveled to Fort Verde and to Fort Apache. In the spring of 1872, Carlos and Gentile traveled by wagon to the Zuñi country, to the Keresan Pueblos of Acoma, and Laguna. From there, they went to Albuquerque and to Santa Fe, catching a stagecoach to Trinidad, and then Pueblo, Colorado. Photographs from this trip are found in the lantern slide collection used by Montezuma for his Indian talks in his adult years (now available in the Collester Collection, the Smithsonian Institution National Anthropological Archives).

## MONTEZUMA AND BUFFALO BILL

Montezuma later wrote of his first encounter with the iron horse, when he and Gentile rode the train from Pueblo to Denver, Colorado.[34]

>…I looked and saw coming, an object without legs and very unlike a human being.
>
>The monster rolled in, puffing and sending in the air large curls of smoke. Steam was shooting from either side. A powerful arm turned the large wheels, while red-hot coal

dropped from beneath it. I stood there in the greatest amazement. Mr. Gentile told me this was an iron horse. My imagination traveled fast to make out the iron horse.

I could not speak English or I should have asked more about it; so I thought "if it is an iron horse a horse must be attached to it," and I came to the conclusion that they burned horses for the power or strength to draw what was behind. I thought it was really alive, for no dead thing could have the power of locomotion.[35]

This was the beginning of extensive travels, poorly documented by both Gentile and Montezuma, including visits to Denver, Washington, New York, Detroit, Grand Rapids, and Chicago. In November 1872, now living in Chicago, the traveling photographer became involved with Ned Buntline, the promoter of Buffalo Bill Cody, and Montezuma joined their first stage production.

William Frederick Cody was born in a log cabin in LeClaire, Iowa, on February 26, 1846.[36] In his teenage years, Cody drifted from job to job, even riding with the Pony Express for a short time. He served as a guide and scout with the Seventh Kansas Union regiment during the Civil War. Afterwards, his skills as a tracker, rider, and marksman rapidly made him in demand, and by 1866, he was, at age twenty, serving General William T. Sherman, Commander General of the Military Division of the Mississippi. Over the next decade, Cody came to know many famous names of the era, including Wild Bill Hickok and George Armstrong Custer. He even scouted for the Tenth U.S. Cavalry in 1867, the very same year Richard Henry Pratt was appointed to this unit (Chapter 3).

Cody was first called Buffalo Bill in 1867, although it was not until he started killing buffalo for the Kansas Pacific Railroad that the name became widely known.[37] Cody was an excellent shot, but part of his prowess in buffalo hunting was due to the method he adapted from the Indians. Using a fast horse, riding bareback, he approached the head of the herd, shot the leaders, and crowded the animals to run to the left in a circle. He then picked them off one by one, twenty to forty at a time. The buffalo were so readily available and so many were killed at a time for the railroad contractors that only the hump and hindquarters were used, the rest left on the prairie. The name "Buffalo Bill" spread across Kansas, was reported throughout the country, and by 1890, became Cody's trademark.

Cody was recognized for his bravery, reliability, and endurance. On one occasion, delivering dispatches, he rode 300 miles in about fifty-eight hours.[38] By 1868, General Philip Sheridan had appointed Cody as Chief of Scouts for the Fifth Cavalry. He had exceptional knowledge of the country, using trails and routes others did not know. By now he had the look that was to become famous: long, flowing hair; a wide mustache that curled upwards at each end; a small goatee on his chin; fringed buckskins and a large sombrero (the forerunner of the ten-gallon hat).

At Fort McPherson in Nebraska, Buffalo Bill met Ned Buntline. Buntline was the pseudonym of Edward Zane Carroll Judson, author of hundreds of novels (writing as many as six per week), most of which were the so-called dime novels of the late 1800s. Out of this meeting came *Buffalo Bill, the King of Border Men*, the first installment appearing on December 23, 1869, in the *New York Weekly*. It appeared in book form later, in 1881, under the title *Buffalo Bill and His Adventures in the West*. A year after meeting Buntline, in 1870, Cody met another principal in his first stage show, John Burwell Omohundro, "Texas Jack." Texas Jack served in the Confederate Army and came north in the first big cattle drive from Texas to Nebraska. During this time period Texas Jack and Buffalo Bill were hunting buffalo and guiding hunting parties for rich and important people. Considerable publicity followed Cody's successful conduct of a hunt for Grand Duke Alexis, the twenty-one-year-old son of the Russian Czar, Alexander II. In between these activities, skirmishes with the Indians continued. On May 22, 1872, Cody was awarded the Medal of Honor for his bravery during an encounter near Fort McPherson. However, the Medal of Honor was being given out indiscriminately in those days, and it was soon withdrawn anyway because Cody was employed as a civilian scout, not a soldier.[39] It was later reinstated by Congress, but not until after his death.

Cody resigned as a government scout in December 1872 (temporarily, because he was to periodically return) having served four generals and taken part in seven expeditions and fourteen battles against Indians.[40] He had formed friendships with royalty, generals, and the wealthy. During that previous year, Buntline was urging Cody to go on stage; there was money to be made. Texas Jack was all in favor of this venture, and after resigning their positions, Cody and Texas Jack went to Chicago to join Buntline.

Arriving in Chicago, the two frontiersmen discovered that Buntline had no script. Not a major obstacle for Buntline, locked in his hotel room for four hours, he wrote *The Scouts of the Prairie*, or *Dove Eye, the Lodge Queen*, based on the latest Buffalo Bill serial, *Buffalo Bill's Last Victory*.

*The Scouts of the Prairie, and Red Deviltry As It Is!* (the final title) featured Buffalo Bill and Texas Jack. Montezuma, at age six, first appeared in the December 16 performance, playing *Azteka*, in a comical scene III.[41]

> My little stunt was to appear on the stage in little Indian garb with bow and arrow. Ned Buntin [sic] appeared in drunken state and hails me: "Who are you?" I replied, "I am the President of the United States." As he goes from me I shot him with my bow & arrow and hit him. Mr Gentile was the advertising agent and ticket collector.[42]

The show was a popular success despite critical reviews. It is speculated that Gentile's involvement in this show was a consequence of Gentile's friendship with an Italian ballerina, Giuseppina Morlacchi, who played the role of Dove Eye, the Indian maiden in the show. The show had its impact; Morlacchi fell in love with Texas Jack Omohundro and married him. Morlacchi studied dance at La Scala and introduced the cancan to America. The *Chicago Tribune* portrayed her as "a beautiful Indian maiden with an Italian accent and a weakness for scouts."[43] Gentile capitalized on the show, selling pictures taken with members of the

*Montezuma—Age 6*

## The Scouts Programme!

Messrs. CODY, JUDSON, OMOHUNDRO & NIXON..........PROPRIETORS
Manager.........Col. E. Z. C. Judson | Scenic Artist.........Frank D. Hill
Gen'l Director.........Jno. Burke | Properties and Effects.........Jno. Burke
Stage Manager.........W. J. Halpin | Costumes.........Mrs. Burke
Armourer.........W. J. Speck | Music.........Carlo Paul

The New Sensation Drama, written by NED BUNTLINE, and founded on some of the most thrilling and interesting incidents of his great New York Weekly Indian Stories, entitled

# SCOUTS OF THE PRAIRIE

## And Red Deviltry As It Is!

### CAST OF CHARACTERS:

BUFFALO BILL—by the Original Hero..........Hon. W. F. CODY
TEXAS JACK—by the Original Hero..........J. B. OMOHUNDRO
CALE DURG..........NED BUNTLINE
DOVE EYE..........M'LLE MORLACCHI
Mormon Ben..........Mr. Wentworth
Sly Mike..........Mr. Walters
Phelim O'Laugherty..........Harry Gilbert
Carl Pretzel..........Walter Fletcher

### INDIANS.

| | | |
|---|---|---|
| Wolf Slayer | | W. J. Halpin |
| Big Eagle | | W. H. Ferris |
| Ar-Sa-ka | Pawnee and Indian Chiefs | Grassy Chief |
| Ato-pi-tan | | Prairie Dog |
| Au-na-ka-wa | | Water Chief |
| Te-ke-tis-pu-ta | | Big Elk |
| Kit-ka-hi-ona | | Great River |
| Chuh-Kah | | Seven Stars |
| Black Eye | | |
| Nat-tah | | |

### Synopsis of Scenery and Incidents:

[smaller descriptive text, partially illegible]

# PRAIRIE ON FIRE.

Magnificent Scenic Effects; Life-like Illustrations of a Great Western Prairie, as seen when on Fire. Immensely Grand; K. P. Railway Train in a Herd of Buffalo—Clear the Track.

To be preceded by the short but Territory Laughable Farce of

# A KISS IN THE DARK

Mr. Pettibone..........Harry Gilbert
Frank Fathom..........Harry Wentworth
Mrs. Pettibone..........Jennie Logan
Mary..........Mrs. Burke
Unknown..........Miss Jackson

## MATINEES WEDNESDAY AND SATURDAY!

50 Cents.........Children.........25 Cents

D. H. ELLIOTT. (Gen'l West. Agent Kan. Pac. R'y.,) Trav. Agent for this Combination.

cast, and it was after a few performances that Montezuma joined the cast on stage.

The dialogue, of course, was of minor importance. Struggling to learn the lines, Buntline told Cody to read the cues. "Cues be damned," Cody exclaimed, "I never heard of anything but a billiard cue."[44] In New York, the *New York Times* suggested that if Buntline actually spent four hours writing the play, it was difficult to see what he had been doing all that time. But it was a dynamic, action-packed show, and audiences loved it. The *New York Herald* was years ahead of defining "camp" when it said: "Everything is so wonderfully bad it is almost good."

The action and the stereotypes, presenting and embellishing scenes and stories from real life experiences, produced the genre of the Western with horses, guns, heroes, and villains. Audiences in the East were thrilled to have their imaginations and emotions stirred; philosophy and literature were not necessary.

The company traveled to St. Louis, Cincinnati, Louisville, Indianapolis, Toledo, Cleveland, Pittsburgh, and Franklin, Pennsylvania, and by now, Montezuma was identified as the Apache-child of Cochise. After Franklin in March 1873, Gentile and Montezuma were no longer part of the show. Montezuma and the Buffalo Bill Wild West show were to cross paths again, in a controversy that followed a wreck of one of the show's trains, and Montezuma, years later, strongly objected to Wild West shows. It is relevant to our story, therefore, to recount the history of the show after 1873.

## BUFFALO BILL'S WILD WEST SHOW

Buntline was no longer part of the stage show after 1873. John M. Burke, the manager of Texas Jack's new wife, Guiseppina Morlacchi, became a key figure: advance man, publicist, manager, and total devotee of Buffalo Bill. Wild Bill Hickok joined the troupe in 1874, but only lasted a year, pulling pranks and enjoying confrontations that he easily solved by physical force. For the next ten years, Cody spent most of the year with his theatrical activities, but amazingly in the summer he returned to the prairie to serve as a guide or army scout, activities that certainly enhanced his stage presence as the real thing.

On June 10, 1876, Cody joined the Fifth Cavalry as a scout, meeting General Sheridan at Laramie on June 14. Cody and Sheridan traveled to the Red Cloud Agency in Dakota, and while there, General George Crook fought the Battle of the Rosebud on June 17, and Custer and his troops were wiped out at Little Big Horn on June 26. During this time period, Montezuma's cousin, Mike Burns, served as an aide to Captain Hall S. Bishop who was with General Crook's troops. In July, troops had marched to Hat Creek, Nebraska, where in a skirmish Cody killed and scalped the only Indian casualty, a Cheyenne chief named Yellow Hair.[45] This encounter was exaggerated and its veracity challenged, but it became part of the Buffalo Bill myth.

Buffalo Bill's Wild West was launched in 1883, a show on a large scale featuring marksmanship, riding, roping and tying, wagons, nearly 200 horses, fifteen to twenty buffalo, elk, steers, mules, ponies, and about 100 Indians. By 1885, the show took a shape that was to be essentially unchanged until it ended. The show hit big-time revenues in 1886, when one-night stands were abandoned for extended stays. Annie Oakley (Phoebe Ann Moses) joined the show in 1884. She chose the name Oakley from the shooting grounds in Cincinnati where she first met her husband, her opponent in her very first shooting contest. They remained married until their deaths in 1926, twenty days apart. Annie Oakley traveled with Buffalo Bill for seventeen years, the highest paid performer after Cody. She could out-shoot everyone. Complimentary tickets to the theater were called "Annie Oakleys," because they were punched in the center just like the cards Annie Oakley perforated with shots from her rifle.

The Wild West began with music from a cowboy band and the Grand Processional Review, with Indians coming first in full regalia, then Mexican *vaqueros*, followed by the cowboys, then the Sioux warriors, ending with Buffalo Bill. Annie Oakley started the program, wowing the audience in only ten minutes. A race across the arena was followed by the accurately enacted Pony Express. Buffalo Bill re-created his famous encounter with Yellow Hair, then the cowboy skills of riding and lassoing were featured. Buffalo Bill demonstrated his marksmanship, and the entire troupe presented attacks on a stagecoach, the repelling of Indians, riding and roping of wild steers, a buffalo hunt, and finally, the rescue of settlers in a cabin under attack by Indians. The profit in 1885 came to $100,000. From 1887 to 1892, the Wild West was a triumph throughout Europe, performing before huge crowds in England, France, Spain, Holland, Scotland, Italy, and Germany. The troupe of 640 members was a sensation in Germany, where the efficiency of its special railroad train and kitchens taught the German Army some important lessons (German officers were constantly present, taking notes).

In 1893, the name of Buffalo Bill's show was changed to "Buffalo Bill's Wild West and Congress of Rough Riders of the World," in keeping with a new highlight on horses and riding created for the World's Columbian Exposition in Chicago. The show, with its Sioux and Cheyenne Indians, and now including Russian Cossacks, Arabs, and Syrians, opened in April 1893. The crowds were enormous. The show took place on fifteen acres with a grand-stand seating 18,000 people opposite the fairground's main entrance for the Exposition. Remember the Wild West had been out of America for nearly five years, and the popularity of the Show and Cody's reputation reached an all-time high; for 186 days, the show was the hit of the Exposition, clearing $1 million profit. One of the favorite attractions was Cody's camp, always open for exploration by the public, and which now contained Sitting Bull's cabin, dismantled, shipped, and reassembled, complete with bullet holes. The show Indians especially enjoyed riding the carousel ponies on the merry-go-round in the Midway, their whoops and yells always attracting spectators.

The Indian images presented by the show persist to this day. The humanitarian reformers and leaders such as Commissioner of Indian Affairs Thomas J. Morgan, Richard Pratt, and Carlos Montezuma objected strongly to the portrayal and glorification of what was, in their view, savage behavior. It was especially galling when alumni of the Carlisle Indian School participated in the show.[46]

The show continued to be successful for years, until 1915, adding new acts reflecting events of the times. In 1897, it traveled over 6,000 miles and appeared in 104 cities, and in that year, Cody, Wyoming, was established, a town whose development remained a passion for William Cody. In 1899, the show traveled over 11,000 miles. On October 28, 1901, leaving Charlotte, North Carolina, the second section of the show's train had a head-on collision with a Southern Railway freight train, No. 75, at four o'clock in the morning. It was a straight track at the site of the collision, and both engineers managed to reduce their speeds to eight miles per hour before they jumped from their locomotives. It was an error on the part of the freight train crew, and Engineer Lynch, fearing retribution from the men of the wrecked show train, took to the woods and disappeared on a northbound train.[47] Only two of over 100 horses survived. Not a single person was killed. Annie Oakley was severely injured and her career was over (although some claim the real problem was inadvertent imprisonment in a hot bath for a prolonged period of time). Oakley retired at the age of forty-one, although she continued to make theatrical and shooting appearances until the year before she died. After fifty years of marriage, her husband, Butler, and Oakley died in the same year, 1926, and were buried side by side in Ohio. From 1902 to 1907, the Show played in Europe and then returned to America, continuing to be popular until at last Cody retired in 1915 after five years of farewell tours.

Buffalo Bill was a kind and generous man, giving his money away freely and investing poorly. A brave and courageous man, Buffalo Bill was above all a showman. By voice and deed, he regarded everyone compassionately and equally; he was fair and honest in his dealings with both Indians and Whites, earning affection and respect.[48] Though accused of abusing the Indians in his show, investigations repeatedly cleared all charges, and there is no evidence from the Indians themselves of complaints.[49] William Frederick Cody died January 10, 1917, in Denver, and on that day the world's attention was directed to him, not the world war. At the time of his death, his worth was $65,000.

In June 1885, the Sioux chief, Sitting Bull, now fifty-four years old, joined Buffalo Bill's Wild West. After the defeat of Custer, Sitting Bull and about 160 followers (Hunkpapa Sioux nomads and warriors of the plains) retreated to Canada. Most of his band returned to the Dakota Territory, and five years later Sitting Bull surrendered. After two years in custody at Fort Randall in South Dakota, he was sent to the Standing Rock Reservation. By this time,

Sitting Bull was virtually alone in his belligerence against Whites. Cody wanted Sioux Indians for his show, and with persistent effort and pressure on the secretary of the interior, he secured permission to recruit not only warriors but Sitting Bull as well. Sitting Bull was widely advertised and was a hit of the show, riding nobly and alone into the arena in his buckskin, paint, and feathers to endure being hissed and booed as a villain; he appeared from June to October 1885. The year of Sitting Bull and Annie Oakley, 1885, the Wild West appeared before more than a million people in forty cities, turning a profit of $100,000. Sitting Bull used his public exposure opportunity to communicate with the commissioner of Indian affairs and in a personal appearance with President Cleveland to express his concerns and unhappiness with the conditions at Standing Rock Reservation.

Like all who came to know and work with Cody, Sitting Bull developed a strong friendship with Buffalo Bill, a friendship that was to pull Cody into the confrontation that resulted in the Wounded Knee Massacre.

*Sitting Bull and Buffalo Bill*

### GHOST DANCERS AND WOUNDED KNEE CREEK

Carlos Montezuma fell in love with a young Yankton Sioux woman, Zitkala-Ša, in 1901 (Chapter 9). She grew up during the desperate years when the Sioux were confined to reservations, the Ghost Dance religion spread among Indians throughout the West, and the last U.S. military campaign against Indians ended at Wounded Knee Creek. Zitkala-Ša emerged from this period of history with a firm hold on her Indian culture and heritage, and battled with Montezuma who was a product of the assimilation philosophy (Chapter 3).

Native-Americans were organized by tribes, and the Indian conflict was a process of conquest tribe by tribe. The United States Indian Peace Commission was created in 1867 by Congress to address Indian unrest in the West.[50] Negotiations with tribes were placed in the hands of a group of civilian and military leaders who had the authority to meet with chiefs and create treaties, and in the process, produce reservations. A primary aim was to secure safe conditions along the railroad lines being constructed throughout the West, as well as the trails used by settlers and merchants. The major treaty with the southern tribes in the West was signed at Medicine Lodge Creek, Kansas, in October 1867, and with the northern tribes at Fort Laramie in 1868. The Fort Laramie treaty created the Great Sioux Reserve west of the Missouri River in the Dakotas.[51]

The discovery of gold in the Black Hills in the southwestern portion of the Sioux Reserve challenged the Fort Laramie agreement. After the defeat of Custer in 1876,

Congress unilaterally gave the Sioux an ultimatum. No further food and supplies would be provided unless the Sioux Reserve was reduced in size. A special commission secured the signatures of a sufficient number of chiefs to make the new arrangement seem acceptable.

In 1870, there were twice as many Indians as White settlers in the Dakota Territory, but by 1880, Indians were outnumbered by Whites, six to one. Pressure on the Indian reservations increased. This pressure was heavily supported by the railroads and local merchants and farmers. The success of a railroad was dependent upon local business and traffic, not the cross-country lines.[52] Local traffic required White settlers and merchants, and a growth in population. Tribal lands were an obstacle to economic growth and prosperity. Thus, a confluence of interests produced a majority in Congress. Southerners concerned about a concentration of railroads in the North, supported railroad expansion in the West. Agrarian reformers were seeking land for settlers. Western politicians responded to local business and economic pressures. These various and diverse interests were localized, either in issue or region. The philosophy of assimilation (Chapter 3) that went hand in hand with a reduction in Indian lands, gave these groups a national, global theme, one that also attracted the eastern reformers and humanitarians.

By the late 1880s, Indians were confined to reservations. The bulk of the eastern tribes had been removed to lands in the West,[53] and western tribes had been confined by military force. The allotment process was now at work causing a loss of land (Chapter 3). Treaties were made only to be broken or re-negotiated. Indians had little concept of buying and selling, and they were slow to learn the meaning of a treaty, although they learned rapidly that a treaty was not viewed as a sacrosanct agreement by the Whites. The Sioux had lost millions of acres, and Sitting Bull was emerging again, this time as a strong voice for the preservation of the tribal lands. In October 1887, Sitting Bull traveled to Washington with sixty Sioux leaders and effectively united the group against accepting the government's offer (at a very low price) for millions of acres in western Dakota. The Senate appointed a committee with Henry Dawes as chairman to visit the Sioux and make a recommendation. For Henry Dawes, one of Lincoln's pallbearers, Indians were to provide him with a national platform and a popular cause. The committee's report, now Senator Dawes's Sioux Bill, passed in April 1888, and established the current Sioux reservations. The bill provided for the disbursement of "useless and unnecessary Indian lands" and the establishment of a fund (from the sales of the land) to be used for education and the purchase of cattle.[54] In 1889, unified Sioux opposition disintegrated, and a deal was made as General George Crook convinced a large majority of eligible Sioux voters to accept new reservations. Conditions on the Sioux (and essentially all Indian) reservations reached a low point of poverty, dependence upon government rations, hunger, disease, and idleness.[55]

Today the population of American Indians is about two and one-half million, increasing from its nadir in 1890–1900.[56] Of the total population in all fifty states, two and one-half million people (0.9 percent) reported in the 2000 census that they were full-blood American Indians, and an additional 1.6 million people reported that they were partially American Indian.[57] American Indians migrated from Asia approximately 25,000 years ago. The native population in North and South America eventually numbered in the tens of millions, perhaps as high as seventy million. In 1500, the

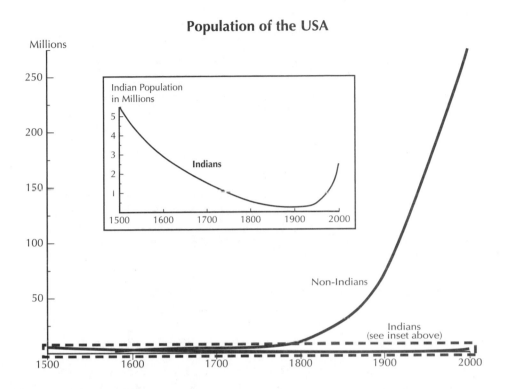

## Population of the USA

American Indian population of the continental United States was about five and one-half million. The population of the rest of the world in 1500 was around 500 million. Life expectancy before contact between the Indian and non-Indian populations was about the same in the two hemispheres of the world. Those that survived infancy with its high mortality rate could expect to live forty-five to fifty years.[58] Contact, of course, brought to the Indians smallpox, cholera, chicken pox, scarlet fever, mumps, measles, diphtheria, influenza, typhoid fever, and the plague (and to this must be added warfare and alcoholism); tuberculosis was an exception, having been carried from Africa to Asia to the Americas.[59] Other diseases that were present before White contact, although with low prevalence, include tularemia, rabies, amebic dysentery, hepatitis, herpes, pertussis, and poliomyelitis.[60]

Beginning in the 1500s, repeated waves of epidemics had devastating effects. From a total of about seventy million Indians in North and South America, the number rapidly declined to only four to five million. By 1800, the Indian population of the United States was only 600,000, and the nadir, a little under 250,000, was reached by 1900. The scale of Indian depopulation was enormous, about a 95 percent decrease. During this same time period, the non-Indian population of the U. S. was growing rapidly, reaching over seventy-five million by 1900. It has been argued that the mammoth change in Indian population left White policy makers with the firm belief that Indians would disappear in the twentieth century.[61] Along with all the other factors that led to the reservations system, one can add the rationalization that a dwindling population would need less and less land.

▶   ▲   ▲   ◀

THERE WAS A SOLAR ECLIPSE on January 1, 1889. A Paiute sheepherder in Nevada, named Wovoka, ill with fever during the eclipse, received a vision (in fact, he believed he went to heaven), and proclaimed himself either a Messiah or a prophet, although many, including the Sioux, believed him to be the Messiah.[62] Wovoka was already a respected shaman among the Paiute. Growing up, he lived with the Wilson family, acquiring his English name, Jack Wilson, and learning the tenets of Christianity.[63] He began to preach "Ghost Dances," a ceremony revealed in his vision, dedicated to the coming (relatively soon) of a time when dead Indians (the "ghosts" being their spirits) would arise, live Indians would not die, the buffalo would return, and most importantly, White men would disappear. The belief in his power was sealed among the Paiute when during a time of drought he accurately predicted the onset of rain. The Ghost Dance religion, combining elements of Christianity with Indian heritage, was actually pacifistic in nature, grounded in Christian ethics, objecting to aggression, fighting, and war (these were not necessary; all that was necessary was to be good and pure because the end was near). The Sioux version, however, was decidedly antagonistic towards the Whites.[64]

The circular, side-stepping to the left Ghost Dance was not a new dance; it was derived from traditional Indian dancing, but it was faster (indeed, frenzied) and carried on for days until exhaustion and trances led to visions and communications with ancestors. The dance was accompanied by songs that began as spontaneous creations from individual dancers with the more powerful prophecies becoming part of the opening and closing ceremonies. The word spread rapidly, and soon visitors from adjoining tribes, then from distant tribes, were visiting the Walker Lake Reservation in Nevada to learn of the teaching and become converted. The Ghost Dance religion rapidly became part of virtually every western tribe.[65] This swift spread was significantly aided by the returning students from the Indian boarding schools who could overcome the barrier of different languages by their ability to read and write English.

Sioux leaders traveled to Nevada by train, spent a week learning the message and the movements and songs of the Ghost Dance, and returned to find a receptive audience. The summer of 1890 proved disastrous for Sioux crops; heat, wind, and lack of rain brought a new round of hunger and desperation. In the second half of 1890, the Indians on the Sioux reservations were Ghost Dancing and wearing Ghost Shirts—cloth, sacklike shirts painted in bright colors and covered with traditional designs. Indeed, it was the ghost shirts that first caused alarm among army and government officials. The Sioux Indians believed the ghost shirts were bulletproof, and U.S. officials worried over why the Indians needed bulletproof shirts.

Sioux is the shortened and changed (by the French) version of the Ojibwe word, *Nadvesiu*. The Sioux were originally forest people in the upper Mississippi River area. The eastern Sioux are the Santee Sioux, speaking the Dakota dialect. The Yankton and Yanktonai speak a Nakota dialect. Those who were driven into the plains and acquired firearms and horses, developed over 100 years into the Teton Sioux with a way of life that centered around hunting and the buffalo, and speaking the Lakota dialect.[66] This group of Indians was known as the *Dakota*, a word meaning allies, as well as the *Sioux*, a name that means enemy. Thus, the Dakota and the Sioux were the same people, a loose confederation of seven tribes: Oglala, Brulé, Hunkpapa, Miniconjou, Sans Arc, Two Kettle, and Blackfeet.[67]

The impact of the decimation and loss of the buffalo on the Sioux cannot be overrated. Buffalo contributed to food, clothing, housing, and ultimately to social and individual behavior and customs. The decade from 1880 to 1890 was a stressful time for all Indians, but especially for the Sioux, as the old lifestyle was changing. Warfare was no longer possible. The rituals, celebrations, and mournings associated with raids and hunting no longer had meaning. Even diet and clothing had to change. Within a decade, the Sioux were no longer free bands of hunters and warriors, but a confined, captive people under the supervision of U.S. Government agents. However, the Sioux had not yet abandoned their struggle with White men.

Ghost Dancing took place in dance camps, teepees with hundreds of men, women, and children on the creeks that were tributaries of the major rivers, the Grand, Moreau, Cheyenne, and White.[68] There was a rapid and progressive commitment until the dance camps were active day after day in the fall of 1890. Sitting Bull at least saw Ghost Dancing as a form of protest against the White man.[69] He supported its spread and practice on the Standing Rock Reservation. The dance camps throughout the Sioux reservations (except among the Yankton and Blackfeet) became increasingly fanatical and belligerent. Attempts by agents to suppress the dances were confronted and turned away by warriors armed with guns. The surrounding settlers were justifiably alarmed, especially in view of the size of the Sioux population:[70]

| Reservation | Population in 1889 |
| --- | --- |
| Standing Rock | 1,700 |
| Cheyenne River | 3,000 |
| Lower Brulé | 1,000 |
| Crow Creek | 1,000 |
| Pine Ridge | 7,800 |
| Rosebud | 4,000 |
| TOTAL | 18,500 |

By November 1890, the government was sufficiently concerned that President Harrison ordered the War Department to suppress the movement. General Nelson A. Miles, commander of the Division of the Missouri, ordered troops (half of the U.S. Army) into the Sioux area. In a carefully orchestrated move, cavalry and infantry simultaneously entered the Pine Ridge Agency and the Rosebud Agency at dawn on November 20, 1890.[71] Within weeks, the mobilization was complete, and the Indians were now confronted with the presence of an awesome number of troops. Ghost Dancing, however, was not suppressed, but incited to an ever greater level of activity.

There was an impression, fostered by the agent of the Standing Rock Reservation, James McLaughlin, that Sitting Bull was a primary force in the movement and that his arrest would halt the Ghost Dancing. Remembering that Buffalo Bill and Sitting Bull were friends, General Miles authorized Colonel Cody (who still carried his rank with the Nebraska militia) to secure and deliver Sitting Bull to the U.S. Army.

Returning from England with the Wild West show, Cody immediately met with Miles and was soon on his way to North Dakota by train. Agent McLaughlin feared the precipitation of a conflict, but Cody simply wanted to meet with Sitting Bull and persuade him by force of their friendship to talk with General Miles. Arriving at the Standing Rock Reservation, Buffalo Bill filled a wagon with presents, mainly sweets. Even the local military officers were opposed to Cody's interference; they tried to prevent the mission by drinking

## Sioux Reservations

Cody under the table, but it was Buffalo Bill who was able to get up in the morning and drive his wagon out to meet Sitting Bull.[72] McLaughlin, however, succeeded; an order from President Harrison recalled Cody before he could reach Sitting Bull's camp.

Events rapidly led to conflict in December 1890, when Short Bull, the leader of the Ghost Dancers at Pine Ridge, sent a message to Sitting Bull that the coming was now very soon (Spring 1891), hastened by White interference, and that Sitting Bull should come to the Pine Ridge Agency to be present at the moment of the coming. In response to Sitting Bull's request for a pass to leave the reservation, McLaughlin mobilized the Indian police to arrest him. On a cold night in the early dawn, December 15, about forty Sioux police surrounded Sitting Bull's cabin. Placed under arrest, Sitting Bull, in the midst of a gathering crowd of supporters, suddenly resisted. The Chief of the Indian Police, Bull Head, was shot by the leader of Sitting Bull's followers, Catch-the-Bear. Although mortally wounded, Bull Head managed to fire a shot into Sitting Bull's chest, followed by a shot from Sergeant Red Tomahawk to Sitting Bull's head. Soon, six Indian policemen and eight Indian followers of Sitting Bull were dead.

When the shooting started, Sitting Bull's horse (a gift from Buffalo Bill) that had been saddled by the Indian police for his transport, prompted by the cue of the gunshots, went into his Wild West routine, sitting down with one hoof in the air in the midst of the battle.[73] The horse was believed to be either Ghost Dancing or possessed by the spirit of Sitting Bull. After the altercation was over, the horse was obtained by Buffalo Bill and ridden by him during the Wild West shows at the Columbian Exposition in Chicago in 1893.

Cody could probably have prevented this violent death of Sitting Bull. Emotions at that time among both the military and the Indians in North and South Dakota were at an intense nervous pitch, and some confrontation was likely. Sitting Bull's death played a role in instigating the Massacre at Wounded Knee Creek. Many of Sitting Bull's followers fled to the camp of Big Foot on the Cheyenne River, a gathering of about 300 ardent Ghost Dancers. On December 17, 1890, the army decided to arrest Big Foot. Hearing of Sitting Bull's death, Big Foot broke camp, intending to move south. On the way to Pine Ridge, the band of Indians met a large body of troops (probably not by chance because they had been under surveillance) from Custer's old regiment, the Seventh Cavalry, under the command of Major Samuel Whitside. The Indians (less than 400 total, mostly women, children, and old men), taken to a cavalry bivouac on Wounded Knee Creek, camped in more than 100 teepees under the guard of about 500 troops and heavy guns.

The next day, December 29, 1890, the Indians were surrounded by the troopers now under the command of Colonel James W. Forsyth, and were in the process of being disarmed amidst anger and protests. The first shot is believed to have been fired by an Indian, incited by Yellow Bird, an old medicine man. But immediately everything opened up. When the two sides separated, the heavy guns placed on a ridge above the camp fired into the Indians. The conflict quickly turned into a series of smaller battles. The number of Indians dead, counted three days after a blizzard had passed, reached 153. It is estimated that there were another twenty to thirty removed earlier from the site.[74] White casualties numbered twenty-five killed and thirty-nine wounded. The Indian wounded were collected and treated under the supervision of the Pine Ridge Agency physician, Charles A. Eastman, a Santee Sioux who received his medical degree one year after Carlos Montezuma.[75] Wounded Knee was a tragic conflict that neither side planned nor wanted.

After two more weeks of tense encounters and isolated skirmishes, the last military Indian campaign ended with the formal surrender of the Sioux at Pine Ridge on January 16, 1891, and a week later the troops dispersed after the largest military review (3,500 troops) since the Civil War. Buffalo Bill was there, the last day of his government service. Twenty-five Ghost Dance leaders were taken as prisoners. Later that year, they joined an additional seventy-five Sioux Indians in the Wild West show when they left for Germany. General Miles and Commissioner Morgan both believed this would be an excellent method to isolate the Ghost Dance leaders and to change their attitudes toward White society. A year later upon their reentry into the United States, eleven of the prisoners were returned to prison, but within seven months all had returned to their homes.[76]

Ironically, the Sioux performed the Ghost Dance in the Wild West show, the only remnant of the Ghost Dance religion that quickly was discarded when the coming failed to arrive. The Ghost Dance religion was the last Indian movement that did not accept some accommodation of White society.

THESE WERE THE PEOPLE, and these were the conditions that surrounded the youth of Zitkala-Ša (Chapter 9).

## CHAPTER THREE

# Richard Henry Pratt,
# The Carlisle Indian Industrial School,
# Assimilation and Allotment

RICHARD HENRY PRATT was a remarkable man, but not a complicated man.

Painfully honest and ruthlessly efficient, those who agreed with Pratt saw him as a man with energy, ability, determination, and dedication; those who disagreed with him saw him as an arrogant, stubborn zealot. Pratt was an optimist and unshackled by self-doubt. He believed he was "supremely right."[1] Pratt faithfully lived according to his principles, worked without compromise to accomplish his goals, and was always clear and honest about his objectives and the reasons for them. In the last decades of the nineteenth century, Pratt embodied and articulated the policy of total assimilation of the Indians. He created, organized, and supervised for twenty-five years the Carlisle Indian Industrial School, a school dedicated to transforming the Indian into a copy of the European-derived White man—the philosophy and process of assimilation. Pratt became Montezuma's mentor and hero; assimilation was Montezuma's credo until late in his life.

## BUFFALO SOLDIERS

Pratt was born December 6, 1840, in Rushford, New York, the first of three sons of Richard and Mary Pratt. When Pratt was five years old, the family moved to Logansport, Indiana. Only four years later, Richard Pratt, Pratt's father, earned a fortune in the 1849 California gold rush, but was robbed and murdered by a fellow prospector on his journey home. Young Pratt was forced to leave school at age thirteen in order to work various jobs to support his mother and two younger brothers. At age seventeen, he began to learn a trade in an apprenticeship with a tinner.

At the outbreak of the Civil War, Pratt promptly enlisted at age twenty-one on April 18, 1861, eight days after the bombardment of Fort Sumter. Over six feet tall and with a smooth-shaven face pitted by smallpox, he was an imposing figure on his horse as he fought with the Second Indiana Cavalry in Kentucky, Tennessee, and Georgia. He left the U.S. Army on May 29, 1865, as a brevet Captain, newly married ten days earlier to Anna Laura Mason. The Pratts would have four children: Mason, Marion, Nana, and Richenda (born twelve years after Nana).

Pratt opened a hardware store in the family hometown of Logansport, Indiana, but business was not good, and he applied for a commission in the regular army in March 1867. He was appointed second lieutenant in the Tenth U. S. Cavalry, a newly organized regiment of 103 Black enlisted men recruited from recently freed slaves. Although a lieutenant, Pratt was addressed as Captain because of his "brevet" rank given for his service during the Civil War. To confer by brevet means an honorary rank, without pay.

Six Black regiments with White officers were authorized in 1866. In 1869, they were reorganized into two infantry regiments (the Twenty-fourth and Twenty-fifth Infantry) and two cavalry regiments (the Ninth and Tenth Cavalry). These men (and one woman, Cathy Williams, who after serving as a cook and laundress for General Philip Sheridan and his staff in the Civil War successfully enlisted and served under the name of William Cathay),[2] compiled a highly credible record in the Indian Wars of 1866–1890. They are now honored by a monument and library at Fort Leavenworth, Kansas. It is part of their legend that the Indians gave the Buffalo Soldiers their name because their tight, curly hair and fighting spirit reminded them of the buffalo.

*I'm just a Buffalo Soldier*
*In the heart of America*
*Stolen from Africa, brought to America*
*Said he was fighting on arrival*
*Fighting for survival*
*Said he was a Buffalo Soldier*
*Win the war for America*

Bob Marley, N.G. Williams; 1983

Pratt's army duty as a young officer placed him in daily contact with two minority races. In addition to his Buffalo Soldiers, Pratt was in charge of the Indian scouts, mainly Cherokee Indians who were English-speaking and educated in Cherokee tribal schools. Their excellent character and performance made a formative and lasting impression on Pratt. As Pratt and his regiment moved from post to post over an eight-year period (1867–1875), he maintained command of the Indian scouts at each post. His regiment fought against the Kiowa, the Comanche, the Cheyenne, and the Arapahoe Indians. Pratt's experiences with Black soldiers and Indian scouts profoundly stimulated his philosophical development. He became convinced early in his life that it was against the Constitution to segregate Blacks and Indians, that citizenship included the right for equal opportunity.

General Philip Sheridan, who succeeded General Sherman as Commander of the Military Division of the Missouri, proposed that the major Indian offenders in the recently concluded Red River War of 1874 (actually a series of skirmishes) be placed in isolation in Florida. Lieutenant Richard Henry Pratt, then at Fort Sill, Oklahoma, was assigned, probably at his own request, the task of first selecting and then conducting seventy-two Kiowa, Comanche, Cheyenne, and Arapahoe warriors to Florida (plus the wife and daughter of Black Horse, a prominent Comanche). He was anxious for a change, but already he believed he could bring about the reformation of the prisoners, at least the young warriors. Pratt rode on the scene at an auspicious moment in time. Indian resistance had succumbed to settlers, the U.S. Army with its rapid-fire weapons, buffalo hunters, railroads, and disease. The problem was shifting from conquest to interaction and management.[3]

Pratt's military experience to this point was not without difficulty. In 1872, he was subjected to a court martial for refusing an order to make him officer of the day, simply because it was not his turn. His principled independence was manifest even at this young stage of his career. Indeed, he was found guilty, but given a light sentence in view of the trivial nature of the offense, and the proceedings did no subsequent harm to his career. Pratt seldom admitted a mistake, but fortunately his stubbornness was combined with a strong commitment to honesty and justice. These traits produced many conflicts during his military duty, and this experience undoubtedly was instrumental in his seeking a position where he would be the authority figure, free to exercise the strength of his convictions.

The Indian prisoners in leg irons and their military guards traveled by wagons 140 miles from Fort Sill to Caddo Station, the western terminus of the nearest railroad line, and from there to Fort Leavenworth, Kansas, by train.[4] Pratt and his prisoners left Fort Leavenworth on May 17, 1875, and arrived at Fort Marion in St. Augustine, Florida, on May 21. Fort Marion was named after General Francis Marion, a Revolutionary War soldier from South Carolina. The fort was originally the Castle San Juan de Pinos, built by the Spanish in the 1580s. The modern walled fort, Castillo de San Marcos, complete with drawbridge and moat, was constructed in the period 1672–1756 out of sawed coquina stone blocks. The name was changed in 1820 when it became American property.

Immediately upon arrival, Pratt made it clear that this imprisonment was an opportunity for the Indians to learn a new way of life. By the mid 1870s, Pratt was convinced of the Indians' ability and intelligence, and further convinced that only the environment had to change to allow them to duplicate the experience of American immigrants. By now Pratt believed that equal opportunity for Indians was denied in the process of locking them on reservations. He viewed Blacks and immigrants as successful examples of amalgamation into American society. Inherent in this belief was his conviction that ultimate success required complete eradication of their aboriginal cultures. In the early 1870s, this view of assimilation of the Indians was a new and emerging opinion, but within a decade it became the prevailing policy.

As the jailer for the St. Augustine group of Indians, he was able to test his belief that Indians could be taught the values and practices of White society. Pratt rapidly made this prison a unique one. The military guards were replaced by Indians, and discipline was administered by a court of Indians. Pratt and his Indians soon became a community project. St. Augustine, then as now, was a town of many retired wealthy people, and a fashionable resort destination for influential northerners. Pratt, throughout his career, had a way of ingratiating himself among the wealthy, especially among women seeking a cause or an activity. Before long, the women of St. Augustine were teaching the Indians English. Pratt's future projects were aided by the many influential people who visited St. Augustine and were impressed by his prison and his prisoners.

By the end of 1876, the Fort Marion Indians, their hair cut and wearing army clothing, were working in sawmills, orange groves, and on construction jobs. The Indians, drilling in military formation and selling their own handmade souvenirs, became a tourist attraction. Well-known visiting artists and writers made this Indian experience known to the rest of the nation.

In February 1877, Pratt proposed a more extensive program. He suggested that the older prisoners be returned to the reservation, but the young men be given a more thorough education.[5] He especially wanted this education to take place in the East, to produce individual role models. Pratt campaigned for the wives and children to join his prisoners, but even in this, his dedication to his conviction was apparent. He feared that without proper training of the wives and children, family reunions at the reservations would persuade his prisoners to return to their old ways.

## THE HAMPTON INSTITUTE

General Samuel Chapman Armstrong commanded a Black regiment in the Civil War. His success led to his appointment in 1866 as an agent in the Freedman's Bureau. In 1868, with the support of the American Missionary Association, he opened the Hampton Normal and Industrial Institute, a school for freed slaves in Hampton, Virginia. Born on the island of Maui, the son of missionaries in the Sandwich Islands, Armstrong intended to follow the examples of missionary schools, teaching vocational training, not higher learning. Manual work, Armstrong believed, was the pathway to discipline and character. His intention was to select the most promising Black individuals, who could then return home to educate others. With the demise of the Freedman's Bureau, interest and financial support for Hampton declined, but Armstrong successfully obtained charitable contributions. Although Hampton eventually became a college, in 1878 it only provided the equivalent of an elementary education.

In the summer of 1877, Pratt was notified that his prisoners would be released to the Indian Bureau. Pratt convinced twenty-two to stay in the East and arranged for seventeen of them to go to Hampton. Armstrong insisted that Pratt be temporarily assigned to Hampton as part of the agreement to accept his prisoners. Taking leave before his intended return to the frontier, Pratt began an eighteen-month stay at Hampton in April 1878. But the charismatic Armstrong deserves recognition for much of the initial success of the Hampton Indian experiment. He even enticed President Hayes, Secretary of the Interior Carl Schurz, and other cabinet members to take a trip by steamer to Hampton to see the Indians. On the boat trip Pratt had time to become known to these influential people and to share his vision for Indian education.

It was at Hampton that Pratt first developed the idea of placing Indians with farm families, a practice which became known at Carlisle as the Outing Program. He individually arranged for the placement of the seventeen former prisoners, usually with his own personal appearance in a community, along with a well-dressed Indian student to overcome the image of "hostile savages."

Armstrong agreed, perhaps at Pratt's urging, to accept fifty students from the Nez Perce tribe. The Nez Perce, 431 people, were currently being held prisoner at Fort Leavenworth. Here Pratt met Chief Joseph in May 1878, but failed to convince him to send the children—the only time in his life he was unsuccessful. In September 1878, Pratt was sent to recruit thirty-four Indian children for Hampton among the Cheyenne and the Sioux. The response was so great, that he requested an increase in the quota, and he returned with forty-one boys and nine girls.

General Armstrong tried to convince Pratt to establish an Indian school at Hampton, but Pratt believed that the Indians would be too isolated, as they were already being segregated from the Black students and the White community. But also, Armstrong and Pratt had similar personalities, and two authorities under one roof could prove to be a problem, especially for Pratt because Armstrong was undisputedly in charge of Hampton. Furthermore, Pratt did not want the educated Indian to return to the reservation, which was the Hampton policy; he wanted to totally assimilate Indians into White society.

## THE BEGINNING OF CARLISLE

Eighteen months had gone by, and General William Tecumseh Sherman, Commander of the U.S. Army, wanted Pratt to resume his military duty obligations. But by 1879, President Hayes and Secretary of the War, G. W. McCrary, were interested in Indian education. After a century of bribery and warfare, the government was turning to a policy of assimilation, a systematic effort to educate, civilize, and Christianize the Indian population. McCrary and General Armstrong suggested to General Sherman that an army officer, obviously Pratt, be detailed by the secretary of war for service in Indian education.

By February 1879, Pratt had developed his idea of a separate school for Indians and already had Carlisle in mind. Pratt traveled in May to Washington to present his case to the Secretary of Interior, Carl Schurz, a German immigrant. Pratt used Schurz's successful progression from immigrant status to a cabinet post as a model of what could be done.[6] He asked for the abandoned Carlisle Barracks in Pennsylvania to open a new Indian school, a plan supported by Armstrong. Fortunately for Pratt, those in charge (Schurz, McCrary, Sherman) believed in the policy of assimilation, and they were impressed with the energy and dedication of young Pratt.

Schurz ordered Pratt to bring the Indian Commissioner, Ezra A. Hayt, to his office and to repeat his presentation. Hayt was impressed and proposed that the initial student body be 100 to 125 pupils. Schurz decided that if the War Department would provide the Carlisle Barracks, an Indian school could be established immediately. Schurz sent Pratt to see McCrary at his home.

Secretary McCrary fully supported this as a War Department contribution. Amazingly, all of this was done on the same day, a time when one could go from office to office, drop in, and talk with the one in authority, and if the day were over, visit them at home. On that same day, an opinion was requested of the Judge Advocate General, who determined it would take an Act of Congress to transfer government property from one department to another. Before the day was over, the appropriate act was written by McCrary, designating Carlisle Barracks or any other vacant military post or barracks to be superintended by one or more U.S. Army officers as an Indian school.

By that time, the House and Senate were adjourned, but the bill was introduced the next morning, May 6, 1879. Pratt was astounded that things could happen so quickly, and was quite willing to hurry back and forth from office to office throughout the day, and to various houses in the evening, accomplishing his objective. Upon saying goodbye, Sherman said, "I declare, Pratt, you remind me more of Stonewall Jackson than any man I ever met." Pratt answered, "General, that is the biggest compliment I ever had and I shall remember it as long as I live."[7]

With the bill before both houses of Congress, Secretary McCrary authorized by War Department order the establishment of the school and support from War Department funds, although the Carlisle Post was itself temporarily transferred to the Department of the Interior. It would be another three years before the bill was passed, becoming law on July 31, 1882, officially establishing the Carlisle Indian Industrial School. The favorable report from the Committee on Indian Affairs read: "The experience at Hampton furnishes a striking proof of the natural aptitude and capacity of the rudest savages of the plains for mechanical, scientific, industrial, and moral education, when removed from parental and tribal surroundings and influences."[8] The report cited the fact that in many of the treaties of 1868, the Government had agreed to provide schools and teachers for Indian children, and the Indians had pledged to send their children to these schools. Furthermore, the report gave government approval to the practice of removing children from the reservations to separate them from tribal influence. At the same time, however, the report supported the return of educated Indians to reservations.

The idea, of course, was that eventually the educated would outnumber the non-educated. This did not take into account the fact that for many years the educated would be a distinct minority, subject to considerable economic and cultural pressures back on the reservation, problems that we will see reported in the personal experience of Zitkala-Ša (Chapter 9). Thus over the next forty years, the impact of the educated minority was not great. Many notable examples never returned to the reservation, becoming successful in White society, but overall, this was a small number. Those who returned were caught in the turmoil of transition, buffeted by poverty, the hostility of fellow Indians, and their own treasured perceptions of Indian heritage and culture.

## CARLISLE, THE FOREMOST EXAMPLE OF ASSIMILATION

Carlisle, Pennsylvania, was settled by Scotch-Irish immigrants in 1751. It was named after the county seat of Cumberland County, located right on the current border between England and Scotland. The Carlisle Barracks served as a supply depot and arsenal during the Revolutionary War.[9] After the war, it became an army school for artillery personnel, and then was little used until 1838, when the School of Cavalry Practice opened. During the Civil War, the Confederate Army occupied the town and barracks in June and July 1863. Upon their withdrawal, the Confederate forces burned most of the buildings. The post was rebuilt after the war and used to train cavalry recruits until April 1871. At that time it was the Army School of Instruction for Cavalry Recruits. It was abandoned partly because of a religious petition from the local community objecting to Sunday dress parades. Sherman, confronted with the petition, moved the school to St. Louis, recognizing that it would be less expensive anyway because the troops were serving in the West. When Pratt visited Carlisle in 1879, he found empty barracks, with three caretakers, a sergeant and two privates.

Carlisle is twenty miles southwest of Harrisburg, in the midst of fertile farmlands. Washington and Philadelphia are each only 100 miles away. The Carlisle Barracks consisted of twenty-seven acres, with twelve acres of land not occupied by buildings. Built in typical army post fashion, it contained a parade ground at the center of two-story, long white barracks in narrow rectangles, each with a double-decked porch facing the parade ground.

After a quick visit to Carlisle, leaving Mrs. Pratt in charge, Pratt was off to Dakota to recruit Indian children. The Interior Department ordered Pratt to choose his first students from the Sioux, the largest group of Indians with treaties specifying education. The original plan was to recruit thirty-six Sioux children from the Rosebud agency, thirty-six Sioux from the Pine Ridge agency, and forty-eight from the Oklahoma Indian Territory tribes. However, recruitment efforts by Indian agents were unsuccessful, as the Indians were still angry and hostile. True to his nature, Pratt took charge.

After an initial rejection, Pratt made a personal and impassioned presentation to the chiefs at Rosebud, the whole process taking many hours. The chiefs were wary of White trickery, and Pratt found the effective response. He relentlessly argued that the problem was that the chiefs could not read or write. If Indians were to learn to read treaties and agreements, then they could be sure the government was being honest. The message was successful. Spotted Tail, Chief of the Brulé Sioux, selected five of his children for Carlisle. White Thunder chose two of his, and two each came from Milk and Two Strike. Once word spread that the chiefs intended to have their own children educated, Pratt was deluged with requests. He accepted sixty-six children and two stowaways from Rosebud and sixteen from Pine

Ridge, a total of sixty boys and twenty-four girls. The event was celebrated by The Giveaway, a ceremony still practiced today, highlighted by the parents of the departing children expressing their pleasure by giving horses and goods to those in the tribe who were poor and needy.

The first part of the trip to Carlisle was by boat down the Missouri River to Yankton. Pratt discovered that the boys were smoking store cigarettes from a trader on the boat. He purchased the entire supply of 4,000 cigarettes. He told the boys that once they got to Carlisle smoking would not be allowed, but until then he and the boys would enjoy the cigarettes until they were gone. Pratt never smoked again.

Pratt and the Indian children reached Pennsylvania at midnight on October 6, 1879, to be greeted by hundreds of town people at the small railroad station in Gettysburg Junction, just south of Carlisle. The entire crowd walked with Pratt and the children the two miles to the Carlisle Barracks.[10] Pratt was then off to Wichita, Kansas, to meet his assistants who had recruited fifty-two more pupils from the Indian Territory. Along with eleven former students from Florida and Hampton, this made a total of 147 students (109 boys and thirty-eight girls) in the first class that began on November 1, 1879. Within four months, Pratt had the school organized and functioning at such a level that it was already impressing visitors, including Secretary Schurz and members of the House Committee on Indian Affairs.[11]

Pratt's first teaching staff consisted of three of the women who had helped him at Fort Marion, Miss S. A. Mather, Miss C. M. Semple, and Miss Perit (Pratt never used any first names), and Alfred J. Standing, a friend he had encountered in the Indian Territory, who had been in charge of a boarding school at Fort Sill, and was the Indian agent at the Yankton Agency. Standing was the assistant superintendent for most of Pratt's years at Carlisle. Obviously, they had a shared philosophy and outlook. Christian principles and abstinence from alcohol and tobacco were employment requirements. By January 1880, Carlisle had a staff of twenty-one teachers, and by 1893, sixty-two, a number that was maintained throughout its years. The teachers were mostly unmarried women.

Marianna Burgess arrived at Carlisle in 1880 at age twenty-seven. For the next twenty-four years, Burgess was the superintendent of printing, overseeing the Carlisle weekly newspapers.[12] Burgess was the lifelong companion of Annie Ely who supervised the Outing Program until 1904. Burgess and Ely were Hicksite Quakers, a branch named after Elias Hicks who caused a rift with "Orthodox" Quakers in 1828. The two women went on to work with the Quaker Indian program in California, and Burgess remained a favorite of Montezuma's and many of the students.

*Richard Henry Pratt*

Ely wrote Montezuma in 1901 in a remarkably open fashion as if Montezuma were a confidant and totally aware of the depth and nature of her relationship with Marrianna Burgess. "Miss Burgess and I still struggle on together, thinking more and more of each other each year, until we have lived out 22 years side by side. We are more like one family than any other two here except the married couples."[13]

*Marrianna Burgess and Annie Ely*

*Pratt and Faculty*

Until 1914, the appropriations for Carlisle uniquely allowed expenses for train transportation; thus Carlisle was the only non-reservation school that was able to recruit students from all over the United States and Alaska.[14] The student population eventually reached about 1,000, and over its thirty-nine-year lifespan, about 8,500 students attended Carlisle.[15] Montezuma's cousin, Mike Burns, arrived in September 1881.[16]

*Teachers' Quarters*

One of Pratt's very first actions was the hiring of two barbers to cut the Indians' hair, both boys and girls. Long hair was a problem for cleanliness, but more importantly, short hair was essential for the assimilation of a new identity. The simple act of a haircut became a traumatic experience for many of the students; in many tribes, the cutting of hair was associated with mourning. Within a week, the first pupils had haircuts and cloth uniforms. Uniforms represented an important method to counteract Indian individualism. The boys wore blue uniforms; the clothes provided by the government were of such poor quality that Pratt purchased old Civil War uniforms. Later, the uniforms were made by the girls in their sewing classes. The girls wore dark blue flannel dresses for winter and light colors for the summer, with dark blue cloaks lined in red.

*Mike Burns at Carlisle*

Indian names were replaced with names selected by the students from lists written on blackboards.[17] Later, it became common to use translated or shortened forms of the original Indian names. New names were both practical, as many Indian names could not be pronounced by the teachers, and part of the process of learning possessive individualism (the personal acquisition of goods and property). Government policy emphasized the need to provide surnames that would allow lines of inheritance when Indians became property owners. Ota Kte (Plenty Kill), a twelve-year-old Sioux boy, was a member of that first class in 1879. He was given the name Standing Bear because his father was Standing Bear, and he chose the name Luther from the list on the blackboard.[18] Another Standing Bear, Henry, was also a Carlisle student, and later, a consistent and strong supporter of Montezuma.

*Wounded Yellow Robe, Henry Standing Bear,*
*Timber Yellow Robe*

*Three months later—Timber Yellow Robe,*
*Henry Standing Bear, Wounded Yellow Robe*

The school year began on September 3, and ended in early March, to be followed by the outing sessions. The initial term of study was three years, but Pratt often tried to keep students longer. In 1883, the term was extended to five years; many stayed ten years, and indeed, it would require two five-year terms to finish the full course of instruction, equivalent to ten grades of education. Carlisle emphasized both academic and vocational training—trades for the boys and domestic skills for the girls. The wake-up bell rang at 5:30 A.M., the call to breakfast at 6:15. The day was divided half for school and half for work, the two groups exchanging places after lunch. The day's work ended at 5:30. Organized in military fashion, the students marched with their individual companies back and forth to every activity.

Military regimentation was applied to every aspect of life, partly to solve organizational problems but also to teach order and discipline, viewed as essential elements of civilization. The handwriting of Carlisle alumni is very impressive, uniformly reflecting the orderly and handsome Palmer Method of penmanship.[19] Evenings were busy with study hours, music instruction, health discussions, and prayer meetings. Pratt was himself in charge of a Saturday-night English-speaking meeting that he usually ended with a rousing speech. Every Sunday, Pratt conducted a personal inspection of the school, including every student room. Church services and prayer meetings were frequent. The campaign of Christianization was aggressive and pervasive, with a great deal of time dedicated to implanting a sense of sin and guilt. The student response to constant Christian proselytizing was uneven, often simply endured and often mixed with traditional beliefs.

Indian student resistance to the assimilation process took many forms.[20] There were many determined runaways. In December 1902, a group of Yavapai boys left the Phoenix

*The Carlisle Detention House*

Indian School and made it home to the Verde River Valley despite freezing temperatures with snow and rain.[21] The best estimate of the number of Carlisle runaways is about 1,850, with about a third successfully avoiding capture and return.[22] Setting fires, stolid non-responsiveness, the assignment of mocking nicknames to authorities and teachers, and clandestine storytelling and cultural acts were general and prevalent manifestations of resistance, often leading to punishment. Pratt usually dealt with returned runaways by punishing or expelling them, and confiscating any money in their savings accounts; only a total of 271 students were expelled.[23]

Punishment was an integral component of the effort to teach discipline and order. Physical punishment, often excessive and degrading in many of the western schools, was commonly practiced.[24] In most schools, students were punished for speaking words of their native languages. The commissioner of Indian affairs officially banned Indian vernacular in all government supported Indian schools in 1888.

Disobedience resulted in physical punishment, extra chores, or humiliating acts such as cutting the school grass with scissors. Everything at Carlisle was kept pristine by student labor. At Carlisle, the old stone powder magazine, constructed by captured Hessian soldiers in 1777, was used as a detention house. The inside has smooth brick walls arching to form a high ceiling; there are no apertures to allow the entry of natural light.

After one and one-half to two years at Carlisle, a student was sent out to live and work during the summer with a family, known as the Carlisle Outing, if he or she requested it. An agreement with rules of conduct was signed by both the student and the patron.[25] A monthly progress report was required of the patron. As with everything else, the process was personally supervised by Pratt, including visits to assess patrons and their environments. Eventually, 600 to 800 students were on outings each year, 948 in the peak year of 1903, receiving board, lodging, and a small payment for their work that accumulated thousands of dollars, most of which was deposited in student saving accounts, another lesson designed to teach possessive and rugged individualism.[26] The students lived as part of the families, mostly Quaker farmers. After a few bad experiences, Pratt refused to send students into cities. There were very few negative incidents. The success of the program can be seen in the fact that there were more patron applications than students available. Each year about 200 students stayed with their placement families and attended public schools.

Other schools were not successful in copying the outing system; most didn't try. One problem was the pull of the reservation when it was nearby. Another was the wary attitude of westerners, still influenced by the times of raiding parties and warfare. Carlisle's success, to a significant degree, could be attributed to its location in the heart of the Quaker farming country.

The Carlisle barracks had no suitable agricultural land. Pratt used money that had been donated to purchase ten acres adjoining the school in 1880 and rented, with Congressional appropriations, 109 acres of farm land east of Carlisle in 1887. This land was later purchased with charitable contributions. In 1900, he rented and then purchased another 175-acre farm. The total holdings eventually reached 307 acres. The school farms were used mainly to supply produce for the school. By the end of his years as superintendent, seventeen buildings

*Superintendent's House*

had been erected and an additional seventeen were remodeled. The thirty-four buildings—five of stone, eighteen of brick, eleven of wood, all painted or stained a soft yellow with white wood trim—formed a rectangle around the former parade grounds that served as drill field, campus, and recreational fields. This large central square contained a white bandstand in the middle, and directly to the side was Pratt's house, with its extra-long bathtub and bed.[27]

During the 1880s, a centralized heating system and electric lighting were installed, mostly with private funds. Water was purchased from the Carlisle Water Company for $240 per year. Pratt added a new gymnasium and a dormitory for girls. Most of the renovations and additions were paid for by contributions. By 1887, Pratt had collected about $80,000 for the school. In the 1890s, Pratt reduced his money-raising efforts, as he believed the school should be government supported.

A graduate of Carlisle was equivalent in education to about two years of high school. This was augmented by half of each day being devoted to training in carpentry, shoemaking, printing, blacksmithing, tinsmithing, farming, and other trades such as masonry, wagon making, painting, carpentry, cooking, tailoring, and for the girls, cooking, sewing, canning, ironing, child care, and cleaning. Surplus goods were offered to the Indian Bureau for use at other agencies. The spring wagon, the Carlisle wagon, became known throughout the West. Carlisle emphasized the mechanical arts, but in contrast to the outing system on farms, Pratt never succeeded in establishing apprenticeships in trades. In 1915, teaching of the trades was severely curtailed, and limited to blacksmith, carpenter, mason, painter and farmer. The Indian Bureau believed only those trades would be of use upon returning to the reservation.

The Carlisle school weekly newspapers were a powerful instrument for spreading the Carlisle idea and name. The slogan on the masthead read, "To Civilize the Indian; Get Him Into Civilization. To Keep Him Civilized; Let Him Stay." Copies went to every member of Congress, all Indian agencies and military posts, and to most American newspapers. But these publications also provided ammunition for those who opposed Pratt.

The Carlisle experience was not lucrative for Pratt. Because he lived at the school he was not paid a quarters allowance. His sole income was his meager army pay.

*Richard Henry Pratt*

Supplementation of his pay required Congressional legislation to provide an amendment to the Indian appropriation bill. Despite Pratt's reluctance to pursue this avenue, his supporters introduced the amendment for a supplement of one thousand dollars. This was approved in a divided vote, but only after angry debate that harmed Pratt and Carlisle, a depressing experience for Pratt.

Pratt believed in abrupt transition, replacing the old way with the new way. Pratt had no sympathy for easing transition from one culture to another, no desire to preserve any part of Indian life, no sentimental attachment to the past. In his harsh judgment, Indian culture and tradition were worthless. On the other hand, his total lack of regard for Indian past life was balanced by his absolute belief that if properly educated, Indians would be successful in White society.

Today it is hard to appreciate that many Americans in the 1800s did not believe Indians were capable of learning, that Indians represented a barbarism incompatible with education. Pratt and Carlisle were viewed as experiments by many, and ultimately Pratt and Carlisle were instrumental in changing prevailing opinions and attitudes about Indians.

Carlisle's existence was in a major way due to Pratt's ability to charm and persuade donors and influential people. Pratt and the school received endless visits from prominent people: writers, philanthropists, legislators, activists, and journalists. They saw an example of successful assimilation: Indians living in harmony with the surrounding White community; Indians who looked and acted like White people; Indians from over seventy tribes exhibiting no evidence of tribalism; Indians living with White families in the successful outing program; Indians living, working, and being educated without waste or corruption. They did not see any evidence of Indian culture or heritage or any overt evidence of unhappiness in the midst of the military discipline.

THE FINAL CHAPTER of Pratt's memoirs was dictated to his daughter in 1923 at age eighty-two.[28] The story in his memoirs of the World's Columbian Exposition in Chicago reveals his drive, his creativity, and his perseverance.

The Carlisle band was formed and playing within four months of the school opening, including Luther Standing Bear on the cornet. As the band became proficient, concerts were given in the public square of Carlisle. Soon the band had engagements throughout the country during the summer months. By 1892, the band had thirty-two boys, dressed in uniforms of red coats and blue trousers.

*The Carlisle Band, Dennison Wheelock, Conductor*

In 1892, the four hundreth anniversary of the discovery of America was celebrated with large parades in New York on October 10, and in Chicago on October 20. Carlisle was represented in both parades; the expenses were provided by donations from friends of the school. In New York, 270 boys and fifty-two girls marched, carrying an elaborate silk banner emblazoned with "United States Indian Industrial School, Carlisle, Pennsylvania," and under that, "Into Civilization and Citizenship."[29] The boys marched in four companies, preceded by the band. The girls marched as one company bringing up the rear in blue uniforms with sailor hats.

In Chicago, only the boys marched carrying the same banner, this time divided into ten platoons. Each platoon represented a characteris-

*Luther Standing Bear*

tic of the school, for example, one platoon with books and slates, another agricultural, carrying implements and agricultural products from the school farms. Others represented carpentry, bakery, blacksmithing, shoemaking, harness making, tinsmithing, and tailoring. Led by the band, they marched six or seven miles to the start of the parade, then marched in the parade, executing military movements in front of the official grandstand, then back to their barracks.

Pratt believed this experience energized the school and motivated a strong desire to visit the Columbian Exposition.[30] The city of Chicago organized the World's Columbian Exposition to be a world's fair celebrating the achievements that followed the voyage of

Christopher Columbus.[31] Nostalgic exhibits of the past were mixed with wondrous predictions of the future. Alexander Graham Bell talked from New York over the nation's first long-distance telephone line.

In early 1893, Pratt promised that any student who saved enough money from their summer's outing could spend a week at the Exposition. He estimated that with a special low rate from the railroads, as they had provided for the parades, $20 per student would provide transportation, hotel and food expenses plus $5 spending money. That summer's work experience was so successful, Pratt estimated that 500 students would be eligible for the trip.

Unexpectedly, the Pennsylvania Railroad quoted a price of $16.50, the regular fare, for transportation rather than the $7 they had charged for the parade. Pratt went to see the passenger agent personally, but could not negotiate a lesser fare. He then visited a vice president of the railroad, who had previously expressed interest in the school. Pratt, citing his army experiences in the Civil War, offered to use two freight cars, which he would prepare with seats using the school mechanics. The vice president immediately recognized that this was not wartime, and the railroad could not be responsible for transportation in that fashion. He offered to present Pratt's case to the company executives that very same day. Later that afternoon, Pratt returned to learn that the railroad would lower its fee to $10. Pratt said thanks, but this was still impossible for the school. Leaving the executive offices, he dropped in to apologize to the passenger agent for going over his head. The agent, mollified by the apology, asked precisely what he wanted. Pratt outlined his needs for 550 students and employees: a train of ten passenger coaches, two baggage cars, and one sleeping car, leaving Carlisle at midnight on Sunday, returning from Chicago at midnight the next Saturday—a total fee of $3,500. The passenger agent instantly agreed. (Pratt didn't reveal how the agent made this straight with the vice president.)

Now that he had transportation, the next challenge was to pay for the stay in Chicago. The Exposition charged a daily admission fee of fifty cents per person, and would not forego this requirement despite Pratt's pleas with the administrators. No problem, Pratt had a proposition. The Indian boys and girls, in a battalion of 300, would provide a daily parade and drill, lasting an hour, anywhere the administrators wished to place them. The band would play for an hour or two every day, at any bandstand they would designate. He further offered a daily performance of orators and individual musicians. He concluded this offer by agreeably allowing the Exposition to charge for these performances, thus providing an opportunity for the Exposition to make money from the Carlisle performances. One of the three administrators offered his opinion, that Pratt was not seeking free admission, but offering a money-making opportunity that should be seized. By a vote of two to one, Pratt's proposition was accepted. Pratt refused the Indian Bureau's invitation to participate in their typical Indian exhibition, adamant in his determination to avoid aboriginal displays, although the Bureau exhibit also featured a schoolhouse and models of classroom behavior with delegations of students from government schools.

Next, Pratt solved the housing and food problem. Several hotels had been built, but not close to the Exposition, and these hotels were having difficulty attracting business. One hotel had been foreclosed and never opened. The South Pier Hotel was one and one-half miles away, near a streetcar line that ended at an Exposition gate. The entire Carlisle party would fill the hotel. Pratt negotiated with the holder of the mortgage, securing the use of the hotel for $200 per day. Nearby, was a large restaurant also enduring poor business. The proprietor agreed to provide breakfast, a lunch to carry, and a dinner—all for fifty cents per person per day. The basis of Pratt's negotiation was the demonstration that at Carlisle, food cost a little over thirteen cents per day per person; thus the proprietor should be able to make at least twenty-five cents per day per student—about $125 per day. Breakfast would be very early and dinner very late, not conflicting with other customers. The proprietor agreed, but then exclaimed, "Wait, I can't do that, I forgot the cost of waiters." Pratt replied, "You won't need waiters. The Carlisle girls are all trained in waiting tables and washing dishes. In fact, I will bring students who are good cooks, and take care of that too."

Next, came the streetcar company, where he arranged for a series of cars to carry the 550 members of the group from the street in front of the hotel directly to the Exposition. The cars came to the spot at the appointed time. The Carlisle students were lined up on both sides of the tracks, and the cars were filled and moving in two minutes' time.

At Carlisle, Pratt organized the purchase of paper boxes and cups to hold three meals for the train trip there and back. He purchased several thousand folding paper lunch boxes for the noon lunches. Cups and water cans were made in the Carlisle tinshops.

On Sunday, October 1, 1893, the train left for what Pratt described as "a jolly journey." The Pennsylvania Railroad provided 600 copies of a map of the Exposition. Not surprising, Pratt organized the Exposition as a military campaign, and nothing was missed. The students wore their uniforms, each with a yellow satin badge bearing the words: "United States Indian Industrial School, Carlisle, Pa, Excursion World's Fair, October, 1893." Each had a map and a memorandum book with an attached pencil for the required daily observations, to be submitted to teachers upon their return. Pratt negotiated a steamboat ride one night to watch fireworks from the lake. The only mishap occurred when one of the Apache boys persuaded one of the girls to take a ride on the lake in an Indian canoe. Neither had ever been in a canoe, and they had to be rescued when the canoe capsized, the girl requiring extensive resuscitation.

When the Carlisle expedition returned, the final cost came to $19.50 per person.

## REACTION TO OFF-RESERVATION SCHOOLS

In 1880, the Federal Government brought thirty-one Sioux Chiefs to Washington, D.C., including Red Cloud, Chief of the Oglala Sioux, and Spotted Tail, Chief of the Brulé Sioux. After the Washington meeting, the chiefs came to Carlisle. Spotted Tail asked for a meeting of the Sioux children together with Pratt. Spotted Tail expressed his objections to the military uniforms and drilling, and complained about the sleeping accommodations and the food. According to Pratt, Red Cloud said nothing and the complaints were addressed satisfactorily.[32] In another account, all the chiefs spoke out angrily against Carlisle.[33] Spotted Tail at first wanted to take all the Sioux children back to the reservation, but eventually took only nine of his family home at his own expense. Pratt reported that this was against the wishes of Spotted Tail's children and the rest of the Indian delegation. There is some evidence[34] that Spotted Tail and Pratt were in dispute regarding the salary of Spotted Tail's son-in-law, who worked at Carlisle. However, official documents indicate that some children did want to return home. Indeed, two sneaked aboard the train and were sent back to Carlisle.[35]

The publicity surrounding the episode with Spotted Tail rapidly died down, but it was used as part of the criticism directed against Carlisle and against the assimilation efforts. Pratt viewed reservations as a system of isolation and segregation. Isolation and segregation were against his principles, his very core of beliefs. He saw Carlisle and similar schools as pathways to integration. Hence, returning to the reservation was not an appropriate goal. In his view, an Indian on a reservation was a prisoner. Freedom came with education. The Indians, the immigrants, and Black Americans were all examples, in his view, of people who should travel the same path. Eventually prejudices and discriminations would yield to the full benefits of American society.

From 1880–1885, Pratt was center stage; after 1885 a network of humanitarian, philanthropic groups became interested in Indians. Pratt saw a busy life and hard work as a system of refinement and selection, ensuring the rise and success of the best individuals, but critics accused Pratt and his system as being deliberately and excessively harsh. Pratt's critics included those who regarded the reservation as the best method and site for "civilization," those who believed the Indians were unchangeable primitive savages, those who profited from the reservation system, Indian parents who objected to separation of family, and Indians who wished to preserve the old ways.

Continuing the reservation system required government support, as obviously the old tribal lifestyle would be impossible. The freedom to hunt was gone. Indians were now either subjugated militarily or starved into submission. The "formerly energetic and aggressive warriors became enervated and dispirited recipients of the dole."[36] Finding a new way of life was both a logical and appealing conclusion for those responsible or interested in the Indian. Pratt demonstrated that this was possible, but he was more than willing to sacrifice culture and heritage in order to gain a rapid transition. He viewed culture and heritage as obstacles to transition, partly because he saw Indian culture and heritage under the rubric of "savagery."

Before 1880, Congress provided about $130,000 per year for Indian schools; by 1890, the sum had reached over $1.3 million, by 1900, about $3 million. The number of schools had increased from 106 to 307.[37] All the off-reservation boarding schools were opened between 1879 and 1898. The second after Carlisle was the school in Forest Grove, Oregon, later moved to Chemawa, near Salem, followed by schools in Chilocco, Oklahoma; Genoa, Nebraska; Albuquerque, New Mexico; Easkell, Kansas, and Grand Junction, Colorado. Between 1890 and 1893, another eleven schools were established. All were patterned after Carlisle, intended to be training schools in "civilized" communities away from reservation influences. By 1898, there were twenty-four off-reservation schools; all except Carlisle were in the West. Only Carlisle reached 1,000 students (in 1900); the rest had enrollments of 100 to 500. By 1900, student enrollment in all the schools had increased to 21,568 and nearly 18,000 of these students were attending a boarding school, either on-reservation or off-reservation, but the total number of Indian school-age children was about 40,000 to 50,000.[38]

Obviously the effort was not coming close to meeting the task. By 1892, half of the Indian population was receiving some education, but only because of reliance on schools supported by religious groups. Appropriations were not sufficient to build new structures, not even enough to keep current buildings in repair. After the Carlisle Bill was finally passed, no other military post was ever converted to a school. The ability to do so was dependent upon future legislation providing funds; this never happened, and no military officers were ever assigned this duty. No other schools developed a successful program like the Carlisle Outing Program. Carlisle's physical nearness to philanthropic people and organizations and successful farms proved important. The on-reservation schools struggled with "relapse"—the return to the tribal way of life—either nightly with day schools or during vacation periods and visits from parents and friends at the on-reservation boarding schools.

Certainly on-reservation schools were necessary, whether they were day schools or boarding schools. Transporting thousands of Indian children to off-reservation boarding schools was an enormous expense. Not surprising, western legislators objected to providing funds for eastern schools, preferring to develop their own local reservations. Some western legislators even preferred to spend nothing on education, believing in the inferiority of the Indian race, for example, Senators Preston Plumb and John Ingalls, both of Kansas.[39]

Competition for Indian students in the late 1880s became intense, as the number of boarding and reservation schools grew. The on-reservation boarding schools, usually located at agency headquarters, emerged as the favored method to wean young Indians from the influences of old habits and traditions. As the on-reservation schools increased, Indian agents and agency teachers actively recruited students to stay at home. The problem became even more intense in the 1890s when the government contracted with religious denominations to operate reservation schools. Missionary zeal added to the efforts to erode tribal traditions and eliminate tribal culture.

Conflicting emotions about removing children from their homes led to exaggerations and accusations that were not unfounded. Off-reservation schools had the especially difficult problems of disease and death away from home (about 220 died at Carlisle).[40] Tuberculosis and trachoma, a damaging infection of the eyes, were very prevalent in the boarding schools with their highly contagious environments. It was common for parents to refuse to enroll their children; agents resorted to force using agency police and extortion by withholding rations. Angry and violent confrontations were not uncommon.[41]

Being a teacher in these schools was not easy.[42] There was always a high level of movement and attrition, reflecting dissatisfaction with unpleasant locations, homesickness, personality and power clashes (especially with teachers being predominantly female and the bureaucratic authority being thoroughly male), and relatively primitive living conditions in a strict Victorian social atmosphere.

The various philosophical positions, self-interest, and differing opinions all conspired to prevent a uniform federal policy. There was growth in the number and support of the off-reservation boarding schools, which educated children away from the tribal environment, but as noted, these schools served only a small percentage of eligible children. The conflict between the principle of education away from the tribe and the desire to keep Indians isolated on reservations was never resolved. It was recognized that it would be best if the graduates of the educational programs were given positions of teaching and administration on the reservations, but this was not carried out, and there was an insufficient number of positions anyway.

The off-reservation schools, especially Carlisle and Hampton, generated detailed surveys of former students that presented a favorable picture. Of course, these reports served a political purpose, and it is difficult not to question their objectivity. Politicians who visited reservations and witnessed educated individuals who had returned to the reservations and reverted to old ways (often overcome with poverty) interpreted this as a failure of the education, not a failure to address the transition or a failure to improve the reservation environment.[43] No one addressed the inner conflict in each individual who tried to bridge the old culture and heritage with the new education. Some publicized this conflict, such as Zitkala-Ša (Chapter 9), but no one offered a plan to support this transition, certainly not to blend the two forces—a foreign and unacceptable idea to most Whites, and especially Pratt. "The old systems must give way. They are slavery. We are for freedom. To emancipate the

Indian from ignorance we must emancipate him from reservations."[44] However, transition was not easy. As a simple, but often unappreciated example, contrast the "civilized" world of a geometric organization of lines, corners, and squares coupled with measured time compared with the space and openness of the Indian world.[45] Add to this a total change in language, dress, and food. Returning to the reservations, students from the off-reservation schools were struck by now existing cultural differences between them and their parents and friends. "Living in two worlds" became a common theme and expression among these students. Tribal pressure was constant and powerful in the form of ridicule, ostracization, and expectations to partake in traditional ceremonies and activities. Efforts to be economically self-sufficient were frustrated by the level of poverty, the lack of equipment and jobs, poor climate and soil, and the conflict of individualism with tribal philosophies of sharing and communal hospitality. These problems applied to men and women alike; the lessons of "domestic science" were hard to apply to tepees or cabins without tables, beds, or utensils. The average student with industrial training found that:

> *"He is a carpenter in a land without lumber, a painter with nothing to paint, a tailor where clothes are fashioned from flour sacks, a shoemaker among moccasin wearers."*[46]

For a short while, it seemed the government was moving to a solution, but the failure to provide adequate funds gradually allowed a greater role for churches and religious groups. A plan to place Indian children in White homes received consideration and there was great interest in the program by families and small educational institutions, but absolutely no funds were provided.[47] The failure of assimilation, however, was not just due to inadequate funding. The process was complicated; it was not a simple on and off mechanism, being *appropriately* obstructed by the retention of a treasured heritage.

In 1885, The House appointed a committee to investigate appropriations for Indian schools and the problems of educated Indians returning to the reservations. The House committee's report in 1886 attacked Carlisle and highlighted the poor performance of those who returned to the reservation.[48] The committee advocated on-reservation schools, both government and church supported, and questioned the practice of removing children from their homes. The failure of returning students was ascribed to educating them in an advanced, civilized setting, stating that students educated close to home would not be shocked by conditions ("barbaric practices") upon returning. Perhaps reluctance to attack reservation conditions significantly reflected an underlying conviction that life on the reservation represented "barbarism" and "savagery," not the problems of changing lifestyle and poverty.

Carlisle's budget and Pratt's $1,000 salary supplement came under attack, and only a defense by supporters and the Indian Rights Association allowed appropriations for Carlisle and Hampton to continue. Pratt wrote to Montezuma in March 1892: "No congratulations have I received from any quarter, not excepting those from good Senator Dawes, fill me with more real pleasure than yours. You know entirely what you are talking about. The others do not. If I can have the approval of my Indian friends, I am willing to take all the condemnation that can come from the white man's side. I am in the midst of a bitter fight and am being personally slaughtered on the floor of the House of Representatives. My salary is stricken out of the Appropriations Bill because I have dared to assert the truth and to public opinions exactly in line with those of your letter. I am not daunted nor uneasy about the future. Carlisle will live in spite of its enemies."[49]

In fact the dispute and debates revealed that the majority of Congressional legislators supported Indian education. Unfortunately, this support was only expressed in moments of crisis, not with a positive, proactive agenda.

## INDIAN REFORMERS

By 1885, there was a surge of humanitarian interest in the Indian, to an important degree, fostered and stimulated by Pratt and Carlisle. Rather than increasing public and governmental support of the off-reservation boarding school approach, with Carlisle being the prototype, as Pratt hoped, this new wave of interest focused on the reservation. Federal policy reflected this new pressure and promoted the reservation school principle. Religious contract schools on the reservations were increasing in number, with the Catholic Church receiving the largest part of federal funds, and providing significant money on its own.

A significant stimulus for this new interest in Indians was *A Century of Dishonor*, by Helen Hunt Jackson, published in 1881, four years before her death.[50] The book presented to the public a recounting of the misadministration and misbehavior by the government as well as White individuals interacting with Indians, and called for reform. Although the book is often categorized as a disorganized polemic, it is an effective and well-researched account of tribal histories, including the Delaware, Cheyenne, Nez Percé, Sioux, Ponca, Winnebago, and Cherokee. It struck a humanitarian chord. Jackson sent every member of Congress a copy of her book at her own expense.[51] *A Century of Dishonor* reflected the Christian pervasiveness of the times, exemplified by this line from the Introduction written by Julius H. Seelye, President of Amherst College: "…and it was only as Christian influences taught him his inner need, and how this could be supplied, that he was led to wish and work for the improvement of his outer condition and habits of life."[52]

The Ponca Tribe, transferred against its will from its reservation along the Missouri River to the Indian Territory (Oklahoma), was a small tribe of about 700, but it had a big impact.[53] The Ponca reservation of 96,000 acres in the Dakota Territory had been guaranteed by an agreement in 1865. Three years later, in the Fort Laramie Treaty, the Peace Commission (Chapter 2), without consulting the Ponca, gave the reservation to the Sioux, the Ponca's traditional enemies. The government's solution was to remove the Ponca to the Indian Territory in 1877. A miserable journey and many deaths (one-third died) certainly did not appease the Ponca, and in 1879, one of the chiefs, Standing Bear, took a small part of the tribe north, settling down in Nebraska with the Omaha Indians. Standing Bear was pursued and arrested, but citizens of Omaha, encouraged by General George Crook, the local military commander, took up the Ponca cause. Crook was keen on avoiding another round of negative publicity for the military, having been sensitized by the uproar that followed the Sand Creek Massacre in Colorado in November 1864 (700 Colorado and New Mexico volunteer militia led by John M. Chivington raided a village of Cheyenne and Arapahoe Indians, killing about 150, mostly women and children). A famous writ of habeus corpus drawn up by two prominent lawyers of Omaha was upheld in the U.S. District Court, and Standing Bear, by now well known throughout the United States, was released from federal custody in Fort Omaha.[54]

Thomas H. Tibbles, an assistant editor of the *Omaha Daily Herald* and former itinerant preacher, toured the country to stir up support against the reservation system and to raise money to support the expected Supreme Court hearing, together with an Omaha

Indian woman, Bright Eyes (Suzette La Flesche, sister of Susan La Flesche Picotte, the first American Indian physician), whom he eventually married, as well as Standing Bear. It was a presentation of the Ponca story in Boston in November 1879 that stirred Helen Hunt Jackson, an author of novels, short stories, and poetry, to begin her short career of publicizing the problems of the Indians. That same Boston presentation spawned one of the first Indian humanitarian organizations, the Boston Indian Citizenship Committee, a group that was to enlist Massachusetts Senator Henry Dawes in its cause, ultimately leading to his appointment to the Senate Indian Affairs Committee. Finally, the Supreme Court declined to review the District Court decision, and Congress appropriated funds to indemnify the Ponca and to provide land in either the old or new reservations according to their wishes. In 2003, the Ponca Tribe of Nebraska, having been terminated in 1966 and restored in 1990 (Chapter 13), had 1,300 enrolled members, but only thirty lived on the 159 acres of tribal land.

Congress established the Board of Indian Commissioners, a volunteer group of ten prominent philanthropists, in 1869, to oversee the Bureau of Indian Affairs, especially the expenditure of appropriated funds, as part of an effort to control the misuse of funds by the agents. The first Chairman of the board was William Welsh, a wealthy Philadelphian and uncle of Herbert Welsh who would found the Indian Rights Association thirteen years later. The idea was to have an influential body of men to work with the secretary of the interior, but independent of political pressures. The board existed for about sixty years, effectively casting its imprimatur of Protestant Christian evangelism on Indian policy and influencing public opinion. Keep in mind, that until 1890–1900, most of the European immigrants to the United States were Protestants from Great Britain and Northern Europe.[55] To understand the assimilationist movement it is necessary to appreciate the dominant norms and values of the times. American society in the late nineteenth century was deeply religious and the idea of cultural pluralism that is a hallmark of today was a new concept not yet considered. Paternalism was a natural expression of high-minded and zealous Christian men and women, statesmen and prominent philanthropists. It was a sincerely felt responsibility to provide what was best, in this case, their own way of life. To debase the motives of the reformers is to avoid considering the thinking of the age. Eventually these humanitarian reformers won their way in Congress.

The Women's National Indian Association, first organized in 1879 as the Central Indian Committee of the Women's Home Mission Society of the First Baptist Church of Philadelphia, was a good example of an emerging sensitivity to the Indian, now that the period of warfare was over. By 1884, this association had thirty-eight affiliated organizations throughout the East and Midwest. In 1883, the name was changed to the National Indian Association. In 1884, the organization joined forces with the Indian Rights Association, withdrawing mainly to charitable and missionary activities, leaving the political arena to the Indian Rights Association.

The Indian Rights Association was organized December 15, 1882, by Herbert Welsh of Philadelphia, initially as a group of thirty to forty men committed to arousing public awareness of Indian problems and seeking Congressional action to provide education and citizenship.[56] Herbert Welsh's inherited wealth allowed him to devote his life to his personal interests, largely a career as a reformer dedicated to American Indians, an interest that was sparked by a visit to the Sioux in the Dakota Territory. The major organizations devoted to Indian reform (the Board of Indian Commissioners, the Women's National Indian

Association, the Indian Rights Association, and the Conference at Lake Mohonk) were like-minded allies in the cause of assimilation and allotment. Indeed, the participants in each organization were often the same people.

Welsh and the Indian Rights Association were initially dedicated to creating private ownership of land, providing a Christian education, and gradually reducing government rations in the belief that this would force individuals to become workers in the American Protestant tradition. The only salaried employees of the Indian Rights Association were a clerk in the Philadelphia office and a lobbyist in Washington, both under the tight control of Welsh, who dominated the association for twenty-two years. The Indian Rights Association published an enormous number of pamphlets, newspaper articles, and speeches describing reservation conditions. This was creditable information because it was based on facts from the organization's own investigations, almost always personal inspection trips by Welsh or the Washington lobbyist. Its information and recommendations became valuable, often the only material available to legislators, and effective in arousing public opinion. Indeed, all of the organizations dedicated to Indian reform in the last decades of the nineteenth century published and circulated huge amounts of literature, with a measurable effect on public opinion and legislators. The Indian Rights Association viewed Pratt as a great moral force, and respected his contribution, but disagreed with his ideas of abrupt termination of the reservations, supporting instead a gradual transition as well as reservation schools and civil service reform for the Indian service. The association also supported the return of educated Indians to their reservations.

Despite its meager revenues ($6,000 to $11,000 per year), the Indian Rights Association was a powerful force, principally because of the indefatigable dedication and energy of Herbert Welsh.[57] The association grew in size reaching the peak of its influence in the early 1890s, with perhaps nearly 1,500 individuals or families. Many members were women, also members of the Women's National Indian Association. Its primary thrust was mainstream Christian assimilationism, but the association became involved with countless disputes and causes, and often protected Indian groups against White interests. Targets for action were selected from an endless list of problems, often brought to Welsh's attention by Indian service personnel, army officers, missionaries, and Indians themselves. Welsh gave priority to issues associated with land and resources, the improvement of personnel in the Indian service, and the development of education and appropriate laws. The association waged many battles, from major issues such as the Land-In-Severalty Act of 1887, to multiple small causes such as its campaign on behalf of Apache prisoners of war, even for scholarship support for a single individual. From 1882 to 1904, the Indian Rights Association accomplishments and access to government officials produced a remarkable record, one that earned it recognition by American Indians and workers in the Indian service as a court of last resort. By 1904, the association had shifted its views, giving up on allotment and working together with Indians to protect Indian land and tribal interests, a change that was consistent with the new social emphasis in America from Protestant individualism to public welfare.

Interest and growth in Indian reform activity increased with support of the Land-In-Severalty Act. (Severalty is defined as exclusive and individual ownership of land.) When this act was passed, humanitarian interest declined, as there was a belief that reform had been accomplished. The Indian Rights Association was most influential in the passage of this key legislation.

## THE PROCESS OF ALLOTMENT

Westerners were by and large interested in only two things: protection against Indian raids and access to more land. Humanitarian influence on policy was an eastern phenomenon. Because the Land-In-Severalty Act provided additional land for Whites, and money to support the reservations, there was little, if any, opposition of the westerners to the easterners. Because the eastern leaders filled a vacuum, they achieved a position of advisors and experts on Indian affairs for Congress and the Indian Bureau. Most importantly, they saw the Indian problem from only one point of view, that of the Protestant Christian; they did not understand a culture and family life so fundamentally different from their own experience. However, they spoke for the majority of White, late nineteenth-century America, which was not yet a pluralistic country. A strong motivation among these people at this point in history was the underlying idea that successful conversion and assimilation of the Indians would reaffirm the conviction that the American Christian way was the right way. It was an obligation to give Anglo-Saxon Christian civilization to the Indian, and native religious practices were persecuted by almost everyone involved, including missionaries, Indian service employees, and even the humanitarian reformers. Assimilation, therefore, served not only the purpose of solving the problems of the Indian reservations, but it could also be therapeutic for the committed individuals who were influential in government. We look backward today on the policy of assimilation with cynicism, but at the time assimilation was a fervently believed philosophy that was significantly religious.

Albert K. Smiley, a Quaker appointed to the Board of Indian Commissioners in 1879, created the Mohonk Conference of the Friends of the Indian.[58] Smiley expanded the customary one-day board meeting, mainly with representatives of missionary societies, to a three-day meeting at his resort hotel on sixty-foot-deep Lake Mohonk (an Indian name meaning Lake of the Sky), near New Paltz, New York (ninety miles north of New York City).[59] The hotel, a sprawling Victorian castle with its thousands of acres, is now the Mohonk Mountain House, a National Historic Landmark. The resort, still owned and operated by the Smiley family, can accommodate 500 guests.

The first meeting of The Mohonk Conference was in October 1883, and the conference continued to meet every fall until 1917, often a gathering of more than 150 individuals. This became the largest meeting of humanitarians (essentially all easterners) interested in Indians: missionaries, representatives of philanthropic societies, editors, ministers, government officials, and members of Congress, although continuity and direction came from a small core of dedicated, like-minded, religious men and women, such as Merrill E. Gates, President of Rutgers College (and later Amherst), Lyman Abbott, Editor of the *Christian Union*, Senator Henry L. Dawes, Herbert Welsh, Secretary of the Indian Rights Association, Alice C. Fletcher, a noted ethnologist, General Eliphalet Whittlesey, Secretary of the Board of Indian Commissioners, Samuel A. Armstrong, Head of the Hampton Institute, Thomas J. Morgan, Commissioner of Indian Affairs under President Harrison, and Amelia Stone Quinton, President of the Women's National Indian Association and previously an active organizer for the Woman's Christian Temperance Union.

This conference was able to have an impact on government and the public by effective and aggressive publicity of its annual platform. The Indian Rights Association and the Mohonk Conference represented the high mark of paternalism, a Protestant ethnocentrism that would take years to diminish. However, we should remember that these were educated, sophisticated, energetic, and dedicated people—who often with great sacrifice did what they sincerely believed to be right and needed to be done to improve the quality of Indian life. In their view, it was necessary to Americanize the Indians; this meant a focus on rugged individualism and Christianity with a total disregard for Indian culture, heritage, and religion. Many of the individuals made extended tours of investigation in the West and produced periodic reports of actual conditions on the reservations. The evangelical Protestantism of these individuals and the times cannot be underrated. Even those who held government office during these years, such as the commissioners of Indian affairs, were Protestant religiously oriented men.

Pratt rapidly grew disillusioned with the Mohonk Conference; it specifically avoided the on- or off-reservation school controversy. Pratt eventually quit attending. He saw it as a lot of ineffective talk leading to paper bullets.[60]

Between 1884 and 1887, the various groups united in an attempt to influence Congress to pass legislation for citizenship, allotment of land, and the jurisdiction of U.S. laws over tribal autonomy. The citizenship emphasis was sparked by a Supreme Court decision in 1884. An Indian, named John Elk, living in Omaha, Nebraska, tried to register to vote and was refused. The Supreme Court upheld the refusal.[61] The court established that an Indian could not become a citizen by abandoning tribal allegiance, without the consent and cooperation of the U.S. Government. In other words, it would take an Act of Congress to give Indians the rights of citizenship. This further defined the principle that Congress was responsible for Indian welfare, as wards of the government. The power to govern Indians was established in *U.S. v. Kagama* in 1886 by the Supreme Court, upholding Congressional legislation that established federal jurisdiction over certain major crimes.[62]

These rulings galvanized the humanitarian organizations to demand immediate citizenship, rather than waiting for full education. A rush toward citizenship and land allotment quickly followed leading to the Land-In-Severalty Act, also called the General Allotment Act (or the Dawes Act) of 1887. The idea that citizenship should follow proper education was rapidly abandoned in favor of immediate attainment of land and citizenship with education to follow. This was accompanied by renewed support for on-reservation schooling.

THE LAND-IN-SEVERALTY ACT of February 8, 1887, the Dawes Act, provided the following system of allotment of currently held reservation land:[63]

- 160 acres (called a quarter section, this amount of land is a half-mile square) to each family head.
- Eighty acres to each single person over age eighteen, and to each orphan over eighteen.
- Forty acres to each single person under age eighteen.
- The deed (a patent) issued to each allottee to be held in trust by the government for twenty-five years for the owner and his heirs, not to be sold or encumbered.

- After allotment applied to a tribe, the members had up to four years to make a selection of land, but the secretary of the interior could make a selection if the Indians failed to do so.

- Citizenship conferred upon allottees and Indians who have abandoned their tribes, thus subject to laws of the state or territory.

- Reservation land remaining ("surplus" lands) to be sold to settlers with proceeds to be held in trust by the government to be used for education and "civilization" of tribal members.

- Exemption of the Cherokee, Creek, Choctaw, Chickasaw, Seminole, Osage, Miamie, Peoria, Sac, and Fox in the Indian Territory, and the Seneca in New York.

Allotment, the acquiring of private property, was not a brand new proposal. Allotment had actually been viewed for a long time as a means of granting Indians independence from tribal authority. Various attempts were made to introduce and pass general allotment legislation in the 1880s, as allotment was increasingly seen as a strategy to end large reservations that served as reservoirs of "barbarism," and to separate Indian individuals from tribal leadership. Allotment also opened large amounts of "surplus" Indian land, especially in the West, and for that reason, westerners were major supporters. Of course, the Mohonk Conference and the Indian Rights Association were solidly behind allotment. There was some opposition. Concern was raised that after thirty to forty years, the unprepared Indians would be left with no land. But doubt and opposition were swept away by the enthusiasm of the supporters who believed that their plan would compensate Indians equitably for the land lost.

The perceived advantages of the Dawes Act included the creation of Indian private property owners, achieving the power of the vote, confining tribes to an even smaller base, and making more land available for White settlement, cattle grazing, and railroads. But there were problems: it was compulsory, it was premature in the absence of education and improved economic conditions to prepare for land ownership, and there was no regard for Indian preferences. At its heart was a basic conflict: Indians believed in communal ownership of land; White societies believed in individual ownership.

## American Indian History

| Removal and Reservations | Assimilation and Allotment | Reorganization | Termination | Restoration and Recognition |
|---|---|---|---|---|
| 1880 | 1934 | 1954 | 1970 | |

The allotment process was a method of assimilation, according to its supporters, but only in an ideal sense—the idea that ownership of private property was an essential part of civilized life. The law became an act of idealism. The thinking ran like this: The allotment of a parcel of land would set into motion an inevitable sequence of events making Indians assimilated; ownership of land would be an incentive to work; tribal rule would be eliminated; communal land holding would end, and the individual would be removed from the harmful effects of tribal and camp life. And there was always the supposition that many Indians would become farmers or stockmen almost instantly with this simple act. In reality, most of the land involved was not farming or grazing land, and, of course, a way of life is not instantly changed (the Indians who toured with Buffalo Bill joined old warriors in mocking any Indian who tried to farm). In addition the level of poverty made it impossible to acquire the equipment and supplies required, and insufficient funds were provided for this purpose. But at its heart, the allotment philosophy was the same as Pratt's: the elimination of the tribes, the reservations, and the Indian way of life. For the Indians, the allotment experience was demoralizing. Those influential men in White society who liked to be viewed as the Indians' friends ironically contributed to the dissolution of Indian self-respect and autonomy by rejecting any accommodation or blending of White and Indian values. The well-intentioned plans were not geared to an Indian heritage and outlook. Indians emphasized a communal rather than an individualistic spirit, sharing rather than personal accumulation, and a use of nature that did not include exploitation for profit.

The act did not spell out how the land was to be selected. In operation, the allotments were taken, not always side by side, on reservation lands, and the Indians were essentially confined by the law to this land for twenty-five years. Thus there was little change, and the allotment process did not end the isolation of Indians. The Dawes Act allowed the Indians to become even more confined and pressured by Whites near and around them.

What the Dawes Act did accomplish was the loss of Indian land from 1887 to 1934, most of it by 1921. During this time, 118 reservations (138 million acres) were opened for allotment; by conservative estimates, eighty-six million acres (more than 60 percent) were lost.[64] Others have provided even higher estimates. Most of this came from land left over after allotment, so-called "surplus" land, but some represented leases and sales by the Indians to White people after the twenty-five-year trust period ended. For many tribes, the twenty-five-year trust period was shortened by the Burke Act of May 8, 1906, that allowed the secretary of the interior (in practice, the Indian agents) to provide individual patents in fee (a certificate like a deed) freeing the land from the protection of the government trust and allowing individual sales without waiting twenty-five years.[65] What was left as reservation land, according to a 1939 government report, was unproductive land, incapable of providing for self-support.[66]

The Dawes Act was a consummate failure; it neither protected Indian lands nor produced long-term benefits for individual Indians. Had the Dawes Act led to true assimilation, the loss of land would not be a major issue. Fortunately, for the preservation of Indian culture and heritage, both Pratt's approach and the allotment approach failed to assimilate the Indians. Although the allotment process made the old way of living harder, it did not eliminate it. Thus the loss of land continues to be a major sore point. Simply viewing allotted Indian reservations on a map doesn't present an accurate picture because, unlike the appearance of homogeneous, contiguous Indian land, it is actually a checkerboard of land plots owned by both Indians and Whites. Furthermore, the process of allotment intensified and complicated the involvement of Indians with the federal bureaucracy.

The handling of individual trust fees and arrangements was a massive job, requiring even more Indian Bureau employees. Those Indians who had sold or leased their allotted lands were thrust into a new dependent relationship for their economic affairs. Those

Indians who became land owners struggled with marginal lands and lack of supplies and equipment. The allotment policy had produced just the opposite of what it intended—a state of poverty and economic dependency. Tribes that had once been self-sufficient were now totally dependent on the market economy of White Americans. Rather than eliminating the Bureau of Indian Affairs, the allotment process strengthened it; its bureaucracy grew larger and more necessary in order to handle the complications of allotment. The effects of allotment continue to produce problems today. Federal regulations require that allotment property be passed equally to heirs. Over 100 years later, many allotments now have up to fifty owners, and land-use decisions must be approved by 51 percent of the co-owners. This continues to be a bureaucratic quagmire. Some Indians now own parcels of land that have to be measured in feet, not acres.

CARLOS MONTEZUMA TOTALLY accepted and enthusiastically promoted the philosophy of assimilation, which is not surprising given his immersion in the prevailing Protestant environment of the times.

The objectives of assimilation and allotment were derived from a fundamental conflict between the communal life and customs of American Indians and the Protestant focus on individualism and Christianity, based strongly on the Puritan work ethic. The fervent reformers believed that the force of Christianity could bring about changes within one generation. They viewed the Indian culture and way of life that differed so markedly from their own as heathen and pagan. This was an approach and a philosophy that amalgamated evangelical Protestantism into what it meant to be an "American."[67] Montezuma was a product of these times, the last decades of the nineteenth century, a time during which American culture was dominated by Protestantism.

The "rightness" of the American way could be seen every day in the decades after the Civil War in the tangible material prosperity that spread over the country. The dynamic growth of Chicago reviewed in Chapter 7 was symbolic of the entire country. This obvious success of American civilization was seen by White Protestants as evidence of "God's way," which of course was also their way. Difficult or undesirable conditions and situations in life would certainly be transcended in man's continuing progress. This was a philosophy also to be found in Freemasonry (Chapter 10) and it is not surprising that Freemasonry was very popular and prominent around 1900, and educated Indians like Montezuma eagerly became Masons.

The prevailing ethos of the late 1800s was articulated in a famous article entitled "Wealth," published by Andrew Carnegie, one of America's richest entrepreneurs and philanthropists, in the June 1889 issue of the *North American Review*.[68] Property was regarded as sacred ("…upon the sacredness of property civilization itself depends"), and its possession by individuals was to be protected by government. The purpose of competition was the accumulation of wealth, and this process benefited society because it ensured the survival of the fittest. This is the capitalist system of individualism, "the best and most valuable of all that humanity has yet accomplished." Finally, the use and disposition of property by the wealthy were responsibilities under God (wealth being a divine gift), and this included appropriate philanthropy dedicated to those who were willing to help themselves ("…one of the serious obstacles to the improvement of our race is indiscriminate charity"). These beliefs are easily discerned in the efforts of the nineteenth-century Indian reformers directed to assimilation and allotment. Anglo-Saxon Protestants believed they had a divine commission to be their brothers' keeper. This, then, was the basis for the White attitude toward the Indian "savages" at this time in history, making the elimination of a different culture a righteous mission.

The failure of assimilation and allotment was due to the simple insistence of White reformers to support a policy that was foreign to the traditions and hearts of American Indians. Despite their loss of political power and autonomy, American Indians were still able to put forth a significant cultural resistance.[69]

What happened to the citizenship granted with the allotments? In practice, nothing changed. The reservation and reservation life were still administered by the government and the Indian agency. The land, supplies, courts, schools, and roads were still under the administration of the Indian Bureau. Because the land was being held in trust by the government, use of the land was under the supervision of the Indian Bureau. For example, the Bureau did not allow Indians to cut and sell timber off their own land. Living on the reservation, there was nothing to vote for. The allotment process did not change the reservation environment of enforced idleness, poverty, disease, and hopelessness.

Although the length and kinds of leases were altered over the years, the principle of leasing both allotted and tribal lands was established in 1891. In 1891, Senator Henry Dawes amended his act, permitting the leasing of an allotment for a period of three years for farming and grazing, and ten years for mining—by reason of "disability." The leases were subject to regulation by the secretary of the interior, which in effect gave authority and power to the local Indian agent to arrange leases.[70] This act also permitted a tribal council to lease surplus tribal lands in those reservations created by treaty, not by Congress or executive order—five years for grazing and ten years for mining. This opened the door for widespread leasing agreements between Indians and Whites, even though they were, strictly speaking, often illegal.

In 1894, leasing regulations were further loosened. The leasing of tribal lands of any reservation was now permitted, and farming (five years) was now allowed.[71] And with allotted lands, inability was added to disability as a reason to allow leasing. Inability, for example, could be an individual without horses or tools.

By 1895, it was apparent that allotment was not accomplishing any major changes, and attention turned to conditions on the reservations and reorganization of the Indian Bureau. Dawes himself referred to the law as an experiment; failure was due to moving too fast and the selling of the "surplus" lands, pushing the Indians into more confinement and isolation.[72] Leasing was the final undermining. In his view, it was a wise policy, but poorly administered. The Indian was left not thoroughly a ward, and not wholly a citizen.

Fortunately, the incongruous segments of nineteenth-century American society (Indians being one) did not disappear, and indeed, their number multiplied in the twentieth-century evolution of "Americanism" that gradually recognized and respected multiple ways of life. The shift away from Protestant dominance was rapid after 1900, fueled by the increases in scientific and technologic knowledge, and sparked by the social discontent and response to the problems created by industrialization and urbanization (well illustrated by the story of Chicago told in Chapter 7). American Protestantism splintered into a kaleidoscope of thought, ranging from orthodox fundamentalism, which can be viewed as a reactionary movement, to liberal philosophic idealism, with many creeds in between. The Protestant emphasis shifted from the individual to social action and reform, a shift that was to have a notable impact on Montezuma.

## PRATT AND ALLOTMENT

Pratt, of course, believed in the primary importance of education. He certainly favored citizenship and elimination of tribal allegiances, but only after educational preparation. He further saw the folly of assigning every Indian the same occupation. Once underway, Pratt saw that the allotment system did not eliminate the reservation, and by 1892, viewed it as a "flat failure."[73] He did favor leasing, seeing the money as a way to gain education or to leave the tribe.

In these years, the single-minded and righteous Pratt grew cantankerous in his opposition to other groups, the Indian Bureau, and legislators, including attacks on the churches for their missionary work, seeing them as aggrandizement rather than true efforts in education (also, their on-reservation location was a thorn in his side). The religious contract schools were an inexpensive way for the Indian Bureau to extend education. Because the religious schools were on-reservation, they represented major competition for students for Carlisle. Thus all religious groups were Pratt's opponents, but especially the Catholics since they represented the majority.

Montezuma, writing in 1892 from the Western Shoshone Agency where he was a physician employed by the Bureau of Indian Affairs, continued to be a staunch supporter of Pratt, the product of an ineluctable bond that would last a lifetime.

> I am fully aware of your position through the press. ...Stand up and face the foe, for you have one Apache in an ambush ready at any moment to rush and present the Indian question black and white. It is disgusting to see how the government ignores the efficient workers in the Indian service, which only exposes their ignorance of what they ought to know better, especially on reliable opinions. It shows plainly that there is an organization behind the House, which opposes the freeing of the Indians from their reservation bondage of degradation and ruin to that of enlightenment and education (Catholics).

> I believe from the bottom of my heart, if there is anything that will change a man—even as Indians—from degradation and ruin, it is the *true* and *undefiled religion* of God. But what is not true, you might just as well deal out poison to the Indians for his ignorance and superstition, will sooner or later wipe them from our midst without they being made a slave under the crown of Rome.

> If the government is so economizing, why not appropriate sufficient money for transportation of Indian children to the East? The children themselves in few years will be self-supporting, have command of the English language and they will have some idea of the world, and I do not think they will ever return to camp life, but will be a man, not a savage; a citizen, not a pauper. While, if the Indian children remain on reservations and attend the day schools, they will lack the above opportunities; at the age of fifteen and sixteen they are married; another family to be added to the ration list, which means expense to the government for years to come as they will be idlers, beggars, gamblers, and paupers.

> Capt, if the choice of my life remained with my mother and father or myself, I would not be writing to you. Ignorant and at the very lowest depth of an uncivilized life of which the

reservation budget bestows would have been my fate. So, you see I believe [in] compulsory education for the Indians. We have enslaved the Indians in ignorance and superstition long enough and have fed and clothed them without any recompense. Some radical change must come soon or they will be an obstacle in our midst. We have experimented with the Indians by bullets and reservation system, they are expensive and failures. I know of no way by which the Indians can become like the whites only by the same process which the whites give to their children and that is "education." This has never failed to improve any nation. The Indians of today can never prosper or grow great, if they are hid away from the outer world and its sunshine of enlightenment.

Our Christian civilization ought to be ashamed that it cannot educate a nation inside of four centuries. … *I will stand by you.*[74]

Pratt forwarded the letter to Senator Dawes, saying, "…the enclosed, which, under all the circumstances, is no less gratifying to me than any I have received within the past few weeks from people occupying high stations in the land."[75]

Appropriations to sectarian Indian schools began to decline in 1892, but not significantly until 1897 when Congress declared governmental policy to be against appropriations for education in sectarian schools. Existing schools were allowed to persist but with progressive reductions until 1901 when contracts with religious schools were ended.[76] However, religious contract schools continued to draw financial support from the Indian trust funds, and it wasn't until 1917 that total federal support was withdrawn.[77]

By 1899, 3,800 students had attended Carlisle, but only 209 had achieved a level at which Pratt provided a diploma of graduation. Thereafter, about forty to fifty students graduated each year (reaching a total of 761), usually requiring a stay of five years, and often more.[78] Luther Standing Bear finished four years in 1883, received an allotment of 640 acres in South Dakota in 1907, became a U.S. citizen and eventually lived in California acting in movies with Douglas Fairbanks and William S. Hart.[79] Pratt was successful in placing a handful of his students in various colleges, but only a few persisted the course.

## THE DEMISE OF CARLISLE

The vast majority of Carlisle students returned to their reservations. It was hard for these young people to resist the pull of family and tribe coupled with the promise of free land and rations. Criticism of Carlisle was significantly derived from the prevailing impression of student performance when they returned home.[80] Government surveys indicated that more than half did well. They were temperate, self-supporting, and living in decent houses, but those that did poorly created, then as now, more than their share of publicity and attention. Critics, such as Zitkala-Ša (Chapter 9), would also argue that even those apparently doing well struggled with their transition state. This experience did not surprise Pratt. It only strengthened his belief that the Indians must leave the tribes and be assimilated into White society.

The growing belief that off-reservation schooling had failed to accomplish its mission had its roots in false expectations. To be sure, government support and funding did not approach a total effort, but assimilation activists promoted the idea that the transition would be complete and rapid, perhaps within one generation. One important reason this could not be accomplished was the simple fact that the students did not respond in a passive manner, but most exercised a process of pragmatic adaptation, adopting some aspects of White society and rejecting others, an active process that saved a part of the heart and mind for tribal culture and heritage. Expecting a total and complete transformation of hearts and minds proved to be unrealistic. Lost in any summary of the Indian boarding school experience are the thousands of individual stories, ranging from heady success to tragic failures and even deaths.

Gradually in the 1890s the rules of civil service were extended to the teachers at Carlisle. This interfered with Pratt's personal management of the school, and his opposition drew serious reaction from government officers, including the Indian Bureau. Governmental Indian leadership came to view Pratt as tyrannical in his control of Carlisle.

| President | Secretary of the Interior | Commissioner of Indian Affairs |
|---|---|---|
| Rutherford B. Hayes, 1877 | Carl Schurz, 1877 | Ezra A. Hayt, 1877<br>Roland E. Trowbridge, 1880 |
| James A. Garfield, 1881 | Samuel J. Kirkwood, 1881 | Hiram Price, 1881 |
| Chester A. Arthur, 1881 | Henry M. Teller, 1882 | Hiram Price |
| Grover Cleveland, 1885 | L. Q. C. Lamar, 1885<br>W. F. Vilas, 1888 | John D.C. Atkins, 1885<br>John H. Oberly, 1888 |
| Benjamin Harrison, 1889 | John W. Noble, 1889 | Thomas J. Morgan, 1889 |
| Grover Cleveland, 1893 | Hoke Smith, 1893<br>D. R. Francis, 1896 | Daniel M. Browning, 1893 |
| William McKinley, 1897 | C. N. Bliss, 1897<br>E. A. Hitchcock, 1899 | William A. Jones, 1897 |
| William McKinley, 1901 | E. A. Hitchcock | William A. Jones |
| Theodore Roosevelt, 1901 | E. A. Hitchcock | William A. Jones |
| Theodore Roosevelt, 1905 | E. A. Hitchcock<br>James R. Garfield, 1907 | Francis E. Leupp, 1904 |
| William Howard Taft, 1909 | R. A. Ballinger, 1909<br>Walter L. Fisher, 1911 | Robert G. Valentine, 1909 |

Increasingly at odds with governmental policy and the Indian Bureau, Pratt, now an embattled reactionary often thought about leaving Carlisle after 1896. When McKinley became president, William A. Jones, a man with whom Pratt had a good relationship, became commissioner of Indian affairs. After McKinley's assassination, Theodore Roosevelt became president, a man with a long history of a critical attitude toward Indians, especially to off-reservation schools, and a personal dislike of Pratt. Pratt and Roosevelt first came into conflict when the Indian commissioner sent Roosevelt to investigate Pratt's complaints against civil service intrusion in 1893. Roosevelt concluded that the trouble was Pratt not the civil service law. Good relations between Pratt and Jones rapidly changed as Jones adopted Roosevelt's more critical attitude. Another Roosevelt favorite and another one of Pratt's targets, Francis E. Leupp, succeeded Jones as commissioner of Indian affairs. Leupp, previously a lobbyist for the Indian Rights Association, actively adopted a policy that favored reservation day schools and the cultivation of Indian heritage and culture. His appointment in 1901 marked the beginning of the decline in influence and dominance of the Protestant Christian reformers.

Pratt became a major in July 1898 and a lieutenant colonel in February 1901, whereupon he offered to retire immediately if he were appointed brigadier general (with its significantly better pension), an offer that was refused. In January 1902, he was notified that he was about to be promoted to colonel. Pratt again offered to retire if given the rank of brigadier general, but this was again rejected on the grounds that he had not been on active duty since he was a captain.

During Pratt's last two years at Carlisle, he became increasingly belli-cose and antagonistic toward his superiors. Carlisle was more and more out of step with the emerging policy of gradual change along with recognition of the importance of Indian heritage. Pratt grew crusty. By now the Bureau and government leadership were waiting for an excuse to order his retirement. Pratt provided this excuse on May 9, 1904, in a speech to the New York Ministers' Conference when he again attacked the Bureau (the speech was highlighted in several leading newspapers). His senti-ment and thoughts were not new, but on June 15, 1904, Commissioner Jones informed Pratt by letter that he was dismissed by order of the secretary of the interior, and with the approval of the president, he would be replaced by Captain William A. Mercer on July 1, 1904. Pratt was given the retired rank of brigadier general.

In his farewell remarks, Pratt said, "segregated, supervised, and schooled on reservations remote from contact with

*Pratt at his Desk—Last Days at Carlisle*

*Anna Laura Mason and Richard Henry Pratt
Fiftieth Wedding Anniversary, 1915*

our people and industries, notwithstanding all the influences of whatever sort that may be doled out to them there, they inevitably continue dependent and undeveloped people. The Bureau is a barnacle, an unnatural, unphilosophical attachment to the ship of State."[81]

After retirement from Carlisle, Pratt lived in various places, including Rochester, New York, Philadelphia with his daughter, California with his son in San Diego and a daughter in

Berkeley, and several hotels in Washington in order to be near the action; he met constantly with legislators, administrators in the Indian Bureau, and fellow workers in the cause. He traveled extensively visiting old places and friends. Eleven years after he left Carlisle, the peripatetic and indefatigable Pratt wrote Montezuma: "Mrs. Pratt and I passed our 51st Anniversary yesterday. …[we will] spend several days at Atlantic City as a sort of a honeymoon."[82] Until his death, he bombarded officials and elected legislators and executives with letters and speeches consistently promoting the views he held his entire life. Hardly a month went by in the next eighteen years that didn't see one or more letters exchanged by Pratt and Carlos Montezuma.

Montezuma, of course, was outraged by Pratt's dismissal. He wrote to the commissioner of Indian affairs: "It is a wrong step, a disgrace to the administration, and a backward movement for the Indian. Your duty is to re-instate him, or prove his utterances false, after his long experience in the Indian service. With all of my heart I concur with him."[83] He further wrote to President Theodore Roosevelt:

> I speak in behalf of my people, the Indians throughout the country. In silence I have looked upon you as a great father at Washington to my people, but I am much surprised and dumbfounded at the position you have taken in permitting the dismissal of the foremost student of Indian affairs in the service of the Government, General R. H. Pratt, from the position of Superintendent of the Carlisle Indian School. He was considered by the educated Indians of our country as the one man in the Government service possessing exceptional ability to deal with the Indian problem, especially the education and civilization of the young. His dismissal is unjust to the wards of our nation, who deserve the rare talents, wide knowledge and accurate judgment he displayed in Indian matters. It is a dark blot in your administration, a backward movement for my people. There is not a wigwam throughout the country that can smoke the pipe of peace with you for such an act of injustice to our veteran leader, General R. H. Pratt. Remember, we educated Indians feel keenly the mistake you have made. It is not too late for you to right this wrong by reinstating General Pratt, and then we shall again smoke the pipe of peace with you."[84]

A month later, Montezuma wrote to Pratt: "I am in bewilderment why I do not hear from the White House or from the Commissioner."[85] A few years later, Montezuma described Theodore Roosevelt as follows: "I cannot for the life of me see what there is in Roosevelt to admire or to make fuss over. To me he is ugly, beastly, coarse and ungentlemanly. His smiles, his patting on the back, his preaching, his flattery and his take-you-in-his-confidence may suit some people but to me the devil does the same thing. He is not sincere."[86]

Montezuma did hear from Commissioner Jones who wrote: "In fact I believe if Genl. Pratt had resigned from the service three years ago his standing would be much better than it is now. I cannot avoid the impression that his physical ailments have affected him mentally, as this is the only way that I can account for his conduct in the last year or two."[87]

Montezuma never heard from the president, but he never wavered in being Pratt's champion. It is not surprising to learn that when Montezuma was on the platform at the Carlisle commencement in March 1905 Superintendent Mercer blocked his scheduled speech.[88]

PRATT'S SUCCESSOR, WILLIAM A. MERCER, in keeping with the Indian Bureau's current views to incorporate Indian culture into school programs, initiated a Department of Native Indian Arts in February 1906 and rejected Pratt's ideas of complete assimilation. Mercer was selected to be the new superintendent because of twelve years of service as an Indian agent, his views that were in harmony with the Bureau, and because he was a good friend of the new commissioner. He lasted three years. He encouraged Pratt supporters to leave and expanded the football program, but most notably he relaxed discipline. Student guards, for example, replaced daily and nightly supervision. Three years later, Mercer requested a return to active duty, amidst rumors of moral impropriety.

During Mercer's years as superintendent, Montezuma continued to work towards the restoration of Pratt. His letter campaign was formidable, to anyone and everyone who might influence the process. His article printed in the *Philadelphia Public Ledger* on July 22, 1907, was entitled: "Carlisle Indian School Drifting From Its Moorings. A Severe Criticism of the Policy Now Pursued at the Institution—General Pratt's Fundamental Principles Cast Aside and Their Purposes Frustrated." The article expressed Montezuma's total support of Pratt and revealed the depth of Montezuma's acceptance of the philosophy of assimilation:

> When at the last session of Congress the effort to destroy the Carlisle School by preventing the usual appropriations for its maintenance came to naught, there was great rejoicing among the real friends of the school and of the Indian People. But they realized that in any event the school would not perish for want of material sustenance. This, at least, was something to be thankful for. These same friends, however, are not unmindful of the fact that there are more ways than one of terminating the existence of this grandly conceived and heretofore successful institution. In this connection the present superintendent of the school is pursuing a policy, which deserves the severest condemnation, as the facts will show.

> Employees older in the Indian service than the school itself are to be removed from the Carlisle Institution and their places taken by others, not for any justifiable reason, but simply because they bore a substantial part in the success the school had attained to under its old-time management. No duty rests upon the friends of the school to minimize the effects, which necessarily must follow these changes in its working form. If the ultimate purpose of the present administration is to put an end to the school as a practical and permanent aid to the Indian cause, no surer method could be adopted than the one being pursued in the unwarranted dismissal of old and faithful employees who, by their habitual adaptability to the needs of the school, cannot be disposed without irreparable damage to the institution. The best proof that they are not being removed for the good of the service is that they had been connected satisfactorily with the former management during its long and most successful career.

## Carlisle's Peculiar Work

The Carlisle School is not like the ordinary college or university, which is, to a great extent, like a large business corporation where changes may constantly be made in department officials and principal officers without detriment to the work of the institution. Such organizations have to educate and train only the youth of civilization the whole course of procedure being, practically, to offer a field for the further development of mental faculties, which already, by heredity and primary training, are fairly well cultivated.

Given sufficient resources, the founding of colleges and universities is generally quite a matter of formality, but with Carlisle all was so different. It had its origin in the thought of one single individual that a way could be found to practically attract the Indian people toward the pursuits of civilization; that something in the nature of an industrial training, together with opportunities for the cultivation of the mental faculties, could be offered to the Indian boys and girls by the establishment of a school especially designed for that purpose. The germ of this beneficent conception of the founder was that there was nothing in a name, but everything in the man; that the Indian was what environment had made him—different from other races as they were different from him only because of the surroundings in the midst of which they lived; and that those only were the Indians best friends who, discarding the untenable theory of making a "better Indian" out of the aborigine, were able to see that the true idea was not to make the Indian better, as such, but, eliminating all that was signified by the word Indian, to take hold of the man and transform him from the plight in which environment had placed him to a condition reflecting the results of civilized influences.

## Before and Since Pratt's Times

It is easy, therefore, to see that an institution conceived as Carlisle was conceived, founded as Carlisle was founded, and successfully conducted for more than 20 years on the theory upon which it was conceived and founded, cannot be perpetuated except by a continuance of the methods which many years of success have shown to be the only methods adapted to fulfill the purpose for which the school was established.

Any other course adopted and pursued is only a sure way of bringing the school to an untimely end. There are a few propositions relating to the present Carlisle School management that may be considered self-evident. First, those who are in charge either have the interest of the pupils at heart or have they not. If they have but one desire and that to do the best that can be done to accomplish the purpose for which the school was founded, then they should not be influenced by personal feeling or motive in selecting assistants to carry on the work.

Second, it is also self-evident that up to the time the founder of the school was removed, without cause, from his position as superintendent, the school in every way had demonstrated the truth and practicability of the theory upon which it was established. The attendance at that time was increasing regularly and the results accomplished by that part of the school work known as the "outing system" were highly gratifying and constituted one of the most satisfactory features of the superintendent's annual report to the Secretary of the Interior. And yet, with a heart throbbing with deepest feeling, we suppose, for the Indian boys and girls the present superintendent without ceremony or cause, strikes off the official head of the woman who was the very life and soul of the "outing system." Mockery, nothing else. And it is useless to mince words or try to give this act of the superintendent even a color of consistency.

## Departures From Old Standards

Judging from the way things are going, the present management all along has been suffering great irritation from the fact that it is everywhere brought face to face with the fact that the school as formerly conducted was a great success. The condition of things was such as to disarm criticism and, therefore, in order to satisfy the desire for a change of some kind the new management was driven in the necessity of making extreme departures from the courses that had been so long adhered to in carrying out the purpose for which the school was established.

First, there was to be something in the military line that could excite the interest of the Indian boy and their first step to this end was to appeal to his pride in dress by supplying him with a blue uniform with bright buttons, which would hold his interest while he was being initiated into the technicalities of military drill and tactics. As a justification for this departure, the Indian Commissioner went into the psychology of the Indian's make-up where he discovered what he termed "a well-known fighting tendency" out of which raw material he could see the making of good soldiers.

The Indian girls would make good nurses, not for any well-defined reasons that could be given, but as a feasible method of doing something that had never before been put in operation at the school.

Owing to previous environment and ignorance of the ways of civilized life, there was every reason for believing the Indian girls to be deficiently equipped for the duties of caring for the sick, but this did not have any weight with the Commissioner, inasmuch as his attention was directed more to the matter of making a change in the school work than to consistency of action.

## Indian Music and Art

Next came an excursion into the unexplored domain of alleged "Indian music." The fact that there was no such thing embraced in any justifiable application of the word "music" did not serve to check the enthusiasm with which the Commissioner set about to make the work of collecting Indian songs and making them a part of the course of instruction to the Indian boys and girls. Another step closely connected in kind with the Indian music departure was taken when the Commissioner constructed what he thought as well of as to call "Leupp's Indian Arts Studio," a building to be used for teaching the Indian boys and girls to do the things that their ancestors used to do in aboriginal days—diametrically opposed, of course, to the purpose for which the school was founded, inasmuch as there could not possibly be any connection between Indian basket making and beadwork and the preparation of the Indian boys and girls for participation in the affairs of civilized life.

If these departures are to be adhered to as a part of the future work of the school at Carlisle, then the management is possibly acting consistently in getting rid of all employees who were so closely and usefully identified with the former superintendent. It could hardly be expected that a force of one-time earnest workers in carrying out the real object of the school, and who had the success at heart, could be completely turned about and successfully employed in a direction entirely at variance with methods to which they had formerly been so closely allied. Better let them go than turn them into mere machines to carry on the work, which apparently has been mapped out under the new order of things.

The Carlisle School for more than 20 years, in addition to the work accomplished in preparing its pupils for participation in the industrial and educational work of the country, was a powerful factor in proclaiming to the people that the Indian, when properly taught and trained in the midst of civilized surroundings, became a man among men without any distinctiveness as an Indian or otherwise, and this was one of the things which the founder foresaw as one of the results which would follow the establishment of the school. It was not difficult for him to anticipate what would follow as a matter of course if the true purpose of the school was strictly adhered to in his management. The founder also clearly comprehended that all work in pursuance of the erroneous idea of "making of a better Indian" would result in nothing toward the solution of the Indian question.[89]

THE BUREAU SELECTED Moses Friedman, the assistant superintendent of Haskell Indian School in Kansas, to replace Mercer. He had considerable experience as an industrial teacher in the Cincinnati school system before entering the Indian service. Moses Friedman succeeded Mercer as superintendent in 1908. Because Friedman was not a military officer, the Indian Bureau now had to pay the superintendent's salary. This added to Carlisle's money problems, because the Bureau had not raised salaries commensurate with the increase in prices in the first decades of the 1900s. But in 1907, Warner, the football coach, received $4,000 for only a few months' work, and a rent-free house on the school grounds. The poor salaries of the general staff compared with the high salary for the football coach conspired to lower morale and staff quality. W.G. Thompson, one of Pratt's long-time Carlisle employees, wrote to Montezuma in 1907: "The school had degenerated into a school of professional athletes. …The welfare of the individual as well as that of the community must step aside to gratify the desire of Major Mercer and 'Pop' Warner (the coach) to win, and create a large account to use as they wish, without supervision from Washington. …it is a common saying at Carlisle that if you are an athlete you can do as you please, stay out nights, get drunk—anything."[90] Montezuma authored a column printed in the *Chicago Sunday Tribune* on November 24, 1907, that itemized the football wrongdoings at Carlisle.[91] Two years later, Clara Spotted Horse wrote to Montezuma from Carlisle: "…I guess you read of the last game at St. Louis. Wheelock made some good plays. That was not Wheelock. Wheelock was here that day no wheres near St. Louis. Frito Hendricks went by that name. …It seems Warner does those things that are not right only degrading the standard of Carlisle."[92] Montezuma passed the letter in 1909 from Clara Spotted Horse on to the famous football coach at the University of Chicago, Alonzo Stagg, who promised to consider the impropriety.[93] As Montezuma succinctly put it: "The Carlisle football team is as crooked as a ram's horn."[94] Although it would take another five years to remove Warner, the reaction had started.

The halcyon days were over. When Pratt left, the railroads withdrew their practice of giving Carlisle reduced rates, tremendously increasing the expense of transporting students. In 1909, the commissioner of Indian affairs assumed the responsibility of making staff appointments to Carlisle according to the civil service laws, and the low salaries ensured teachers of low quality. Even the school diet was affected, as meals became meager and unbalanced. Montezuma never faltered in his criticism, writing in 1909: "Roosevelt & Leupp did not start right upon Indian matters. If they were real friends of the Indians, they would never in the world have dismissed Gen. Pratt from Carlisle, whom I consider the best friend of the Indians in United States and the next mistake was turning that Grand Carlisle School into professional athletic school, a curiosity shop and make the people of the United States believe there is such thing as Indian art & music, which you and I know there is no such thing from the definition by Webster."[95]

Friedman's reign was filled with scandal and problems. By now the physical condition of the buildings was badly in need of upgrading, and structural improvements proved to be Friedman's only positive contribution. In contrast to Pratt, Friedman was a poor organizer with no leadership ability. Carlisle rapidly became an unhappy, rebellious school. Western reservation schools were sending their incorrigible students to Carlisle. Problems of intoxication, pregnancies, and runaways increased. A Congressional investigation in 1914 further discovered a misuse of funds, leading to a subsequent trial. Although Friedman was not found guilty, he and the school never recovered. Oscar S. Lipps, one of the four current supervisors of Indian schools, replaced Friedmann. He had risen through the Bureau ranks and was a competent and energetic administrator. Lipps' first job as temporary superintendent was to restore discipline. This he did, sending three girls to prison, a drastic example that worked. He restored morale and respect, earning a full appointment as superintendent in May 1915.

Outwardly, Carlisle seemed to be doing well. The band now numbered sixty pieces and was invited to every noteworthy event. The newspapers were flourishing; the activities were numerous; the students were healthier and better educated (by 1916, only boys fourteen and older and girls sixteen and older with at least three years of schooling were being admitted). The Carlisle baseball, track and field, lacrosse, and football teams had become very successful, attracting publicity and proving to be financially lucrative (for example, baseball players were being paid to play for other teams during the summer).

Louis Tewanima and Jim Thorpe brought international acclaim to Carlisle. Tewanima, a Hopi Indian, finished ninth in the London Olympics marathon in 1908, and was a record holder in races of eight to fifteen miles in length. Jim Thorpe, a Sauk Indian ("Bright Path") of the Sac and Fox Nation, arrived at Carlisle in 1904. In the Stockholm Olympics in 1912, he won the decathlon and the pentathlon. In 1911 and 1912, Thorpe, five feet eleven inches tall and 185 pounds, was a football All-American halfback. He played professional baseball for seven seasons and professional football for nearly fifteen years, and never missed a minute of play because of injury. Thorpe has often been recognized as the greatest athlete in history; he even won a ballroom dancing contest in 1912.

The Carlisle football team played its first game in 1894. For the first five years, the coach was a volunteer, and although the opponents included respected colleges, high school and YMCA teams were also on the schedule. Although Carlisle was not a college, many of its students were of college age. The games were at first rather informal, and because Carlisle lacked a decent playing field, the only home game was usually the first game of the season. The season of 1896 was a turning point; the team played Yale, Harvard, Princeton, Pennsylvania, and Pennsylvania State—the best teams in the nation. Red and gold became the official colors, and Frank Hudson and Isaac Seneca became Carlisle's first All-Americans. The season ended in Chicago before 15,000 spectators under lights, and Carlisle defeated the team considered to be the champion of the West, the University of Wisconsin. Pratt's initial reluctance turned to strong support as he saw the good publicity and the good

*Carlisle Football Team—1914*

*Back Row:*   Ranco, Hawk, Morrin, Hill, Pratt
*Middle Row:*   Martell, Willet, Welmas, Callac, Bush, Lookaround, Gillman
*Front Row:*   Broker, Wolford, Burd

image the team presented to White society. In 1899, Pratt hired Glenn Scobie ("Pop") Warner to be the first paid coach at $35 per week, and the following year he became athletic director and coach of all sports. He left in 1904 to coach at Cornell, but he was lured back in 1907, with an offer of $4,000 per season to take Carlisle into the big time.

Pop Warner coached the Carlisle Indians from 1899 to 1914, except for the 1904–1906 seasons.[96] The greatness of the teams can be attributed in large part to this innovative coach.[97] Called "Pop" by his teammates because he was older when he was a freshman at Cornell, Warner was the first to use the huddle and numbered plays, the spiral forward pass, to teach the lineman's three-point stance, and to refine blocking to knock over opponents not just move them; he even invented shin guards. He emphasized physical endurance and precise execution. Warner became a legendary coach, spanning forty-four years at Iowa State, Georgia, Cornell, Pittsburgh, Stanford, and Temple. The Carlisle athletes were tough and fast, and loved playing. The football team played all over the country; they especially liked to beat the Army team.[98] Using about fifteen young men with an average weight of 170 pounds, the Carlisle Indians repeatedly conquered teams that outmanned and outweighed them. The 1907 team, Thorpe's first year as a football player, lost only one game. Thorpe played in 1907 and 1908, returned home, then returned to play in 1911, and 1912, when he was first team All-American. In 1912, the team won twelve, lost one, and tied one—playing the best teams in America.

The football team played a major role in the downfall of Carlisle. The Carlisle Athletic Association, presided over by Warner, managed income from football. The popularity and success of the team led to significant revenue. Although the accounts were periodically checked by school officials and the Bureau, the money itself could be spent by the school's superintendent without supervision. After Pratt, football income replaced charitable donations.

To be sure, much of the money was wisely used, but in addition athletes were provided gifts, better diet and lodging, and money, and White ballplayers were paid to be part of the team. Discipline was most lax with the football players. Alcohol abuse and thefts were hidden from publicity. But the rest of the school was very much aware of this special treatment, and it was a major factor in the unhappiness and declining morale in the school. The Congressional investigation of 1914 recommended that Warner resign as athletic director and coach. Under Lipps, athletics were returned to their rightful position and treatment.

In 1917, Lipps left Carlisle to become Chief Supervisor of Indian Schools. The new superintendent was John Francis, Jr., the fourth and final superintendent. By now the Bureau was looking for a way to end Carlisle's days. The Board of Indian Commissioners had released in 1918 its report of a study of students returning to the reservations, concluding that the average returning student returned to the reservation way of life and that conditions on the reservations were the major cause.[99] Commissioner of Indian Affairs, Cato Sells, was given an opportunity when World War I attracted Indians into the service, and the number of students at Carlisle became too low to provide adequate funds based on the per capita appropriation. Sells, knowing the War Department needed more hospitals, offered to return Carlisle to the War Department, which still retained ownership. Francis resigned to enlist in the army, and the Carlisle students and supplies were rapidly distributed to other Indian boarding schools. On September 1, 1918, in a morning ceremony on the parade grounds, the flag was slowly lowered. The flag was handed to Major A. C. Bachmeyher who reattached it, slowly raised it, and Carlisle officially became U. S. Army Base Hospital No. 31. Today, Carlisle is the home of the U.S. Army War College. During its thirty-nine years of existence, the Carlisle Indian Industrial School had about 8,500 pupils from over 100 tribes.[100]

TODAY, FOUR OFF-RESERVATION BOARDING SCHOOLS are still operated by the Bureau of Indian Affairs, all highlighting Indian culture and involving tribal leaders in decision-making. Chemawa Indian School on more than 400 acres in Salem, Oregon, is a four-year high school, serving over sixty tribes from sixteen states. This school, founded in 1880, has had over 30,000 students in its history.[101] Riverside Indian School in Anadarko, Oklahoma, founded in 1874, is a twelve-grade school, serving over 400 students from sixty tribes. Flandreau Indian Boarding School is in South Dakota, and Sherman Indian High School is in Riverside, California. The Haskell Institute opened in 1884 in Lawrence, Kansas, became a junior college in 1970, the Haskell Indian Nations University, and a four-year college in 1993. The Haskell 320-acre campus contains the American Indian Athletic Hall of Fame. Its student body represents over 160 tribes from thirty-seven states.

What would have been the future of Carlisle if Pratt had changed over time, accepting the growing regard for tribal culture and heritage, remaining to select and guide his successors?

Perhaps Carlisle would have evolved into a true collegiate experience, a training ground for Indian leaders and an example of pragmatic adaptation without surrender. But Pratt asked too much. His students had to give up their families, their homes, their friends, their customs, their heritage, their beliefs. Obviously many could not and many did not want to forfeit their personal and communal identities.

Pratt had a low opinion of the Indian's heritage; but he had an unshakable belief that individuals of all races and backgrounds could succeed given a good environment. For Pratt, Carlisle was a mission. He was aware that many eyes were on him and Carlisle, and he believed that Carlisle would have a great impact on future government policy and appropriations. Carlisle was not a total failure. It was a spearhead in raising public consciousness regarding Indian problems, demonstrating that Indian education could be effective. It forced government attention to Indian problems. It was a major force in changing the public's image of the Indian. Although Pratt wanted to exterminate Indian culture and heritage, his efforts in fact contributed to a desire to perpetuate and develop the Indian. Had the Carlisle model succeeded as a general Indian policy, the cost would have been enormous— the loss of a distinctive and enriching contribution to American life by Indian culture and heritage. In 2001, the Oregon state legislature passed a law (similar to legislation in Nebraska) that enables tribal language speakers without college degrees or specific teacher training to become certified to teach native languages in public schools.

The first decades of the 1900s revealed that the off-reservation school system had not substantially changed the problems and lifestyle on the reservations. Certainly some of the returning students tried to contribute to a process of change, but obviously these students could not accomplish change by themselves. The closing of Carlisle reflected a shift in Indian policy from assimilation to gradual change. Rapid assimilation was recognized to be unrealistic; the separation of children from their families was increasingly seen as unjustifiably cruel; and most importantly, an appreciation for the uniqueness of Indian culture was growing. A new emphasis was emerging to draw upon and build upon Indian heritage, a process of gradual development, not transformation. The Indian schools began to construct teaching programs around individual tribal customs and heritage. Nevertheless, the off-reservation schools retained their basic structure of discipline and regimentation. By 1925, the educational effort shifted to reservation day schools and public schools.

In 1928, a comprehensive private evaluation by the Brookings Institution of Indian policy and Indian life on the reservations, commissioned by the secretary of the interior and financed by John D. Rockefeller, Jr., was published as *The Problem of Indian Administration*, commonly known as the Meriam Report, after its director, Lewis Meriam.[102] The report was an indictment of the off-reservation schools, and it stressed the importance of maintaining education within the context of family and community, emphasized the utilization of Indian culture and heritage in teaching programs, and promoted the use of public schools. The Meriam Report described the impoverished state of most Indians. It blamed the allotment policy for producing the loss of good land and retention of marginal land. The Meriam Report resulted in many reforms (although it took many years), but it still accepted the principle established in 1831 by the Supreme Court that the Indians were dependent nations in a wardship relationship with the federal government. It bluntly pointed out that the government had repeatedly not provided sufficient funds to support appropriate policies and services.

PRATT DIED IN 1924, the same year that Congress gave citizenship to all Indians born in the United States. After his daughter, Nana Pratt Hawkins, died, the family provided the Pratt papers to the Yale University Library. The Pratt papers contain about 300 letters sent to him in 1920 on his eightieth birthday from former students, brimming with affection, often addressed with the salutation, "Dear Father." Many treasured the Carlisle experience, the pride of belonging to a successful group of people who marked progress with accomplishments and achievements. They had warm memories of Pratt, always mindful of his authority, but impressed with his fairness, his caring, and his commitment.

Pratt was a champion, a champion of justice for those oppressed by a dominant culture. To be sure, some view him as a villain because he was dedicated to the rapid and absolute eradication of Indian culture, but he was an important historical moral force that contributed to changing the lives of Indians. Pratt helped to create the climate of opinion that made the efforts of succeeding decades possible. The assimilation effort did introduce new attitudes, skills, ideas, the use of English, and some cultural change. This was not accomplished without conflict, but conflict always spurs resistance, and out of that resistance, there arose a heightened sense of Indian identity, especially a pan-Indian identity. Prior to 1900, Native-Americans were tribal-centered, separated by the lack of a universal language. Boarding schools produced a cadre of Indians who could read and write English, the unifying tool that made an effort to find a common ground beyond the tribe possible, a process in which Montezuma played a major role. Ideas could now be carried over railroads and highways; leaders could now exchange thoughts and extend their influence beyond a tight localized circle. Although not his intention, Pratt contributed to the effort to develop an Indian future within American society by producing educated Indians who could act as leaders, interpreters, and communicators.

On April 23, 1924, Richard Henry Pratt died in the Army Hospital in San Francisco four months after his eighty-third birthday. He was buried in Arlington Cemetery and joined by his wife three years later. His headstone is large, reading on one side:

FRIEND AND COUNSELOR OF THE INDIANS
FOUNDER AND SUPERINTENDENT OF
THE CARLISLE INDIAN SCHOOL 1879 – 1904

Pratt would have been proud of this stone, especially the inscription at the base on the other side that reads:

ERECTED IN LOVING MEMORY BY HIS STUDENTS AND OTHER INDIANS

(When I stood before Pratt's grave, with the soft sounds of *Taps* from a distant funeral passing through the air on a fine, summer morning, a Black Arlington groundskeeper approached me and asked about Pratt, saying: "I like to learn about the people buried here." I told him about Carlisle and the Buffalo Soldiers, and he said: "He couldn't've had any prejudice.")

## CHAPTER FOUR

# Montezuma's Youth:
# Through Good Friends and
# by My Personal Effort

IN LESS THAN a year's time, Carlo Gentile and Carlos Montezuma saw a lot of America. Leaving Arizona in November 1871, they passed through Albuquerque, Santa Fe, Trinidad, Pueblo, Denver, Washington, New York, and Detroit. After their travels, Gentile and Montezuma settled first in Grand Rapids, Michigan, but soon they were living on the west side of Chicago. Gentile worked in Fulton's Gallery on West Madison Street, and the job provided lodging in the Fulton household.

In 1872 we came to Chicago where I began to learn more of the habits of civilized life. It was on the west side of the city where I first appeared with my long hair falling on either side of my face. I wore no hat and was noticeable on account of my nativity. I was cared for by a lady whose acquaintance I made in Grand Rapids, Michigan.

Mrs. Lydia Caldwell whose friendship we gained at Grand Rapids moved to Chicago. She was full of business & was a hustler. She conceived the idea of having a gallery and to go into partnership with Mr. Gentile. I was moved to her home in West Lake St until she broke up house keeping.

In 1871, I was taken from the most warlike tribe in America and placed in the midst of civilization at Chicago. My greatest wish was to understand the "paper-talking" as it was interpreted to me. I often saw boys and girls going to and from the school house. I had no idea that all had to be taught—but I had a little suspicious idea of the house.

By this time I was well known among the boys attending the Tilden School. After school hours I played with them. One day some of the boys coaxed me near the school. They could not take me any further than the fence which surrounded the school. I was suspicious of the building. I remember full well that afternoon while busy playing marbles with the boys some one touched my shoulder. Who was it but Miss Winchell, principal of the Tilden School [Miss Harriet Winchell was at the Samel J. Tilden School for 51 years, 44 as principal[1]]. I looked up with a frightened amazement. She smiled at me and said few words and left me. It was about a week after this incident, the boys crowded around me at the gate of school and the bell was ringing to call the children. One of the larger boys bodily shoved me inside of the school yard and took me into the school. Being shy I did not know what to do but one of the teachers took my hand and had one of the boys take me up to the principal. Miss Winchell asked me questions and all I could say was "yes" and nod my head. My English was very imperfect. She gave me a small note and made me to understand to take the note to Mr. Gentile. So that afternoon I made a bee line to Mr. Gentile's gallery and proudly fulfilled my mission. He smiled and went with me to get the slate and a pencil and a few other things as the note called for. With the package under my arm and placed on the horse car to my boarding place. I was anxious for tomorrow to come. I was up early next morning to go to school with the rest of the boys. I was placed in the lowest class. I was willing to learn and do the same thing as the rest of the children. I remember the children singing. I sang too. I did not know the words but I carried the rhythm and made as much noise as the rest. In a short time I caught on and learned fast.

At this time I knew not my A,B,C's. I could not count, nor understand letters. It was but a few months before I could repeat the Lords Prayer, sing "precious Jewels," with the scholars; say my A, B, C's and count one hundred, besides writing and describing different objects.

I learned as fast as any of the whites for the reasons that the teacher delighted to instruct me. I left this school and went to another one. Here was the best teacher I ever had in public school. This lady seemed to comprehend the nature of any circumstance and guided me all she could. I made good advancement in my first reader, by taking my books home at night so that I could be instructed there also. Most of the reading I committed to memory.

On Saturday nights I slept with boys who sold newspapers, and early on Sundays we went together to the news office for our papers. I could not tell the difference between them but my friend separated the Times and Tribune, by running a string between the two. Barehead with thick black hair and childish voice, I was an attraction. I sold as many papers as any of the boys. I made my spending money in this way. Some of my playmates attended the Sunday School. I was taken into one of them. I could not understand the preaching or any of my teachers. Only the music seemed to charm me. After my first visit to the Sunday school I wanted Sunday to come every day so that I might hear the music. Canon Knowles was the pastor. He took an interest in me that I can never forget.

Mr. Gentile placed me in charge of Mrs. Baldwin. I remember that sad 4th of July. Childlike I did not want to leave my playmates. At least I wanted to play with them on the 4th. Not so, with a valise that had all my belongings I reluctantly followed Mr. Gentile to his office. From there Mr. Baldwin took me with him to his home, corner 42nd St and Cottage Grove Ave. Everything was done to make me enjoy the fireworks but I thought of the west side. This motherly home was the turning of my life. No mother could have watched over her own son as I was cared for by Mrs. Baldwin. I had to toe the mark and be truthful in all things. I left the first school and principal Miss Winchell, but she followed my career with interest of love until her death several years ago.

With Mrs Baldwin I attended the Oaklawn School. My teacher at this school was Miss Mary Perry, now Mrs. Brown. We see each other now & then.[2]

In 1875, Montezuma was featured in an article in the *Chicago Tribune*.[3] Carlo Gentile was identified as the photographer at the corner of State and Washington, directly across the street from the site upon which The Reliance Building would open in 1895 and house Montezuma's downtown medical office. Montezuma, called "Monty" by Gentile, was described as a boy with a broad face, high cheekbones, swarthy skin, black hair, and "brown eyes that dance with fun." He appeared to have a bright, intelligent manner. The *Chicago Tribune* quoted Gentile: "Monty fraternizes amicably with boys of his age and is expert at all games. In marbles he is so successful as to accumulate them by hundreds. He can play cards, chess, and checkers with remarkable skill. He is good-natured and obliging, is perfectly truthful and honest. He does not suffer at all from any prejudice against him as his force of character soon commands the respect of his schoolfellows. He is bold as a lion and can thrash the average boy of 13, so that he is not imposed on. His vocabulary is larger than that of children of his age, and the quickness of his parts is such that he is considered a boy of bright promise. Mr Gentile will send him to dancing school next winter, and he will finish his education in Europe, probably in Italy, as he shows a taste for music."[4]

Europe was not to be, however, as Montezuma suffered a chronic respiratory illness of unknown nature in 1875, causing Gentile and Montezuma to separate for the first time, allowing Montezuma to attend a country school in Galesburg, Illinois, until 1877. Montezuma lived with the C. J. Ferris family, and later reported two years of pleasant memories of farm work and walking two miles to school.[5] "I had two cows to milk. I grew so fast and was so careless of my health that I was taken down with congestion of the lungs. Three doctors gave me up, but they did not know how tough an 'Injun' is, and I pulled through under the tender care of Mrs. Ferris."[6] During this time Gentile remained active in Chicago with his photography and acquired a new skill, making composite photographs.[7] A famous picture of his portraying General Sheridan and his military staff was published in the September 1877 issue of the *Philadelphia Photographer*. This led to exhibits and awards in New York City, prompting Gentile to move with Montezuma to New York.

*1874—Age Eight*

In the spring 1877, I went to Brooklyn to school. I was by this time sufficiently advanced to study grammar, geography, arithmetic, and history. At this school I always stood at the head of my class. I did this by staying at home nights to study, not by playing at corners as did some of the white children.[8]

Gentile and Montezuma boarded with Mrs. Baldwin in Yonkers, who in her correspondence for years after, addressed Montezuma as "My Dear Boy" and signed her letters as "your Mother." This was the same Mrs. Baldwin who cared for Montezuma in Chicago, 1871–1873. Years later, Montezuma recalled his time with Mrs. Baldwin: "She cared for me with a mother's watchful care. As I review my past life, I cannot but acknowledge that this was my salvation—my turning point. I should have been lost except for her kind treatment and maternal advice. I will remember her last advice at the door when we parted, 'Always be a good boy. You will always find friends.'"[9] In 1898, Mrs. Baldwin wrote to Montezuma in Chicago:

I laughed to myself and thought of the time in Chicago of the time I would give you a half dollar and a little pic [*sic*] in order that I might keep you at home for a time. How I would worry when you were away to[o] long at play figuring something would happen to you. Gentile would say let him go, he will come back when he gets hungry. ...[10]

Gentile's new business was an art store selling prints of his photographs.[11] According to one account, a financial disaster struck Gentile in the fall of 1878 as a fire destroyed his New York store and almost all that it contained.[12] However, no mention of such a fire could be detected in New York newspaper files.[13] Nevertheless, Gentile and Montezuma moved to Boston where they met a missionary who put them in contact with the Baptists. Gentile decided to seek a more stable home for the boy, and after two or three months in Boston, Montezuma was on his way to Urbana, Illinois.[14]

The American Baptist Home Mission Society had its headquarters at 28 Astor House in New York City. George W. Ingalls was the Director of the Indian Department that had as its slogan "For Christianizing and Civilizing the Indians of Our Country."[15] Ingalls personally selected a placement for the eleven-year-old Montezuma, the household of Reverend William H. Stedman, pastor of the First Baptist Church in Urbana, Illinois. This placement was supported by the Young Men's Christian Association (YMCA) and Ingalls wrote on October 16, 1878, to the President of the YMCA of the Illinois Industrial University (later to be renamed the University of Illinois):

> I promised the vice-president of your Asso. A brief sketch of Montezuma, the Apache Indian boy I left in Urbana to get an education.
>
> He is from the Pinal Mountain Band of Arizona Apaches, and is about 11 years old, having been found and taken charge of by a Mr. C. Gentile, in the year 1871. Mr Gentile then in Arizona prospecting for Gold. Until recently a photograph artist of Chicago, Ill.
>
> The boy was about 5 yrs old Mr. G. thinks when he got him. He has had an oversight of him ever since until within two weeks when he consented to place him in my charge that he might become a useful man.
>
> The circumstances under which he was found are these. The Pinal Mountain Apaches were at war with our Government and had committed many and serious outrages (provoked however by bad white treatment) and the Pima Indians employed by our soldiers attacked the Indian village of Montezuma's people at night, when most of the able bodied Indians were away and killed many of the old people, some getting away. It is supposed Montezuma's mother was among the killed because he never saw or heard of her afterwards. He with his two sisters, one younger and one older, were sold to whites.
>
> His sisters to a man now in Sonora Mexico. He to Mr. Gentile for $30.
>
> Until he came to Mr Gentile he had been raised in a grass house and seldom with outer covering for his person than a breech cloth. I will have soon and send to you a photograph of him and his two sisters taken soon after he was first found. He and his people never had been accustomed to use knives or forks, but to eat with their fingers instead. He nor his people had then ever had any of the advantages of civilized life and were among the most vicious degraded Indians in our country. Without any knowledge of a supreme being and treated their women little better than of cattle.
>
> I want Montezuma to become, first a Christian and then to be a Physician and with a good education and love of Christ in his heart, to go back to his people and labor for their good as a Christian or Missionary physician. I want him to have a knowledge of some trade perhaps as carpenter or other useful trade, a knowledge of farming so he can direct such branches of industry among his people.
>
> While bright in some studies he seems slow when put at work and must be trained and have patience exercised towards him, for his race are disinclined naturally to hard work. He is truthful and as far as I know of good habits—a little too mischievful [sic] perhaps. Rev Wm Stedman has consented to give him a room and board at very low rate in consideration of his doing some few duties around his place and will inform you of the terms. Please lay his case before your Asso and the Young Ladies. Send unto me this place or in the Indian Territory. What your decision is as to a position for him. I will write your Asso on receipt same account of my work in the field to which I go tomorrow.
>
> Your Bro in Christ[16]

In the late nineteenth century, the Young Men's Christian Association (YMCA) and the Young Women's Christian Association (YWCA) were dedicated to the moral welfare of young people.[17] The YMCA was founded by George Williams in London, England, in 1844, starting as no more than a prayer group. The YWCA had a similar start in England and was established by 1859. The purpose was to meet a social need, to provide a place for young men and women caught in the unhealthy social conditions of the newly industrialized cities. Of course, the YMCA and YWCA also intended to apply traditional Christian morality to these young men and women living alone in the cities, as the YMCA and YWCA leaders worked to protect young people from the evils of dance halls, saloons, and brothels. Queen Victoria knighted George Williams in 1894 for his work with the YMCA, and he was buried in 1905 in St. Paul's Cathedral among many of England's heroes.[18]

After the Civil War, the focus of the American YMCAs was Christianity, spearheaded by two prominent evangelists, Dwight L. Moody (headquartered in Chicago) and John Mott.[19] By the 1880s, YMCAs had their own buildings with living quarters, classrooms, gyms, and swimming pools. The history of the YMCA is one of secularization with an emphasis on social service and health, mirroring the change in American society after 1900. Soon the social, educational, and recreational functions overshadowed the original religious thrust. But in 1878, it was still not unusual for the American Home Baptist Mission Society to seek YMCA involvement in supporting Carlos Montezuma.

The Stedmans, with five children, lived on a small farm. William H. Stedman first came to Urbana, Illinois, only four years before Montezuma, in 1874. Stedman was the pastor of the First Baptist Church, located near the University. He took seriously an obligation that he described in July 1909 in an article in the *Urbana Courier-Herald* heralding his plea to join his campaign to build a new church in the memory of the founder of the University of Illinois, J. M. Gregory: "But we know that nobody can accomplish for our Baptist young people what our own Baptist pastors can. We know that the right kind of a man once located on the field, who will be ready to meet the four hundred Baptist students on their arrival, see them properly located and gather them into a church home, set them to work in some line of Christian activity, will not only save them from many of the temptations incident to their surroundings, but will give back to the home church at the end of the four years a great host of strong well-trained Christian teachers."[20]

"I had a great horror of preachers, and in order to provoke me, Mr. Gentile used to tell me that he was going to make a preacher of me. How emphatically I used to say 'No Sir!' But when I arrived with one for a few months I thought that preachers were not so bad after all."[21] The relationships with the Stedman family stood the test of time. Reverend Stedman presided at Montezuma's marriage in 1913, and Montezuma maintained a life-long correspondence with the family, in which he is greeted as Brother Monty (usually spelled Monte by the Stedmans and Montezuma) and signed, for example, your sister, Lucile or Jeannette. During a winter revival meeting in 1880, he was baptized in the First Baptist Church.[22]

> I started my schooling in a public school on the west side of Chicago. I went subsequently to various schools in that city and in Brooklyn, where Mr. Gentile took me. Later I got sickly and was put on a farm near Galesburg, Illinois, and there I used to walk two miles to a country school. Still later—for Mr. Gentile could not always look after me himself—I was put with a preacher in Urbana, Illinois. This preacher had five children of his own, and I made the sixth. But somehow he managed with me. A little money may have come to him

from my friends; it could have not been much. My education up to that time had been rather hit-or-miss, so a number of students set to work and fitted me for the preparatory school of the University.

But I had to work hard, as well as study. I dug in the fields and worked in the garden, and did chores, and in summer I worked on a farm. There was very little free time. However, the preacher, though a very good man of God, happened to be a devoted hunter. When the work was done, he and I would go hunting together. That helped pass the time pleasantly.[23]

## THE UNIVERSITY OF ILLINOIS

Stedman arranged for Montezuma to receive private tutoring from other students. After one year, Montezuma passed the entrance exam for the Preparatory School of the University. This school was a special operation of the University, necessary because of the poor quality of high schools in that time. The average Illinois high school in Montezuma's time had only two or three teachers.[24] Montezuma attended the Preparatory School for one year, and, in 1880, he entered the University at the age of fourteen.[25]

*Montezuma at the University of Illinois*

Religion dominated university experiences before the Civil War, with an emphasis on ancient languages, mathematics, and moral philosophy. It was typical of these Protestant dominated colleges to require daily, and often twice daily, chapel attendance. College presidents were often clergymen. The increasing importance of science and technology in the last half of the nineteenth century stirred a change in the nation's schools despite religious suspicions, but the change occurred over decades and Montezuma's experience was still under Protestant religious influence.

Urbana and Champaign existed as two small villages in the middle of Illinois, side by side on a dusty, treeless, unbroken prairie. They united in a successful campaign to obtain from the Illinois legislature in 1867 a land-grant college, originally called the Illinois Industrial University. The first class entered in March 1868. The opening ceremony was heavy with Protestant prayers and hymns.[26] By 1873, the student body totaled 400, coed since 1870.

The Land-Grant College Act of 1862, sponsored by Justin Smith Morrill of Vermont, provided federal money for state colleges.[27] The funding came from 30,000 acres of federal land sold for each state Senator and Representative to provide an endowment that would ensure the teaching of agriculture, home economics, and engineering in addition to the usual academic studies. The act also required the establishment of a military training program that is now the Reserve Officers' Training Corps (ROTC). Speculators bought much of the land, and most states received very little money, requiring supplemental legislation in later years to provide adequate funding. In 1994, twenty-nine American Indian colleges gained land-grant status, bringing the total number of land-grant institutions to 105.

Many land-grant institutions were trying in the 1880s to eliminate "agriculture, industrial, and mining" from their names. The movement to change the name of Illinois Industrial

University was initiated by students in 1880, who pointed out that "industrial school" had come to mean a reformatory institution, but there was considerable opposition. A bill to change the name passed the House of the Illinois General Assembly in 1884, and then passed the Senate, but only after a fierce battle. On June 19, 1884, the summer of Montezuma's graduation, the university became the University of Illinois at Urbana-Champaign.[28]

In its early years, the focus of the university was agriculture, but by the time of Montezuma's attendance in the 1880s, the curriculum reflected a liberal arts academic education. The University included a College of Literature and Science, a College of Natural Science with a School of Chemistry (Montezuma's choice), a College of Agriculture, and a College of Engineering (the largest). There were about 370 students and thirty on the faculty, about half were full professors.[29] The University had to pay well to attract faculty to what was viewed as an unattractive prairie environment. About 20 percent of the students were women. Tuition was free in the state university and fees amounted to about $25 per year.[30] Today, the 1,500-acre campus serves 26,000 undergraduates and 10,000 graduate and professional students with 2,000 faculty. Urbana and Champaign are separated by a line that passes north to south through the middle of the campus. The campus is an oasis of trees in a land that is still flat as a floor, with cultivated farm land (all soybeans and corn) stretching to every horizon, intersected by widely spaced roads with nary a curve or a hill.

Montezuma entered the University of Illinois at age fourteen and graduated at age eighteen in 1884. Montezuma was enrolled in the College of Natural Science in the pharmaceutical program of the School of Chemistry. Reverend Stedman applied to the YMCA for financial aid.[31] The YMCA found its greatest strength after the Civil War in universities.[32] Devotional meetings were held at the University of Illinois in space provided by the institution on Sunday mornings and one weekday evening. It was the University YMCA that sponsored Montezuma. Montezuma's grades were good enough that in his second year, the University waived all fees.

The School of Chemistry offered four vocationally oriented programs: pharmaceutical, chemical, agricultural, and metallurgical. The courses included four years of chemistry, related sciences,

*The Chemical Laboratory Building (now Harker Hall) at the University of Illinois*

*Student Chemistry Laboratory at the University of Illinois*

English, mathematics, two years of German, and subjects required of University seniors: mental science, logic, political economy, and constitutional history.[33] William McMurtrie, formerly a chief chemist with the United States Department of Agriculture, headed the chemistry department. McMurtrie studied the chemistry of the hog as well as wool fibers.[34] A strict disciplinarian, he was not a popular teacher, demanding prodigious feats of memorization. The School of Chemistry was housed in The Chemical Laboratory, a building constructed for $40,000 in 1877–1878, providing desks and laboratory space for 160 students. It is now the oldest building on the campus, renovated in 1992–1993.

Montezuma was a college student during a time when student demands for freedom and extracurricular activities were opposed by faculty who enforced a nose-to-the-grindstone approach by extensive disciplinary rules with black marks for violations.[35] At this time, the University was led by its Regent, Selim H. Peabody (named after an Arab chieftain in a popular novel), a formal and autocratic individual.[36] Peabody instituted the policy of declaring a "major" interest and a "minor" interest (as opposed to the previous policy of totally elective and random choices), ensuring that a student not only focused on an interest but acquired a broad exposure. Peabody believed in regulating a student's life to maintain a quiet, dedicated group of students. The inevitable conflict between the students reflecting the spirit of the times and Peabody with his strict rules eventually led to his departure in 1891.

A feisty spirit among the students was fostered by the boredom of the surrounding prairie. Student pranks and rowdyism were prevalent during Montezuma's years at the University. In 1881, students put a buggy on the peak of a University building and buried the ashes of a textbook of geometry with fanfare and a cremation ceremony.[37] Fences and boardwalks were uprooted, and on one occasion, the stairs were removed from a building stranding the students on the second floor. Student turbulence reached a peak in 1883, a year before Montezuma graduated. Peabody restored some peace by dissolving the student government, implementing a new demerit system, and maintaining control over the student newspaper, *The Illini.*

Urbana-Champaign contained about 10,000 people, but offered little to relieve the monotony of living on the prairie. The student newspaper noted in October 1883: "Somebody may, can, would, should and must, must, MUST keep the cows off the campus."[38] The faculty suspended students who visited billiard halls or saloons. The University provided nothing beyond the formal and compulsory student hours; the buildings were closed on the weekends and at 6 P.M. on school days. On the weekends, only the library was open, but only from 2 to 5 P.M. on Saturdays. There were no student resident halls. Students lived with families or in rooming houses. Meals were mainly at boarding clubs ($2–$2.50 per week), but meals were often the victim of a tight budget. Students were therefore very fragmented, a real obstacle to socialization.

Students and faculty in Montezuma's years were in two different camps, separated by the old-time college ethos of the University. Faculty members generally failed to attend student programs, even chapel services, which were compulsory for students, and had no interest in college sports.[39] Students created organizations to provide interest and some social atmosphere, literary and dramatic clubs that sponsored oratorical contests and debates, class activities, and sports. A high point of the year was the Intercollegiate Oratorical Contest held in October on different campuses. About fifty-sixty students were granted leave to attend, and the results were awaited with greater interest than that given to the baseball scores of the intercollegiate competition held in connection with the Oratorical Contest. There were multiple specialized societies, such as the Telegrapher's Society, the Chess Club, the Society of Political Education, and the Temperance Association.[40] Nevertheless, the students of 1880–1890 believed that success and some worthy end required hard work, and the aim of education was to acquire the mental tools to follow that path.[41]

Darwin's writings were challenging fundamental doctrine, but Peabody was unshaken, perceiving education as the tool to comprehend the truths provided by God in nature.[42] Montezuma's education was still dominated by the Protestantism of the middle 1800s, to be reflected in his later activities (as a Freemason, a member of the First Baptist Church of Chicago, and his interactions with the Protestant Indian reform organizations). Most students were religious, and the YMCA grew in strength, joined by the YWCA in 1884.[43] The moral code of the campus was puritanical in keeping with the prevailing Protestantism and strongly supported by the faculty. Not only were smoking and drinking opposed, but also card playing and dancing on campus.[44] Dances and banquets were held in nearby commercial establishments, such as the Columbian Hotel in Urbana or the Griggs House in Champaign.

MONTEZUMA DISPLAYED in his college writing a sophistication and vocabulary that reflected what must have been an impressive volume of reading during his teenage years. The school newspaper, *The Illini*, printed Montezuma's essay on Aztec Civilization on March 4, 1881.[45] As an eighteen-year-old teenager, he was already articulating his attitude and feelings about the Indians, in another article with amazingly sophisticated language, entitled "Our Indians," in *The Illini* on March 10, 1884:

> How strange for a people once great and powerful to pass away from the land possessed by them and their fathers; for those who once made others tremble to dwindle away to a weak and helpless race upon the face of a country, and in the eyes of a people, who as a civilized nation is second to none. But such is the case of the North American Indian. His history and apparent destiny will excite the compassion of those who are unprejudiced towards race or color. Strong and hearty in his mountain home, that place he has learned to love, that place which is sacred to him as the home of his fathers, he is forced to leave and take up his abode in a warm, malarial climate as a ward of the nation. His family ties are broken, his pride and interest in his country are gone. He is not a citizen of the country in which he lives, oppressed and subdued, unwelcome by the people whose destiny once lay in his hands, deprived of all that is dear to him and conscious of the fact that his power is gone, now and then striking a feeble blow. ...I do not regret that civilization has extended, that her invisible hand has reared temples of learning, that industry has superseded indolence, that a wilderness should be transformed into the home of the most prosperous people on earth. Nor would I have this beautiful land of ours still the tenting grounds of the savage, but I do regret that he today is not fit to share with us the advantages of a civilized nation. ...Justice and humanity do not require that the civilized should conform to the habits and customs of the savage, but justice and humanity do require that the rights of the weaker party be respected, thereby forming an example which shall touch tender chords created alike in all mankind, and teach the savage that civilization is right. ...Education, science and

intercourse with nations have enabled us to overcome the savage and he is now at our mercy. ...Let us remember that no race of savages that ever peopled the earth has leaped, at a single stride, the great gulf that intervenes between the savage and an enlightened nation. He must pass through those successive stages that lead from barbarism to enlightenment. ...To-day the question is, "What are we to do with those that remain? Are we to permit them to be a class among us, ignorant, debased and corrupted by bad company and intoxicating liquors? Are we to continue to oppress and exterminate them? Is it impossible to better the present reservation system? Is it impossible to show justice and mercy to a race that has been impoverished that we might be made rich?" An unfaithful treatment will but make the evil worse and the burden heavier to bear. Let us take up this work of Indian civilization as earnestly and faithfully as we did the freeing of three million slaves. Let us write a page in our history that will atone for the thoughtless and hasty deeds of the past, that, when read by future generations, it may shed a light which will cause the spots on that record to appear less dark; for the time is fast approaching when the last Red Man shall start on his journey to the great spirit whom he, too, has worshipped. May he reach the harbor safely. Better, far better, that we entail a debt on our posterity than leave them an inheritance of shame.[46]

Montezuma, a handsome and serious young man, graduated on June 11, 1884, in the pharmaceutical program, with a Bachelor of Science degree in chemistry. His handwritten sixteen-page thesis was entitled *Valuation of Opiums and Their Products*.[47] Interestingly, his name is printed on the thesis as Chas. Montezuma, and on his official transcript, he is Charles Montezuma. The thesis describes his experiments (which took two months) to compare several methods of preparing pure morphine compounds. His grades were not dazzling, ranging from 75 to 91, with a preponderance at the lower end.

*Montezuma at the University of Illinois, Near Graduation*

Montezuma was elected president of the class of 1884[48] and secretary, then president of the Adelphic Debate Society. On May 5, 1883, the student newspaper, *The Illini*, reported on an Adelphic Contest. "Mr. C. Montezuma of whom every Adelphic is proud, gave one of the rare treats of the evening on 'Indian's Bravery,' commencing with the impressive scene of Thermopylae, he likened the Indians to that band of Spartans. The most vivid, pathetic, and beautiful picture ever painted in our Hall, was 'Monto's' in his description of the Indians in America before the arrival of the white man. The account of the career of the Indian chiefs so ably described, contained more truth than poetry poetical though it was."[49]

I don't know how it happened that I got through the University. My grades may have been pretty poor. But it is on record that somehow I did graduate and did get the degree of bachelor of science. I specialized in chemistry. As I had been thrown on my own resources, I realized I had to climb a mountain of discipline if I was to be a man among men in a white man's world. That made some of the things I did seem easier. I had already decided I wanted to study medicine.

No. 1580  *Charles Montezuma*

Nativity. Arizona Territory          Age. 16 – 1

Parent or Guardian. C. Gentile          Residence. Chicago.

Entered. Jan 4. 1882          Examination passed in. ✓

### COURSE.

| Year. | Term. | STUDIES. | | | |
|---|---|---|---|---|---|
| 1880 | 1 | English 75 | Trigonometry 75 | Chemistry 78 | |
| I | 2 | English 80 | Aul. Geom 80 | Chemistry 90 | |
| 1881 | 3 | English 75 | F. H. Draw 75 | Chemistry 91 | Taxidermy 80 |
| 1881 | 1 | German 81 | Physiology 75 | Chemistry 75 | |
| II | 2 | German 80 | Microscopy 75 | Chemistry 90 | |
| 1882 | 3 | German 75 | Zoology 80 | Chemistry 90 | |
| 1882 | 1 | German 75 | Mineralogy 76 | Chemistry 77 | |
| III | 2 | German 75 | Physics 78 | Chemistry 86 | |
| 1883 | 3 | German 75 | Physics 78 | Chemistry 85 | |
| 1883 | 1 | Ment. Sci. 80 | Physiography 75 | Chemistry 88 | |
| IV | 2 | Logic 75 | Const. Hist 80 | Chemistry 90 | |
| 1884 | 3 | Polit. Econ. 90 | Geology 78 | Chemistry 80 | |

### REMARKS.

Degree B.S. conferred June 11, 1884
School of N. S.

AUG 28 1979

I went with a letter to a Mr. Fuller, then head of the largest wholesale drug house in Chicago. I asked him for a job. [Fuller remembered Montezuma from his days as a newspaper boy.] I remember very well what Mr. Fuller said, for he disappointed me bitterly, yet gave me great help. "If you are going to study medicine," he said, "you don't want a position in a company like ours. Here you would be nailing up packing boxes from morning to night. I have work of that sort and I could give it to you. But it wouldn't help you. Get in a drug store where you can learn about mixing drugs. I will give you a letter to a man in that business; and another to a physician who may help you about medical school."

As I was leaving with the letters, Mr. Fuller held out his hand with something for me. "Take this," he said, "Use it judiciously." It was a ten-dollar bill! That was only one of many instances of kindness I have had and treasured. Years before, when I was just a boy learning civilized customs, Mr. Gentile left me for a while with a woman who treated me like my mother. And when I left her, she said: "Do what is right; you will always find friends."

How truly she spoke! It is the greatest satisfaction of my life, greater than money or any material rewards, that I have always found friends, and have had their opinion of my abilities to live up to.

I took the letter Mr. Fuller gave me to the physician [Dr. Hollister of Chicago Medical College]. He told me I could enter medical college in the fall and promised to help me financially. "But," he said, "you must help yourself as much as you can."

That left me free on one point: I could go to school when school began again. But I also had to have a job. I called with my letters and references at a number of stores. It proved a discouraging task. "Nice references," one after another told me, "but you have had no experience!" No one would take me.

At last I threw my references away and called at every drug store I saw. And then I did find a pharmacist [C. Pryne Stringfield], quite close [4 blocks] to the medical school as it happened, who listened to me patiently.

"What can you do?" he asked.
"I can do anything." I replied.
"Wash windows?"
"Yes."
"Sweep the floors?"
"Yes," I said. "I am willing to do anything. What I want is just a chance where I can work for my meals and a bed and a little money, and can have a few hours a week to attend school."
"Well," he said at last, "I'll give you a trial on that basis."

I made good and stayed with him for five years, until I completed my course at medical school.[50]

Montezuma entered the Chicago Medical College on June 21, 1884, only ten days after his college graduation. Even though the school did not charge him tuition, it took him five years to graduate, principally because he could not attend classes full-time, even having to return to the Stedman farm for a period of time. Maintaining his job in the pharmacy (where he also lived) throughout medical school allowed him to persist. "Through kind friends my tuition was remitted me at the Chicago Medical College. For five years alternately behind the counter and attending lectures I finally graduated in medicine."[51]

## GENTILE AFTER MONTEZUMA

In 1878, the same year that Montezuma left for Urbana, Gentile opened a new business in Chicago with two studios, the Boulevard Studios at 200 Michigan Avenue, at the corner of Van Buren Street (College of Pharmacy Building) and a branch at 3907 Cottage Grove Avenue. Two years later, Gentile and other Chicago photographers formed the Photographers' Association of America, and he was vice-president. What is certain is that Gentile was fairly successful.[52] By 1885, he had an excellent national reputation, known for his skill in new developments and techniques. Gentile was the photographic editor of *The Eye*, a weekly, semi-literary magazine published in Bloomington, Illinois. In 1884, he purchased the magazine, moved it to Chicago, changing the name to *The Photographic Eye and The Eye*, available for ten cents an issue, $2.50 per year. In 1887, Gentile hosted a convention in Chicago, the Great Convention of American and Canadian Photography.

Gentile wasn't always successful.[53] In 1886, Gentile and Oscar Durante, a young fellow Neapolitan, founded *L'Italia*, an Italian language newspaper. It became very popular and influential, but unfortunately for Gentile, he sold his share to Durante very shortly after its founding. In 1887, Gentile and Giuseppe Ronga began publishing a bilingual newspaper, *Il Messaggiere Italo-Americano*, but it folded after two years.

In 1891, a magazine, the *St Louis & Canadian Photographer*, published the following comment: "We are informed by Mr. Charles Gentile, editor of the Eye, that he was called upon last month to mourn the loss of his wife. She died very suddenly with pneumonia. We believe this makes the third wife Mr. Gentile has been called upon to follow to her last resting place. Our sympathies are extended to the bereaved."[54]

Beginning in 1891, Gentile invested considerable time and money in promoting a building devoted to photography for the Chicago World's Columbia Exposition of 1893. He did exhibit at the Exposition, but most of his efforts were thwarted, and financial difficulties began to accumulate. *The Eye* was receiving criticism, and then another tragedy occurred in his fourth marriage, a young daughter died of scarlet fever.

It has been incorrectly stated that Gentile committed suicide.[55] At the age of fifty-eight, Gentile was diagnosed with Bright's Disease.[56] Bright's Disease is a chronic inflammation of the kidneys that culminates in renal failure. The cause is not infectious; it is due to the production of antibodies against tissue in the kidney (an auto-immune disease), the etiology of which is unknown. In the summer of 1893, Gentile was visited by Montezuma on his way from the state of Washington to his new job at the Carlisle Indian School in Pennsylvania. Montezuma advised Gentile to rest and get treatment for his kidneys, but the inexorable course of the disease brought his death on October 27, 1893, a few days before the World's Columbian Exposition closed. An obituary in *The Eye* said he left a wife and a six-year-old son. Mrs. Gentile wrote to Montezuma on October 27, 1893, the same day of Gentile's death.

> Dear Sir,
>  We got in this morning; tomorrow we will bury him.
>  The Press Club will attend to that. The shock has been too terrible, I could not get in time to see him—he was already dead, I can't realize it! such a good man. I feel so heartbroken so desolate. I wish you could have come I thought so much of you!
>  I received your two telegrams thank you for your kindness. I do not know yet how his business stands, but I think in very bad shape and we are left at present without anything, and don't know who to go to and if you could help us as soon as possible I'll be very much obliged to you.
>  Poor little boy, so young and be an orphan![57]

Evidently Montezuma did not attend the funeral on October 28, 1893 (It would have been difficult for him to afford the trip and to be awarded leave from his position as school physician at Carlisle). He did provide financial aid to Mrs. Gentile,[58] who found her way to California. Montezuma wrote to George Ingalls in 1895: "Mrs Gentile that you knew I understand is in California. Mr. G is dead. He died soon after the World's Fair. Poor man! I did all I could for him and he placed his only child in my care. So you see I am alone."[59] Montezuma became "custodian" for the son who was apparently also named Carlos, but only for a short time, and we know no more about him.[60]

## CHAPTER FIVE

# Becoming a Doctor:
# I Am Ready to Do Anything

ASKING FOR an American physician's help in the early nineteenth century was an act of desperation. At the beginning of the nineteenth century, medical care was directed to the treatment of symptoms (fever, convulsions, pain), and chances were that treatment by a physician would do more harm than good. By 1900, the odds of being helped by a physician were better, but not until somewhere between 1910 and 1912, did a patient have, for the first time in history, a better than a fifty-fifty chance of benefiting from consulting with a physician.[1] Montezuma graduated from medical school in 1889 and practiced in Chicago from 1896 to 1922, the time period during which medicine became a true profession, the earning of a living through the regulated application of a body of specialized knowledge.

## EARLY AMERICAN MEDICINE

In eighteenth-century England, physicians had somewhat of an elite status, being regarded as learned professionals who utilized their minds. Surgeons practiced a craft, working with their hands, and belonged to the same professional organizations as barbers. Because physicians had some stature, they were not inclined to migrate to the colonies; therefore, the earliest American doctors were mainly surgeons. Early American society was not highly stratified, and soon all who practiced any form of medicine came to be recognized as doctors. It was not hard to be a doctor in early America; a little experience, a little knowledge gained from another, and a man could be in business, usually a part-time business, ancillary to some other trade or occupation.

Medical practice in the 1700s differed little from that of the preceding centuries. There was no substantial body of medical knowledge. The cause and contagion of infections were unknown. Diagnoses were inaccurate, composed of the recognition of specific symptoms, such as fever, rather than the cause of the symptom. But there was a beginning. Surgeons were able to set fractures and dislocations, amputate limbs, remove superficial foreign bodies, and lance and drain infections. The bark of the cinchona tree was demonstrated to be effective for the treatment of malarial symptoms; however, the uncertainty regarding the actual cause of a fever and the crude bark preparation with its bulk and side effects combined to restrain its use. It was not until the mid 1800s that quinine, the concentrated alkaloid of cinchona, became available in large quantities.

The 1700s also saw the important discovery of inoculation and vaccination for smallpox. Inoculation was the transfer of a small amount of pus from an infected smallpox patient into the arm of a healthy individual. If the resulting infection were a minor one, relative immunity was acquired against a severe, virulent smallpox infection. Unfortunately not all inoculated infections were minor, and in the mid 1700s, several epidemics could be traced to inoculations. In 1798, Edward Jenner published his discovery that an infection with cowpox would produce immunity to smallpox. Cowpox was a skin disease on the udders of cows that produced skin lesions and a mild illness in dairy cow milkers. Inoculation with cowpox was called "vaccination," after the Latin word for cow, *vacca*.[2] Vaccination against smallpox rapidly became widespread in the United States.

In the years before and after 1800, American society resisted the efforts of some physicians to make themselves into an elite profession. One problem was the general awareness that there was little unique that physicians had to offer. Most illnesses were taken care of in the home under the supervision of the women in the family. The understanding of disease was so limited that specialized knowledge was not only unavailable, it was not needed. There were relatively few commercial medications. Most conditions were treated with the simple measures of good diet, cleanliness, exercise, and fresh air. American families in the 1700s had their own botanical medicines (sassafras, sarsaparilla, dandelion). Recipes for various concoctions were obtained from friends, newspapers, and almanacs. Early in the 1800s, botanical therapy books written for domestic use made the practice seem more professional, although the indications and results were no more validated than the family-derived products.

## MEDICINE IN THE 1800s

In the early 1800s, the United States was not a healthy country. Water supplies were polluted, sewage disposal was haphazard, food was prepared and transported with unsanitary methods, and insects were not controlled. These problems were compounded by city living with poor housing and malnutrition. Malaria was a common problem in the early 1800s, even in northern states. The illness was believed to arise from decomposition in marshes and swamps; the name comes from an Italian word meaning "bad air." Malaria was so common that it was regarded as a part of life. Dysentery from a lack of sanitation was also common, as were pneumonia and influenza. Infectious epidemics, especially cholera and yellow fever, routinely struck with rapidity and produced high mortality rates that in modern times are seen only with warfare. Modern generations don't remember times when epidemics stopped the business of a city and the dead were stacked like cordwood.

The therapeutic zeal of these early American physicians was out of proportion to their medical knowledge. Physicians cared little for the reasons why (the theoretical and experimental basis of medicine), only for the how (actual clinical practice). But this was not their fault; it was a reflection of the limited and unscientific knowledge of the times. Indeed, charismatic, caring physicians did more for their patients than their equally knowledgeable, but dull and insensitive colleagues.

Physicians and patients were quick to invoke religious explanations; illness was a sign of God's displeasure. Epidemics were often viewed as punishments for sin. Medical diagnosis in the early 1800s consisted of recognizing and categorizing various symptoms. Fever was a major diagnosis, but rather than being considered as a manifestation of a disease, it was the disease. There were no thermometers; therefore fever was diagnosed by feeling the patient, the presence of pain, and the complaints of weakness, disorientation, and "feeling" sick. Anything that would improve the symptoms was considered to be affecting (treating) the disease. Therefore anything that reduced fever was good therapy, no matter the actual consequences.

The thermometer is a good example of the time and effort involved before a simple procedure can become a useful tool for the practice of medicine. Hermann Boerhaave in Leyden introduced the thermometer, an impractical instrument at first, being fifteen inches long and requiring up to twenty minutes of rectal insertion.[3] Measurement of body temperature did not become a routine procedure until after Carl Wunderlich, professor of medicine in Leipzig, reported in 1868 several million temperature recordings in 25,000 patients. The thermometer is derived from the need to objectively measure body temperature. Its use required technical refinements to yield a simple, easy to use, and reliable instrument. Body temperature readings had to be scientifically accumulated and correlated with health and illness. Finally, the proper use and interpretation of the thermometer had to be incorporated into medical education.

The first half of the nineteenth century was a time of aggressive, active treatment (so-called "heroic" treatment). It wasn't complicated. The patient was bled, blistered, and purged. The sicker the patient appeared, the more vigorous the treatment. Physicians had to be courageous; the treatment often produced an unconscious patient. Whoever sent for a physician could expect to be treated in this manner. It is not surprising that turning to a physician was a desperate measure, and physicians were regarded with skepticism and some hostility.

Bloodletting was a popular medical treatment in the United States for approximately 150 years, from the Colonial Period into the 1900s. The world history of bloodletting is even older, over twenty-five centuries.[4] Draining blood and emptying the gastrointestinal tract had their roots in the Greek belief that good health depended upon the balance of body humors. Medical treatments, therefore, became attempts to restore equilibrium.

The death of George Washington in 1799 is attributed to the severe bloodletting, purging, and blistering he received in the forty-eight hours after he complained of a sore throat.[5] Bloodletting was the preferred treatment for fever in the early 1800s. The effect was often dramatic because copious amounts of blood, several cups to quarts, were allowed to flow. The resulting hypotension and shock often produced an apparent beneficial effect on the fever; the fever was replaced with fainting, coolness, and sometimes death. One dominant school of thought advocated bleeding until the patient was unconscious. Bloodletting was used for everything, including convulsions, concussions, hernias, wounds, burns, fractures, and of course, infections. The skill of the physician involved the selection of veins or arteries and the method (lancet, leech, or cupping).

After bloodletting, cleansing the stomach and bowels was the next most popular treatment. The emetics used to induce vomiting and the laxatives used for purgatives cannot be compared to modern medicines. They were powerful with immediate explosive results, and often they were poisons. Calomel was the preferred cathartic. Calomel is mercury chloride, a compound that irritates the bowel and with prolonged use poisons the body. It could be carried in a physician's coat pockets and administered with a teaspoon. The doses and durations of use were very large, and its administration was standard practice even in the sickest of patients. Another popular treatment was "tartar emetic," tartrate of antimony, also a poison. These treatments were challenging and destructive, but physicians of the nineteenth century also had tonics to "build up" the body's systems. One of the most popular tonics was arsenic, followed later by strychnine, both recognized today as poisons.

Blisters were produced by chemical or hot plasters. Blistering was recognized to cause convulsions, gangrene, and even death, especially in children. Remember nothing was done halfway. The more powerful the treatment, the better the result. A blister was produced on the site of pain; the fluid in the blister was then drained achieving what was believed to be the removal of harmful materials. Blisters on the forehead or on a shaved head were used for the treatment of fever. Twenty to thirty blisters would not be unusual.

BENJAMIN RUSH WAS ONE of the most prominent American physicians of his time, and his methods of practice were a good example of the unscientific and dangerous state of medicine around 1800. Benjamin Rush was a graduate of the College of New Jersey (now Princeton) at the age of fifteen who then acquired medical experience with five and one-half years of apprenticeship with John Redman, a highly regarded physician in Philadelphia.[6] His M.D. degree was obtained at the age of twenty-two in 1768 from the University of Edinburgh in Scotland. He established a successful practice in Philadelphia and soon became professor of chemistry in the College of Philadelphia. Elected to the Second Continental Congress, Rush was one of five physicians who signed the Declaration of Independence. It was Rush who provided Thomas Paine with the title of his pamphlet, *Common Sense*, that was the rallying call for revolution in the colonies in the early months of 1775.[7] Benjamin Rush was one of the few who took an aggressive, assertive stand against slavery, publishing an anti-slavery pamphlet as early as 1773. Confidant and close friends with both John Adams and Thomas Jefferson, Rush was able to renew the friendship between the two ex-presidents, which resulted in a remarkable correspondence that began in 1809 and extended until Adams and Jefferson died on the same day, The Fourth of July, 1826.[8]

Benjamin Rush, from 1783 until his death in 1813, was on the staff of the Pennsylvania Hospital, the first hospital in the United States.[9] The original building, the carefully preserved Pine Building, still stands, a short walk from Independence Hall in Philadelphia. I have lectured, with an awesome sense of history, in the very same amphitheater in Pennsylvania Hospital where Benjamin Rush convincingly argued that all diseases had one and only one basic cause. His belief was solidified by his experience in the yellow fever epidemic in Philadelphia in 1793. Deluged with sick patients who usually failed to respond to any of his treatments, he turned in desperation to very large doses of mercury (calomel) and jalap (a powerful herbal cathartic). He combined this with bloodletting, and soon believed he could effectively treat yellow fever. He even self-administered his recommended treatment when he himself developed yellow fever. Rush believed that all illnesses, from insanity to the gout, were manifestations of a tension in the vascular system. Rush simplified medicine in his mind and for his students by arguing that extreme bloodletting relieved vascular tension. The fervor of his belief and his high status in the medical profession and society, combined with his warm, enthusiastic personality, were major reasons why bloodletting and purging remained the primary therapeutic methods for American physicians for so long a period. Unfortunately, Rush erroneously believed that the human body contained twice as much blood as it actually does (eight to ten pints), and that effective treatment required the removal of 80 percent of the body's blood. When Rush removed multiple pints of blood, the poor patient had very little left.

In 1803, President Thomas Jefferson selected Benjamin Rush to be the medical tutor for Captain Meriwether Lewis. Rush provided Lewis with a list of health rules to follow in caring for his men and a list of research questions regarding the health practices of Indians.[10]

The Lewis and Clark Expedition relied upon calomel and bloodletting to treat all medical problems, including syphilis. The first bleeding on the expedition was for sunburn.[11] Sacagawea almost died four months after giving birth, while at the Great Falls of the Missouri.[12] It is thought she had a severe pelvic infection. Captain William Clark treated her with repeated bleedings and a poultice made of warm water, flour, pulverized bark, and a dash of tincture of opium. The poultice was wrapped in a cloth and applied to her "region." Perhaps she got better because Lewis discovered a sulfurous spring and he forced Sacagawea to drink as much as she could, having remembered that a similar spring in Virginia was associated with cures. Fortunately she did get better because her death may have significantly altered history. Charles Eastman, the Sioux physician at the Wounded Knee Massacre in 1890 (Chapter 2), served as an Inspector for the Bureau of Indian Affairs from 1923 to 1925. He was assigned the task of investigating the circumstances of Sacagawea's death. Eastman's report concluded that Sacagawea lived to be almost 100 years old, dying on April 9, 1884, at Fort Washakie, Wyoming.[13] Her death, however, is an historical controversy; others have concluded that she died in 1812, at Fort Manuel, at the mouth of the Big Horn River.

Sacagawea was a Shoshoni Indian by birth, from the western side of the Rockies. She was captured in 1800 at the age of ten by a Hidatsas (a tribe at the confluence of the Knife and Missouri rivers) war party at Three Forks, where the three great trout streams, the Jefferson, Gallatin, and Madison form the Missouri. Probably the main reason Charbonneau was hired as a guide by Lewis and Clark was to have his wife, Sacagawea, along to translate for the Shoshoni. Here is the pathway conversations had to follow: Shoshoni by Sacagawea to Mandan by Charbonneau to French by Cruzatte to English, and then back the other way. Lewis and Clark looked forward to meeting the Snake tribe of the Shoshoni, as they would be totally dependent upon them for horses and food in order to complete the portage over the Continental Divide to the Columbia River. In September, 1805, as they were trying to find the pass over the Rockies, and in desperate need of horses and food, they were suddenly confronted by an armed party of sixty Indian warriors. The chief of the party, Cameahwait, turned out to be Sacagawea's brother, and they recognized each other.

IN THE MIDDLE of the 1800s, medical schools replaced apprenticeship as the method of medical education. The standard apprenticeship lasted three years, providing about $100 per year to the preceptor. The first half of the apprenticeship was supposed to be devoted to reading medicine with a doctor; in the second half the apprentice rode with the doctor making house calls. Because there were no standards or regulations, the actual experience varied from being productive and worthwhile to a near total lack of education, due to a half-hearted effort on the part of either student or doctor, or both.

In the first half of the 1800s, medical schools were of simple construction, easy to establish, and this period of history saw a rapid increase in small schools not associated with universities.[14] Except for anatomy, the only teaching method was the lecture. Even surgery, including bloodletting, was taught by lecture. The lectures reflected the state of knowledge of the lecturers, not very complicated or extensive. Most medical schools had three to five faculty members and one classroom. The full course of instruction required two years, but it occupied only four months of each year, and most schools repeated the same course each year. One professor would often teach multiple subjects (every teacher was granted the title of Professor). Practical anatomy was not required for graduation (to avoid public reaction), but virtually every medical school provided anatomy experience with dissection. Cadavers were obtained legally and illegally, and they were often deteriorated. Passing a final examination yielded an M.D. degree. Most students became doctors without ever witnessing a childbirth. Histology, bacteriology, and pathology all suffered from the lack of a microscope. Clinical medicine was still expected to be learned by an association with a preceptor. Medical schools with their lack of facilities and equipment were, therefore, inexpensive to operate and earned money for the faculty (the student fee was $200 to $285 per year in the city schools). For these reasons the number of schools proliferated in the early 1800s. In the 1800s, a popular professor could add to his practice income about $10,000 per year; less popular faculty about $5,000. At this time, a practicing physician earned $1,000 to $2,000 per year.

The students entering medical school in the first half of the nineteenth century were not well-educated.[15] Few cities had public high schools. College education concentrated on the classics, not very helpful for an aspiring physician. It has been estimated that less than 4 percent of men entering medical school had two or more years of secondary education.[16] Therefore admission standards were not high; most schools were willing to provide a short course of instruction to anyone who could pay for it.

Despite these limitations, the increase in medical schools in the early 1800s did improve medical education, but this was because it previously was so irregular and inconsistent in the apprenticeship system. Unfortunately, the therapeutics being taught continued to be the violent and vigorous methods of bloodletting, purging, and blistering—lending these methods even more credibility. The drugs used continued to be the frightening collection of opium, mercury, and arsenic as well as cinchona and alcohol. Finally, the decline in the use of these methods took place in the second half of the 1800s. Nevertheless, bloodletting and the use of calomel persisted sporadically until 1910–1920.

Despite the introduction of new agents, overmedication continued to make consulting a physician a hazardous choice. Chemicals to reduce fever were developed to replace bloodletting. Some were harsh and dangerous, such as aconite and *Veratrum viride*. But by 1820, quinine, extracted from cinchona bark became available in large amounts. It replaced calomel as the physician's favorite drug and was used for fevers of all causes; indeed, any medical problem whose cause was obscure was labeled as malarial by physicians.[17] By 1890, the United States was using 40 percent of the world's consumption of quinine.[18] The side effects were so common they were called "cinchonism," gastrointestinal irritation, nervousness, tinnitus, and in severe cases of overdosage, deafness and blindness. After 1890, antipyrine replaced quinine as an antipyretic, followed by acetanilid, and ultimately, in 1897, acetylsalicylic acid (aspirin).

Opium and morphine were used at the beginning of the twentieth century for almost every illness, with an amazing indifference to its addictive properties.[19] It is not hard to imagine how doctors and patients appreciated the narcotic-induced alteration of the mind. Because oral administration was relatively impotent, soon the method of choice became the hypodermic syringe. By 1910, United States importation of opium far outranked that of European countries. The impact in terms of the number of addicted people has been impossible to estimate. The use of the syringe, the lack of regulations governing the sale of opium, and the widespread use of patent medicines containing opium combined to make addiction a real problem. Physicians were aware of this and turned to other drugs, one of which was cocaine. The nasal use of cocaine became so popular it was instrumental in the rapid development of otolaryngology, the nose and throat specialty.

The second half of the nineteenth century also saw the growing popularity of alcohol. There is a reason why alcohol is still referred to, usually in humor, as "medicinal." Whiskey and brandy in the late 1800s were highly regarded as tonics and were used liberally to treat acute and chronic diseases, even infectious diseases such as typhoid and pneumonia. The most common dose for adults was one-half to one ounce of whiskey or brandy every two to three hours. This most certainly would have produced an inebriated state. Even infants and young children were treated with large doses. Many patent medicines contained amazingly high levels of alcohol, as high as 30 percent, often combined with opium in one form or another. The advances in bacteriology increased the use of alcohol when it was discovered that contact with alcohol was germicidal. For example, patients with tuberculosis were treated with alcohol sprays, inhalations, injections, and enemas.[20]

Until the mid 1800s, hospitals were dangerous places that were best avoided. Industrialization and city living, combined with improvements in hospital hygiene and an understanding of antiseptic techniques after the Civil War, led to a rapid growth and use of hospitals that has persisted. Medical schools established minimum standards, and by 1893 most required three or more years of training. Johns Hopkins in Baltimore opened in 1893 and became the model for years to come, bringing research and clinical care together, and providing specialized training in a university hospital setting. By 1900, medicine became more uniform, more organized, and more recognized as a respectful profession.

## MEDICINE AT THE TURN OF THE TWENTIETH CENTURY

Modern medicine is very complex, an elaborate system of specialized knowledge and technical procedures governed by its own rules of behavior. It is now an enormous arrangement of hospitals, clinics, corporations, private and government health plans, and a vast labor force. It little resembles the system in place in Montezuma's time, the early 1900s. The medical profession today is powerful, the beneficiary of scientific progress that created potent and influential economic entities. But in 1900 the medical profession was not a dominant one, and the medical system did not resemble the bureaucratic Goliath of today.

One hundred years ago, doctors had less income and prestige. The medical profession was not strong, and being a physician was not a guarantee of a good income. Medical care was not a major issue with state or federal governments because the costs were not huge like they are today; political issues, like induced abortion, were not at the forefront; hospitals, pharmacies, and pharmaceutical companies were not powerful corporations like they are today. The financing of research and health care was not the important economic issue it is today.

The American Medical Association (AMA) was formed in 1847, but until it reorganized in 1901 and 1903, it was not a powerful organization. Its early attempts to standardize medical education were totally ineffective. At the time Montezuma entered practice (around 1900), only 8,400 of the approximately 100,000 regular physicians in the United States were members.[21] And only 25,000 belonged to state and local medical societies affiliated with the AMA. Two major changes in structure had a profound effect that ultimately made the AMA a powerful organization. In 1901, the AMA reorganized, making the local county medical society the foundation of its structure; all licensed physicians had to be accepted into local society membership, every member automatically became a member of the state society, and the state societies became the source of delegates to the AMA legislative body, the House of Delegates. Although membership in the AMA at first declined, physicians (especially specialists) were quick to realize that referrals depended on relationships with fellow members in the local societies. In 1903, the AMA adopted a set of principles that effectively left a code of professional behavior up to the local societies, further strengthening the structural organization.

The professional behavior of physicians became an important issue at the turn of the century. When medicine lacked an objective basis (gained only with the growth of scientific knowledge), malpractice suits were unheard of. As medicine became more scientific, physicians' behavior could be judged more objectively. "The number of malpractice suits in the first fifteen years of the twentieth century exceeded the number of suits during the entire nineteenth century."[22] This phenomenon increased the importance and strength of local medical societies, as they were able to secure and provide malpractice insurance at lower group rates and to provide resources for defense testimony in the courtroom. The medical defense plan of the Chicago Medical Society provided legal and financial support to every member, beginning in 1904.

As more and more graduates from medical schools went to work in the cities, they organized local medical societies. A major motivation for organization in the late 1800s was to have a favorable effect on economic competition, with special efforts directed against practitioners such as homeopaths, users of patent medicines, and pharmacists who provided advice and drugs over the counter. In the largest cities, elite organizations composed of well-known and influential physicians were formed to be scientific forums. Many of the members in these societies were connected with medical schools, but often the members were wealthy, of the right family background with the right friends, and they were White, Anglo, Protestants. Indeed, these connections were important around 1900 when Montezuma began practice. It required more than professional competence and a good personality to attract a wealthy clientele. And by the time Montezuma began practice, it was also worthwhile to develop a specialty, to move a step beyond the competitors by having a greater store of a specialized knowledge and experience.

It wasn't until the last decades of the 1800s that a critical amount of medical knowledge had been accumulated that would allow the creation of specialties. This coincided with the concentration of people in the cities, widespread use of the telephone, and improved transportation—all allowing a specialist to collect enough patients to make a living. Surgeons capitalized on the development of antisepsis and anesthesia (nitrous oxide and ether came into use in 1842–1847), and surgical procedures quickly became a major part of hospitals. The ophthalmoscope to examine eyes was invented in 1851, and soon, in 1864, ophthalmology was the first major specialty. By 1900, there were fifteen national specialty medical societies.[23] The American Gastroenterological Association (Montezuma's specialty) was founded in 1897. In these early years of specialties, most specialists continued to function as general practitioners, as family physicians. There is no evidence that Montezuma was a member of the American Gastroenterological Association.

Effective anesthesia allowed surgery to move from crude carpentry to a delicate art. Surgeons now had time to dissect gently and deeply, and the most innermost cavities became approachable (even the skull). As surgery became more complicated and hospitals safer, both physicians and patients recognized the need for good hospitals. The advantages of anesthesia were immediately apparent and adoption was rapid. The story with antisepsis was a little different.

Deep wounds and surgical procedures, even childbirth, were often followed by infection and death. Physicians knew that deep wounds, if closed, would lead to abscess formation, and therefore, healing by secondary intention (keeping the wound open to heal from the bottom up) was a standard procedure, usually accompanied by a rocky course, and all too often, death. For a long time, a hospital was regarded as a place where you went to die. One reason hospitals in the early 1800s were regarded as dangerous places to be avoided was the problem of acquired infections. Physicians were very much aware of this problem, but no one knew how it happened.

Louis Pasteur demonstrated that germs are airborne, and Joseph Lister established that wound infections were the consequence of transmitted germs. At that time, surgeons operated with bare hands, repeatedly wore a bloodstained coat, and instruments were of course not sterilized, often dropped to the floor, picked up, and used again. Lister chose carbolic acid as his antiseptic, but it was not as rapidly accepted as was anesthesia. Carbolic acid was a destructive substance (for wounds, surgeons, and assistants), and many physicians found the germ theory hard to accept. Gradually, better antiseptics replaced carbolic acid. Sterilization, caps, gowns, and rubber gloves became routine, and by 1880, the American Surgical Association was founded. By 1900, bacteriologists had discovered microorganisms to be the cause of tuberculosis, diphtheria, cholera, typhoid, and tetanus. The microscope came into general use in medical education in the 1890s. It was the development of the microscope coupled with the manufacture of chemicals that could stain microorganisms that allowed the rapid progress in bacteriology from 1860 on. But it was not until the turn of the century, that microscopes became a common instrument in a physician's practice. The first ten years of the twentieth century (the first years of Montezuma's private practice in Chicago) finally saw scientific knowledge reach the stage of a critical mass, sufficient knowledge to change the way physicians practice and to have a positive effect on the health of patients.

The importance of the microscope cannot be overrated. Consider the average physician who had never seen a microscope being told that a sickness seen every day in practice is due to an invisible microorganism. This was rejected by many just on the basis of "common sense." The introduction of the microscope to medical education produced a more open state of mind. The final acceptance and application of the germ theory came when specific pharmacologic therapy could be aimed at a microorganism diagnosed by bacteriology.

By the 1880s, when Montezuma attended medical school, most medical schools (but not all) had adopted a three-year curriculum. Schools were introducing laboratory and basic science training into the curriculum. Full-time teachers and scientists who were not clinical practitioners were becoming medical school professors. Scientific achievements (mostly in bacteriology) were creating a respected collection of knowledge; this combined with the growth of specialties to make medicine an increasingly attractive field. The number of medical students increased dramatically. In 1880, there were 100 schools with 11,826 students; by 1903 there were 160 medical schools with 27,615 students.[24] By 1910, Chicago had more medical schools than any other city in the United States. The most expensive Chicago school cost $185 tuition per year; the least expensive, $100.[25]

A more uniform program of instruction followed the creation of the National Conference of State Medical Examining and Licensing Boards in 1891, which called for licensing laws to require diplomas from schools that had minimal standards for entrance and instruction.[26] The Association of American Medical Colleges had been established earlier, but its influence dates from its new name in 1889, and by 1894, it required member schools to have four-year courses of instruction.

The American Medical Association formed its Council on Medical Education in 1904, at a time when there were 158 medical schools in the United States. The Council invited the Carnegie Foundation for the Advancement of Teaching to evaluate medical education, and in 1910, the Flexner Report (under the direction of Abraham Flexner) became the basis for consolidation and reorganization of medical education, bringing medical education into the universities with a uniform curriculum and an emphasis on the basic sciences.[27]

Before the Flexner report resulted in a major improvement in medical education by 1925 as the good schools survived and the poor schools disappeared, the overall quality of the graduates ranged from good to abysmal. The U. S. Army Medical Corps, between 1888 and 1909, failed 72 percent of the physicians taking the examinations for admission.[28] The decline in small and inadequate medical schools did not occur just because of the call for new standards. The increasing need to incorporate laboratory and basic science into medical education required major expenses in equipment and professors. Many schools could not afford to make the changes and simply closed.

**THE CHICAGO MEDICAL COLLEGE**

In the last decades of the nineteenth century, medical schools became the sole pathway to becoming a physician. Carlos Montezuma was the first Indian student to attend the Chicago Medical College, which became Northwestern University School of Medicine.[29] He graduated at age twenty-three on March 26, 1889, losing the distinction of being the first American Indian physician by two weeks. This distinction belongs to Susan La Flesche Picotte, a member of the Omaha tribe, who graduated from the Women's Medical College of Pennsylvania in Philadelphia (now the Medical College of Pennsylvania–Hahneman University) on March 14, 1889. Picotte, a year younger than Montezuma, died at the age of fifty in 1915. Like Montezuma, she was an advocate of assimilation (she attended Hampton Institute), but became a vigorous opponent of the land loss associated with the allotment program.[30] Unlike Montezuma, she confined her efforts to her own tribe and was little known nationally.

The first medical college in Chicago was named for the deceased Benjamin Rush of Philadelphia, and its charter in 1837 actually preceded by a few days the city charter. However, Rush Medical College was not sufficiently established financially and was unable to accept students for another seven years, teaching twenty-two students by four professors in 1843.[31] By 1850, the first medical journal, the *Illinois Medical and Surgical Journal*, appeared, as well as the first medical societies, the Chicago Medical Society and the Illinois State Medical Society. This was a banner year, as the first significant hospital began operations, the Mercy Hospital.

The forerunner of the Chicago Medical College was established in 1859 as the Medical Department of Lind University. By 1860, the first year of the Chicago Medical College, the population of the city was 109,280.[32] Five of the seven principal founders of the Chicago Medical College were active or recent members of the Rush faculty. Most importantly, Nathan Smith Davis and W. H. Byford were involved; their dissatisfaction with the current quality of medical education was already recognized. Remember, most medical schools were business enterprises, not educational institutions. The founders of the Chicago Medical College were intent in their desire to develop a school that would have greater organization, better admission requirements, and up-to-date teaching. The initial development of the school was instigated by Lind University (later to become Lake Forest University). The plan was to have instruction progress from basic studies in the first year, to more complex subjects in the second year, ending the practice of course repetition, and to clinical instruction in hospitals in the third year. To accomplish what was a much greater program compared with other schools, the annual term was increased to five months, from October to March, increasing the requirements compared with all other schools at that time. The first faculty (ages twenty-four to forty-two; the emeritus professor, Rutter, was fifty-eight) were all medical doctors, except Mahla, a Ph.D., and Spafford, a lawyer:

| | |
|---|---|
| Edmund Andrews | Principles and Practice of Surgery |
| W. H. Byford | Midwifery |
| N. S. Davis | Principles and Practice of Medicine |
| Titus DeVille | Descriptive Anatomy |
| H. H. Hollister | Physiology and Histology |
| Ralph N. Isham | Surgical Anatomy and Operative Surgery |
| Hosmer A. Johnson | Materia Medica and Therapeutics |
| F. Mahla | Chemistry and Toxicology |
| David Rutter | Emeritus Professor of Midwifery |
| H. G. Spafford | Medical Jurisprudence |
| M. K. Taylor | Pathology and Hygiene |
| Horace Wardner | Demonstrator of Anatomy |

This was a young and courageous group of men, earnest in their collective desire to improve medical education and to match the best of Europe. They promised a larger faculty (all committed), a longer term, progressive complexity of study, practical anatomy, hospital clinical instruction, and fewer formal lectures (bound to gain favor with prospective students). This truly was a bold venture, demanding more of the students and more of the faculty. It was recognized by other medical people in Chicago as an effort of "reform," and even the faculty considered it experimental. The first class began three months after Northwestern University graduated its first class of five students. The faculty dressed somberly and formally in black, with Prince Albert coats and tall silk hats. Even the students wore suits at all times, with vests, ties, stiff collars, and black Homburg hats.

The Medical Department of Lind opened in October 1859, on the third and fourth floors of a new five-story brick building, on the northwest corner of Market (now Wacker Drive) and Randolph Streets. The entire block was known as the Lind Block. The new medical college had two lecture rooms, a dissecting room, a chemical laboratory, a museum for specimens and skeletons, and a library of several hundred books. Two of the faculty members had previously organized the Chicago City Dispensary, a clinic to treat the poor, already operating in this building for a year. The building also housed a wholesale grocery and an enterprise that made and sold pianos. Hospital instruction was provided in Mercy Hospital (sixty beds), on Wabash Avenue near Van Buren Street.

The first class numbered nineteen juniors and fourteen seniors (students who had already received some education at other schools). Instead of enduring 520 lectures in sixteen weeks (as in other schools), the junior students attended 446 lectures over twenty-two weeks.[33] Most importantly, microscope instruction and demonstration were included in the program at a time when other schools viewed the microscope with distrust. The senior students attended 600 lectures plus clinical instruction. At the end of the first term, nine students were awarded the degree of Doctor of Medicine. Total revenue the first year was $1,950, balancing expenditures. The initial cost for the students was higher than that of other institutions, the faculty clearly stating that their objective was high quality. The fees totaled about $60 per year, at a time when board and room cost $2.50 to $3.50 per week. Tuition was actually the total sum of individual tickets sold to the students for lectures as well as laboratory and hospital instruction. This was the method by which professors earned supplementary income. The system changed in 1879, when a total tuition fee of $115 was required to cover all instruction. A final $20 was charged for the diploma itself. For over fifty years, it was traditional to obtain the signature of each faculty member on the M.D. diploma, easily done since the faculty was not large in size, compared with present day numbers.

The medical college was a success from the start. It rapidly added an optional summer course that including readings, dissections, a weekly lecture, and bedside teaching. The Professor of Obstetrics even arranged for each student to attend a home delivery. Student numbers steadily increased throughout the years of the Civil War. This success coupled with financial problems at Lind University prompted the faculty to purchase and remodel a building on the east side of State Street (now near Cermak Road) in 1863, occupied by the fifth class of eighty-nine students. At this point in time, 1863, the faculty reorganized with a new name, the Chicago Medical College. In that same year, Mercy Hospital moved to a new building at Calumet Avenue and Rio Grande (now Twenty-sixth) Street.

In 1864, the Chicago Medical College was incorporated, under the direction of a board of trustees, made up of the current faculty members, and terminated its official relationship with Lind University, although the College continued to view itself as an academic affiliation of the University (now Lake Forest University). Finally, in 1868, all association with Lake Forest University ended. By now, the faculty considered their College to be the first medical school in America to be dedicated to the highest principles of education and organized accordingly.

In 1867, the College continued its pioneering efforts with new precedents. The academic period was increased from five to six months; the total course requirement was increased from two years to three years, standards of preliminary education were established, and laboratory study was required in chemistry, histology, physiology, and pathology, but in reality, the claims were greater than the practice as instruction was limited to chemistry. After a decade of operation, the Chicago Medical College was providing two to three times as many lectures as other schools, the faculty was larger, the curriculum was more extensive, attendance was required, strict grading was maintained, and hospital instruction was mandatory. The overall organization began to resemble a pattern that was to persist in the United States for a hundred years. The first year was devoted to the basic sciences. The second year combined basic sciences with beginning clinical instruction, and the third year consisted of clinical and hospital instruction. The College was truly at the forefront of medical education in the United States. Overall, however, American medical education after the Civil War was no match for that in European countries.

Northwestern University was chartered in 1851, began its first class in 1855, and by 1859 had a total of thirty-six students. It was founded on the stolid orthodox principles of the Methodist Episcopal Church. The Chicago Medical College and Northwestern University became affiliated in 1870, with respective annual budgets of $4,000 and $28,000.[34] In 1869, Northwestern admitted women for the first time, and in 1870, its affiliation with the Chicago Medical College made it a true university, not just a College of Literature, Science, and Arts. Nathan S. Davis, the president of the medical faculty, was a trustee of Northwestern from its founding, and this undoubtedly played a role in the affiliation. The medical college retained its name, but officially became the Medical Department of Northwestern University. The medical degrees would now come from Northwestern, upon the recommendation of the medical faculty. Undergraduate Northwestern students would be permitted to attend chemistry classes at the medical college, and tuition charges to the medical college were waived for Northwestern graduates (this lasted until 1896), and the University contributed $15,000 for a new medical building at a site provided by the Sisters of Mercy next to their hospital. Accordingly, the president of the medical faculty, Nathan S. Davis, became a "Dean."

Nathan Smith Davis died in 1904, at the age of eighty-seven, a general practitioner of medicine until ten days before his death. As a young physician, he practiced in upper New York and New York City, but always pursued speaking, writing, and teaching, and played a key role in the events that led to the founding of the American Medical Association. In 1849, at age thirty-two, he accepted the position of Chair of Physiology and General Pathology in the new Rush Medical College in Chicago. A year later he became Chair of Medicine, and ten years later left to help found the Chicago Medical College. He was the dominant personality of the College and one of the preeminent medical forces in Chicago, helping to found Mercy Hospital and the Chicago Medical Society.[35] He served as President of the College for four years, and then Dean for twenty-eight years until 1898. He could and did lecture on any subject, and made sure that he not only provided information (all personal opinions as was the style of the times), but also inspiration. However, he found it hard to change. He opposed the introduction of the thermometer and the microscope, and he made fun of the germ theory of disease. An abstainer, he was a loud advocate of temperance. He became the first editor of JAMA, the *Journal of the American Medical Association*, at the age of sixty-six and held that post for twelve years. Davis was a wiry man, with deep-set eyes on a long face accentuated by a large forehead topped with bushy hair, and at the other end, a short beard that he limited to the area below his chin, but stretching from ear to ear. It is not surprising to learn that this gruff, serious man full of his self-importance rarely smiled. But this superficial sternness overlaid the gentleness and kindness present in all great physicians. With his shaggy, white hair and in his black suit (including a coat with tails), white shirt, stiff and standing collar, black bow tie, and silk top hat, he looked like the great man that he was. One would think that Davis and Montezuma knew each other well, but as we will see, a letter from Montezuma suggests that there was little interaction between him and the faculty.

The Chicago Medical College faced a crisis in 1869 when the city of Chicago authorized the widening of State Street, a project that would eliminate the front part of the medical building. A lot was leased from the Sisters of Mercy adjoining Mercy Hospital in return for staffing the hospital and making it a teaching institution. A need for cash to erect a new building was part of the motivation to affiliate with Northwestern. At a cost of about $30,000, the building was ready for the 1870–1871 academic year, on the corner of Twenty-sixth

Street and Prairie Avenue, the site of instruction until 1893, thus including Montezuma's medical school years. A three-story building in brick with stone trim, it matched the Gothic design of the Mercy Hospital. Today, the old site of the Chicago Medical College is occupied by modern buildings, the current home of Mercy Hospital.

The Chicago Medical College building during Montezuma's student years contained two large lecture halls (amphitheaters seating 240 and 260 students—a popular stunt was the "passing up" of a classmate from a front row to the top row, accompanied by foot stomping), dissecting rooms, laboratories for chemistry and microscopy, a museum for anatomical and pathological specimens, and a library.[36] A free clinic was established in the street level basement, and there was also an ice-cooled vault lined with logs to maintain dissection material. Unfortunately this arrangement produced moldy deterioration of the unembalmed bodies. The students at the dissecting table usually smoked or chewed tobacco to endure the odors. The Chicago Fire occurred on October eighth and ninth, 1871. Eighteen thousand buildings were destroyed, making 90,000 people homeless. The Chicago Medical College and

*Chicago Medical College—1870-1893*

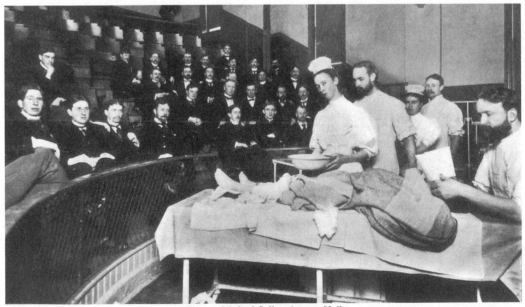

*Chicago Medical College Lecture Hall*

the nearby hospitals were beyond the southern limit of the fire; only one day of class was missed although three-fourths of the faculty lost their homes.

The Chicago Medical College was one of the first medical schools to establish formal entrance requirements. They were not robust. In 1887–1888 when Montezuma was a student, only 23 percent of the 200 to 220 students were college graduates, but then the percentage was much lower in most other medical schools.[37] Medical historians often describe the rowdiness of these early students (quick to fight, individual vs. individual or even class vs. class, and eager to pull stunts like dropping anatomical parts from cadavers into the pockets of visitors) and attribute it to their lack of education, but their dedication and willingness to work hard cannot be underrated (necessary qualities to succeed in medicine, a hard taskmaster).

As noted, Dean Davis was a staunch opponent of the germ theory of disease.[38] In lecturing to classes in 1886, he made fun of microbes and called them a passing fad. However, Montezuma and the medical students of the late 1880s were certainly made aware of the rapid advances taking place. Edmund Andrews, a founding faculty member, became one of the first surgeons to use antiseptic techniques, using Lister's methods. Henry Gradle, Professor of Physiology, presented a series of lectures on Bacteria and the Germ Theory of Disease as early as 1883. In book form, his lectures appeared in numerous languages throughout the world. In 1889, the year Montezuma graduated, Bayard Holmes was lecturing and demonstrating (presumably with a microscope) in bacteriology, and was given the title of Director of the Bacteriological Laboratory.

Montezuma was a student at a turning point, when new methods were being introduced, but old thoughts and practices were still in place. Training in the use of the microscope began in 1871. By 1878, formal study of normal and pathological histology was part of the course of instruction. Tissue preparation by individual students was begun in 1886. And by 1887, a fully equipped bacteriological laboratory was functional. Laboratory work in bacteriology was still optional, not required, at the time of Montezuma's graduation, and it is not certain if every student was exposed to the new knowledge. Montezuma's student notes reveal, however, that he was familiar with the use of a microscope, and his lecture notes, ten years later, indicate that he taught students the importance of a microscope.[39]

By 1890, instruction was provided in nervous and mental diseases, ophthalmology and otology, orthopedic surgery, diseases of bone and joints, dermatology, histology, physiology, gynecology, pediatrics, obstetrics, laryngology, physical diagnosis, and bacteriology; the faculty had grown to twenty-nine, and the total enrollment was 214. However, the professor of chemistry (not a clinician), the registrar, and the janitor were the only full-time and salaried positions.[40] In 1889, the course of instruction was extended to seven months per year, and four years overall, first as an option, then required by 1892. With the increase in course time, the summer course ended in 1876. A postgraduate course for practicing clinicians was initiated in 1880, a course Montezuma was to attend in 1895.

Every medical specialty taught in the Chicago Medical College had its corresponding clinic, either in the nearby hospitals or in the basement dispensary. The dispensary was treating 15,000 patients per year in 1890. Students, divided into small groups, saw patients under the supervision of two instructors. The pedagogical style, however, was not that of today. The instructor was clearly the Doctor in Charge.[41] The physical exam consisted of a few questions, palpation of the pulse, a perusal of the tongue, and a quick listen with the stethoscope. This traditional educational approach was challenged in Montezuma's time by

Frank Billings. Billings graduated from the Chicago Medical College in 1881, expanded his medical knowledge in Europe in 1885–1886, and returned to demonstrate the techniques of bacteriology, and in particular, the tubercular bacillus. In 1886, he was named Lecturer (and later, Professor) of Physical Diagnosis at the Chicago Medical College, and the students soon were being taught to perform a careful examination from head to toes before formulating a diagnosis. Montezuma's student notes indicate that he participated in Billing's clinic.[42] As a member of the attending staff at Mercy Hospital, Billings became a prominent internist and the personal physician of many of the wealthiest and most influential families in Chicago. Billings resigned in 1898 after his requests for financial aid for the school were rebuffed by Northwestern; he went on to be a important figure in the medical development of Rush and the University of Chicago, ultimately having a major impact on the city of Chicago and achieving national and international influence and acclaim.

In 1860, Nathan S. Davis introduced a new monthly medical journal, the *Chicago Medical Examiner*; for $2 per year, the subscriber could read original articles, clinical reports, book notices and reviews, and editorials—similar to medical journals today. Although owned by Davis, the journal did reflect the Chicago Medical College because most of the contributions came from the faculty and alumni. In 1875, the *Examiner* merged with the *Chicago Medical Journal* (the journal of Rush Medical College) to form the *Chicago Medical Journal and Examiner*. This journal expired in 1889 before Montezuma could benefit from its reading—perhaps a victim of competition from the American Medical Association's new journal, the *Journal of the American Medical Association*, begun in 1883. Especially since the editor of this new weekly journal was Nathan S. Davis.

Surgery was the first specialty in Chicago medicine. One of the most important early surgeons was Christian Fenger, a Dane who arrived penniless in 1877.[43] A tireless worker, Fenger applied his knowledge gained as a pathologist in the autopsy room to his surgical dissections in the operating room, and he was one of the first to emphasize clinical microscopy. He spoke eleven languages and read many foreign journals. His disciples became the most noteworthy internists and surgeons in Chicago of the early 1900s. One of them, John Benjamin Murphy, became world renown treating tuberculosis with thoracoplasty and artificial pneumothorax (Chapter 17). Montezuma must have known about these great teachers and practitioners, and probably heard presentations by them at his hospital or at medical society meetings.

In the early 1900s, about 25 percent of practicing physicians considered themselves specialists.[44] The practice of fee splitting (sharing part of a specialist fee with the referring physician) was widespread in the first decade of the 1900s.[45] But free clinics were an issue of controversy in the city of Chicago.[46] By 1880, the medical schools and teaching hospitals had created a large number of free clinics in order to provide teaching material. The Chicago Medical Society claimed that this was a ruse to funnel patients into the practices of the faculties, obviously an issue of economic controversy. But not all free clinics were associated with medical schools or hospitals. By 1907, there were forty-four clinics in Chicago, sixteen connected with hospitals, nine with medical schools, and thirty free standing.[47] In only six were all treatments and medications free, and therefore, the Chicago Medical Society had a point in believing these clinics (which were not reluctant to advertise for patients) represented competition for private physicians. This debate did not go away as more and more clinics opened, especially after World War I. The Chicago Medical Society continued to fight for a stringent limitation of free care to only those who could not pay.

In 1891, the relationship between the Chicago Medical College and the University was reorganized, establishing the new name of the Northwestern University Medical School. "Chicago Medical College" was carried as a subtitle on announcements (but not on the diploma) until 1910, even though in 1906, the Chicago Medical College ceased to exist as an independent corporation. In 1893, a new five-story building was occupied by Northwestern on South Dearborn Street at the corner of Twenty-fourth Street, with laboratories designed to accommodate the new developments in medical science. This was joined a few months later by a new clinical building, named Davis Hall (Davis was still the Dean and a generous financial contributor to the new building), and the block was filled in by the Wesley Hospital.

DESPITE THE FACT that the Chicago Medical College was at the forefront of medical education, a pioneer in new emphasis and dedication, we must assess it with the proper perspective. Because medical education in the United States was so relatively primitive and the extent of medical knowledge so limited, it didn't take much to be at the forefront. And even marching in the front, viewed with today's eyes, there was much to be desired. In the 1880s, one traveled to Chicago Medical College by walking or in a buggy or streetcar drawn by a horse, along an avenue lined by open, dirty ditches. By the time of Montezuma's graduation, the College's building was dilapidated, and there was insufficient space to meet the demand for increasing laboratory work.[48] Dissections were carried out at night under the dim light of gas jets. The building was only twenty years old, but it had obviously suffered from neglect. Because all the teaching (except chemistry) was provided by men with busy private practices, little attention was given to the care of the facilities. Descriptions of rooms in these years note the dirty and dusty conditions; it was just then that the importance of cleanliness was becoming appreciated. The teaching by these men was done in their spare time, and the teaching income was supplemental to their main sustenance, their private practices. Thus, the didactic teaching was often a process of repetition, learning by rote memory. The microscope was a relatively new instrument, and it is likely that both normal and pathological histology relied upon memorization from lectures and books.[49] The clinical lectures must have been better, more practical and to the point, based upon the experiences of the teachers. But even here, memorization was the method, directed toward passing the periodic quizzes. Success (and graduation) depended upon the accumulation of extensive lecture notes, the regurgitation of which was expected at examination time. Although there wasn't as much to know as there is today, the student was expected to know all of it, and well. Clear and logical reasoning was learned mainly by sharp observation of the examples provided by the teachers. Physicians, until about 1900, were incredibly knowledgeable about many things, often experts in diverse fields such as botany or geology or ornithology. But this was because the volume of medical knowledge at that time did not require the full occupation of the physician's time and brain. Today, a significant portion of a physician's leisure time is devoted to continuing education, a requirement made necessary by the constant and rapid expansion of medical knowledge.

In 1891, the text of Norman Walker's presidential address to The Carlisle Medical Society (the same Carlisle on the border of England and Scotland that was the namesake of Carlisle, Pennsylvania, and the Carlisle Indian School) summarized his assessment of American medical education after a long journey visiting schools and hospitals throughout the United States.[50] Recognizing the British contempt for the medical profession in the United States, he found little reason to change that attitude. He estimated that only a fifth of the students could see or hear a presentation in a Chicago lecture hall, and that any layman attending a British course in physiology would know more than the majority of American students. Walker was very critical of student quality, indicating that only one-third would have passed the British anatomy examination that was required prior to beginning dissection. He pointed out that lectures were largely descriptions of a professor's own experience in practice, many students graduated without ever looking through a microscope, and the students themselves were of an inferior social position (an American might consider the last criticism a compliment).

## MONTEZUMA, THE MEDICAL STUDENT

The typical medical student in the 1880s had to have a job. Besides paying tuition, enough had to be earned to provide for room and board because most students did not have family resources. Medical students cleaned the private practice offices of the faculty, delivered newspapers, lit street lamps, worked in restaurants, or cleaned buildings. Montezuma began medical school on June 21, 1884, at the remarkably young age of eighteen, and the Chicago Medical College, recognizing his uniqueness, did not charge him tuition. Nevertheless, he often had to return to the Stedman farm to work as a farm hand. This was possible because the medical school curriculum occupied only six months of the year. His collegiate decision to pursue a pharmaceutical program paid off because he was successful in obtaining work and living quarters from C. Pryne Stringfield, a Chicago pharmacist. From 1887 until Montezuma graduated, he lived at various locations near his medical school (87 Twenty-ninth Street, 1619 Indiana Avenue, and 2616 Cottage Grove Avenue) and worked in the pharmacy.

Even during his early years as a student in Chicago, Montezuma presented many lectures on the Indians, to a variety of groups ranging from ladies' clubs to church organizations. He obviously was pleased to share his personal convictions, a view that is apparent in a hand-written manuscript of a speech entitled, "The Indian of Tomorrow," presented to the National Woman's Christian Temperance Union in Chicago, 1888.[51] It was obviously carefully copied from notes because it is neat, carefully spaced, and without changes or corrections. This was probably his standard speech in those years, no matter what the forum, and the language is impressively eloquent for a young man in his early twenties. The speech articulated the Protestant assimilationist philosophy of the times:

> What of the morrow for the Indian? The subject is a significant one, not only to persons who are merely familiar with his history, but especially to those who feel deeply on questions involving human rights. We say "significant" because its consideration carries us back to the time when neither the native now called Indian nor any person for him took any thought of the morrow.

> For him at this time, his abiding place, his home, his country, was a world in itself, where, excepting such tribal conflicts as were in the nature of things inseparable from aboriginal life, there was none to question his mode of life or dispute his claim. It is too late now to

serve any purpose by going into the matter of right and wrong concerning the early and recent relations between the aborigines of this country and the other races, the invaders of the Indian's domain. The barbarous trespassers upon the estate of this native son, the ruthless onslaught upon his home and fireside, the demoniacal attacks upon him and his household, the desperate resistance which he finally came to make against his annihilation, together with the horrible scenes attending his indiscrimination, visitations of revenge upon the despoilers of his birthright—all are buried in the ashes of the past, and having once constituted one of the inevitable steps in the evolution of the human race must necessarily as time goes on grow dimmer and dimmer and eventually become so obscured by distance as to seem altogether insignificant in point of human history as thousands of other sanguinary epochs in the world's movement.

To a certain extent, the conclusion of the subject may be summarized by saying that wherever today are to be seen Indians living, moving, and having their being in a manner so thoroughly in keeping with the ways of modern life as to attract no attention in a racial sense, there you may behold the "Indian of Tomorrow."

The connecting link between the Indian of the past, or present, and the Indian of the future is the process by which he shall be transformed—a process, in fact, by and only by which mankind is able to pass from a low and insignificant plane of existence to a higher and more potent sphere of life.

It is worthy of remark (and notice of it cannot be evaded when we have before us the question of the Indian's development) that we are obliged to approach the threshold of the discussion "broom in hand" equipped so to speak, for the sweeping away of the cobwebs of misconception which envelop the Indian as an individual. While generally, the possibilities of advancement for all classes of the European races are taken for granted without qualification or exception, this Native American is so stamped and branded with the name "Indian" that he practically travels a road so beset with pitfalls, stumbling blocks, and unevenness of footing that he is consigned to the dual work of clearing his own pathway. Where other men need only to bear the burden of the journey itself over his course as he makes the journey, having come out of his contest with the pale-face without home, without fireside, with scarce a place to lay his head in a country once entirely his own, he finds himself designated and distinguished as a lazy worthless member of a class of people who are good only when dead.

The Indian came out of the final struggle for self-preservation without houses, cattle, or land. Not only this, but, thus reduced, he finds himself without any of the mental development which accompanies the growth of individuals in civilized life. In all those matters relating to human conduct and a knowledge of men and things acquired from experience and education, the Indian, when finally forced to succumb to superiority of numbers, appears only as a child, so far as concerns mental development.

While this is a perfectly natural condition when looked at intelligently it is nevertheless worthy of remark that the disadvantage which he thus labored under because of his puerile condition has been the subject of consideration for improvement in his life and surroundings.

There was no reason why the Indian should develop mentally during the period of his aboriginal life, as he lived for the physical alone and was able to supply those demands by the exercise of his bodily capacities only. All that was required to supply the wants of nature was provided in abundance, and all he had to do was to put forth his hand to pluck and eat, and when hunger was satisfied, his activities for the time being came to an end. There was no social organization of the character so common in civilized communities—no schools, no churches, no courts, no prison, no hospital, no asylums, no saloons, no teachers, no pupils, no judges, no lawyers, no sheriffs, no doctors, no books, no reading or writing, no education and consequently, no learning or mental development.

When we consider therefore that all persons, Indians not excepted, come into the world a mental blank, and attain to whatever intellectual growth they may reach only as the result of surroundings and influences upon the faculties with which they are endowed, it is easy to understand that the Indian's mental caliber was in inverse proportion to his physical development—that though he was an adult in appearance he was mentally a child. In civilized life it is the rare exception to see such a disproportion between the physical and mental development of an individual as to excite surprise. Children and adults have a mentality at least in matters of common knowledge, substantially in harmony with the physical growth, and the result is that when they come in contact with each other in the affairs of life, they meet more or less on an equal footing, each knowing something of human nature and of the ways and conduct of men, and are thus they might otherwise become the victims.

Thus unprepared to protect himself against the numerous cheating devices of which the pale-face was possessed, the Indian was easily made the subject of many kinds of spoliation. He was deceived, cheated, buncoed, and robbed from every direction, and by the same means was in a chronic state of destitution, because of which he in turn was regarded as worthless. He was looked upon not as a victim, but as an Indian, who by reason of the fact was distinctly different from other men. What the Indian needed at these times was protection against imposition. The government was lacking in practical knowledge of them. He was misunderstood and misjudged, and the misconception was permitted to become a part of the country, so-called knowledge of the Indian. For decades he had been paraded and pictured in the light of curiosity, as though he were born to live for all times, to stalk abroad as a painted, beaded, blanketed, and feather-bedecked creature upon which the morbid spectators might feast their curiosity.

The "Indian of Tomorrow," however, has to meet the never-varying laws of the natural world. All development in organic life involves a struggle with the seemingly adverse forces of nature, and in this evolutionary process man comes in for a liberal share of hard knocks. The almost limitless power of resistance which the rugged, gnarled oak comes, finally, to possess, is attained only after years of battling against wind and storm. So has it been with rugged man in all ages. Growth is a struggle. In other words, without the struggle there is no growth. So that, after all, those forces against which we must contend are beneficent, rather than adverse, as a rule even though they sometimes destroy.

Owing to this power of mobility, and in proportion to his freedom of action, man comes to contend with nature's forces in every conceivable form, and therefore, in keeping with his experience, he acquires a complexity of organization superior to that of all other forms of life. Thus, apparently, is man able to realize more out of life, as it is, than does any other creature, and thus, out of the struggle with multitudes of opposing forces, comes to him a corresponding abundance of opportunity. As with the oak, so with individual man. Nature furnishes him with nothing to lean upon. Nature is wiser than he. She knows how to prepare him for an advanced condition in life, and sends out her forces on every hand to give him battle, that he may be strong, giving him the world for his field of operation.

With a consciousness of these facts, how clearly appears the necessity that this nation give to all those in its keeping the widest sphere of action. Wherever the Indian is so situated that he is not compelled to exert himself for sustenance, he is being injured both in body and in morals. His existence becomes artificial. Nature would force him to exertion and to battle, that he might eat and live a full life and learn and enjoy. Nature would keep a strict account with the young Indian. She would pay him in proportion to his labors, and according as he developed the power to cope with his fellow-man in industry and skillfulness, so would he receive of the good things the world has to give. Every day that the Indian, or any other creature, is kept under guardianship is a day cost which should have been put to individual effort. The sooner he has to meet the storm and tempest of life's battle, the sooner will he develop the power to resist its forces and to keep his equilibrium.

The Indian, individually, is entitled to the privilege of waging his cost. For existence in civilization just as much as other men are. He also owes it, as a duty to the country, as well as to himself, to get out and get to work, and begin to grow like other men. The question is not what he can be taught and what he can accomplish under certain conditions, but rather, is he out among men? Is he existing and climbing and getting on, surely, even though slowly? There is no reason why he should be housed and nursed. The proposition seems foolish the moment we look upon him simply as a man. Forget the past for the sake of the present. Close the books that tell of war and strife, hatred and death, and give attention to the demands of peace which "hath her victories no less than war." And the Indian will naturally and legitimately be given his place in civilized life and will assume that place, where he can reach forward with that hopefulness which others seem to possess.

The Indians must become their own emancipators. There is none to carry the burden for them. The fundamental principle embraced in the theory of the non-reservation school is that a change of environment furnishes the key to the solution of the Indian problem. It is strange to behold how persistently the nation has closed its eyes to this fact while at the same time we have only to read, to think, to look about us, no order to see on every hand that it is, and always has been, the shifting, the moving from place to place, and the going and coming of the people of the world, that has brought us to the state of civilization which man has obtained throughout the earth.

The stationary people, the races that cling to the spot of their birth, that adhere to tradition, that shrink from contact with other races are the non-progressive, the least civilized, and the least among mankind. Everywhere is the truth proclaimed that would you rise, would you grow, would you advance, would you realize that possibilities within your grasp, then—out with you, Mongolian, out with you, African, out with you, Caucasian, out with you, Indian, into the great world, where everybody meets everybody, from every nation and country. For all the earth, land, and sea is man's habitation. He alone is a true friend of the Indian who has come to realize that the reservation or any substitute thereof, is a sad and dreary environment with which to surround a human being, and that while with its bounds no man can hope to realize the glorious possibilities which are the heritage of freedom.

In spite of all these things, and surrounded as he has been by all manner of hindrances and misfortune, the Indian of tomorrow is living here and there, a few at least, in almost every northern and western state and territory, having risen above the circumstances which handicapped his people until he is one in civilization, in business and public affairs, with his pale-face brother.

He can be found in every profession, industry, and calling; educated, world-wise, and able to compete with individuals of civilization generally. The Indian of tomorrow, as a result of the same influences that develop men generally, will be the Indian with the man part of him made manifest by effective action in the affairs of the world, and so marked in all respects like other men of character and accomplishment, that the Indian part of him will no longer be a matter to excite curiosity. The Indian of tomorrow, by virtue of his struggles of today, will not be treading a pathway beset with the same kind of pitfalls as in the past. He will be marching and keeping step with all other members of the world's vast army of workers, where neither he nor they will think of wars and strife, hatred, or revenge. The Indian of tomorrow will be, not an unfortunate savage, clothed in the accouterments of his former benighted condition, but the Indian redeemed, transformed, and raised to the plane of manhood, which he long since would have occupied had the man part of him been discovered and by intelligent treatment been developed.

The Indian as he is known in story and song, as he has been pictured in fireside tales and in one-sided history, will not be recognized in the Indian of tomorrow. The Indian, with his traditions, his superstition, his long hair, his racial distinctiveness, and his aspect of contrast with the civilized man, will not be seen in the Indian of tomorrow.

And, in all this transformation, uplifting and civilizing, there will be nothing to regret. What he was in his native condition was only a natural part of his close association with nature alone. His conduct and action were the results of a yielding to demands of necessity, rather than habits acquired from following inclination. His was a life on that lower plane upon which men gladly turn their backs accordingly as they succeed in rising to higher things. No part could contribute to the well-being of the man of civilization. Those who know the Indian's character feel justified in saying that the Indian himself does not desire to perpetuate the recollection nor rehearse the scenes and incidents of his former life, being content to take on the new life, free and unburdened of everything connected with his unprofitable past.

*The Indian of tomorrow will be, however, in some respects at least, the Indian of today, in that he will be highly endowed with a sense of what is just between man and man, will have a keen sense of appreciation of kindness extended to him, and for many generations yet to come, he will continue to be un-emotional. His hopes lie in the possibility of becoming a full man, and not that he may be made simply a "better Indian."*

The Indian of tomorrow will be, however, in some respects at least, the Indian of today, in that he will be highly endowed with a sense of what is just between man and man, will have a keen sense of appreciation of kindness extended to him, and for many generations yet to come, he will continue to be un-emotional. His hopes lie in the possibility of becoming a full man, and not that he may be made simply a "better Indian."[52]

Montezuma's attitude and philosophy were in perfect harmony with Richard H. Pratt's thinking. Barring a clash in personalities, it was inevitable that the young Indian and the older White man would become friends and partners "in the cause." The exact time when Montezuma first met Pratt is unknown, nor is it known what circumstances brought about this meeting. Perhaps the meeting took place in Chicago, but it is probable that Montezuma, still a medical student, visited the Carlisle Indian School. We do know with certainty that Montezuma's correspondence with Pratt began during his medical school years. Montezuma initiated the correspondence by asking Pratt for a report on how the Apache students at Carlisle were progressing.[53] On at least one occasion Montezuma was invited to participate in a program presented by Pratt in the winter of 1886–1887 in Philadelphia and New York, probably delivering his speech entitled "The Indian of Tomorrow."[54] He also accompanied Pratt and 130 Carlisle students to New York City in February 1887, and at the age of twenty-one, recounted his life story during a program that featured student performances.[55]

## GRADUATION

Graduation at the Chicago Medical College required satisfactory performance in examinations (written exams, an "Eastern custom," began in 1876) and a thesis. No record or copy of Montezuma's thesis can be found. The public was invited to commencement exercises, and many came, obviously viewing it as a spectacle.[56] Dress was the usual black formal suit (not replaced by academic garb until the 1890s). That evening, an elaborate dinner was at the home of Nathan S. Davis or at a hotel, highlighted by original lyrics sung by the class, praising and making fun of faculty members, a tradition still common in the annual medical shows at most schools today.

Some of Montezuma's classmates went on to become prominent individuals in medicine. Joseph Bolivar DeLee became an American giant in obstetrics, still active and respected when I began my education in obstetrics and gynecology. His book, *Principles and Practice of Obstetrics*, first published in 1913, was a standard used by practitioners and students worldwide through many editions. C. H. Mayo of Mayo Clinic fame was in Montezuma's class. Isaac A. Abt, graduated two years after Montezuma and became one of the first important and great pediatricians.

A month before he was due to graduate in 1888, Montezuma wrote to Richard H. Pratt at Carlisle: "My graduation in medicine is coming near (March 29th). I want to know what you think I might to do in order that I might be useful to my people. I am ready to do anything or wait until I can. Yours in the Cause."[57]

Pratt offered Montezuma a position at the Carlisle Indian School. "When you graduate if you have no immediate and pressing work in view, my notion is you had better come here and take hold with Dr. Givins for a while and get practical training. I can pay you something and this will be as good a point to spy out the field and strike from as any one could have. Joshua and one other of our boys will take a little run across the Atlantic and visit her Majesty's Kingdom April to June. I have had it in my mind to try to arrange for you to go along. A party of Canadian Indian youth from Shingwauk Home at Ste. St. Marie are going over under the care of Rev. Wilson the Supt who wishes to raise money to enlarge and also to show English people what we are doing in America and contradict Buffalo Bill's Wild West. The trip will broaden those who go and be well worth the time it costs. How would you like it? I can probably help you into something in the line of your desires, and will."[58]

Montezuma may have been excited over the prospect of visiting Europe, but Pratt later reported that the trip to England was abandoned. By then Montezuma had even more upsetting news to report to Pratt.

On March 26, 1888, Carlos Montezuma wrote to Richard Pratt and told him: "The Faculty have decided not to permit me with a diploma on account of my backstanding and for my welfare. During the past years in this college no interest was taken in me by any of them, aside from my presence in classes. But at this meeting they forgive me practical training by being among them here for six months then …I really do not know what to do. If I should come with you my intention is to attend the Medical College in Philadelphia or New York. Over time I can get a diploma. I do not think they did a fair thing with me. My idea is they have a prejudice[d] personal feeling towards me. But I do not know. I long to be with you in this important work for the Indians. If you think that I should remain here until September or be with you all, please notify me at once."[59] In a personal interview in 1921, Montezuma said that he was unable to finish medical school on time because he could not spare the time from the work he was required to do in the pharmacy.[60]

On that very same day, Montezuma wrote Pratt a second letter. "I have heard what some of the faculties [sic] plans are. Dr. Dudley expects to have me at his house to do the work about his house, which I don't think will help me. I understood I was to help him in office work, but such is not the plan. Now I really think it was to prevent me from being with you that made them keep my diploma back. I shall not give them any satisfaction. My intention is to graduate in one of the eastern colleges. This coming year. Yours in the cause."[61]

Pratt must have responded immediately because his return letter is dated only two days later, and handwritten instead of his usual typewritten correspondence: "My dear Carlos— I have yours telling me of your failure to graduate and asking my advice. I understand how bad you feel. You have but one worthy course and that is to hang on there, come joy or sorrow, come life or death, and wring from your college the diploma you are after. Compel them to give it through your own gains, your success, your worth. Don't attempt to climb any other mountain but that one. Once on top of that one and in fellowship with all who have climbed it you will have a chance to make them glad for your grit, your success, and all the faculty as well, and I your friend, as well as many others, will rejoice and hope and pray that figuratively, and even literally speaking it may be another case where the stone the builders rejected will become the chief head of the corner. Governed by lofty principles and industriously patiently waiting you may then go and reach the highest honors and place in your chosen profession, so that your chaps with whom you did not graduate, your professors who are doubtless right and wise in their action and all who ever graduated or who may hereafter graduate from your alma mater and even the profession of the whole could in the future and take off their hats to the little Apache boy who was sold for thirty dollars ('thirty pieces of silver') but to whom God gave a mission in one of the great emergency's [sic] of the world which he filled so worthily and which was so high that it stood as a land mark on the shore for all time. The crucifixion of Christ bought eternal life to man. Then rejoice my good Carlos that you are considered worthy of a little crucifying and may the good Father ever have you under the shadow of his wing. Your faithful friend."[62]

March 28 .88

My dear Carlos—

I have yours telling of your failure to graduate and asking my advice. I understand how bad you feel.

You have but one worthy course and that is to hang on there, come joy or sorrow, come life or death, and wring from your college the diploma you are after. Compel them to give it through your own gains, your success, your worth. Don't attempt to climb any other mountain but that one. Once on top of that one and in fellowship with all who have climbed it you will have a chance to make them glad for your grit, your success, and all the faculty as well, and I your friend, as well as many others, will rejoice and hope and pray that figuratively, and even reverently, speaking it may be another case where the stone the builder

A powerful letter, and it had its effect. Montezuma stayed the course, and graduated March 26, 1889, at the age of twenty-three, twelve days after Susan La Flesche Picotte received her M.D. degree from the Medical College of Pennsylvania. Montezuma graduated just before a period of great change in medical education. He left the Chicago Medical College before the major emphasis on laboratory experience in physiology, pathology, and bacteriology was established. The replacement of part-time teachers with full-time teachers having specialized expertise did not begin until the 1890s. Nevertheless, these changes were underway in his early years of practice, and must have had an influence through his consultations and interactions in the hospital and at meetings.

Pratt was pleased and now once again was thinking of the future for a twenty-three year old new physician. "Gradually your eyes have been opened and you now know what an education is. How much time and patient effort it takes to get all the Indians to understand this is a part of our great task. Some, like yourself, must have a liberal education, or else all will stand in lower walks of life. I met Dr. Hill, of the Presbyterian Indian Mission work in Washington, and he told me he had recommended to the board, that you be employed and sent to one of their Missionary fields in the Territory. I only offered you Carlisle as a refuge and a place to strike from, supposing you would want a larger field. It was my judgment, too, that a brief experience in our Hospital work would better fit you for dealing with the particular diseases to which Indians are most subject. However, that will come to you in time.

Having given more than ordinary time to your medical training, you may be all right in that. You are in good lines to work your way forward to the highest position you are capable of, and I think you had better undertake it. Faithfully your friend."[63]

Upon graduation, Montezuma lived at 2616 Cottage Grove Avenue and opened an office near Chicago Medical College, but had little business. It would have been nearly impossible to attract paying patients to a physician who was a very youthful twenty-three year old with no family or business connections and little experience. His clinical exposure was limited to medical school demonstrations; he served no internship; he spent only one year before graduation with Dr. Dudley and his extensive notes indicate that his experience was limited to obstetrics and gynecology[64] (Dudley was Professor of Gynecology at the Chicago Medical School). The year's experience did produce a solid friendship with Dudley that Montezuma maintained when he returned to Chicago in 1896. Montezuma was forced to continue to work as a pharmacist as in a letter to Pratt in August, five months after his graduation, Montezuma complains: "My intentions have been to work more for the Indian than in the past, but I am so confined in the store."[65]

Thomas Jefferson Morgan was commissioner of Indian affairs from 1889 to 1893. He was a Baptist minister and professional educator who totally supported the philosophy and practices of assimilation.[66] Morgan would regard Montezuma as an outstanding model of what could be achieved. After five months as a physician in practice, Montezuma received a letter from Morgan, asking if he was interested in a position as a physician in the Indian Service. "My friend, Captain Pratt, tells me that you have finished your medical studies, and have entered upon the practice of your profession. He speaks of you in very high terms as a man of intelligence and perseverance, and it has occurred to me that you might like a position as physician among your own people at some Indian Agency. ...I have recently appointed Miss La Flesche, who graduated from the medical school in Philadelphia, and subsequently had some hospital training, as physician among her own people, the Omahas."[67]

Montezuma wrote promptly on August 12, 1889, accepting Morgan's offer, "Nothing else would give me a greater pleasure than to sacrifice my past experience for the elevation of a nation that you have at heart. I have been thinking several weeks how could I situate myself so as to help my people, or rather that has been ever since I was old enough to appreciate my surroundings. That was why I was corresponding with our friend Capt. R. H. Pratt. I would have applied for a position before this, but I did not like the idea of being an office seeker. But now, as you have kindly induced me for a position, I will most cordially accept any position that you might think best to offer, not with any selfish motive but for the sake of my so long neglected race. For my part, I am willing to do anything which will reform them and also to do all I can to set them a good example. ...I remain yours for justice in the Indian Affairs."[68]

You are hereby appointed to the position of Clerk and Physician at the Indian School at Fort Stevenson, Dakota, at a salary of $1,000 per annum. ...You should report to the Superintendent of the school as soon as possible. The expense incident to reaching the school must be borne by yourself. Very respectfully, T. J. Morgan, Commissioner.[69]

MONTEZUMA STARTED WORK at Fort Stevenson with enthusiasm and optimism on September 20, 1889. He initially viewed this as an opportunity to help his people, but it didn't take long for him to become disillusioned.

## CHAPTER SIX

# Yours in the Cause:
# Working for the Bureau, from North Dakota
# to Nevada to Washington to Pennsylvania

MONTEZUMA WROTE TO Captain Richard Pratt on June 21, 1892: "I have come to the conclusion, that I could do more for the Indians in the east than in the bondage system of a reservation. The White people can appreciate the Indian question more to see the *real living proof* than the ignorant and superstitious Indians can appreciate my labor in their behalf. Though I be one of their own race. Not only this, but if one of them can be educated to the highest standard, why send him on a reservation to be stunted in his progress with the environment of a reservation life? Capt, understand me not to say these few remarks to show my discouragement. No, far from it! I am willing to serve my people in the line of my profession wherever I am placed in the Indian service. Your Apache friend, Carlos Montezuma, White Rock, Nevada."[1]

Indian reservations, as experienced by Montezuma, developed over a period of time that began 100 years before Montezuma's graduation from medical school. During the conflict with the English during the Revolutionary Period, the Colonists made a deliberate effort to secure the friendship of the Indians. Agents were appointed to live among the tribes, charged with reporting Indian movements and arranging trade. In 1786, Congress established two districts, one north of the Ohio River and one south, with a "superintendent" over each under the supervision of the secretary of war. As westward expansion progressed, this system incorporated tribal holdings, now called reservations, grouped into superintendencies, with each superintendent reporting to the commissioner of Indian affairs.[2] The reservations were placed in the charge of "agents" reporting to the district superintendents. In the mid 1800s, the office of superintendent was abolished and the agents became directly responsible to the commissioner. The Indian school system, however, retained the title of "superintendent." Each off-reservation school was under the supervision of a superintendent, who like the agents in charge of the reservations, answered directly to the commissioner of Indian affairs. Schools on reservations were, like everything else on the reservation, under the control of the agents. The agents were unofficially often addressed as "Superintendents."

### Congressional Acts That Established the Reservation System

1793: President authorized to appoint agents to live with the Indians.
1818: President nominates and Senate approves all Indian agents.
1824: Bureau of Indian Affairs created by the secretary of war.
1832: Office of Commissioner of Indian Affairs created by Congress.
1834: Bureau of Indian Affairs established by Congress.

1849: Bureau of Indian Affairs transferred from the War Department to the Department of the Interior.

1873: Established five inspectors, nominated by the president and confirmed by Senate, to visit and report on the agencies.

1878: Indian police authorized.

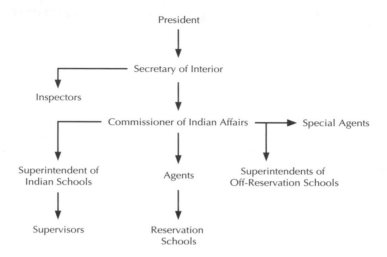

## FROM CHICAGO TO NORTH DAKOTA

In November 1889, the twenty-three-year-old Montezuma wrote to Amelia Stone Quinton, President of the Women's National Indian Association: "It always gives me a pleasure to do anything which will promote the welfare of my people or correct the wrong ideas of the whites [about] the Indian people. I have at last reached the first step in my aim of life. ... My first recollection of a desire to tell my people many things which would do them good was back in my childhood soon after I was taken away from my parents (1871). Having such a desire I tried in everyway to prepare myself. At times things seemed dark...when turned out into the world on my own resource without a relative to give me a kind word, but through God's mercy, I was placed in kind hands. ...After my university course, I entered a drug store in Chicago and at the same time continued my medical studies at the Chicago Medical College for four years. In my last year at the college, I had the honor of being with Prof. E. C. Dudley, M.D., whose kindness I shall never forget. Having thus come up through the Common School, University, Druggist, and a Physician, I began the practice of my chosen profession in the city where 19 years ago I was brought as a non-existing being, fresh from an Apache Camp. During the last few months of my practice, several offers were given me to go elsewhere, but I refused them, not because of any selfish motive, but my idea of working among the Indians is even then denominational. The forepart of September I was gladly surprised by a letter from the Hon. Com. T. J. Morgan asking me whether I would accept an offer in the Indian Service. I promptly replied I would. A week or two after-ward, I received my appointment to the position of Clerk and Physician in this school.

The 21st of September [1889] found me at Fort Stevenson where I was greeted by the Supt. George E. Gerowe. It is surprising to know that there is a School such as this (way interior to a barren region). Our nearest railroad station is Bismarck, 75 miles south. Our nearest station is 10 miles distant by stage. The next day, being Tuesday, I was awakened half past six by the school bell. Half an hour longer found me in our morning service, where all are gathered together to sing, hear the word of God, and ask his guidance and blessing. This last for twenty minutes. When I hear [the school bell] the 107 children rise and march to their breakfast. Perfect order is kept from the little 'tots.' ...around the table, standing with bowed heads, thanks are given in unison for this another meal to the giver of all good and perfect gifts. Order for the day is given by the Industrial Teacher and Matron.

When I reached my office, I found many waiting, some came for medical aid, some to see the new Doctor, and others to see whether I was really an Indian. They knew I did not belong to this tribe on account of my appearance and dress. Of course, they called me a Sioux because they hear more of that tribe than any others.

The school consists mostly of three tribes. Araick Aree [*sic*], Gros Ventres, and Mandans. These tribes are located in the Fort Berthold Reservation, 17 to 18 miles up the river."[3] Fort Stevenson was an abandoned military fort converted into a school for the children of the Fort Berthold Reservation located in the northern part of North Dakota. The reservation was occupied by three tribes in 1900 that numbered: 416 Arickara, 459 Gros Ventre, and 243 Mandan.[4] Although they were farming people with crops and cattle (4,000 head of cattle in 1900), they were dependent on government rations because of poor crop years in this semi-arid land. Their health was described as very bad, and their housing, unsanitary. Many refused to send their children to the school. Today, the Fort Berthold Reservation borders Lake Sakakawea (the North Dakota spelling version of Sakagawea) that is formed by the Garrison Dam on the Missouri River. The name of the lake was chosen in poor taste by the U.S. Army Corps of Engineers in that the lake covered the best land held by the Indians.

"Being bush since my arrival, I have not had a chance to visit their homes, but what I see of them are those who visit their children. Some of them look respectable, but a great improvement is still desirable. The feathers, blankets, moccasins, and tongue remain with them. In this school, the Supt. George E. Gerowe and the employees are all who have an interest in the Indians and object as to make *the* school of the west. If this the object, it means work. I assure you and whatever is in my power to do shall be done. I am glad to impress upon these young minds the duty of life, from what experience I received during my 19 years among civilization. Oh! That I could awaken them. Believe in a better life than that they are living from day to day. ...Yours in the cause of Indians' works, Carlos Montezuma, Physician to Fort Stevenson School."[5]

*At Fort Stevenson—Age Twenty-four*

Montezuma, as a twenty-four-year-old young man, shared his idealism and his philosophy in a speech he presented to the students at the Fort Stevenson School:

As you look around in the midst of your school work, your mind turns home to mother and father. And you ask yourself, why have not my mother and father been educated here when they were young. If you went home, and asked them, their reply would be: "I have not had the chance." It has been but a few years since I feared the white people; a few years back no friends offered me their hands. I lived and roamed on this wild prairie from my youth up. Such has been the history of a nation, which you and I belong. It is a sad story. But a story that ought to inspire you to a nobler and higher aim to manhood and womanhood.

Not very long ago, the Indians were considered by the white people the same as the wild deer and could never be tamed nor they be educated. If they were, they would die in a short time. These ideas were among the cowboys and those who had misdealings with the Indians. But, some of the white people in the east thought, if we were divided off to ourselves somewhere, where we could hunt, fish, have our war dances, speak our own language, and have soldiers to look over us, we would be all right. So they did. Ft. Stevenson was once a military fort where soldiers were kept to protect the white people form those wild, savage Indians. Ft. Berthold Reservation is a tract of land which is so long and so wide, outside of that lines the Indians are not allowed. This plan was better than nothing. The Indians were kept this way until the present time.

There was a regular army officer who was stationed in one of the frontier forts. He was ordered to take certain bad Indians from the Indian Territory. After being with the Indians sometime, he gradually mastered their ways and satisfied their wants. He taught and helped these poor Indians. His interest in the Indian question increased so much so that he wrote to the Department for aid in his school. While in charge of this small school, he noticed that education means more than teaching them their A. B. C's. It means to bring them face to face with civilization. Having this idea he requested an Indian School to be established in the East. After a continuous pleading, Carlisle Barracks was granted to him. This was the first experiment. Very soon the school was known from east to west and was looked upon as a marvelous undertaking. Having some influence at Washington, where the Representatives of this country gather to promote its welfare, while there he would invite Senators and congressman to visit his school. In this way he showed them what can be done with you and with me.

Today we celebrate the outcome of what was accomplished through the influence of Indian education. Education does not mean to learn from books only, but we know we are made or built up to manhood and womanhood as to our surroundings.

For example, Mr. X says he never attended any school when a boy. But he can read, write and make a living for a large family. He is educated just as much as that young man who has graduated. One is educated by books while the other by practical experience. So you will agree with me that Dawes Bill is not sufficient. It only places you and me on an 80 acres lot. Without knowledge, without money, without tools, without a horse, you look around and ask yourself where am I to get the plough to cultivate my soil and the oxen to draw my plough, and the seed to sow, and where can I find a friend to show me how to use these and teach me so to be a man.

The answer to these questions is right here at Ft. Stevenson school. What the Dawes Bill does not provide you have an access to it in the government schools. Where you are taught in the care of yourself, in the care of animals, in the plowing, sowing and reaping; in the cooking, sewing and sweeping; in the prayers and reading and in the Sabbath rest worship. From all of these you learn what life is and ought to be, to be prosperous and successful.

The Indian Bureau three years ago decided that all instructions given in Indian schools must be taught in the English language, that no other language must be taught. This is another advantage for us Indians, as it is with English speaking people we have to deal. We cannot be civilized through the agency of an uncivilized tongue. So your advancement depends upon your ability to read English, speak English and write English.

The government may aid and send teachers to instruct you. This is not enough. Boys and girls remember that you have a part. Your part is to devote with all your might what is given you to do. Whether it be hard or easy, you must help yourself. Then gradually, you shall be equipped for life's struggle and competition, and once equipped you shall be free. And I shall not be [?] back or elsewhere for any cause whatever.

I noticed the other afternoon there lay stretched on the stage a sick student, going home— maybe to die. It looks discouraging but it is our honor to die in an honest undertaking. But do you know children, I would rather die in the struggle for my manhood and the welfare of my people than to remain in ignorance with health. We cannot do no more than run the race as far as we can, God will finish the rest.

Children, Let the heart within you throb for the betterment of yourselves and of a nation which you claim. You are a part of the American family. Children, to be educated for the responsibilities that will surely come to you as a citizen of this country.[6]

But there was an undercurrent of trouble, a clash between the superintendent and Montezuma that was already heard in Washington. Commissioner T. J. Morgan issued a strong rebuke on December 14, 1889: "I have requested Supt. George E. Gerowe to hand you this letter. You are advised that the position you hold is that of clerk and physician. The duties of clerk are as important and necessary to the welfare of the school as those of physician. You are expected to perform all the duties usually incumbent upon the clerk under the direction of the Superintendent in addition to the duties of physician. You are further expected to comply with all the regulations of the school as laid down by the Superintendent, willingly, promptly, and faithfully. Anything less than this will be unbecoming a conscientious employe[e]. Mr. Gerowe as Superintendent of Fort Stevenson School is the superior officer, and all employe[e]s are expected to work in entire harmony with him.

I have a great deal of interest in you personally, and have sought to aid you in every way possible. I appointed you Clerk and Physician at Fort Stevenson expecting you to prove yourself entirely competent to perform its combined duties. I shall expect good reports from Supt. Gerowe in regard to your work both clerically and professionally. I have written thus at length in order that you might know fully what the Office expects from you, and also to clearly define your relations to the Superintendent of Fort Stevenson School under whose directions you must perform your duties and to whom you are responsible for faithful, efficient, and conscientious service."[7]

Less than a year after arriving at Fort Stevenson, the conflict between Gerowe and Montezuma reached a fevered pitch. Montezuma wrote to Commissioner Morgan on May 14, 1890: "I was emphatically told by Supt Gerowe in a fit of anger yesterday that I must leave this school at the end of this quarter or he will. I most humbly as a Christian submit the charges which may be given to your office for a careful consideration. I have been wronged like many of the Indian instructors which have left this institution. I have consciously endeavored in every way both by example and precepts to elevate the Indian people whom I have at heart. But *prejudice, distrustful feeling* and lack of encouragement from the Superintendent will always lead an Educated Indian downwards. Such is my position at this place. As a peaceable Christian Indian Physician who has a love for his people and an ambitious desire to benefit them for a nobler aim of life, may I have the honor to request for a transfer or shall I remain at my post. I leave myself in your power for a consideration, your humble servant."[8]

Gerowe had forwarded a list of complaints about Montezuma to the commissioner:

- The Indians are dissatisfied with the school.
- The pupils dislike Montezuma.
- Montezuma is incompetent as a clerk.
- Montezuma is impudent.
- Montezuma does not conduct himself properly.
- Montezuma is filthy.

Morgan requested Montezuma to address these complaints: "Under date of May 14th, Mr. George E. Gerowe, Superintendent of Fort Stevenson School, again asks that you be removed from the Service for incompetency. As I am interested in your welfare and desire your success, I enclose herewith copy of the statements made by the Superintendent, and shall expect a prompt reply pending which no action will be taken looking to your immediate removal."[9]

Ten days after receiving Morgan's request on June 17, 1890, Montezuma replied in a long rambling letter, seventeen pages long, with less than his usual precise and correct grammar, probably affected by his strong emotions, also reflected in his underlining of words for emphasis: "I have the honor to submit the following explanations to your letter. …I entered this school on 21st of Sept as a Clerk and Physician. I found the children in a bad condition as I reported, but never gave an explanation why (to present a reflection on the Superintendent). 'Sores' as George E. Gerowe put it, were nothing serious but merely chronic eczema, characterized by itching. And crust forming. From the history of the cases since Dr. Ducketts valuable service, the children received this annoying skin affection from the *filthy camp life*, which I understood from the Supt himself that he permitted them (the children) to remain home longer then the Inspectors instruction. Thus coming from the camp to the school, remaining here *without change* of *clothing* and *without any help* they were made worse. These same children were not assorted, but occupied the same bed with the healthy. Sequel: they gave it to each other. I found out also that their *beds* were *not changed* for some times and to my surprise *not one sheet* could be found on the beds but slept between the folds of the blankets. As this affliction is an exuding one, it would naturally smear the bed at night. I discovered the *bath room* was a *filthy place* with *three* (3) wash tubs for 67 boys, and when through *wiped on their dirty shirts*. The *clothing never brushed* from their appearance and Camp going was permitted.

When confronted with such an appalling spectacle of cleanliness, I ordered new clothing; have the children wash and sleep separately; the bed clothing to be washed and sheets be supplied for every bed and have them changed every week; the bath tubs to be increased, clothes be brushed, and never permit a single child to go to camp, but have their parents come to them. To the above request, new suits were supplied to the boys sometime afterward, but never kept clean as I wished. Sleeping and washing separately lasted but a short time. Bath tubs have been increased now and then, the towels lacking, and supplying the boys beds with sheets only lasted long enough for the Inspectors benefits. Going to the dirty camps not strictly forbidden. I have again and again emphatically asked that the above requirements be enforced but at the date of his complaint such thing never occurred. *Under* these *conditions*, no *Physician* can *never* [sic] *cure* eczema though it be 'under the same climatic influences and same diet.' He says, 'one would be surprised.' I am well aware non-professionals would be surprised because of their ignorance. In the same school 'under the same climatic influences and same diet,' we have 45 girls. Only one or two have been affected with the same disease. Why? Because, my orders were complied with by the matron.

I over Supt George E. Gerowe, as a physician who ought to know, the condition of the children at the present is good. During my service (9 mos) not a single death and do not expect one for some time to come. What better record can I give?

I cannot go into details of a man who has no knowledge whatever of Practice of Medicine, but I challenge any conscientious Doctor who will do any better under the same circumstance in which I am situated.

'The dissatisfaction of the Indians against the school' was told by Dr Best, the reservation Physician, who was a personal friend of Supt. Gerowe endeavored to get him my place soon after my arrival here. I would rather have the Indians words than the Dr.'s.

'The Pupils dislike me.' Supt gave me a hint of this. I said 'before I believe it. I would take a vote.' Those who dislike me dislike me without a cause. Supt has taught long enough to understand human nature, that children will snarl against you the more you try to benefit them for the time being, but later in life, they will appreciate your labor. Just so, with the children here. I require from them more than any employee, because I love and have a great interest in their welfare. I shall repeat what I said to Supt. 'Do you know I would lick every pupil who comes to me with a complaint against an employee who is endeavoring to benefit them and who knows what is for their best. If you do not, you will encourage them to come again. I come here not to be ruled by the untutored Indian children, but I come with love and 19 years of discipline in the white man's way. I come to teach them in nothing else.'

'My incompetency in the office.' I am debarred from the official letters and many things which a clerk should have an access by a combination lock. Without going into details of the past quarters. 3rd quarter 1890 was near by myself. Supt has been here one year and half, his knowledge of the books and papers is so better than mine. I hope he does not expect an Indian to be more intelligent than himself.

'My impudence.' I have a perfect right to express my opinion up on a subject which I have at heart and to my professional affairs. I have quoted some of my impudence.

'My conduct.' My conduct while here has been that of a Christian physician as such I should be respected, not so, as I will state further on.

'*My Filth.*' I am really surprised to have such an erroneous language to proceed from a person who pretends to be a Christian and a minister of the gospel. But knowing his temperament and the time of this writing, I can excuse some of his errors. I have worked with prominent Doctors, acted as a Clerk in a Drugstore for seven years, and experimented in laboratories. Never in my life has such a blame thrown to my face, but rather I was credited for my neatness. I am not ready to accept a mad man's testimony.

Aside from answering the above charges, I respectfully ask that I be permitted to state my condition at this school with Supt George E. Gerowe. Little did I think such would be the state of affairs after a few days acquaintance with the Supt. My first intimation of his prejudice[d] feeling toward me was a few months. One day, he asked, 'How would I like Dr. Best position. There is $200 more in it.' Another time, Dr. Best was down one Sunday. After he was gone Supt asked me if the Doctor mentioned about exchanging positions. Being an Indian and my keen observations to the condition of the school made the Supt and employees suspicious of me. And all eyes were upon me. Of course, comments were freely given to each other. The matron repeated something like this: 'I would not trust the Doctor alone with my seven years old daughter.' To several of the employees and Supt. Again detectives were put on my heel. The girls were prohibited to come to my office and on my account boys and employees were not allowed inside of a yard. The above mentioned Matron (Mrs Mitchell) I am glad to say, she confessed to me all of these and apologized for doing me wrong. She left this school as a mother to me.

Sometime in December just before his first complaint, Mr. Emmerich, Clerk of Ft. Berthold Reservation, was released from duty. He stopped on his way home. Mr. Gerowe thought it would be a fine thing to have him so he asked me whether he could help. I for courtesy sake granted him the privilege. Knowing the clerks disposition I occupied most of my time in the drug room. Not a day passed that I did not ask Supt. if he had anything for me, the reply was always negative. I think he reported that I lacked the interest of a clerk. It is not so, as I told him face to face. There is nothing in the clerk line that I cannot accomplish. If I am as worthless as Supt Gerowe pictures me, you would do me justice by complying to his request.

At the table or somewheres, this clerk (Mr. Emmerich) spoke about me for a joke. 'That he caught me sitting on the bed with a certain girl.' Supt took it up in earnest and spoke to me of it and also mentioned what the matron said. Supt believed everything against me. He went so far as to get the matron to write to you against me. I never saw such a suspicious person. Can such a person run an institution like this where love should reign.

I enclose you herewith letters dated May 14 same date as Supt's but never mailed as I wished Mr Gerowe to see it. A week later I presented the letter as a gentlemen and said, 'Mr. Gerowe, I wrote this letter after our quarrel. Considering the matter over, I thought best not to send it for both parties sake, but let us settle this as two Christians.' Not until persistent reasoning, he consented to write for my transfer. But from your communication he never kept his word. After his failure for my removal he has misused me.

I may mention the children that were transferred to Carlisle school. He never consulted me relative to their health. They were kept secret to me until at the last moment. If he did they would have never gone as healthy. Of course they were examined and some found unhealthy by the School Physician.

This Spring, Supt was suddenly taken down by a constitutional attack. In the acute stage I attended him. Like everything with him easily discouraged. Just at the time of his convalescence, he called for the Berthold Doctor. …The latter doctor consulted me. I presented the case before him. He concurred with what I have done and I dictate to him what to do. He followed my advice and the Supt was made better in few days. (His (Supt) mind was affected that was all.)

I may mention another case. The Principal Teacher went off in the 3rd week. Cause (ill health). If Supt consulted with me, I could not consciously agree with him. The above cases placed me in a very awkward position before the department. Other schools and here. All I ask is harmony, one that will stick by me in every undertaking to promote the Indians.

Since May 14th the School is in a better condition. My long persistent pleading is being carried out as good as can be expected under the circumstance. The premise has been cleaned and as the Principal Teacher is away I have charge of the boys. They are three cases of eczema on hand. In a few weeks all will disappear from our midst.

If I am so inefficient in the Practice of Medicine, presenting false reports to the department, disliked by the pupils under my charge, incompetent in the office, ungentlemanly in conduct and so filthy as George E. Gerowe presents me, I full deserve his request. As a self made and educated Indian who has labored over a mountain of obstacles from his youth up to his present position, earned by his independent persevering efforts and now in the field for his people's welfare, I ask, should he not be encouraged and aided in every way to be more useful, instead of teaching the Indians to have prejudice[d] feeling against him, and trampling him down. Is not such a person disloyal to the Government under the Indian Service and deserved to be carefully investigated? Consider and do with me as you think best. Your humble servant."[10]

Morgan's reply, only four days later, was abrupt: "You are hereby appointed physician at Western Shoshone Indian agency, Nevada, at a compensation of $1,000 per annum, to take effect when you report for duty at the Agency, which you should do as soon as practicable as the position will be vacant after today. Show this letter to the Agent to identify you when you reach the Agency."[11] Pratt explained: "The Commissioner stated to me that you made out the best case but it was necessary to make a change and so he sent you elsewhere."[12]

Montezuma's troubles at Fort Stevenson can without a doubt be attributed to George Gerowe because in April 1891, the physician who succeeded Montezuma listed a familiar litany of problems and complaints in a letter to Montezuma that began: "Though we are strangers, I feel that we are friends because we have both suffered from the damnable insinuations of our Christian friend Gerowe."[13]

## FROM NORTH DAKOTA TO NEVADA

The Western Shoshone Agency served about 550 Shoshone and Paiute Indians eighteen miles from White Rock, Nevada.[14] The Indians fished in Pyramid Lake and worked for neighboring farmers and ranchers. Despite the presence of the lake, water was scarce, and only 200 acres were irrigated. Montezuma reported for duty on July 21, 1890, and promptly requested a horse because his duties required visits, in addition to emergency calls, to different villages three times a week that were ten to thirteen miles from the agency. All expenditures had to be requested from the agent, who in turn, forwarded the request with his recommendation to the commissioner. A horse was purchased for $75, nearly a full month's worth of Montezuma's wages, but his request for reimbursement for his travel from Fort Stevenson was denied.[15] Only two months later, Montezuma was forced to request a second horse, finding his circuit of thirty miles per week plus daily visits to the Indian camps to be too much for one horse.

"… Sunday morning, I was suddenly summoned to an accidental case of shooting of one of our Indians while hunting antelope. The distance was 50 miles through canons [*sic*], brushes and large rocks. Part of the way the road or trail was taken, but mostly through a shorter way over a rough trail, no road whatever. Monday afternoon I found my patient at the bottom of a cannon [*sic*] several thousand feet from the level of the surface. After relieving his pain, adjusting his wound and giving orders what to do, I left the poor Indian to nature's care."[16]

In one year at the Western Shoshone Agency, Montezuma treated 260 cases, delivered eight babies, and reported seventeen deaths (two by falling in a mining shaft).[17] "On my first arrival the Indians were shy, they mistrusted my position. They saw that I was like them but to be a white man's doctor out of an Indian, they could not explain, unless the devil jumped into me and changed me as I am. I admit it takes the devil to make an Indian medicine man, but I differ with them with respect to the intelligent physicians of the whites. By gradual wedging through thick and thin with the faithful support of the Agent we have overcome most of their wrong ideas of the white man's medicine. Still they cling to their old habits of isolating the sick out in the cold without food, clothing and proper care. One ration day, I was suddenly called to a serious case of accidental hemorrhage of a woman that had miscarriage. I found her lying at the back end of our town well with a dozen or more women jabbing over the affair. There she sat in the snow, half soaked with water, with her body cold as ice from loss of considerable blood. After perservering with her, she was finally persuaded to come to my office where I could care for her. Indian women are so timid that they rather die than to ask aid from the Indians or from 'the white doctor.'"[18]

Montezuma's relationship with the agent, William J. Plumb, must have been a pleasant change after Fort Stevenson because Plumb consistently approved Montezuma's requests along with a laudatory comment or two. Nevertheless, Montezuma continued to be appalled by reservation conditions, unloading his feelings in letters to Richard Pratt and apparently for the first time complaining that the Indians perceived him as a White man. Pratt responded: "…I understand very well what you stand face to face with now. It is not, as you know, my way. I would have had you continue among the whites and become part and parcel of the civilized portion of the country, and leave to others of our own race the duties that you now perform. However, you are there, and I trust that in all respects you will be what the Indians call you, a white man, not only white in conduct outside but white in the inside."[19]

Montezuma's frustrations eventually compelled him seven months after his arrival to request the erection of a hospital, a request to Agent Plumb that revealed Montezuma's reaction to the Indian's system of medical care. "I have had the honor in my quarterly reports to call the attention of the Hon. Commissioner of Indian Affairs to the necessity of erecting a building for hospital purposes at this Agency, but I fear that through the great mass of business that must come before the Hon Commissioner, my reports have escaped his attention. Hence, I desire through you to present to the department some of the urgent reasons why such a building should be erected, at an early day.

First, the curse of savage life is the medicine man, he is the oracle and well nigh omnipresent. I visit a patient who is troubled with pneumonia, leave medicine with directions when to be taken, orders to keep him from exposure to cold are given, and to nursing, etc. My back is no sooner turned than in steps the medicine witch who begins his diabolical incantation. He, to show his contempt for the white Doctor, strips him naked and plunges him into the cold water, throws my medicine out of doors, the patient dies and the white Doctor is to blame for it. This is not an isolated case, but has happened several times as you know. Many times I have been refused admittance to the presence of the sick by these fiends, and such is their hold on these people that even the most intelligent yield to their threats when out of sight of the Agency.

Second, even if these people were free to and willing that the Agency Physician should treat them, the miserable, and squalid hovels which many of them live in renders it impossible to do justice with them, especially in the winter months. But the hope of these people all lies in the school children and there is very little hope for them unless they can be freed from the influence of the medicine men. This can only be done by being able to treat them away from home and its baleful influence. Many of them come to me voluntarily for medicine but I know from the condition of the child their parents refuse to allow them to take it or make them throw it away. This can be remedied only by erection of a hospital, so that the patient can be under the control of the Agency Physician.

The medical fraternity have reached that conclusion that diseases can be checked or controlled by the surrounding condition of the patient. And from past personal experience I have noticed that most all deaths occurred by complications due to exposure or want of proper care and I believe all Agency Physicians will bear me out in this statement.

If such be the aim of the Department towards enlightening and alleviating the diseases of the Indian race, I affirm you or me as Agent and Physician to this Agency, were we to overlook such an important factor we would not be worthy of the position which we occupy before the government. Knowing the deep interest that you take in the welfare of these people, I respectfully ask that you forward this communication to the Hon. Commissioner of Indian Affairs with such recommendations as in your judgment may seem best."[20]

Montezuma's request was strongly supported by Agent Plumb who emphasized that Montezuma's work was discouraging and "the results are far from satisfactory to work constantly (as the Doctor does) and find himself thwarted by Agencies that he has no power to control."[21] But even Commissioner Morgan was discouraged and frustrated as he revealed in a letter to Senator Henry Dawes.

"I enclose for your private information copy of a letter from the Physician at Western Shoshone Agency, Nevada. Dr. Montezuma is a young Apache Indian. He graduated first from the State University at Champlain [sic], Ill., and then from a medical school in Chicago. He was then appointed by me as physician. As you will see, his letter evinces intelligence as well as heart.

Of course his pitiful appeal in behalf of the humane treatment of the unfortunate sick under his care will be in vain. I have plead and urged and begged for money for hospitals, but have been refused, and I am helpless.

I do not send this communication to you officially nor, with any expectation at all that it will accomplish anything. I simply lay it before you that you may see how an Indian looks at this matter and that you may divide with me the sorrow, which I know you feel as well as I, that we must turn a deaf ear to such calls of humanity."[22]

Montezuma never tried to work with the medicine men, but consistently and constantly belittled and antagonized them. This in fact was the official policy of the Indian Bureau. Agency physicians were instructed to use every effort to overcome the influence of the medicine men.[23] The problems, the frustrations, the conflict between Montezuma's message of assimilation and the old tribal ways—all combined to stir Montezuma to find a way out. As always, he turned to his idol and supporter, Richard Pratt. After two years at the

Western Shoshone Agency, Pratt continued to provide his counsel: "Reservations make Indians of white men, and of course early make Indians again of young Indians, unless they are sustained by a great deal of education and business, such as you have. ...If you could be sure of place and opportunity to make a living in the higher and better influences of civilization, I should say do it, but until you do see that, better cling to what you have, and save, save, save, so that you may sustain yourself, if necessary, through the period of acquiring practice."[24]

Montezuma tried to be patient. "Dear Capt, Two years ago today, at about five o'clock in the evening you could see a young man introducing himself as Physician appointed to the Agency after walking eighteen miles from White Rock. As he had never followed an Indian trail since his childhood you can imagine how he felt too. How can you and I disagree on the Indian question, if our experiences and our object be the same. It is prejudice, jealousy, selfishness etc. that separates harmony of minds, but minds of love to promote the welfare of the Indian can never separate. I shall do as you command, relative to my leaving the service or not, and watch out for a better chance in the east, and save all I can while I hold my present position."[25]

During his second year at the agency, Montezuma continued to be unable to accept Indian ways, but he was encouraged by some acceptance among the younger generation: "Fandangoes, where the Indians concentrate all their superstitious customs, have been the cause of many deaths. The dance begins at sundown and continues until late in the morning. Overheating themselves in the craze and breathing in the dirty dust during these long hours, have caused them to catch cold and gradually turned into pneumonia, to which most of our Indians are victims. The dust affects their eyes and throat. Much blindness can be traced to this savage custom. Indians from a distance at this time have introduced immoral diseases. It is gratifying to note that our enlightened Indians are generally losing their confidence in the medicine man. The old, ignorant and superstitious ones still imagine the practice of the howling brute to be good. But with time, and as the younger generation takes the places of their parents, our hopes will be fulfilled and the labor we are doing for them will be rewarded."[26]

Montezuma busied himself with a plan to form an association to help Indian students returning from boarding schools to work among White people or on the agencies. He sent letters to every agency requesting the names of returned students or those who could speak and read the English language. In September 1892, he received many replies, listing many Indians by name, and estimates that surprisingly indicated that the majority of Indians on the reservations could speak English and many could read English. This idea did not die with Montezuma, but its only manifestation could be found in heart-felt letters to young Indians.

Montezuma was not enjoying life on a reservation. He complained: "I dislike this lonely business. It may look nice to others, but it is hard on me who likes civilization."[27] Finally, Montezuma decided he needed to be in a location that was less barren and destitute, "more civilized," and he inquired about vacancies at other agencies. On December 2, 1892, after two and one-half years at the Western Shoshone Agency, Montezuma accepted by Western Union telegram an appointment as physician at Nespelem on the Colville Agency in Washington, at a compensation of $1,200 per annum, effective January 9, 1893.[28]

## FROM NEVADA TO WASHINGTON

The Colville Reservation, formed in 1872, was large, containing 2.8 million acres, which included a large amount of agricultural land.[29] This area in northeastern Washington, extending west from the Columbia river, was the reservation for many tribes, including the

Coeur d'Alene, Spokane, Nez Perce (Joseph's band), Kalispel, Methow, Okanagan, Nespelem, San Poil, Lake, and the Colville. The allotment process (Chapter 3) was not yet underway during the time Montezuma served as Agency Physician.

In January 1893, Montezuma reported to Nespelem, the headquarters for the Colville Agency Physician. He was congratulated by Captain Pratt, who cautioned him: "You will see your opportunities. There may be a need. Be a man and be a physician. Make people respect you, make them want you."[30] But once again, Montezuma had a rocky start as he found his office to be practically a bare room, prompting a letter of requests to the agent in charge.

"On my report for duty I found everything in disorder and discouraging. The Doctor should have respectable shelving for his drugs. This was temporarily accomplished by few rough boards at hand. There is no sign of a chair in his office. There should be curtains or blinds in the drug room where he is expected to examine patients. Some kind of a table I have no doubt can be made after the mill is in working order. Office desk is lacking. No physician can get along without one. The physician's room is entirely bare. The most important request I wish to present before you is a riding horse including a saddle, blankets, and bridle for the same. By my experience of four years in the service I do not think we 'physicians' do justice to the Indians of whom we are laboring to elevate by sitting in our office. We should visit every camp and show our interest in them by our presence. This can only be done by means of a horse...."[31]

The agent for the Colville Reservation was not nearby; Major Hal J. Cole was located at Fort Spokane. He forwarded Montezuma's requests to the commissioner, but not without the comment that the previous physician never complained, and that physicians in this agency had always furnished their own horses and equipment. Although the Bureau eventually fulfilled Montezuma's requests, Montezuma continued to be unhappy.

He wrote directly to Commissioner Morgan: "I am greatly discouraged and disappointed with my new surroundings. I thought when I selected this place that I would be surrounded by influences, which would be for my betterment, but I am mistaken. I would a thousand times rather have my old place back again than to remain here. I left Western Shoshone Agency not because I wished to but I yearned for enlightenment. I sacrificed friends in order to leave it. [This was undoubtedly true as Montezuma was to maintain a warm and friendly correspondence with the Western Shoshone Agent and his family, as well as others from the agency.] But I have come very short of my anticipation. Once more I ask your guidance as a lonely Apache who is trying to seek a higher scale in life. Are there any more vacancies in school service or agencies? If so will you please wire them to me...."[32] Montezuma's signature to this letter is poignant with meaning. He signed it, "Charles Montezuma." During the short time he was at the Colville Agency (six months), Montezuma appeared to be so filled with a desire to be part of White Protestant civilization, that he took to calling himself Charles, the anglicized version of Carlos that he used a decade previously during his years as an undergraduate student at the University of Illinois.

Montezuma's despair is palpable in an emotional and very long letter written to several young Indian students, written with sloppy handwriting that was very unlike his usual style. He reported that "It is very disgusting to see an overgrown, lazy, and worthless baby (Indian man) with his leggings, moccasins, long hair falling on either side of his neck, his arm laden with trinkets, highly colored blankets wrapped around his body to his chin, waddling behind his poor wife—like an ant carrying a larger load then herself—who has been out all morning in snow over three feet deep, to get enough shrubs to keep the fire going for this miserable Indian to gamble. It makes my heart ache and I often wish there was no government to feed and clothe such good for nothing beings. My dear friends, this is no exaggeration, but every day occurrence in all reservations."[33]

Montezuma's experiences were not unique, nor did they reflect his own idiosyncrasies or a difficult personality. From 1897 to 1901, William J. McConnell, an inspector for the Department of the Interior, documented the poor health conditions on the reservations, and the poorly paid medical service personnel who had inadequate equipment and medicines and were mostly uninterested in their jobs.[34] Efforts to improve Indians' health didn't begin until 1908, sparked partially by the Sixth International Congress on Tuberculosis held that year in Washington, at which the Commissioner of Indian Affairs, Francis E. Leupp, presented a report on the state of Indian health. Unfortunately, increased appropriations and efforts were severely curtailed by World War I.

Montezuma's time at the Indian agencies was not all work and no play. He reported to Pratt that he enjoyed the gun and rod. He hunted deer, ducks, and prairie chickens, but complained that he caught only a few trout in the Nespelem River that flowed near his house. Montezuma finally resolved to leave the Indian service, to locate in a civilized community, to show the White people that an Indian could compete in the medical profession. He poured his heart out to Richard Pratt, signing these letters as Carlos.

Conferences on a vast range of subjects were being organized to be held in conjunction with the World's Columbian Exposition in Chicago scheduled to open in May 1893. Somehow Montezuma became a member of the advisory council organizing these meetings and began to correspond with other reservation physicians, gathering data to prepare a presentation that he planned for Chicago, on the subject of the effect of climate on health.[35] When Pratt learned that Montezuma had requested a leave of absence to attend the Columbian Exposition and to scout practice opportunities in Chicago, he quickly suggested that Montezuma apply for the position of School Physician at Carlisle that serendipitously had just been vacated in June 1893. The transfer was granted, and on July 6, 1893, Montezuma was granted twenty days leave for travel to begin his new duty at the same annual salary of $1,200.

## FROM WASHINGTON TO PENNSYLVANIA

Montezuma served as the School Physician at the Carlisle Industrial School in Pennsylvania from July 1893 to December 1895. He immersed himself without complaint in the routine of the school. Besides his medical duties, he made inspections, lectured the children about being on the grass, and worried about his financial affairs.

In January 1895, he became a medical examiner for an insurance company, a method many young physicians used to earn extra money taking medical histories and performing physical examinations on candidates for life insurance.[36] Montezuma tried to invest some of his money, purchasing investment certificates, but he was repeatedly in arrears with his payments. Part of his money problems can be attributed to his generous practice of providing notes to Miss Luckenbach to allow the bearers (colleagues and older students) to draw funds (from $7 to $20) against Montezuma's school account. He purchased the "International Cyclopaedia" from Dodd, Mead & Company in New York City, but here too, he was delinquent with his payments.

*Carlisle Hospital (still standing)*

*Montezuma and Carlisle Students*

These were the halcyon days of Carlisle. Montezuma as team physician accompanied the football team to its games. This was in the first two years of football at Carlisle, and the games were nearby. He was responsible for teaching "Hygienics."[37] He attended the Lake Mohonk conferences in 1893 and 1895, and presented short talks that must have delighted his listeners in that they upheld the Protestant ethic and the philosophy of assimilation.

As representative, a most unpromising specimen, of the Apaches, I entered Chicago twenty-two years ago. It was about the time that General Howard was on the trail of my father. Since then I have had the grand chance of standing side by side with the white man's son in gaining a liberal education. I have had four years' service as agency physician in North Dakota, Nevada, and Washington. I am now at Carlisle. This experience has afforded me a full chance to come face to face with my people. Therefore the views that I may express here are convictions derived from the most intense personal interest, personal observation, and study. The reservation is a demoralizing prison, a barrier to enlightenment, a promoter of idleness, gamblers, paupers, and ruin. If you were to isolate your children on barren soil, away from any civilized communities, among the ignorance and superstition of centuries, would you expect them to be cultured and refined? Could you put them among idlers, beggars, gamblers, paupers, and make them industrious and self-supporting citizens? No: rather you would place them in the midst of the most refined, cultured, and educated communities among English-speaking people, where they might see all phases of civilized life, not for five years only, but for all their lifetime. Five years of schooling is not education enough for an Indian boy any more than for a white boy. To accomplish their civilization, compulsory education is necessary for the Indian, not on reservations, not near them. If the choice of my life had remained with my father or mother or myself, I should not have been here tonight. Ignorance and the very lowest depths of an uncivilized life would have been my fate. You are sympathetic and philanthropic. Your sympathy and philanthropy are misused, when directed to teaching on the reservations. Your effort should rather be to open those reservations, people them with settlers, so that the Indians may have the example of good white men, and in this way bring in the light of civilization. Teach the Indians particularly to earn their own bread in God's appointed way by the sweat of the brow. That means liberty, manhood, and citizenship. You do wrong in undertaking to cancel your obligation to the Indians by giving them large money annuities, food, etc., taking away the need of persistent effort and holding them in pauperism. Against that I protest. Help the weak and feeble, but do not administer to idleness. It is not climate or civilization that is killing my people; it is the bondage of ignorance. Your duty is to educate them and their people how to live in a better way. They must be surrounded by that which is the highest and purest in our two races. Carlisle knows how to accomplish this through her motto, "From Barbarism into Civilization and Citizenship." In behalf of the down-trodden races for whom I speak, and as a member of one of those tribes who look to you for help and instruction, I say with the woman of old "Entreat us not to leave thee, or to return from following after thee; for whither thou goest we will go; and where thou lodgest we will lodge; thy people shall be our people, and thy God our God."[38]

...Captain Pratt has not loaded me to come here and fire at you. He knows that I stand independent. If you want to civilize Indians, I believe the fundamental idea is to have them with you, side by side. ...You give a savage, ignorant, uncivilized Indian a hundred sixty acres of land, and protect him for twenty-five years! You had better protect the white man instead of the Indian, or at the end of that time the Indian will be minus the land.[39]

Pratt sent Montezuma on summer trips to western Indian reservations to recruit children for the school. His performance on one occasion, sending unhealthy children to Carlisle, earned Montezuma a rare rebuke from Pratt. "Please do not repeat your carelessness in Michigan last year. We must not be shipping back your pupils at once. If I can not trust my doctor, who can I trust?"[40]

*Montezuma and Nurses at Carlisle*

In the fall of 1895, just a year before Montezuma decided to move to Chicago, he presented a lecture to the Cumberland County Medical Society at an afternoon meeting in the town center of Carlisle.[41] The talk described his favorite treatment, menthol prepared in various ways as a remedy for just about every medical condition. We will save his detailed description for Chapter 8 because it continued to be a mainstay of his practice.

On November 22, 1895, Montezuma resigned as physician at Carlisle and in the Indian Service, effective January 8, 1896, to avail himself "of a favorable opportunity for entering private practice in Chicago."[42]

"...fully convinced that personal development consists in rubbing against the world without pampering, I resigned from the Indian Service to prove that I, a lone Indian born in savagery, could make my way by myself, unaided, in the world alongside white men. And if I could, so could my people. From that time, 1896, I have done it. My people can do it. Any man, black, red, yellow, brown, or white, can do it against obstacles, if he will. But he must do it himself; it cannot be done for him."[43]

## LESSONS FROM THE RESERVATIONS

Montezuma's first years as a young physician, six years and four months from age twenty-three to age thirty, were devoted to service with the Bureau of Indian Affairs. This experience must have made him a better physician. After graduating from medical school, physicians today spend several years in further training, either in general medicine or in a specialty. But the educational process never ends. There is the necessary learning of new advances and techniques that requires constant reading of the medical literature, attendance at educational conferences, and interaction with colleagues, but just as important (if not more) is the steady accumulation of experience. Medical practice requires constant decision making, and often all the facts needed to make a decision easy and straightforward are not available. Yet a decision must still be made, in a process called medical judgment. Medical judgment is constantly improved, refined, and made more effective by the personal experiences of the physician, learning from each and every patient encounter. That is the fundamental reason why older physicians are in general better clinicians. And that is why Montezuma was a better physician when he left the service of the Bureau of Indian Affairs than when he entered. Indeed, in the late 1800s, with the availability of only a very limited amount of medical literature and few teaching conferences, a physician learned mainly through experience. Montezuma accumulated an experience that was notable in its variety and breadth.[44] He took care of injuries, treated conditions like measles, gonorrhea, bronchitis, rheumatism, conjunctivitis, tuberculosis, menstrual abnormalities, and eczema. He extracted teeth and delivered babies. Montezuma administered ether and chloroform to provide anesthesia for the reduction of compound fractures and for extensive suturing, and he used cocaine for local anesthesia. He developed the sensitivity and compassion derived from dealing with dying patients. And most importantly for his future philosophy and thinking, Montezuma saw firsthand what life was like on the western Indian reservations from 1889 to 1893.

Towards the end of the nineteenth century, American Indians, now locked on reservations, had become completely dependent on federal programs. A traditional way of life, including the methods of achieving economic well being, had essentially been destroyed. Indian political, religious, and social customs were being effectively suppressed. Instead of assimilating into White society, Indian communities had sunk into a dispirited existence on the dole, which was barely sufficient to sustain life.

Montezuma's reactions to the Indians themselves were consistent and non-changing, strengthening his own philosophical position. "The intention of The Government is good toward the Indians, but feeding and clothing abled [sic] bodied men and women and keeping them from the outside world of enlightenment is a sin. ...The reservation system is demoralizing damage to the Indians or anybody else. ...In order to bring the Indian papooses under the influence of our Christian civilization, we must take them away from their home surroundings and foster them among the civilized communities, where they can use all of their faculties to our ways."[45]

Montezuma's time on the reservations forged his resolve to succeed in White society. Not even working in the "more civilized" environment of the Carlisle School would be sufficient, "...a living example of what the Indians can be among the whites is better than returning them to camp life to disgrace their nation."[46] Montezuma's reservation experience committed him to a higher mission than being just a physician, "that is to prove to white people there is the same stuff in the Indians as there is in the white people, it only requires the same environment."[47] This unyielding, unwavering rejection of the reservation system and tribal culture would cost him the love of Zitkala-Ša (Chapter 9).

"If you wish to succeed in life, you must devote most of your time to one object."[48] Montezuma henceforth would devote himself to the elimination of the Bureau of Indian Affairs. In his view, this was an essential step in the process of total assimilation. "The best way to solve the Indian question is to put them in a civilized community. Educating Indian children five years and sending them back to their camp life without any encouragement is like having them to quit for a while their wild habits and then letting them go back to them again. This is not education, but rather a pittance on the part of the Government and a blind to the Indians."[49]

AT THE AGE of thirty, Montezuma, a Yavapai assimilated into White society, was committed to demonstrating that he would be an example, proof that the process of assimilation was the right solution for the Indians. Because the reservation system was an obstacle to assimilation, he would fight for its abolition. Because the Bureau of Indian Affairs supported and maintained the reservation system, he would turn from being a Bureau employee to a major opponent and antagonist of the Bureau.

A ROUND 1900, CHICAGO was a noisy, smoky, bustling, exciting, prosperous town. It had become a large and sprawling urban complex in the historically short, but dynamic, span of sixty years. Montezuma first saw Chicago in 1872 (the year after the Great Fire) at the age of six. By 1896, when Montezuma returned to Chicago, the city had changed considerably. It was a city of energy and human spirit, of young people from incredibly diverse cultures looking to make something of themselves.

**BEFORE THE GREAT FIRE**

Chicago sits on a flat plain, smoothed by the action of the glacial lake that finally retreated to form Lake Michigan. This level land is only slightly higher than the lake, a problem for architects and builders, and the clay deposited by the glaciers is difficult to drain, a problem for public comfort and health. On the other hand, the flatness made it extremely easy to lay out streets, place trolley tracks, and build railroad lines.

The site of Chicago was near a one and one-half-mile portage only six miles upstream from the mouth of the Chicago River. At high water levels, the portage was very short, even canoeable; at low levels, the portage was a difficult trip through swampy conditions. It connected the Des Plaines River and the Mississippi River system to Lake Michigan and the St. Lawrence River system. The name "Chicago" was derived by French traders from an Indian word, "Chicagoua," the place of the wild onion; the flat marshlike land was filled with wild onion plants.[1] The area was part of the colony of New France because of the explorations of Jacques Marquette and Louis Joliet. Later ceded to the English, the territory became part of the United States after the Revolutionary War. To guard this location, the federal government built Fort Dearborn in 1803 (the site is at the southwest corner of the Michigan Avenue bridge over the Chicago River). It was destroyed by the Potawatomi Indians in 1812, then rebuilt and occupied until the 1830s. The population of Chicago was only sixty in 1831. The last Indian uprising occurred in 1832 when Chief Black Hawk (the namesake of the Chicago professional hockey team) led a group of Sauk, Fox, and Kickapoo Indians from Iowa across the Mississippi in an effort to regain their western Illinois lands. The fighting did not take place near Chicago, but the publicity spurred a wave of American immigration to the area. Within a few years, the Potawatomi Indians were forced to move across the Mississippi River, and most are now located in Kansas and Oklahoma.

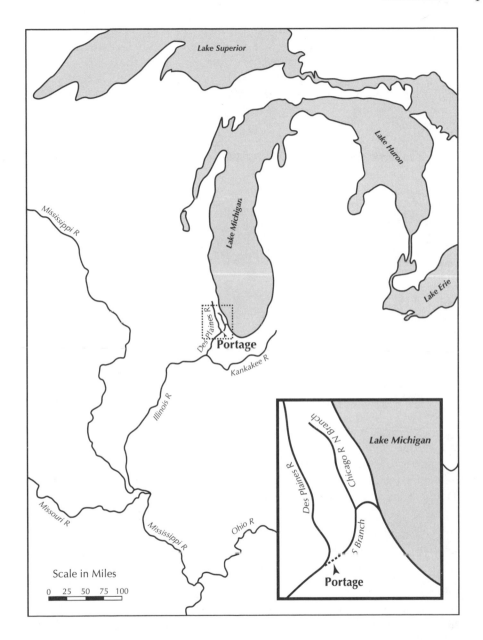

Chicago became a city in 1837 when the population reached 4,000. The opening of the Illinois and Michigan Canal in 1848 joined the Great Lakes and the Mississippi River, ensuring the commercial prosperity of the young city. The majority of the workers laboring to build the canal were Irish immigrants, who settled in an area that came to be called Bridgeport, an area that remained the center of Irish life and politics even in 1900. The canal ran 100 miles from Bridgeport (only thirty blocks from the center of Chicago) to La Salle and Peru.

The canal, together with the building of roads and railroads that began the year the canal opened in 1848, combined to make Chicago a hub of wholesale trade. The mouth of the Chicago River, previously obstructed by a wide sand bar with shallow water, was now a legitimate port with a deep channel protected from drifting sand by two long piers, the north pier extending over half a mile into Lake Michigan. During the Civil War, Chicago became a national center for the meatpacking, grain, and lumber businesses. At the same time, the manufacturing industry grew. Burgeoning employment opportunities accounted for a rapid expansion in population, Americans and a large number of foreign-born immigrants, halted only temporarily by the Great Fire of 1871.

For over fifty years, railroads provided the fastest mode of transportation in the United States. The tracks of eastern and western lines converged at the meeting place of land and water transportation, the center of Chicago where the canal came together with the Great Lakes and the Chicago River. Chicago rapidly became a bustling port and business district, loading and discharging grain, wood, animals, and passengers of all kinds, either changing trains to continue east or west, or to seek opportunities in the city. The western lines came to Chicago to connect with transportation by the eastern lines, which were forced to maintain lower fares and charges because of the competition provided by Great Lakes shipping. Soon Chicago was at the center of a railroad map that looked like spokes in a wheel. By 1857, almost 100 trains entered and left the city every day.[2] Novels that featured Chicago in the late 1800s, like *Sister Carrie* by Theodore Dreiser, were fond of describing the first images of the city seen through the windows as a train passed through flat and empty prairie land to a smoky metropolis. In the last decades of the 1800s and into the early 1900s, Chicago was characterized by a sooty sky, a consequence of its industries, buildings, and homes that consumed bituminous coal. Even the Sioux Indians with Buffalo Bill's Wild West show called Chicago "Sotoju Otun Wake," smoky city.[3]

Streets covered with wooden planking began to appear in 1844, and wooden sidewalks gradually became prevalent in the downtown area.[4] Limestone blocks began to cover the downtown streets after 1855. By 1871, the streets were lit by gas street lights, and the poles carried telegraph wires, but only eighty-eight of Chicago's 530 miles of streets had been paved.[5]

Getting around Chicago in the years before the Great Fire was not easy. There were few sidewalks, and the streets were either muddy or dusty, filled with debris, stray animals, manure, garbage, and lined with ditches containing sewage. Human waste was deposited in what were called "privy vaults," actually just holes in backyards and cellars. The roadside ditches were intended to be washed by rainfall into the Chicago River. The river was also a common sewer for the packing plants, tanneries, and the other factories that lined the banks. Streets and sidewalks covered by wood often trapped water, garbage, and manure. The smell of the city was unmistakable.

The construction of sewer lines had to solve a major problem: the water level, the level of Lake Michigan, is only fifteen feet under the flat ground of Chicago. The solution in the 1860s was to raise the level of the streets; the new space under the streets now allowed for sewer lines, water pipes, and gas mains.[6] Not all buildings were placed on new, taller foundations, and for years, Chicago's sidewalks went up and down. The first sewage system used pipes down the center of the streets, collecting storm water and waste from buildings. The pipes drained by gravity into the river, which was dredged to handle the increased volume of drainage (the dredged material was used to elevate the streets). It took twenty years to raise Chicago ten to twelve feet higher.

Although the new sewage system made Chicago drier and somewhat healthier, it made the river and drinking water worse. The river was too sluggish to clean itself. Theodore Dreiser wrote in 1898 that "if the Chicago River had a voice equal to its odor," it could provide its own report. But "if the Chicago River waters did not speak any faster than they flow, we should never get the report."[7]

The collecting site for Chicago's water was at the shore of Lake Michigan, and the obvious solution was to build a tunnel to an intake crib far out in the Lake. The first Chicago water system was completed in 1866. A two-mile brick-walled tunnel, five feet in diameter, was built thirty feet below the lake by Irish immigrant workers using picks, shovels, and mules. Water was pulled from the lake bottom at the intake by the pumping station. The water system was connected to the Chicago Water Tower with its 138-foot standpipe to create water pressure. The medieval-style Old Water Tower and Waterworks pumping station were saved and maintained on Michigan Avenue in downtown Chicago as a nostalgic reminder of the Great Fire.

Unfortunately the water system did not totally solve the problem. Every increase in river flow, from rain or spring floods, drove sewage far enough out into the lake to enter the Chicago water intake. The solution was to reverse the flow of the Chicago River. The first attempt included deepening of the canal and the installation of a pump at the Bridgeport terminus. Indeed, the flow of the river turned to the south in July 1871, and in 1872, a second intake tunnel was built, now six miles into the lake. A southward flow, however, lasted only one year. Accumulating sediment stopped the flow, and it wasn't until 1900 that the flow in the Chicago River was permanently reversed.

Horses powered city transportation in the 1800s. Horse-drawn cars running on rails in the streets had a top speed of six miles per hour, but usually went slower. It took an hour to travel about thirty-two blocks (four miles).[8] The packed cars were heavy, and the work exhausted the horses; each car required about seven horses per day to keep it going. Many horses died on the city streets, over 10,000 per year. The delivery of freight depended upon horse-drawn wagons. There were ice wagons, furniture wagons, pie carriers, flat beds, enclosed wagons for baked goods, and the police patrol wagons complete with warning bells, irons for prisoners, and rescue equipment.

Potter Palmer was rich when he retired at age forty-one, leaving his dry-goods business on Lake Street to Levi Z. Leiter and Marshall Field. Palmer tired of vacationing, and returned to Chicago to become a real estate developer and even wealthier. His plan was to develop State Street as a commercial center. He had quietly purchased about a mile of frontage.[9] In 1868, State Street was paved, but poorly, and it was muddy, narrow, and lined by pawnshops, saloons, and boardinghouses. Palmer succeeded in obtaining a city ordinance to widen State Street, and he built about thirty stores and business places along the new, wider lines. Some property owners refused to cooperate, and until after the Great Fire, State Street zigzagged through The Loop. Palmer's objective was to create a handsome, safe shopping area that would attract women, extending the system of advertising, guaranteed satisfaction, and free deliveries that he employed in his first dry goods store. Palmer built a six-story, block long building on State Street and convinced Leiter and Field to rent this prime block in the new downtown shopping district; the store opened in 1868. A few blocks south on State Street, Palmer built the eight-story Palmer House Hotel; the largest building in Chicago at that time was a wedding gift for his wife.

The rich capitalists of Chicago had begun to build their mansions on the South Side, especially on Prairie Avenue. However, the people of Chicago lived side by side before the Great Fire, with the rich not far from the poor. There were no tall tenement houses; the poor lived in small cottages and shanties, usually built two to a lot, one in front, the other in back. Large numbers of immigrants began to arrive in the 1850s, and by 1870 over one-half of Chicago's population was foreign-born, the largest group being German, followed by the Irish and the Scandinavians.[10]

## Meat, Bread, and Wood

The meatpacking business started with hogs.[11] Civil War contracts for salted pork made it profitable for farmers to grow corn to fatten their hogs then ship the hogs by rail to Chicago. The first packing plants in Chicago were limited to pork because only fresh beef was being sold in local markets throughout the United States. Thus at first, in the mid 1800s in Chicago, pork was packed only in the winter to avoid deterioration of the meat, and live cattle were received from the West and shipped live to the East. The Union Stock Yards opened in 1865, only four miles southwest of the center of Chicago. Constructed by railroad engineers as a small city, it had its own sewer and drainage system (the first in Chicago, but it emptied into the South Branch of the Chicago River), streets paved with wood, pens that could handle over 120,000 animals, and rooms cooled with ice to permit pork packing year around. The Yards were linked to all the major railroads, and a canal connected the Yards with the Chicago River. A commuter line ran from downtown Chicago to the Stock Yards, and soon the Yards were Chicago's major tourist attraction.

The reaper, a steel cutter and collector of grain, was invented by Cyrus McCormick on his father's plantation in Virginia. McCormick patented the reaper in 1834 and sought a location for a factory that would be closer to American grain production. In Illinois he found that grain could not be harvested before it decayed (within four to ten days) because of a lack of laborers. He built his first factory on the mouth of the Chicago River, and by 1860, he was making over 4,000 reapers a year, at $120 each that could be paid over time.[12] McCormick was the first to use extensive advertising and to back his product with an unconditional, money back guarantee. He died in 1894, leaving his son to preside over the International Harvester Company, which was formed in 1902.

The reaper changed the commerce of grain.[13] Large four-story structures for the storage of grain were built next to the McCormick factory at the mouth of the Chicago River (the first grain elevators). Movement of the grain was powered by steam engines, connecting the incoming grain in railroad cars with the outgoing path into the large shipping boats of the Great Lakes. Before 1850, grain arrived in Chicago in wagons, transported in sacks, loaded and unloaded by hand, and bought and sold sack by sack. With the development of railroad transport and steam-powered grain elevators, grain could now be bought and sold by the quality of a lot rather than individual sacks (in other words buyers and sellers did not exchange precisely the same grain, but the same amounts of similar grade and quality). The Chicago Board of Trade became the first modern commodity exchange, where grain and animals could be bought and sold like stocks and bonds.

Wood traveled in the opposite direction of grain. Lake boats brought finished lumber from northern Wisconsin and Michigan to Chicago, and railroads took the wood to the farmers for houses, barns and sheds, fences, wagons, and a source of heat and energy in the treeless prairies. The land around Chicago also contained few trees; nevertheless, the city became a lumber center and used white pine for its houses and buildings, the fuel for the Great Fire. The trains returned to Chicago filled with agricultural products and livestock, and the boats returned to the lumber country filled with provisions and equipment purchased in Chicago.[14]

Chicago entrepreneurs moved quickly to acquire vast forest holdings in Wisconsin and Michigan to feed their lumber industry in Chicago. The lumber industry extended along the banks of the Chicago River from the McCormick Reaper Works at the mouth on Lake Michigan to the canal at Bridgeport. Old pictures show the banks of the river covered with piles of drying lumber stretching for miles in either direction, waiting to be sold. The entrance to the canal was at Twenty-second Street; it was a site marked by many diagonal channels off the river. Along the channels were wharves to receive the boats loaded with lumber; each wharf was connected to a railroad siding to receive and then deliver the products from the planing and saw mills in the North. The lumber trade stimulated the establishment of nearby industries, making furniture, pianos, wagons, and ships. It was possible for a group of homesteaders on the prairie to receive by train from Chicago a ready built town of houses, stores, taverns, churches, and a courthouse.[15] By 1870, over 200 lumber boats arrived in Chicago every twelve hours.[16] The ships headed up the river to Bridgeport, passing thirteen miles of docks and piers and twenty-four swinging bridges (by 1898, there were fifty-two draw- or swinging bridges).[17] Imagine the havoc the swinging bridges, pivoting on their piers on small islands in the middle of the river, created with traffic as these boats passed up the river. Being "bridged" was a common frustrating experience, and one reason that development first favored the South Side of Chicago. There was a surge of enthusiasm for overcoming the bridge bottleneck with the opening of tunnels under the river in 1869 and 1871 for pedestrians and vehicles. This was only temporary, however, as the tunnels proved to be too small, and they began to leak. The lumber industry began to decline after 1880, and by the middle of the 1890s, Chicago was no longer the major lumber supplier for the West. Competition from new forests served by railroads made direct shipments from mills possible, eliminating the need to pass through Chicago, and the white pine forests of the Great Lakes area finally vanished, totally consumed, replaced by yellow pine from the South and fir from the Pacific Northwest.

Montezuma lived in Chicago when the city gradually lost its position as a center of commerce. The development and rapid use of automobiles and trucks eliminated the centralization of various industries that was created by the railroads. The output of the Union Stock Yards, which had plateaued at a very high level in the 1880s continued to be very active during Montezuma's years in Chicago, then began to decline in the 1930s, and by 1960, all of the major meat packers had closed their Chicago factories. The change with lumber and grain was more rapid, as grain production, elevators, and milling moved north and west in the late 1800s, and white pine shipped to Chicago by boat was no longer a prime building material by the middle 1890s.

## THE GREAT CHICAGO FIRE

Around nine o'clock on Saturday evening, October 8, 1871, the same month and year Montezuma was captured by Pima warriors, a fire broke out on the West Side of Chicago in the cow barn of Mrs. Patrick O'Leary. Keeping pigs, cattle, and chickens was legal in the city of Chicago until 1890. Mrs. O'Leary's cow was housed only one mile from the center of the city. Spread by strong winds, the fire burned for two days, consuming the entire center of the city and leaving homeless 90,000 of the 300,000 population, destroying four square miles with 18,000 buildings, and killing about 300 people.[18]

A long drought in the summer of 1871 and dry hot winds proved to be a bad combination for a city at great risk for a fire. Almost every building in the city was built of white pine from Wisconsin and Michigan, and the few brick and marble buildings downtown had combustible roofs. Even the streets with their wooden pavements and wooden sidewalks were a fire hazard. By October, the wood in Chicago was totally dry.

On the evening the fire started, a hot wind was blowing towards the concentration of the wood structures in the southwestern portion of the city. The popular story that Catherine O'Leary's cow kicked over a kerosene lamp while being milked is still quoted today. An official inquiry concluded that the O'Leary family was asleep when the fire started.[19] And twenty-nine years later, a reporter admitted that he and his colleagues had concocted the story.[20] But the fire did start in the O'Leary cow barn at 137 De Koven Street, only a quarter of a mile west of the river. If not for the wind, it might have been contained. But soon, the lumber yards and factories along the South Branch of the Chicago River were burning, and flaming debris was blown across the river to start fires in the heart of Chicago, spreading north and east to destroy most of the commercial and governmental structures in a swath that measured about four miles long and one mile wide. Terror and confusion reigned in the streets as people joined animals in flight. Many were fortunate to reach the lakefront where they stood in the water and watched the fire.

The steady winds of thirty miles per hour reached gusts of gale-force produced by convection whirls, tornado-like rotating columns of superheated air.[21] The force of these convection whirls was responsible for casting burning debris into unburned areas. The Waterworks pump house was built of stone with a slate roof, but a burning timber crashed into the roof and started a penetrating fire that consumed the interior. The Water Tower was barely damaged, but without the pumping station to keep it filled, pressure for the city's water supply for the fire fighters lasted only a few minutes. The fire spread to the South Side, and then to the North Side, burning itself out on the prairie just beyond Lincoln Park. When the sun rose Monday morning, the fire was still raging. Soon the industrial complexes on both sides of the river were destroyed, but the direction of the fire was northeast, and the Union Stock Yards and packing plants were spared.

Tuesday morning dawned on a desolate and destroyed center of the city. Seventy-three miles of streets and buildings were destroyed; however, firemen managed to save the O'Leary cottage. Fifty-eight companies were driven into bankruptcy; only half of the insurance money that was owed was paid.[22]

## CHICAGO AFTER THE GREAT FIRE

Chicago's recovery was so fast, it was spectacular. By the end of October, the water system was working again, and most of the natural gas and public transport systems were operating. Palmer rebuilt the building housing the Marshall Field Store, which is still at its site on State Street; a new and larger Palmer House was built using the original plans that were buried in the basement under sand and clay in the first hours of the fire; and McCormick built an even larger reaper factory in a new site (now in Blue Island, near Western Avenue and 123rd Street). The first phase of rebuilding lasted about two years, with a rapid restoration over the surviving water, sewage, and transportation systems. The second phase began after 1880 and created the basic structure of Chicago today; by 1900 when Montezuma was living and practicing medicine in Chicago, there were 1,400 miles of paved streets lit by street lamps, about 1,000 miles of streetcar lines, an efficient waterworks and sewage system, the Sanitary and Ship Canal, over 200 acres of parks, and over twenty skyscrapers.[23]

After the fire, horses continued to dominate the streets. Growing crowds in the downtown streets combined with the clip-cloppity of horses and the clangorous clanging of streetcar gongs created an increasing level of noise. Pictures of downtown intersections in the 1890s show four to six horse-drawn streetcars (with open sides in the summer), five to ten horse-drawn wagons and carriages, pushcarts, and hundreds of men in dark suits and black hats and women in long skirts (hems to their shoes) in a hubbub of activity. People were concentrated into the skyscrapers of the relatively small downtown area, The Loop, and by the late 1890s, traffic jams of people, horses, bicycles, and vehicles were a common sight. In 1900, there were more than 3,000 messengers on bicycles in The Loop delivering important documents and telegrams. The streets and sidewalks contained watering troughs for the horses, newsstands on most corners, letter boxes for the posting of mail, police and fire alarm boxes, benches to wait for streetcars, and even water fountains provided by the Woman's Christian Temperance Union.[24]

After 1880, the horse-drawn streetcars were replaced by eighty-two miles of lines for cable cars, similar to those in San Francisco today, with the cables powered by steam engines (faster than horse cars at nine to ten miles per hour). By 1901, downtown, and everywhere by 1906, electric streetcars, the trolleys that operated until 1957, replaced the cable cars.[25] By the early 1900s, the horses were gone, and streetcar lines extended far out into the surrounding open country, in anticipation of future suburbs.

When the Great Lakes glaciers began to melt, the exit of the meltwater through the St. Lawrence River valley was blocked by ice. The flow was forced to the south creating a mile-wide valley known today as the Chicago outlet, the path taken by every major transportation system that serves Chicago. As the ice continued to melt, the St. Lawrence River opened and the flow was no longer southward; the Chicago River joined Lake Michigan in draining to the east. The Chicago River extends one mile inland from Lake Michigan then splits into the twenty-four-mile-long North Branch and the ten-mile-long South Branch to divide the city into North, West, and South sides. In early Chicago, gutters drained into sewers that dumped their contents into Lake Michigan or the Chicago River. Theodore Dreiser described the Chicago River in 1898: "Nowhere along its shore within the great city limits is there a foot of unoccupied ground where a tree may find root. No branch or blade of green graces its shores. No bountiful springs rise from point to point and feed it. Its tributaries are dark, stone-arched sewers which empty their subterranean blackness into it in continuous stream."[26] It was finally realized that the city's high rate of typhoid fever, cholera, and dysentery was due to impure water.

Chicago sits precisely on a continental divide separating the Great Lakes and St. Lawrence River system from the Mississippi River Basin. This divide is a ridge about eight feet high, located twelve miles west of the lakeshore. This geography was altered in January 1900 when the Sanitary and Ship Canal, dug over eight years to a level below the surface of Lake Michigan and paralleling the old Illinois and Michigan Canal, opened and reversed the flow of the Chicago River from Lake Michigan to the Illinois and Mississippi Rivers, changing the direction of the flow of sewage.[27] The new canal from the south branch of the Chicago River to Lockport twenty-eight miles to the southwest cut twenty-five feet deep through the

# Chicago

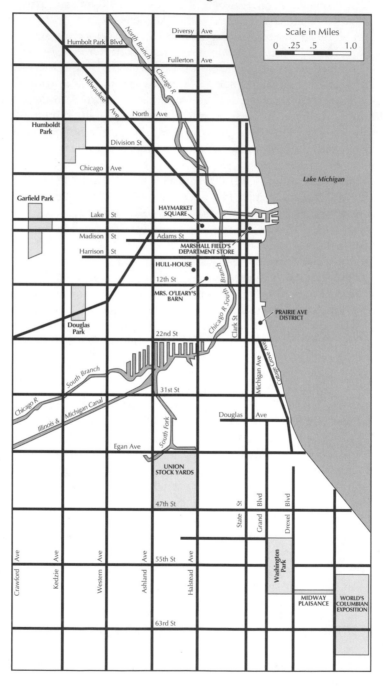

continental divide. This 160- to 306-foot wide canal (larger than the Suez and Panama Canals) together with a dredged and deepened Chicago River permanently reversed the flow of the river, making its confluence with Lake Michigan no longer its mouth of discharge. The enormous size can be appreciated by comparing it to the old Illinois and Michigan Canal, only six feet deep and sixty feet wide. Locks at the mouth of the Chicago River and at Lockport control the flow. Two more artificial rivers were opened in 1910 and 1922, draining the northern communities into the North Branch of the river and reversing the flow of the Calumet River, providing drainage systems to the west for nearly all of Cook County. Chicago's new drainage system was challenged by other states, but the federal courts supported Chicago in its claim that pollution was dissipated before reaching other cities. It wasn't until the 1930s when the U.S. Supreme Court ordered a reduction in the amount of water being diverted from Lake Michigan that Chicago's sewage was treated prior to entering the flow into the Des Plaines River (today fish are living once more in the Chicago River). Sterilization of the city water supply was begun in 1912 and completed in 1917. Typhoid fever joined cholera and smallpox in disappearing.

## The Skyscraper

By 1900, downtown Chicago, known as The Loop, was a modern, high-rise city built on an area cleared by the Great Fire. The name "Loop" came into fashion in 1897 when elevated train tracks formed an overhead loop encircling a thirty-five-block area. Some of the buildings are still standing, such as the Public Library, the Newberry Library, and the Auditorium, but many have vanished, including the twenty-two-story Masonic Temple. In 1892, the Masonic Temple, across the street and only two blocks north of Montezuma's downtown office, was the highest building in the world. The Palmer House is only two blocks south from Montezuma's first downtown office. The lavish Palmer House lobby in Montezuma's time was an important public meeting place. Men gathered in the lobby to make business deals, buy or sell at a broker's exchange, hear the latest news, and talk politics. The Loop, as it does today, contained governmental and commercial offices along with retail and wholesale businesses, clubs, theaters, restaurants, and hotels. Its appearance was enhanced when downtown utility lines were all placed below ground by 1900. Outside of The Loop, the city was noted for its characteristic small lots (25x125 feet) that contained structures ranging from one-story cottages to brick or wood tenements to elaborate mansions. And further out were the new suburbs. The skyscraper was instrumental in the development of suburbs. The vertical concentration of working people in the downtown area required a horizontal expansion of the city in order to provide residential housing.

Underneath The Loop, there exists a tunnel system that extends forty feet under nearly every street in downtown Chicago.[28] The concrete tunnels are about six feet wide and seven feet high with side walls that curve into an arched ceiling. The tunnels were officially constructed to carry telephone cables, but narrow gauge railroad tracks were secretly installed. Construction began in 1899, and by 1906, freight service with electric locomotives was established delivering packages and mail to Loop building basements and servicing the coal burning boiler rooms. The Chicago Tunnel Company maintained this service and complex (with sixty miles of track, 149 locomotives, and 3,000 freight cars), unknown to most Chicagoans. The tunnels were not abandoned until 1959 when they were disrupted by subways, but they are still there.

The gathering places of Chicago at the end of the nineteenth century were mainly privately owned commercial establishments: hotels, department stores, and railroad stations. These buildings were lavishly appointed and decorated to attract crowds, and they contained all sorts of services (barber shops, hairdressers, newsstands, restaurants, ballrooms). The department stores especially benefited from the improved ventilation, lighting, and space in the new iron and steel structures with electricity and elevators. Public transportation packed people into the downtown area, and shopping became a form of recreation for women. The railroad stations provided any service a traveler could need and served both commuters and long distance travelers. By 1913, 746 commuter trains were serving about 125,000 riders per day, and the lines were operating on tracks that had been either elevated or lowered to provide safer and faster travel to and from suburban stations.[29]

Any building ten or more stories tall and served by elevators was called a skyscraper. The pioneering efforts of Chicago architects like William Le Baron Jenney (who worked out the engineering of carrying a building's weight on a steel frame), Daniel Hudson Burnham, John Wellborn Root, and Louis H. Sullivan produced greater profit for building owners by allowing an increase in urban density on the same plot of land. These architects built a new Chicago, beginning in the 1880s, in place of the five- and six-story buildings that were built rapidly in the years just after the Great Fire. The rebuilt Chicago of the 1870s was demolished to make way for a bigger and better downtown of skyscrapers; Montezuma's first downtown office building, The Reliance Building, was an excellent example of this process (Chapter 8). The Great Fire remained a powerful influence, however, in that fireproofing was always a prime consideration, and the new buildings required new methods and materials for fireproofing. Anchoring increasingly tall and heavy buildings on the flat Chicago land with its high water level and shifting soil was another challenge for the architects and engineers. In less than a decade, the builders of Chicago solved these problems and created structures supported and held together by frameworks of steel, allowing the outer walls to have no function other than maximal ventilation and lighting.

Burnham and Root became good friends, prime builders, and influential citizens of Chicago.[30] Root was gifted in music, drawing, sports, and social skills (he was the creative designer of the pair); Burnham was visionary, organized, and a driver (he was the business manager, organizer, and promoter, but also an important contributing architect, of the partnership formed in 1873). The stone gate at Thirty-ninth and Halsted Streets, the main entrance to the Union Stock Yards, was one of their first commissions.

Tall buildings cannot function efficiently without elevators.[31] Elisha Graves Otis developed the first safe passenger elevator, powered by steam hoists and using his patented automatic safety brake. Otis died before the age of the skyscraper, but his sons continued the development of the elevator. The next innovation was power by a hydraulic system, driven by the water pressure in the city's water pipes, introduced in New York by the Otis Company and in Chicago by the country's other major elevator company, owned by William E. Hale who built and opened in 1895, The Reliance Building, which housed Montezuma's first downtown office. The elevator, the telegraph, and the telephone made it no longer necessary for businesses to be near the ground floor or on-site at warehouses and factories. A fifteen-story building could house several thousand tenants, concentrating business managers with white-collar workers and services such as doctors, lawyers, and dentists. Real estate managers and investors quickly learned that the higher spaces were brighter, quieter, and capable of bringing in high rental fees. Architects were motivated to produce tall buildings with as many large windows as possible to bring light into every rentable space; vertical rows of large bay windows are characteristic of the early Chicago skyscrapers. High-strength steel columns and beams, riveted together, made it possible to create the space that would allow big windows.

Chicago buildings had a foundation problem because the solid limestone layer was ninety to 150 feet below the ground, covered by sand and clay with a water level only fifteen feet below the surface.[32] Buildings could not be supported, therefore, with large stone basements. The problem was solved in three phases. The first five- and six-story buildings were supported by large pyramids of stone, supporting the building at their apex and distributing the weight through a wide base sitting on a concrete bed. As buildings became taller and heavier, the required size of the pyramids became an obstacle. Twelve stories were the limit. Root provided the next development: distributing the weight of the building and allowing uniform settling by placing the building on a concrete pancake, two feet thick and reinforced with steel, basically a concrete and steel raft. The floating foundation had its limits, however, and the really tall buildings required the "Chicago Caisson." The caisson, developed in the 1890s, consisted of a column excavated to bedrock, and then filled with reinforced concrete to provide a weight-supporting pillar.

The Great Fire demonstrated that even iron would yield to the enormous heat of a massive fire. The Chicago skyscrapers were fireproofed by covering the iron with terra-cotta, the same clay product used for pots and tiles. External terra-cotta sheathing and the supporting structure of an iron cage fire-proofed with terra-cotta significantly reduced the weight of a building, compared with stone and masonry buildings, allowing higher constructions to be supported by Root's floating foundation. Louis Sullivan formulated the famous architectural philosophy that form should follow function, but the Chicago architects of the 1880s and 1890s were forced to practice this philosophy because the capitalist owners of the buildings made sure that money was limited and directed to required functions, with little, if any, left over for artistic expression.

The new skyscrapers created a new workforce; this was a time of a great increase in new middle-class occupations, a good time for an Indian doctor to establish a practice. The concentration of business and service offices into the downtown buildings, combined with new office technology like typewriters and file cabinets, attracted young, unmarried women to downtown Chicago. The first typewriter was invented in Milwaukee and sold in 1874 by the arms manufacturer, E. Remington & Sons, for $125.[33] The typewriter brought women into the business office, previously an all-male world. In fact, the first typists were trained by the typewriter companies and the purchase of a machine brought the "typewriter" (a young woman) and the typewriter. By 1920, over 50 percent of the clerical work in the country's business offices was being performed by women.[34] The typewriter was followed by the dictating machine, the accounting machine, the addressing machine, and the calculating machine.

During Montezuma's time in Chicago, the downtown offices were staffed with young women who were White, native-born, and unmarried, with a constant turnover as they were expected to and did leave when they were married. The pay was relatively good, but less than that of male clerks, another reason business offices welcomed the new female workforce. In addition, their rapid turnover hindered organizing efforts for better working conditions and higher pay. Before and after 1900, young women from small towns and farms were flocking to Chicago by train to find work. As Theodore Dreiser described it, speaking through Carrie Meeber in *Sister Carrie*, these were young women lured by the possibility of new wealth and possessions and exposed to new sexual temptations and seductions, who worked under harsh conditions controlled by a strict and powerful management.[35] There were new jobs for men too. The establishment of a new urban commercial culture increased opportunities in the service industries (banking, transportation, newspapers, healthcare, and government). The foreign-born were concentrated in industry and lower forms of service (newsstands, grocery and candy stores, bakeries, laundries) while the new professions attracted native-born Americans to the city.

At the time of the Great Fire, the hurrying crowds of people in downtown Chicago were almost all male.[36] Women began to be seen without male escorts on Chicago's downtown streets in the late 1880s. By 1900, daytime in downtown Chicago had become a women's world, workers and shoppers.

## Shopping in Chicago

Marshall Field and Levi Leiter re-established their department store after the Great Fire in the new building on the site of the original store on State Street. Marshall Field became the exclusive owner in 1880 of Marshall Field & Company, both a wholesale and retail supplier of a wide assortment of goods. The retail store, which today is still located in the block between Washington and Randolph Streets, was the largest such store in the country in 1900, employing 9,000 workers and containing fifty-three elevators, a medical clinic, and a post office. Marshall Field followed the business practices of Potter Palmer, and went to the extreme of proclaiming that the customer is always right, and his store was enormously successful in marketing its goods to middle- and upper-class women. Other department stores along State Street, like Lehmann's, served all classes with goods that appealed to everyone, but Marshall Field deliberately catered to wealthier women. Field made shopping in his store an enjoyable experience, indeed, a form of entertainment. The store contained nicely furnished lounges and rest rooms, restaurants, a parlor with a library, a nursery, meeting rooms for women's organizations, telegraph and telephone services, and even stenographers. The customer was encouraged to browse and dawdle. This was the female equivalent of the downtown clubs attended by the husbands. Field died of pneumonia in 1906, but not before becoming Chicago's richest man by investing in many of Chicago's successful companies.

The commercial businesses of Chicago served not only the metropolitan area, but the entire country. Aaron Montgomery Ward started his mail order business at the time of the Great Fire, and he was back in business six months after the fire.[37] By 1876, the Montgomery Ward Catalog had 150 pages, by 1893, over 500 pages and the company was receiving over 15,000 orders per day. Richard Warren Sears started with a mail order business based in Minneapolis that sold watches through the mail.[38] His first employee was Alvah Curtis Roebuck. This business was aided immeasurably when standard railroad time was established in 1883; everyone needed a watch.

Railroads created the system of time we use today.[39] Prior to railroads, travel was slow and at the mercy of the weather and seasons. Railroad travel was fast regardless of weather and season and when every geographical area in the country established time by the position of the sun, it meant that trains had to travel through hundreds of local times. Keeping two trains from using the same piece of track at the same time was just one of the difficulties.

In 1883, the railroads instituted "standard" times, creating the four time zones in each of which every clock reads the same. Although this was not officially established by the U.S. Government until 1918, the country quickly adopted railroad time to regulate commerce and social behavior.

Sears sold his watch company, and in 1892, he and his partner organized a competitor for Montgomery Ward. In 1894 the Sears, Roebuck & Company moved to Chicago. Rural mail delivery was established in 1896, and consequently the large mail order enterprises could reach out to practically every family in America. The arrival of a new catalog was a memorable family occasion, and the old catalogs were put to good use. I remember my grandfather precisely cutting the old catalog pages into four equal squares to fit the little box in the little house in back of our Ohio farmhouse. I also remember that the softest pages in the catalog were the yellow index pages. Alvah Roebuck sold out to Richard Sears in 1895, and Sears retired in 1908 at age forty-four, when the catalog contained 1,000 pages and 35,000 orders per day were being processed.

## The World's Columbian Exposition, May–October 1893

Chicago won the national competition for the right granted by Congress to host a fair commemorating Columbus's landfall in 1492. The opening date was delayed a year to allow Chicago to get ready, but even then, just as with Olympic cities today, it was a frantic race that just made it. The chosen site, Jackson Park, was eight miles south of downtown Chicago, on bare and swampy lakefront land that abutted the railroad tracks to the west. Trains took passengers from The Loop to the fairgrounds in twelve minutes. Burnham and Root were the supervising architects, but most of the architects chosen to design the buildings were from the East and noted for favoring a return to classical styles. This was a deliberate decision on Burnham's part in order to produce a national fair and to avoid a provincial Chicago look.[40] Three days after the architects met to begin the project, Burnham's partner, John Root, died of pneumonia, leaving Burnham, at the age of forty-four, alone as the overall supervisor of the fair.

Construction of over 200 structures, drainage of the land, the creation of canals and lagoons, and the planting of over a million plants began in 1891. The buildings were not meant to be permanent. Framed of wood or steel, their outer facades were made of staff (plaster molded with jute cloth to resemble any type of masonry) and were painted white, creating an impressive image of solid classic (Roman and Greek) buildings, the White City. Only one building was built to be permanent. The Palace of Fine Arts with a $1 million gift from Marshall Field became the Field Museum, which moved into its own building in 1921. Gifts from Julius Rosenwald of Sears, Roebuck made it possible in 1933 to open the abandoned Arts Palace building as today's Museum of Science and Industry.

Chicago was still plagued with impure drinking water, but the fairgrounds had Pasteur filters on the drinking fountains, two water treatment plants, and an efficient sewage treatment system. The absence of typhoid fever at the fair was a convincing argument that the city of Chicago had to do something about its contaminated water. Burnham's success led to commissions to develop city plans for Cleveland, San Francisco, and Manilla, and ultimately to the plan for Chicago completed in 1909, some of which was carried out, principally removing the railroad tracks along the lakefront to create the public land and parks that exist today.

## World's Columbian Exposition

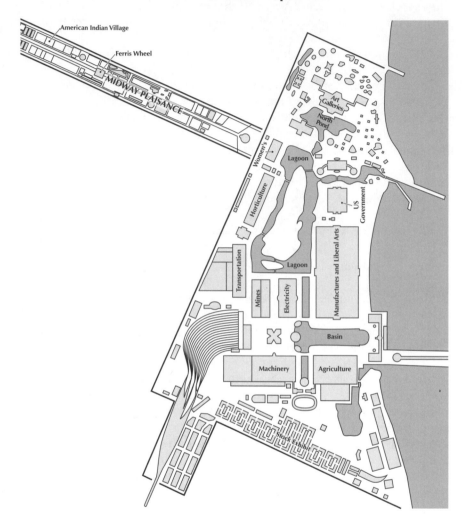

The World's Columbian Exposition, covering 633 acres, opened on May 1, 1893, presenting to the world exhibits of American accomplishments in science and technology. In addition, most countries throughout the world had their own exhibition buildings. The White City encouraged the spread of neoclassic architecture throughout the country; although not original in design, it was a model of how people thought a city should look. The fair was a spectacle of electricity, generated by an on-site steam plant, with electric transportation, lights, and new household appliances, business machines, farm equipment, and even the electric chair for executions. The fair demonstrated the power and benefits of electricity, using three times the amount of daily electricity currently being consumed in the city of Chicago, to vast numbers of people who had never seen an electric light. In the six months it was open, approximately 27.5 million people visited the Fair, traveling hours by train and taking days to arrive from foreign countries, paying an admission fee of fifty cents for each individual over age twelve, and twenty-five cents for children six to twelve. On one day alone, October 9, 1893, over 700,000 people came to the fair on "Chicago Day," when schools, businesses, and factories closed on the anniversary of the Great Fire. However, the admission numbers do not account for multiple entries, so that the actual total number of people was probably considerably less, perhaps near 12 million.[41]

George Washington Gale Ferris, a bridge designer, has a wheel named after him.[42] The wheel, 140 feet high, 250 feet in diameter, ringed with 3,000 electric bulbs, was the landmark of the fair. The thirty-six cars were enormous, each holding forty people; one revolution took twenty minutes (for fifty cents). A total of 1.4 million riders earned only a small profit for Ferris and his investors because of the high costs accrued with its fabrication in Pittsburgh, its transport to Chicago, and its erection on the fairgrounds. The wheel was systematically dismantled in 1894, and a year later, erected at a small amusement park on North Clark Avenue. Faced with legal expenses incurred by court battles with local property owners who opposed the presence of the Ferris Wheel Park in a residential area, combined with declining popularity in a time of a depressed economy, the wheel accumulated a debt that led to its transfer in pieces in 1900 to a junk dealer for $1,800.[43] George Ferris died of tuberculosis in 1896. His famous wheel was re-erected at the St. Louis Louisiana Purchase Exposition in 1904, and than dynamited into small pieces in 1906.

The exhibit buildings (the Court of Honor) around the lagoons were impressive, but it was the mile-long Midway that attracted working families.[44] Most working and rural families, however, came from nearby because the trip could account for a major portion of a typical income at that time. Two weeks in Chicago would cost at least $55 plus train fare.[45] An organized trip (train, meals, and hotel) from Massachusetts for ten days cost $125. Nevertheless, many working individuals and families raised the money or used their savings to see the marvelous Exposition.

The Midway was the world's first amusement park, the forerunner of the entertainment parks of today. It had the exotic (foreign ethnic villages), the amazing (Harry Houdini and his wondrous escapes), the ridiculous (two-headed pigs), the fakes (the Irish Blarney stone that was previously a piece of Chicago's pavement), music (Scott Joplin playing ragtime), the risqué (belly dancers)—a little bit of everything. Many of today's familiar products were introduced at the Exposition: Cream of Wheat, Juicy Fruit gum, Cracker Jacks, Aunt Jemima Syrup, Pabst Beer, soda pop, hamburgers, the first picture postcards. Dvorak composed the *New World Symphony* in honor of the Exposition.

*World's Columbian Exposition Ferris Wheel*

The Indian Bureau presented exhibitions of typical Indian life, but also featured a schoolhouse and models of classroom behavior with delegations of Indian students from government schools. The Columbia Exposition actually marked a change in the public perception of Indians, from a frontier threat to a nostalgic reminder of the American past as portrayed in the exhibits and the Buffalo Bill Wild West show.[46] This in fact would be one of the influences that undercut the policy of assimilation, as the need to eradicate native culture based upon the belief that Indians were a threat diminished.

All but two of the fair's buildings were destroyed in a great fire on July 5, 1894, during the strike against the nearby Pullman Co. The Columbian Exposition was followed by a profound recession in the nation's economy that lasted until 1897.[47] There were many causes for the downturn in the economy. Railroad overexpansion suddenly ceased and entered a period of contraction. The national trade balance had abruptly changed to an excess of imports. Agriculture accounted for a decreasing share of the national wealth and was experiencing a decline in agriculture prices and thus decreasing purchase power. Foreign investments were being withdrawn because of European banking problems. And the public lost confidence in American banks and the U.S. Treasury's gold standard. By the end of 1893, banks and businesses were closing. Massive unemployment generated significant labor unrest throughout the country. Chicago was hit harder because so many workers who had jobs during the fair were suddenly unemployed. By January 1894, unemployment in Chicago reached 30 percent, and in some industries, over 50 percent.

## Ordinary People Living and Working in Chicago

Because the Lake Michigan shore line has been extended into the lake by landfill, and swampland and wetlands have been either filled or drained, all according to the Burnham plan, Chicago is larger today in area than it was in 1900. In 1900, everything was more concentrated; 90 percent of the total population (1,698,575 people) lived in the central area of the city compared with less than 45 percent today.[48] Even though residential buildings were smaller, more people were packed into the space, an average of twenty-five for each 25x125-foot city lot. Thus, it was common for people to walk.

Although many people walked to work, school, and to appointments with their doctors, public transportation was available at five cents per ride. For many workers, however, sixty cents a week for transportation was a substantial percentage of their wages. There was a 500-mile network of streetcars, and downtown Chicago was served by the El, the elevated railroad, still operating today. The streetcar started with individual cars pulled by horses, converted in 1882 to a cable system, and although electric cars were introduced in 1890, many lines still used horses or cables until 1906. The El was available to the South Side in 1892, the West Side in 1895, and the North Side in 1900. Many of the bus routes in Chicago today follow the same paths as the original streetcars. Rail service to the suburbs (as far as Evanston and Hyde Park) was operating by 1903.

People and goods moving in and out of Chicago in 1900 preferred to travel by rail or water. In 1903, seven million passengers passed through Chicago railroad terminals, together with freight accounting for about 1,000 trains per day, and in 1900, 16,976 ships arrived and departed.[49] The roads to the country were used mainly by farm wagons, with some buggy and bicycle traffic for business or pleasure. The Schwinn Bicycle Company was established in 1896, and by 1900, Chicago was the center of bicycle manufacturing.[50] A bicycle could be purchased from the Sears catalog for $12 to $15. Bicyclists were instrumental in pressuring the city to use smooth paving on its streets, preparing the way for the automobile. After 1905, the bicycle faded from the streets of Chicago.

City traffic in 1900 consisted of many bicycles and pushcarts, about 50,000 horse-drawn vehicles, and only 377 registered automobiles.[51] In 1908, horse traffic was still predominant, with 36,778 one-horse vehicles and 16,900 multihorse vehicles. This amounted to one vehicle for every thirty people, compared with one for every two people today. Streets were free of parked vehicles (horses were allowed to stop at the side for only a short time). Outlying streets were usually empty. Downtown, the streets were jammed—top vehicle speed was less than ten miles per hour. Even the fastest vehicles (the few cars and the electric street cars) moved no more than twenty miles per hour, a speed that was considered reckless, and therefore, rarely seen. Occasionally, traffic would be halted for long periods of time in The Loop at bridges or railroad crossings. There were no stoplights, appearing first in 1914 in Cleveland, Ohio, or lane makers, only an occasional policeman. The busiest streets were those with streetcars; the drivers of horse-drawn wagons would take advantage of the steel rails, which provided a faster, smoother ride. Taxis were used mainly for transportation to and from railroad stations. Downtown was busy during working hours; the streets were usually clogged with a mixture of people, horse-drawn wagons, and streetcars. The streets were noisy, and it was dangerous. Countless tragedies occurred as lives were lost to runaway horses, falling freight from wagons, vehicles (trains, trolleys, and cable cars) moving through unregulated traffic and pedestrians; over 400 hundred people a year were killed on the streets of Chicago.[52]

About 43 percent of Chicago's streets had some sort of paving in 1900. Paving included wood blocks, crushed stone, bricks, and stones. Only 3.5 percent of the streets were covered with asphalt because it was poor footing for horses. The wear of traffic caused rapid deterioration of the paving, and even the paved streets were rough and dusty. In bad weather, the unpaved streets could be impassable. Street lighting was prevalent, employing a variety of methods (gas, gasoline, and electric powered lamps). But the streets beyond downtown were usually very empty after dark. Most of the streets were lined with sidewalks, made mainly of wood. The sidewalks often covered spaces used for coal storage and even toilets.

The cost of living in 1900 Chicago was approximately 5 percent of the cost in 2000.[53] Prices reflected this difference; meat cost ten to fourteen cents per pound, a loaf of bread was five cents, and milk cost six cents a quart. The average rent paid in tenements was $8 to $10 per month with heat provided by a coal stove; each bath cost twenty-five cents. The mayor and the Health Department were pushing for more free public baths. A single man could live in a hotel for twenty-five to fifty cents per night. A house in a good neighborhood could be rented for $25 to $60 per month. A first class letter could be mailed for 2 cents, and an umbrella cost $1.25 (an umbrella can be purchased today on the first floor of the Marshall Field store for $20 to $30).

One thing that hasn't changed is the climate. Winters are cold, with occasional heavy snowfalls, and there is a reason Chicago is known as the "windy city." The prairie winds are enhanced by being forced through channels created by the straight streets lined with tall buildings. Summers develop a heat embalmed with a humidity that is so thick it feels like it could be sliced like a loaf of bread, a humidity that spawns thunderstorms. The weather changes rapidly with shifting clouds that mix storms with days of bright sunshine and fresh clarity. As far as the weather goes, Chicago is a city of superlatives. It can be the hottest, or the coldest, the wettest, or the driest. Like the weather, Chicago was a city of contrasts: millionaires in mansions and poor people living in slums, parks with careful landscaping and streets with horse manure, the temperance center of the world and one saloon for every 200 people.[54]

Men have always liked old-fashioned saloons, enjoying the camaraderie of other men. In the neighborhoods that surrounded downtown, the saloon was a place to go for gossip, political discussions, making phone calls, and seeking employment; the saloon could also be used as a post office.[55] The saloons often hosted weddings, dances, and meetings for ethnic groups and labor organizations.[56] The saloonkeeper, usually one of their own in the ethnic saloons, served his customers by providing these services in return for 5-cent-drafts of beer and 10-cent-shots of whiskey. This was an easy business for an immigrant to start, usually funded by the supplying brewer. The role of the saloon in the neighborhoods was so important that saloonkeepers became involved with the political parties, and many were aldermen sitting on the City Council. The free lunch in saloons started in Chicago in the early 1870s.[57] This practice was attacked by restauranteurs, the Health Department, and by businesses and industries that were rightfully concerned regarding their workers' efficiency after a barroom lunch. In 1917, the City Council of Chicago prohibited free lunches in saloons.

In the early 1900s, Chicago was a thriving city and a concentration of medical science and knowledge. It was very much a new American town, a place for new developments and a minimum of traditions—a good place for someone different, like an Indian doctor. It was a rowdy town, characterized by a recognition that "anything goes."[58] This reached its apex in the gangsterism during the prohibition era of the 1920s. The near South Side of Chicago, between South State Street and the river, in 1900 contained what was known as the "segregated district," or the Levee. This was an area in which brothels and gambling houses were permitted, receiving only occasional perfunctory police raids. Government officials tolerated prostitution and gambling until social pressure after 1910 produced official closure of the segregated district.

The transformation of Chicago from a pioneer village in 1831 to a vibrant industrial and commercial city in the late 1800s, especially after the Civil War, brought the usual problems associated with long hours of work, crowded living in unsanitary conditions, and a growing poor segment of the population. Although child labor had declined, dirty sweatshops (workplaces in which workers work excessive hours for low wages under unsafe or unhealthy conditions) were increasing in the 1890s.[59] Workers had little choice but to live in tenements with few windows and bathrooms. The wonders of the Columbian Exposition in 1893 were in stark contrast to living conditions in the city. It wasn't until 1907 that effective action at the state level was taken to regulate living and working conditions. The downtown shopping, business, and entertainment center of Chicago was surrounded by a ring of factories and housing for workers, many being newly arrived immigrants. Further out, there was a semicircle of suburbs, extending from Lake Forest in the north to Hyde Park in the south. Movement to the suburbs was not exclusively a middle-class phenomenon; well-paid workers were also moving beyond the belt of industry that surrounded downtown Chicago.

In 1900, the manufacturing industry employed 210,687 men, 44,961 women, and 6,973 children (fifteen years and younger).[60] The average worker in 1900 Chicago worked sixty hours per week, and often more.[61] A typical family of five required about $600 per year to meet their basic needs. A lower-class working man could rarely earn enough money to support a family, and therefore all family members, including the children, usually had jobs, many peddling goods from a pushcart. Around 1900, Chicago was filled with thousands of street peddlers. Immigrant men often got their start in America (a curbside education) with carts and boxes filled with produce and goods. Italians and Greeks dominated the fresh produce trade; Germans were mobile fixers and repairers; Jews concentrated on recycling clothing and junk.[62] The mobile vendor was useful and convenient for housewives who needed to shop every day, until cheap refrigerators and automobiles became available. The immigrant peddler was a city neighborhood institution into the early 1900s when the outward movement of people into suburban areas produced an unwelcome environment for the peddler. In 1913, Maxwell Street was designated an official peddlers' market, and the street peddlers became sidewalk vendors at this marketplace for the poor until 1994.

Factory workers and construction laborers earned sixteen to twenty-five cents per hour (about $570 per year). An individual with a trade, such as a bricklayer, earned fifty cents per hour (about $1,200 per year). Firefighters earned $840 per year; female secretaries about $900. Chicago city schoolteachers earned $500 to $800 per year. The middle class, less than half the population, consisted mainly of professional people (including physicians), owners of small businesses, and higher paid clerical personnel; a comfortable middle-class income was about $1,200 to $3,000 per year. For many Chicagoans, the show windows in the stores along State Street were only a place for entertainment, dreams, and longings.

In the first years of his private practice, Montezuma encountered the workers of the city, many of whom were immigrants. In 1900, 98 percent of Chicago's population were White; 34.5 percent were foreign-born; and 77 percent were either born abroad or had at least one foreign-born parent.[63] Most came from Northern European countries, especially Germany, Ireland, England, and Scotland. Southern and Eastern European immigrants did not begin to come in large numbers until 1900. Only 24 percent of families owned their own homes. Social activities for these working families were centered within their own ethnic groups, with dances, picnics, street festivals, and meetings at local clubs and organizations. Clerks and stenographers working in the downtown area lived in boardinghouses and flats (apartments of several rooms confined to one floor), and traveled by streetcars to popular dance halls on weekend nights. Baseball became very popular in the 1890s; the West Side stadium used by the White Stockings was easily reached by public transportation, and workers from all over the city came to watch the games at twenty-five cents a seat. Finley Peter Dunne covered the White Stockings for the *Daily News*, and coined the term "southpaw" for left-handed pitchers because the pitched ball from left-handers came to the plate from the South Side of Chicago.[64]

LIKE THE INDIANS at this time in history, these ethnic groups were subjected to considerable pressure to undergo a thorough assimilation into American society. Although the immigrant was often presented to Indians as an example of successful assimilation, in fact ethnic groups in their new American city environments held on to their customs and culture as an important way to maintain their identities and their values.[65] It was, and still is with immigrants today, the method by which some security, meaning, and pleasure could be found in a hard and often hostile life in which discrimination was commonly encountered. The food, music, and traditions of the Macedonian people were an important part of my immigrant family's life in Ohio, and these ethnic customs are still part of our lives today. There is a fundamental similarity in the experiences of immigrants and the history of the Indians during the time period when the dominant forces in American society had little tolerance for multiple cultures. Indeed, Richard Pratt wrote to Montezuma in 1906: "I want to especially congratulate you on your article in December's 'Tomorrow,' which I have just read. It is clean, clear-cut, logical and timely. I do not entirely agree that the holding on to German and French songs by those who come to us from those nations does not interfere with their becoming thorough Americans. I think all the facts would indicate that they have not entirely 'burned the bridges behind them' and become really, truly, thoroughly and permanently Americans—that the keeping up of their national songs has some material influence in pulling them back to their old homes, and that, should there be a reasonable excuse, they would pull away from America back to the Father-land."[66]

Although the Protestant ethos at the turn of the twentieth century recognized the cosmopolitan origin of American people, it was committed to a single idea. The dominant society of America at that time was unified in a belief in the American way: democracy, capitalism, brotherhood, and freedom. It was acceptable for an individual to be different, but everyone would eventually experience assimilation into the American way of life. Until the recent decades after 1900, the diversity among immigrants and Indians was expected to be temporary. The goal of assimilation was a homogenous culture of like-minded individuals, with no place for independent and different *groups*. Cultural pluralism did not begin to emerge in America until after 1920, too late to influence Montezuma's life and thinking.

IMMIGRANTS HAD MEAGER POSSESSIONS, rented their living space, and had few clothes. A willingness to work was their major asset. Montezuma's first downtown office was at 100 State Street, and only five blocks away a Department of Health report three years before Montezuma opened his office described a damp, dark cellar room with thirty-one bunks in 4x7-foot wooden cubicles, another cellar room with fifty double bunks, no ventilation, and an inoperative toilet.[67] The large number of immigrants created a housing shortage; single-family houses were packed, one family to a room.[68] In the 1890s, landlords moved the wooden houses to the back of the lot and built new brick tenements, five-stories high, containing as many as six flats, housing up to 150 people, especially in the West side ethnic neighborhoods.[69] As expected, the most crowded areas had the highest mortality rates from infectious diseases; typhoid fever continued to be a problem. The mortality rate with labor and delivery of pregnancy was exceedingly high, and the highest mortality rates were in children under the age of five. The crowded living conditions, poor plumbing, poor garbage removal, and inadequate sewage systems created optimal conditions for epidemics of infectious diseases. The neighborhood next to the Union Stock Yards had the highest tuberculosis rate in the city.[70]

The Union Stock Yards thrived after the Great Fire, to a significant degree reflecting the development of the refrigerated railroad car that permitted the processing of beef in Chicago with subsequent delivery to the rest of America and the world. By 1893, nearly 20 percent of Chicago's population depended on the meat industry for employment.[71] Prior to 1900, the stockyard labor force was primarily composed of Irish and German immigrants, after 1900 the immigrants were largely Slavic. On the South Side of Chicago, the odors from the slaughtering and packing establishments in the Union Stock Yards were prevalent, injuries were frequent, an average of twenty-three accidents per day in the Armour plant,[72] and exposure to infected meat was common.

The Union Stock Yards, the site of about 100 individual companies, were four miles from the center of the city, extending from Thirty-ninth Street south to Forty-seventh Street and west from Halsted Street to Ashland Avenue. The Stock Yards were connected to the Illinois & Michigan Canal by a channel, the South Fork, the famous "Bubbly Creek" in Upton Sinclair's *The Jungle*, with visible gas rising from decaying packinghouse refuse. The area was surrounded by wooden two-story houses, stores, and saloons—criss-crossed with train tracks—an area of ethnic neighborhoods with 40,000 people (over 57,000 by 1920) known as Packingtown. There were over 500 saloons, twenty-three per block along Ashland Avenue where the workers came for lunch. The saloons came to be very important for communication across ethnic lines and for labor organization.

The Stock Yards area could be found by the smell, an olfactory bouillabaisse of butchered meat, blood, animal dung and urine. Tourists, as many as 10,000 per day during the Columbian Exposition, came through an imposing stone entrance, one of the first commissions for Burnham and Root.[73] In the yards, thousands of sheep, cattle, and hogs in constant movement produced a cacophony of squeals, grunts, and bellows—virtually every animal had arrived the night before by train. The collection, selling, and butchering would empty the pens by the end of the day.

In 1893, approximately 25,000 men, boys, and girls, and some women processed about fourteen million animals, generating about $200 million, with a generous portion going to the two giants of the industry, Philip Danforth Armour and Gustavus Swift.[74] The Armour and Company butchered hogs in a building that covered 140 acres along with a forty-acre cold-storage area.[75] The packing industry pioneered the methods of mass production and the assembly line. A hog entered the process by having a hind leg chained to a large, turning wheel. The wheel carried the hogs upside down to an overhead railway. After first being killed by having its throat cut, it continued down the track pulled by gravity, its blood to be used in fertilizer collected in a trough. The hog was then dipped into a vat of boiling water to soften and loosen its bristles. Removed from the vat, the hog was pulled by a ring through its nose for a ten-second ride through a scraping machine. Hitched again to an overhead rail, the hog descended to a gang of six cutters who worked rapidly, each with a specific task. Cleaned and halved, the carcasses were then hung for twenty-four hours in an enormous chilling room cooled by rail-shipped ice. The whole operation took ten minutes—ten minutes of loud noises, blood, and gore. After being chilled, each carcass was butchered with cleavers, a task that took thirty-five seconds per hog. The cuts were then sent to be pickled, salted, or smoked, placed in boxes and barrels, and loaded on to trains. The pace was deliberately fast, directed by hard-driving foremen shouting orders in a half dozen languages. The work was hard and dangerous, but there was no shortage of job-seeking immigrants, many of whom were hired on sight each day from the hundreds waiting at the gates desperate for employment.

The beef house was quieter. The cattle moved without protesting into narrow chutes and were bludgeoned with sledgehammers. The side of the pen was raised, a chain attached to one of the hind legs, and as in the hog house, the animal was lifted by a hoist and sent down the line. First the animal was bled to death, then decapitated. Immigrant workers labored constantly to push the blood into drainage holes, but the men always worked on a floor covered with muddy blood, hard work that was even harder in the winter. An assembly line of men moved among the carcasses, each with a specialized task, scraping, gutting, cleaning, and cutting about eighty cattle per hour. The beef was sent directly to refrigerator cars (at first, specially designed, enclosed cars with strategically placed spaces at both ends of the cars filled with ice and brine), an invention by an engineer commissioned by Gustavus Swift that eliminated the need to transport live cattle beyond the packing plants. Because of the refrigerator car, the processing of beef surpassed pork packing in 1889 as Chicago's largest industry, and Swift owned the largest beef-packing plant in the Union Stock Yards. The Union Stock Yards attracted allied industries. The residue from the packers was transformed into glue (horns, hoofs, and sinew), oleomargarine (fat), sausage casings (intestine), pork and beans (utilizing previously unusable meat), fertilizer, hairbrushes, and buttons. The intention was to waste nothing. Besides increasing profits, this effort reduced the amount of pollution that had previously been dumped into the Chicago River.

The work was irregular, determined by the size and timing of animal shipments, and the pay was low. The availability of unskilled immigrants and later Black migrants allowed the packers to keep labor costs at the lowest possible level. Common laborers earned from fifteen to eighteen cents per hour.[76] The women managed the family household, supplementing the meager income by providing room and board for about $10 per month for two to three boarders, family and boarders all usually squeezed into four rooms. Weddings, funerals, and doctor's bills were major expenses to be met only by significant sacrifice. The campaign to reform working conditions and product quality in the packing industry was unsuccessful until it gained national prominence, significantly aided by President Theodore Roosevelt when he read *The Jungle* by Upton Sinclair in 1906.[77] The Union Stock Yards closed in 1971, after the meat packing business moved farther west. Today, the meatpacking industry located in the rural parts of the West, especially Texas and Nebraska, is still a dangerous occupation for its workers, and it continues to employ new immigrants, provide very low pay, and avoid union organization.[78]

The first steel rail made in America was produced in Chicago on May 24, 1865.[79] But it wasn't until the 1880s that a period of record railroad building fueled the growth of Chicago's steel mills, near the town of Pullman, on the Calumet River. By 1901, the plants of the United States Steel Corporation covered the lakefront from the Calumet River to the Indiana border (Marshall Field was a major stockholder). The ore came by boat from the Lake Superior region in the north; Appalachian coal came by train to Ohio's Lake Erie ports, then by boat to South Chicago. The workers also arrived by boat or train, mainly Slavic immigrants from Eastern Europe. By 1930, the Lake Calumet harbor had replaced the mouth of the Chicago River as Chicago's port.

### The Capitalist and the Worker

The early development of Chicago can be attributed to an impressive collection of retail and manufacturing entrepreneurs. Eventually their companies became targets of the labor union movement, and Chicago became a center of class conflict. The Socialist Labor Party, the original organization, the Workingmen's Party formed in 1874 was renamed in 1877, was an important political force in Chicago in the late 1800s, influenced by anarchist ideas, and dominated by German workers. Working conditions in the various industries provided the motivation for the workers; the owners, like George Pullman, were just as dedicated to blocking the organizing of their workers. In the late 1880s, anarchists were agitating for confrontational acts that would terrify the capitalist owners. The extreme rhetoric did indeed create fear among the capitalists. In 1886, the Socialist Labor Party focused on the campaign for an eight-hour day. Picnics, marches, a strike, and talk of bombing culminated in the Haymarket Affair.[80]

In the first week of May in 1886, a series of events led to a turning point for anarchism, a movement dedicated to complete freedom, requiring the abolition of laws, government, and class structure. On May 3, a battle between union and nonunion workers as well as the police took place at the McCormick Reaper Works after a strike for an eight-hour day began on May 1. On the night of May 4, about 2,500 workers gathered in a rally called by anarchist leaders in Haymarket Square, near Randolph and Des Plaines. Police entered Haymarket Square at the end of the meeting when only a few hundred workers were left. A bomb was thrown and shooting broke out, leaving seven policemen dead and sixty-seven injured. Eight anarchists, leaders of the movement, were arrested, tried a month later for causing the deaths by their political activity, and seven were sentenced to death by hanging, one to life imprisonment. The state supreme court upheld the decision. One prisoner defiantly committed suicide the day before the scheduled hanging igniting a dynamite cartridge in his mouth. Two requested clemency and were granted life imprisonment. On November 11, 1887, four of the leaders (Albert Parsons, August Spies, George Engel, and Adolph Fischer—all German immigrants but Parsons who was from Alabama and all former members of the Socialist Labor Party) were hanged in front of nearly 200 witnesses. In 1893, the Governor of Illinois, John Peter Altgeld, pardoned the three men in prison, and denounced the unfair trial, a move that brought considerable criticism and abuse from the newspapers and the business world. The person who threw the bomb was never caught. The Haymarket Affair was a temporary setback for the labor movement, and it was the beginning of a new attitude towards anarchists. Henceforth, anarchists would be viewed by city, state, and federal governments, business and labor organizations, and civic and religious groups as bomb-throwing radicals that must be opposed and suppressed. For the next thirty years, anarchists often had their rights to free speech trampled. Carlos Montezuma, a product of American Protestant assimilation, would have been vigorously opposed to anarchism; he truly believed in the "civilized" social order that surrounded him. Montezuma's fight for Indian rights was always within the context of organized society, not against the basic structure itself.

George Mortimer Pullman built the town of Pullman, to house 12,600 of his employees.[81] His company produced the luxurious sleeping cars that were leased and staffed by Pullman to railroads. The railroads collected extra fees for their use, fees that went directly to the Pullman Co. By 1900, Pullman's Palace Cars had no rivals, and the line expanded to include a dining car, an observation car, and a parlor car. The company also manufactured freight cars, regular passenger cars, and streetcars, along with the steel that was used for the cars. The site Pullman chose for his manufacturing plant and his town was marshland on the northern shore of Lake Calumet (now near the Indiana border at 111th Street).

Pullman, Illinois, was built to be a 100 percent company town (everything was owned by Pullman), controlled for profit (even the church was for rent) and for supervision and manipulation of the Pullman Company workers. Completed in 1884, the town of all-brick buildings and houses, like the Pullman Company, was self-sufficient The town had its own sewage system, newspapers, stores, and even the pastor of the church was a company man. Saloons, political activity, and labor organizations were forbidden. On the surface, the town and company were models of success, but the paternalistic feudalism of George Pullman stirred individual resentment, often expressed in the saloons of neighboring Roseland and Kensington.

Thousands of tourists visiting the Columbian Exposition took a side trip to marvel at this model city. A year later, 1894, the workers of the Pullman Company went on strike, not only against their working conditions and the loss of wages that was a consequence of the 1893 depression, but also against the tyranny of the company town. When business decreased, Pullman reduced wages by as much as 30 percent, but he did not reduce rents or utility rates in the town. Supported by the American Railway Union, headed by Eugene Debs, the strike spread and eventually tied up the railroads of the entire nation.[82] Violence prompted federal intervention; conflicts between federal troops and workers and a federal injunction ended the strike. A federal commission investigating the strike called for an end to Pullman's paternalism and prompted the State of Illinois to file suit to force the Pullman Company to divest itself of the town. Pullman died in 1897, and one year later, the State of Illinois won its court battle. The town of Pullman became an ordinary industrial town and was annexed by the City of Chicago. Pullman became a state landmark in 1969 and a national and Chicago landmark in 1971–1972.

Montezuma's Chicago was a battleground between capitalist owners and ethnic workers. The Pullman strike led to the formation of the Socialist Party of America. Daniel De Leon, a native of Curacao, a Dutch-owned island off the coast of Venezuela, and a law professor at Columbia University in New York until he devoted himself to politics, emerged as the leader of the Socialist Labor Party in the 1890s, advocating strict Marxism and militant organization of workers. In Chicago, the Socialist Labor Party was dominated by German immigrants in the 1870s, but later was prominent in labor agitation with Slavic workers. By the 1920s, the labor movement had achieved a substantial improvement in working conditions.

## Jane Addams and Hull-House

Jane Addams arrived in Chicago in 1889 at the age of twenty-nine and opened a settlement house in a poor immigrant neighborhood one mile west of State Street.[83] Her motivation can be traced to time spent in Toynbee Hall, the world's first settlement house, in the slums of London. Addams established a house for young women, renting for $60 per month a dilapidated but solid brick mansion built in 1856 and belonging to Charles J. Hull, at 800 S. Halsted Street on the corner of Halsted and Polk. The volunteer workers in the settlement houses lived with the residents, and Hull-House, furnished like a comfortable middle-class home, became a living example and center of instruction for young immigrant women. Some of the teachers were John Dewey, Susan B. Anthony, Clarence Darrow, and Frank Lloyd Wright. The reform-minded women who lived in Hull-House found a support system that substituted for a family, an alternative to a traditional marriage, and links to other reformers and their organizations.[84] The charismatic Jane Addams received the Nobel Peace Prize in 1931 for her pacifistic activities before and after World War I. Addams died in Chicago on May 21, 1935.

Upper middle-class educated men and women began the settlement house movement to help working people with the problems generated by industrialization and immigration into cities. In many settlement houses, the philosophy was identical to the assimilationist movement directed to Indians: forced acculturation with eventual dissolution of ethnic neighborhoods and groups.[85] Later, the supporters of this thinking turned to restriction of immigration as a policy. Jane Addams and her famous settlement house in Chicago, Hull-House, was supported by the wealthy people of Chicago and widely respected and admired. Although not immediately, eventually Hull-House was regarded as a place where new immigrants were "understood," and their cultures respected and nourished. Like other settlement houses that focused on immigrants, the Protestant women of Hull-House had to be secular, recognizing that immigrants strongly resisted changing religions. The Hull-House reformers were also political activists, and they joined forces with other organizations to bring about legislation, such as the 1893 Illinois anti-sweatshop legislation that established an eight-hour day for women and children working in industry, and in 1903, a strong child labor and compulsory education law.[86]

Settlement houses were often affiliated with universities, serving as sites for socioeconomic studies and investigation. The University of Chicago supported a settlement house in the stockyard district and Northwestern University had one on the North side. Hull-House did not have a formal affiliation, but worked closely with the academic staff at the University of Chicago, especially the Department of Sociology. The interaction between the settlement houses and the university professors, it is argued, influenced each other in the development of new social philosophies and policies.[87] Sociologists have debated the exact role the settlement houses played in the emerging pluralism, but surely Hull-House represented a beginning for an alternative response to forced assimilation and acculturation, specifically the support of ethnic and cultural diversity. Nevertheless, during the time Montezuma lived in Chicago, the settlement house movement espoused Americanization through assimilation, and did not encourage ethnic groups to maintain their cultural pride.[88] It wasn't until after Montezuma was gone, after 1930, that a new regard for diverse cultures challenged the philosophy of assimilation that dominated American life during the years of Montezuma's adult life. In the immigrant neighborhoods, ethnic community centers replaced the settlement houses.

Hull-House, a complex of over thirteen buildings, yielded in 1963 to the University of Illinois in Chicago, except for two of the original buildings which are operated by the University as the Jane Addams' Hull-House Museum. The Hull-House original mansion has been restored to its early look and is a national and Chicago Historic Landmark. Today, the Hull-House Association continues settlement house work in multiple sites in the city.

## CHICAGO IN THE EARLY 1920s

Until the twentieth century, the country's values, goals, and politics were derived from small groups of people: professional people, teachers, preachers, and artists (like the reformers promoting the assimilation of Indians) and most importantly, the economic giants (like the capitalists in Chicago) created by the wave of industrialism after the Civil War. By the 1920s, the size and vigor of large groups of workers at various socio-economic levels were influencing politics, economics, and, with the increasing availability of leisure time, even popular culture. These forces were setting into motion new ideals and attitudes regarding minorities, race, religion, and sexual behavior that continue to evolve today.

By the 1920s, Chicago was the goal for immigrants from Southern and Eastern Europe, African-Americans from the South, and middle-class, young, White people from rural areas and small towns in the American Midwest. These new workers liked to party, and the entertainment industry in Chicago thrived—movie theaters, dance halls, burlesque, vaudeville, museums, and of course, jazz, the folk music of the city. The Loop remained the center of activity. State Street was firmly established as the premier retail center for shopping. Many of the largest movie theaters and nightclubs were along Randolph Street between State and Clark. Cheaper department stores on State Street were south of Adams, and burlesque shows and dance halls were located south of Jackson on State Street. Cheaper theaters, dance halls, and clubs, along with cheap lodging houses, second-hand clothing stores, missions, and dingy restaurants, could be found west of the river on Madison Street, an area that attracted unaccompanied men. Many of the finest restaurants were near the intersection of Clark and Madison Streets.

The Eighteenth Amendment, the Volstead Act, became effective on midnight of January 16, 1920, prohibiting the importing, exporting, transporting, selling, and manufacturing of liquids containing more than 0.5 percent of alcohol. Prohibition was expected to reduce crime, poverty, and poor health. The law was flagrantly violated, and the supply of alcoholic drinks became the source of vast revenues for organized crime. The racketeers were especially prominent in Chicago, and their names became familiar to everyone: the O'Banions, the Gennas, Bugs Moran, and the most powerful of all, Al Capone.[89] The neighborhood saloons were closed at the beginning of Prohibition, but they were quickly replaced by illegal speak-easies (entry required speaking a code word through a slot in the door), hidden in basements and office buildings, admitting only those with membership cards, and remaining open by paying protection to police and city officials.[90] Doctors and druggists became frequent suppliers of high quality liquor, to be used, of course, for medical purposes. The social experiment was a failure, ending in 1933.

The United States entered World War I on April 12, 1917. With its large German population, Chicago was a center of anti-war protests and organizations, and this served to intensify anti-German emotions in the city. For several years patriotism and loyalty were major political issues. The war stopped the flood of European immigrants to Chicago, and the demand for unskilled labor, especially in the packing industry, produced a doubling of the Black population between 1915 and 1920. The packers also recruited Black workers as strikebreakers. The Black community was concentrated east of State Street, extending from Twenty-sixth Street to Forty-third Street, encompassing South Park Avenue and the site of Montezuma's home office, causing him to move in 1922.

Large-scale Black recruitment and migration to Chicago with its accompanying tension in the labor market culminated in the Chicago Race Riot of 1919.[91] The disturbance was ignited by the stoning and drowning of a young Black man who drifted while swimming in Lake Michigan at the Twenty-sixth Street beach on July 27 into an area reserved for Whites. The police refused to arrest the White man who threw the stone, and Black indignation erupted into violence between Whites and Blacks. It should be emphasized that the beach incident only provided an opportunity for an escalation of the violence that was actually already ongoing between Black strikebreakers and Irish workers.[92] The state militia entered the city on the fourth day of fighting and remained for nine more days. Even Blacks working at the Palmer House were beaten and killed. By the end of the riot, thirty-eight were dead, 537 injured, and 3,000 families were homeless (Blacks and Whites).

CARL FREDERICH BENZ and Gottlich Wilhem Daimler working separately and independently designed and built the first successful automobiles in 1885 and 1886, and horseless carriages became a familiar sight in Europe in the 1890s. In 1900, only 8,000 automobiles were registered in the United States.[93] Ransom E. Olds built the first popular car, the Oldsmobile, a two-seater with a one-cylinder, three-horsepower engine; 425 were sold for $650 each in 1901. Henry Ford founded his company in 1903, with the Model A selling for $850. The Model T Ford (the "tin lizzy") was introduced in 1908, with a four-cylinder, twenty-horsepower engine that could go thirty miles on a gallon of gasoline at a speed of thirty-five miles per hour. The world's first auto assembly line began production of the Model T in 1914, and by 1924 half the cars in the world were Fords. The Model T was selling for $290, and over fifteen million were sold until the last one was produced in 1927.

Montezuma, looking down on State Street from the large bay windows in his downtown office, first saw crowded streets with horse-drawn vehicles, then cable cars giving way to electric trolleys, and by 1920, he saw long lines of small automobiles that looked like marching black ants. Although the automobile began to appear on Chicago's streets in the 1890s (America's first automobile race covered 100 miles from Jackson Park to Waukegan, won at a speed of seven and one-half miles per hour), it wasn't until the first decade after the turn of the century that it became fashionable among the wealthy to own an automobile, and in the second decade the automobile became widely affordable.[94] The automobile was promoted as a solution to common problems in Chicago, factory and locomotive smoke in the air and horse manure on the streets, not to mention the daily problem of collecting the carcasses of the expired horses. The small, quick automobile was at first also seen as a solution to traffic, darting in, out, and around slower vehicles, especially streetcars confined to their tracks. By 1910, the streets were clogged with parked cars, and by 1920, traffic jams consisted of automobiles, now affordable by most working people, and trucks, cheaper to maintain than horses.

CARLOS MONTEZUMA LEFT CHICAGO in December 1922 after living continuously for twenty-six years on the near South Side. He saw the change from a city dominated by horses to a city filled with automobiles. He interacted with immigrants who were at first from Northern Europe and then Slavic and Mediterranean people. His own neighborhood became a community of Black migrants. Right before his eyes, American life changed from a Protestant-dominated monoculture into an emerging pluralistic society. Industrialization, the growth of science and technology, and increasing secularization all collaborated to bring about a shift from individualism to social concerns and public welfare. These changes in this dynamic period in American history are reflected in Montezuma's life as over time he became more and more concerned with his tribe and all Indians.

## CHAPTER EIGHT

# Montezuma in Private Practice:
# Do Not Fail Me, Doctor!

CARLOS MONTEZUMA WAS not a bleeder, a blisterer, or a purger. He practiced medicine during a pivotal time in medical history, when medicine became a profession, organized medicine became powerful, and individual physicians gained respect and authority. However, Montezuma never became wealthy.

## THE PRACTICE OF CARLOS MONTEZUMA, M.D.

Before 1900, the middle and upper classes were usually treated in their homes. Without appropriate connections, the young physician had to rely on an office practice, composed primarily of patients who could not afford house calls.[1] Physicians at the top of the social scale enjoyed prestige and wealth. These physicians were usually from prominent families to begin with and had completed their medical education in Europe. In addition, these physicians often held professorships in the better medical schools. The physician conducting an ordinary practice relied on his office patient volume and struggled to make the professional connections that would provide him entrée into the upper classes. It wasn't until the first decade after 1900, when Montezuma practiced in Chicago, that the accumulation of scientific knowledge and the improvements in communication and transport combined to make office practice more respectable and more lucrative.

In rural America, individuals were self-reliant and accustomed to dealing with illnesses. As society became more urban, individuals came to rely on the specialized skills of strangers, and the doctor was no exception. The growth of cities and the building of roads made doctors available and their services less expensive. Telephones had a major impact on medical care. Doctors could now be reached rapidly, and appointments made so that office hours became a practical method of practice, improving the chance of seeing a doctor for the patient and increasing the number of patients for the physician. The increasing availability of physicians coupled with a relatively large number in practice (medical schools continued to proliferate) produced a very competitive market. The average physician's annual income around 1900 was between $1,000 and $1,500; a federal employee averaged about $1,000.[2]

When Norman Walker reported on American medical education to his British audience in 1891 (Chapter 5), he also reported what he had observed about American physicians.[3] He described a typical day for a general practitioner with office hours from nine to eleven, two to four, and again in the evening from seven to nine. Between these hours, the doctor visited his patients in their own homes, driving his own buggy (implying that only Americans would drive without a groom). House calls, about four per day, and office visits were charged from $2 to $5. The charge for pregnancy and delivery was $25 for physicians with the highest reputations, $10 for most. Walker noted that the American general practitioner was willing to do almost any surgical procedure. Overall, the average American physician was not well founded in anatomy, physiology, and pathology, but he was a storehouse of remedies and treatments in an empiric approach to diseases, not wasting time in pondering over diagnosis.

When Montezuma started practice in 1896, medicine bore little resemblance to medicine today. But during the twenty-six years of his practice, a considerable change took place. In 1800, diagnosis depended on the observation and interpretation of a patient's symptoms. By 1910–1920, diagnostic tools were available to support the role of observation. The stethoscope, the ophthalmoscope, and the otoscope made carrying the doctor's black bag worthwhile. Laboratory technology was now available, including the microscope, x-ray machines, thermometers, blood pressure machines, chemical tests of blood and urine, and the electrocardiogram, providing results that could be perused in consultation with colleagues. Soon vaccines were available for diphtheria, tetanus, and typhoid. Progress in science and technology was providing a new stature for physicians, the holders of specialized knowledge. This had an impact on income as well; from 1900 to the mid 1920s, physician income increased about five-fold.[4]

In 1900, physicians still had to earn their stature by their interactions with patients; there was less of an institutionalized automatic recognition that comes with the M.D. degree as there is now. Authority comes easily to physicians. Patients struggling with an injury or illness, and especially if threatened with death, defer to the judgment of one with special knowledge that can or might help. The physician is unique in bringing a special personal relationship to the patient in the process of utilizing his or her store of knowledge. It is not just a pure administration of knowledge. The process requires individualization, applying the knowledge in a modified form based on the physician's experience and the physician's familiarity and understanding of the individual patient, a process called "medical judgment." In the past and even now, this relationship recognizes the authority of the physician. Although less paternalistic, the physician of today still functions in a position of respect and authority. And indeed, some degree of authority is necessary in that an injured or sick individual often is not fully capable of objective reasoning and decision-making. But one aspect of a physician's authority makes it less than total: the physician's judgment is not an order; it can be, and often is, ignored. A physician's advice is not a command, although it is often something that would be unsafe to disregard. The strongest force behind a physician's authority is the consequence if the physician is ignored.

Physicians had become less isolated by 1900. Hospitals became indispensable. Anesthesia and antisepsis made it no longer dangerous to go to a hospital; indeed, white and starched uniforms became a hallmark of the new cleanliness. The licensing system for physicians was significantly strengthened when a license became a requisite for hospital privileges. The emergence of hospitals and specialization encouraged good will among physicians to enable access to patients and facilities. Montezuma always maintained his office practice near his medical school and the hospital of his training, Mercy Hospital. Undoubtedly, he favored the use of Mercy Hospital for his patients throughout his years of practice.

Physician organizations became more effective. The membership and influence of local and state societies rapidly increased. Professional societies provided prestige and contributed to the regulation of economic competition (soliciting referrals, gaining appointments to hospitals and medical schools). Educational activity by a practicing physician also produced community prestige and contacts for referrals. Thus practicing physicians had multiple motives to be associated with a medical school. Montezuma was a lecturer in the Postgraduate Medical College, a school that no longer exists, and was on the faculty of the College of Physicians and Surgeons, affiliated with the University of Illinois, supervising medical students in the medical clinic on Tuesday and Friday mornings from eleven to noon.[5] He was also on the faculty at the Chicago Hospital College of Medicine (this school merged with Jenner Medical School in 1912 to form the Chicago Medical School that later affiliated with the Mount Sinai Hospital).[6] He presented practical lectures on his specialty, gastrointestinal disorders. For example, on one occasion he demonstrated his method for the analysis of stomach contents after removal by aspiration.[7]

In 1900, Chicago had over 1,200 physicians and sixty-two hospitals.[8] Tuberculosis and respiratory infections were the leading causes of death. The city's Department of Health was very active, inspecting buildings, milk and food products, checking the water supply, and promoting vaccinations and public health measures, such as an anti-spitting campaign. In the early 1900s, patent medicines fell into disfavor. Physicians were now organized and could act through the American Medical Association to campaign against nostrums. The *Journal of the American Medical Association* stopped printing advertisements for patent medicines in 1905. In addition, the pharmaceutical industry recognized that the public was increasingly relying on physicians for their drugs. These efforts were helped tremendously by muckraking journalists who delighted in exposing useless medicines as well as quack physicians. In 1906, Congress passed the Pure Food and Drug Act, the beginning of federal drug regulations. However, therapeutic agents were still few in number.

The scientific accomplishments of Pasteur and Koch had an enormous impact on medical practice. An understanding of the basis for infectious diseases led to effective public health measures and antiseptic surgery. Improvements in water purification reduced typhoid outbreaks, and milk processing decreased infant mortality. But it would not be until after 1935 that sulfa drugs, the first anti-bacterial drugs, became available. The office physician continued to be mainly a diagnostician. Nevertheless, by 1900, the development of bacteriology surely made Montezuma conscious of the need to maintain cleanliness in his interactions with patients.

Montezuma knew how to use a microscope. He knew about Robert Koch and the tuberculous bacillus.[9] He knew that germs caused infections and he knew the principles of antisepsis (the use of agents to kill germs) and asepsis (the use of techniques to avoid contamination and contagion). The subject was just beginning to be taught at Chicago Medical College when he graduated. Following graduation, it is unlikely that he was exposed to the new ideas during his years working for the Indian Bureau, prior to entering private practice. In the 1890s, however, the new science was prominently being featured in journals and at medical society meetings. By 1900, Chicago was a center of medical education. Montezuma must have been influenced by this exposure. In his notes for a talk (perhaps to medical students) without a date, entitled, "The Adulteration of Certain Commodities Ordinarily Used As Food," he described problems with milk: "The adulteration of milk is so easy a matter that a physician should always be careful in prescribing cow's milk as an alternative for mother's milk. ...The sanitary records of this country, England, France and

Germany afford numerous histories of epidemics of the acute infectious diseases, such as typhoid and scarlet fever, diphtheria, dysentery, cholera and other dreadful scourges, by the addition of contaminated water to milk. Instances are cited in which the virus of these diseases was conveyed in milk simply by washing the utensils with water taken from wells located near privies. Facts are gathered from the Lancet and Medical times and Gazette."[10] Montezuma was obviously reading current medical journals, and his notes indicate that he used a microscope as he talks of the microscopic examination of milk to identify "pus cells."

THE CHICAGO MEDICAL SOCIETY was formed in 1850, and by 1890 had 560 members, and nearly 1,000 by 1900.[11] By the 1890s, the programs contained subjects from many specialties, and bacteriology was being featured. The Society provided other benefits as well. Montezuma's membership form noted that in return for the annual dues of $5 he received protection against malpractice suits and blackmail, membership in the Illinois State Medical Society, and a subscription to the *Illinois Medical Journal*.[12] In addition, he was automatically a member of the American Medical Association.[13]

In the early 1900s, specialty societies began to emerge producing many branches affiliated with the original Society, and each held their own educational meetings. Most specialists belonged to a branch society as well as a specialty organization. In Chicago, medical writings could be studied in the medical department of the Newberry Library in the 1890s, and in 1906, The John Crerar Library was established with $2 million obtained from the will of a wealthy railway magnate. Physicians also had their own social organizations, the most prominent being the Physicians' Club of Chicago.

The practice of bloodletting had disappeared in Chicago by 1885.[14] Modern medicine began with the burst of bacteriologic discoveries that by 1900 identified the organisms that caused tuberculosis, pneumonia, cholera, bubonic plague, typhoid fever, diphtheria, and others. Many Chicagoans (for example, Edmund Andrews and Frank Billings at Chicago Medical College) had visited Europe and returned to teach the germ theory to their colleagues. Cleanliness and pure water were long advocated by physicians and government officials, but the acceptance of the germ theory of disease provided an understandable rationale that gave public health measures meaning and support. Cholera last appeared in Chicago in 1873, and by the turn of the century, public efforts were responsible for declining mortality rates from infectious diseases. Antiseptic techniques had become routine in hospitals by 1880, and presumably, in physician offices. Asepsis (basically clean hands and clothing), as well as rubber gloves, was a routine procedure in the 1890s. Montezuma was aware of the new developments in bacteriology by the time of his graduation, having been exposed to the teachings of Henry Gradle and Bayard Holmes, Chicago Medical College faculty who were two of the first Chicago physicians to accept and promote the new discoveries. Most assuredly, by the time he entered private practice in 1896, Montezuma was familiar with the causes and prevention of infectious diseases because of the rapid acceptance of this new science. And he also knew that despite improvements, infections were still the leading causes of death.

Bacteriology was fervently opposed by homeopaths, a group of practitioners that reached peak numbers in Chicago around 1900. Homeopathy was founded by S. C. F. Hahnemann of Philadelphia in 1796. Homeopaths believed that if a large dose of a drug produced symptoms similar to a disease, then small doses would cure that disease. Homeopaths were not interested in the causes of diseases, but rather emphasized the cures to be found in the administration of small doses of drugs. The public appeal of this approach when contrasted to the heroic, drastic measures (bleeding, blistering, and purging) employed by regular physicians until 1900 is readily apparent. Because the new science of bacteriology identified the microbes causing diseases but had yet to offer specific, pharmaceutical cures, it is understandable that the homeopaths found this new emphasis hard to accept. Surely Montezuma had to contend with homeopathy, because by 1905, Chicago was a national center for this practice of medicine. Homeopaths and other irregular practitioners held staff positions in hospitals, until disappearing after 1910.

WHEN MONTEZUMA BEGAN HIS PRIVATE PRACTICE, his challenge was to attract patients in a competitive environment (including physicians of all kinds with tremendous variations in training and education, patent medicines, and even then, lay practitioners) by using his knowledge and personality. This competition was a powerful force in causing physicians to use methods and treatments that would yield obvious short-term effects, easily recognized by the patients. Montezuma had his special salve. Patients who moved away from Chicago wrote to Montezuma and requested that he send his special salve. He mailed it to his relatives at Fort McDowell.

Montezuma's salve was a mixture of Vaseline (Vaseline is a purified petroleum jelly, developed by Robert Chesebrough when he was a chemist in Brooklyn in 1870) and menthol, a preparation that became familiar in later years, as Vicks VapoRub. Montezuma described the various ways he prepared menthol to treat about any medical condition he encountered in a lecture on October 22, 1895, that he presented to the Cumberland County Medical Society at an afternoon meeting in the Courthouse located in the center of Carlisle, just a year before he moved to Chicago.[15] The meeting was on the second floor, in the large courtroom itself, with eight members of the Society sitting in the black and white pews.[16]

Seven years as government physician and surgeon on the frontier, among soldiers, miners, cowboys and Indians of various tribes; remote from brother physicians and proper help, I was compelled to depend upon myself to use the best methods at my disposal to alleviate pains and sufferings. The one that has been most valuable to me, I will endeavor to give to my listeners this afternoon.

My first notice of menthol was behind the drug counter as a clerk in Chicago, at that time, it was prescribed by eminent physicians.

Menthol as found in the market is a colorless, prismatic crystal, having the strong and pure odor of peppermint. It produces warmth in the mucus membrane and on inhalation it gives sensation of soothing coolness. It is sparingly soluble in water, readily soluble in

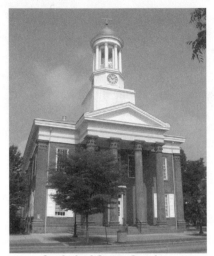

*Cumberland County Courthouse*

*Cumberland County Courtroom*

alcohol, ether, chloroform and oils. It melts at 43°C, boils at 212°C and volatilizes at the ordinary temperature.

Menthol belongs to the class of camphor and is obtained by repeated distillation of Japanese oil of peppermint. Its chemical formula is $C_6H_{20}0$. It is unofficial in this country. I do not know the reason why, unless it is for the want of a better knowledge of the drug or for its expensiveness; but it is retained in the British Pharmacopeia and is extensively used there.

Menthol acts as an antineuralgic, antiseptic, anaesthetic and stimulant.

It has been used for the eye, ear, & skin diseases with much efficiency; lung, nose and throat diseases by inhalation, it has been most beneficial. In some of the hospitals of this country it has been used as surgical dressings.

I believe the object of our coming together as professional brothers & sisters is to help each other in our personal experiences, taking for granted that we have the theories of medicine.

Lung troubles among the Indians are greater than their neighbors—the whites. It is not because the Redman is weaker in the lung than the white man. It is not so. It is because they are ignorant of their new life from their savage state.

On the frontier where my patients were thirty or forty miles apart, it would be useless for me to apply hot linseed poultice or mustard plaster in acute case of pneumonia, and have these ignorant people to change it every twenty minutes and the mustard plaster. That requires perfect care & watching. In my discouraging work I tried the raw meat, the fat pork, the onion, the hot linseed poultice with mustard to allay inflammations was of no avail; but at last I made a plaster out of Vaseline and menthol. To my surprise, it fulfilled my long want to take the place of all of the above mentioned applications.

Now, I am satisfied that after you have tried the method you will have faith in the menthol plaster. I always carried these two articles in my saddle bag, and made the plaster and bandaged it to the suffering patient with great relief in a few minutes. This plaster can be kept on the patient for a week without losing its virtue, which I believe is better than a nurse to change a poultice every twenty minutes, since there is danger of exposure by the change.

There is another very important medical virtue in the plaster from the menthol, and that is the patient inhales the menthol unconsciously. It is a sedative on the lining membrane of the air passage and a stimulant effect upon the congested condition of the bronchioles. As a powerful germicide & antiseptic, it kills the microbes of infection and prevents its dissemination.

In my hospital work at the school where I have twenty or more every year I am gratified to say, it has never failed me in its action.

I believe an inflammation or congestion is the same in every part of the body; whether it be in the mucus membrane, synovial membrane of the joints, superficial surfaces or in the bones. It must be treated in the same routine treatment, only in a modified method.

This same plaster will answer the same purpose in relieving the pains & scattering the congestion in rheumatism, bruises of all kinds and neuralgia. The menthol liniment, I generally use a dram of menthol to half and half of alcohol and olive oil to make two ounce solution. The headache solution is the same, only you can add more menthol if you think best. Be careful of the eyes. Rub thoroughly over the congested blood vessels.

In skin diseases I have found menthol most valuable, for example in measle eruptions use the menthol in olive oil and leave out the alcohol, and make it half a dram to eight ounce mixture. In Erysipelas, strong solution of menthol mitigates its spreading. In poison ivy, it has been my main remedy, and also in heat rash where there is intense itching.

In earaches, two drops of the strong solution in sweet oil has taken the place of the unique hot water remedy & laudrum.

In acute rhinitis, influenza and other affections of the nose and throat, menthol by means of spray or brush application has always been advantage to me.

My two years wholesale treatment of such cases has convinced me of its special virtue more than ever.

I agree with Mr. J. Lennox B. that it stimulates to contract the capillary blood vessels of the passages of the nose and throat, always dilated in the early stages of head cold and influenza.

It arrests sneezing & rhinal flow. It relieves, and indeed dissipates, pain and fullness of the head by its analgesic property, so well known by its action when applied externally to the brow in case of Tic Douloureux.

By menthol inhaler when nasal discharge is excessive, it is checked; when deficient and thickened, in hypertrophic rhinitis, its healthy character is restored.

In eye diseases it is used for its antiseptic & sedative effect. In my hospital work I can testify its beneficial effect in simple conjunctivitis.

Internal use, it acts as oil of peppermint, and I am unable to give my testimony only at present, still, I use it in my cough mixture exclusively.

Surgically, I have used the plaster after [I] apply the iodoform dressing in order to equalize the temperature and its antiseptic property, over which I apply oil silk to retain the moisture, and thus protect the exposure of the wound. I have in few exceptions failed to have union by first intention as some of my colleagues will testify, who are in this room today.[17]

Unfortunately Montezuma didn't patent and promote his salve, otherwise he could have been rich. Menthol is an alcohol obtained from peppermint oil (or other mint oils). It is an antipruritic, cough suppressant, decongestant, and topical anesthetic. For many of us, one of the most memorable smells of our childhood is that of Vicks VapoRub. Vicks was developed by Lunsford Richardson, a druggist in Selma, North Carolina, who combined petroleum jelly and menthol just like Montezuma did. The commercial promotion of the product began around 1907 by Richardson's son, in Greensboro, North Carolina. H. S. Richardson named the product after his brother-in-law, Joshua Vick, who was a physician. Today, Vicks VapoRub contains 2.6 percent menthol, 4.8 percent camphor, and 1.2 percent eucalyptus oil. BenGay, a salve for aching muscles and joints, was introduced in the early 1900s, a combination of menthol and methyl salicylate. Montezuma's salve and other menthol preparations predated the commercial products by many years and constituted a principal weapon in his armamentarium. A Yavapai man told me in 2002 that his grandfather always talked of "Montezuma's metholatum."

Whiskey continued to be regarded as a tonic during Montezuma's time. During the years of prohibition, the Internal Revenue Service required physicians to maintain a log of prescribed whiskey with dates, amount prescribed, patient names, and diagnoses. Montezuma's prescriptions gave the patient sixteen ounces of whiskey with instructions to take one teaspoonful three times a day.[18] His log (U.S. Internal Revenue permit number 2441) contained two to four prescriptions for whiskey per month.[19] The indications were wide ranging, from a general tonic for nonspecific weakness to chronic conditions like diabetes mellitus and renal disease. Of course, the only medical impact of this treatment was the alcohol effect on the central nervous system.

MONTEZUMA MOVED from Carlisle, Pennsylvania, in December 1895 into an apartment at 3444 Wabash Avenue in Chicago. Richard Pratt told him that "We were all sorry to see you go in one way, and yet some of us were glad in another way. I think the common sense verdict of all your friends is that you have done right."[20] But the going was slow and Montezuma was discouraged, until once again a chance encounter had an impact on his life.

One day, as Montezuma was walking slowly along State Street, a hand clapped him on the back. "How are you, Monty?" exclaimed Fenton B. Turck, a former classmate and now director of his own clinic specializing in gastrointestinal problems.[21] Learning of Montezuma's difficulties in establishing a practice, Turck promptly offered him a position in the Turck Clinic, and the two physicians worked together for the next seventeen years. Montezuma developed his expertise as a gastroenterologist essentially by means of an apprenticeship with Fenton Turck. When Turck moved to New York City in 1913, Montezuma continued to work in the specialty clinic.

The primary method of treatment that Montezuma learned from Turck was colonic lavage. Turck described his method with the results of his studies on both animals and his patients at a meeting of the American Medical Association in June 1899, and again at the Mississippi Valley

*1896—Age Thirty*

Medical Association in Chicago on October 3, 1899; both presentations were subsequently published in the *Journal of the American Medical Association*.[22] Turck and Montezuma introduced hot or cold air into the colon to "produce what has been well styled gymnastics of the colon."[23] They also used large volumes of water, hot water with temperatures increasing to a high of 131°F alternating with ice-cooled water to 41°F. They even inserted a flexible cable high into the colon to produce "mucosal massage" by electricity. These methods were used to treat a

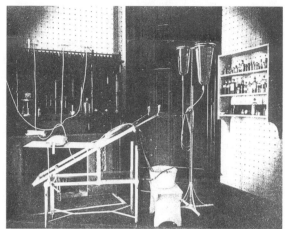

*Turck's Special Table for Colonic Lavage*[24]

host of diagnoses, including chronic liver disease, diabetes, kidney problems, early stages of appendicitis, and even typhoid fever. Colonic lavage still has its advocates today (to "cleanse the large intestine and eliminate toxins") but for good reason, not among the medical profession. Turck's objective was not to cleanse the gastrointestinal tract, but to stimulate it. This vigorous treatment was best applied with the hips markedly elevated, and for this purpose, Turck had constructed a special table.

Turck was well-published in the medical literature. He reported the use of the gyromele for the diagnosis of stomach disorders. The gyromele was an instrument inserted down the esophagus into the stomach. The distal end could be rotated allowing application of the intake to a specific location in the stomach, guided by palpation or fluoroscopy. The gyromele allowed direct application of reagents to the gastric mucosa or the aspiration of tissue or localized contents. The Turck clinic provided microscopic examinations of sputum, feces, urine, blood, and stomach contents. Montezuma used this method and even lectured on the analysis of stomach contents aspirated with the gyromele.[25] Turck used the gyromele in his animal experiments; throughout his career he combined practice with scientific investigations in the laboratory.

In later years, Turck concentrated on the mechanisms involved with cardiovascular shock and fatigue. After leaving Chicago for New York City, Turck established a research laboratory at 428 Lafayette Street in an old colonial mansion; he saw patients in the mornings in his home office at 14 East Fifty-third Street.[26] Twenty years later in 1933, Turck published a book containing a description of his work, entitled *The Action of the Living Cell, Experimental Researches in Biology*.[27] For over thirty years, Turck argued that a common mechanism of disease involved the release of a toxin from individual diseased or injured cells, a toxin that he called cytost. He was especially convinced that this toxin was the cause of shock (cardiovascular collapse with a fall in blood pressure). Turck performed hundreds of animal experiments in his laboratory, investigating this hypothesis, and his clinical practice (stimulating the gastrointestinal tract) was consistent with this belief. His basic mechanism involving a toxin was very close to what we know today. Septic shock does follow the release of active substances from white blood cells fighting an infection, but cleansing the gastrointestinal tract did not and does not affect the pathophysiology. Turck believed that stimulating the gastrointestinal tract released a small amount of his cellular toxin, and this would produce a beneficial effect by increasing the activity of normal cells throughout the body. He even postulated the existence of an antitoxin, an insight that previewed the immunology of the future. Turck had an inquiring, scientific mind that deserved respect; a presence that must have had a salutary effect on his apprentice, Montezuma.

## MONTEZUMA'S OFFICES

Only two months after moving to Chicago, by February 1896, Montezuma had established his private practice of medicine in two locations. He now lived at 3016 South Park Avenue, and held office hours out of his home from eight to eleven in the morning, and again from seven to 8:30 in the evening (telephone South 544). Montezuma rented this three-story house, sharing it with C. W. Baldwin, for $50 per month.[28] Baldwin was a dentist who later maintained his office in a house across the street.[29] For the rest of his life, Montezuma was never far from Mercy Hospital, always living and working within walking distance. He was familiar with Mercy Hospital (and this would include the professional staff) from his medical school days, and understandably, he preferred the use of this hospital for his patients. In 1901, he moved just a little south, to 3135 South Park Avenue (telephone Douglas 2080). At first he apparently lived on one floor of this house, renting at $40 per month.[30] But eventually he owned this second house, because in 1913 he received a notice from Cook County for $13.20 in taxes levied on personal property in the South Town.[31] South Park Avenue is now the eight-lane Martin Luther King Boulevard.

Montezuma didn't have far to go to his church, the First Baptist Church of Chicago, the church that he attended even during his medical school days.[32] Montezuma's first house (3016 South Park Avenue) was on the west side of the street, one block and across the street from the First Baptist Church. The block is now entirely filled with a city public high school. Today the First Baptist Church is the Olivet Baptist Church, and the building is still a handsome, well-built, cream-colored stone structure on the southeast corner of Martin Luther King Boulevard and Thirty-first Street. The house that Montezuma owned (3135 South Park) was right next door to the church, but now the site is an empty grassy area associated with a series of twenty-two-story apartment buildings.

*First Baptist Church During Montezuma's Life, As Seen Today*

These were relatively large houses, and Montezuma used the extra rooms for boarders and visitors, often Indians traveling to and from Washington. He frequently provided a place to stay for young Indians, like Louise Blue Sky from Minnesota, a young woman just out of school who could not find work in Chicago, became sick, and recovered in the Montezuma household.[33] Reservation Indians coming to Chicago to seek jobs would come to Montezuma for help. He usually took them to the Indian Warehouse, run by the Bureau of Indian Affairs, the shipping point for goods being sent to western reservations.[34]

In the middle of the day, Montezuma saw patients in his downtown office at 100 State Street in the Reliance Building. By the time Montezuma established his State Street office, almost no one lived in the downtown area. It was now a place for

*1903—Age Thirty-seven, in his State Street Office*

shopping, business, and entertainment. Montezuma could walk the thirty-five blocks to his downtown office from his home in thirty to forty minutes, or he could walk five blocks and ride the State Street streetcar, a fifteen- to twenty-minute ride.

Montezuma's downtown office was in the very center, the heart of the city, in The Loop, catty-corner from the Marshall Field Company. It was a choice location in a wonderfully elegant building on the southwest corner of State and Washington (now 32 North State Street), directly across the street from the site where Carlo Gentile operated his photography store in the late 1870s. It must have been a deliberate decision by Montezuma to locate his downtown office where it would be readily and appropriately available for the middle- and upper-class women shopping at Marshall Field's. His office was on the fourteenth floor (Suite 1400), next to the top floor, a location known to require higher rental fees. Seeing patients for only one hour at midday in a high-rent office makes it extremely likely that Montezuma shared the office with other professionals; his rent was only $10 per month.[35] Nevertheless, the highly respectable location of this office motivated Montezuma to use only this address in blue on his white stationery and prescription pads. For ten years, he received all of his mail at 100 State Street.

William E. Hale, the owner of the Hale Elevator Company, purchased in 1882 the First National Bank of Chicago building that existed at the corner of State and Washington. Hale commissioned Burnham and Root, and specifically John Root, to design a sixteen-story (fifteen stories plus a basement, ground floor and a mezzanine) new structure to be named the Reliance Building after the Hale family business, The Reliance Company, which was to be located on the thirteenth floor of the new building. In 1890, the upper two stories of the existing building were supported with jackscrews, and the ground and mezzanine floors were demolished. A new basement and ground floor formed the foundation for the new tower, and in 1891, the Carson Pirie Scott & Company, a department store, moved into

*The Reliance Building—1900*

*The Reliance Building—2003*

this space, to move one block south eight years later into its own building designed by Louis Sullivan. Root died in 1891, and Charles B. Atwood, hired by Burnham as Root's replacement, completed the project. When the leases expired for the occupants of the upper floors, construction resumed, and the Reliance Building opened in March 1895, the first building in Chicago to be totally supported by an internal, riveted cage of structural steel.

The building was immediately successful, but years later began a long decline to a state of serious deterioration. After declaring the building a Chicago Landmark in 1975, the City of Chicago purchased the building in 1993 for $1.2 million, and was responsible for a meticulous and faithful restoration that was completed in 1996. All the windows, except for one small segment on the eighth floor, were replaced; the original cornice on the flat roof was reduplicated in aluminum, and 2,000 pieces of terra cotta were replaced. The original dark pink granite on the exterior of the first floor that came from a no longer worked quarry in Scotland was exactly matched. Replication of the mosaic floor in the lobby was made possible by the discovery of a buried 3x4-foot piece of the original floor. The building was purchased by Canal Street Hotel in 1998 and today houses the Hotel Burnham and the Atwood Café, named after the architect who finished the project.

The building today looks like it did in 1896 when Montezuma rented office space, although it undoubtedly has more bathrooms. The upper floors are wrapped in a skin of cream-colored glazed terra cotta, the first building in Chicago to do so, with each upper floor of large flat and projecting bay windows (the "Chicago window") separated by a horizontal Gothic style ornamental design. The out-of-view south and west walls are of brick. The ground floor (the storefronts) consists of bronze and highly polished granite surrounding wide glass windows, with the edges and junctions of the granite marked by ornamental bronze in the same theme as found inside. The building is 200 feet high, with fifty-five feet of frontage on State Street and eighty-four feet on Washington Avenue. It stands on Root's floating foundation—a twenty-four-inch layer of concrete reinforced with iron "I" beams and railroad rails, sitting on a twelve-inch concrete slab.

The building was designed to house doctors and dentists in the top seven to fourteen floors. Examining old pictures of the building, it is apparent that there were many dentists, and they enjoyed painting their names on the office windows to be read by the public on the streets below. The lobby entrance is on State Street. The marble and mosaic in the small weather space between the doors, the vestibule, is repeated in a narrow lobby. Lavish and handsome lobbies were a characteristic of Chicago buildings of this period, designed to make an immediate and lasting impression on visitors. The walls are multicolored and marbled; the floor is an intricate and colorful mosaic of small pieces of marble. The left wall is filled top to bottom with ornate ironwork that frames four elevators, now enclosed, but once open cages behind the metal work. A set of narrow stairs made of ornate ironwork is at the far end of the lobby.

Today, the upper nine floors, well lit by the large windows, have been converted to 103 hotel rooms and nineteen suites. Exiting the elevator on one of the top floors, you enter a small lobby with a high marbled ceiling that contains, along the left side, narrow stairs (little more than one person wide with marble steps that have scalloped smooth surfaces and edges worn by countless footsteps over the years) replicating the same ornate metal work framing the elevators on every floor, and connecting floors seven to fifteen. There is a quietness that is only encountered in these old high-ceilinged buildings with carpeted floors. The upper

floors of the Reliance Building are carpeted with brightly colored patterns duplicated from the original carpet.

The hotel room doors, which used to be the office doors, are large, with gold-lettered numbers on the opaque glass in the upper half, and a letter slot in the mahogany of the lower half. The halls are trimmed in mahogany with patches of cararra marble and "Florentine" patterned glass. Next to the elevators on each floor, in a tiny alcove on the wall, is an old hand crank telephone (circa 1900), and it works; Montezuma's telephone number was Central 257. The walls of this building that once witnessed medical and dental complaints, illnesses, and pain now see vacationers, business people, and romantic trysts.

The Reliance Building was (and is again, thanks to the City of Chicago) a splendid structure, one in which poor and middle-class patients would be impressed and wealthy patients would be comfortable. The patients could even shop on the ground floor before or after their appointments in one of Chicago's finest department stores. Later Woolworths was next door, the seventeen-story Boston Store at the next corner, Charles Stevens and

Brothers and Mandel Brothers stores across the street, and the new Carson Pirie Scott & Co. building one block away.

It is likely that Montezuma's office in the Reliance Building was the only one housing a professional person who was not part of the White majority segment of society. The fact that he scheduled only one hour a day in this office indicates that he was not overwhelmed with middle- and upper-class patients.

AFTER TEN YEARS in the Reliance Building, Montezuma moved in 1906 to 72 Madison Street (sometime in 1912 it became 7 West Madison Street), one block to the south on the southwest corner of Madison and State Streets, across the street from the Carson Pirie Scott & Co. Building. Displaying his affinity for new buildings, Montezuma opened his second downtown office in the brand new Chicago Savings Bank Building, a building similar in architecture to the Reliance Building. He rented his office from another physician, Milton H. Mack, paying him $18.28 per month for the space, his share of the electric and gas bills, and the services of a "girl."[36] The building is now a National Historical Landmark and is one of the few buildings built around 1900 that was until recently in its original condition.[37] In 1997, the structure, now called The Chicago Building, was converted to dormitory residences for the School of the Art Institute of Chicago. The building is fifteen stories high, with two basements, supported by a structural steel framework enclosed in dark, reddish-brown, unglazed terra cotta and featuring on the Madison Street side the Chicago-style bay windows. The original cornice still surrounds and decorates the edges of the roof. The original marble lobby with its brass fittings opens on the long side of the building on Madison Street. The building was designed by the architectural firm of William Holabird and Martin Roche. Montezuma's downtown office after 1906 was on the eleventh floor (Room 1108) of the Chicago Savings Bank Building. His midday hours were a little longer, from 12:30 to 2 P.M., and his telephone changed from Central 257 to Central 3285.

*The Chicago Building—2003*

Montezuma received his mail for twenty years at his downtown offices, but in March, 1916 he closed his office in The Loop. He frugally continued to use his remaining stationery, carefully crossing out the office hours, telephone number, and address of his Chicago Savings Bank location. His mail was directed to his home at 3135 South Park Avenue.

For just a few months, Montezuma worked out of an office on the West Side (1811 South Loomis Street), a neighborhood of densely packed three-story houses. Montezuma's office was on the corner of South Loomis and Eighteenth Street, now the site of a small branch of the Chicago Public Library. In 1917, Montezuma opened an office at 2541 South Trumbull Avenue that he called his "Suburban Office," with hours from 3 to 5 P.M., telephone Rockwell 406. He maintained this suburban office, about four miles due west from his home, for three years. The area is now a Hispanic neighborhood, but the street of his office has not changed that much. It is lined with three-story narrow brick houses, with only a six-foot-wide space between each house.

*2541 S. Trumbull Avenue*

In the last eight months of his life, Montezuma and his wife lived at 2720 South Michigan Avenue, only four blocks north and four blocks west from his house on Park Avenue (an automobile dealer occupies the site today). He opened his last office at this address on May 3, 1922 (telephone Victory 6483). He told Richard Pratt that they had to move because of the change in his surroundings,[38] most assuredly referring to the fact that the area east of State Street, including South Park Avenue, had become Chicago's Black community.

IT IS UNLIKELY that poor patients made their way to Montezuma's handsome downtown office, but it is very likely that lower socio-economic class and immigrant family patients consulted Montezuma in his home office on South Park Avenue. Montezuma's home office was only a few blocks from Lake Michigan (the area is now extended by landfill to contain Lake Shore Drive), about ten blocks from the part of Prairie Avenue where the Chicago wealthy entrepreneurs built their mansions, and about two miles from his downtown office. But, the Union Stock Yards, surrounded by working-class communities, were only ten blocks to the south.

Mrs. Yonkers is a good example of at least one group of patients Montezuma encountered in his home office. Because of her poverty she was forced to move frequently, but on

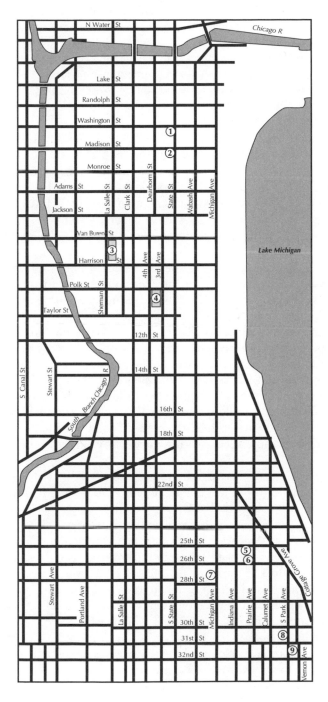

① The Reliance Building
1896 – 1906

② The Chicago Savings
Bank Building
1906 – 1922

③ La Salle Street Station
"20th Century Limited"

④ Dearborn Station
"Navajo" to Phoenix

⑤ Mercy Hospital

⑥ Chicago Medical College
1870 – 1893

⑦ 2720 S Michigan Ave
May – December 1922

**Home Office on S Park Ave:**

⑧ 3016, 1896 – 1901

⑨ 3135, 1901 – 1922

Scale in Miles

0      1/8      1/4

at least one occasion she lived on East Thiry-fifth Street, only a few blocks from Montezuma's home office. Her letters indicate that she attended Montezuma's church (probably a good source of patients for Montezuma). In a series of letters, with poor spelling and punctuation, from spring to fall in 1899, she revealed her own economic struggle and Montezuma's compassion and generosity.[39] She wrote to Montezuma in March: "I have tried to keep track of all you have given me so will do right by you for your kindness. I will come Tuesday night to see you." She asked for fifty cents because she had nothing to eat in the house and did not know what to do.

That summer, 1899, she informed Montezuma, "...I got a Position down town and I have not got a cent in the House. I walked way down town for two days and I can not walk any more. [I have] nothing to eat if you will kindly let me take enough money just for car fare for a week I will return it as soon as I get paid. ...I tell you doctor when you have no money or anything to eat you certainly have not got very much ambition to work. ...I would not ask a favor if it was not for my little children and then I work in a laundry and home to wash all day and then walk home. I cannot stand it. It is a kindness I will never forget and perhaps I can help some other poor unfortunate like my self that is in need." By August, things were critical and Mrs. Yonkers was trying to place her children in a home. "I am so sorry to have to bother and worry you so very much. But you know my Cousin Tomosio. I have not had a cent of money, only those 30 cents you sent me. If you could let me take a little for the children. ...I would not ask it Doctor if it was not for my little children."

"I owe the Lady for this [week's] rent and she is pressing me for it and here I have not even got a cent to buy my poor little children enough to eat with. ...If you could spare a couple of dollars to give to the Land-Lady. ...If you could help me to get my children in a Home for a few months until I could get started a little I would thank you very much kindly." She asked Montezuma for a letter to help place her children in the "Home." "I am very sorry to bother you so much if you could let me take 30 cents I would thank you very much. I wish I knew Doctor what to do about the little ones. If I could get them settled this week I could get a good position as house keeper with some wealthy family. as they will pay me $6 a week."

The "Home" consented to take her children for one month, and she asked Montezuma, "Doctor if you could let me take a couple of dollars to get the two little [?] a pair of shoes as they have none to go out with. I will try and settle with you as soon as I get paid. I would not ask it but I can not take them in their little bear [sic] feet."

A month later, "I thank you very much for your kindness Saturday night. If you knew how glad I was to receive that money as we had nothing in the house for two days. If you can spare 25 cents if so as to get some Bread for tomorrow. ...Doctor I am very sorry to impose on your kindness so much but I hope God will reward you some day. I am sure you deserve it for your great kindness. Now I have only worked one-day all last week and I earned $1.50. Well, you see I can not get a long on and I realy [sic] do not know what to do I have to pay Rent. ...I will tell you Docter [sic] I worked for a number of Lady's from the Church and I certenly [sic] tried to do all in my Power to pleas [sic] them but it was impossible. I find that when you realy [sic] have to work the nonChristian People are the best to work for."

Finally the last word on September 30, 1899, in Montezuma's letters from Mrs. Yonkers: "We have not a bit of coal in the House and it is so cold. Let me take 35 cents to get something to eat for the little children over Sunday. I have now a [?] to pay you back your money that you were so kind to let us have so often. But will not receive any until the 7th of the month. I have received a Position as demonstrator for Sprague-Warner and Co. and am in hopes now I will get along. It will be hard until I receive some money but I will pay you first on my word and honor."[40] Mrs. Yonkers is just one example of many, Whites and Indians, in Montezuma's correspondence, indicating his readiness to provide financial support to patients and acquaintances, surely one of the reasons Montezuma never accumulated significant wealth.

## THE WRECK OF THE WILD WEST SHOW TRAIN

The first eighteen years of the twentieth century marked the heyday of Wild West shows.[41] There were dozens of such shows and most provided employment for Indians. Luther Standing Bear was one of Carlisle's first students, and in 1902, he joined Buffalo Bill's Wild West show as an interpreter, traveling to Europe and earning Richard Pratt's wrath: "Luther Standing Bear went off with 'Buffalo Bill' and lost his character."[42] Later, in 1912, he moved to California, worked in the movies and published four books about the Sioux.

In April 1904, the Buffalo Bill Wild West show was performing on the East Coast and preparing for another tour in Europe. A train was dispatched to Rushville, Nebraska, to bring a band of Sioux Indians to Jersey City to join the show. On the night of April 7, 1904, Luther Standing Bear was riding with a group of Sioux Indians on that Buffalo Bill show train operated by the Chicago & Northwestern Railway Company. Years later, Standing Bear recalled the collision in his autobiography: "On the morning of April 7, 1904, I was sitting in the last car of the train. It was very early, but we were all up and dressed. I was riding in such a position that I could look out the rear door and see the railroad track winding in and out. Several of the men were singing and I joined in. One man who was sitting next to me did not sing, but seemed very quiet as if worried about something. We were rounding a curve, when suddenly I saw a train behind us coming at lightning speed. Then came a terrific crash. There was not even time to cry out. When I opened my eyes again, the seats were piled up on top of us and the steam and smoke from the engine were pouring in on us in great clouds."[43] The force of the collision was so great that the speeding locomotive, number 1101, was engulfed by the coach that contained the Indians.[44] Amazingly, only three Indians died; sixteen were hospitalized in Phoenix Hospital in Maywood, Illinois.[45]

The railroads had extensive medical systems in place. High injury and mortality rates in 1900 required more than 6,000 railroad surgeons.[46] The railroad surgeons had their own specialty, complete with national organizations and journals. This effort was largely directed to the hazardous life of the workers and to protection against lawsuits. Montezuma took this system on.

*Montezuma—1905, Age Thirty-nine*

Two weeks after the wreck, Montezuma wrote to the commissioner of Indian affairs: "I think it is not the right thing or policy to allow the Railroad physician to attend the Indians at Maywood. It would strengthen the Indians' case were they to have an outside physician and surgeon. Now, may I ask you for your approval to take them in charge."[47] He added in another letter that very same day: "I have been silent in reference to the catastrophe at Maywood, but not inactive here. From what information I have personally observed they will need your good service. Having nothing personally against Mr. Asay from whom you may have received a request to litigate for the Indians. Do you not think he would be partial to the 'Buffalo Bill Show' as his brother is connected with the concern. Think over the matter. The Indians have claim against the 'Show' as well as against the railroad. Please supply an interpreter who will be discreet and honest as well as capable for these Indians. The present interpreter is not entirely disinterested in my opinion as derived from obvious circumstances."[48]

There is no record of Montezuma receiving official permission to intercede. Indeed, Commissioner William A. Jones replied on April 30 that he was not prepared to act upon the request. He further stated that the Pine Ridge Agent was looking out for the interest of the Indians.

John R. Brennan, the Pine Ridge Agent, submitted his report to the commissioner of Indian affairs on May 2, 1904. "I have the honor to enclose herewith a copy of agreement made between the representatives of the Indians, namely J. R. Brennan, of the one part and representatives of the Chicago and Northwestern Railway Company, of the other part, in reference to a settlement for the injuries received by said Indians on April 7th, 1904, on the Railroad of said Company near Melrose Park, Cook County, Illinois. Mr. Beathe, U.S. Attorney, myself, representing the Government, and Mr. Richards, representing the Railway Company, have investigated this matter as fully as possible, and have concluded that the amounts fixed in the contract are reasonable ones under all the circumstances. The Indians will get their money at once without any expense or delay. It was hard to determine what the values of the lives of the three dead ones were. But taking everything into consideration considering also that the Indians themselves are satisfied with these amounts, we concluded to recommend them. Two of the dead Indians had never done any work. One of them Iron Tail, had done some work. The measure of damages in this State, as I suppose in all States is based upon the ability and willingness of the deceased person to work. I send you herewith a description of the injuries of the Indians, so you can see how near we are right in our estimates. Upon the approval of this contract by the proper officers representing the Government, the matter will be ready to close up. I assume the Railroad Company will want somebody representing the Government to sign releases, and will also want each of the Indians and the representatives of the dead ones, to sign releases.

Luther Standing Bear: Scalp wound fully healed. Dislocated hip, right side. Sprain of left collar bone. Contusion left side. Dislocated nose. Will fully recover.

Has-No-Horses: Fracture right shoulder. Contusion right chest. Wound in left leg, sinus leading down to the bone. Said by Doctor to be an old wound. Dislocated left hip. Will recover.

Charge-The-Enemy: Contusion of head—healed. Contusion chest. Knee bruised. Bad sprain of left ankle.

| | |
|---|---|
| Mrs. Comes Last: | Scalp wound—healed. Badly bruised. No permanent injuries. |
| Tommy Comes Last: | Right eye bruised. |
| Mrs. High Bear: | Compound fracture left forearm. Fracture lower end of femur of left leg. Right limb sprained and bruised. Back bruised. Scalp wound. |
| Short Step: | Face and neck badly burned. Will probably heal. Right hand badly scalded on back. Left ankle bruised. Claims to spit blood. |
| William Blue Cloud: | Right leg amputated just above the knee. Burned underneath chin. Left elbow cut and scalded. Backs of both hands badly burned. |
| Goose Face: | Fracture of right hip joint. Socket of left hip fractured. Both hips dislocated and bones broken. Ankle out of joint. Will probably be crippled. |
| Turning Bear: | Sprained left ankle. |
| Kills First: | Fracture of right leg about juncture of lower and middle thirds. Both hands scalded. Doctor says will heal without disability. |
| Long Bear: | Both hands scalded. Puncture wound in left leg. Burned on back. Nose, lip and ear slightly burned. |
| Pawnee Killer: | Burn and contusion right foot. Contusion head. Bruised on back and abdomen. Pain when passing urine. Left leg bruised. |
| Little Elk: | Puncture wound left leg above ankle. Back and right shoulder bruised and burned. Internal pain. Left side bruised. |
| Martin Poor Elk: | Bruised on left side. Some internal pain. |
| Little Iron: | Sprain of left ankle. Slight bruise of left hand. Head bruised. Contusion of chest. Hearing of left ear slightly affected. |
| Chief High Bear: | Fingers thrown out of joint. Contusion of back. Pains through back |
| The names of the dead Indians are: | Phillip Iron Tail<br>Comes Last<br>Kills Ahead"[49] |

The agreement between the Chicago & Northwestern Railway Company and the Indians listed the following financial compensation in consideration for the release of all claims or demands against the railway, and agreed to pay all bills for nursing, care, food, lodging, and medical attention incurred at the Phoenix Hospital, and all other bills for expenses reasonable up to the time of discharge, also free transportation for each to Rushville, Nebraska:

| | |
|---|---|
| "Luther Standing Bear | $1,250 |
| Has-No-Horses | 1,250 |
| Charge-The-Enemy | 300 |
| Mrs. Comes Last | 100 |
| Mrs. High Bear | 1,250 |
| Short Step | 500 |
| William Blue Cloud | 2,500 |
| Goose Face | 2,500 |
| Turning Bear | 150 |
| Kills First | 500 |
| Long Bear | 500 |
| Pawnee Killer | 250 |
| Little Elk | 250 |
| Martin Poor Elk | 150 |
| Little Iron | 210 |
| Chief High Bear | 270 |

**For dead Indians:**

| | |
|---|---|
| Philip Iron Tail | 2,000 |
| Comes Last | 1,500 |
| Kills Ahead | 1,500"[50] |

TOTAL $16,930

Montezuma disagreed with this settlement and became involved in a dispute that resulted in a letter from Judge Edward F. Dunne, of the Circuit Court of Cook County, sent on May 6 to Commissioner Jones: "We, the undersigned are in receipt of a letter signed by Luther Standing Bear, High Bear, Has No Horses, and Charges Enemy, a committee of Indians representing the injured Indians and the relatives of the deceased Indians that were killed and injured in the Chicago & Northwestern Railway Company's tracks near Melrose Park, April 7, 1904. The substance of the communication from the Indians is a protest made by them against the consummation and carrying out of an agreement of settlement claimed to have been entered into by the Railroad. ...The Indians express themselves as highly dissatisfied with the proposed settlement and intimate that they are being unfairly treated. They have asked us, in the communication to interest ourselves in their behalf and to prevent the carrying out of the proposed settlement. E. F. Dunne, G. Frank Lydston, M.D., Carlos Montezuma, M. D., Honoré J. Jaxon."[51]

Montezuma submitted his own medical report in which he obviously overstated the permanence of the injuries (for example, contusions were said to be permanent). He submitted his own "estimate of pecuniary damages" per the request of the commissioner. His total for the survivors amounted to $51,250 in contrast to the $11,900 in the agreement engineered by the Pine Ridge Agent and the railway company.[52]

"...permit me to say that my natural dislike of litigation has caused me to deduct in each case a large percentage for the sake of lending whatever influence may attach to this estimate, to the avoidance of litigation; and that my life-long experience as a man of Indian blood brought into exceptionally beneficial relations with the white man's civilization, and therefore inspired by warm friendship for the white people, has caused me to stand with special firmness in this matter, on the ground of friendly but exact impartiality. Just as on other occasions I have stood between the white man and the Indian, when one or both were bewildered, so also in this case, I stand firm in the position that no difference should be made between a white man's injury and an Indian's injury; that the Indian and the white man are of the same human flesh and the same human blood, and subject to the same human capacity to receive pain and suffering from external conditions, and that when such conditions bring injuries in the way of pain and disability and disfiguration, as a consequence of the fault of others, the financial equivalent of that injury should be estimated from the actual circumstances, and not from prejudice of color or race.

From the standpoint of actual circumstance, I wish to call your special attention to two considerations: one is that these men are the picked men of the reservation, and that the loss to themselves and their families is therefore so much the greater. The other is that on an Indian reservation there are no artificial means of travel, such as serve to help out people who are injured in our great cities, and that the loss and inconveniences to reservation dwellers, arising from physical injury, is therefore in this respect also so much the greater.

...In regard to the question of disability, it is to be noticed that the answers given by the Indians are for two reasons very apt to be misleading to their own very marked disadvantage: First, because their natural pride and scorn of suffering incites them to make light of their injuries; Secondly, because the unaccustomed ease of their present surroundings causes them to imagine that they are much stronger than they really are. When they once resume their natural and active life, they will be apt to find themselves very much less capable than they formerly were.

I trust that these considerations will have their due influence in determining the stand taken by you in regard to these cases. I know that the spirit of justice and fairness displayed by you will appeal to and awaken the same spirit in the representatives of the Railway Company and will induce them to abandon that appearance of the strong throttling the weak, merely because he is strong, which seems to me to mark the Company's present propositions to you."[53]

On May 28, 1904, the acting commissioner of Indian affairs answered the letter from Circuit Court: "I am in receipt of your letter of May 6, protesting against the settlement arranged for on behalf of certain Indians of the Pine Ridge Agency injured in a railroad wreck at Melrose Park, Illinois. You jointly state you are in receipt of a letter signed by Luther Standing Bear, High Bear, Has No Horses and Charges Enemy, a committee representing the injured and the relatives of the deceased; that the substance of that communication is a protest against this settlement, and that they are highly dissatisfied therewith; and that they intimate that they are being unfairly treated; that they have asked you to interest yourselves in their behalf, and to prevent the carrying out of the proposed settlement. You ask that I look into this matter carefully, and that you be given a chance to point out its inequity, and that no steps be taken in the way on consummating this settlement until you can present the Indians's[*sic*] side of the case.

This unfortunate incident has been a matter of careful investigation on the part of the Indian Office and received considerable attention at the hands of the Commissioner of

Indian Affairs personally. The interests of the Indians were placed in the hands of the Department of Justice and their personal welfare looked after by the Indian Agent. Considerable expense and trouble was [*sic*] taken to investigate all phases of this matter, and after most careful consideration I can see no good reason for not approving the settlement made on behalf of these Indians. An attempt to collect for personal injuries in the courts involves delay and expenditure for attorneys [*sic*] fees, expenses on behalf of the claimants, with no certainty that the damages that might be secured through judgment would exceed the amount proffered by the railroad company. As a matter of information it would be of considerable value in considering this case to know how long the average case of this kind stands on the calendar of the court before which it will be brought until final judgment is secured and the money collected.

I am of the opinion that the settlement should stand, and shall use all my endeavors to have the Indians accept the same in satisfaction of all claims against the company."[54]

Montezuma lost yet another battle with the Bureau of Indian Affairs.


## MONTEZUMA AS A PHYSICIAN

Imagine for a moment that you are a patient, seeing Dr. Montezuma for the first time. Arriving after a long walk, or in a horse buggy, and later by streetcar followed by a short walk, you ascend the two or three steps that abut the sidewalk along South Park Avenue. The door announces his name and office hours in gold letters. Opening the door, a short hallway leads to the waiting room, and you are surprised to see two Indians in full traditional regalia sitting in the corner awaiting advice and counsel from Montezuma before resuming their journey to visit Washington bureaucrats. The walls of his study hold various Indian artifacts collected by Dr. Montezuma; there is no hiding the fact that he is an Indian. There were only eight American Indians counted in Chicago by the 1900 census.[55] Entering his consultation office, you are greeted by a short man (five-feet, six-inches) with a thick, stocky (but not fat) body.[56] His skin and eyes are dark; his hair is straight and jet-black. His voice is deep, soft, and gentle, and like modern Yavapai Indians, his voice has a lyrical rhythm that is pleasant and easing. His fluency with English is impressive, and he is noticeably courteous. His demeanor and speech immediately create a sense of caring and respect. He is a handsome man. Dressed in his dark blue serge suit, white shirt either with a black tie or a small collar buttoned tight around his neck or, as he usually preferred, with a small, white bow tie, with his clean skin and hands, except for his dark Indian appearance, Montezuma looks like every other Chicago doctor. Montezuma would never make a house call, even in the middle of the night, until he was well dressed in his collar and cuffs.[57] He was always careful to represent himself well, not allowing even a single opportunity for a derogatory thought or comment to be directed against an American Indian. He was consistent and serious in his decision to represent his people.

Montezuma characterized himself in filling out a form for "The National Cyclopedia of American Biography," as conscientious and industrious in his profession.[58] He didn't drink or smoke and described himself "as a temperance man."[59] How do you judge the quality of a physician who worked in the distant past? In 1921, Montezuma told this story in a personal interview with a journalist: "I remember an incident from my early days in Chicago when I was trying to establish a practice of my own. I wanted this for my office, and I wanted that. I thought I must have each item, or fail. And I lacked the amount, several hundred dollars, to buy it. I took my problem to a physician whom I knew, one of the wealthiest physicians in the city at that time. He listened to what I had to say; then he said: 'Yes, Montezuma, what you say is all very well. The fixtures you want for your office might help you a little, at first. They would impress some of your callers. But don't you see, that would be all they'd do. You have a good mind. That's what counts. My young friend, merit will see you through!' I never forgot his words. I have tested their truth time and again as the years have passed. And I have learned that merit comes slowly, not in a day or a year, but gradually, the unconscious accumulation of honest effort."[60]

It is worthwhile to appraise the nature of the interactions between the

*Around 1915—Age Forty-nine*

doctor and his patients. The story of Lilian M. Grandy is very revealing. She wrote to Montezuma in July 1898 from Briggsville, Wisconsin, where she was vacationing.[61] Even though she was not in Chicago, she continued to consult with Montezuma, seeking his counsel through the mail. She told him that she was passing clots of blood about the size of a large walnut. "What is the matter with me? I am waiting for the medicine you said you would send. Do not fail me, Doctor." On August 3, she informed Montezuma that she received his medicine. "Doctor – I cannot help but think that I am in the condition I feared for several days, I have had terrible pains and a discharge with clots now and then. And I really think I am growing larger, and my breasts are sore and seemed larger. Of course that just may be my imagination. I am waiting so anxiously for the pills that you said would bring me around this month. It will be 4 months this 15th that I had my last sickness. Oh Doctor, you do not know how I worry. I do hope the pills will come soon. I will pay you when I return. The discharge is colored sometimes just a little clear bright red blood passes and then there will be small clots, not very much but some. I have a great deal of pain. If I am not in the *one* condition, I must be wrong some way."

Montezuma's letter with pills arrived August 10, and on August 11, she wrote: "But I have not taken any as according to directions I had better not." She was still passing some clots, and she described her vaginal discharge: "I can hardly describe it. It looks more like flesh." The occasional gushing of bright red blood frightened her: "I am obliged to wear a napkin all the time. Doctor can you tell me what is the matter. I was never like this before, and can hardly understand it. I shall be back the last of this month? I thank you very much for your kind and encouraging letters. Yours in friendship, L.M.G."

The next letter is not dated: just "Tuesday Morning" on stationery with an American flag and she told of an amazing event: "You will be surprised to hear from me again so soon. Well doctor, I do not know whether you will be surprised to hear what I am about to relate." She recalled how last Saturday she was in dreadful pain, and indeed: "while on the chamber I really thought I was paralyzed with pain. Finally I had one and there was a thud in the chamber and oh doctor how can I tell you, but when I could get up there was a little baby. Will God ever forgive me. I am too wicked to die and too wicked to live. Ah! I put the little thing in a box and went out in the grove and buried it. Doctor—God, and myself alone know what I suffered. …Doctor, one thing worries me now. There was no flow before it came. …I have not flowed any since, not any discharge to speak of. I am very much worried. I had a dear friend die some time ago. She married, had a miscarriage at three months and the afterbirth did not come, and she being young did not know. Blood poison set in and she died. I do not have any pain to speak of. …It is just 4 months today the 15th since I was sick last. I do not know why but I felt confident I was that way. Doctor I did not see anything that I tho't could be an afterbirth. Of course I do not know what it would look like but it does not seem to me I flowed enough. I shall be back in about two weeks now if all is well. I shall go to work but God help me with a heavy heart. No one knows what my feelings are. I must close now. Doctor tell me do you think I am all right. …Please let me hear from you soon. Are you surprised. Yours respectfully, L.M.G."

Miss Lilian Grandy miscarried at about sixteen to eighteen weeks of pregnancy when the baby was about six inches in size. When Montezuma was the physician at the Western Shoshone Agency in 1891, he prescribed an ergot preparation to treat a miscarriage, a treatment that he learned during the year he spent with Dr. Dudley just before his medical school graduation.[62] Ergot is a complex of alkaloids derived from a fungus that grows on rye grass. The medical profession had known since around 1820 that ergot could contract the uterus, although the most active alkaloid was not isolated and purified until after 1930. By the end of the nineteenth century, ergot was widely used to treat postpartum hemorrhage (for years, a major cause of maternal mortality). Montezuma probably mailed Miss Grandy ergot tablets, which would prevent one of the main complications of miscarriage, hemorrhage. Notice that he carefully instructed Miss Grandy not to take the pills immediately; he obviously did not want to cause a miscarriage. The other major complication associated with a miscarriage is infection, but antibiotics were still a dream. Retention of the afterbirth (the placenta) is a major cause of both hemorrhage and infection, and Miss Grandy was entirely appropriate in recalling the sad case of her friend and worrying about the completeness of her own miscarriage. Ergot tablets would contract the uterus to aid the emptying process and complete the miscarriage. What is impressive about this correspondence is the willingness of Miss Grandy to confide in Montezuma about an event that at that time would have been regarded as something very private. The correspondence indicates that Montezuma was able to develop and maintain strong and confident relationships with his patients.

We are able to know little more regarding Montezuma's medical practice. The patient notes available in the Montezuma collections appear to be Montezuma's scribbled notations, probably taken during patient interviews.[63] Examination results, diagnoses, and treatments are usually missing. We do know that he saw patients of all ages, made house calls, and often used his methods of intestinal irrigation and colonic lavage, using hot and cold water, five gallons at a time!

## MONTEZUMA'S FINANCES

Montezuma lived a comfortable life. He lived in a nice house and was able to provide accommodations time and time again for visitors and friends passing through Chicago. He dressed well, went to the movies, and at least on one occasion he took Jeannette Stedman, Reverend Stedman's daughter, to the opera, who observed: "but the old saying is: In New York it is how rich are you? In Boston what do you know? Philadelphia—who was your grandfather? But in Chicago, What do you wear!"[64] Montezuma maintained his Masonic activities, belonged to the Press Club of Chicago, was generous with money and gifts sent to his Indian relatives, and could afford to take a month-long vacation in Arizona almost every year. Nevertheless, Montezuma was never what could be considered rich or wealthy. In the first fifteen years of his practice, Montezuma was doing relatively well financially, as judged by his membership in multiple organizations, subscriptions to several medical journals, and purchases of medical books. But by 1914, money was tight. He closed his downtown office in 1916; he closed his suburban office around 1920, and in the last two years of his life saw patients only in his home office.

By the 1850s, bloodletting and purging had given way to less violent remedies, and the economics of medical care had evolved into a fee-for-service system. Montezuma's medical records indicate that he saw slightly more men than women, and his fees ranged from $10 to $100.[65] An ongoing problem that was prominent in Montezuma's practice was the significant amount of care he provided on credit, leading to a large number of unpaid bills. Montezuma had learned a lesson about collecting his money. "The best time to get your money from a patient is when he is very sick. If you present your bill after he gets well, he will tell you 'to go to the place where it does not snow.'"[66] In making this statement, Montezuma was using his medical practice experience to argue that Indians should strike when the iron is hot, to demand freedom and citizenship while fighting in World War I.

Money became a problem for Montezuma in the last ten years of his life. His patient volume declined at the same time he was writing hundreds of letters, paying for travel, lodging, and meals at national meetings, and supporting the production and mailing of his monthly newsletter, *Wassaja*. Beginning in 1914, he would write gripping sentences on the bills that he mailed. "I am in need. Do for me as I have done for you." "Be a man. Can you do anything for me as I have done for you. I have faith in you and we are on the square. Let me hear from you. Do not fear. I am in need at the moment." "As man to man may I ask that the above amt. be settled."[67] He continued to earn a small amount of money by charging $2 per month to rent rooms on the upper floors of his house.[68]

There were times when there was no available cash, causing Montezuma to go a day without eating.[69] The rent for Montezuma's downtown office was often in arrears, and even a $2 payment from a patient was noteworthy and highly appreciated. He wrote to his wife who was on a summer trip in Michigan: "I order menthol for tomorrow, but I have not enough money to pay for it. I will get along some way, hoping I can get some money before it will be delivered to me." "Took in two dollars today. The menthol did not show up at my city office. That much I escaped to pay out, so I am all right with the world so far." Montezuma purchased menthol, five pounds at a time, for $14.[70] "Today I have only 2 cents. …I have to live on my *looks* and [?] until I get some money."[71]

For many years, Montezuma supplemented his practice income with small honoraria from his lectures. During his years in practice in Chicago, Montezuma presented many lectures on the Indians, to a variety of groups ranging from ladies' clubs to church organizations to civic and business meetings. The lectures were variations of the same basic speech. He gave it different titles, such as "The Indian Problem from an Indian's Standpoint" given to the Fortnightly Club on February 10, 1898. The speech was received so well that it was printed as a pamphlet and distributed to interested Chicagoans.[72] A similar version was published in *Current Literature* in April 1898, entitled, "An Indian's View of the Indian Question."[73]

The annual reports of the Commissioners of Indian Affairs, Indian Agents, school officials and the missionaries usually create the impression that the Indians are all improving.

An anxious friend of a patient inquired of the doctor as he passed from his morning call: "How is the patient?"

"Improving," was the reply.

Next day she asked again:

"How is the patient this morning, Doctor?"

"Improving," he said.

And several times again she inquired with the same answer.

Some days after her last inquiry, she heard of the patient's death.

One of her friends asked her:

"What did the patient die with?"

She replied:

"I guess she died with 'improvement.'"

It is a high time that a red flag or some other danger signal be hung up on the present Indian policy or the Indians will all die with "improvement."

The Indians of today are not the Indians of the past. They have been cut loose from the advantages of barbarism and thus far have not profited by civilization. This makes the Indians of the present more degraded than their forefathers ever were.

I go back to my childhood and behold coming forth from his wigwam, the stoic warrior of mountain, plain, and forest, he was the child of nature, and a true American. Erect in form and strong in presence, his head was carried high, was mantled with long black hair and decorated with the feathers of the bird that soars above the storm. These were tokens of strength, prosperity and happiness. The brow told of purpose, of conscience, of independence, of liberty; the penetrating eye measured the depth of human nature and spoke louder than words. The massive jaw and the clear-cut, firm lips told of natural strength and character; the beads that ornamented his proud neck placed there by the hand of a woman, were tokens of her pure devotion and love for him when far away.

This man took in the pure breath of heaven and defied the germ of disease. A strong and steady arm drew the bowstring and brought in the wild game for food and clothing. The girded loin sustained hunger, thirst and fatigue from early dawn into the darkness of midnight. Strong and elastic limbs and fleet moccasined feet, which distance never tired, overmatched the panting deer.

But the times have changed, and the Indian has changed with them. The picture fades away; the warrior sings the last chant, droops the high brow, abandons personal hope and gazes with yearning heart into the faces of his children.

...Do you know that your whole effort has been and now is crowding them into depths of a state worse than barbarism?

...My convictions come from intense interest, from personal observation. I have put all my thought into it. Most people have a wrong idea of the reservation; it is not an early paradise, nor a land of milk and honey, where the pipe of peace is continually smoked. It is a demoralized prison; a barrier against enlightenment, a promoter of idleness, beggary, gambling, pauperism, ruin, and death.

[Many of the paragraphs are the same as found in the talks Montezuma gave at the Lake Mohonk Conferences in 1893 and 1895, Chapter 6. He concludes with:] I wish I could collect all the Indian children, load them in ships at San Francisco, circle them around Cape Horn, pass them through Castle garden, put them under proper individual care in your public schools, and when they have been matured and moderately educated let them do what other men and women do—take care of themselves. This would solve the Indian question; would rescue a splendid race from vice, disease, pauperism, and death. The benefit would not be all for the Indian. There is something in his character which the interloping white man can always assimilate with profit.[74]

The Grand Rapids Public Library offered him expenses plus $5 or $10 honorarium in August 1906.[75] He continued to deliver his staple speech that he developed while still a medical student a decade before, but his repertoire expanded. In January 1909, he received an invitation to lecture at the Lowell Institute in Boston, and his response provided a choice of three titles:[76]

1. The Indian of Tomorrow
2. Public and Governmental Misconceptions of the Indians
3. What It Is To Be An Indian

In 1909, he presented "The Indian of Tomorrow" to a large audience at the Chicago Art Institute. This was the same lecture that he gave to the National Woman's Christian Temperance Union in Chicago, eleven years earlier as a medical student in 1888 (the full text is in Chapter 5). After giving the same lecture to the Illinois Woman's Press Association, also in 1909, the talk was printed and sold in pamphlet form by the National Woman's Christian Temperance Union.[77] By 1914, he had a collection of nearly 200 hand-colored, glass lantern slides "showing the conditions of the Indians of 40 years ago to the present time. Many of the pictures cannot be duplicated as my guardian, Mr Gentile, took them at the time of my capture over 40 years ago."[78] (170 slides can be viewed in the Collester Collection, Smithsonian Institution National Anthropological Archives. How Doris Collester of East Riverdale, Maryland, acquired the slides is unknown.) His list of talks now included: "Missionaries Among the Indians," and "What Indians Must Do." Despite different titles, however, every talk had the same fundamental message: "Sons of the aboriginal Indians, do you know we have been driven from the heritage of our fathers from generation to generation until we can not take another step! What are we going to do? We must decide for ourselves very quickly. Are we to disappear as the buffaloes or rise above the horizon of the twentieth century and respond, 'We are here!' The sound of your own voice at the roll call will be at the end of the final battle to gain your freedom by your individual self."[79] The Lawrence (Kansas) Daily Journal-World said: "Dr. Montezuma is a splendid speaker—would be called one on any rostrum between the oceans—on any subject he might elect to speak from."[80]

Newspaper reproductions of Montezuma's speech at the annual meeting of the Society of American Indians in 1915 ("Let My People Go"—Chapter 13) and the appearance of his monthly newsletter, Wassaja, in 1916 (Chapter 14) produced a wave of publicity for Montezuma that stimulated a sharp increase in requests for his lectures. Most organizations did not provide an honorarium, but judicious use of the ample expense money could leave some left over. For example, in 1916, Montezuma lectured in upstate New York for $50 in expenses (he spoke for nearly two hours to 1,000 people at the Roycroft Convention in East Aurora, New York[81]), and a trip to Kansas City featured several talks; one addressed the 800-member Kansas City Knights of Columbus for $25 expenses.[82] This flurry of engagements prompted Montezuma to sign with The Mutual Lyceum of Chicago, a booking organization that charged 25 percent of negotiated fees.[83] A talk at the Wicker Park Woman's Club was arranged for $30. This activity seemed to have eased his financial state, so critical in 1914, because once again he was able to vacation in Arizona in 1917, and this time he was accompanied by his wife. But soon the demand for Montezuma waned, and in the last few years before his death, there was very little extra money.

Montezuma calculated in the fall of 1921 that he had only $473 available cash.[84] Despite this shortage of cash, he still made a $50 payment to the Masons![85] He also always paid his dues to maintain his membership in the Chicago Illini Club and the University of Illinois Alumni Association. The good news was that the mortgage on his house was essentially fully paid (at $25 per month); in August 1921 Montezuma decided to pay off the remaining balance of $31.[86]

Montezuma told his wife that he expected to make $200 in October 1921 (a sum that would have been very respectable in 1900, but did not reflect the substantial five-fold increase in average income for physicians by the 1920s[87]). His life was busy in his last few years, but not with patients; on one occasion describing his day he reported only one patient at 9:30 and another between 10 and 11 o'clock.[88] Another time he told his wife, "Today I had three patients that is doing pretty good. Tomorrow I will have just as many."[89] In 1913, standard fees for general (not specialty) care were $3 to $5 for an office consultation, $5 to $15 for a house call, and $5 to $25 for a night call.[90] Then as now, it required more than a few patients a day to make a good living.

In July 1922, six months before his death, Montezuma purchased three vacant lots in Harvey, Illinois ($88 for one, and the other two for $40 each). Perhaps because of a foreboding sense of the short time he had left, he recorded the deeds in the name of his wife, as "Mary K. Montezuma."[91] Thirty years later in 1952, when Marie was living at 2219 Prairie Avenue in Blue Island and now widowed for a second time, she sold the lots for a total of $1,000.

It is possible that Montezuma's tight finances in the last years of his medical practice were due to a decrease in patient volume because of his political activities during World War I (Chapter 16). This activity, especially along with the investigation by the Bureau of Investigation, could easily have been unfavorably perceived by the public as unpatriotic. However, no evidence can be found directly linking Montezuma's politics with his practice income, and his tight finances began in 1914, three years before his political activities attracted federal attention.

Most of Montezuma's patients came from the surrounding neighborhood, and a change in this neighborhood must have affected his medical practice. After 1910, Montezuma's neighborhood dropped lower on the socio-economic scale, and after 1915, his home office was in the middle of a rapidly growing Black community. [92]

It is also likely that Montezuma continued to practice in a fashion that was appropriate in 1900, but did not adjust with changing times. A possible reason for this is that the time he devoted to his political activities hampered his continuing education. In 1911, testifying in the House of Representatives (Chapter 12), Montezuma told the Committee on

Expenditures in the Interior Department, "I am known as the stomach and intestinal man of Chicago. I have gone deeper into that than any man in the United States, I guess, especially the nonoperative treatment of appendicitis."[93] The clinical term "appendicitis" was first used in 1886, accompanied by an urge for early surgical treatment.[94] The localization of tenderness at a particular spot on the abdomen, McBurney's point, was described in 1889, and by 1894, early diagnosis and operative treatment were being championed.[95] By 1911, clinicians should have been aware that when the diagnosis of appendicitis is made, the treatment is always surgical. It is better to occasionally operate on a normal appendix then to allow an inflamed appendix to rupture and produce very serious—indeed, life-threatening—infectious consequences. This was even more the case in 1911 when antibiotics were not available.

The decrease in Montezuma's patient volume in the last ten years of his life probably reflected the impact of all of these forces, and when he died, all that he had to leave for his wife were his files, his collection of Indian artifacts, the payment (amount unknown) from his life insurance,[96] and his house.

# Zitkala-Ša:
# Let Me Wish the Day's Sunshine
# May Enter Your Soul—I Am Your Friend

CARLOS MONTEZUMA and Gertrude Simmons Bonnin (Zitkala-Ša) were in love. They almost married, but never did because they could not reconcile their philosophic differences. Gertrude Simmons Bonnin was a writer, a musician, a public speaker, a Congressional lobbyist, and a female Indian leader in a time dominated by men.[1] Despite the fact that she was of a new generation, a product of the assimilation effort, she was one of the first influential people to insist on a modern sense of tribalism, the root of her basic conflict with Montezuma.

Gertrude Simmons was born to Táte I Yóhin Win (Reaches for the Wind), a Sioux of the Yankton band, who could remember a visit to her village by Lewis and Clark in 1804.[2] Born on February 22, 1876 (the year of the Battle of the Little Big Horn), Gertrude was her mother's ninth child from three White men; only five of the children survived infancy. Gertrude was from the third marriage, to a man named Felker, but her mother, also known as Ellen Simmons, gave her the name Simmons from the second marriage.[3] Felker was booted from the home by Ellen before his daughter's birth when she could no longer tolerate his abuse of Dawee (David). Gertrude's half brother David Simmons, who was to be the next most important relative in her life, was twelve years old at the time of her birth. Zitkala-Ša (Zit-KAH-la-shah) is the Indian name that Gertrude selected for herself, around the age of twenty-four. It means Red Bird. In her formal correspondence with the Indian Bureau and politicians, she identified herself as Gertrude Bonnin. Gertrude Simmons was listed as Gertie Simmons Bonnin (her married name), No. 209 on the Indian Census Roll taken in 1930 on the Yankton Reservation. Her number for allotment and identification was AL-594-609. In her private life, she and her husband were known as Gertie and Ray. But in her writings, she signed herself as Zitkala-Ša,[4] and Zitkala-Ša is the name she used in her correspondence with Carlos Montezuma.

## A YANKTON SIOUX

Gertrude, as a child, lived only a half-mile from the Indian agency at Greenwood on the Yankton Reservation in Dakota. The Yankton tribe of the Sioux had ceased military activities in 1859 when they accepted a 430,000-acre reservation. Gertrude's early years were a time in which distrust and dislike of the White man were common themes among the Yankton elders, passed on to Gertrude by her mother.[5]

Gertrude grew up in a village dominated by women, children, and old men. Warfare and disease had winnowed the population of young men. The first eight years of her life were relatively tranquil, filled by her mother with an emphasis on the old Sioux lifestyle.[6] However, Quaker missionaries had targeted the Yankton Reservation, gathering up children for education in the East. The Quakers totally supported the policy of keeping young children away from the reservation to enhance the process of assimilation. David was sent to White's Manual Labor Institute in Wabash, Indiana. He returned three years later, was granted a land allotment in 1892 and never again left the reservation.

Gertrude went with the Quakers to White's in 1884 at the age of eight. Despite her mother's and David's admonitions, her imagination was fired by Quaker stories of grand sights, and especially, red apples.[7] Ultimately David supported Gertrude's argument with her mother, believing in the importance of education. After three years at school where she was subjected to the usual Indian boarding school system of assimilation, she returned to her mother, but from age eleven to age fifteen she was buffeted by a loyalty to her mother and her tribal culture and a longing for more education. During this time she spent a few months in 1890 at the Santee Normal Training School in Nebraska. Finally, she returned to White's for three more years, graduating in 1895 at the age of nineteen. Her commencement speech attacking inequality for women prompted a Quaker woman to pay her tuition at a Quaker school, Earlham College in Richmond, Indiana.

Gertrude's early college years despite being the only Indian student were good years. She was popular and productive, and she developed her natural talents for writing, speech, and music. She played both piano and violin, often performing in the community. In the late nineteenth century, speech in college featured truly heralded and acclaimed oratory. Gertrude won the college oratory contest in February 1896 of her freshman year. This entitled her to participate in the state contest in Indianapolis, where she was not only the sole Indian, but also the only female contestant. Cheered on by her Earlham fellow students, despite being the last speaker in the program, she presented her winning, ten-minute Earlham speech, "Side by Side."[8] Beginning with a historical recounting of early Indian "barbarism" and warfare, the speech moved to the slow growth of civilization that culminated in the unique freedoms of America, and finished by outlining the responsibilities of America towards the native peoples. She argued that the Indian people possessed an admirable culture with fine human values before the appearance of the White man, and that American principles appropriately should provide the Indian people with equal opportunity, justice, and love. "We come from mountain fastnesses, from cheerless plains, from far-off low-wooded streams, seeking the 'White Man's ways.' Seeking your skill in industry and in art, seeking labor and honest independence, seeking the treasures of knowledge and wisdom, seeking to comprehend the spirit of your laws and the genius of your noble institutions, seeking by a new birthright to unite with yours our claim to a common country, seeking the Sovereign's crown that we may stand side by side with you in ascribing royal honor to our nation's flag. America, I love thee. 'Thy people shall be my people and thy God my God.'"[9] This was a speech that would have been admired by both Carlos Montezuma and Richard Henry Pratt.

As the winners were to be announced, a white sheet banner was lifted by a student group, containing a caricature drawing of an Indian girl, crudely labeled with the word, "squaw."[10] This made the experience even more delightful when Gertrude was awarded one of the two prizes.

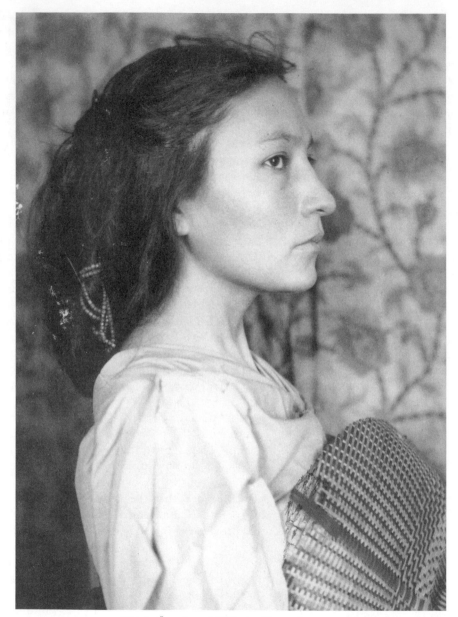

*Zitkala-Ša—Around 1900, Age Twenty-four*

Gertrude was welcomed back to the college campus with a major celebration, virtually the entire school turning out. Buoyed by the experience, but plagued with guilty feelings toward her mother (remember that her mother never budged from her old-way beliefs, and especially her attitude toward Whites), her energy was consumed. She collapsed and had to recuperate with a family in Knightstown for the last six weeks of school. In retrospect, this can be viewed as the first physical evidence of a life-long conflict: her desire for success and enjoyment of higher education vying with an intense loyalty to her Sioux culture, with the pot kept boiling by the unrelenting pressure of her mother, who despite her marriages to three White men spoke only the Dakota language. Frustration and physical symptoms came from the fact that Gertrude could find no compromise; it was either the Indian way or the White way. Her physical problem would recur throughout her college years, forcing her to leave Earlham after two years, before she could complete her work for a degree. The symptoms she reported listed stomach complaints, weariness, low spirits—likely the manifestations of her ongoing inner conflict and struggle.

It was at this time that Gertrude began to think, as did Montezuma, Charles Eastman, and others, that her success in the White world could serve as an example for both Whites and Indians of what could be accomplished.

Seeing a return to the reservation as a surrender, she resolved to teach at an eastern Indian school. In 1897, at the age of twenty-one, Gertrude was hired to teach at the Carlisle Indian School. Pratt, the singular and irrepressible superintendent of Carlisle, was initially attracted by her oratorical and musical skills. It doesn't take much imagination to consider that Pratt at first viewed Gertrude as a model for his goals, the acculturation of young Indians. Her speaking, writing, and musical skills were testimony to her own successful transition. If he knew of her inner conflict, of her intense loyalty to her Indian culture, he would never have hired her.

Gertrude was delighted with her first impressions of Carlisle, describing it as a quaint little village. Teaching was a vehicle for her, not her passion. She was willing to function as a teacher, believing the position would provide her opportunities for professional development and emergence in White society. She was a soloist and an orator (recitation from *Hiawatha*) with the Carlisle Indian Band.[11] For Pratt, her talents were examples, a model. For Gertrude, her talents were tools by which she could demonstrate the worthiness and abilities of Indians.

Gertrude almost immediately contacted literary societies from Washington to Boston. For example, she was invited to speak and play the violin at a meeting of a Washington literary club, at which President McKinley would be present.[12] Contacts at these literary meetings led to the publication of her first article, "Impressions of an Indian Childhood," in the *Atlantic Monthly*, in January 1900. This was followed by articles ("The School Days of an Indian Girl" and "An Indian Teacher Among Indians") in the February and March issues. It was with these articles that Gertrude chose the name Zitkala-Ša, and it was her professional name that became known in eastern social and literary circles. These articles, later published in 1921 in a collection of her stories,[13] were the first publication of an autobiographical story by an Indian, describing the difficulty of being an Indian growing up in White society. In April 1900, *Harper's Bazaar* described her work in a column, making readers aware that she was attracting much attention in eastern cities.

Pratt's reaction was initially supportive, recognizing that the first article described the problems and the poor quality of life on the reservations, and the level to which an educated

Indian could arise. But the increasing angry tone toward White society and the obvious pride in being an Indian in the later articles were not in harmony with Pratt's belief in total assimilation. Pratt published a bitter review of one of her stories in the April 12, 1901, issue of *The Red Man and Helper*, the Carlisle newspaper. Pratt attributed her ability to her White education, and she was remiss for not being grateful. The story itself was "immoral," portraying the inability of a Sioux warrior, educated at an off-reservation school, to return to his culture.

In Pratt's eyes, Zitkala-Ša had changed from the shy Gertrude Simmons to the aggressive and popular Zitkala-Ša. Pratt sent Zitkala-Ša west at the end of the spring term, to recruit students for Carlisle. A long train ride home to Yankton provided ample time for Zitkala-Ša to anticipate the emotions of her family reunion. Yankton, and in particular her mother's lifestyle, were now seen with new eyes, influenced by her eastern experience. The poverty of the reservation struck her hard, and it was not just her now biased personal point of view, because life was undeniably and obviously difficult on the reservation. Her brother, David Simmons, had been out of work for two years, replaced by a White man in his position as assistant government clerk at the agency, and was now trying to support the family by farming.

In the last decades of the 1800s, the Yankton Sioux were under great pressure, for their land, and against their culture. The chiefs had been replaced with appointed representatives expected to approve government proposals. The Treaty of 1858 granted Yankton communal ownership of 430,405 acres, and now the allotment plan was underway. By the end of 1892, the appointed council of "leaders" had ceded all Yankton lands to the United States as individual people accepted allotments with little if any protest. Many of the Yankton had returned from eastern schools and approved this apparent move away from the old ways. In 1891, the appointed Yankton leaders, the Speaking Council, prepared a constitution that delegated decision-making power to the government Indian office. David Simmons signed this constitution, although he later was a leader in the fight to revoke the constitution and establish a true Yankton government.

Most of the Yankton accepted two parcels of land, one near the Missouri River for a home site and one farther west for farming. For many years, the Yankton families moved between these sites, spending the summers camping on their farmland and the winter seasons at their home sites. By 1900, this pattern of life had ended as more and more Yankton leased or sold their land. The Yankton Reservation in southeastern South Dakota along the Missouri River and the Nebraska border now consists of 36,561 acres and contains about 6,000 Yankton, Yanktonai, and Assinibone Sioux, all speaking the Nakota dialect. Today, there are 7,178 enrolled members in the Yankton Sioux Tribe.

In the summer of 1900, Zitkala-Ša could easily see the encroachment of White settlers. The poverty of her family stood in marked contrast to the White homes, and fueled Zitkala-Ša's underlying anger and resentment toward the Whites. In her American Indian Stories, she poignantly wrote about her temporary abandonment of her culture.[14]

In the rest of the country, Casey Jones died at the throttle of his "Cannon Ball" express, saving his passengers' lives; William McKinley, the Republican, beat the Democratic candidate, William Jennings Bryan, in the presidential election; Dr. Walter Reed discovered that yellow fever is transmitted by the mosquito; and *The Red Badge of Courage* by Stephen Crane was a bestseller. A bill to make lynching a federal crime was defeated, but Brigham Henry Roberts of Utah was expelled from the House of Representatives on charges of polygamy. There were 8,000 automobiles on the road, but eighteen million horses and mules were still in use. Kodak's Brownie Box Camera sold for $1, and film for six pictures cost ten to fifteen cents.

RETURNING TO CARLISLE was a reinforcing experience for Zitkala-Ša. She was now thoroughly dedicated to the preservation of her heritage, seeing that the White teachers were devoted to their own values and cultures and were determined to bury Indian notions and beliefs. Not surprising, neither Pratt nor Zitkala-Ša could compromise their positions that clearly represented opposing causes. There is no doubt, not even after all these years, that Zitkala-Ša could be irascible; her self-righteous attitude was not easy to deal with, a worthy match for the opinionated Pratt.

Upon her return to Carlisle, Zitkala-Ša fell in love with Thomas Marshall, a Lakota Sioux from the Pine Ridge Reservation, a man she had originally met when they had been together as students at White's, and who was now a sophomore at nearby Dickinson College.[15] Marshall and Zitkala-Ša become engaged, but within months after Zitkala-Ša left Carlisle for Boston, Marshall died of measles. This sad experience together with the growing militancy of her philosophy led Zitkala-Ša in a new direction, again with Quaker support.

In late 1900, Zitkala-Ša enrolled in the New England Conservatory of Music in Boston.[16] Except for the death of Thomas Marshall, there followed a happy year, filled with music, intellectual company, good friends—all expressed in her letters to Montezuma.[17] Nevertheless, this good life did not tempt Zitkala-Ša; she had already decided to return to Yankton. When her Quaker sponsorship ended, her financial support depended on her success as a writer. In 1901 she published "The Trial Path" and "The Soft-Hearted Sioux," and her book, *Old Indian Legends*. "The Soft-Hearted Sioux" is especially meaningful, dealing with an eastern educated man who could not escape being between two cultures upon his return to the reservation.[18] These stories incurred Pratt's wrath, expressed in sharp and accusatory language. This vocal and loud difference between Pratt and Zitkala-Ša occurred at the same time during which Montezuma and Zitkala-Ša were trying to establish and maintain their relationship. Surely it must have been difficult for Montezuma, a Pratt protégé.

## A LOVE AFFAIR

It is accurate to describe the thirty-five-year-old Montezuma and twenty-five-year-old Zitkala-Ša as being in love.[19] Their love was fostered by a basic motivating force in each, a desire to be an example of what an Indian could accomplish in White society, and by a shared distrust and dislike of the Indian Bureau developed by their personal reservation experiences.

Montezuma spent two and one-half years at Carlisle, 1893–1896. It is not known how Montezuma and Zitkala-Ša first met. Montezuma left Carlisle before Zitkala-Ša arrived, but he frequently returned to visit the school, and they could have met on one of these visits. The relationship most likely began when Montezuma accompanied the Carlisle Band (as "team doctor") on a tour of eastern cities in March 1900.[20] At each performance, Zitkala-Ša recited "The Famine" from *Hiawatha*. Although Mrs. Cook also accompanied the band to act as chaperone for Zitkala-Ša, Montezuma and Zitkala-Ša had plenty of opportunity to get to know each other.

The evidence of their love can be found only in Zitkala-Ša's letters of 1901. Alas, Montezuma's letters to Zitkala-Ša are lost, and their story must be reconstructed unilaterally from Zitkala-Ša's letters, carefully saved by Montezuma, all written with a bold hand on 5x7 plain paper, each page numbered, four to five words to a line using em dashes instead of commas and periods, with liberal use of exclamation points.[21] Her salutations range from a polite "Dear Friend" to "My Sweetheart" at her emotional zenith, to simply "Montezuma," and even worse, no greeting, when she was stirred with anger. Her closings similarly ranged from a simple "Goodbye" to "Lovingly" and "Goodnight Dear Heart," but an abrupt "Zitkala" or just the letter "Z" when she was short of patience.

They had so much going for them, both successful, well-educated, intelligent, sharing the bond of being rebellious members of a minority in the White world. Yet they were never certain about their relationship, to the point of keeping it a secret; no mention appears in public writings or writings of others. In the beginning of their correspondence, Zitkala-Ša asked Montezuma "to use plain envelopes, for your name on the envelope is too conspicuous."[22]

The eventual parting of their ways was the result of a fundamental conflict in their most passionate beliefs. Zitkala-Ša went back and forth, from loving to anger, even taunting Montezuma with lists of others striving for her love. In February 1901, in the midst of her courtship with Montezuma, Zitkala-Ša was writing of her decision to return to Yankton to teach, but more importantly, of her belief that the Indian culture must be and should be preserved. Montezuma, of course, was a devotee of Pratt, not about to change his mind that the reservation system and the old ways must go. Montezuma would not and could not abandon his private practice and return to a reservation. His unhappy and frustrating reservation experience sealed that attitude.

THIS WASN'T THE FIRST TIME MONTEZUMA was spurned in love. Several years earlier, in 1898, Tena Knox was a patient in Montezuma's hospital; somehow he made her acquaintance, perhaps even before her hospitalization, but to his surprise she was discharged and returned home to Clyde, Kansas, without telling him. He expressed his love in a letter, a letter that surprised Tena Knox. She wrote him on October 7, 1898, addressing him as "My Dear Friend." "Your letter was just received and it is true that I left without seeing you but not without leaving messages for you, for no matter how heartless you may think me, I did feel your kindness to me during my illness at the Hospital. ...But harder than all these is the knowledge 'my brother' loves me. It is impossible for me to love. I am sorry that I have caused you this pain and wish that I had been more prudent that it may never have come to this, but it seems my life in Chicago was all a mistake anyway. And I hope you will forgive me."[23]

Undeterred, Montezuma wrote back, pouring out his love and his heartache. Tena Knox responded, the second of her two letters in the Montezuma collection, "Dear Doctor Montezuma, Oh, what have I done to cause all this sorrow. Your letter reached me today and I hardly know how to answer it. I only know that I have unconsciously been the cause of a sad disappointment and it grieves me that it is so. For tis hard when we know we have wounded those we respect so highly. Yet I realize I have been too thoughtless. I had never thought of you as really loving me, and the last few months I was there when it seemed everyday our duty must be my last, and at last when every day was all I could do to keep up, I looked for your coming for you were always so happy and I would think 'I must keep up' and I was looking not at the real meaning of your visits. Oh, I can never forgive myself for being so thoughtless and so seeming false though God knows I did not mean to be trying to win your love. …there is only one man in the world I can love, if we never meet again it will be for the best, but if it is God's will we will meet. …I cannot tell you my grief over this trouble I have caused you. Sincerely your friend, Tena Knox."[24]

ZITKALA-ŠA INTENDED to return to the reservation to harvest more stories for her writing, and in her writings to demonstrate Indian values and culture. In one of her first letters to Montezuma in February 1901 she said, "As for plans—I do not mean to give up my literary work—but while the old people last I want to get from them their treasured ideas of life. This I can do by living among them. Thus I mean to divide my time between teaching and getting story material."[25]

In the preface to her 1901 book *Old Indian Legends*, Zitkala-Ša wrote:

> These legends are relics of our country's once virgin soil. These and many others are the tales the little black-haired aborigine loved so much to hear beside the night fire. …And now I have tried to transplant the native spirit of these tales—root and all—into the English language, since America in the last few centuries has acquired a second tongue.
>
> The old legends of America belong quite as much to the blue-eyed little patriot as to the black-haired aborigine. And when they are grown all like the wise grown-ups may they not lack interest in a further study of Indian folklore, a study which so strongly suggests our near kinship with the rest of humanity and points a steady finger toward the great brotherhood of mankind, and by which one is so forcibly impressed with the possible earnestness of life as seen through the teepee door. If it be true that much lies "in the eye of the beholder," than in the American aborigine as in any other race, sincerity of belief, though it were based upon mere optical illusion, demands a little respect.
>
> After all he seems at heart much like other people.[26]

Montezuma, like Pratt, wanted nothing from the past. He was totally committed to assimilation. He could not share Zitkala-Ša's view that there was an Indian heritage worth preserving. But Zitkala-Ša didn't "agree with Col. Pratt about the great superiority of non-reservation schools. The old folks have a claim upon us. It is selfish and cruel to abandon them entirely."[27]

Montezuma and Zitkala-Ša were planning a meeting in Chicago. "As for stopping in Chicago—I would not plan for more than one day. Were it possible to arrive in the city in the forenoon—then go on in the evening. Don't bother about a room for me as I should want to see your office anyway. …readjust yourself to new surroundings in good earnest but do not forget the sunshine in the broad out of doors—Does it not say—Cheer up—Cheer up! Each new day demands new victories—Today my friend let me extend a hand for your new awakening! Let me wish the day's sunshine may enter your soul—I am your friend."

*out of doors — Does it not say — Cheer up — Cheer up! Each new day demands new victories — Is — my friend — let me extend a hand for your new awakening! Let me wish the day's sunshine may enter your soul — I am your friend Zitkala-Ša*

In March 1901, Zitkala-Ša's stories were still causing a stir at Carlisle, but Montezuma was more appreciative. Zitkala-Ša wrote: "Dear Friend, Your understanding of my story pleases me. Your prophecy is correct. Already I've heard that at Carlisle my story is pronounced 'trash' and 'I—worse than Pagan.' Certainly people are welcomed to their opinions. I must cling to my own. You have long kept Col. Pratt as your friend—do not lose him on my account. He has revealed himself to be fully small and bigoted. For all his imposing avoirdupois. …If my work does not stand on its own merit neither the King's horses nor the King's men can hold it long together. It is just this spirit in me, which offends the Col.— who has said I was too independent! I won't be another's mouthpiece—I will say just what I think. I fear no man—some times I think I do not fear God. But I do respect the Indians' spirit within me for whose being or going I cannot account. The 'Atlantic Monthly' wrote me a note in praise of the story. An intelligent literary critic says my writing has a distinguished air about it—others say I am covering myself with glory! Oh—but so many words: What do I care—I know that all the world could not take a liberal view of my work—But in spite of other varied opinions I am bound to *live* my own life! …I won't argue nor fight. That is not my purpose. I merely say what I think and there is the end!"[28] As a measure of Zitkala-Ša's growing reputation, her story "The Soft-Hearted Sioux" appeared in the March 1901 issue of *Harper's Magazine* that also included an article by Woodrow Wilson and short stories by Bret Harte and Edith Wharton.

## ZITKALA-ŠA'S EARLY WRITINGS

| TITLE | PUBLICATION | DATE |
|---|---|---|
| "Impressions of an Indian Childhood" | *Atlantic Monthly* | January 1900 |
| "The School Days of an Indian Girl" | *Atlantic Monthly* | February 1900 |
| "An Indian Teacher Among Indians" | *Atlantic Monthly* | March 1900 |

(published as a book in 1901: *Old Indian Legends*[29])

| | | |
|---|---|---|
| "The Trial Path" | *Harper's Magazine* | March 1901 |
| "The Soft-Hearted Sioux" | *Harper's Magazine* | October 1901 |
| "A Warrior's Daughter" | *Everybody's Magazine* | 1902 |
| "Why I Am a Pagan" | *Atlantic Monthly* | December 1902 |

(published as a book, with additional stories and essays, in 1921: *American Indian Stories*[30])

But Montezuma's praise couldn't change her plans. "Oh— I really can't stay more than a day in Chicago—I would not feel justified to be the cause of your patients' deaths— by causing you to neglect them. What if I could not stop off at all?" And later: "As for stopping off in some city—Don't say 'please'—It is not becoming. Do not bother about a room anywhere. My visit would be only a few hours. I'll tell you the day some time in advance so you may kill off the patients who otherwise might linger to demand your attention on that day."[31]

Montezuma's letters were apparently long and effusive in promoting (perhaps prematurely) a marital union. "The dual spirit of your letter confuses a poor reader like me. If the length of time required to peruse a letter denotes an interesting reading than I say your epistle is decidedly 'interesting.' If when all the sentences are in sets, pairs—an affirmative and a negative to counteract the first—means a show of kindliness—then your letter was very kind. Was it really worthy of you? I cannot say. First you said—'Practically we can do as *we* please.' Then later— 'If God wills we are not to marry we shall still remain good friends.' Do you intend I should infer that *you please* to blame God for a cold philosophical love you mean to put on me? Cold love is impossible. It is like trying to warm your hands by the crystal brilliancy of an icicle! Warm loving, growing affection is capable of shaming a frozen heart! But dearie me! I do not care about plunging headlong into the abyss of an avalanche. Such measured love may serve well enough in a purely competitive business but hardly suffices for wedlock. Is it possible then to want what we do not truly love? Yes—I can conjure up conditions where such would be quite plausible. For instance—a fine horse to draw your wagon! Feed your horse, shout its pretty name! You love that horse, don't you! Feeding and stroking won't buy me! I am now puzzled for what you would marry me. Were you planning Charity Hospital under the guise of matrimony? There are plenty of Charity Institutions in the cities whither proper lack of pride and respect would take me! But for one lifetime at least I am not so totally depraved as to accept charity—private or public! I do not want to demoralize you! I had no thoughts of limiting your ambition. Perhaps the Indians are not human enough to waste your skill upon! Stay in Chicago. Do! I consider my plan a more direct path to my high ideals. It will be a test of character but I shall not stay away for cowardly fears. If I succeed—it is genius. If I fail—it was due time to undeceive those who credit me with genius! In the meanwhile I am what I am! I owe no apologies to God or men!"[32]

"You suggest seeing my mother. It were useless for she has no influence upon me. But that is out of the question now. I myself being satisfied that you do not love me enough. I shall never tell you in so many words whether I love you or not. If my giving you the preference to a long list of applicants—conveys no measuring to you. Words would be sounding metals only. Race has little to do in the man who is to win me. Shall I turn to elaborate details to convince you—I had a more subtle reason for choosing you than mere material convenience and family?

On my list are these—
1. a well-known German violinist
2. a Harvard professor
3. a Harvard postgraduate
4. a well-known writer of today
5. a man of a prominent New York family
6. 4 western men scattered from Montana to Dakota

Why, I have not sought anyone of them. I have not counted any of last year's nor those previous for it would be too long a list. I write all this stuff to show you that there are other men who can give me as much as you could. I do not care about a doctor's profession more than those of the others. In truth music, art and literature are more in line with my own. I raise both hands to the great blue overhead and my spirit revels in a freedom no less than the vast conclave! I am free! I am proud! I am chosen! I caper to no world of pigmies nor a pigmy God! You say this is idealist. In your heart you call it an insanity I suppose. But better my spirit by whatever name you choose to label it than being a perfect slave to public fads and farce religions. It is more practical for the time being. To be a slave but practical drudge does not sound well in my ear. But here's to your health, long life, and prosperity! I would respect you no matter how much you differ from my way of thinking. But as soon as you drop your own honest conviction to chatter the parrot's part—then my respect and interest are lost. So my friend—we agree to disagree. I cannot stop in your beloved chosen city! I shall pass through because I have to. I am decided I shall leave either Monday or Tuesday— a week from today." And in an added warning: "Do not attempt to meet me. I am gone entirely out of your reach."[33]

Did Montezuma and Zitkala-Ša view their differences as we see them now? Was this an insurmountable obstacle or a source of stimulating discourse? Are Zitkala-Ša's comments in her letters meant to be amusing? I think not. Zitkala-Ša constantly challenged Montezuma in his position, his views, his unwillingness to join her on a reservation. The conversation in her letters was not for fun, it was intended to accomplish their union on her terms.

She called Pratt "pigheaded," and Montezuma, "sweetheart." How different Montezuma's life would have been if he had bent a little. Her letters of April and March 1901, contain many challenging paragraphs, paragraphs that must have built further stubbornness in Montezuma, rather than conversion.

Zitkala-Ša seemed to anticipate the impact of her letters, because outbursts of differing opinions or emotions were usually followed by an apology. Just a month later, Zitkala-Ša was once again pressing her request for Montezuma to join her on the Yankton Reservation, "Just to be frank—I want to stay a year in Dakota for my mother's sake. She's over eighty and cranky (like me) and I owe it at least one year to care for her. I've been wondering what your mind is now regarding a Government position."[34]

Montezuma's reply was a box of candy, a strategy that was, on some occasions, effective. "My best-est-dear—At last the sweets have arrived! How I wish you were here to eat the chocolates."[35] But the debate was not slowed. "Sweetheart—I read what the Helper had to say about Hampton's statement that civilization is not reached in a hundred years. History of the Pale-faced voices shows that to be true. Today is the Product of twenty centuries of recorded time and no one knows how much unwritten ages! I resent Carlisle's talking of you as it does. Its talk—boasts—of you as a savage Apache and now an honorable physician in Chicago—the result of Education!! I guess if the character was not in you— savage or otherwise—education could not make you the man you are today. It was not that you were Indian—nor that civilization was an irresistible poser—but because in an unusual measure the Spirit of a Universal God was and is in *you*! ...Education has developed the possibilities in me were they not there—no school could put them in! Dear, I hear you say— 'Oh, Oh! Now don't get cranky!' But I wish to see larger than trifling details in a question like that of the powers of years to produce the flower of civilization. It is a sad thing to see one's race practically prisoners of war—Bound like babies—and must have a permit for every move! It is heart-rendering to see a government try experiments upon a real race—If like physicians they would first try big vivisection, their wonderful theories on lower creatures like cats and dogs, then the Indian, I might not feel it so keenly at times! Say—try starving out life by feeding insufficient unfit food to cats, then having found the best death rate, try it in earnest upon the old Indians on these Reserves. As it is it is cruelly long! ...Enough—Let me tell you of pleasanter things. This evening I found the first wild rose I have seen this year. I brought it home—thinking to send it to you—but it is so withered and shriveled up—I must wait till another time when I can press one in proper time. I wish you were here or I there with you this evening. Well perhaps we may meet sooner than we know. I may not feel equal to staying till November in Yankton. In that case dear—I would come to you. Would that be all right? Now I must say Goodnight—Happy dreams to you. May the great Spirit guard you for me—my well chosen one. Yours, Zitkala."[36]

The very next day, Zitkala-Ša reached out to Montezuma in response to criticism of her at Carlisle. "See the Helper! This is the way Pratt loves me! Ah! But he is pigheaded— and little divine. I must live my life. I must think in my own way (Since I cannot help it). I must write the lessons I see. ...You are not ignorant of the fact that I have many many admirers—but since How I turn to you for the first time for a word of courage. Shall I continue in my work or shall I keep still? If I had no confidence in you—I would not write this letter. I will recover from this nausea caused by the crude inability of those who would be critics of my art. But I am ill this moment. Ah—I rise. I lift my head! I laugh at the babble! I dare—I do! I guess I am not so sick after all."

They continued their debate by mail, she in Boston, he in Chicago, as Montezuma suggested that she only visit her mother, not live with her. "O Yes I think of you some times— I hope you don't object. You know even a cat may look at the King! I wish I could make reply to your philosophy but being neither a pugilist (like Col. Pratt) nor a debater (like you) I have to be content to do what I feel without explaining or justifying myself. I must live because I must—not because why. If a well robin sings he does not heed the cat who says 'Yes you use your throat in a skillful manner but I could use mine to better advantage when I taste you.' Nor does the bird care if a kind hearted mortal is enjoying his warbling. He is unmindful of praise and blame alike. He sings because he must. Not because why! …The robin that taught me this lesson lodged on a tree near my window—not because it knew I was an appreciative audience. Another one tree was the best one for him, but because he was a universal creature fliting from tree to tree. He does not willfully choose a single tree and there stay aloft until he dies. Sure he builds a nest in a single tree but he flies to a hundred others too! Since you claim all America as your universal home, I don't think you are very consistent when you avoid the reservation for a dwelling in a city. Just now you are partial to a city. You are not doing as broad a thing as you think in thoughts. While my robin visits a forest of trees where he sings his little life out to the earth and sky, he returns again to his nest. …I have a mother who loves me because it is a mother's instinct to love her child. In turn I love her because it is a part of a child's make up to love its parent. Neither mother nor child loves because why, but because God made them so—because they must. Now while I feel the Universe is my stamping ground, that earth is not too wide nor the sky too high for my soul to live in. I am drawn by instinctive fire to my old mother. Visit her only? That is cruel and heartless. I must live with her and show her each day a practical demonstration of my love for her. She will never realize what cost it may mean to me who has acquired so many artificial tastes that they have become my second nature. But I must not consider the appreciative capacity of my audience. Learning thrift and business faculty are mighty convenient things in this greedy world—since we must live in it—but I think love and kindness measure more actual living— a more outspreading growth of one's soul—than their reverse. …I think a word of cheer that I might give my mother's heart far more potent in a thousand years from today than the mere reaching of a countless, heartless, senseless herd of people. Still if there is the least good to be gained by this appealing to a multitude, it is a secondary matter not wholly unworthy of consideration. Is it possible then to combine these two? Is it within a single person's power to be loyal to a feeble helpless mother and still not be the better able to appeal to a thousand mothers—or parents. For being kind to those nearest first? I am going to try to combine the two! I am going to my mother because she cannot come to me. I can write stories and have them published in the East for the so-called civilized peoples. This is combining the two. This shows you my mind on the subject. I won't try to reason for you. You know your own heart best. Follow your highest conceptions—that is all we can do. You ask if you could make me happy. I don't know. If you considered it—worth your while and should try to do so— I imagine you might be able to make me happy and many others too. You say you love me— but I am no judge—others say that to me. How am I to know which one is true. For surely all cannot love me alike. To tell you the honest truth I am a delusion and a snare. You should love one more able to give you as much and as largely as you give of your heart. However if you finally agree with me that life is lived most when we love and that to be happy individuals—you would have to come to me in Yankton. You could do a vast deal of good by filling the position of Agency physician better than any of your predecessors. But remember I do not ask you to do it. You must do it from choice. If that you cannot—then you don't love me enough—after all. I would forgive you though and keep your friendship sacred in my heart. Truth is worth any cost—If by this letter I prove that you love me in that you were mistaken and do not feel such a vital sentiment for me. Which ever it does prove—is truth. That is what we both are seeking. We must abide by that. I have said enough in one letter. I stop this for until I have your reply. Then in my next letter I shall be better able to say whether you shall be permitted to meet me at the station or whether it would be wiser to pass through without your knowledge. I am quite equal for either."[37]

The steadfastness, independence, and strength of Zitkala-Ša's commitment deserve admiration. She truly rebelled at the idea of becoming a Chicago physician's wife in White society. "I guess it seems odd to you to find another as stiff necked in old opinions as your willful self! I have no desire to make definite plans for my future life. I am too independent. I would not like *to have to obey* another—never!"[38] Her resentment of Montezuma's desires and ideals emerges in her letters. This resentment must have further strengthened her commitment, because surely she knew the poverty of the reservation; she already knew she did not thoroughly enjoy the profession of teaching; she knew she would leave behind the intellectual and artistic aspects of life she so enjoyed, and she worried about the irritating pressures to be experienced with her mother and family. Marrying Montezuma seemed like an easy way out, how tempting it must have been—but how she should be admired for seeing that it truly was not the easy way out, that it would require excessive compromise on her part. "Oh—I am not encouraging since I am not. I am only guessing. By the way I hope you still forgive me for answering your letter before the proper week of silence. That is your rule—Is it not? If you do not like letters too close in succession I'll wait two weeks next time or even all summer if that would meet your approval. Seriously is there no reason that would make you think it by far a grander thing to live among the Indians; to give a little cheer to the fast-dying old people than to be a missionary among the whites? Consider this well— for upon your reply—my mind is likely to be changed. Earning more money is a fair inducement but surely not the highest. It is not my highest, at any rate. It is only little over two weeks when I shall be westward bound. I trust you are well and very happy as you usually appear to be. What is 'Wassaja'? A 'teaser'? I got a few Indian things from my poor old mother. I am proud to have the things but they made me want to weep to see that my mother really loves me. And thinks of me at times. I wish I could talk to you instead of writing. I do not know how to write a letter."[39]

MONTEZUMA COLLECTED Indian objects. He viewed these pieces as historical relics, not as present day symbols of an ongoing heritage. The study in his home was adorned with his collection of Indian artifacts, but it was a museum of his heart, not of his brain. Both Zitkala-Ša and Montezuma valued Indian culture, but Montezuma as a proud nostalgia of the past, Zitkala-Ša as a present day reminder of Indian uniqueness. They did agree on one thing. Both wanted the benefits of American life (technology, healthcare, education) for their people; they disagreed on the process.

Perhaps Zitkala-Ša's old and ailing mother played a part in this love story of conflict. Zitkala-Ša proposed that Montezuma become the agency physician for at least a short while to allow Zitkala-Ša to be with her mother. Zitkala-Ša was driven by her life-long guilt to heal the rift between mother and daughter, rooted in Zitkala-Ša's involvement in White society. Was Zitkala-Ša testing Montezuma's love by her demand for him to return to the reservation, or did she know that this was totally unacceptable, and a method to provide Montezuma with a way out of their relationship? Probably both. She was not what Montezuma wanted her to be. He would not live as she wanted him to live.

Nevertheless, Zitkala-Ša agreed to stop in Chicago on her way to the Yankton Reservation and her mother. This may have been a response to an encouraging and support-ive letter from Montezuma after more criticism of her from Carlisle. "Moles are all of sizes, strange but true. A strong bodied man with a mole heart must really do heroic work at stir-ring the earth and ferreting out earthworms for his food. But how many generations must glide by before nature turned compassionate at last gives the blind brats in human shape a second sight. Till then like Col. Pratt will make mountains out of mere rocks by the way. What folly to argue with them about a matter beyond their best comprehension. Speak to them about the crimson sunset flooding the brown hills with glory and they reply that all is darkness and life is only in ferreting for earthworms! Bah! In my heart I have charity for the mole-hearted creatures. I believe they are evolving toward a perfect divine idea. They are crude now in this particular stage of their evolution. I blame them not for being in the hands of an All-Maker who is moulding them like clay! And I have sufficient faith that in God's own time He will perfect the pottery is busy with. I have re-covered from my first sense of illness upon reading the crude, spiteful little scribe. …For two days I was actually sick. People around began to worry. I thought that I was in for an attack of malaria fever. No it was not that. I was well as soon as I saw my mistake in taking things too much to heart. Is not the mind a most wonderful thing? …My friend, you were loyal to our race to speak a liberal mind in behalf of me of the least of the Sioux tribe. Perhaps that will give a new idea to Col. Pratt. Since straws show which way the wind blows! But do be cautious. Do not lose the Col. for your friend. I don't like fighting at all. I will speak my mind but never a breath in argu-ment or heated controversy! Life is all too brief to waste time in such a beastly occupation."[40]

Even before the westward trip to Chicago, Zitkala-Ša and Montezuma were discussing the possibility of a pan-Indian organization. In Montezuma's plans, as was certainly the custom of the times, the organization would be composed only of men. "Your idea of an organization seems a plausible project. Why do you think the men are able alone to do it—and in a queer after thought—suggest the Indian women should have theirs too? For spite, I feel like putting my hand forward and simply wiping the Indian Men's committee into nowhere!!! No—I should not really do such a thing. Only I do not understand *why* your organization does not include Indian women. Am I not an Indian woman as capable to think on serious matters and as thoroughly interested in their race as any one or two of you men put together? Why do you dare to leave us out? Why? Some times as I ponder the prepon-derance of men which are so tremendously out of proportion with the small results I laugh. It is all some waste of time than we pause to realize. …Your last two letters rather made me feel that I had better stop in Chicago overnight anyway. We can talk then!! Let us promise to sit on opposite sides of a table and if we get very very much enraged than we use pencil argument! We must not come to blame in our intense respect for one another. Do you agree? I went in to see about my train. I leave Boston Wednesday 1 P.M. and shall arrive in

Chicago Thursday (May 9) 5:25 P.M. If you are not there—I shall go on my journey."[41]

The meeting in Chicago was heralded with a hastily written stern warning. "Did I not tell you to beware of me? I say I am a delusion and a snare. Do not be too sure of me for I am the uncertain quantity—perhaps may prove to be the 'Minus' one too. I swear I am not yours! I do not belong to any body. Do not wish to be! First I like roaming about too well to settle down anywhere. Second I know absolutely nothing about house keeping. I would be restless and a burden—See? I can help you most as a friend—but never otherwise. Oh well—we will talk to better advantage in a few days. …Now—my friend—do be careful. I must warn you again. I am uncertain!! Hoping to see you Thursday."[42]

Chicago's downtown railroad stations (only the Union Station at Adams and Canal still stands and functions today) were busy places. The trains had great names: The City of New Orleans and The Panama Limited to New Orleans, The Green Diamond, The Silent Knight, and The Zipper to St. Louis, The Twentieth Century Limited, The Admiral, and The Knickerbocker to New York, The James Whitcomb Riley and The Buckeye to Cincinnati, The Hoosier and The Tippecanoe to Indianapolis, The Texas Chief to Houston, The Antelope to Oklahoma City, The Olympian to Seattle, and The Hiawatha and The Black Hawk to Minneapolis.[43] Zitkala-Ša left from the South Station (completed in 1899) on the Boston & Albany Railroad for a 200-mile trip to Albany, New York. At the Union Station in Albany, she connected with New York Central's Twentieth Century Limited; she departed Boston in the afternoon and arrived twenty-eight hours later at Chicago's La Salle Street Station.

THE TRYST IN CHICAGO must have been emotionally satisfying and fulfilling because over the next few months, Zitkala-Ša's letters reached their most loving and tendersome level. Writing from a train out of St. Paul on the way to the Fort Totten Indian Agency Industrial School in North Dakota where she spent several days and wrote many letters before going on to the reservation in South Dakota, Zitkala-Ša said: "Oh—you do not know how it affected me to find you had not used my purse for my ticket. I felt like burying my face in both my hands and weeping. It was hard to accept it even from you—But I do not want to hurt you so I shall try to hold uppermost in mind the pleasure it may have afforded you to do it. Last night I placed my beautiful red rose on part of my pillow. This morning I awoke but my rose would not be aroused—you were and are now wonderously kind to me. I know it—and appreciate it too. How comes it to pass—I wonder. So long I've wandered hither and thither—careless of others as they were of me. I fear there is some error in all this— …Did you know last evening I wished I had not to leave you? As I think of you I desire for you only. Life's best gifts. I wish you to leap forward not so much in what is generally termed civilization but into true nobility! Upon the strength you have gained may you be enabled to go the yard yourself—though I am sure you are now far more than your best friends know. If my letter is saturated with the odor of cigars do not imagine I did the smoking. Some how the gentlemen are careless in our car (though it is not a smoker!) I heard one say—'Where is the Smoking Car?' and I said in my heart—'Where are gentlemen?' With my best love, Goodbye, Yours."[44]

Her letters, however, while indicating a commitment to marriage in November, still contained uncertainties. "I think it is unfortunate that you have been so deeply impressed by those who condemn me for 'my moods.' Perhaps it would be better for you if you should agree with them more than you have done here to me. I know that you must be satisfied with me after a time. Sometimes I even think of sending you a check for my ticket which really you should not have given me. As you did without asking me about it. And then release you from binding yourself to such a one as I am. I am not responsible enough to pretend to occupy any body's heart. I get weary of people who cease striving to please after they think they are sure of their game. See—I am not so sure that November will wean anything out of the old routine after all. I suppose the sweets win over the spelling match— on the way since your last two letters have mentioned them but today brings nothing, not even a letter. I had a letter from my old mother and she has affected my whole thought again. At least one year I must *give* her! If you do not wish to wait for me a year—marry when and whom you choose! I must do what seems to me my first duty. I feel that I must be saying some hard things but I cannot pad them with feathers. Perhaps such a revelation would show you how unworthy I am of your devotion. In an indirect way it may be a kindness to you. I remember you said you were proof against heartbreak. I thank God for that! But I can not help being *myself*. I should indeed feel badly to lose you as my friend but I am not capable of any effort to be agreeable. Forgive me—I pray you. I wonder what you are doing! What you have written for the Redman!! Probably I should not agree with it for I usually find the sentiments in the Carlisle paper contrary to mine! …Here is a pansy I've had in my room! Sincerely from one who does not know her own mind."[45]

Montezuma kept the pressure on with boxes of sweets and daily letters. "I was so glad to get *my daily* letter this afternoon— It is such a source of strength in many more ways that you have ever heard me say. You please me much about your views of helping my cousin. She will be *your* cousin then! I like to have you tell me what you do each day. It puts me in better harmony with you. My dear heart—sometimes I have a great notion to return to Chicago before going to Yankton Agency. But that is only fleeting. I face many hard conditions at Yankton when I go there. At times I shrink from them and feel like pleasing myself chiefly—But ho! I must try to be brave—no one knows the briefness of his or her own life! And I must *do* what I can in the now. Sweetheart—you are brave and your bravery has matured strength which is admirable. I know you *can* make me happy and I hope I may at least gladden your heart a few days out of a year! I know so little about keeping a house in running order that the undertaking is perfectly appalling to me. And from sheer cowardice I almost back out of the experiment. I call it experiment because the affair is strangely *new* to each of us. Now just imagine how convenient it would have been had you been married before! Or I! My cousin would not only be a companion but she could help me in puzzling problems for she is quite a housekeeper. I smile as I picture you fastening screens to the windows and doors of your house. By the way how do the half dozen blades of grass grow now? You get tired and must be very sleepy when night comes. I appreciate your writing me under such trying circumstances. I am well but some how the heat has made me inactive. I cannot think and wish to sleep night and day. I wish I were with you this evening! I wish we could dine together again. I am not casting any reflection upon the people who are entertaining me. …But for all the association I prefer my own beloved. I wish you success each day and real rest each sleep! May I grow more wanting of you—my highly esteemed."[46]

But the very next letter in June 1901 reflected Zitkala-Ša's ambivalence, and for the first time, mention of "the other fellow." "My dear Montezuma, There are several reasons which places the going to Arizona entirely out of the question. Especially since your last letter do I think I am right not to go. …You pleased me by saying there would be a piano in the house. But what do you mean about a brief courtship? Do you suppose it was ended when I said I would give you the preference? That is annoying to say the least. I've a big mind to marry the other fellow and let you find elsewhere the properly prolonged courtship. I set aside the stated month November! Hereafter that time will be indefinite. Just take the dose. I will not consider any argument. Only time will be the prime factor in bringing out the proper outcome of this. Yesterday the stage driver from Oberon said he would bring the box today. I'll not wear it here for I do not like to create talk."[47] Presumably, this last refers to an engagement ring, soon to become infamous.

Zitkala-Ša emphasized to Montezuma in June 1901 her wish to keep talk about marriage strictly between the two of them. "You are right in believing I do not like display. It is my wish to have our wedding informal and very quiet. There will be plenty of time if the world does not come to a sudden end—after the event, for outsiders to hear about it. I may tell my mother, but no one else. I have often wondered within my heart why you did not choose to honor me with your ring. Perhaps you took my joke in earnest. I said I did not wish to be stamped so I could continue to have fun! Still I want you to do what you want to. For my part I should have been proud to have been trusted to wear the usual symbol of love. I have not a single picture of you. I wish I had one! Don't you think it would be nice of you to send me one? This string of wants sounds selfish, I fear, but it grows out of my affection for you. I should not want them if I wished to keep you out of mind and heart. As soon as I go to Yankton I shall begin to make the beaded cushion covers I promised you. It will be my pleasure to make such with my own hands. …That will be my fancy work when I come to live with you! Dear—I want to be kind to you. I want you to be happy and if it is in my power I would like you always to have reason to be proud of your wife 'to be' as she is already of you. Yesterday I received a letter from my publishers asking me to write *another* volume of stories! I shall gather all I can and do the writing when I am in our own home. Sweetheart—would it not be a great work to write *many* volumes of Indian legends? I like to have you tell me of your doings. I marvel at your ability to run a scheduled time! That is wholly beyond my comprehension. I am glad you gave the physicians something to think about. I have been pondering the question of our organizing. Sometimes I think the times are not ripe enough. Then again by the day that there are more educated individuals—old arts will be partially if not wholly lost! Such a puzzle. An organization needs a few million dollars to begin on! Perhaps tomorrow I can write my view of it. By then I trust my thoughts will be focused and clear! Do you remember this rose? It was yours dear and I've kept it a long time. Now I send to you. Affectionately, Zitkala"[48]

"I am glad to hear of your gradual march of triumph into the new life. A house with lawn and flowers surely is a splendid index of a splendid character. That is another feather in your cap! My, your success will eventually fill your cap with so many feathers I'll have to call it a 'war bonnet,' 'Montezuma's war bonnet!' What a striking title for your biography. By the way The Atlantic Monthly has just accepted a little scribble of mine—'Why I am a Pagan.' I imagine Carlisle will rear up on its haunches at sight of the little skyrocket! Ha ha!"[49]

"I have yours asking if it is possible for me to go to Arizona with you. I will not finish this letter today but shall take a few times to consider your proposition. My feeling is that it is best not to. I'd rather you would give me my Arizona in the form of an engagement ring. I do not wear common jewelry but I think the only two I should ever prize would be the engagement ring and wedding ring. I want to give you a duplicate to the plain wedding ring and shall expect you to wear it too. Of course it would be a little larger to fit your finger. I have written only one letter to my mother since I saw you. Then I only told her I was here at Fort Totten! She does not know my plans nor will till it is done. I have not told my brothers either. I am kin to them according to marriage. I am truly a stranger to them. I do not wish to tell my personal affairs to strangers. When you marry me remember it does not in any way bind you to my so called home folks. I want to help mother because she is not able to look out for herself—but my brothers who have always looked after their affairs whether or not it affected me good or ill are welcomed to so continue! Outwardly we are good friends but last year saw the last gifts I mean to make them. I bear no malice but I choose to be independent of all of them. If I can convince my cousin to come in the fall to Chicago I'd come with her. We could run around the corner to some Justice of Peace and be married quietly the evening of the arrival. Then when the announcement cards are sent I'll send some to my brothers; and that will be soon enough. I'd like to see you dear, but never at Yankton Agency unless we were to live there! You had better not come to see me. Perhaps it will be just as well to wait till I come to you! As for writing up your life for publication, I can best do it after I live with you a while! I think it would be best to wait for a year or two before I undertake to write about you. Don't you? I am just seeming to wake up! So gradually—I hope it is 'slow but sure.' For a while I went by the force of my own momentum without any conscious effort or ambition.—Now as I say, I feel the spirit stirring for a little utterance. Dear busybody how are you tonight? I think I could really put my arms around your neck were you in reach."[50]

"Dear can't you ever understand that my mother does not care whom I marry? Proud of you for son! Nonsense! She would no more appreciate you than ṣhe does me! There do get it into your head to leave out the home folks who are strangers to me."

"I am *glad* indeed, to read such favorable reports of your cases. Of course you forget to tell me about those that die! (Dearie— I just could not resist teasing you a wee bit.) Tricked hearts make a wicked world—and suffering is the consequence. Some cases appear as if the innocent were suffering for another's wickedness—but suffering can be eliminated by knowledge. So it is ignorance suffering for past follies. No one person can revolutionize the world in this regard—but—by each looking strictly after his own spiritual as well as material affairs will evolve the problem. I think true kindness is one of the finest traits of one's character. But free giving is not always the real kindness I judge in your case, it was a real kindness to help as you did. Still it is possible to question it—even there. Life is not worth living if it does not demand some little effort on our parts, to continue in it. It is not what we give for nothing, but what we inspire others to try to do that is the best the most valuable gift we can offer to humanity at large. And even to our best friends. ...I am interested in studying life in any form, in any race. Of course I am chiefly occupied in my race—yet to be an all-round thinker I am compelled to study all races. ...I see progress but I am rather reluctant to waste my time in speaking of these things; in writing about them perniciously. 'There is a right time for everything under the sun.' And one great wisdom is to learn the art of recognizing these times! I think thus! I am not telling you what you are to do but I am telling you about my ways of working. Dearie—you have an assumed place in God's mind in the universe from which no one can encroach upon your place by a hair's breadth. So have I—We want to realize that it is a bigger place than the whole United States, which our existence must affect. Not so much because of our nationality nor mode of dress, but because we must reflect like mirrors the all powerful maker, our source. The more we keep our crystal windows free of the mist of vices, the better reflection we can gain. Let us strive after a universal understanding of life. Let us not be centered to run along in the narrow groove of nationality. I am proud of your success, dear—and wish that your highest dreams may even be self excelled. Goodnight my own dear heart."[51]

Sometime in June 1901 Zitkala-Ša wrote an emotional letter, flowing straight through her pen without corrections or rewording. "Dearest heart—It is as you say; the greater part of civilization is a complication of desires! Is it to be lamented? In reply to your statement of a supposed case—the primitive Apache has the present enlightenment to start from and therefore will progress more rapidly than an other race here to fore. Let me ask you a question. Here is a class of college men— will a child reach the same class more quickly in actual studies, because he sits in the room with college men? Gray matter in the brain (if that is the seat of the God spirit) is alike in every child, but for that reason alone we could not ask a five-year-old to do the work of a grown up. There is difference of years—and while the things we spend years to learn may have little or no intrinsic value till they are absolutely necessary for living in this temporary world. Now these conveniences for a shifting temporal world are called by various names. To master them is called civilization—The majority of men and women are hopelessly treading drudgery mills and that is civilization? To be compelled to work when you do not wish it—is drudgery—not civilization! That is about what Carlisle would gain in the end—success in making drudges. I prefer to be stone-dead rather than living-dead! The intellectual class of the so called civilized is a small minority! The majority are drudges—after so many centuries if the Anglo Saxon can produce so small a flower—by what magic do you expect a primitive Indian race to become civilized—and not drudges!? *I* do not wish to see them drudges for that is worse than their own condition. I would rather have them all intellectual artistic men and women but if I place them as primitives as you do—I would have no right to expect so much—save the right of being disappointed. Rome was a civilization quite superior in some things than this modern one here. Rome held captives and slaves the flaxen haired savages of Europe. From these self same slaves springs the Anglo Saxon. ...I did not do away with the centuries it has taken them to grow to the present state! But I do expect the Indian to compete with the highest minds in every branch of pursuit of today—And this is my reason—I consider the Indian spiritually superior to any race of savages, white or black—I call the Indians simplicity of dress and freedom of outdoor life—wisdom which is more powerful than that of the hot house flower of which your large city can boast! I believe his own self respect and honor to keep unwritten laws—so that a man's house was safe if a stick was crossed over the tent flap—of far more worth intrinsically than written laws and compilations by inspiring fear of physical punishment. Morally the Indian in his own state is cleaner than those city dwellers! If they did wear their birthday clothes—what of it! Do not the painters and sculptors resort to the semi nude figure when they wish to copy the greatest combination of graces? To a race who were accustomed to nudity it was as proper as the seeing of human clothes racks of new wear clothes to civilized eyes! If the Indian race adapts itself to the commodity of the times in one century it won't be because [of] Carlisle! But because the Indian was not a degenerate in the first place! I will never speak of the whites as elevating the Indian! I am willing to say higher conceptions of life elevate the whole human family—but not the Indian more than any other. Until Col. Pratt actively interests himself in giving college education to Indians I cannot say his making them slaves is anything other than drudgery! And drudgery is hell—not civilization! If Carlisle expects the Indian to adapt himself perfectly to 'civilized' life in a century she must admit that the Indian has powers which entitle him to a better name than Primitive! And by virtue of this development he can compete with all so called civilized peoples in a short time. On the other hand if she declares the Indian a superstitious savage she must allow him centuries—as the other savages have required—to mature to the prevailing customs. You know how Carlisle scoffs at all Indianism. …Her belief compels her to yield to Hampton's idea. If you have faith in the Indians becoming 'civilized' it is not because you agree with Carlisle! Nor Hampton—but being Indian you know the material which warrants your faith. And the material is not Primitive—nor can be represented by a small band like the Apache!"[52]

"As to the ring, will you place it in a candy box? People here are so abnormal about knowing every body's affairs that I do not wish them to pry around the small box."[53]

One can imagine Montezuma's style: sweets in boxes and sweet-talking in daily letters. Later we shall see that Montezuma addressed his letters to his wife with the salutation, "Dutchie," or "Dovie." But this was a style that began to wear thin with Zitkala-Ša. "Dear you are good noble and an ideal sweetheart (only I think you might not be so extravagant in calling me strange names!) I would rather have your confidence—You intellectually, and here and there a little evidence of your big heart than good for nothing names! I am queer?"[54]

That summer she explained the origin of her name. "I have a half brother whose name is Simmons. Once my own father scolded my brother; and my mother took such offense from it that eventually it resulted in a parting—so as I grew I was called by my brother's name—Simmons. I have it a long time till my brother's wife—angry with me because I insisted upon getting an education said I had deserted home and I might give up my brother's name 'Simmons' too. Well—you can guess how queer I felt—away from my own people—homeless—penniless—and even without a name! That I choose to make a name for myself and I guess I have made 'Zitkala-Ša' known—for even Italy writes it in her language!"[55]

"Your letters are much appreciated at this end—be assured. Still you know I do not care for too much sweets. It is much more when actually lived! Don't you too think so? …I wanted to write to you tonight—You are good, kind, true, and strong—I value each trait highly. Some times when I think of our plan for next Fall I fear I do you wrong. I seem so unfit for making a home cheery for anyone."[56]

"I wrote you a long letter yesterday which by the way served to kindle this morning's fire. I told you in trifling details the nightmare this summer is to me for—under certain traits, they were magnified till a larger view of the purpose of life was wholly obscured. …Mother's queerness adds to the pathos of the situation. Your evasive reply to my request—made me think hard of giving you all up. I felt rather desperate and cared little indeed if I never wrote again. I do not care anymore this morning what I do but at least I won't bother you with my 'mosquito bites.' I do not alter a word of my last letter but I say stick to your past and your own conscience. I am not coming to Chicago, nor do I count upon your coming west. I am not worth the sacrifice. …So don't fool yourself by a juggling with words—At any rate we are obliged to postpone our plans for it would be folly for either to harbor a secret unhappiness by complying half-heartedly with the other's wish. And in the meanwhile, should you meet with another more like your self, then do not pause a moment on my account. I am equal to thinking about and bearing what falls in my lot. I may not hang them on my wall as readily as you can, but I can stand them in my own way. So do not apply for the position of Agency. Since you cannot do it with the proper spirit. Physician, I have a plan for myself this year. This moment's idea. I do not return east but remain here. You will hear in plenty of time how or where my course is laid."[57]

Perhaps the complaints of too much sweetness prompted an angry retort from Montezuma. "Please don't get cross with me for then you will lose control of me entirely. I have had a difficult summer with a cranky old woman by the merest accident my mother. I have just exactly *all* I can bear and a whit more would make me jump the traces all together. I have felt pretty nigh desperate more times than my pride would permit my telling. I can stand a great deal—just so much but not again beyond a certain measure. And I tell you the measure is already full and well pressed to the rim. This very night that I write—I have been needlessly tortured by mother's crazy tongue till all hell seems set loose upon my heels— and I feel wicked enough to kill her on the spot or else run *wild*. You sensible folk whose nerves are cast iron and are not susceptible to the influences of others idiosyncrasies have not sufficient imagination to know how excruciatingly painful it is to a sensitive wretch to have 'to grin and bear' all the yelping ferocity of human brutes. The only thought I am capable of is 'I must clear out of her sight,' where I am to go or where—What I am to do—no one knows. Nor do I."[58]

WHAT HAPPENED in August? Was it just the conflict with her mother? Did that conflict crystallize her thoughts? Zitkala-Ša returned the engagement ring and unleashed a barrage of challenges to Montezuma. "As for our former relation I have nothing more to say. It is gone. But I will be as good a friend as I can. If you will permit me to be. If not, than this is the last letter." On August 21, 1901, without even the courtesy of a salutation: "So you— who ventured comment upon a brief courtship—can scarce hold out one prolonged? You were hurt because the ring was returned; and so soon would have given up the pursuit? Where is your determination, which dauntlessly wins whatever you chose to seek? And if you were hurt—remember I was before you—so misery was not alone yours. Perhaps Montezuma, N[ichols] has written you of a ruby ring I wear. Your silence added fuel to my fire and there! I told you fairly in the start that you were not alone in the race—You say you love me. Others boast the same. How shall I know which is deepest, truest, and genuine? But at last—I have concluded to try you once again. You may return my ring if so it pleases you. However I shall not be able to go to Arizona. You go alone—and when you return we shall come to some more definite point. Montezuma, you had better not wait too long to answer this letter. See. Sincerely, indeed, Zitkala."[59]

"Now I must insist once again upon your securing the position of Agency physician in some sorry country. I say this for my mother's account. I simply cannot leave her out of my plans without feeling like a criminal as she cannot help herself; and my brothers are seen more selfish than I am. If you cannot comply than we shall postpone the day while I teach here and take care of my mother. Montezuma—I think you are making a poor bargain with me.

You should have given me up and thanked your lucky stars for a narrow escape. If we marry—it will be when you have carried out my wish—not before. At any rate while my mother lives. What do you say to that?"[60]

"Why do you always take so much for granted and do things upon the impulse. You are arranging your furniture in the house and doing things in the most assured manner upon my 're-consideration' which is not a promise one way or the other as yet. Constant wishing to hurt you, I confess I feel too selfish and too sinful to assume such stern responsibilities till this morning I do not want to marry anyone. I do not know how alone though I may try to be sincere in my dealings with individuals. I think I prefer to work alone as I have done hither to. Dr, don't love me. Just consider my lack of love and pity me. Just be a good strong friend to me—don't write to me about myself that is too dry a subject. Let time work its result. I have received both boxes. Give me plenty of time for my final decision. And then whatever it is, I'll try to abide by it ever after."[61]

The wedding was to be in November, but by October, Zitkala-Ša's mind was set, the engagement ring was returned, and she made clear the involvement of Raymond Telephause Bonnin, a Yankton Sioux with a French father. Raymond was twenty-one years old in 1901 when Zitkala-Ša was twenty-five, and most likely the reason for the change in tone in the August letters. "What makes you assume the supposition that I was going to marry you in Nov? Did I not break up all the old plan? I have only reconsidered the case—as yet giving you no definite reply—Yet you write me such positive letters—that I'd like to surprise you with the frank statement of the facts. I am well. I do *not* wish any financial aid. I do not come to you this month—nor any other—for the simple reason of our non-congenial temperaments. I have a friend out here who claims all I can give by the laws of natural affinity. In a few days I shall return your ring to you! There I've written plainly because you have made me *cross*. If in my openness there is naught to forgive—I beg of you to do it. I can always respect you as a friend—but never more. Let me wish you success in your chosen world and work—Mine lie in places 'barren and foreign' to your acquired taste. Goodby, Z."[62]

And so Montezuma refused to travel to Yankton, Zitkala-Ša refused to go to Chicago, and she married Raymond Bonnin in May 1902. Zitkala-Ša's return to South Dakota marked the end of any possibility of a life together, both underestimating each other's stubbornness and commitment. Letters that summer indicate Montezuma's hope that reservation life would convince Zitkala-Ša to come to him. Life with her cranky old mother was not easy, applications for employment were unrewarded—yet in August, Zitkala-Ša returned Montezuma's engagement ring. The ring went back and forth at least once, perhaps more, accompanied by the same old arguments on each side in a correspondence that went on for eight more months.

Montezuma even tried economic arguments. Zitkala-Ša was unrelenting. "Just before I begin the day's labor in my private office which I've at last rented here in the hotel—I would drop a line to you in noisy Chicago. My friend—you would, after knowing that another holds my regard—allure me with home and supply of daily necessities. I would be untrue to my own idea, to you—for you deserve a true and undivided love—and to the third party also. It would be wrong for me to yield to your persuasion and I can not accept more in that sacred line than I could give in return. You would grow dissatisfied Montezuma and then would follow sad days. I have lands here that are estimated at $5,000 and as there is talk of paying off the Indians who can take care of themselves, I shall not be in need of a home for I shall have enough to start one at the least. This is not counting my share in my mother's land which is said to be about $2,000. So with eight thousand for rainy weather—I can pass the present days with my odd writings and western interests. I have other confidence to make to you. Once while yet in school I had a chum. She was an Indian Territory girl and soon after returning was married. She died a month ago leaving behind a request that I take her two year old baby girl. I have not decided what to do. I feel strongly inclined to take it but have so much work in hand that I hardly see how to arrange her keeping. I have been waiting to see what you say about the ring and the meanwhile wear it as a friendship ring. I do not wish to hurt your feelings needlessly or I would suggest paying you its money value. Than I might always keep the token of one so loyal to me as I believe you to be."[63]

One can imagine the angry Carlos Montezuma. In the Montezuma Collection, there is a small pamphlet of a few pages (really an advertisement) for the Chicago Roentgen X-Ray Laboratory. Scribbled on this pamphlet, with no date, in his own handwriting, is the following:

Miss Gertrude Simmons
(Zitkala Sa)
Yankton Agency
So Dakota

Madam —

I am sorry that you have some Indian blood in you.
The less you write of *my people* with the poisonous tank of your heart and unbalanced condition of your mind, the better. *Am I a cast iron man devoid of all human reasoning and feelings?*

Indian blood,
Carlos Montezuma[64]

Did he send it to her, and was it returned; was this his example to be transcribed to his stationery, and why did he save it? It seems that he did mail this angry outburst to Zitkala-Ša because her letter of January 1, 1902, says goodbye: "My dear Dr. Montezuma, If you are so sure you are my superior, that I am a fake—do not resent losing so worthless an acquaintance. I feel sorry for you that your own indiscretion centered your regard upon such a wretch as I am! (God is my only judge!) He knows me and my struggles better than my best and truest mortal friend! In his eyes I would be doing you a greater wrong to marry you than to have done as I have. Do not think I made my reply in a trifling mood—for there are many by the way; and it was not the easiest thing I've done—to live up to my best judgment. Do not feel reckless and revengeful! Live on in your brave way. Live up on your highest conception of God's creatures. I am striving but oh—dear—it is hard—so hard—I wish sometimes that I was dead. Z."[65]

Montezuma responded with anger when Zitkala-Ša reported that the engagement ring was lost. "Did I not once return that infernal ring? Who used his powers of persuasion to cause me to wear it again? You did—you upright blameless man! Have you forgot how you contradicted me every time I told you I thought it useless to consider matrimony? If you have forgot I guess Mrs. Cook [Mrs. Cook was the chaperone on the Carlisle East Coast trip in March 1900 that included Montezuma and Zitkala-Ša] could remind you of some of your conduct toward me not so long ago. And I think she would not blame me and let you stand with a halo on! I got your two letters today. Ten miles is quite away for daily delivery of post, but you perfect creature took no thought of another's feelings. You wrote cruelly wickedly in the manner of a low Italian day-go."[66]

"I had the misfortune of losing the ring, and while I regretted the loss…I regret it more than I don't have it to send it to you! I gave you the chance to name the price that I might refund your affection in money but you let that chance go by—leaving me to infer that your delicacy and genuine feeling for me would not take it back and so were still. *Now*—(after I told you months ago I had met another) now that I am married you write as you do! That is unlike you! It is base and cowardly. Z."[67]

"Why do you seek a hold upon honesty where you insinuate honesty is not? Why I ask! Wounded self—love turns vicious. Never true affection as exemplified in the crucification of Christ. You are neither a follower of Christ nor of God as you professed. If this does not open your eyes—nothing ever will. I am proud—fearless and as independent as *you* are—more than you pose to be. I can walk into the Realm of the Muddy Waters—defying your feeble forces any day. I have tried to tell you I meant no harm to you. I meant no robbery. I thought a gift unasked was a gift. Especially as you never made any mention of ever reclaiming it. And now you fume about like a chicken with its head cut off—knowing nothing of what you strike against! Are you a real Brave to the core? Then be calm. Speak to me as I deserve to be spoken to. And I will show you what stuff I am made of. I would make every effort to satisfy your mercenary demands—I have no deposits and depend upon my daily work—which is not always as regular as yours. But I so much regret this great misunderstanding between us. Montezuma—I am mortal as you are. If you would have charity for your errors—have some for others. Have some for me. I ask of you this once. If you do not heed me—I shall not be susceptible to any force. I only wish to be treated as a woman, as a mortal seeking to live honestly, not devoid of errors."[68]

Yankton Agency
S.D. July 26 1902
Sir—
I shall pay the cost of the lost ring by degrees as fast as possible if you will kindly forward
me the bill of sale.
Mrs. Gertrude Bonnin[69]


July 29, 1902
Mrs. Gertrude Bonnin
Yankton Agency
So. Dakota

Madam
In reply to yours of 26th I would say the ring is over 60 years old and not purchased lately.
A friend who was precious to me passed it onto my hands with her last words "never allow
this ring be worn by another, unless it be *the one.*"
I have heard her to say it was worth over $90 on account of the cut and the genuiness makes
it value and not the size.
It will be satisfactorily to me for you to replace the loss as your letter of July 26. $75 is
the evaluation.
Carlos Montezuma[70]

About one year later, Montezuma turned the matter over to a lawyer who wrote to
Zitkala-Ša. But the controversy was soon dropped; the ring remained lost and unpaid for.
Montezuma was probably influenced by a strong letter from an old Carlisle friend, Jessie W.
Cook, now working at another Indian boarding school, the Sherman Institute in Riverside,
California, who wrote on June 11, 1903: "I consider your influence at Carlisle has been very
uplifting and all have a high regard and admiration for you. I am so sorry to know that you
intend doing something that is going to bring you into ridicule, and will, in a measure injure
your influence. You know how much I have been with Zitkala and that she confided in me
her every act. I knew how devoted you were to her. I know when she became engaged to
you, and I would have been glad to see that engagement culminate in marriage, but she is a
girl of moods and many minds, and you know all women have the privilege of changing their
minds. She wrote me when she lost your diamond, and she was sick over it, and wanted to
know what she could do. I wrote her that however badly you might feel at her giving you
up I was sure you were too honorable to make her any trouble about the ring. ...I had
supposed it was passed over until this morning when I read your lawyer's letter to her. Now
my dear friend, let me beg of you to let the matter drop. It is impossible to do a thing of
that kind and keep it secret, and the moment it gets out you will become a laughing stock.
So far no one knows that you were engaged, at least I have never heard it, and I am quite
sure if it were known outside I should have heard it. Don't you see that it will simply make
your sorrows public, and the public always laughs at a man who tries to take a revenge like
that upon a girl. They will say, 'Oh, if he is that kind of a fellow the girl was lucky to get rid
of him' and it won't do you a bit of good, but a great deal of harm. Of course, if your practice is not good and you really need the money that will surprise people too. For we have
all supposed you were doing a good business. ...Believe me doctor, I write as your friend.

Don't let the lawyer carry this on. Even he is laughing at you. I can see it in the wording of his letter, and I am sure you would live to regret if very much."[71]

Within a short time, perhaps a year, Zitkala-Ša considered and rejected a life with Montezuma. Zitkala-Ša, steadfast, independent, and blunt in her objectives, permitted little room for hypocrisy between the two of them. She was deeply aware of the opposing belief systems driving their lives; she feared subjugation of her heritage and values as a member of White society; she was driven by guilt to be with her family; she must have feared Montezuma's strong personality and his own drive to dominate. Zitkala-Ša recognized both emotionally and intellectually that the two were incompatible, that Montezuma would try to tame her spirit. She was very much in touch with herself and knew that a role like the loving, supporting wife Montezuma was seeking would stifle her independence and activism.

Finally the correspondence ended. But it was to resume eleven years later when Zitkala-Ša and Montezuma were reunited by a cause, the Society of American Indians. In the meantime, Zitkala-Ša became Mrs. Gertrude Bonnin.

## LIFE AS GERTRUDE BONNIN

Raymond Bonnin was twenty-two when Zitkala-Ša, age twenty-six, married him in May 1902. Their son, Raymond Ohiya (Winner) Bonnin, was born seven months after their marriage, and shortly after the birth, Bonnin was offered a position as a clerk on the Uintah Ouray Ute Reservation in Utah. In 1903, the Bonnins traveled to Whiterocks, on the Uintah Reservation, about one million acres of land, 140 miles east of present day Salt Lake City, home of the Uintah Ute band and the Northern Ute people of western Colorado. They lived at Fort Duchesne, the army base on the reservation, for the next fourteen years.

In Utah, a significant loss of land was occurring through the allotment process leading to outright sales. Conditions on the Uintah Reservation were worse than in Yankton. Bonnin was one of five clerks at the Uintah Agency, in charge of purchases made by the agency and the delivery of goods. Bonnin proved to be an effective advocate for the Indians, acting as their lawyer and seeking appropriate prices and quality. Receiving no responses to her requests for employment, Gertrude nevertheless became involved with the agency school.[72] Using a neglected shipment of brass instruments, Gertrude became the music teacher, forming a school band by fall 1904. She organized a basket-weaving class, using the skills of the elderly grandmothers. She lectured on hygiene and healthcare. But the Bureau continued to ignore her requests for employment, even the letters sent to Commissioner of Indian Affairs Leupp by the agency superintendent.

In spring 1905, an agency teacher unexpectedly resigned, and Superintendent Mercer hired Gertrude at $600 per year. Nevertheless, the Bureau appointed another teacher, but fortunately he failed to appear, and Gertrude was given a permanent appointment in March 1906.

In fall 1906, the Bonnins returned to Yankton to be with Ellen Simmons when she died at about the age of seventy-one. Even in death, Ellen Simmons expressed her anger by willing her allotment to her elder son from her first marriage, Peter St. Pierre. Gertrude's letter to her brother suggests that St. Pierre had turned their mother's mind against any children born of her union with a White man, thus even David was excluded from the will.[73]

The Bonnins returned to Ft. Duchesne, but found that another teacher had been hired in Gertrude's absence. This was not a good time for Gertrude. With no employment, her only duties were being a wife and a mother. Even her interest in writing waned. Surrounded by a people being decimated by poverty, ignorance, and disease, the commitment of her youth was severely tested. She turned to the company of Whites and the Latter Day Saints Church, although a search of the Mormon records confirmed that the Bonnins never formally converted to Mormonism.[74] She continued to spend hours among the Ute women teaching cooking and healthcare. In 1909, she converted to Catholicism, a consequence of spending a winter at the Standing Rock Reservation in North Dakota and being favorably impressed by the Benedictine priests working there. These years saw the beginning manifestation of a general tendency to be suspicious and non-trusting of other people. She preferred to work alone, indeed allowed no others to share in her control of her classes.

In 1913, Gertrude had another noteworthy accomplishment. On Feburary 20, 1913, *The Sun Dance* premiered in Vernal (a White settlement twenty-five miles from the Uintah Reservation), an opera written by Gertrude and Vernal's music teacher, William Hanson. Hanson published an account of *The Sun Dance* in which he described Gertrude as a popular lecturer with two long braids of hair hanging to her knees, dressed in buckskin, beads, and feathers.[75] He was impressed with her commanding stage presence that featured a "musically charming and convincing" voice.[76]

The opera was a love story of a Sioux man, Ohiya (her son's name), who is committed to complete the Sun Dance to prove his worth for his beloved Winona. Hanson wrote the actual music, but it was based on traditional Indian melodies provided by Gertrude and played for him on her violin. Hanson's original lyrics were rewritten by Gertrude to conform accurately with Indian life. Hanson trained the orchestra and chorus. Gertrude enlisted Indians to make authentic costumes, and even elders to perform part of the Sun Dance. The opera was well received, requiring a third unscheduled performance, and multiple performances throughout Utah in 1914, including the Provo Opera House and the Salt Lake Theatre. In 1935, Hanson, who was now a professor, revived the opera at his school, the Brigham Young University (he wrote the music for several of the school's traditional songs). In 1937, the opera was selected by the New York Light Opera Guild as the American opera for the year and performed in 1938, a week after Zitkala-Ša died, in New York City to good reviews in Hanson's opinion, but to disappointing reviews according to others.[77] Although Zitkala-Ša must have disagreed, Hanson obviously believed that he was the owner of the opera, listing only his name on the title page of the manuscript (available in the archives of Brigham Young University) and granting the rights to Brigham Young University in his will.[78]

*Zitkala-Ša—1913, Age Thirty-seven*

At this time, Gertrude and her busy life led to a marital rift. Working on *The Sun Dance* provided long months of absence in Salt Lake City, immersed in music. Raymond accused her in April 1913 of caring for Asa Chapman, a clerk at the agency with whom Gertrude often talked about books and ideas.[79] This led to a loud exchange, culminated in Gertrude and her son leaving the house to stay with a neighbor. Soon rumors spread that Raymond had beaten her, an allegation that was strongly denied by both Raymond and Gertrude. This created trouble at the agency for Raymond, and ultimately a humiliating and embarrassing experience for both that brought them back together.

IN MAY 1913, Gertrude traveled to Ohio to visit a friend. She must have called Montezuma, perhaps from a train station, because the next day she sent him this letter (still writing on plain 5x7 paper):

My dear Dr. Montezuma,

The real joys in life we get only in little "nips"—as you said last night. With some of us those "nips" are few & far between. But really some times the thing we desire had we got it may have proven anything but a joy. In all sincerity I want to say that you had a narrow escape—but you escaped. I was not worthy because I did not recognize true worth at that time.

Permit me to say that I am one of your admirers—It does not really matter one way or another to you—because I am not great as you are. However, I wish you to know that I would like to be counted as one of your friends. I humbly beg your forgiveness for my gross stupidity of former years—which was not relieved by my misfortune to lose what I could not replace. I have never passed through Chicago since that time & I could not go through now without putting forth an effort—no matter how hard—no matter if you might have refused to see me—I had to try to see you.

You are generously kind to welcome me & I wished we might have had an opportunity to talk but we couldn't. So I am taking this liberty to write to you.

I am going to Westerville, Ohio to visit a dear friend of mine Miss Maud Russell. Should you care to say anything to be kind to me you may write me there. I seem to be in a spiritual unrest. I hate this eternal tug of war between being wild or becoming civilized. The transition is an endless evolution—that keeps me in a continual Purgatory. My duty as mother & wife—of course keeps me in the West, but now I can hardly stand the inner spiritual clamor to study to write—to do more with my music—yet *duty* first! Rip Van Winkle slept twenty years! But my sleep was disturbed in half that time. I wonder if I may sleep again,

Gertrude Bonnin[80]

Her letter articulated her eternal tug of the Indian ways against civilization, perhaps stirred by the success of her opera *The Sun Dance*. A month later, in June 1913, Gertrude traveled east to place Ohiya in a Benedictine boarding school in Illinois and to visit friends in Boston.

Of course both Bonnins wanted their son to receive a good education, but did Gertrude also want to relieve herself of the burden of motherhood? On this trip, Gertrude wrote once again to Montezuma. Her letter is long and rambling, dwelling at length on her renewed interest in playing the piano. "I am returning to Utah because Mr. Bonnin insists upon it. …I should count it a special favor if you would send me copies of your lectures and articles published should you feel so inclined now & then. I will not be in a position to receive any letter—even though it might be ever so impersonal—as I know you would have made it."[81]

At least the friendship was re-established. In 1922, a year before Montezuma died, Gertrude even had an enjoyable visit in the home of Montezuma and his wife. Montezuma informed Pratt: "…The other day, whom did I receive a telephone from, but Mrs. Bonnin. She is in Chicago on a lecture tour under Women's Federation. You can imagine I was surprised for I imagine she had cut off with me. We made arrangement that she spend last Sunday with us. She came and we had a splendid visit."[82]

GERTRUDE CONTINUED to write Indian stories, but they were never published. The Bonnin writings and documents were provided to Brigham Young University by a probate lawyer, where they are now available in the Harold B. Lee Library. A selection of her unpublished stories, some poems, and the libretto of *The Sun Dance Opera* were published in 2001.[83]

Gertrude joined the advisory board of the Society of American Indians in 1914. Within a year, the Society was calling for social and educational community centers on Indian reservations patterned after Zitkala-Ša's women's classes in Utah. In 1915, Zitkala-Ša established such a center on the reservation, even successfully recruiting agency funds. In the July–September 1916 issue of the *American Indian Magazine, the Quarterly Journal of the Society of American Indians*, Zitkala-Ša published a long poem, "The Indian's Awakening." It was a reflection on her life, with despair at the loss of her early idealism, recognition of a failure to make a change, and then the awakening of her spirit, the urge to again identify with her Indian heritage and to drive her people to accomplishment. All of this was made possible by venues opened by the Society of American Indians. She signed her name Zitkala-Ša, a name she had not used for fifteen years.

> *I snatch at my eagle plume and long hair.*
> *A hand cut my hair; my robes did deplete.*
> *Left heart all unchanged; the work incomplete.*
> *These favors unsought, I've paid since with care.*
> *Dear teacher, you wished so much good to me,*
> *That though I was blind, I strove hard to see.*
> *Had you then, no courage frankly to tell*
> *Old race-problems, Christ e'en failed to expel?*

*My light has grown dim, and black the abyss*
*That yawns at my feet. No bordering shore;*
*No bottom e'er found by hopes suck before.*
*Despair I of good from deeds gone amiss.*
*My people, may God have pity on you!*
*The learning I hoped in you to imbue*
*Turns bitterly vain to meet both our needs.*
*No Sun for the flowers,—vain planting seeds.*

*I've lost my long hair; my eagle plumes too.*
*From you my own people, I've gone astray.*
*A wanderer now, with no where to stay.*
*The Will-o-the-wisp learning, it brought me rue.*
*It brings no admittance. Where I have knocked*
*Some evil imps, hearts, have bolted and locked.*
*Alone with the night and fearful abyss*
*I stand isolated, life gone amiss.*

*Intensified hush chills all my proud soul.*
*Oh, what am I? Whither bound thus and why?*
*Is there not a God on whom to rely?*
*A part of His Plan, the atoms enroll?*
*In answer, there comes a sweet Voice and clear,*
*My loneliness soothes with sounding so near.*
*A drink to my thirst, each vibrating note.*
*My vexing old burdens fall far remote.*

*"Then close your sad eyes. Your spirit regain.*
*Behold what fantastic symbols abound,*
*What wondrous host of cosmos around.*
*From silvery sand, the tiniest grain*
*To man and the planet, God's at the heart.*
*In shifting mosaic, souls doth impart.*
*His spirits who pass through multiformed earth*
*Some lesson of life must learn in each birth."*

*Divinely the Voice sang. I felt refreshed.*
*And vanished the night, abyss and despair.*
*Harmonious kinship made all things fair.*
*I yearned with my soul to venture unleashed.*
*Sweet Freedom. There stood in waiting, a steed*
*All prancing, well bridled, saddled for speed.*
*A foot in the stirrup! Off with a bound!*
*As light as a feather, making no sound.*

Through ether, long leagues we galloped away.
An angry red river, we shyed in dismay.
For here were men sacrificed. (cruel deed).
To reptiles and monsters, war, graft, and greed.
A jungle of discord drops in the rear.
By silence is quelled suspicious old fear,
And spite-gnats' low buss is muffled at last.
Exploring the spirit, I must ride fast.

Away from these world ones, let us go,
Along a worn trail, much traveled and,—Lo!
Familiar the scenes that come rushing by.
Now billowy sea and now azure sky.
Amid that enchanted spade, as they spun
Sun, moon and the stars, their own orbits run!

Great Spirit, in realms so infinite reigns;
And wonderful wide are all His domains.

Hark! Here in the Spirit-world, He doth hold
A village of Indians, camped as of old.
Earth-legends by their fires, some did review,
While flowers and trees more radiant grew.
"Oh, You were all dead! In Lethe you were tossed!"
I cried, "Every where 'twas told you were lost!
Forsooth, they did scan your footprints on sand.
Bereaved, I did mourn your fearful sand end."

Then spoke One of the Spirit Space, so sedate.
"My child, We are souls, forever and aye.
The signs in our orbits point us the way.
Like planets, we do not tarry nor wait.
Those memories dim, from Dust to the Man.
Called Instincts, are trophies won while we ran.
Now various stars where loved ones remain
Are linked to our hearts with Memory-chain."

"In journeying here, the Aeons we've spent
Are countless and strange. How well I recall
Old Earth trails: the River Red; above all
The Desert sands burning us with intent.
All these we have passed to learn some new thing.
Oh hear me! Your dead doth lustily sing!
Rejoice! Gift of Life pray waste not in wails!
The maker of Souls forever prevails!"

*Direct from the Spirit-world came my steed.*
*The phantom has place in what was all planned.*
*He carried me back to God and the land*
*Where all harmony, peace and love are the creed.*
*In triumph, I cite my Joyous return.*
*The smallest wee creature I dare not spurn.*
*I sing "Gift of Life, pray waste not in wails!*
*The Maker of Souls forever prevails!"*[84]

Zitkala-Ša's election in 1916 as secretary in the Society of American Indians required a move to Washington, a move agreed to by Raymond. Perhaps he recognized that Zitkala-Ša in her restored zeal would never go back to a domestic life. The Bonnins moved frequently, but always lived in rented spaces in the center of the city. Raymond applied for active service in the army and was given a second lieutenant's commission. He eventually became a captain during World War I. The Society was run by males, the day-to-day work was done by women, serving as clerks. The Society women voluntarily remained in the background, a general socio-political status for women at this time in history. Zitkala-Ša was a new force, seeking power and influence, directing her attention and writing to issues of land and leadership. Drive and desire she had, diplomacy she lacked.

## AN AMERICAN LEADER

In the early 1900s, there was a growing population of educated Indian young people. In 1911, Fayette McKenzie, a sociologist at Ohio State University, organized the first meeting in Columbus, Ohio, of the American Indian Association, quickly renamed the Society of American Indians. The purposes of this group included national organization with a united voice and continued support for assimilation. The leading figures were all successful products of assimilation (doctors, lawyers, preachers, and teachers), and understandably they supported this approach and turned away from Indian tradition and heritage.

The pan-Indian movement and the Society of American Indians in particular will be examined in greater detail in Chapter 13. To complete the story of Zitkala-Ša in this chapter, we will briefly consider the political activities that occupied the last twenty-one years of her life. Zitkala-Ša was by herself in the first two years in Washington, D.C., as Raymond was serving his wartime active duty.

Woodrow Wilson was elected president in 1916, campaigning with the slogan, "He kept us out of war."[85] Only five months later, the United States declared war on Germany, and a month later, Congress passed The Selective Service Act requiring every American male between the ages of twenty-one and thirty-one to register for the draft. The war and the draft would affect the focus and efforts of the pan-Indian movement.

The Society of American Indians was meant to be the voice of the Indian directed to White society. By 1913, it had 200 active members and over 400 associate members. But dissension was common as these highly educated American Indians all had strong opinions about objectives and priorities. Opposition to and abolition of the Indian Bureau were at the forefront. Montezuma was a leading agitator against the Bureau, believing that the Bureau was tied to the reservation system and that time had proved that this system preserved not only the old ways, but poverty and ignorance as well. Many of the Society members worked for the Bureau and their loyalty was questioned. Leaders of the Society opposed Montezuma's call for an abrupt end to the Bureau, believing gradual movement away from the Bureau was necessary to allow emerging Indian systems for independent governance and living. Soon Montezuma lost patience with the moderate stance of the Society. His famous "Let My People Go" speech at the 1915 annual meeting (Chapter 13) highlighted its failure to act. Another dividing issue was the growing use of peyote in tribal rituals.

Certainly Zitkala-Ša could not play a conciliatory role. She had never been a team player, and did not have the personality for it. Zitkala-Ša was handicapped by her difficulties in working with groups; she was a distrustful, suspicious, and very anxious woman. Her chronic health complaints (heart palpitations, weakness, and fatigue) were most likely psychosomatic in origin. Zitkala-Ša repeatedly wrote romanticized accounts of Indian heritage, and this emphasis on past culture ran contrary to the assimilation objectives of many of the educated Indians. Montezuma went so far as to publish a critical article in the *Chicago Record Herald* in 1913 reacting to the performance of *The Sun Dance*.

In 1916, Zitkala-Ša sought to moderate Montezuma's criticism of the Society of American Indians, asking him to be understanding and work within the Society.[86] Montezuma always had ample time assigned to him at Society meetings, in later years the work of Zitkala-Ša. She correctly saw that Montezuma was a valuable member of the Society, but his outspoken, aggressive views were also a distinct threat.

Zitkala-Ša was in conflict with Marie Baldwin, the Society treasurer. Baldwin was a supporter of assimilation; indeed she was a spectacular model of its success. Baldwin was the daughter of Jean Baptiste Bottineau, a Chippewa of the Turtle Mountain Band in North Dakota. His father, Pierre Bottineau, was a famous guide who at one point was involved with the Lewis and Clark Expedition. Bottineau became a very wealthy man dealing in Minnesota real estate and fur trade. He moved his family and fortune to Washington D.C. and became a prominent lobbyist in Congress and at the Indian Bureau, especially as an advocate for the Turtle Mountain Band. He was a strong supporter of eastern boarding schools such as Carlisle. Marie Baldwin's life was patterned after her father's. She graduated with bachelor and masters degrees in law from the Washington College of Law. In 1916, Baldwin was one of only two Indian women lawyers in the United States. Baldwin worked for the Bureau, as an accountant clerk in the Education Division. She was a highly educated, intelligent, successful woman, and in her success, believed assimilation was the right pathway.

Baldwin and Zitkala-Ša were very similar in many ways, including opposition to the use of peyote. But conflict was almost immediate. Perhaps Baldwin objected to a newcomer to the Society rapidly gaining influence and leadership. But the main difficulty between the two women was the exact same disagreement that had existed for years between Zitkala-Ša and Montezuma. Baldwin and Montezuma shared a close friendship with Philip B. Gordon, a Chippewa and Catholic priest. All three agitated for immediate dissolution of the Bureau and rapid and total assimilation. Baldwin differed only in her need to defend Bureau workers who were Society of American Indians members from the attacks of Gordon and Montezuma. Zitkala-Ša favored a more gradual approach and maneuvered to limit Baldwin's role in the Society. By early 1918, Zitkala-Ša succeeded in driving Baldwin out of the Society of American Indians. To be fair, Zitkala-Ša had good reasons to become exasperated with Baldwin; Baldwin's financial reports were often late, and she refused to make the membership list accessible.[87] Arthur C. Parker, while president of the Society, complained that "Both have been petty and spiteful," and lamented: "And no women will ever make a good Secretary, bad as I was in some ways. Women officers will scrap."[88] Zitkala-Ša assumed the duties of secretary and treasurer, sealing Baldwin's exit by suggesting that Baldwin's handling of the treasury was not totally honest.[89]

AFTER THE INDIANS were successfully confined to reservations, dozens of religions arose. Like the Ghost Dance Religion, their quick demise suggests that they were a reaction to the rapid deprivations of early reservation life. The Native American Church, a fusion of Indian tradition and Christian religion centered around the use of peyote, was more pervasive and lasting. Peyote was used widely to induce brightly colored visions on an individual basis in the southwest, originating in Mexico and spreading northward.

The new religion began in the 1880s, probably in western Oklahoma among the Kiowa and Comanche, and between 1880 and 1930, it spread to most of the tribes. A central feature is a group ceremony using peyote, involving chanting and meditation. Not surprising, White missionaries were vigorously opposed to this new religion, as were many Christianized Indians. Despite efforts to outlaw the use of peyote, the Native American Church was incorporated in 1918, and in 1944, the organization became the Native American Church of North America, which today is the largest Indian religious organization. James Mooney, the famed Smithsonian ethnohistorian, traveled throughout Oklahoma in 1891 participating in peyote ceremonies. Seeing an opportunity to unite Indians in the peyote religion, he wrote the charter for the initial incorporation of the Native American Church in 1918.

Zitkala-Ša opposed peyote use, viewing it as pernicious as alcohol.[90] This obviously was in conflict with her usual support and defense of Indian heritage and culture. To a significant degree, this position was due to the fact that her views of culture and heritage were defined by her Sioux experience and life. Peyote was used by the Ute, and from her years living on the Uintah Reservation, she thought the Utes were primitive and superstitious in comparison with the Sioux.

The Society of American Indians at their 1916 conference adopted a resolution supporting the passage of the Gandy Bill by Congress outlawing the trade and possession of peyote. The bill passed in the House, but failed in the Senate. The following year, Zitkala-Ša worked with the Woman's Christian Temperance Union and the Anti-Saloon League to successfully fight for a Colorado state law prohibiting peyote.[91] In that same year, Arizona Congressman Carl M. Hayden introduced a bill in the House to revise liquor traffic laws as they applied to Indians, and peyote was included. The bill passed the House in early 1918. In February, the Senate Subcommittee on Indian Affairs held extensive hearings on the Hayden Bill. Among a large number of witnesses testifying against peyote were Richard Pratt and Gertrude Bonnin.[92] Zitkala-Ša was the only witness who spoke as an Indian, and to emphasize this, she appeared in full traditional native dress, as she usually did for her speaking engagements.

Unfortunately, zeal replaced accuracy. Zitkala-Ša was even presented as a granddaughter of Sitting Bull and a graduate of Carlisle.[93] Perhaps Zitkala-Ša did view herself as a descendent of any and all Sioux leaders. Certainly she promoted this public image as a means to enhance her impact, and it is appropriate to call the clothing she wore at her presentations a costume.[94] At the hearings, the inaccuracies were exposed by James Mooney, the distinguished ethnologist and peyote devotee who had investigated and chronicled the Ghost Dance Religion in western tribes, still today one of the most respected works in ethnohistory.[95] Even Zitkala-Ša's native garb was identified as not that of the Sioux. But Zitkala-Ša rose to new heights in her oratory in response, arguing against peyote, using vivid stories (anecdotal but effective) to illustrate her points. Nevertheless, the committee members persisted in referring to her inaccuracies in their questions, but again Zitkala-Ša was impressive in her responses, drawing the praise of the chair, Senator John Tillman, who told her that she was "one of the most intelligent witnesses we have had before us."[96] These hearings were a personal triumph for Zitkala-Ša establishing her presence as a Washington lobbyist, but Mooney's link to peyote severed the government support for his fieldwork, and he died three years later without completing his study of the peyote religion.[97]

The committee recommended passage of the anti-peyote bill, but it failed again in the full Senate vote. Since 1960, the use of peyote has been protected in the courts under First and Fourteenth amendment rights. The American Indian Religious Freedom Act Amendments of 1994 established that the use, possession, or transportation of peyote by an Indian for bona fide traditional ceremonial purposes in connection with the practice of a traditional Indian religion is lawful.[98] Otherwise mescaline and peyote are illegal substances in the United States.

ZITKALA-ŠA ALWAYS HAD a good relationship with Arthur C. Parker, who in 1917 was the president of the Society of American Indians and editor of the Society magazine. She complimented him: "No one is blessed with the clear vision; terse expression; and untramelled composure, that you are,"[99] and Parker supported Gertrude Bonnin in her argument that the offices of secretary and treasurer should not be separate (her successful campaign to boost Marie Baldwin out of office). In 1917, the Society magazine emphasized the patriotism of American Indians serving in the war, probably in hopes that this would influence Congress to pass legislation granting Indians citizenship. The 1917 annual Society conference was not held, apparently in deference to many members away in war service, but an underlying reason was the fear by the officers that they would lose control of the organization, as dissension was increasing, not decreasing. Parker, the president, was frustrated and chose to minimize the society, and strengthen the *American Indian Magazine*. His aim was to have a strong board of editors under his direction to assume a leadership role in the pan-Indian movement, in place of the Society. Parker was especially wary and weary of the time spent arguing over abolition of the Bureau and peyote. He certainly did not want Indians in favor of those issues to gain control.

Zitkala-Ša supported Parker's views on peyote, but she had become won over to Montezuma's position regarding the Bureau. She was a faithful subscriber to *Wassaja*, Montezuma's newsletter. In 1918, Parker wanted to again avoid an annual conference, but

Zitkala-Ša prevailed to have the meeting in Pierre, South Dakota (in Sioux country). Parker did not even attend as increasingly he did not have the time or money to devote to the Society, and Charles Eastman was elected president as Zitkala-Ša was confirmed as secretary and treasurer.

Although the annual conference re-elected Parker as editor of the *American Indian Magazine*, Parker told Zitkala-Ša that "Under the circumstances, I am afraid it will be difficult for me to serve as editor since the making up of a magazine is a work that can only be done in one office. ...I have the feeling now that it will be best for you who are at the head of things to grip the editorial reins."[100] Parker believed it was most efficient and practical to house the magazine in the office of the secretary-treasurer, the official business office of the Society. Zitkala-Ša referred his decision to President Eastman, and Zitkala-Ša became the editor-in-chief of the *American Indian Magazine*. The Society was now in the hands of Sioux leadership: Eastman as president and Zitkala-Ša as secretary-treasurer and editor of the magazine.

The 1918 meeting of the Society of American Indians was not a success. Only twenty-five active members attended, including Montezuma. Only Montezuma, Coolidge, and Gordon remained of the founding members. The poor attendance was blamed on timing and the war. However, apathy surely played a role, as the Society was having little impact on federal Indian policy. Even its effort to save Carlisle school from closing failed. After the war, Zitkala-Ša and the Society focused on the effort to gain citizenship. Zitkala-Ša promoted a Society effort to have President Wilson include Indian representatives at the Versailles peace conference. Actually, the idea originated with Montezuma.[101] This met with no response, and it was yet another failure for the Society of American Indians.

1918 also saw the agenda of Montezuma gain prominence in the Society. The 1918 conference passed a resolution calling for immediate abolition of the Indian Bureau. This had the unfortunate effect of alienating another segment of the Society, an important and dedicated faction, those members who were also Bureau employees. In addition, many older Indians were alarmed that elimination of the Bureau would leave Indians without protection and support, because there was no alternative in place.

The 1919 annual conference was placed in the planning hands of Montezuma and Gordon. By now Zitkala-Ša viewed Montezuma and Gordon as allies, and her time was occupied running the Society and the magazine from her home in Washington. Having reached a position of control and influence, Zitkala-Ša did not produce a record of success and happiness. Rather than seeking compromise and developing issues that would unify, Zitkala-Ša continued to promote Bureau abolition and the elimination of peyote, and to focus on citizenship. Tribal factionalism, opposition to Society policy, and her own distrustful and suspicious nature combined to produce declining membership and personal disappointment.

The ninth annual conference met in Minneapolis, Minnesota, in October 1919. The focus was on citizenship legislation. Attendance was better than the previous year, partly because the pro-peyote faction chose to participate. This led to a contest over the presidency between Eastman and Thomas Sloan, an advocate for the religious use of peyote. Despite Zitkala-Ša's efforts, Sloan was elected by an overwhelming margin. Stunned, Zitkala-Ša rose to refuse her nomination to be re-elected as secretary-treasurer. The Society then nominated her husband, Captain Bonnin, but he too refused the nomination. Thus the Bonnins withdrew from the Society. This was not without some benefit for the Bonnins. The Society was being supported at considerable financial expense from their home, and Zitkala-Ša had come to recognize that the Society was accomplishing little.

THE BONNINS REMAINED in Washington. Upon returning from the war, Raymond prepared to become a lawyer (although he never gained formal admission to the bar). Both Raymond and Zitkala-Ša viewed this as important as their attention turned to protection of Indian land rights, an issue in constant dispute as the allotment process continued to operate, now for forty years. It did not end until John Collier became commissioner of Indian affairs under Roosevelt. Collier was a social scientist who had served as an officer of the American Indian Defense Association for ten years.[102] He called for the end of the allotment process, viewing the consolidation of land under community ownership and control as an important method to preserve Indian societies.

*Gertrude Bonnin—1921, Age Forty-five*

| President | Secretary of the Interior | Commissioner of Indian Affairs |
|---|---|---|
| Warren G. Harding, 1921 | Albert B. Fall, 1921<br>Hubert Work, 1923 | Charles H. Burke, 1921 |
| Calvin Coolidge, 1923 | Hubert Work<br>Roy O. West, 1928 | Charles H. Burke |
| Herbert C. Hoover, 1929 | Ray L. Wilbur, 1929 | Charles J. Rhoads, 1929 |
| Franklin Delano Roosevelt, 1933 | Harold L. Ickes, 1933 | John Collier, 1933 |

Zitkala-Ša became involved as a field researcher with the Indian Welfare Committee of the General Federation of Women's Clubs. In 1923, Zitkala-Ša, Matthew K. Sniffen (secretary of the Indian Rights Organization) and Charles H. Fabens, (lawyer for the American Indian Defense Organization) wrote a thirty-nine-page pamphlet entitled, *Oklahoma's Poor Rich Indians: An Orgy of Graft and Exploitation of the Five Civilized Tribes—Legalized Robbery*, published by the Indian Rights Association. This pamphlet was the result of their investigative effort, filled with statistics and true personal vignettes. The reaction was loud, and although ultimately ineffective in the short-term, it was noteworthy for being a major factor in exposing corruption in Oklahoma and leading to the formation of the Meriam Commission.

In February 1923, Zitkala-Ša was named as a member of the National Advisory Board of the American Indian Defense Association, largely because of her friendship with John Collier.[103] Because of this friendship, Collier assured Zitkala-Ša a place in the Indian reform movement in the 1920s.

In 1926, Zitkala-Ša organized an all-Indian movement, the National Council of American Indians. In response to the Indian Citizenship Act of June 1924, she now sought to organize the Indian vote. Zitkala-Ša was president of the National Council of American Indians from 1926 until she died in 1938. Raymond was the secretary-treasurer. The headquarters were in the Bliss Building, the site of the Indian Bureau and the American Indian Defense Association. Despite support from Collier and the American Indian Defense Association, Zitkala-Ša had difficulty attracting members. Nevertheless, the organization and its newsletter gave Zitkala-Ša a legitimate platform from which she could act as a spokesperson for the pan-Indian movement. She and Raymond traveled extensively, visiting reservations and gathering information. In her last years, she was an active watchdog over Congress, well-known to the Bureau of Indian Affairs, and testifying before the Senate subcommittee of the Committee on Indian Affairs many times. She became a nationally known lecturer. Using her writing skills, she repeatedly described reservation problems and conditions in letters to newspapers, legislators, and in newsletters.

Finally, in 1932, the Bonnins and Collier had a falling out, for sure a clash of like personalities, but Collier emerged triumphant as he was named commissioner of Indian affairs under Roosevelt in 1932, bringing an end to fifty years of allotment begun under the Dawes Act.[104] The Indian Reorganization Act (IRA) of 1934 (the Wheeler-Howard Act) incorporated most of the recommendations made in the Meriam Report; it provided for the revival of tribal government and traditions, promoting the adoption of tribal constitutions.

The granting of full citizenship to Indians in 1924 signaled the end of the philosophy and policy of assimilation and allotment; land ownership was not necessary for citizenship nor was conformity to Anglo customs a requirement. This reversal of federal policy was formalized by the Indian Reorganization Act of 1934, prohibiting further allotment and affirming the right of Indian self-determination and governance. It emphasized the support of reservation day schools. The Indian Reorganization Act provided for the voluntary adoption of a tribal council system of representative, constitutional government and for the organization of tribes as business corporations to manage tribal resources. It authorized the restoration of land to tribal ownership and made provisions for the purchase of new land. It also stipulated that qualified Indians would henceforth be preferred for appointments to vacancies in the Indian office.

Collier aggressively promoted self-determination. However, many tribes, including the Yankton Sioux, voted not to accept the Indian Reorganization Act, mainly because Collier had not and was not consulting Indian peoples. The Indian Reorganization Act was viewed, especially by the Bonnins, as yet another instance of federal policy dictated by the Bureau of Indian Affairs. Opposition by the

*Gertrude Bonnin—1930, Age Fifty-four*

Bonnins was focused on the Yankton Band, and the Yankton voters turned down a new constitution. The Bonnins offered a constitution that gave rights to all tribal members wherever they lived; Collier insisted on reservation restrictions. Here, it is noteworthy that the Bonnins had a broader view, giving recognition of Indian identity no matter where individuals lived, and they refused to recognize that Collier had much to offer. This debate continued for three years, coming to an end when Zitkala-Ša died and Collier abandoned his effort with the Yanktons. Unfortunately, this was another example of a failure to make progress because of an inability of Zitkala-Ša to compromise, to work together. To her very end, Zitkala-Ša opposed all government mandated programs, no matter how progressive or enlightened.

In the midst of this conflict with Collier, Gertrude Simmons Bonnin (Zitkala-Ša)— writer, musician, public speaker, Congressional lobbyist, and Indian leader—suddenly died at age sixty-two in Georgetown Hospital in Washington, D.C., on January 26, 1938. Zitkala-Ša lived in the reservation and assimilation era, a time of transition from the remembered past to the difficult present, a conflict between tradition and acculturation.

She was one of the strongest and earliest proponents of Indian self-determination. A note-worthy figure, she:

- was a prime mover in the initiation of the pan-Indian movement
- brought Indian issues before the legislature and the public
- was instrumental in the developing definition of tribalism and Indian identity
- was an indefatigable fighter for protection of the Indian landbase and culture
- kept the pan-Indian movement alive between the demise of the Society of American Indians and the beginning of new organizations (the American Indian Federation and the National Congress of American Indians).

Zitkala-Ša is buried in Arlington Cemetery with her husband, Captain Raymond Bonnin, who died four years later. The large headstone reads:

GERTRUDE SIMMONS BONNIN
"ZITKALA-ŠA" OF THE SIOUX INDIANS
1876 — 1938

## CHAPTER TEN

# Freemasonry:
# Call Me Brother

TEARS WERE ROLLING down Montezuma's cheeks, when upon his acceptance as a Mason, he said to the members of his Lodge: "I have much to thank you for, you take me by the hand and call me brother. It ought to be the ambition of every good man to be a good mason."[1] Virtually all educated American Indians in the first decades after 1900 eagerly became Masons. Montezuma became a Master Mason, a member of Blaney Lodge, No. 271, and later Dearborn Lodge, No. 310. Why the attraction? Understanding what Montezuma and other middle-class American Indians gained from this interaction requires an understanding of Freemasonry, but to provide a straightforward history of Freemasonry is difficult. It is not for a lack of written material. There is a vast literature on the subject; however, it is a different world with its own terminology, filled with conflicting historical arguments, convoluted thinking, and emotional advocacy and antagonism. Nevertheless, an objective assessment reveals the attraction for Montezuma and the impact Freemasonry had on him.

Freemasonry is the largest and oldest international non-denominational organization in the world.[2] It is devoted to three fundamental principles. First, belief in a Supreme Being is required for membership. Second, treatment of others is based upon tolerance, understanding, and respect. And third, the organization supports charitable activities. The financial obligations of Freemasonry are funded by initiation fees, Lodge fees, and charitable contributions. The fundamental structure and exotic ceremonies of Freemasonry have existed almost unchanged since its founding; however, local jurisdictions commonly create and maintain modifications.

Amazingly, the origin of Freemasonry is unknown because for many years its secret existence was maintained and written records or accounts strictly avoided. The most favored belief places its roots in the craft of stonemasons and builders who worked on the castles and cathedrals of the Middle Ages. The legendary history of Freemasonry is traced to the tradition and lore of English, Scottish, and possibly Irish working masons who, unlike most people in the Middle Ages, traveled extensively, from building site to building site.[3] The origin of the word "Freemason" is explained in at least two ways. First, ancient masons taught their craft only to the freeborn, and these craftsmen were called Free Masons, individuals who had full citizenship and were free of obedience to one city or area, and thus able to travel.[4] In the second explanation, a Freemason is a more skilled mason who works with freestones, softer stone used for the carved facades, in contrast to the rough-masons who laid the hard structural stone.[5]

Another speculation explains Freemasonry by linking the organization with a medieval crusading institution of soldier-monks founded in Jerusalem in 1118, The Order of the Poor Knights of Christ of the Temple of Solomon in Jerusalem, or the Knights of the Temple of Solomon, or even the more familiar name, the Knights Templar.[6] The Knights Templar swore to a triple monastic vow, including chastity, poverty, and obedience (combining these with the military vocation of knighthood to protect pilgrims to Jerusalem). Their original quarters were at the site of Solomon's Temple. The organization became very wealthy as the ruling classes supported them with generous gifts of land and valuables, and eventually it operated as a financial banking institution throughout Europe. Incurring the wrath of organized religion, specifically Pope Clement V, the members became persecuted and hunted. Living a secret life on the run, it is argued, they developed a mutual protection society using passwords, symbols, and signs derived from their previous secret activities. Even the Lodge of Freemasonry in this explanation is traced to nothing more than a system of lodging to provide a hidden place of sustenance. In the Templar system of organization, the overall commander was given the title of "Grand Master." Perhaps the two explanations come together in the claim that Knights Templar who fled to Scotland kept their order alive by joining a guild of working masons.[7]

The *recorded* history of Freemasonry began in 1717 when four individual lodges formed the Grand Lodge of England. Another possible explanation for the word "Freemasonry" is that prior to becoming public in 1717, the organization existed as "Secret Masonry," and after 1717, as "Free Masonry." Lodges that previously may have been active trade associations became with cessation of castle and cathedral building mutual benefit organizations with an emphasis on charity. It seems logical that wealthy and educated individuals were solicited and welcomed for their material and intellectual contributions. Initially, Masonic Lodges consisted only of working masons. As others were admitted, they were designated as accepted or *speculative* Masons as opposed to working or *operative* Masons. The Grand Lodge of England was the first recognized organization of speculative Masons, and marked the beginning of control by noncraftsmen. The development of additional degrees and greater hierarchy led to a schism between older (the "Atients") and newer members that was resolved in 1813 by a reunification and the formation of the United Grand Lodge of England.

Freemasonry began in an old English milieu that was Protestant and Anglican. But it is isolated and separate from organized religion; its religion is a universal one. Freemasonry rejected atheism, but also refused to adopt a specific religious belief—a middle ground that left room for thinkers in almost any direction. The primary membership requirement is a belief in a Supreme Being, but men of all religions can be members with the objective of constant self-improvement and dedication to charity. Indeed, discussion of religion and politics is forbidden in Masonic Lodges. Although the rituals and ceremonies are emotional, the connection with stonemasonry provides a structure as rational as geometry. The geometric metaphors illustrate order, harmony, and clarity.

One characteristic that has attracted members is the fact that Freemasonry holds itself autonomous and separate from the rest of surrounding society. The conferring of Masonic degrees takes place only in private Lodges, and each Lodge is independent and self-sufficient. The ceremonies and rituals are sworn to secrecy by the members, but they have been the subjects of hundreds of books. Although the details have been recorded for outsiders, it is still claimed that only the insiders have a true understanding of the secret symbols, an understanding of the meaning within the context of the rituals enacted within the lodges. The secrecy then is really a sense of privacy and individuality.

The definition of a Lodge is a simple one, a body of men, but enhanced by the presence of spiritual beliefs in humanity, truth, justice, art, beauty, and religion. This is a new meaning, evolved from the original that simply indicated a place to eat and sleep for those united in a secret organization. Although, it continues to indicate a secret meeting room, it is a Lodge only when the members meet as Masons. Long ago, the building or room was irrelevant, but today the meetings in American cities are in impressive Masonic Lodges, often called Temples in the past because much of the symbolism in Masonic ceremonies is an allegory of the building of King Solomon's Temple. Commonly there is an inscription in the stone over the entrance, for example, "The Scottish Rite of A.F. and A.M." A.F. and A.M. stands for Ancient, Free and Accepted Masons and is used by both the Scottish and York Rites. A Grand Lodge is the administrative body in charge of an area (the local jurisdiction), for example, there is a Grand Lodge in each state of the United States. The local lodges are known as "Blue Lodges," and are presided over by the Worshipful Master, an old English term for an honorable leader. The Grand Master is the official in charge of the Grand Lodge.

The Masonic Temple on the corner of Randolph and State Streets in Chicago, designed by Burnham and Root, was only two blocks from Carlos Montezuma's first downtown office. When opened in 1893, it was the tallest building in the world with twenty-one stories plus a gabled attic, and it remained the tallest building in Chicago until 1911. Later considered old fashioned, the building was demolished in 1939. The building featured a central light court surrounded by shops on the first nine floors, with offices and sixteen lodge halls on the upper floors. Many of the Masonic Lodges of Chicago used the building, but Montezuma attended meetings of Blaney Lodge No. 271 (the number designates the location in the sequence of lodges granted charters within a state), at 912 North LaSalle Street. After 1913, Montezuma was a member of the Dearborn Lodge, No. 310, located at the Midway Masonic Temple, 6115 Cottage Grove Avenue, near Montezuma's home on South Park Avenue.[8]

Masonry became public when the first Masonic text was published in 1722, *Robert's Constitutions*, which was very Christian in orientation. It described the history of masonry and architecture as the roots of Freemasonry. This work, known as the Old Constitution, traced the evolution of stone building from its Biblical origins, culminating in the Freemasonry ceremony that gives prominence to the building of King Solomon's Temple. It further provided behavioral charges, a guide for routine etiquette that ranged from paying your bill at an inn to working only at that where you are expert. Regard and promotion of each member's welfare were important duties. The Old Constitution sternly admonished that the secrets of Freemasonry will not be directly or indirectly published, discovered, or revealed. Up until this point in time, Freemasonry was believed to be entirely about working masons, but *Robert's Constitutions* was published for the use of the emerging membership of non-working Freemasons. It was rapidly replaced by *The New Book of Constitutions of the Antient and Honourable Fraternity of Free and Accepted Masons*, by James Anderson, known as *Anderson's Constitutions*. Both documents articulated a historical provenance derived from the working craft of masons.

*Anderson's Constitutions*, although first published in 1723, only a year after *Robert's Constitutions*, was an approved guideline even earlier, rapidly replacing the Old Constitution.

Its purpose was to present the Masonic past and a guide to behavior, and it rapidly established a tradition that linked working masons with leisurely, scholarly, and even aristocratic members.

The historical tradition according to *Anderson's Constitutions* starts with Adam and Eve, created after the image of God, the Great Architect of the Universe.[9] Adam is assumed to have had knowledge of geometry, a noble science that came to be the foundation of masonry and architecture, allowing the building of cities, and more significantly, civilization. The grand building event was the erection of Solomon's Temple. A name of great significance in Masonic ritual is Hiram. Many of the craftsmen building the Temple were sent by Hiram (or Huram), King of Tyre. He sent his namesake, Hiram (or Huram) Abiff, the most accomplished mason of the time, whose murder would become the central feature of Masonic legend and ritual. History is depicted as the efforts of man to achieve again the perfection attained by Solomon and Hiram Abiff. Individual Masons are expected to work toward the acquiring of skills and knowledge that allow the perpetuation of civilized societies.

Masonry rapidly became fashionable, as scholars, businessmen, tradesmen, and clergy, and even the noble and powerful, enjoyed the Lodge as a respite from politics and the pressures of their lives. Freemasonry changed its focus from the construction of stone temples to building spiritual temples. The fraternity was changed into an organization open to all men (although the members' vote for a candidate had to be unanimous) and dedicated to morality and wisdom, expressed symbolically through the tools and implements of stonemasonry. However, the closed nature of the organization and the high fees (the fees today are not as high as they were relatively in the past) certainly made it unavailable to men in the lowest ranks of society. Middle-class men were attracted to the organization not only because it provided economic and intellectual contacts, but membership also allowed interaction with those from the highest levels of society.

In the first decades of the eighteenth century, English Masonry was visible as a series of meetings, marches, and dinners involving appropriate dress, badges, and jewels (used to indicate the rank and office of various members). The basic structure, history, and ritual had been established. By 1730, Freemasonry rapidly expanded on the European continent. This coincided with the development of the Third Degree, creating the Master Mason, and the emphasis on religious neutralism that avoided political opposition. It was (and still is) this spirit of freethinking about religion that attracted (and still does attract) opposition from organized religion. At this time, too, charitable activity became established as an important part of Freemasonry, as a voluntary and anonymous function.

In the second half of the eighteenth century, the Royal Arch Ritual, consisting of the fourth to thirty-second degrees each with its own title from Secret Master to Grand Inspector General, was added. The name of this ritual comes from a central myth of ancient Egypt, the imaginary arch made by the course of King Osiris, the Sun, from the vernal to the autumnal equinox. The seven signs of this passage correspond to the steps required by a Mason to earn this degree (only Master Masons are eligible). The system of the Royal Arch Ritual is attributed to a French origin that drew heavily on the noblemen involved in the Crusades. It was argued by a Scotsman, Andrew Michael Ramsay, who developed Freemasonry in France, that the original Masons were not workers in stone, but the Crusaders themselves.[10] Many of the strange words encountered in Masonic ritual can be traced to French origins. This system with its expansion of degrees and ritual is called Scottish Masonry, popular in the United States as the Ancient and Accepted Scottish Rite of Freemasonry. The thirty-third degree is an honor conferred by a Lodge in recognition of a member's outstanding involvement and contributions.

The ritual and ceremony can be easily found in a multitude of books. They are complex, requiring a large amount of script with symbolic words to be learned by heart, integrated with symbols taken from the working tools and implements of stone masonry (square, angle, chisel, level, and compasses), gestures, hand positions and grips, passwords, and various postures and movements.[11] The symbols and emblems were originally drawn on the floor of the Lodge. Floor-cloths replaced this method, eventually leading to portable tablets called tracing-boards or lodge-boards. The boards depict by symbols the lessons that are part of each degree of Masonry. Degree is a designation granted according to the customs and terminology of Freemasonry. It is simply a stage or level of membership. An Entered Apprentice is given the First Degree; a Fellow or Brother (of the Craft) follows the Second Degree. A Master Mason has received the Third Degree, a position that emerged later. Each degree is a step from ignorance to knowledge, from darkness to light, the emphasis on constant self-improvement. The First Degree is the first stage of the ritual; the tracing board portrays a checkerboard floor, the sun, moon, and stars, and three columns with a ladder, Jacob's Ladder, offering a pathway to a better life. The symbolic tools of the Apprentice are tools of action, the gavel, the chisel, and the twenty-four-inch measure. The Second Degree board shows a winding staircase leading to the middle chamber of Solomon's Temple, the destination of Jacob's Ladder in the First Degree. The tools of a Fellowcraft Freemason in the Second Degree are tools of testing, the level, the plumb-rule, and the square. The tools of the stonemasons became symbols of ethical values. The square, for example, represents honesty, and the level, equality.

At the conclusion of the First Degree, the candidate is presented with a Masonic apron, always a pure white lambskin. Individuals often purchase a white cloth apron to be used for public display, for decoration with Masonic badges and symbols. The square represents living on this earth with honor and integrity. The compass symbolizes spiritual life, and "G" stands for geometry and God, intertwining the revered science with a belief in a Supreme Being. Even the floor is symbolic, a checkerboard in black and white that indicates the vicissitudes of life.

The Third Degree board features a coffin, skull, and crossbones, symbolizing death and rebirth. The Third Degree symbolism is a universal one, manifested by the American Indian Ghost Dance Religion as well (Chapter 2): death, a catastrophic event, followed by a restoration to a desired original state. The ceremony in the Third Degree is centered on an allegory with the Lodge representing the Temple of Solomon and a search for the Word. The symbolic tools are tools of design and creativity, the instruments of the old stone craftsmen. The Word was known only to the master builder of Solomon's Temple, Hiram Abiff. Hiram was killed by fellow builders before the Temple was completed for not revealing the secret Word (a common mythologic ritual of human sacrifice at the opening of a temple). Buried by his assailants, he was raised by Solomon and reburied in the Sanctom Sanctorum (the central sanctuary of the Temple). The enactment of his burial and raising, with the candidate playing the role of Hiram, is a key scene in the dramatic ritual of the Master Mason, obtaining through this ceremony the secrets of a Master Mason, including the symbolic Word (symbolic of acquiring knowledge of oneself). In the legend, the working party sent out by Solomon to find and re-bury Hiram Abiff agreed that their first words would constitute the substitute for the Word. The Master's Word came to symbolize an ongoing, never ending quest for the wisdom of the ancient world, untarnished by succeeding human problems and perceptions. In the legend, the workmen who found Hiram's body could not lift it because his flesh came off in their hands. Thus the Masonic ceremony features the "lion's grip," a ceremonial embrace of fellowship with five specific points of contact between the candidate and the Master Mason.

In the Royal Arch ceremony (the York Rite), candidates are blindfolded, partially undressed, and encircled with seven coils of a rope that unites them with each other. They pass under a Living Arch, formed by the joined hands of members; they kneel and crawl, and respond within the scripted words and signs. The interpretation of this symbolic ritual is very personal. Certainly it is not meant to be literal, and it is this personal and private interpretation of the symbolism that is the only real mystery in Freemasonry.

Masonic funerals are an expression of affection for a departed brother. The ceremony is conducted by the member's Lodge if it is requested by the member or his family, and it is an addition, usually a prelude, to any regular service, either secular or religious. Or the involvement may consist solely of attending the service. If buried away from home, local Lodges perform the ceremony. The general Masonic funeral service is suitable for all faiths, but the Knights Templar service is specifically Christian. The funeral service, like all Masonic rituals, is a traditional ceremony, but the details vary according to local standards.[12] The attending Masons wear their aprons and a sprig of green in their coat lapels to symbolize immortality. The Master and members exchange memorized readings, throw the dead man's apron into the grave, and finally, pass around the grave three times, casting their green sprigs into the grave and saluting the dead man with an arm stretched out straight. Buffalo Bill had one of the largest Masonic American funerals in history. Masons from Phoenix attended Montezuma's burial.

## AMERICAN FREEMASONRY

Benjamin Franklin was Grand Master of Pennsylvania and produced the first American reprint of *Anderson's Constitutions*. American Freemasonry was essentially British for several generations, and was one of the methods by which a group of men, mainly merchants and professionals, distinguished themselves from the common people as a benevolent elite. Before the American Revolution, prominent Masons in white stockings and gloves often marched in seaboard cities, displaying their Masonic aprons and jewels.[13] Many prominent leaders, including many signers of the Declaration of Independence, were Freemasons.[14]

After the American Revolution, the original body of American Masons came to be viewed as anti-egalitarian. Freemasonry changed as the organization spread into the interior of the land, attracted military officers, leaders in commerce, and a more populist membership. Freemasonry as an organization reflected and aided the change from a hierarchical society before the Revolution to a more republican society.[15] American Freemasonry from 1790 to 1826 became a powerful and prestigious organization. This growth involved many who lacked political power and social distinction, and this new membership, the real builders and bakers in American society, chose to call themselves "Ancients," to make a distinction with the older Colonial group, paradoxically called "Moderns."[16] The organization reached nearly every small town in America. Freemasonry reached such a peak of popularity and respect during the years after the American Revolution, that nearly every large structure erected (even the U. S. Capitol) was begun with a dedication ceremony presided over by Masons. The ceremonial ritual anointed bridges, the Erie Canal locks, state houses, monuments (Bunker Hill and Concord Minutemen), university buildings (the Universities of Virginia and North Carolina), and even a variety of churches. The Masons of Chicago presided over the laying of the cornerstone for the Chicago water pumping station on March 25, 1867. When the water tower was repaired and preserved in 1913 in response to an appeal by the Chicago Historical Society, the worn inscription was replaced by the insertion of a bronze tablet that reads: "Laid by the Masonic Fraternity March 25, 1867. Jerome R. Gorin, Most Worshipful Grand Master."[17]

As American business and professional people began to assert some social class distinction, Freemasonry became a popular method to acquire social and cultural self-identification. American Freemasonry has been distinguished as a social force in each Lodge's local community, with a network of local political and economic power and influence. Nevertheless, Freemasonry ideals were retained, an identification with virtue, learning, and religion, and especially the principle of universal love and equality of men before a Supreme Being. However, the organization increasingly embraced Christianity, and the members of the Knights Templar explicitly aligned themselves with the Christian religion.

The liberal cosmopolitan nature of the English, Scottish, and Irish Lodges that welcomed foreigners and Jews was not typical of eighteenth-century American identity, exemplified by Jeffersonian Republicans. Although early American Masons were virtually all Protestants, Masonic rituals drew the ire of Protestant churches and organizations. The result was predictable. Protestantism became a more overt and acknowledged feature of American Freemasonry Lodges compared with European Lodges. By 1825, American Freemasonry had become the largest non-denominational organization in the United States.[18]

As American Freemasonry grew and spread, the various degrees and ceremonies multiplied, ultimately yielding the two major rites that exist today. The York Rite traces its origin to the Lodges in England, in the eighteenth century. It consists of the degrees of the Royal Arch, the Council of Royal and Select Masters, and the orders of the Commandery of Knights Templar—all intended to amplify the basic three degrees with themes and symbols derived from the medieval crusades.[19] The Scottish Rite was formed in Charleston, South Carolina, in 1801, and involves thirty-two degrees. The American rites became very complex and required precise wording and performance in its rituals. An individual belongs to a local lodge, the "Blue Lodge," and within the Blue Lodge can follow the Scottish Rite system or the York Rite and the Knights Templars, or degrees can be acquired in both pathways.[20] Freemasonry around 1900 was predominantly White, middle-class, Protestant, and of course, totally male. The Order of the Eastern Star, an organization for female relatives of Masons, duplicated the Freemasonry ceremonies and rituals. The Order of Rainbow for Girls and the Order of DeMolay are Masonic youth groups

By the 1820s, the perceived position and power of Freemasonry in America began to attract opposition and rejection. Anti-masonry was sparked in 1826 when William Morgan, a Mason in Batavia, New York, was intent on publishing a book that revealed Freemasonry's secrets.[21] Morgan was abducted, carried to Fort Niagara on the Niagara River between the United States and Canada, and never heard from again. A series of trials resulted in five men receiving jail terms that ranged from one month to three years, but an anti-masonry outcry was galvanized, sweeping the country over the next two years. New newspapers were formed and joined old newspapers in pledging to the cause. The first third party in American history was born; the Anti-Masonic Party collected nearly 350,000 votes in the presidential election of 1832. The fundamental argument, with a strong component of evangelical Christianity, was that Freemasonry's secrecy, exclusivity, and power were incompatible with American life. Furthermore, the American emphasis should be on the public good, not individual accomplishment. The anti-masonic movement nearly destroyed Freemasonry as membership plummeted, and by 1834, mission accomplished, the anti-masonry movement had dwindled away. The flurry of activity successfully changed public opinion and demystified Freemasonry. Only a small cadre of hard-core members remained in Freemasonry. The motivations, methods (agitation and use of the media), and public dynamics of the anti-masonry movement were to emerge again later in the temperance and abolitionist reform movements.

American Freemasonry revived after 1840, and the additional degrees became enormously popular again. By 1880, American Freemasonry was again a respected and prestigious organization, and by 1910, 7 percent of White males were members, by 1920, 10 percent.[22] Nearly half of all the Freemasons in the world today are in America, but membership declined in the 1920s, and Freemasonry has never again achieved the popularity and prestige it had just before and after 1900.[23]

After World War I, American Freemasonry became more of a civic organization.[24] The war was a catalyst for broadening the scope and vision of Americans and hastening the social change from the nineteenth-century emphasis on the individual to a new concern for public welfare. American Freemasons became more interested in using the power of their organization to address social problems. That is not to say that American Freemasonry joined with those in various trenches (such as the working people involved in labor conflicts). Indeed, American Freemasonry was quick to attribute social disruptions to radicalism and to promote the American system. American Freemasonry was slow to accept the new wave of immigrants, Catholics, and Jews, and to separate itself from the Ku Klux Klan.[25] The Freemasonry view of public service was a promotion of "Americanism," (the ideals of the old Protestant, middle class). But slowly and surely American Freemasonry became less isolated and more involved in civic issues, especially public education. Freemasonry became more of a private organization with a commitment to charity. It still commanded respect, but no longer encouraged or inspired reverence. The rituals became more symbolic, and the tight embrace of Christianity was loosened. Increasingly, lodges developed educational and social programs aimed at the family. This change paralleled the national shift in emphasis to broad group issues as American culture became more secularized and less religious, a shift that Montezuma could perceive in his own Masonic Lodge and in the city around him.

## FREEMASONRY AND AMERICAN INDIANS

Arthur C. Parker, noted Seneca scholar, anthropologist and ethnologist, director of the Rochester Museum, and president of the Society of American Indians from 1916 to 1918, was a prominent Mason and was awarded the esteemed thirty-third degree in the Scottish Rite, an honor granted to those who have made outstanding contributions. Parker published a thirty-six-page monograph in 1919 entitled *American Indian Freemasonry*, in which he argued that the essence of Masonry lies in the practice of its moral and philosophical teachings, not the legend or the allegory, but the moral and truth they represent.[26] He defined *inherent* Masonry as an inner potential in men who are capable of becoming Masons and *inductive* Masonry as that into which inherent Masons are led, to be taught the special principles of Masonry by the rites derived from the experience and wisdom of ancient brethren.

Parker identified four fundamental beliefs of the Iroquois that he believed qualified them as Masons, beliefs that Parker claimed were held by all Indian tribes. Parker emphasized a belief in one Great Spirit: "The Great Architect of the Universe to the Indian was the Maker of All."[27] Parker characterized Indians as truthful, charitable, considerate, and stoical—attributes of virtue and morality. He pointed out that Indians believed that conduct in the present life influenced a future life. And finally, Parker stressed a belief in universal kinship, a brotherhood of relationships similar to that of a fraternity. This belief extended to all parts of nature and became manifest in the complex social organization present in all tribes, highlighted by sharing and hospitality.

Parker traced the history of ceremonial societies and fraternities among American Indians. Specifically he mentioned the lodge rooms of the Zuni and the cults and societies of the Pawnee and the Navajo. Parker found a counterpart to the symbolism so prominent in Freemasonry in the symbols and sacred words given to animals and nature. "The Masonry of the Indians as builders and as philosophers dealing with moral truths grew out of their experiences with nature and with the actions of human kind."[28]

Recognizing that Indians did not erect great traditional stone buildings, Parker associated the greater complexity in social organization of eastern American Indian tribes with their more elaborate dwellings. Tools of stone and bone produced beautiful objects, treasured by archeological museums. Surely, said Parker, this is testimony to a sense of balance and harmony similar to that of the ancient Masons. In the making of these objects and dwellings, the Indian had his own "form of the plumb, the level, the square, and the compasses."[29]

Parker described the religious rites and legends of the Iroquois, finding the elaborate constructions not pagan, but "heroic." Parker recounted at length the Seneca legend in which Red Hand takes on a similarity to Hiram Abiff. In its denouement, the Bear grasped the hand of the Leader who, though slain, was to be raised. With a strong grip, Red Hand was raised to go on a quest for a "mystic potence," which when gained, allowed Red Hand to found an Order to know the order of the universe, and to preserve the bonds of faithful brotherhood with its mysteries and chants. Parker concluded: "...who shall say that the Senecas have not the thread of the legend of Osiris or that they have not an inherent Freemasonry?"[30] "There is an intimate connection between archeology and Masonry. The archeologist finds the lost cornerstones of history and with his trowel unearths records that history has failed to write. The archeologist gives us new knowledge of our ancient brethren wherever they were distributed over the earth. ...Every relic that is found on the sites where once lived the primitive peoples of the world is a lost letter, syllable or word."[31]

Middle-class, educated, American Indians around 1900 were practically all Masons. The initiation fee was substantial for the times, $50 to $100, with annual dues of $6 to $12.[32] Parker's explanation in 1919 was surely an elaborate and emotional rationalization, but it is not difficult to objectively discern multiple motivations for American Indians to seek Freemasonry. Membership in a White, male, Protestant exclusive organization must have been viewed by this group of Indians as demonstrable, palpable evidence of successful assimilation (with its social respectability) into American White society. Indeed, Masons themselves believed that their fraternity had played an important role in spreading civilization,[33] an idea certain to appeal to the assimilation philosophy. The ceremonial rituals provided a sense of orderly progression to achievement of honor and knowledge for those who were willing to develop their abilities and fully bring their energy to bear. This idea must have been extremely attractive for a group of men who were forced to struggle to establish themselves in American society and who had embraced the philosophy of American individualism. The higher degrees and official positions in American Freemasonry offered new badges of status, rewards that proclaimed position and identity in American society. Membership further provided opportunities for business, political, and educational networking, opening lines of communication that would ordinarily be closed. And finally, American Freemasonry upheld the practice of not allowing within the Lodge any civic or personal distinctions or competitions that would cause fraternal conflict. Of course, this was relatively easy in that American Masons tended to share the same beliefs in social and religious ideals. Nevertheless, the humanitarian, tolerant, friendly, and respectful atmosphere enforced within the private world of the Lodges must have been a welcome respite from direct and indirect racism educated American Indians encountered in their daily lives. Indeed, the Lodge, a congenial place, could be an asylum from the trials and tribulations of outside life. For an individual without family, like Montezuma, the Lodge must have been a home, a place that provided the kind of support usually found at home with family. In a Lodge, "we are all brothers."[34]

THE FRATERNAL ATTRIBUTES of Freemasonry were surely an attraction for Montezuma. Carlos Montezuma entered Freemasonry at the age of forty, ten years after he returned to Chicago. He learned about Freemasonry from Charles B. Gibson, a physician in Chicago and Master of Blaney Lodge, who had been friends with Montezuma ever since his first year at the University of Illinois in 1881.[35] Montezuma applied for membership on September 12, 1906, was named an Apprentice Mason on August 7, 1907, received the degree of Fellow Craft on September 25, 1907, and became a Master Mason on December 4, 1907, in Blaney Lodge No. 271.[36] He served as Chaplain (Senior Deacon) in 1912 and 1913. Sometime after 1913, he affiliated with Dearborn Lodge No. 310.

Masonic ceremonies feature a theatrical performance following established and memorized phrases and leading candidates from station to station with a flourish and under the eyes of watching members. The ritual (really a pageant) involved prayers and incantations with physical interactions that were symbolic and sometimes rough, intended to emphasize ritual and even to frighten candidates. One can imagine that Montezuma's ability as an impassioned speaker at public occasions was unleashed in the secret gatherings of the Lodge where props and costumes created dazzling theater. Montezuma "put in many nights at Dearborn, assisting in conferring of degrees, posting candidates, etc. He was noted throughout the fraternity for his wonderful visualization and renditions of a certain part of the second section of the third degree—in this particular work he had no compare and its like will probably never be seen again."[37]

Montezuma's involvement with Freemasonry must be viewed as evidence of his commitment to what he called "civilization." "It is the duty of the Government to aid him [the Indian] in every way in making the change from his former mode of life to the conditions of civilization."[38] "Civilization," however, was the middle-class Protestant ethic of the times, and the moral lessons taught in Freemasonry were in harmony with the prevailing Protestant middle-class culture. Admittedly there were the respectable virtues of honesty, temperance in all behavior, and industry, but these virtues were expressed in rugged individualism, the pursuit of wealth, and the Protestant religion. This was certainly consistent with Montezuma's social Darwinism in his dedication to the abrupt termination of the reservations and Indian culture, casting Indians into White society to allow the survival of the fittest.

American Freemasonry in the nineteenth century believed in the power of individual will to work towards perfection. This was the philosophy of social reform until industrial growth and urbanization made it clear that individualism was not sufficient. The conflicts between capitalists and labor could not be solved by brotherhood and love. In the twentieth century, Freemasonry changed from its focus on the individual to an emphasis on social issues and problems. Montezuma would change his own philosophy when he joined the battle to save the Yavapai land, a fight initially at the individual level, but over time increasingly at a tribal level. This change was consistent with the changes Montezuma was experiencing in American society and Freemasonry.

# CHAPTER ELEVEN

# Rediscovering the Yavapai:
# They're All Related to Me

IT TOOK HIM thirty years, but Carlos Montezuma did return to those places that were still alive in his memories from childhood. Beginning in 1901, Montezuma returned to Arizona in the early fall of nearly every year. He rediscovered his relatives, his tribe, and reconnected with the land of central Arizona. "Most of the Mohave Indians are related to me and they are scattered all over Arizona territory, but most of them are living at Ft. McDowell and the San Carlos Reservations."[1]

When the Land-In-Severalty Act was passed in 1887 (Chapter 3), Montezuma, identifying himself as an Apache, immediately wrote directly to the secretary of the interior asking, "under what condition and in what locality am I entitled to land."[2] The letter was referred to the commissioner of Indian affairs who responded: "...you would be entitled to an allotment of land with the Apaches, when their reservation is divided, if you should be located thereon at the time, or you can make settlement upon any vacant and unapportioned lands belonging to the United States, and become entitled to eighty acres, if unmarried, and 160 acres if married."[3] Montezuma then asked for a description of what lands were unoccupied in the Indian Territory, Kansas, Arizona, and California. "I wish to secure a place where I can do most good to any people who have been trodden down, especially the Apaches. I think there can be derived some good out of them. ...Yours in the Cause."[4] The acting commissioner informed Montezuma that he would have to seek his desired information from local land districts, and that temporarily ended Montezuma's quest for land. Pratt consoled him: "You will certainly be entitled to your distributive share of land when the Apaches take up theirs in severalty."[5]

## REDISCOVERY OF THE YAVAPAI

Montezuma went to California in January 1900, accompanying the Carlisle football team to play the University of California at Berkeley. On the return trip, he visited Phoenix, Albuquerque, Santa Fe, and stopped at the Haskell Institute in Kansas. Richard Pratt paid his expenses in return for a report on southwestern Indian schools. Upon his return, Montezuma dutifully reported to Pratt even before going to sleep: "I feel it my duty to thank you and to express my candid opinion of our trip. It was my anniversary trip—a lapse of thirty years from captivity into liberty—a change of one generation. I need make no mention of the boys and their management. They all deserve praise. Throughout the trip we were of one mind to show the best side of Carlisle. We did it. For your Football Team to go three thousand miles to compete with one of the best educational colleges on the coast and defeat them against odds [Carlisle won by a safety, 2–0] was as effective as generations of gradual assimilation of the Indian into civilization. ...Phoenix, Arizona is a pleasant place. ...I noticed they are not afraid of Apaches as formerly. I was surprised to know fifty miles from here I was captured near the Four Peaks. ...Though Haskell has many advantages it does not come up to Carlisle. None of the schools have 'the outing system' nor do they seem to take any interest in that direction. All they seem to think of is to get as many pupils as possible to maintain their schools. That is poor policy. When you are dealing with future men and women, get them out among the people and not confine them in convent-like methods (Indian schools). I lost a chance to sleep. I hope my words were not wasted. I expressed what was in my heart at that moment. Again I thank you for your kind favors."[6]

But it was not until 1901 when Montezuma was thirty-five years old that he decided to reconnect with his roots. He prepared for the trip, still thinking he was an Apache, enlisting Michael Burns to help seek out relatives and places of his childhood. He asked Burns about remaining elders that might remember his family and especially his capture by the Pima warriors. Burns wrote on February 20, 1901: "My Dear Cousin, ...You mentioned about whether Thumbo was able enough. I must say that he is, if he had taken sick since I left him and his family at San Carlos. This was a year ago last Sept and now going on 2 years. I understood that Thumbo's camp was away towards the road to where the enemies came to the main camp of yours. Do you still recollect that a party of Indians just had arrived from North and held a great talking that night. Nearly all the men were called to and it was the reason that no one was out towards the road to watch any raiding parties during that night. But I am sure we can find the place and can gather Indians of the same tribe and relatives of ours to go with us, and would be very glad with you especially. But I am still trying to find out about your baby brother and had never heard anything about the baby until from your inquiry."[7]

A month later, Burns told Montezuma his version of the death of Montezuma's mother: "...It was me that told you about the death of your mother by Indian scouts from Carlos and overtook her near Tonto Basin after crossing the Salt River, on the Black River while on her way to this place [Camp Verde]. To where she was told about you was seen here by some other Indian women and on hearing she was so crazy to see you, so she started away from San Carlos Agency without proper leave of absence from the Agent. If she had gone and explain the whole facts to the Indian Agent she might given a written pass and could come here and return homeward again without being hurt, and she might could live til yet. But no Indian could go away without being reported by Indian Police who were told to watch the Indian camps and count the Indians every morning. There are but 3 old men living at this old Military Post, who are the oldest settlers but they are away and could not see them to ask whether they know anything about older times. ...I must say to where you was captured. It is almost direct East from Phoenix and almost direct north from Florence. It is in the rough mountains of Superstition. The Four Peaks stands north east of Phoenix. North of the Salt River. ...I would be glad to join your party."[8]

Montezuma asked the San Carlos Indian Agent to help him in his quest: "I expect to be at San Carlos Agency the first part of the coming month (September). It will be my first trip to my native home since 1872. Many of the old Indians who remember the raid (by the Pimas) at Four Peaks are dead but I understand an Indian whose name is 'Thumbo' still lives on your agency. May I ask your kind favor to notify him that I am coming and that I want

**Arizona Territory**

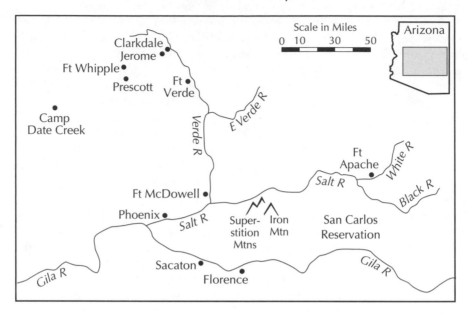

him to take the trip with me to the four Peaks and show me the place where I was captured 29 years ago by the Pimas. Also I want to look for the record of my Father 'Co-cu-ye-vah' and my mother. I understand my mother was killed by Indian police on her way to Fort Verde. I hope to give you a very interesting story of my self. I will come in the interest of the Carlisle School."[9]

Never having a surfeit of money, Montezuma convinced Richard Pratt to provide expenses for his planned trip. Pratt told him that summer that he could send Montezuma as an agent to recruit students for Carlisle. He could not send Montezuma's companion, but he would arrange the benefit of any cut rates he could obtain. Pratt arranged for a ticket to San Carlos on the Atchison & Topeka Railroad and even provided $100 for expenses.[10]

The summer of 1901 was the time of Montezuma's courtship of Zitkala-Ša (Chapter 9), but she turned down his invitation to join the Arizona trip. "I have yours asking if it is possible for me to go to Arizona with you. I will not finish this letter today but shall take a few times to consider your proposition. My feeling is that it is best not to. I'd rather you would give me my Arizona in the form of an engagement ring."[11] It's a good thing Zitkala-Ša chose not to go because by the time Montezuma was in Arizona, the relationship was already in its stormy phase.

Burns replied from Camp Verde on July 15, 1901: "So I must say that I was so disappointed to hear that you could not come out until fall and I can not be with you in that time. And I had left off many good offers just on your account to go out in the country with you, and would be too glad to go and also visit some of my old camping places. So you can come on the train from Chicago to San Carlos. You must change trains at Bowie Station to Carlos on the Northwest and Gila valley RR to Globe and you can hire an interpreter there and the old people are there and you select them to go with you. …Hoping you will succeed in finding out about your family more clearly than I can obtain."[12]

In order to find and visit his childhood sites, Montezuma ultimately relied heavily on his cousins, Charles, George and Richard Dickens. These cousins were the children of Su-ke-yal-vah (Susie Dickens), the sister of Montezuma's mother, who avoided capture on the night of the Pima raid in October 1871.[13] She died at the age of 108.[14]

THIS TRIP IN SEPTEMBER 1901 must have been a moving experience. We can recount it only in letters from Montezuma to Richard Pratt. The first was written on September 23 and mailed from the San Carlos Agency: "This is my third day at the Agency. In regard to my relatives, Father died half a mile from the Agency bullring. Mother was found dead along side of a trail with a bullet hole. So I have no near relatives. I found a second wife of my father's, whom I recollect twenty nine years ago. Also I found my mother's sister's daughter. I expect to go to the place where I was captured in a day or two. Col, San Carlos reservation is like all reservations. A hot bed of everything but that which will elevate the Apaches. I am sorry to say, the returned pupils of Carlisle have not the best of reputation. Whiskey is the cause. What can we expect! Put an Angel on a reservation, the angel will not be an angel very long. We must not fight against natural results. It is not natural to cage my people."[15]

*Iron Mountain*

Montezuma did make it to the top of Iron Mountain, the site of his capture in October 1871, known to the Yavapai as Mard-ho-jar-may-joe.[16] It takes only a little imagination to see Montezuma standing on the site of Iron Mountain and falling like a rock into his past. Old memories must have washed over him, as for the first time, he made a full circle of his life. "Last evening I returned from that long anxious trip to the place where I was captured in the Superstition Mountains, which is part of the Pinal Mountain range. It is about eighty miles from the Agency, northwest. To get there we passed over couple trails and it took us three days. The first night after leaving the Agency we camped at an Indian grass hut on the foothills near Globe. You can imagine my first experience at Indian camping. I ate their cooking and slept on the ground. The novelty of it is all right but to live and die that way is not comfortable. I endured five nights of sleeping on the ground quite well, but I was really glad to get into bed last night. The plateau is called Iron Mountain. It was a very steep peak. The tallest in the range. You can imagine when I tell you it took us one good hour to get up on the top. When we got up there I was somewhat like Rip Van Winkle. I thought that the grass huts I saw under trees would be there but there was nothing but a bare ground. I thought the small trees would be as small as ever; the trees that I played under would be to me now as it did then. I imagined the grass that protected me under foot would seem to me now as it did then. I imagined the grass that protected my tender feet would still protect. But no. It has all changed! The small bushes have grown to be trees, the trees then are dead and those standing look old and weather beaten. The grass has been trampled under by cattle. Even the mountain looked larger and higher. I was telling this to my guide. He laughed and said, 'I guess they grew, those mountains.' A relative who escaped that awful night was along—he showed me the place where my house stood and the rest of the huts. The next day he came to the place and found about seventeen killed. I found a bone and two fragments of bones, four stones that ground their grass with. We went down and came over night on the mountain. Tomorrow morning I will take the train for Phoenix and visit the school and also go to the Pima village and at the same time in the house where I was held."[17]

Charles Dickens, when interviewed years later, remembered Montezuma standing silently and thinking, then motioning and saying: "Right down there, by that rock wall, is where the Pimas nabbed me that night."[18] Montezuma collected pieces of pottery and found an old bow; it was falling apart, but he took it home.[19]

The drive to the Iron Mountain trailhead covers seventy-six miles north from Highway 60 on a rough forest service road. The trail to Iron Mountain starts at an elevation of 4,883 feet. A hike of one hour takes you a mile to the southeast of the peak, a climb of 615 feet. The peak of bare reddish rock thrusts straight up to its highest level of 6,056 feet. The landscape defines a chaparral, a dense thicket of low-growing shrubs and trees. There is no shortage of wood. Pinyon pine trees dot the slopes, many as high as fifteen to twenty feet. There are several kinds of junipers, including the large Alligator Juniper, some with trunks a foot in diameter. Cottonwood trees are concentrated around the spring a half-mile down the eastern side at an elevation of 5,150 feet. The space is filled with madrone, manzanita, quinine bushes, and even large gooseberry bushes. The elevation is too high for cactus; only an occasional prickly pear is found. The ground is covered with grass and scattered century plants can be seen all the way to the top of the peak, Sotol agave at the lower elevations and Parry's agave at higher elevations (*Agave parryi*, the mescal prized by the Yavapai years ago). You can see for miles in the desert air. There is a pleasant quietness in which individual birds can be easily heard. Montezuma returned to this place many times in the rest of his life, and it is easy to feel and sense why he did.

*Iron Mountain Peak*

From Sacaton, Montezuma again wrote Richard Pratt: "I am having the real dream of my life and at the same time I thought I had a splendid group of children from this Agency but at the moment I fall flat as anything in my anticipation for pupils. ...And being so near where I was sold by the Pimas, I took the time to come up here and I am well repaid for coming as I am received by the Pimas with warmth and gladness for some remembered me being with Mr. Gentile on our way down the valley from Adamsville. Off Adamsville (this was where I was sold for $30.00) fortunately I met the young Mexican boy (Santiago Lorma) whom I played with thirty years ago about this time."[20]

*Pinyon Pine Tree at Iron Mountain*

Sunday morning early, several of us started from Sacaton and reached Adamsville about noon. We drove through the forsaken place. We saw no one. But being anxious to find out something I commanded the buggy to stop. The first living being we saw was an old man. I beckoned him to come to us and when he was in speaking distance I asked him a question. His answer was "no save Americana." But he called out a young man to speak for him, which brought out several other young men. The young man acting as our interpreter I began: "Ask the old gentlemen, how long he has been living in this place." The old gentlemen replied, "forty years." (Pointing in the direction where I supposed the adobe house stood, and then using my two hands to represent ten years, I flipped them down and up three times and used one or two fingers to represent years, making altogether 31 or 32 years) "Ask him, if he remembers about 31 or 32 years ago there lived over yonder a man who took pictures."

The old man looked down a moment and then suddenly raised his head and replied, "Yes."

Now ask him if he remembers the little Indian boy he bought from the Pima Indians. This small boy was captured from these mountains (pointing to the Superstition mountains fifty miles away). Before I finished the question, these sons of his were saying: "Montezuma, Montezuma!"

He looked up at me and said, "Yes."

And I smiled and pointing to myself, I said, "I am that Indian Boy."

Quick as a flash those boys and the gray headed father rushed forward with extended hands and bid me welcome which was equal to a greeting for a lost son's return after many years of absence.

At this moment a man jumped off from his horse a short distance away and was tying his horse. The father looked and said, "There is the boy who used to play with you."

Before the man reached us I recognized him at once. He was thunder struck and smiled with joy to see once more the orphan boy he befriended in his childhood days.[21]

"Florence was my next visit. As I remembered being in a Catholic Church. I went to the old Chapel to see if I was on record in their books. Sure enough there was my name and date Nov 17, 1871. So you see I am insured for Heaven."[22]

The *Arizona Republican* described him on that visit: "He was dressed in canvas hunting garb, somewhat soiled, and had just returned from the mountains north of Silver King, a locality of peculiar interest to him for reasons which will appear further on in this article. He is a man of medium stature, stoutly built, with an oval face, regular features and the thick, black shock of hair characteristic of the Apache. He has the easy carriage and address of the refined easterner. …Dr. Montezuma has given much patient effort to tracing his family history, and on his recent trip to Iron Mountain, a spur of the Pinals—with the assistance of a Mohave-Apache who made his escape at the time of the massacre—he succeeded in locating the spot where the tragedy occurred, nearly all the evidences of which have been removed by relic hunters. However, the doctor brought back with him an old bow that had evidently done service in that sanguinary encounter, which he will carefully preserve."[23]

Michael Burns actually did not make this trip, and wrote to him later in October 1901: "I had written a letter in reply to your request to direct the way that you could reach San Carlos Agency and to where you could see some of your few remaining relations in that tribe of your father and mother. So I had happened to notice a paper one day in Prescott and read a piece which was taken from the 'Silver Belt' of Globe where it said about your visit through Globe and out to your old ruin camping place. The Party consist of Antonio and a supposed an 'Apache Indian.' I saw him often at San Carlos but I could hardly take him to be an Apache Indian. He looks more like a Cherokee and half negro. But at any rate, he has been most everywhere in the country as an Apache Indian. But you was not exactly an Apache. We are just called Apaches. You must remember that there are different classes of an Apache family. The White Mountain, the Chiroduras, San Carlos, Tontos. These three or four speaks the same tongues and a little different in some words and their ranges a part from one another, mostly in the northern or eastern part of Arizona. We were called an 'Apaches Indian,' when are collected at San Carlos Agency. But there are two more families which are called the Mojaves and Yumas. These two tribes speak the same. Our tribe used to roam from Silver King all along the mountain ranges to near Haupais or to San Francisco Mountain. Those you had seen at Camp Verde were the northern Mojaves and from Prescott to near Phoenix. And Yumas used to roam west of Prescott. When these two tribes are gathered, they were many. They were once the valley were full of them at Camp Verde in 1873–74, they had some fights with the San Carlos and the Tontos on the way to San Carlos Agency. The Mojaves and Yumas drive the Apaches in the mountains, killed 271, and destroyed nearly all they had left in their camp until the soldiers stopped them, and the Apaches killed 3 and surrendered some."[24]

Montezuma also tried to meet Charles H. Cook, a Presbyterian missionary in Sacaton (the first school teacher on the Pima reservation), but was unsuccessful. Cook remembered Montezuma: "…In the meantime I will try and find out something more about your capture and the place of it which I understand is a very steep high mountain, perhaps not very far from San Carlos Agency or Globe. Some one told me that a Maricopa, who has but one eye, brought you here. …I remember seeing you in 1871 when you were probably about 5 to 6 years old and purchased from these Indians by a Chicago photographer."[25]

In future years, it was Montezuma's practice to invite several people to join him on his annual visits to Arizona. In 1910, he arranged a trip "with five or six of my good, jolly masonic fellows."[26] He depended on his relatives for the logistics:

My cousin Hiram,

I am coming to Arizona again this September—leaving Chicago about the 15th of September, that will get me in Arizona on the 18th. I will bring with me 5 or 6 of my good friends. So you all will have two months or 60 days to get that many good horses for us. You can talk with Charley Dickens and have that many horses ready. Tell me how many saddles and guns to bring or anything we will need on our trip.

We want to go to McDowell to talk with Mohave Indians for 2 days—then go to Florence where I was sold—you want to see the place and so does Charley—then we want to go where I was captured (Iron Peak) and then we want to take a good week's of hunting. You know the good place. Afterwards we will go slow to San Carlos, Ft. Apache, Cooley Station, Petrified Forest and then to Holbrook. Where you will take the horses back and we take train for home. Remember we will leave saddles and guns for part pay for doing so much for us but these good friends will treat my relations like they do me. And they have money to buy baskets and Indian moccasins etc. Get the women to work make baskets for us.

Hiram, Charley and several others who want to come with us—we will have great good time of our life. Bring that horse you said you give me. Shall I bring saddle for the horse?

Your cousin
Carlos Montezuma
"Wassajah"[27]

IN 1913, Montezuma was joined in his annual Arizona vacation by a group of notable friends, including Reverend William H. Stedman, John M. Oskison, a Cherokee and an editor of *Collier's Magazine*, destined to be vice-president of the Society of American Indians in 1916, John T. McCutcheon, the noted cartoonist of the *Chicago Tribune*, W. Kirkpatrick Bryce, a lawyer from New York, Charles B. Gibson, a physician from Chicago, P. H. Hayes, a lawyer and fellow Mason from Phoenix, George N. Morgan, a classmate at the University of Illinois and now an attorney in Chicago, and W. H. Grindstop of Phoenix. Montezuma enticed his companions with the promise of a week-long hunting trip. John Oskison published a detailed account, "With Apache Deer-Hunters in Arizona," in the April 1914 issue of *Outing*.[28]

Montezuma's invitation promised that they would go to the Fort McDowell Agency, "where we will see the Mohave Apaches—the real primitive Indians of the West. They will entertain us where we shall have a chance to fish, swim, and live out of doors. They will provide horses for us on a great hunt and sightseeing trip among the most picturesque scenery of Arizona. One week or ten days, the Indians will show us how to hunt and show us where battles were fought between them and Pima scouts and soldiers forty years ago. …Every step of the way we will be guided by the Indians, all of them related to me."[29] With only 250 to 300 Yavapai at Fort McDowell in 1913, most *were* undoubtedly related to Montezuma.

Four men in the hunting party were first to arrive in Phoenix, where they were met the next day by Charles, George, and Richard Dickens, and the tribal chief, Yuma Frank, accompanied by friends, making a total of fourteen Indians. The Indians packed newly purchased supplies in their wagons, and the group made its way to Fort McDowell. John McCutcheon's artistic talents were utilized to paint a board eight feet long that read: CHARLES DICKENS' STORE. The visitors helped the Indians mount the board, running front to back on the roof of the small one-story structure.

Charles Dickens estimated that about twelve Indians would be participating in the camping trip, including Michael Burns, who with his family had moved in 1913 to Fort McDowell. So supplies were provided for eight White men and fifteen Indians. The first day of the hunt, the hunters discovered their party now numbered nine White men and twenty-seven Indians!

The first night of the hunt was enjoyable around a large campfire until a storm with high winds, rain, and thunder drove the men to shelter. The next day they rode into the hills west of the Verde River, scouting for deer as they rode. The Indians killed several deer, the White men, not a single one; they did bag some quail and rabbits that Stedman enthusiastically cleaned. Oskison was convinced that "all of the rocks in the world must have been piled up on the hills of Arizona at one time."[30] The group listened to "Monty's poetic improvisations concerning the old care-free life of his people until we began to believe that civilization is a horrid mistake."[31] On the fifth day of the hunt, Montezuma joined three others in a search for deer, but his only weapon was a pair of binoculars. Montezuma planned the day's campaign, a plan that included flanking movements to trap the deer.

They worked hard that day, and Oskison observed that Montezuma "is heavy and short, but there is a wonderful power stored in his stocky frame."[32] By 1913, Montezuma was wearing suspenders to hold his trousers over a mildly protruding abdomen. They walked a long distance, fighting the rocks and the canyons, and never even had an opportunity to fire a shot. On the last day, a deer was shot and the kill was assigned to Oskison, even though he admitted: "Mine was the second shot—Heaven knows where the bullet went."[33]

## Yavapai Dancing

The Indian Bureau vigorously suppressed Indian dancing. All things Indian—music, art, clothing, religion—were regarded as obstacles to assimilation. Indeed, Indian dancing was an affront to the evangelical Protestantism at the end of the nineteenth century and the beginning of the twentieth century, regarded as pagan, heathen behavior associated with savages.

Just eight months before the 1913 hunting trip in Arizona, Yuma Frank had written to Montezuma: "…Every Indians, from birth to the oldest age are looking upon you as our protector of our earthy rights. We further present our rights that had been forbidden by this Agent, against our custom of dancing. I will try at first to explain the character of the dances. It has no ceremonies or other superstitions believe within the dance. It is clean, gentlemanly, and respectable. We do not often practice this custom of dancing. Only we call for the dance on National Holidays and other Holiday. It is suggested for dance for the purpose of pleasant gathering. We all love the pleasure of dancing just as much as whites or other nationality."[34]

The Fort McDowell superintendent, Charles E. Coe, was especially focused on the elimination of tribal dances and rebuffed the requests of Yuma Frank. In September 1913, Montezuma requested a favor of Commissioner Sells and received permission for the Yavapai to hold the dance in his honor.

> I leave to Camp McDowell, Arizona Sept twentieth to visit my play grounds of forty two years ago.
>
> I want to ask you an exceptional favor. I have always been opposed to Indian dances, because they demoralize the Indians. That is when the Indians take a whole week to get ready, devote one week to dancing and one week to get over the effect.
>
> There is a different case. Mohave Apache dance lasts only one night. It is religious rites, reminder of past memories and songs of rejoicing. The Mohave Apaches are very peaceable & do not wish to antagonize any one. For that reason they ask me to write to you and get your permission for them to hold a dance of jubilee for my honor and friends.
>
> I therefore ask that you permit them to celebrate in the old way of showing their thankfulness.
>
> I have heard great deal about you since you took hold of the helm of the Indian ship. For your encouragement they have been of the best from men who know what they are talking about and Indians who have heart-interest in their race.[35]

Granted permission by Commissioner Sells, the Indian community had a dance of welcome the first night at Fort McDowell during the 1913 hunting trip, involving the whole tribe, numbering about 270 at that time. The dance lasted all night long. Reverend Stedman, now seventy-two years old with graying chin whiskers and a bald head, was the first to crawl into his sleeping bag. Montezuma and Oskison gave up sometime after midnight.[36]

The dance stirred angry responses directed to the commissioner from Charles E. Coe, the Superintendent of the Salt River and Fort McDowell Reservations, and a Presbyterian missionary in Scottsdale, George H. Gebby. "It seems strange that a man of his education and attainments should encourage the perpetuation of such practices if he knows how they retard the progress of the Indians."[37] "I am prepared to state that the Doctor's representation was wholly in error. This dance is a social dance and when it was formerly permitted among these unmoral and half-civilized people it was often accompanied or followed by fights, jealousies, and domestic difficulties. ...It is my opinion that having lived from boyhood among other reservation conditions, he does not understand his own people or know the peculiar reservations conditions here any better than any other Chicago physician."[38]

This controversy brought censure on Montezuma for encouraging old ways. The very next year, the Fort McDowell Yavapai urged Montezuma to request permission for a dance at the Reservation's Fourth of July celebration. Montezuma did so, but Commissioner Sells refused to grant permission, and he continued to do so in response to annual requests.

> ...Dancing by the Indians is a matter that has given the Office much concern. As you know dances which are essentially barbarous in their nature, such as the Sun Dance, and other dances that have specifically harmful features, have been heretofore prohibited; but even the dances which are in themselves innocent and harmless are sometimes perverted with mischievous results, and I am advised that the latter condition obtained among the Indians at Camp McDowell before indulging in this pastime was wholly eliminated in 1912.
>
> Last year at your solicitation permission was granted by this Office, over the protest of the Superintendent in charge of the Indians at Camp McDowell, to hold a dance of jubilee in your honor upon the occasion of your return to that reservation. That dance was recognized as an exception, but even in that instance an adverse report was made to the Office by one in close contact with the Indians. Local conditions very materially influence the permissibility of sports and pastimes for the Indians, and I feel that the Superintendent's judgment in this matter should not be overriden without substantial reasons; therefore I feel that I cannot authorize the dance this year although it would be a pleasure to grant your personal request were circumstances different.[39]

## THE BONES IN SKELETON CAVE

The Skeleton Cave Massacre occurred on December 29, 1872. Mike Burns, who was captured about two weeks before the massacre by Captain James Burns, accompanied the army troops to the hiding place of a band of Yavapai, a cave on the north side of a canyon that is now flooded by Canyon Lake. The Indians refused to surrender; seventy-six were killed, many of thirty-five still living died later, and eighteen women and children were taken to Fort McDowell.[40] All of Burns' relatives were killed. The dead were left behind.

Workers discovered the cave during the construction of the Roosevelt Dam from 1905 to 1911.[41] Some of the bones were looted, but the discovery stirred memories of the episode in Mike Burns. He proposed to Montezuma that they retrieve the bones in Skeleton Cave. "...Could we get around in some way so that there could be something done in towards helping us to gather the bones of our people in that cave for burial? Just lately I have been thinking about writing to our representatives who is Carl Hayden from Phoenix and Mark H. Smith of Tucson if they could get money set aside for purpose to get parties of Indians to gather their dead relatives so that the bones be put in boxes for to bury them and head stones be placed over and the date when they met death on what occasion occurred. I wish you will give me some good and strong ideas on forming the words in writing to the Government representatives or who are at the heads of making the laws. It looks shame for leaving those human bones lying there, and no respect shown, or effort to put them away, as all human beings especially in the midst of a civilized country as this United States."[42]

Montezuma liked the idea: "...so they will not do very much to burying the bones of our relatives at Bloody Cave. If you want that done, you Indians can go there and do the work yourselves. When I get there we will take that trip and do it ourselves. That is the best way, but I will speak about it to others and see whether we can get Government to defray the expenses. ...But as I say, let us all go up there when I come & dig the bones out, put them in boxes & bury them nicely. I would not say too much about it because scientists are searching for such things to take away for themselves. I am glad you brought this up and it would be no more than proper for us to do the work."[43]

In 1920, Montezuma led an expedition to Skeleton Cave that included Mike Burns and the Dickens brothers. They collected the bones, returned to Fort McDowell, and arranged for their burial in the reservation cemetery. Only two years and three months later, Montezuma was buried in this cemetery, immediately next to the Skeleton Cave Grave.

*Skeleton Cave Grave (in foreground)*

## MONTEZUMA'S EFFORT TO ENROLL IN A TRIBE

Montezuma's attempt to enroll in a tribe began in the summer of 1915 when he was forty-nine years old and ended with denial by the Commissioner of Indian Affairs, Charles H. Burke, in the summer of 1922 only six months before Montezuma's death. On August 2, 1915, Montezuma wrote to Assistant Commissioner E. B. Meritt asking about his position as legal heir of his relatives: "...after this raid all of my relatives that escaped with the men who went away to make the Peace treaty with the government at Ft. Thomas were taken to San Carlos Reservation, 1871. After these many years I am the only survivor, all the rest died at San Carlos. In what position am I as legal heir?"[44] The secretary of war received a letter from Montezuma in 1916 in which Montezuma "requests contents of treaty signed by Apache Indians at San Pedro or San Carlos, Oct 1871, men of an Apache camp on Iron Peak, Superstition Mts who had gone to San Pedro to sign a peace treaty when their camp was routed by a party of Pima, Maricopa and Mohave Indians one night in Oct 1871, the boys and girls being captured and old folks killed."[45] Various authorities responded, including the Adjutant General, and no record could be found of any treaty corresponding to Montezuma's request.

Meritt replied asking whether Montezuma was applying for enrollment at San Carlos where his parents were taken in 1871, or as a survivor of the tribe. Either way, he was asked to provide details of his Indian blood and family history. But Montezuma did nothing for five years until 1920, when he told Meritt that his family had died at San Carlos, and he wished to be enrolled as a member of the San Carlos Reservation.

> My father and mother died San Carlos reservation, Arizona. Mother in 1872 and father in 1876. Also my brother 1872. I have been away from my people since 1871. I therefore wish to be filed as a member of the San Carlos reservation. Not knowing the necessary steps to take, I wish your advice and if there [are] papers to be sign[ed], please send them or could the department authorize the Agent at San Carlos to place my name in the registry book as a member of the San Carlos reservation.[46]

In response Meritt outlined the requirements:

> ...You should furnish a sworn statement giving your family history, Indian ancestry, place and date of your birth, places and approximate dates of your subsequent residence, whether you have heretofore made a similar application and action taken thereon, degree of Indian blood you claim, the name of the tribe to which each of your parents belonged, whether or not they were enrolled and recognized members of the tribe, and just what benefits, if any, they received as Indians. Your statement should be corroborated by affidavits of two or more persons who have knowledge of the facts in the case.[47]

In November 1920, Montezuma submitted an application to be enrolled with the Apache Indians of the San Carlos Agency. The application was received and acknowledged by Assistant Commissioner Meritt who incorrectly noted that Montezuma wished to be enrolled at the Salt River Agency. Montezuma by mail had to correct Meritt, pointing out that the application was for enrollment with the Apache of San Carlos Agency. The application contained his sworn affidavit, completed in Maricopa County, Arizona, when he was on vacation, and Montezuma also included his pamphlet, *Let My People Go*, as a declaration of his principles.

Carlos Montezuma being first duly sworn upon oath deposes and says: I am of lawful age and a resident and citizen of Chicago, Illinois. I was brought to said city at about the age of four years by C. Gentile from Arizona. I was christened at the Chapel in Florence, Arizona, by the priest in charge and the record shows: "An Apache boy christened under the name of Carlos Montezuma, November 26th, 1871." My people, at the time of my birth, did not read or write and kept no records from which I can ascertain definitely just when and where I was born but distinctly remember my parents. I am informed by relatives of my parents, that I was born about the year 1867 on Fish Creek near where the Roosevelt Dam is now situated and that my parents were full blood Apache Indians; that my parents were of the Pinal Apache Tribe of Indians and that they are now known as the Mohave Apaches. Our band had been hunted and attacked by United States Indian Scouts. Many of my people were killed and I and my two sisters were taken prisoners by the Scouts who were Pima Indians.

I was taken to the Pima country and later taken by three Pima Indians who claimed the ownership of me to a place seven miles beyond Florence where they sold me to Mr. Carlo Gentile for the sum of $30.00. My two sisters were sold to Mr. Chas. Mason, and were taken to old Mexico, the State of Sonora where they died without issue. [This disagrees with the account of his nephews in Chapter 2.]

My mother in seeking to locate her children, whom she had lost, was killed, being shot by some of the United States Scouts.

My father was known among the Apache Indians as Co-lu-ye-vah and lived until his death, about 1876, at San Carlos agency, Arizona. He was survived by his last wife known as Yu-co-dep-po who now lives at Fort McDowell Agency, Arizona.

The mother of Charles Dickens, a full blood Mohave Apache Indian living at the Fort McDowell Agency, Arizona, is an aunt of mine being my mother's sister and much older than me. She knew me prior to my being taken by the United States Pima Scouts, and she knew all of my parents' family. She knew and still knows of the facts and circumstances of which I here testify, except as to the record of baptism and certain other facts of which I have personal knowledge. Since I have revisited my native country I have met with Charles Dickens, a cousin, my step-mother, Co-lu-ye-vah's widow, Yu-co-dep-po, and others who have verified the facts of parentage and relationship to Charles Dickens. Since my relationship has been reestablished at the Fort McDowell Agency, Arizona, and I make frequent visits to my people and live with them for such periods I can spare from my professional duties.

I have spent a great deal of time verifying the facts herein recited and as to those facts of which I have personal knowledge I swear that they are true and as to those which come to me upon information of others and from records, I swear, as to them, that upon the information obtained I believe them to be true.[48]

The two corroborating affidavits came from two elderly residents at McDowell, To-mol-gah and Su-ke-yal-vah.[49] To-mol-gah, about ninety years old, said she knew Montezuma's father and mother, and that Montezuma was a Pinal Apache (now known as Mohave Apache). Su-ke-yal-vah was Suzie Dickens, an aunt of Montezuma (his mother's sister) and had known him as a boy.

Meritt then directed the San Carlos Superintendent, A. H. Symonds, to investigate the application. The attitude of the superintendents can be appreciated by a statement in a letter from Byron A. Sharp, Superintendent of the Salt River Reservation, to Symonds: "I wish you success in your dealings with this man and am sorry he has chosen to inflict himself upon your jurisdiction."[50]

Symonds suggested that a previous ruling by the Secretary of the Interior Lane applied here: that an individual who lived away from the tribe, gained citizenship, and was independent was not entitled to tribal benefits. Symonds also recounted an episode where Montezuma and a band of thirty Yavapai "invaded" his office and complained about the Bureau. Symonds' report requested that "his application be disregarded," concluding that "…He takes occasion to tell the Government employees, in the presence of all the Indians that he can get together, in a loud, important tone of voice that the white man is simply on the Reservation for what he can get and is not interested in the Indians. …I would therefore brand Dr. Montezuma as a trouble maker of the worst sort."[51]

The Salt River Agency Superintendent, Byron Sharp, was ordered to interview Montezuma's stepmother at McDowell. This he did, and Yu-co-dep-pah swore that she was Montezuma's stepmother and that he was born near where Roosevelt Dam had been constructed. In the meantime, Ernest Stecker replaced Symonds at San Carlos. The San Carlos Tribal Business Committee had been instructed to discuss the matter with their constituents, and in October 1921, the committee voted unanimously to enroll Montezuma at San Carlos. Steckler concluded that Montezuma was by right of birth entitled to enrollment and he requested approval.[52]

Faced with two reports with different conclusions, Commissioner Burke then requested a third superintendent, Charles L. Davis, Superintendent of Fort Apache, the agency bordering San Carlos, to investigate the enrollment request. Davis reviewed the record, interviewed Stecker, and recommended that Montezuma be interrogated under oath, significantly not just to establish his life history, but to present his attitude toward the government.[53] This was never done.

Davis conducted a hearing on March 7, 1922, at San Carlos, interviewing many individuals, who were generally supportive, highlighting the distinction between Mohave Apache and Apache. Three days later, Davis interviewed Yavapai at Fort McDowell, including Little Jack, Sam Axe, Su-ke-yal-vah, and Yu-co-dep-pah. Davis summarized his investigation in a letter on March 20, 1922, to the commissioner.[54] He emphasized that Montezuma was not an Apache, but correctly pointed out that Montezuma did not try to deceive anyone but had himself been confused as well as many others. His final report on April 25, 1922, eight pages of single-spaced typing, highlighted the following questions:[55]

- The confusion regarding his age: four or six when captured?
- Did he intend to live on San Carlos?
- He was already assimilated, why enroll in the tribe?
- Did he still believe in his speech of 1915 to the Society of American Indians?
- Would he become a Yavapai? And if so, why did he want this?

Keep in mind that Davis's conclusions were in the framework of an attitude that viewed tribal membership as entitlement to ward status with the government. An independent assimilated life such as Montezuma's was believed to be incompatible with tribal life; only Indians who needed assistance should be enrolled—thus Davis had difficulty understanding why Montezuma wanted enrollment.

Davis further believed that much of the testimony obtained at San Carlos and McDowell was derived from information planted by Montezuma. Specifically he doubted that Su-ke-yal-vah (Suzie Dickens) was Montezuma's mother's sister. He even thought that Montezuma might have been ten or twelve years old at the time of his capture. Davis concluded that Gentile had been a "showman," and that Montezuma, a product of that experience, was prone to exaggeration. And finally, Davis, as all Indian Bureau officials, personally distrusted and disliked Montezuma and wanted to thwart him.

Undoubtedly, the reluctance in Washington reflected, at least partly, Montezuma's reputation as a troublemaker. Ultimately, two years after Montezuma's request, Commissioner Burke recommended on June 17, 1922, to the secretary of the interior that Montezuma's application be denied.[56]

> ...This case was carefully investigated in the field, and the reports of the Superintendents of the Salt River, San Carlos, and Fort Apache Agencies are transmitted.
>
> The evidence, which is somewhat conflicting and not as satisfactory as could be desired, seems to establish that the applicant is a full-blood Indian of the Mohave-Apache band; that he was born in Arizona in the early sixties, and was, when a child, captured or abducted (about 1871) from his parents by Pima Indians who sold him in 1872 to a white man; that he was never thereafter identified or affiliated with his people, but has been reared and educated among the whites—his status since attaining his majority having been that of a citizen of the United States and of the State in which he resides, with full rights as such.
>
> The further facts are that the so-called Mohave-Apache band, to which applicant claims to belong, is not an Apache band, but belongs to the Yuman family; that this Mohave band was affiliated with the neighboring Apache bands during the period from the close of the Civil War up to about 1874 when most of these bands were captured by United States military forces and taken to the San Carlos Reservation as prisoners of war; that some twenty or thirty years later they were released—some locating at Fort McDowell, Camp Verde, and other parts of the State.
>
> The evidence also establishes that at a meeting held October 28, 1921, on the San Carlos Reservation, the members of the tribal business committee voted for the enrollment of the applicant, though there were three dissenting votes at the meeting held at Rice District for the selection of representatives to the tribal business committee.
>
> Attention is invited to the report dated April 15, 1922, by Superintendent Davis, Fort Apache Agency, who says that the San Carlos Reservation was set aside by Executive Order of November 8, 1871—about the time of applicant's capture; that applicant's parents were later taken there as prisoners of war but his mother remained only a short time and his father left the reservation as soon as released; that the fort or Camp McDowell Reservation was set aside for Indian purposes by Executive Order of September 15, 1903; that this later reservation was more a part of the Pima country at the time of Montezuma's capture than of the Mohave-Apache country; and that the place of birth of applicant was not within or now near to any of the reservations today.
>
> After a most careful consideration of the matter, I am of the opinion that the facts in the case are not such as to warrant the enrollment by blood or adoption of Dr. Carlos Montezuma at the San Carlos Reservation. It is accordingly recommended that his application be denied.[57]

Montezuma revealed in a letter to his lawyer, Joseph Latimer, the depth of his anger and confusion:

My dear Joe,

Well, what do you think of that? The enclosed letters will surprise you as they have me. I was denied, by the Indian office with the approval of the Assistant Secretary of the Interior, of my application for enrollment with the San Carlos Agency.

The letters show up the Light of what we have claimed the Indian Bureau to be. It will go to the extreme to discredit an Indian. It reveals plainly that the Indian office is ignorant of the Apache Indians, even though they try to know something about them. They confess the evidence in my case is conflicting. Why have they not given me a chance to enlighten them? It here tells plainly that they did not approach Indians that knew me in my childhood. Superstitiously the Apache Indians are reluctant to mention the dead, for that reason I imagine the Superintendents who were employed to investigate my case, did not get much out of the old Indians.

At the time of my capture by the Pima Indians (1871), there was no such tribe as the Mohave Apaches. This name was given to certain Apaches since then. Mohave tribe of Indians had their homes on the Colorado River, on the line of California and Arizona, several hundred miles west. My band of Apache Indians were foreigners and foes to those Mohave Indians on the Colorado River.

An old Indian woman gave me the information that I was born up along Fish Creek, somewhere between what is now know as "Fish Creek Station" on the Roosevelt Road, and Weaver's Ranch six miles North of Iron Peak, the place of my capture, in the Superstition Range of Mountains. This was given me at McDowell, Arizona, two years ago.

At Florence, Arizona, where I was Christened, there is a written record in the Catholic Church that I was about four or five years old November 1871. That Christening occurred after I was sold to Mr. C. Gentile. The Indian Office says I was sold in 1872. Is it a wonder that I did not affiliate with my people any sooner? I was forced away and brought East. It was a case where I could not help myself.

...In 1901 for the first time since my capture, I returned to San Carlos and visited Iron Peak. Ever since then I have been affiliated with San Carlos in one way or another. My affiliation with San Carlos Indians may help my request, but there is a stronger tie that binds me to San Carlos, and that is, I belong there.

Another thing seems to trouble the Indian office—that I am a citizen. The Indian Bureau does not like to see the Indians as citizens; they want them to be wards forever. As an Apache Indian, I am proud of my American citizenship, but what has that got to do with my rights as approved by the Indians of San Carlos.

...If I am not an Apache, there is no such Indians as Apache Indians. If the Indian department were better informed they would find out that my parents were the first Indians that were received on San Carlos in 1871. My father and mother, on the advice of soldiers at San Pedro, went to San Carlos on their own accord.

...The Indians on San Carlos are not against me, but it is the infernal Indian Bureau supported by the Invisible interests as shown by the Indian meeting of October 28, 1921.

...The story of my Mother and Father was given to me by my father's second wife (The Apache Indians in their primitive state were polygamists), who accompanied my father to San Pedro and later went to San Carlos with him and my mother. She is living today. Her name is U-ma-dapa. She said that they (three) lived on San Carlos.

...What the Department says of my father and my mother shows that they do not know anything about them. What they have said of my father and mother is only made-up, or a dream.

...You can see that they are trying to bring me in with the McDowell Indians. The truth is that most of the McDowell Indians were enrolled on San Carlos reservation before they went to McDowell. From the Bureau's viewpoint, I am under-rated and do not deserve my request, because of my citizenship, and for actively striving to aid my people nearly half a century. I must confess this beats all. ...Is it true—and I hope not—that citizenship debars Indian enrollment. Does absence debar enrollment? Does a birth away from or near reservation debar enrollment? Does the approval of the Indians of my enrollment with them debar me from enrollment? ...The record of my life from the time of my capture, 1871, has been an open letter to the world. There is no Indian living that has had a wider affiliation with the Indian people than I have, even on San Carlos I am known from the date of its existence.

One must take into consideration that I am speaking of what took place fifty one years ago. Any old Apache Indian who lived in the Superstition Range on the site of San Carlos Agency, and around Four Peak Mountains, will tell you that the Band my Father and Mother belonged to from time immemorial, roamed and lived on the grounds of San Carlos Reservation. That land was the home of my Father and Mother before the whites came.

...Joe, I stake my request on the strength of my pedigree, that my father and mother were San Carlos Indians, (1871), and not on the name of Mohave Apache Tribe. The scientific classification of the Apaches was unknown in 1871.

I have given you these facts as a fighting basis. The question is, how shall we proceed? I leave that with you. I will hunt up data and send to you.[58]

Richard Pratt advised Montezuma: "...I have this view, Doctor, and give it to you frankly as an old friend. You would be stronger if you omitted any involving claim or desire to promote a claim as a member of any Apache group. That course, to my mind, would give you more strength than you have when you put in a claim to the Bureau, which on the face of it shows a desire to become an inheritor among the Indians of whatever property, etc., they may have."[59]

I hardly know what to say. Of course, I know you speak for the best relative to my request to be enrolled with the San Carlos Indians.

Once I thought of applying at McDowell, but after thinking over the matter I was more entitled at San Carlos, because my father and mother lived there and died there.

...I fully realize the stand you take, that it appears as though it was for mercenary object, and that my standard of working for the Indian race may be weakened in seeking to be enrolled at any reservation.

It appears that is the real basis for the department's denial of my request, that I am seeking to better myself.

So far as I know I am entitled to a patch of land. Having that in mind, I concluded it was time for me to accept it, and San Carlos was the place, because of my father and mother. Had I gone elsewhere for my enrollment, the department would have more excuse to exclude me.[60]

In retrospect, Montezuma might have been more successful applying at McDowell, but he applied at San Carlos simply because his parents had lived and died there. However, it is unlikely anything would have overcome the Bureau's resistance to him as an individual antagonist. Furthermore, there is something good in the Indian Bureau's denial of Montezuma's enrollment at San Carlos. It is fitting that he returned to Fort McDowell to die, to be buried in the tribal ground preserved by his efforts.

MONTEZUMA MADE ONE LAST ATTEMPT, just six months before he died, to unravel his confusion over whether he was an Apache. He asked the Bureau of American Ethnology of the Smithsonian Institution, "In what year were the Apaches of Arizona classified? Why were the Mohave Apaches called so, when they were enemies of the Mohave Indians who lived on the Colorado River? ...Before criticizing the classification of the Apaches, I want to know why the original Apaches were called Mohave Apaches. They may be called Pinal Apaches, because they roamed next to the Pinal country, but to be given Mohave Apache as a name is absurd, when the Apaches had no use for the Mohave."[61]

The Smithsonian advised him: "...[we do not] classify the Mohave Apaches with the Apaches, but with the Mohaves, since they talked a language closely related to Mohave although they at times were at war with the latter tribe. The Mohave Apaches are as often called Apache Mohaves, and they call themselves 'Inyavape,' of which the English name Yavapai is a corruption. This name evidently means 'eastern people.' When or how the term Mohave Apache or vice versa was started is not clear. ...It is a poor and misleading nomenclature and should be discouraged in favor of the name Yavapai. I take it that the term Mohave Apache was given originally because the tribe lived east of the river and was erroneously thought to be Apaches, yet spoke a divergent dialect of Mohave."[62]

IN THE LAST twenty-three years of his life, Montezuma rediscovered the Yavapai. He deliberately and successfully traced his personal history through witnesses, relatives, and visits to the scenes of each important event. It is striking that Montezuma repeated this process over and over again, and he brought friends to participate with him in these Arizona pilgrimages. It proved difficult for Montezuma to disengage himself from his lifelong image as an Apache. The Apache image and name were familiar to the American public, and this served Montezuma well in his political efforts. But finally, in the last months of his life, Montezuma did acknowledge that he was a Yavapai.

## CHAPTER TWELVE

# Land and Water Rights:
# Dear Cousin, We Need Your Help

L AND AND WATER RIGHTS for the Fort McDowell Yavapai became a principal issue that consumed a significant portion of Montezuma's time and energy during the last twelve years of his life. The fundamental questions were: what priority do Indians have over water on their land; what volume of water are Indians entitled to; what uses of water are involved; and most of all, does a tribe's right to its land take precedence over flood control and water availability for others, even if it affects many thousands of people?

In 1908, the U.S. Supreme Court ruled that Indian land reserved by treaty included the reservation of water necessary for the irrigation of the land for both present and future needs (*Winters v. United States*).[1] The litigation arose in a dispute with the Assiniboine and the Gros Ventre over water in the Milk River that served the Fort Belknap Reservation in Montana. Specifically, the court ruled that a dam could not be built that would prevent water from reaching an Indian reservation. Furthermore, tribal rights take precedence over state rights when the existence of the reservation preceded the establishment of the state. The Supreme Court reasoned that when the Federal Government established a reservation, it fully intended the reservation to be livable and productive, and this would include enough water to irrigate arid land. Ironically, the Supreme Court ruling that upheld Indians' water rights was significantly due to the allotment policy of the times. Pressure for the decision came from White ranchers and businessmen who were leasing or who had purchased reservation land.[2]

The principle of sufficient water has been consistently upheld since the *Winters* ruling. Indian water rights governed by federal law differ with the water rights governed by law in western states.[3] State laws follow the principle of "prior appropriation," which simply means that water belongs to the first person who diverts it for use. Most importantly, Indian water rights are reserved (a tribe cannot lose its water rights through nonuse) and the amount of water is not only determined by the tribe's initial use, but in fact a tribe is forever entitled to as much water as it needs to provide for the reservation (this can be challenged only if a landowner had appropriated the water prior to the establishment of the reservation). In some instances, Indian rights to a particular source of water have been recognized to predate the reservation (usually in a treaty). The specific uses for the water are not specified; they need only to satisfy the needs of the reservation.[4] Therefore, the water can be used to support game and fish, to irrigate lands, to support home and recreational use, and even for industrial purposes. A tribe can legally sell its excess water. This can be a difficult problem because it is not easy to determine how much water a tribe is entitled to obtain, nevertheless, state and city governments in Arizona currently purchase a significant portion of their water supply from Indian tribes. In reality, therefore, most tribes have open-ended water rights.

Litigation in state courts over water rights was made possible in 1952 when Congress passed the McCarran Amendment.[5] Although the Amendment did not change the *Winters* doctrine, state courts unfortunately have had a history of ignoring the principles of federal water rights, and Indian water rights are part of the trust responsibility that is the obligation of the Federal Government. Of course these principles have taken years since the *Winters* ruling to reaffirm and establish. It was not so clear for the Fort McDowell Yavapai struggling in the first two decades of the 1900s.

## THE FORT McDOWELL RESERVATION IS ESTABLISHED

The Fort McDowell Reservation is twenty-three miles northeast of Phoenix. The Verde River flows through the reservation from north to south, and the reservation is in a fairly level valley at an elevation of 1,200 to 1,500 feet, surrounded on all sides by mountains. From 1910 to 1922, the Federal Government repeatedly attempted to move the Yavapai Indians from their reservation and to use the Verde River water to irrigate non-Indian lands.

### Southeastern (Kwovokopaya) Yavapai History

| Hunter-Gatherers and Some Farming | Conflict and Confinement | San Carlos Reservation | Fort McDowell | Fort McDowell Yavapai Nation |
| --- | --- | --- | --- | --- |
| 1860 | 1875 | 1900 | 1999 | |

Non-Indians seeking Arizona Indian land and water in the 1870s had been pressuring the government to consolidate the Indians. John P. Clum, the twenty-three-year-old new agent on the San Carlos Reservation, brought order to the reservation by establishing a force of Indian policemen and an Indian court, making this reservation a safe location for a large concentration of Indians.[6] Clum was one of the agents nominated by religious denominations, in this case the Dutch Reform Church. Frustrated by bureaucratic obstacles, he left the service in 1877. He founded the famous newspaper, *The Epitaph*, in Tombstone, Arizona, and became the mayor and postmaster.

About 3,000 Indians of several tribes, but mainly Apache, were placed on the San Carlos Reservation in the 1870s. This included the band that made the Yavapai Trail of Tears in 1875 (Chapter 1). The Indians were prohibited from hunting or gathering food in the surrounding mountains, and a daily roll was taken in conjunction with the provision of rations. The rationing system and the control it provided were maintained for over thirty years, until farming was re-established.

A military post was constructed by companies of California Volunteers on the Verde River in 1865 and named after General Irwin McDowell. Initially called Camp McDowell, the name was changed to Fort McDowell in 1879.[7] The garrison at first housed nearly 500 men, later 100 to 200. The Volunteers had entered the Arizona Territory to keep the Confederates out, and then under orders of their commander in California, General

McDowell, they remained to protect settlers (the Arizona Territory was assigned to the California military).[8]

McDowell was born in Ohio, but raised and educated in France before returning to the United States to graduate from West Point Academy. He served in the Mexican War and eventually became commander of the Union Forces at the First Battle of Bull Run where he committed his troops before they were ready.[9] After the defeat, McDowell commanded a division, and then a corps in the Army of the Potomac. He finished his career as commanding officer of the Department of the Pacific with headquarters at the Presidio in San Francisco. McDowell was buried in the San Francisco National Cemetery after his death in 1885.

The first troops at Fort McDowell consisted of three companies of California Volunteers, joined by a company of 100 Pima Indians (led by their chief and now Sergeant Antonio Azul, who was to lead the Pima raid that captured Montezuma in 1871) and a company of 100 Maricopa Indians. Regular army soldiers replaced the California Volunteers in 1866, but Pima and Maricopa Indians continued to be used as scouts.[10] These army troops were a rough crowd; drunken behavior, courts-martial, and cashiering were common events. They regarded the Indians in the countryside as "hostiles," and they shot to kill any Indian, male or female, that ran from them.[11] Their life was difficult. Accommodations were Spartan. They lived in insect-infested adobe structures with sod roofs solidified with horse manure that made it impossible to sleep inside when it rained. Food was scarce, and scurvy was always a problem. Even shoes were insufficient in number, and the troops were often barefoot. The duty was hard work, with troops frequently traveling over 2,000 miles in a month's time. Deserters usually occupied the guardhouse. In the first seven years of the post's existence, there were constant patrols, fighting, and killing.

After twenty-five years, the U.S. Army abandoned Fort McDowell in 1890, leaving behind eighty-six graves in the post cemetery.[12] Two years later, the remains were disinterred, boxed, and shipped to the Presidio in San Francisco for reburial. The only grave that remained was that of George Kippen, a civilian who was the very first to be buried there.[13] The Fort McDowell Yavapai Nation cemetery is at the same site, and Kippen's marker can be viewed today, near and to the north of Montezuma's grave.

After Fort McDowell closed, about 25,000 acres were placed under the jurisdiction of the Department of the Interior on February 14, 1891. The military post included a farm of 240 acres with a four-mile long irrigation ditch, initially established by the soldiers and later leased to private farmers.[14] Nine years later, in 1900, a large number of Yavapai simply walked away from the San Carlos Reservation, to return to the Verde River Valley. The San Carlos agent was very willing to allow this exodus because the area in which the Yavapai were living was being mined for coal; their leaving would relinquish their claim to the coalfields.[15] Many Yavapai (about 200) settled in the area around the old fort; however, Mexican and White settlers already occupied the most favorable land along the Verde River (and also maintained a saloon and gambling house). The Yavapai were forced higher up on rocky slopes.

The Bureau of Indian Affairs learned that these Yavapai were desperately in need of shelter and food.[16] An Indian office inspector reported that the Yavapai were industrious and recommended that land at Fort McDowell be provided for them. In November 1901, the Interior Department designated the Fort McDowell land for Indians. However, continuing opposition by the White and Mexican settlers on the land prevented passage of the required bill. Early in 1903, a group of fifty-seven Yavapai under the leadership of Yuma Frank peti-tioned President Theodore Roosevelt for the Fort McDowell land (it is not known who provided the expertise for the well-worded document).

> We, the Mohave-Apache Indians, living on the old Fort McDowell abandoned military reservation, reach out our hands to you for help. We are now in a starving condition but for three years we have been living in miserable brush tepees on the barren hills obliged to shift for a poverty stricken existence while white and Mexican trespassers upon reserved public lands have occupied and enjoyed all the harvest from the only fruitful lands on the reservation. We left our reservation on the Gila River under passes from the Indian Agent because we had no water with which to irrigate the arid lands and we came to the Verde River, the home of our forefathers from which our people were forcibly removed many years ago, with the solemn promise from General Crook and other officers that if we served them as scouts and soldiers and were true to our trust we should sometime return and this land we love so well should be ours. How well we have kept our compact is well known and is a matter of record in the War Department.
>
> We receive no rations from the Government, neither do we desire aid further than that we be given lands to which we are justly entitled. Our people are strong and are willing and anxious to win their own bread.
>
> We beg that we may call your attention to the fact that both the Secretary of the Interior and the Commissioner of Indian Affairs have recommended that the north half of the McDowell Reservation be allotted to us and we understand that pursuant to this recommendation that lands were withdrawn from settlement for Indian purposes and a bill was introduced allotting these lands to the members of our tribe. We had heard of various rumors to the effect that compacts have been made between the alleged settlers on these lands and those who hope to be with the Territorial Delegate to congress to defeat our claim, and we have been made to understand by these Mexican and White trespassers that they had received assurance from the Delegate that our claims would be ignored and we be sent with our poverty back to the Reservation at San Carlos where our condition can only be infinitely worse than it is now.
>
> It is unjust to the alleged settlers and to us and the country generally that this matter should be delayed. In view of these facts we most earnestly urge that we no longer be left to eke out a miserable existence on the arid hills but that action be taken at once and the bill passed or defeated. We desire nothing more than that we may be enabled to become self-supporting, self-respecting and independent American Citizens.[17]

Yuma Frank (Kuh-pah-la-va, Tearing), Tom Surama, George Dickens (Mack-la-va, Many Feet), and Charles Dickens (Sum-nu-ge-kaw, Crooked) traveled to Washington to present the petition.[18] The expenses were paid by selling wood and baskets, and the trip was made clandestinely because the Indian Bureau officials had refused to give permission for the men to leave the area.

President Theodore Roosevelt sent Frank Mead, supervisor of Indian reservations, to Fort McDowell in the summer of 1903 to assess the situation, a move prompted by grow-ing hostility between the settlers and the Indians.[19] He reported on September 4, 1903, that there were about 184 Yavapai at Fort McDowell and 216 at Camp Verde. Mead's report was very supportive, indicating that the Yavapai were requesting land and a little help to be farm-ers. Mead estimated that about 2,000 acres of land at Fort McDowell were irrigable, and about two-thirds of this land was already being served by irrigation ditches. Thus Mead believed Fort McDowell was a good investment and recommended on September 12, 1903, an allocation of $25,000 to buy out settlers on the land, and another $3,000 to build more irrigation ditches. The recommendation was accompanied by an executive order drafted by the commissioner of Indian affairs:

> It is hereby ordered that so much of the land of the Camp McDowell Abandoned Military Reservation as may not have been legally settled upon nor have valid claims attaching thereto under the provisions of the act of Congress approved August 23, 1894 (28 Stat. L., 492), be, and the same is hereby, set aside and reserved for the use and occupancy of such Mohave-Apache Indians as are now living thereon or in the vicinity and such other Indians as the Secretary of the Interior may hereafter deem necessary to place thereon.
>
> The lands so withdrawn and reserved will include all tracts to which valid rights have not attached under the provisions of the said act of Congress, and in addition thereto all those tracts upon the reservation containing Government improvements, which were reserved from settlement by the said act of Congress, and which consist of (1) the immediate site of the old camp, containing buildings and a good artesian well; (2) the post garden; (3) the United States Government farm; (4) the lands lying north of the old camp and embracing or containing the old Government irrigation ditch, and (5) the target-practice grounds.[20]

Only three days later on September 15, 1903, Roosevelt signed the executive order establishing the reservation. Reverend W. H. Gill, a local missionary, was named agent and resident farmer on September 30, 1903.

The Fort McDowell Reservation totals 24,680 acres, measuring four miles wide east to west and ten miles long in the north-south direction, appearing on a map as a vertical parallelogram with an elevated upper right corner. Even though the forty settlers were squatters and had no valid titles to the land, the settlers were reimbursed for their lands in 1904 (the total cost came to $61,523).[21] By 1905, the Yavapai were the sole occupants of a land that included four irrigation ditches and about 1,300 acres of agricultural fields. From 1900 until the 1970s, the Yavapai population at Fort McDowell was a relatively constant, 250 to 300 Indians. Today, there are about 1,000 Indians in the Fort McDowell Yavapai Nation and about 600 live on the reservation.

Gill, the newly appointed Fort McDowell agent, promptly wrote to Montezuma in 1903 reporting that the ten miles by four miles wide valley was now an Indian reservation. This was a noteworthy achievement, taking place at a time when Indian lands were being lost in the allotment process. And it was good land.

> Mojave-Apache Indian Reservation
> Fort McDowell Arizona
> Oct 26, 1903
>
> Dear Doctor
> Notice the above caption. It is an assured fact. By a proclamation of the President signed Sept 15th 1903, this beautiful valley 10 miles long by 4 miles wide has been turned into an Indian reservation. Of course the settlers on the south half have valid claims but nearly all these are manifesting a desire to sell out to the government so that the prospect now is that nearly the entire reservation will soon be occupied by Indians. There is great

# Fort McDowell Reservation

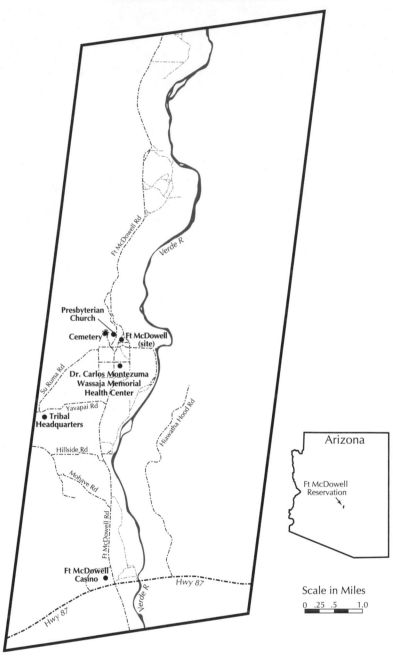

Presbyterian
Church

Cemetery

Ft McDowell
(site)

Ft McDowell Rd

Verde R

Su Ruma Rd

**Dr. Carlos Montezuma
Wassaja Memorial
Health Center**

Yavapai Rd

● **Tribal
Headquarters**

Hillside Rd

Hiawatha Hood Rd

Mohave Rd

Ft McDowell Rd

**Ft McDowell
Casino** ●

Hwy 87

Verde R

Hwy 87

Arizona

Ft McDowell
Reservation

Scale in Miles

0  .25  .5      1.0

joy here in the Indian camps. The settlers have all submitted quietly to the government's decree and all is peaceful. The Indians have gone to work with a will but they do not actually enter upon their lands until Dec 1st as that is the date on which the whites and Mexicans must have removed their property from the reserved lands.

Just here is a point which I wish to press upon your attention. I remember you told me when you left that when I got ready to build a church to let you know and you would help me and get others to help so far as you could. Of course I would like comfortably a place of worship but there is another case even more urgent just now and one which if delayed can never again be taken advantage of. It is this. In the break up here of the settlers, there will be much property disposed of at a very low figure. It consists of horses, furniture, cows, hogs, goats, chickens, corn, wheat, etc. etc. Think for instance of 51 hogs, shoats and pigs for $100. Bees, heavy with honey for $1.00 per colony. Wagons at $15 to $20 etc. Why doctor it is the chance of a lifetime. Cash is urgently needed at once, not a month, three months, or even two months from now, but in less than 30 days.

Or this grand opportunity will have passed away forever. All these things our people must have to get a start in the new life. Think of the loss that will result from delay at this crisis in affairs. …

Now is the time doctor to put in your best blows for your people. …Oh, help our fallen brothers rise! *Help, Help, Help, and now.* Think of our dear people, often hungry and cold, shivering in their wretched brush hovels in the barren hills. Shall we not bring comfort and cheer to these unfortunate and downtrodden people now that it is in our power to do so?

Yours truly
W. H. Gill[22]

There is no record in the Montezuma collections to indicate whether Montezuma responded to Gill's appeal. Gill was doing a good job; he was respected, liked, and effective in guiding the farming activity of the reservation. In 1906, the Indians built the still-standing Presbyterian Church under Gill's direction. Unfortunately, Gill's time at Fort McDowell lasted only four years. Gill decided to remove gambling from the reservation, and in 1907, called a community meeting for this purpose. Austin Navaho left the meeting and returned later with a rifle to confront Gill at his house.[23] Gill, however, had a shotgun, and when both fired at close range, Navaho missed and died immediately. Gill left his fate up to the Indian community, and he was asked to leave.

## FORT McDOWELL vs. THE FEDERAL GOVERNMENT

Agriculture in the desert required the availability and control of water. The Salt River Valley Water Users Association was formed for this purpose in 1903. The association and the Federal Government, under the provisions of the 1902 National Reclamation Act, agreed to build the Roosevelt Dam on the Salt River (constructed from 1905 to 1911), and the Granite Reef Diversion Dam (completed in 1908) below the confluence of the Salt and Verde Rivers. Roosevelt Dam (Theodore Roosevelt Lake) was the nation's first project initiated under the National Reclamation Act. The Salt River was harnessed with even more dams in the 1920s, the Horse Mesa Dam (Apache Lake), the Mormon Flat Dam (Canyon Lake), and the Stewart Mountain Dam (Saguaro Lake). The Salt River is now just a series of reservoirs connected by short stretches of a flowing river. The Salt River water disappears into irrigation canals, and the Salt River that flows through Phoenix is nothing more than a dry riverbed. The Salt River

Project (the SRP, which began as the Salt River Valley Water Users Association in 1903) was established in 1937 as a political subdivision within the State of Arizona, and today it is the nation's third largest public power utility and one of Arizona's largest water suppliers.

In the years following the *Winters* ruling, it became apparent that the Indian irrigation projects, mostly planned and built by the Federal Government, were designed for the benefit of the surrounding White population.[24] It was not until 1928, that the secretary of the interior received a commissioned report from Porter J. Preston, an engineer from the Bureau of Reclamation, and Charles A. Engle, an irrigation expert in the Indian Bureau, that criticized the government's program of irrigation on Indian reservations (Indian money had been used to build irrigation projects not used or wanted by Indians).[25] Even at the site of the *Winters* ruling, the Fort Belknap Reservation in Montana, Bureau of Reclamation projects enlarged the irrigation system and funneled most of the water to off-reservation ranches.[26]

Patrick T. Hurley, a rancher and founder of the Salt River Valley Water Users Association, brought suit in 1905 in the District Court of the Third Judicial District of the Arizona Territory seeking the right for members of the association to use Salt River water for irrigation.[27] The Federal Government intervened in the case seeking to adjudicate the water rights of both Whites and the Indians. The litigation did not end until 1910 when the Kent Decree (issued by Judge Edward Kent) established the water priorities for the Salt River Valley. As part of this decree, the Federal Government recognized the right of the Fort McDowell Indians to Verde River water, granting sufficient water to irrigate 3,000 acres of land.[28] However, the decree also stated the government's intention to remove the Indians from the Fort McDowell Reservation (this would obviously make Verde River water available to non-Indian farmers and ranchers).

For twelve years after the Kent Decree, the Federal Government tried to move the Fort McDowell Yavapai Indians. The plan was to move the Yavapai to the Salt River Reservation, the home of the Pima and Maricopa Indians, who for years had lived along the Salt and Gila Rivers. According to the Kent Decree, five-acre allotments were to be granted on an individual basis along with water rights. Of course, Yavapai *tribal* ownership of land and water would cease. The Kent Decree ignored the precedent established by the U. S. Supreme Court in *Winters v. United States* in 1908.

In 1910, The Bureau of Indian Affairs stated that the move, with its allotment, would ensure perpetual water rights for the Yavapai individuals. However, there was a technical problem. The Fort McDowell water rights carried Class A priority; the Salt River water rights would be Class C priority. Under the Kent Decree, there were three categories of water rights:

Class A: Reasonable, continuous, and beneficial use of water over a long period of time.
Class B: Periodic use of land after those with Class A rights had their share.
Class C: Uncultivated land upon which no irrigation had been in place.

Thus the allotted land on the Salt River Reservation would have water for the Yavapai only if there was any unused water left.

The Yavapai, therefore, had two problems: First, the change from Class A to Class C priority meant in essence a loss of their water rights, and second, they did not want to be forced to live among their old enemies, the Pima Indians.

## Arizona Reservations

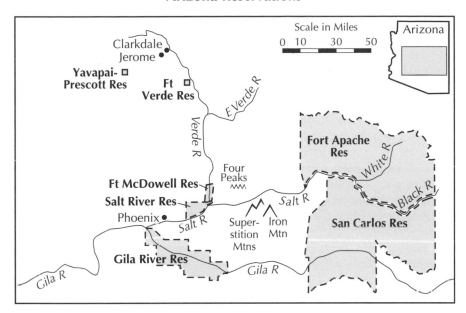

THE ANNUAL FLOODING of the Verde River was a major and recurring challenge for the Fort McDowell Indians, destroying their hand-made diversion dams for irrigation. The conflict over water and land from 1900 to 1920 prevented the use of federal resources to maintain the reservation's irrigation system. The flood of 1911 caused considerable damage. The Bureau of Indian Affairs refused to repair the Fort McDowell irrigation system and used this as an excuse to push the move to the Salt River Reservation.[29] The Yavapai argued for a dam to protect against floods.[30] The government response was that Fort McDowell could farm only 3,000 acres, and that at least 5,000 acres were necessary to justify a dam. Thus the move made more sense. The Fort McDowell Yavapai, therefore, were being forced to confront two threats: a move to the Salt River Reservation and a loss of their water rights or unusable water in the Verde River because the government was refusing to maintain the water control system.

Charles Dickens, Montezuma's thirty-four-year-old cousin, wrote on March 29, 1910: "I have been thinking about writing to you concerning to which I have spoken to you during we met together at Kelvin, Ariz. Lately I learned that our agent have heard from Washington that we are to be move to the Pima Indian Reservation. You will remember that my band oppose to this according to several circumstances. During six years hard struggle, we just beginning to realize in the field of self-supporting race. We oppose to this because we feel we are not capable to take up with unprepared land for farming. The situation of the place is completely desert land; never been farm; even not a wire on it. Dear cousin, we need your help and wish you to see justice is done with us as I have talked with you before. Although we have not talk with agent (Mr. Coe) but I am going to just as soon as I can. I like you to write to the Government and find out about it. I want to hear from you. This is all I want to say."[31]

In 1910, the Fort McDowell Yavapai formally enlisted the aid of Carlos Montezuma, naming him their official representative. Joining Montezuma in this cause was his Chicago attorney, Joseph W. Latimer. Montezuma was granted the power-of-attorney to act with the authority of the tribe, and it is well-recognized that his intervention at this point in time was pivotal in preventing the removal of the Fort McDowell Yavapai Indians.[32] It is not hard to see how Montezuma proved useful for the Yavapai. He was an intelligent, articulate man who could be forceful and powerful in both his speech and with the pen, whereas no other Yavapai had his education and experience. The Bureau expected reservation people to have essentially absolute cooperation and total obedience to Indian superintendents and agents. Montezuma made sure that the Yavapai signed nothing without his approval. Montezuma believed that if the Yavapai accepted allotted land on the Salt River Reservation, the Fort McDowell land that was to be reserved for Yavapai use would be forfeited. Of course, government officials soon came to view Montezuma as a major obstacle and troublemaker. Indeed, he was a threatening figure, being more articulate and educated than most of the Indian Bureau employees.

> We begged hard for this land for homes and the Government purchased it for us. We have been living here six years and think we are making improvements in our condition. We do not like to give up our homes and go to the Salt River reservation. We have some cattle and horses and would have no grazing for them at that place. We make a success of raising poultry. We have a good church here and all our children go to Sunday School and we are trying to have them grow up right. We appreciate the assistance the government has given us in our irrigating ditches but will undertake to keep them up in the future without any help. We have already told Mr. Inspector Norris, who visited our reservation a short time ago, these things. We therefore very respectfully petition you to be allowed to remain here in our old homes at Camp McDowell. We hereby appoint Carlos Montezuma as our representative in these matters.[33]

Charles E. Coe, the superintendent of the Fort McDowell Indian Agency, wrote directly to Montezuma in May 1910 regarding the above petition:

> Chief Yuma Frank and some of the other Indians of this reservation have formulated a petition to the Indian Office, protesting against being removed to lands under the Salt River irrigation system, a copy of which I have mailed to you under separate cover.
>
> In working out this plan the department is trying to provide for the future of the McDowell Indians. At the present time they are not farming more than one-third of the lands that were under cultivation when they were given this place. This is on account of the heads of two ditches being washed out beyond repair and it is only a question of time until they will be unable to get any water in the two ditches they are now using. All the inspecting officials who have visited here since the Verde began cutting away the land have recommended the change to Salt River. Chief Engineer Code has gone over the ground very carefully and reports that when the present ditch goes it will take over $10,000 to get any water.

As you know, the Salt River Valley has made wonderful progress in the past few years. Unimproved desert land can not be bought for less than $150 per acre while orange lands closer in are selling as high as $500 per acre. The lands being offered to these Indians are good bottom lands, where they are assured an abundance of water from the Reclamation Service—this without any cost whatever to the Indians. There seems to be a misapprehension in the minds of these people as to the disposition of the Camp McDowell Reservation if they should accept the Salt River lands, and your letters to Charles and George Dickens lead me to believe you have the same erroneous idea. I have just received a letter from the department, dated April 30, saying that they will be allowed to keep the Camp McDowell Reservation for pasturage, etc.

Some of the Indians are already in favor of the plan and all of them say they would be willing to go when they can not farm here any longer, but of course the proposition can not be held out to them indefinitely. I believe a few words from one of their own people— a business man, such as yourself—will influence all of them to take advantage of such an excellent opportunity at once. Delay is dangerous to their interests and may lose to them the opportunity entirely.[34]

It was Richard Pratt who suggested a course for Montezuma. "This morning I took up the matter of your interest in the McDowell Indians. After some search I lit [sic] a full exposé of the case in Leupp's report of 1905, pages 98 to 103, which is so clear and full and makes their tenure so strong I can see no reason for uneasiness. It is clear to me in Leupp's exposé that they can only be disturbed by act of Congress for the land was in past purchased for them by special appropriation of Congress for their particular use. Get the Indian Office Report for that year (1905) and read. …If this matter comes before Congress then we can fight it. If the Bureau attempts to go against the full and complete acts of both the executive and legislative branches heretofore there is every opportunity to make such a smell as will damn it. All the Indians have to do is to strenuously refuse to move… ."[35]

At this point, Montezuma became intensely involved. He arranged for a Washington-based lawyer, Harry Bright, to represent both Montezuma and the Fort McDowell Yavapai, although Bright's involvement was soon replaced by Montezuma's friend and lawyer, Joseph W. Latimer. A formal protest was presented to the secretary of the interior, who responded on January 27, 1911:

> The receipt is acknowledged of your communication, dated November 8, 1910, protesting against the proposed removal of the Camp McDowell Indians to the Salt River Reservation, Arizona, and requesting, instead, that they be allotted at Camp McDowell and that a new modern dam be built for them there.
>
> In response you are advised that it has never been the intention of the Government to force the Camp McDowell Indians to remove to the Salt River reservation against their wishes, though the Department is satisfied, after careful investigation, that it would be to their best interests to so remove. As such removal would involve the expenditure of about $45,000 for water rights for these Indians, it may readily be seen that the Government would save money if the Indians stay where they are, and, in fact, is only considering their best interests in suggesting that they remove to Salt River.
>
> Something over $9,000,000 has been expended on the Salt River project, and it is extremely improbable that any further expenditures in that vicinity will be considered on any new project which would benefit but a small number of Indians, such as the dam which you propose be constructed.

The Department wishes also to point out to you that it is very unlikely that the Government will consent to the expenditures of any further funds for repairs to the present dam and ditches in use by the Camp McDowell Indians.

In conclusion you are advised that if the Camp McDowell Indians accept the opportunity offered them to participate in the benefits to be derived from the Roosevelt dam waters, it is not the intention of the Department that they will be deprived of the use of the Camp McDowell lands for pasturage and timber; nor will the Salt River Indians be entitled to any share in such lands.

As the matter now stands, the Indians who do not wish to remove to Salt River will not be compelled to do so by the Government, but the Department reiterates its belief that those who do not accept allotments of the irrigable lands at Salt River are standing in their own light, and it is hoped that they will soon see where their best interests lie.

R. A. Ballinger
Secretary of the Interior[36]

Montezuma immediately responded to the secretary, in a letter dated only three days after Ballinger's letter:

...After a thorough investigation of the question in Arizona by myself, consulting with the leaders of the tribe and the tribe themselves, and further consultation with eminent men in full position to pass judgment on such a question, I thoroughly disagree with your department that it is to the best interests of these Camp McDowell Indians to move, and I positively know *it is not their wish to move*.

...If there be a saving to the Government of $45,000—as you state in your letter—if these Indians are not moved, then, if the Government could be convinced that the condition of these Indians could be immeasurably improved for them to have an expenditure of a small amount right at Camp McDowell, we could accomplish a double purpose of saving the Government money and making it possible in making valuable citizens of these Indians.

The dam that these Indians want, and which the engineers assure us would furnish the agency with all the water it could possibly need, we are prepared to show, by competent engineers, would cost less than this $45,000 expense which you claim it would cost the Government to move them. We earnestly and sincerely believe that your department has been unintentionally mislead [*sic*] in reference to the removal of these Indians of the Camp McDowell agency being to their interest and advantage, and, if you care to give us the opportunity, we would be more than pleased to submit to you, in whatsoever form you may suggest, full evidence of the desires of these Camp McDowell Indians, and also more complete information, which we believe would convince your department that it is not only contrary to the best interests of these Indians to move them to the Salt River reservation, but that, with a comparatively small expenditure of money, they can be immeasurably benefited by being left on the Camp McDowell reservation, where in a short time they will become producers instead of wards.

These Indians are not a lazy, shiftless and immoral band, but are industrious, pastoral people; and history shows that their parents were invaluable to this Government in the settlement of the South-Western country, their scouting and their faithfulness alone being responsible for the rounding up of the Geronimo band of renegades in the 80's. All they need is a little help from the Government to put their farms in condition where they can be cultivated, and this particular band of Indians will soon become good citizens of this Government, and are yearning for this time to come, and, in fact, have made great progress when we consider the untilled condition of much of the land which they occupy.

We know that you, as the head of your department, are a fair-minded man, and are acting upon information which you believe is correct, and that you are therefore sincere in your position; but we are anxious to show you the grave error that would be commited [*sic*] if these Indians were moved, and we want to assure you that whatever we are doing on their behalf, we are desirous and anxious at all times to have your approval and approbation.[37]

Montezuma arranged for John H. Stephens, a Democrat and representative from Texas, 1897–1917, and chairman of the Committee on Indian Affairs, to introduce H. R. 6294 in Congress that would provide for allotment of twenty acres on Fort McDowell for each Indian; the remaining land would be sold by the secretary of the interior and the proceeds used for repair and construction of dams on the Verde River.[38] Montezuma wrote in January 1911 to Charles Dickens: "I have spent about $100 at Washington to have our bill presented before the house. I *sent the outline of the bill to Yuma Frank. Read it to him and the rest of the Indians* and tell me what they think about it. I was told that it was impossible to ask more than 20 acres each irrigated lands for the Mohave Apaches. That will take most of the land that can be irrigated. The rest of the land you can use as pasture for your stock, etc."[39]

Montezuma's involvement inspired R. G. Valentine, the commissioner of Indian affairs, to issue a directive to all superintendents and agents on December 23, 1910, that quoted U. S. law preventing any agreements to be made with any tribe of Indians or individual Indians unless approved by the secretary of the interior and the commissioner of Indian affairs. "…it is believed to be in the interest of good administration not to permit any contracts with any agent or attorney to be entered into with Indian tribes or individual Indians not citizens of the United States without departmental authority previously granted. Superintendents and Indian agents are hereby directed not to allow the negotiation of such contracts with the Indians under their charge, unless explicitly advised by the department or the Indian Office that prior authority therefore has been granted."[40]

Charles Dickens complained to Montezuma: "I am sorry to tell you about your letter. Mr. Coe and the inspector both come to me and Mr Coe ask me who write you. I say no body write me yet since I came home from Ray. Well Mr. Coe say to me I got your letter and he say he saw a letter from Chicago. He want to see the letter and Mr. Coe he take my letter in my pant pocket and both read your letter, and the inspector he tore apart your letter. 8 men saw that Mr. Coe take my letter out of my pant pocket, he got no right. Mr Coe bring inspector down here and asking me how many letter from you and he want all the letters to see. I say I got only one letter from you. We want you to report this to commissioner and tell him that Mr. Coe he take my letter in my pant pocket and tell him Commissioner that we said Mr. Coe is now mistaken by this time asking a letter who from. When you write to the commissioner and ask him did he told Mr. Coe to go around the Indian camp and asking about letters. We all agree that the inspector is alright but Mr. Coe he bring down here and take my letter, both read it. You find out right away about that and let us know at once."[41]

Yuma Frank had the same experience: "…Mr. Coe is always trying to opened your letter when ever we get letters from you but I don't let him to opened any letters, and compelled him to let him read. He want to know what you got to say bout the Indians. Mr. Coe he is not the kind of man to take charge. He don't seem to know his business. We might just as well go without Agent. They won't do things for anyhow. …Not a thing has been done since Mr. Coe took charge, but simply attempted on forcing Indians to move to Salt River. …Trying to close everything unless we said, 'we will move to Salt River,' but we are not going to move at all. Only six Indians going to move. But rest not going. …I depend on you what to do. Write soon and let us know."[42]

Acting Commissioner of Indian Affairs C. F. Hauke wrote Montezuma in March 1911 that if the Yavapai agreed to move to the Salt River Reservation, then the Indian Bureau would consider the possibility of allowing them to retain Fort McDowell land for farming and ranching.

> …After careful consideration the Office is still of the opinion that it would be to the best interests of the Indians on the Camp McDowell Reservation to move to the Salt River Reservation and accept allotments there. Careful investigation by experienced field men shows that it is not practicable to irrigate sufficient land on the Camp McDowell Reservation to afford allotments to the Indians there; that at the outside about 1300 acres only could be furnished with water, which would not be sufficient, and that owing to the treacherous character of the stream from which the waters should be taken, the irrigation and diversion dam would be subject to damage during times of flood. Something over $9,000,000 has been expended in the project from which waters are obtained to supply available lands on the Salt River Reservation. The project there is an assured one. If the Indians from the Camp McDowell Reservation will move to and accept allotments on the Salt River Reservation, it will practically mean a guarantee to them of a permanent water supply, while if they remain on the Camp McDowell Reservation the facilities for obtaining water at best are precarious.
>
> It should be understood at this time that the present plans of the Office do not contemplate allotments to Indians of the lands now embraced in the Camp McDowell Reservation and the Indians should understand if they agree to move to and accept allotments on the Salt River Reservation they will be given irrigable lands there; being allowed also to use the lands within the present Camp McDowell Reservation in common for agricultural, grazing or timber purposes. The Office does not expect to insist on the removal of these Indians to the Salt River Reservation, but will point out to them why it will be to their material advantage to go there. Sufficient irrigable land on that reservation will be retained to afford allotments at least of 5 acres with assured water rights which will be in the nature of a standing invitation to these Indians to go to the reservation and select allotments there wherever they care to avail themselves of this privilege. It will prove to the material interests of these Indians, of course, to remove to and accept allotments on the Salt River Reservation at the earliest practicable date, and for your information it may be said that recently, the Superintendent of the Camp McDowell School advised the Office that forty-two of these Indians had not only agreed to but had actually gone to the Salt River Reservation and selected the lands there wanted in allotment. This action on the part of the Indians is very gratifying to the Office, mainly because it is an indication of the fact that the Indians themselves are beginning to see in which direction their best interests lie.[43]

The Indian Bureau plan, however, did not recognize the Yavapai rights to the Verde River water. In addition, the government was refusing to repair and maintain the water control system at Fort McDowell. The Indian Bureau obviously thought that a lack of water would force the Yavapai to agree to the move. To make the situation more acute, the Fort McDowell day school was closed in an attempt to put pressure upon the Yavapai; the children were forced to go to the Phoenix Indian School with a promise of their own school if the Yavapai moved.[44] Montezuma promptly replied to Hauke, sending a copy to Senator Robert L. Owen. Owen was a Cherokee, who graduated from Washington and Lee University, served as the Indian agent in Muskogee, and in 1907 was one of the first two senators from Oklahoma, re-elected in 1912 and 1918.

> …You state that 1300 acres of land in Camp McDowell *can be irrigated*—this with the timber and grazing land in the reservation, which need not be irrigated, will make ample allotment for the Mohave-Apaches, and is exactly that for which we are contending.
>
> We feel gratified that you should so closely agree with us when you state that 1300 acres in this reservation can be irrigated. We are reliably informed that more can be successfully irrigated, but take it on your own statement, and we can make an allotment giving to each Indian—man, woman, and child—more irrigated acreage than you offer in Salt River reservation, and with the timber and grazing land added to this we have just what we want and that for which we are contending.
>
> Also your statement confirms our contention that the cost is comparatively light, as it must be with only 1300 acres to irrigate. Your contention that the "treacherous character of the stream from which the waters would be taken, the irrigation and diversion dams would be subject to damage during times of flood"—is not substantiated from reports of competent engineers who have examined this location for us with the view of ascertaining the practicable establishment of irrigation. They report it is amply practicable; that there is a natural formation that makes it a comparatively cheap proposition, and one in every way reasonable; and at a cost far below what your own Department estimated would cost the Government to move the Mohave-Apaches to the Salt River reservation, namely: $45,000.
>
> From a stenographic report of a conference between Chief Yuma Frank, with three other Mohave-Apache Indians, and your Inspector E. B. Linnen, held at Sacaton, Arizona, February 22, 1911, said Inspector Linnen urged upon the Mohave-Apaches to take five acres of land in the Salt River reservation, stating they would not have to move there, but that the Government was giving them this five acres *in addition to its present purpose* "to give each man, woman, and child ten acres of farming land and forty acres of grazing land, making a total allotment of fifty acres to each member of the tribe of the Camp McDowell reservation land;" and the Inspector urged Chief Yuma Frank to tell his tribe that the Government would allot the Camp McDowell land as above quoted, on which they could live, but in addition wanted to give each Indian five acres in Salt River reservation which they could "rent out." This proposition was repeatedly urged upon Chief Yuma Frank by Inspector Linnen in a conversation, the typewritten report of which occupies over four pages single space.
>
> Your letter to me of March 11, 1911, states emphatically: "It should be understood at this time that the present plans of the Office do not contemplate allotments to Indians of the lands now embraced in the Camp McDowell reservation."
>
> For what purpose do your agents and inspectors so flagrantly misrepresent the facts? Is this what your Department countenances as fair treatment to these Indians? Is this an illustration to you that your agents upon whose information you form your conclusions are, to say the least, using peculiar methods in urging this tribe to follow its "best interests" and move to Salt River reservation?
>
> We care not what may be the selfish interests of individuals to have these Mohave-Apaches move to the Salt River reservation and give up natural rights which they have in the Camp McDowell reservation, a place they live, where they have for years resided and still wish to reside, and we recognize the sincerity of the chief officers in the Department of the Interior in believing that it is for the best interests of these Mohave-Apaches to

move, but we want to repeat that we have written before—your information that these Mohave-Apaches want to move is erroneous; that if you will, unbiased, examine the conditions you will agree with us that it is not to their "best interests" to move; that you are being misled as to those who have consented to move, and that your information as stated to me in your letter of March 11, 1911, that "forty-two of these Indians had not only agreed to but had actually gone to the Salt River reservation and selected the lands there wanted in allotment,"—is entirely untrue—but that the facts are that every subterfuge to get these Indians to move to Salt River reservation against their avowed declaration to stay at Camp McDowell, is being used by your subordinates in Arizona.

Why this great haste to move these Indians? Your Department we should think would be glad to cease with such tactics as your Inspector Linnen used February 22, 1911 (heretofore set forth), and let these subjects be freely, openly, and fairly discussed, and then a decision made after full consideration of all sides.

The evident desire of some of your officials to hurry this matter when no reason on earth can be advanced for the necessity of haste, forced an appeal to Congress, and, as you know, the matter is there pending.

Why do you permit your inspectors and agents to continuously urge upon these Mohave-Apaches immediate selection, moving, and allotment in this Salt River reservation, when you have been officially notified that they do not want to go, and also when you further state in your letter to me of March 11, 1911, that your Department has as yet no legal authority to place any Indians on this Salt River reservation except "Pima and Maricopa Indians"? I refer to that paragraph of your said letter reading as follows:

"In order that there may be no misunderstanding, however, on your part in connection with this matter, you are further informed that the Executive Order of June 14, 1879, created the Salt River reserve for the use of the 'Pima and Maricopa Indians' and before allotments can actually be made on the Salt River reservation to the Indians now on camp McDowell reservation, it will be necessary to procure a modification of the Executive Order referred to so as to authorize the Secretary to locate thereon such other Indians as he may deem advisable. The matter has by letter of even date herewith been submitted to the Department for transmission to the President in order to procure the necessary enlargement of the Executive Order of June 14, 1879."

The Mohave-Apaches do not want to be wards, and with a little Government help (less than your Department states will cost you to move them to the Salt River reservation) they would be in a position right at Camp McDowell to demonstrate their fitness to become citizens; and with a fair hearing we devoutly believe their wishes and their welfare will not be trampled under foot by moving these Mohave-Apaches from a land in which they are contented and where nature assists them in their happiness and good, to a land of surroundings foreign to their every mode of life for generations, and people with other Indian tribes who for generations have been their sworn enemies.

Respectfully
Carlos Montezuma
Authorized Representative of Mohave-Apache Indians
Camp McDowell Reservation[45]

Hauke replied a month later: "Nothing is found in your letter which would cause the office to alter the opinion expressed in its letter of March 11, 1911, of the advisability of allotting the Camp McDowell Indians 5 acres of irrigable land within the Salt River Reservation, and that it would not be feasible for the Government to attempt to construct an irrigation project to cover the irrigable lands within the Camp McDowell Reservation."[46] Hauke further informed Montezuma that the executive order of June 14, 1879, had been amended and that the secretary of the interior was now empowered to settle any Indians on the Salt River Reservation.

In October 1911, Latimer, Montezuma's attorney, compiled a summary of the McDowell "situation," and sent it to members of the House Committee on Expenditures in the Interior Department, members of the Committee on Indian Affairs, and key senators. Montezuma was on his annual trip to Arizona, choosing to make this trip instead of attending the inaugural conference of the organization he helped to found, the Society of American Indians (Chapter 13). A letter from Latimer found him in Arizona and informed him: "...I feel I have conducted a clean fight in McDowell and have surely and unequivocally trapped the Indian Department, and am convinced a continuation of just such work is the only feasible and sensible manner of successfully eradicating the tremendous evils of the Bureau. This fight has cost me a very large amount of time and some personal money and I am at a loss to figure where proper remuneration can be raised."[47] Indeed, by 1914, Latimer was forced to take a position with the Climax Container Company in Chicago, "Manufacturers of Single Service, Liquid Proof, Paper Containers for Milk, Oysters, Butter, Oleomargarine, etc."[48] In 1918, he opened a private law office in Cleveland, Ohio, in 1921 he was in San Francisco, and in 1922, Latimer's law office was on Wall Street in New York City. Latimer's respect and affection for Montezuma never vacillated. "Your good loyal friendship has always been one great big ray of sunshine—maybe I will make you proud of me yet!!"[49]

Montezuma was not just vacationing in Arizona in the fall of 1911; he put his time to good use. He summarized his activities in a long letter to the congressman from Illinois, James M. Graham. Graham emigrated from Ireland at age sixteen, became a prominent lawyer in Springfield, and was the Democratic representative from the Twenty-First District in Illinois from 1909 to 1915, and the chairman of the House Committee on Expenditures in the Interior Department, the home of the Indian Bureau.

> I left Chicago on the morning of Oct 3rd and arrived in Phoenix on the morning of the 8th.
>
> Several days before leaving Chicago, Brosius of the Indian Rights Association called at my office on his way from Arizona, where he had visited the Pimas and the McDowell Mohave Apaches. He spoke discouragingly of the Pima situation and agreed that McDowell Mohave Apaches should be granted their request to remain where they are and to support themselves.
>
> ...Being furnished with names of newspaper men out there interested in irrigation, Sunday evening I called on Sam Small of the Phoenix Sun and Mr. Scott of the Arizona Republican.
>
> Mr. Small was much interested and was in favor of doing all he could to air the wrongs of the Indians in Arizona fearlessly. He spoke very nicely of you as his personal friend. He then went on and gave me his newspaper work in Washington, he has some opportunities to come in contact with senators and representatives. He called back Senator Dawes and other good friends of the Indians. After our talk we found each other striking the same note on the Indian question.
>
> I assure you we have a good friend in "the Phoenix Sun" in the person of Mr. Small. [Montezuma then recounted a similar meeting with Mr. Scott of the Arizona Republican.]

Monday, I called on Jeff Adams, an old settler who lived at McDowell. He said that he was friend of the Indians but for their best interest he believed that they better accept the government's offer down at Salt River reservation. He spoke of the treacherous condition of the Verde River and the easy method of irrigation by the Roosevelt Dam water if they accept the Indian Bureau's offer. Having special interest there he could not express himself otherwise.

…Looking around the city while in Phoenix I called on Mrs. Gill at the Indian School. She was the wife of the man who transacted the purchases of the McDowell Agency from the settlers there for the Government and who did so much for those Indians. She was in favor that the Apaches move to Salt River reservation and retain McDowell as pasture lands. Then I asked her "and give up their water rights?" "No," she said. I explained to her that would be the case if those Indians move. "That was another proposition," she said.

Monday afternoon I made a short visit to Mr. McClintock, Postmaster of Phoenix, an old friend of mine. He too claimed to be friend of the Indians and then went on to tell me "that McDowell Indians had no more rights there than any other Indians. The settlers and the Pimas had that land first. It was the good will of the Salt River Valley people that keeps those Mohave Apaches on Ft. McDowell. Those Indians make no use of that land. They are better off with five acres at Salt River reservation and use the Roosevelt Dam water for irrigation." I guess he believes the Indians have no rights anywhere.

Tuesday I spent the day at McDowell where I met Chas Dickens. Here I called on my friend Mr. Fuller, a civil engineer. He had been at McDowell. He informed me that a dam could be built for the McDowell Indians. He asked me: "Who are the party that is fighting against your Indians remaining at McDowell?" "That is what I am after," I said. "Well, confidentially, I can tell you that it looks to me as though the irrigation project people are the ones."

Thursday morning I took the train for Mesa which is 15 miles south. Before leaving Thursday morning I called on Mr. Cooke (I think that is his name) an old irrigating project engineer. He was very conservative and was not definite as to his views on the McDowell situation.

On the same day I called on Mr. Harris who did a great deal of engineering for the Government on the Roosevelt Dam. I asked him whether a dam could be built on the Verde River for the McDowell Indians. He said, "Yes." Then I asked what it would approximately cost. After some figuring and looking over pamphlets he said he was not sure but guessing as near as possibly he thought it would cost $300,000.

By wagon I arrived at McDowell Thursday Evening. I stayed with the Dickens. Friday we went up the Verde River not far from the upper end of the Reservation line and looked over the amount of lands that could be irrigated if a proper dam was in operation. Three Chicago friends [two were Gibson and Morgan] were with me besides Indians. Nearly three thousand acres was my calculation. The brush dam improved by your suggestion irrigated nearly one thousand acres. A modern small dam could irrigate three times as much more land.

I was informed by the engineer consulted that the amount of water taken from the Verde by these Indians would not alter the flow of the Verde river down to the Salt River valley.

Remaining two days at McDowell and looking over the reservation has not altered my stand I have taken for my people… .[50]

Montezuma also kept Richard Pratt informed. The relationship between Montezuma and Richard Pratt remained steadfast and never wavered. Strong testimony to the depth and sincerity of the respect and affection between the two men is the fact that in May 1912 Richard and Mrs. Pratt stopped to visit Fort McDowell on their way home from California.

The purpose was no more than to share with Montezuma Pratt's own personal observations. "My rushed visit to McDowell gave me much to think about. …I found a tuberculory school teacher with a tuberculory wife, both light weights and from Texas so not large in race sympathy, and not able to impress the Indians even if capable. So time most vital to progress is being wasted. I did not go to any camps but Dickens and did not go above the Agency but can easily see how it is. I should like much to see you and talk it all over with you. …It seems to me we might with all the influence we can get there to push the development of McDowell resources. It did not seem to me they were much concerned to do that. On a fair day to work on their ditches under construction they were idle in their camps. I admit all the discouragements of uncertainty and the Government's crooked action, but the best way to overcome all that is industry and utilization of what they occupy and contend for. …but if they could be brought to go ahead in a self reliant way and show their love for their Fort McDowell child in spite of the attempts to get them to abandon it, don't you see how far more difficult it would be to oust them and how immensely stronger their friends would be in contending in their behalf."[51] These words must have strengthened Montezuma's resolve to continue to urge the Fort McDowell Yavapai to work hard at their farming.

Despite Pratt's disparaging comments and Montezuma's correspondence that contains many requests for money from his relatives, it is difficult to criticize Montezuma's cousins for an unwillingness to work or for failing to fulfill their promises to pay him back. For example, Charles Dickens wrote to Montezuma in July 1912: "I am working again for Olson & Graf with 18 men from here [on Granite Reef dam and ditches] and I am going to stay this job until you come & hunt deer. …All McDowell Indians raise a big crops this year. Each men make many sacks of grains and putting lot of corn and melons and pumkins [sic]. I hope you come soon & stay with me for two months. Cousin, I am pay all up on my bill on wagon and I buy more wagon and I buy Buggie for $59.00 and I buy saddle & horse to [sic]. I pay horse & saddle & harness for $70.00 and I run a little store to [sic] at my place. While I am going away my brother Sam Dickens gone run for me."[52]

By this time, Montezuma's position was crystal clear in his own mind. "Commercialism has sprung up and the Indians are the victims. Take for example, the Reclamation Service, the Conservation of National Resources of the Government, and real estate…all of this I believe has forced the Indians to give up lands, timber, and their water rights without the Indians' consent. I do not believe that 5 or 10 acres of irrigable land is sufficient when by rights they own more."[53] But Montezuma and Latimer were arrayed against a formidable collection of individuals, and all had vested interests. W. H. Code was the chief engineer of the Indian Irrigation Service. He had previously worked for the Consolidated Canal Company of Mesa, headed by A. J. Chandler, one of the largest landowners in the Southwest and president of the Mesa Bank. Benjamin A. Fowler, W. J. Murphy, and J. P. Orme were other wealthy landowners. Murphy controlled the Arizona Improvement Company, operating a system of canals for irrigation.

A RESOLUTION OF THE CONTROVERSY was sought through the means of a Congressional hearing, the Hearings Before the Committee on Expenditures in the Interior Department of the House of Representatives on House Resolution No. 103 to Investigate the Expenditures in the Interior Department.[54] The hearings lasted twelve days in June 1911.

Chief Engineer Code argued before the committee that the *Winters* ruling did not apply to reservations established by executive orders. However, this ignored the fact that the Pima, Maricopa, and Yavapai Indians had been living in the area of the Salt, Gila, and Verde Rivers and using the water for many years before White men appeared. Indeed, the Hohokam people had been farming with irrigation canals along the Salt and Gila Rivers hundreds of years before the appearance of Whites.[55] Thus both *Winters* and the principle of prior appropriation were ignored by Engineer Code.

Montezuma was joined at the Congressional hearings by his Chicago-based lawyer, Joseph W. Latimer, and Chief Yuma Frank, George Dickens, and Thomas Surama from Fort McDowell. The hearings started with ex-Commissioner Francis E. Leupp on the stand who expounded on his views of the Indian problem.[56] Leupp was followed by the current commissioner, Robert G. Valentine, and in an amazing demonstration of the friendly attitude of the chairman of the committee, James M. Graham of Illinois, Joseph Latimer was allowed to interrogate Valentine (for six days!) during which the Fort McDowell controversy was reviewed. Then it was Montezuma's turn, and in an interaction with the friendly chairman, his testimony covered two days and filled forty-eight pages in the transcript of the hearings. He told his life story, shared his opinions on reservations, Indian schools—all the subjects in his writings and lectures for the past fifteen years. The hearing concluded with the three Yavapai representatives who emphasized their strong desire to stay at Fort McDowell. They made a good impression as well dressed, hard working men (the committee was impressed by their callused hands).

| President | Secretary of the Interior | Commissioner of Indian Affairs |
|---|---|---|
| William Howard Taft, 1909 | R. A. Ballinger, 1909<br>Walter L. Fisher, 1911 | Robert G. Valentine, 1909 |
| Woodrow Wilson, 1913 | Frank K. Lane, 1913<br>John B. Payne, 1920 | Cato Sells, 1913 |
| Warren G. Harding, 1921 | Albert B. Fall, 1921<br>Hubert Work, 1923 | Charles H. Burke, 1921 |
| Calvin Coolidge, 1923 | Hubert Work<br>Roy O. West, 1928 | Charles H. Burke |
| Herbert C. Hoover, 1929 | Ray L. Wilbur, 1929 | Charles J. Rhoads, 1929 |
| Franklin Delano Roosevelt, 1933 | Harold L. Ickes, 1933 | John Collier, 1933 |

Secretary of the Interior Fisher concluded at the end of the hearings that the effort to provide allotments on the Salt River Reservation was a *mistake*. Fisher wrote to Joseph Latimer: "It may clear the ground somewhat of misunderstanding to state at the start that both the department and Indian Office consider the idea, in any form it may have taken either of plan or of action, of general allotment for the Camp McDowell Indians on the Salt River Reservation or on land adjacent to it rather than on the Camp McDowell Reservation, to have been a mistake."[57] This battle in the twelve-year war was won. The Yavapai Indians were agreeable to accepting allotments on the Fort McDowell Reservation that would retain their water rights. However, H.R. 6294 (Representative Stephens' bill for allotment of Fort McDowell) was referred to the Committee on Indian Affairs and never enacted. Fortunately, the protests from Montezuma and Latimer prompted the new Secretary of Interior Walter Fisher to order a survey to determine the feasibility of constructing a dam and an irrigation system on the Verde River, the idea being that more land would be available for irrigation and thus the Indians would not have to move. Indeed, the survey was accomplished late in 1911, concluding that a $72,380 expenditure would provide 3,000 additional acres of irrigable land.

Richard Pratt wrote to Charles Dickens on August 27, 1912: "Mr Latimer has sent me copies of the letters from the Secretary of the Interior, telling that they are going to allot your lands at once. I want to congratulate you on the success of Dr. Montezuma's, your, and Mr Latimer's fight to hold on to your property. It has been a great success and due entirely to Dr. Montezuma's 'bull dog' tenacity and the able support he has had from Mr. Latimer. Dr. Montezuma and Mr. Latimer have worked for you and your people without pay and have spent a great deal of money in doing that, as you know, Dr. Montezuma has made several expensive trips to Fort McDowell and other trips to Washington. As a member of your tribe, Dr. Montezuma is entitled to his allotment and it will be your duty as well as I believe your pleasure, to see that he gets one of the best. I think in addition to that, the Government ought to pay Dr. Montezuma a good amount of money to pay more than he has expended for having saved the Government from doing a wrong thing and bringing upon itself additional censure because of its bad treatment of its Indian wards. Mr Latimer is also entitled to your consideration. Just how you will give that is the problem. Allow me as your friend and a friend of your people to suggest that it has been the custom of many of the Tribes for several hundred years past to adopt into the Tribe and give them full tribal rights, white men who have been their useful stanch [*sic*] friends. This would be small reward for the service Mr. Latimer has rendered you and yet that would be a graceful, nice way for you to show your gratitude. I write this to you entirely without the knowledge or suggestion of either Dr. Montezuma or Mr. Latimer, but of my own free will and because I know so much of the circumstances."[58] But Pratt did send a copy of the letter to Montezuma.

After the fall national election in 1912, the mail was busy with letters to Washington suggesting and promoting candidates for the position of commissioner of Indian affairs, to be appointed by the new president, Woodrow Wilson. Latimer's involvement in the Fort McDowell fight gained him sufficient publicity and friends that his name was put forth. Although Latimer claimed to not take seriously the possibility, he did write Montezuma to ask Richard Pratt for a letter to the president urging the appointment.[59] Of course, he was not considered by the government to be an appropriate candidate.

## MONTEZUMA, THE PIMA, AND THE MARICOPA

Montezuma tried to become involved with land and water disputes at other reservations, including the Pima, Maricopa, and Papago Indians. Frank A. Thackery, superintendent of the Salt River Reservation, provided his point of view of this controversial activity in an article printed in the journal of the Chilocco Indian School of Oklahoma.[60] He reviewed letters sent by Montezuma in 1912 and 1913 to Pima, Maricopa, Lehi, and Santan Indians on the Gila River and Salt River reservations that included blank forms to grant power-of-attorney authorizing Montezuma to act in various matters, including land and water rights. Montezuma followed this solicitation with another letter requesting total support, stating, "I cannot risk my reputation unless all of them are back of me." Montezuma had obtained a copy of a protest sent to the commissioner of Indian affairs, signed by many of the Indians of the Salt River Reservation. This protest complained that Pima and Maricopa Indians had been compelled to sign a petition to grant Montezuma full power to act in all matters concerning the reservation and that those supporting Montezuma represented those against progress.

Montezuma was stymied in Washington; nothing could be decided until President Wilson appointed a new commissioner of Indian affairs. The previous commissioner, Robert G. Valentine, had resigned in response to a politically inspired Congressional investigation that charged him with improper conduct.[61] In the meantime, Montezuma wrote repeatedly to the Pima: "If the allotting agent comes out there and urge you all to be allotted—do not agree to anything until they give everything in writing how much land they are going to give to each Indian. Before you sign any papers let me see the papers first. Tell the allotting Agents to write to me or have Mr. Coe write to me. Stick and say that you all have chosen me as your representative."[62] Richard Pratt was fond of telling Carlisle students that the postage stamp was a great example; all it had to do to accomplish its objective was to stick to the envelope. "Sticking to it" became a common Pratt-Carlisle theme. Soon students and Pratt supporters, including Montezuma, adopted this theme, often shortening its expression to "stick to it," or just "stick."

"I want to tell these chiefs that every Pima in Salt River Valley must stick together and do not quarrel among themselves. This is no time to fight with each other. We (Pimas) must be of one mind and say that we want our land divided or allotted in the right way—10 acres irrigated land to each Indian, then divide the rest of the land so much for pasture land and so much for timber land. By doing this the Indians get all their land equally divided among themselves. Another important thing to find out before signing papers for the Government is whether you get the water rights free for 5, 10, 15, 25, 50, 100 years or forever."[63]

"Tell the Chief and the Pima Indians that I do not blame them for getting uneasy and want to know what I am doing for them. Ever since I took up the Pima work, things have been unsettled. The men at Washington were too busy with elections to pay any attention to anything I may ask. The Government was uncertain whether the Democrats would get in power and the Commissioner of Indian Affairs Valentine was having trouble of his own and everything looked unfavorable for me to do anything. That was the reason why I have been slow and now we know the new President has been elected by the Democrats and there is no Commissioner of Indian Affairs. …I am sorry that some Pimas do not believe in me but in time they will see that I am not working for myself but for the best interest of the Indians."[64]

Montezuma's motives cannot be questioned. No evidence can be found of self-aggrandizement, only a consistent and pure theme of compassion and empathy. "Nothing would give me more pleasure but to work and help you all I can to get your rights. I feel as though I am one of you. …There is a grand and noble picture in your act of appointing me as your representative. I remember 40 years ago I was among you as a small boy captive. I feared you as gods—awful enemies. Few of the old men and women may remember me. And the same belief you all had for the Apaches who roamed the Superstition range of mountains. Forty-five years time has changed our thoughts for each other. Today we are brothers of the same blood. We are under the same cloud of trouble and we must help each other. And now you have that great confidence in me to take your affairs in charge. It makes the tears come to my eyes, for you all could not do any more to show our brotherhood than in the act of appointing me as your representative at Washington. In return I assure you all, you need not have any fear that I will act for myself. What I will do will be as you say with the help of God as my guide."[65]

And increasingly the Pima Indians turned to Montezuma for help. "…But now we are going to tell you that the Salt River and Pimas Reservation Arizona are perty [sic] bad. Because when the Surveyor come here and survey on this land and put in some kind of pipe post in the ground, they said If any body will take this pipe out of the ground will be throught [sic] in the Phoenix jail. We are going to tell you that one of the Indian are throught [sic] in Phoenix jail now by taking out that pipe post. …All of the Indian want you to stand for the Indian. We are wanted to find out about this pipe post."[66]

Finally, President Wilson appointed Cato Sells commissioner of Indian affairs in June 1913, nine months after Valentine's resignation. The small town (a few thousand people) of Sells, in Pima County, directly south of Phoenix about twenty miles before the Mexican border, is named after Cato Sells. Sells, a native of Iowa, moved to Texas in 1907, established the Texas State Bank and Trust Company, and devoted himself to Democratic politics.[67] He was an early supporter of Wilson and was responsible for large campaign contributions from Texas; his reward was his appointment as commissioner. Sells was a dedicated prohibitionist and assimilationist. During Sells tenure as commissioner, the first Indians reached the end of the twenty-five-year trust period for allotted land (Chapter 3). Whites wanted these lands and states were eager to impose taxes upon this land. Sells imposed a ten-year extension on the trust period, but at the same time more vigorously pursued activation of the Burke Act to remove federal controls over "competent" Indians. He did this by announcing that all adult Indians of less than one-half Indian blood would be assumed to be competent. In addition, "incompetent" Indians would be allowed to sell their land. As a result, the Indian Bureau significantly increased the number of individual deeds that were granted after 1913. But Sells strongly believed that many tribes, especially those in the Southwest, still required federal protection and maintenance.

Sells made a strong first impression, especially on Richard Pratt. Pratt advised Montezuma: "The commissioner is a splendid fellow and has taken hold of his big job with a great deal of vigor."[68] "I am satisfied he is a good and true man and means to do big and good things for the Indians and to be above any of the picayune and pestiferous acts of the last administrations."[69] "He is by all odds the ablest, and I think is going to be by far the best Commissioner of Indian Affairs we have had within my knowledge, now running over 46 years. His conception of his duty, the knowledge he has already obtained in regard to the affairs of his office, his attitude on education and his intentions, are to me even better than I, myself, could have conceived or have enjoyed, notwithstanding all my long experience. He is an able lawyer, and therein he has tremendous advantage. He is clean in his habits and thought. He needs to have his hands held up by all of us. He works harder than any man I have known in public office in Washington, because he is determined himself to get into the merits of every case and to see all sides, and to conclude only after he has such knowledge."[70] These strong words motivated Montezuma to proceed slowly to avoid antagonizing the new commissioner and beginning on the wrong foot. He did, however, have Latimer send a summary to Sells of the Fort McDowell affair that culminated in the decision by the previous secretary of the interior to proceed with allotment of Fort McDowell and to erect an irrigation dam.

When Montezuma appeared for a meeting with the Indians on the Salt River Reservation in 1913, during his visit to Arizona that included the hunting trip described in Chapter 11, Superintendent Thackery sent the Indian police to follow the commissioner's directive of 1910, and ask Montezuma for proper authority to negotiate with the Indians. Montezuma was brought to the superintendent's office, where in the presence of witnesses, Montezuma was informed that without proper authority, a meeting would not be permitted and was provided at his request a written statement to that effect.[71] Upon returning home, Montezuma described the confrontation to Richard Pratt:

You know that I did not go to Arizona for no other mission than to hear what the Indians had to say. They had written to me to make them a visit and thinking I would not interfere with the Indian department I made dates to have a meeting at Lehigh [Lehi], Sacaton, and Blackwater. I felt free to do this because I was going there to do philanthropic work. I did not think one moment that any one could have any objection.

At Lehigh [Lehi] we had a large meeting. I had Oskison take down what the different chiefs said. At the close another faction wanted to speak to me. They asked me what business I was there for and if I was sent by the Government. I told them I was there because I had the interests of the Indians at heart and that I have been doing this for many years. That the Government did not send me to them but I am doing this work to help the Government to do the right thing for the Indians. Many other questions they asked and I answered them and made them to understand that I am trying to help all Indians forward and not backwards. The next day several Pima Chiefs took me to Sacaton 4 miles northwest of Sacaton the Agency. As I got off the wagon Indian Policeman shake hands with me and handed a paper of instruction to read. I knew what it was and I told him that instruction did cover my position but he told me that I better see the Agent first before the meeting. Mr. Gibson and myself went with the policeman to Sacaton. The Supt invited us into his office.

He asked me "What are you here for?"
"Justice for the Indians," I replied.
"Have you any authority?" he asked.
"No" was my answer. He referred to instruction.
I said, "Yes, I know that instruction. Once before that question came up in my case with Com. Valentine & Secretary Fisher and they decided that instruction did not cover my work for the Indians. I am working for charity & no money involved."
"You have your secretary with you?"
"No Sir!" I said.
"I cannot have you hold meetings to speak with the Indians unless you have an authority from Washington," he said.

I replied, "Had I known this I would have been provided with an authority but I thought my reputation was sufficient. This was the first time I have ever been questioned whenever I have spoken to the Indians. I do not forget the Supt of the Indian department. I generally act as peace-maker and not a disturber."

"I cannot allow you to speak," he again said.

"Then have that written on paper and sign it," I asked. He dictated to his stenographer and wrote what he pleased and gave it to me. I took it and walked out assuring him that I would not hold any meetings.

We went back to the meeting & had the police interpret what the Supt had said and then told them not to make any trouble for if they did, it could be blamed to me.

I wanted to visit Blackwater for there I was kept by the Pimas after taking me from the mountains and also visit the Montezuma ruins & Adamsville where I was sold. Few of the Chiefs took me to Blackwater where we staid [sic] over night. Next day they took me to Adamsville & Montezuma ruins. We came back & had dinner at Blackwater & back to Sacaton for the night.

Every step of the way we were shadowed by Indian policemen. I left Sacaton Sept 29th for McDowell.

This story sounds petty but the Supt. Telegraphed (no doubt) to the Commissioner & the reply telegraph I received after I got back to Chicago.

It appears as though I was there for a selfish purpose and to make disturbance among the Indians. Knowing me as long as you do, you know that making trouble was the last thing in my mind.[72]

According to a description of the confrontation with Thackery by one of Montezuma's hunting companions, John Oskison, Montezuma was accused of being a "trouble-maker and a contract-seeker. [We] were bundled off the reservation as meddlers!"[73] In response to this confrontation, Commissioner Cato Sells telegraphed Montezuma:

ADVISED THAT YOU HAVE HELD MEETING WITH PIMA INDIANS FOR PURPOSE OF PROCURING POWER OF ATTORNEY TO REPRESENT THEM YOU WILL BE REQUIRED TO COMPLY WITH INDIAN OFFICE CIRCULAR FOUR NINETY SEVEN PLEASE CONFER WITH SUPERINTENDENT THACKERY AND TAKE NO ACTION THAT IS NOT IN COMPLIANCE WITH INDIAN OFFICE REGULATIONS[74]

Montezuma was treading lightly with the Pima and the Maricopa. He repeatedly explained his caution to the chiefs: "To tell you the truth I have not sent the papers that you all signed to have me as your representative to Washington yet. I am studying the whole situation before I do it. It will not be right for me to say anything against your superintendent or the Commissioner of Indian Affairs until I am authorized to do so."[75]

Montezuma finally communicated directly with Commissioner Sells. The letter is long, emotional, and lacking in the kind of facts one would need to impress the new commissioner. He sent copies to the Pima, asking that it be read to as many as possible.

I am going to speak to you freely and frankly because I appreciate you as a man who holds the rein of the destiny of these Pima and Maricopa Indians and know that you really wish to do the best thing for them; but you can not do anything for them unless you have their right condition brought to your attention for consideration.

There is something radically wrong with these Indians or they would not go outside of the Indian Reservation for aid. They have appointed me as their representative to speak for them and to intercede for them and try to help them out of their struggle for their rights. The writer tried to ascertain the true conditions of the Pima Indians and attempted to meet various members of the tribe in this matter, but in so doing was ordered through instructions from Washington, *off* the Reservation and was forced to depend thereafter upon individual statements.

In 1871 the writer was an eye-witness to their life of plenty, freedom and no care. They lived in peace with all coming settlers. There was no question as to their rights. Their storehouses were filled to overflowing, corn and all sorts of vegetables abounded as well as their "staff of life"—the mesquite beans and cacti. They had herds of cattle and horses, swine and domestic fowls flourished in their hands. The Gila River majestically swerved through a vast forest of bamboos or canes of a mile wide on each side of the river. The river supplied them with fresh water to drink and for irrigation.

If I understand the original object of the Indian department, it was not instituted for commercial purpose or to do any injustice to the Indians, much less to impose or permit settlers to enter on their rights without their consent. Its ultimate intent was to help them to be one with us. It was a noble philanthropic branch of the Government and not a means to forward selfish interests.

If there is a tribe of Indians that the Government ought to deal justly and generously with, it is the Pima and Maricopa tribes. Their plea is to retain what belongs to them and not anything more. Their title to the land upon which they live is a heritage from God, in the name of justice, by rights of priority of possession and by a legal grant from the Government for reward as being always at peace, and their great service rendered the government in the days when the Apaches were dangerous elements in Arizona. It was at this time the writer was taken captive by them (this is the Pimas). They spared my life. I would be ungrateful and unworthy of my race, the Apaches, and my benefactors, the Pimas, if I refused to help them in this hour of their distress.

Forty-four years ago they were good Indians; water was plentiful for them to irrigate their land. They were industrious, lived happily and independent. Surely to them it was "a land of milk and honey."

About twenty years ago public sentiment was aroused in their behalf. They were starving and in a destitute condition on account of the water of the Gila River was being diverged by the new settlers above them. They never dreamed that this would ever happen, but the fact is it did. Philanthropy came to their aid, the Indian Rights Association bestirred themselves in their behalf, the Indian Department took them under their wings and the press favored them for a little while. They were at ease, because they had great faith in the government so they gave themselves into the hands of the Indian Bureau, thinking that they would be cared for and protected for all time to come. They believed that as they treated the Government right, the Government would serve them the same way. But alas not so! In time the invasion by selfish greed interests bedimmed these Indians' title to their rights, *and the poor Pimas and Maricopas are nowhere.*

And to-day they are not prancing up and down the Gila River as of yore; they are living a mere existence of poverty and despair. O cursed and that damnable system! It has ruined that free and innocent people to an "Indian Bureau pecked creatures." They know no man but the Agent or Superintendent who frowns at them, rides around them in his automobile with a supernatural air and tells the Indians that he talks with Washington. It is sad and pitiful to see these sons and daughters of freedom bow to this man God In America.

No one that has taken heart interest in their welfare, can consciously praise the past treatment of these Indians. Slowly with the settlement of Salt River Valley, within a decade, these once independent and peaceable Indians have witnessed a dwindling away of their land, forest and means of subsistence.

They have been treated as though they were not human, but they are human and as such they have come to realize that something must be done to protect them of their water rights, money, land, forest, and education. They are lost and do not know what to do.

From various investigations facts have been shown that these Indians have suffered, have been cheated, their money misappropriated and the Indian department was silent on the matter. Many things were passed as laws without any voice from them, and their lands were taken from them without legal authority.

In the beginning of creation of the Indian Department of the Government it had oneness of purpose of looking after the interest of the Indians. To-day the department has branched off into other interests, namely: the Forestry Reserve, the Reclamation service, the Irrigation project, Natural Resource project, etc. In other words it has come to pass in the Indian Department that the Indians' interests are secondary matters to their legal rights.

No one who has studied the interests of the Indians can overlook that there are some special interested people in the background, who are appendages of the Indian Bureau and with them are in a conspiracy to help each other, and let the Indians take care of themselves.

As these branches of the Indian department progress the Indians look on with credulity as these projects move together with the selfish interests of the pale-faces-machine within machine, working from one hand into another in rapid succession, slight hand performance, making these Indians to believe that these hirelings are wonderously working out everything for the Indians' best interest. It bedazzles the Indians. In one sense it looks as though these grafters had an understanding among themselves, "while the Indians are dizzy, let us do them and do them good."

In delaying with these Indians justice seems to be dethroned. Progress without a heart seems to have taken its place. It is plainly manifest that there is no sympathy and no consideration for these Indians. It is a cold and crooked manipulation to get their land. "System, carry out the system" seems to be the pass word in dealing with the Pimas and Maricopas. In their cries they have no redress. It is "Mr. Indians, you do as I say or go to jail until you make up your minds to do as I say." They are ruled by fear and tyranny. When the poor Indians try to defend themselves from forced injustices, mistreatment and intrusion on their rights, they are told to accept and not say a word. Obey Washington through its agents or be put in jail until they make up their minds to follow the instructions from the Great Father. To the Indians, it is like holding a pistol to their heads and saying "money or your life." I cannot, I will not and I do not believe this administration wishes to follow in the same trail of the former administrations of Leupp and Valentine in dealing with these Indians.

There are interests and interests. True, but it is clear that the Indian Bureau should look after the Indians' interests. These Indians are being pushed against the wall and deprived of rights that the Government gave them years and years ago. With the government heretofore granting to them at least 160 acres of land now within the Salt River Valley, and to-day the Government is attempting to transfer these Pimas and Maricopas into the Salt River district with a doubtful 10 acres of irrigated land.

Well then, if the aim of the Government is for fair delaying and just allotments for these Indians why not divide their land to them "pro-rata,"—so much irrigation land, so much timber land, and so much pasture land? In other words allot it so that they will get all of their land among themselves.

These Indians are being pushed against the wall contrary to their wish. It is not right.

There is no just credit of dealing with them in the past why should this administration try to make the last worse than the first?

The Indian is a man. As such he comes within the protection of the Constitution of the United States. Their voice must be heard and not disregarded. Therefore, I ask you as a great man and as a friend to human kind to help the Pimas and Maricopas as you would yourself.[76]

Montezuma tried to resolve the situation by obtaining official authorization. His strategy was to be appointed as a representative of the Society of American Indians and to ask the leaders of the organization to obtain a permit from Washington to hold meetings with the Pima and the Maricopa. Arthur Parker, the secretary-treasurer of the Society, provided a written statement appointing Montezuma to study reservation conditions in Arizona, and he wrote to Commissioner Sells.[77] However, Sherman Coolidge, the president of the Society, told Montezuma that Commissioner Sells was opposed to the idea.[78] But Montezuma insisted: "I regret to say the department does not understand me. During all my dealings with the Indians have I ever interfered with the Indian Bureau. If they understand me they would know that I am helping them to deal rightly with the Indians and not to make any trouble. When those Indian Superintendents thought I was not doing just the right thing does not make it so. They did me wrong and I acted like a man, that is why they are so sensitive. For myself, I do not ask it but when I am working for the Indians, it is the duty of the Society to back me up. Again I ask a letter from the Society, approved by the Commissioner of Indian Affairs to permit me to check to those Indians and in that way harmonize the friction now existing in Arizona. No man can ask any more or less than this for the best interest of all concerned."[79] The Society, not wishing to aggravate Commissioner Sells, ignored Montezuma's second request.

Although Pima Indians continued to write to Montezuma with various complaints (diligently forwarded by Montezuma to the Indian Bureau), the controversy over land slowly diminished as the Bureau pursued the allotment process on the Salt River Reservation. "…you know that I did not try to make trouble for you, but I did try to tell you what was best for your interest. …I wish you to know any land owned by the Pima and Maricopa tribes, when your allotment is finished and you have land left, that land that is left belongs to the tribes and cannot be sold without the consent of the tribes. Look out for that and do not sell away the land that is left over. Indians who were not on your side said most everything to scare you. That was why they called you 'Montezuma.' I guess you heard that I was going to make money by my talks to you Indians. You know that is not true. What I have done for you Indians has been done free and from my heart. What I am doing now is to free all Indians and get all Indians to be citizens."[80]

## THE FORT McDOWELL YAVAPAI DO NOT MOVE

Nothing was happening at Fort McDowell. Montezuma continued to urge resistance, telling his cousin, Mike Burns, who had moved with his family from Camp Verde in the north to the Fort McDowell Reservation: "…Mike, the way things look Washington is trying to starve the Apaches from McDowell & make you move to Salt River Valley. Washington is willing to leave you all allotted of pasture land on McDowell. That will not do. Some one wants the water rights of the Verde River that belongs to the Apaches. The Apaches will be tried to fool them to move to Salt River. When the Apaches do that then they will lose the rights of the Verde River. So be careful what the Government will try to do with you. Just stay where you all are and never make a move. Ask for the dam and be allotted on McDowell. Sign no papers until I see it and advise you all. Stay together and we may turn out in the long run... ."[81]

Montezuma complained to Commissioner Cato Sells: "I was assured that you have the welfare of the Indians at heart and it is impossible for me to believe that these Mohave-Apache Indians of Camp McDowell, who are relatives of mine and for whom, without the slightest remuneration, I have worked for three years, will now have ruthlessly set aside their rights granted them by the former secretary of the Interior, Hon. Walter L. Fisher. The delay in a decision from you since our complete letter to you under date of April 16th last causes me deep anxiety, and I am writing you this letter personally lest our communications with the facts therein set forth have not been brought to your personal attention."[82]

In November 1914, the Fort McDowell Yavapai lost their chief, Yuma Frank, who was succeeded by Montezuma's forty-six-year-old cousin, George Dickens. From the edge of his grave three days before he died, Yuma Frank sent Montezuma a stirring message:

> ...Now I am sick and I am not able to live. I am pretty sick now. All the Indians come to my Camps and see me today. Remember when I died George Dickens take my place and you can help him as I do help you. ...Please always saying to the Government: Build a dam for McDowell my peoples. Please, Brother, help all you can. ...Brother Montezuma, remember me and I always remember you too, and I am keep my words in your book. Also tell my friends, Mr. Latimer, I am not able to live longer, so good-by and shake my hands with this letter, and when I am died Chas. Dickens will let you know at any time.[83]

*Yuma Frank—1914*

My dear Chief,

Your sad letter in your sickness reached this day. No better man that ever lived than you and I hope when this reaches you, you are better and that you have been cared for in the best way. We all have to die and if we face God, who made the mountains and all of us to live, know that we have been true and faithful to our people, He (God) will take care of us when we leave this world for the home we are to live after we are dead. You have fought a good fight. You have seen the country taken away from your people and now you have stood up as a brave man for the interest of your people to seek the small shot McDowell for them. True, you have worked hard to be faithful as a Chief to your people, and if you die, die happy, that we those who live, we will work just as faithful as ever to carry out what you had in your heart. But I hope that you will not die, but you will live long enough to see your people have a home on McDowell and that the government will build a dam and give each Indian so much irrigated land and the rest as timber and pasture lands. That will take all the land in the four (4) miles wide and twelve (12) miles long. That is what Mr. Latimer and myself are trying to get for the McDowell Indians. I do not know how you are sick but I will send you salve to take or rub where you are sore and cough medicine if you cough and medicine for strength. Take the medicine as it says on the bottle. How I wish I could be with you, so that I can help you as much as I can. I had hoped to come to Arizona this year but having no money I could not come.

I am pretty sure the Commissioner of Indian Affairs is coming to McDowell. If he comes to Phoenix, have him to come & see you and then you can ask him to construct the dam & see that your people are cared for after you are gone. He will listen to you because he is a good man and will come to you because you are sick and cannot come to him. I know he will do what you will say to him. I will send your letter to Gen. Pratt, as he is a good friend of ours, he will speak for us and do what he can for the McDowell Indians, also will Congressman Graham whom you know at Washington. I want you to know Mr. Latimer and I have been busy to get the land & water rights for you McDowell Indians. And I pretty sure you will get it. Your letter will do great deal to help us.

I hope you will not die, keep up good heart and take care of yourself. At any rate that you will see the Com. of Indian Affairs, Mr. Cato Sells when he comes to Phoenix. Have one of your men as Chas. Dickens & George to go to him and ask him at your home. How glad he will be to do that. Look to God and pray to Him & he will bring good health to you. I pray that you may live & enjoy life with us.

Your true & great friend,
Carlos Montezuma[84]

Dear Cousin

I am sorry to tell you about my sister Grace. She is now died last night 6:30 and we very sorry to her and I am feel crying & still I am crying yet while I am writing this letter to and pretty near my mother kill her self, on account Grace. All my brothers was very sorry for Grace died and we buy coffin to Mesa and we put her in. Bury her today. This coffin we buy cash $40 and we paid for it because we all very anxious to Grace. Too[sic] her childrens put in school to Phoenix day before yesterday. Dear Cousin I am sorry to tell you another death. Our Chief Yuma Frank died last week to [sic] on 18th at night 7:30. We sorry to [sic]. Also we buy coffin to put in. Cash $20. Now George Dickens is a chief of McDowell Reservation. I think we alright alright [sic]. Dear Cousin George Dickens send you too [sic] baskets for Joseph W. Latimer. I wish you hand to him. We all well except my sister died & the Chief. We sorry to them.

From your Cousin
Chas Dickens[85]

It was now 1915, no allotments had been made and no dam was under construction. Commissioner Cato Sells finally visited Fort McDowell. He invited Montezuma to join him, but Montezuma couldn't afford the trip, and Sells refused to provide his expenses.[86] Beginning in 1914, on multiple occasions, Montezuma told his cousin Charles Dickens: "I feel very sorry to say that I will not be able to come out to Arizona this year. Money is so hard to get and I must stick to my work."[87] However, Montezuma agreed to meet with Sells in Washington after his investigation. The word from Fort McDowell in letters to Montezuma was that the commissioner told the Indians they would have to move to the Salt River Reservation.

> Commissioner Cato Sells just arrive here McDowell this morning. But Commissioner say first place he wants us to move to Salt River, and get land down there and live down there. But we all McDowell Indians answering back to him and we all say we don't wanted to move to another place and all the Indians say rather stay here. And Commissioner always say we all have to move Salt River. ...and also Commissioner say he cannot do anything for dam and he say cost to [*sic*] much money to built dam. And he say there is about only 3000 acres here. He say if 5000 acres lands here he think it be alright for dam built....[88]

> ...As I told you before and Commissioner say to [*sic*] much money cost to build a dam by the ingneer [*sic*] said and I answer back to him if you cannot do anything for me a dam & I said let that go and I said it is alright for to stay here and build me the brush dam. ...I said about you that you are my cousin and he said he know you very well and he said when he return to east he will see you and told you about what I said to him. And Commissioner say he didn't mean he want me to move but he don't know him self and he said he will see the matter when he return to Washington. ...Cousin we all Mohave Apache say to Mr Sells that we don't want to move to Salt River and also we don't want sign any paper until we hear from you.[89]

By now Commissioner Sells was achieving a new reputation in Montezuma's mind, readily fueled by Richard Pratt: "Confidentially, between you and I, the commissioner of Indian Affairs has about the worst case big head that I have ever known in public life. It is so bad that leaders in his own party note and condemn. There is more energy in the Bureau, but it is all directed Bureau-wards; absolutely none of it towards lifting the Indians into citizenship and independence."[90]

*Charles, Richard, and Sam Dickens*

My Cousins,

I have to smile to think you did just the right thing with Mr. Sells, but he did not do the right thing with you. It shows that some people, maybe Mr. Coe, maybe Mr. Valentine, maybe Mr. Meritt, and maybe Phoenix people, talked to Mr. Sells before coming to McDowell and he had already made up his mind what to do. He seemed that he went to you Indians, to persuade you to move to Salt River. He thought he could do it because he is a big man and to please maybe those people I have mentioned. But you were as smart as he was. The Commissioner thought that you could all move to Salt River when he said that he cannot build a dam for you at McDowell. He did not expect George's answer, "It is all right, if you cannot build a dam for us Indians, we will stay here on McDowell and use brush dam as we have been doing in the past rather than to move to Salt River." I noticed he backed a little bit and gave his reason (and it is a weak excuse of a reason) that it would cost too much. That makes me mad. I would like to show him the Roosevelt Dam the Dick Copper mines and the dam at San Carlos. That will be worth millions for the white people. …Your Indians rights of the Verde River holds good just as long as you remain at McDowell. That is worth more than 5 acres of irrigation land in Salt River. That old promise that if you move to Salt River the Government will permit you Indians to use McDowell as a pasture. Any one that does not understand the wording, it sounds nice, but Mr. Latimer & I found out it was to fool you Indians. It does not say, that you can *own McDowell* but that the *Government will permit* you Indians to *use McDowell* as pasture for your cattle, etc. Now you see that McDowell would not be yours any longer after you move to Salt River and that the Government can take away McDowell as your pasture and you could have nothing to say. Do not be fooled. You stay on McDowell, use your brush dam and work the best you know how and Mr. Latimer and I will do all we can to guide you right.[91]

The Fort McDowell Yavapai made it clear to Commissioner Cato Sells that decisions had to flow through Montezuma. That being the case, Sells did not return directly to Washington, but stopped first in Chicago to meet with Montezuma. Montezuma described the meeting in a letter to Richard Pratt:

Last Friday morning I had the pleasure of having a talk with the Hon. Commissioner at Congress Hotel in this city. Mr. Latimer was with me at the time because he could present matters much better than I could. We greeted each other with smiles and good fellowship. The Commissioner related his visit at McDowell. He was much interested in them and wants to help them. He said: "Those Indians treated me very nicely. After looking over the field for a dam we had a meeting. They shake hands with me and expressed themselves that they were glad to have the Commissioner come and see them. They wanted a dam. I explained to them that it would not pay to have a dam only to irrigate 1300 acres. I saw that there was an atmosphere of disappointment. And then I told them what I thought the best thing to do. You can have McDowell as your pasture land and I will give each Indian 5 acres of irrigation land down on Salt River reservation and have a fence built around the McDowell and will do all I can in seeing them started down at Salt River reservation OK."

The McDowell Indians were not the only ones who were disappointed. The commissioner was made to understand by Chief George Dickens that if the Government will not construct a dam for them, they will remain at McDowell and use brush dam rather than to move to Salt River Reservation and accept the inducements of the Commissioner. And also the Chief made the Hon. Commissioner to understand that they will not desire anything until Dr. Montezuma was consulted first. The Commissioner told them that he will talk with me when he gets back East.

After hearing the Commissioner we spoke of the dam with questions that he answered vaguely. We pinned him on McDowell as pasture land for Chief Dickens Indians whether if they moved down to Salt River reservation, will the pasture be their property.

The Com. said, "Why certainly."

Mr. Latimer praised the Commissioner and said that that offer was more than ever been given to the McDowell Indians.

I spoke up and I said, "if that is your offer to the McDowell Indians, that they hold the pasture land as their own and own 5 acres each on Salt River reservation and use the Roosevelt water, I know I can persuade those Indians to move to Salt River reservation."

We dropped that matter and were speaking of the Maricopa and Pima Indians who occupy lands adjacent to the McDowell Indians if they move to Salt River. Right there the Commissioner spoke up, "Will it not be nice for the Pima & Maricopa Indians have their pasture in with the McDowell Indians?"

"No," I said quickly, "before the McDowell Indians share the pasture with those other Indians, they would stay at McDowell and not move down to Salt River reservation."

That suggestion spoiled our harmony that he first offered. Mr Latimer and I explained that would not work. We separated with the best of feeling knowing it was a conference rather than committing anything definitely.

For your confidential information, we saw through him. Some interested party want to take away those Indians' water rights of the Verde River. That is why a dam will not be built on Verde River and that is why the McDowell Indians are wanted to move to Salt River reservation.[92]

1915 saw the beginning of another problem. The City of Phoenix obtained permission from the commissioner of Indian affairs to build a water pipeline across the Fort McDowell Reservation, diverting water from the Verde River to the city. There was neither permission from the Yavapai nor compensation given. Construction began in 1920, and in 1922, the Yavapai were paid for the water and land lost, another accomplishment spearheaded by Montezuma and Latimer.[93]

The Fort McDowell controversy contained within it the very first noticeable disagreement between Pratt and Montezuma. Pratt clearly placed public welfare, the need for water by the general population, over the Yavapai rights to their own land. "There are two sides to [the] Fort McDowell case. Private ownership must bow before public need and the Apaches lose cast by not utilizing or lamely utilizing especially in the presence of frontier people."[94] "...neither McDowell or Salt River cut any very great figure in their future welfare as compared with the development of their intelligence and ability to take care of themselves or their own property individually. ...if they themselves are not stirred and anxious and persistent to reach that competency, they are not entitled to what they have got and they belong to that class which I so often spoke of at Carlisle, the man who had one talent and went and buried it."[95] Pratt's opinion regarding the Yavapai and simultaneously his advice to Montezuma that he should be tolerant of Arthur Parker and the Society of American Indians (Chapter 13), to give them time and a chance, struck a nerve in Montezuma.

Montezuma addressed Pratt in a fashion that lays to rest any thought that Montezuma was a sycophant: "General, I am surprised that you have crawfished and laid down your staunch and firm ideas. It does not sound like General Pratt but more like the Indian Bureau. Wait until the Indians are educated, wait until the Indians can take care of their property, wait until the Indian can be strong enough to withstand the rascals, wait, wait,

wait. Do not give freedom to the Indians. They are not prepared. Wait! General, I know that sound too well. That is the suction out of Parker, Coolidge, Indian Bureau, Indian Rights Association, scientists, intellects and churches. General have you forgotten the Indians and have gone on the other side? I never heard that from you at Carlisle speeches to your Indian pupils. General Pratt, I am again surprised that you entertain Parker's position. Remember General, you are not to bow to Parker but he is to kneel at your feet on Indian matters. I fear you are being used by those who are unworthy of your support. Coming around to you now is no sign of their sincerity, they should have come to you in the beginning. It is well to gain their confidence but you cannot afford to change your position on the stand you have taken these many years for the best interest of the Indian race."[96] Pratt totally and noticeably ignored this strong admonition by Montezuma.

Pratt believed the Yavapai would retain rights to the Verde River water, but Montezuma was convinced that if the Fort McDowell Indians accepted allotment on the Salt River Reservation, they would forfeit their rights to Verde River water. Montezuma was undoubtedly right because as he repeatedly pointed out, the Bureau of Indian Affairs persistently neglected to put in writing a guarantee of Verde River water for the Yavapai.[97] Montezuma was quite willing for the McDowell Indians to accept land on the Salt River Reservation, but only if they were first allotted Fort McDowell land with its water rights.

RESOLUTION OF THE FORT McDOWELL SITUATION was stalled by World War I. "Mr. Latimer and I will try to do something but war takes up the attention of the country that it is hard to pass anything through Congress."[98] However, Commissioner Cato Sells must also have had difficulty in pushing forward a definitive solution because he was being buffeted by two points of view. There was, of course, the forceful argument being made by Montezuma and Latimer, but the reports from the field were not in agreement. Sells was a bureaucrat, and within a bureaucracy administrators cannot dismiss the conclusions of the workers within the system. Sells received many letters from Superintendent Coe, his successor, Superintendent C. T. Coggeshall, the allotting agent on the Pima reservation, John Baum, and the third superintendent at Salt River and Fort McDowell during this time, Byron Sharp.[99] Listen to some of the adjectives and phrases applied to Montezuma: "a reputation as an agitator and fee gather," "influencing them in a manner prejudicial to their best interests," "will seriously interfere with law and order," "Indian malcontents—the 'Montezuma crowd,'" "one of Montezuma's followers and a mischief maker," "a source of constant trouble," "his henchmen, the Burns and the Dickens families," "against your Administration and the carrying out of your policies by your subordinate officers," and finally, "I believe that in dealing with the malcontent followers of this agitator, Dr. Carlos Montezuma, it will be necessary in enforcing the rules and regulations to sooner or later send one or more of these Indians to Sacaton under a jail sentence."

The field matron at Fort McDowell wrote despairingly to Sells: "Dr Montezuma while on a visit to the McDowell Reservation last year did not hesitate to prescribe axel [*sic*] grease and menthol, for all ailments, for his McDowell brothers and sisters. …In conclusion I beg to state there is hope for betterment, if we can in some way remove the bone of contention, to some other place, where he formerly lived for the past twenty years, the subject in question is Montezuma's Secretary Mike Burns. And we sincerely believe we could get these Indians to move to the Salt River project within the next year."[100] These reports must have dissuaded Cato Sells from any sense of cooperation with Montezuma. Furthermore, Montezuma was repeatedly castigating Sells in his monthly newsletter, *Wassaja* (Chapter 14).

Superintendent Byron Sharp was a committed opponent of Montezuma. Sharp went out of his way to make life difficult for Montezuma, even interfering with one of Montezuma's hunting trips.

> …I had somewhat exciting time in Arizona. On Oct 11th [1917] several of us arrived from the mountains. The next morning I was confronted by a game warden who took me to Phoenix to see the Chief Warden. We did not find him. The next day we called at his office but he was away and would not return for a week. I was not arrested but some people thought I ought to procure license to hunt, $20. I did not see it that way because I did not do any hunting but went with those who did the hunting. I know a brother lawyer Mr. Hayes of Phoenix. I explained the whole matter to him and as he accompanied me once into the mountains and knew I did not carry anything more than a stick, he told me to go where I pleased and he would attend to the matter.
>
> Before I left Chicago I wrote to the Indians to be sure to get their license to hunt and when I arrived at McDowell I wrote to Mr Sharp Supt at Salt River Agency, and invited him to go with us on a hunt and suggested about the Indians and asked for a leave of absence for them. He replied that he could not and that the Indians could go with me. When Mr. Hayes questioned the game warden, he said that there were complaints against Montezuma of bringing people out there and hunting without license and that he had in his pocket a letter written by Dr. Montezuma to Supt Sharp. That was enough to show some one in the Indian Service wanted to trap me and belittle me before the Indians. One Indian told me that Supt Sharp said "Dr. Montezuma is afraid to come out to Arizona. He would be put in jail." He was nearly right but he did not belittle me at all.
>
> …The conclusion is *the Indians will not move to Salt River*. They want to be allotted on the McDowell and they will show the world what they can do. It is not the Indians that are keeping back the progress on McDowell, it is the Indian Office and towns around McDowell.
>
> …George Dickens had nothing when he went on McDowell. Now he has cattle, turkeys and a small store. Against all odds he has these. Other Indians on the reservation have still more and are advancing.
>
> I smile when the Indian Department offers five acres on Salt River and the use of McDowell for pasture. Such offer is a blind, *just to get those Indians to move*. Show me otherwise.[101]

Letters from Montezuma to Cato Sells went unanswered. Senator Harry Lane of Oregon had Montezuma's famous speech, "Let My People Go," that was presented at the 1915 annual conference of the Society of American Indians (Chapter 13) published in the May 12, 1916, *Congressional Record*. Senator Lane insisted that the speech be read, but after five minutes, he interrupted the reading and said, "I ask that the rest of the document be printed in the Record. No one is paying any attention to it. You might just as well go out on the front porch and whistle against the east wind as to read that in here, so far as its receiving any attention is concerned, so I ask that the further reading of it be dispensed with."[102]

Montezuma was told that this Congressional recognition, even though no one wanted to listen to the speech, prompted some unsavory comments from Commissioner Sells. "I am informed that immediately after 'Let My People Go' appeared in the 'Congressional Record' (May 12, 1916), that you called up Senator Jones of Washington and informed him that I had a scheme whereby I expected to make great profits at the expense of the Indians, which scheme was defeated by the Indian Department; and that for this reason I am now fighting the Indian Bureau. Mr. Commissioner, if you are sure and know the matter to be a fact that I did have such a selfish scheme as you stated to Senator Jones of Washington, it is your duty as Commissioner of Indian Affairs to make your remarks black and white on paper and furnish me with a copy of the same. May I ask you to do this for Senator Jones and myself."[103] Montezuma followed this letter with many reminders over the next six months to the commissioner and to his assistants. The only response he received was a promise from Assistant Commissioner E. B. Meritt to call the original letter to the commissioner's attention.

From 1916 to 1920, the Yavapai were constantly pressured to move to the Salt River Reservation, and Montezuma repeatedly counseled them to not give up their land. They held fast. As part of the war effort, the Indian Bureau tried to increase beef production, and as with the Sioux (Chapter 2), the plan was to use the Fort McDowell reservation land for cattle, a plan made without consulting the Yavapai. Montezuma was instrumental in strengthening the Yavapai resolve to not accept this plan and to present the Yavapai position at the Bureau of Indian Affairs. A letter crafted by Montezuma refusing the cattle was signed by thirty-three Yavapai men and forwarded to the Bureau of Indian Affairs by Montezuma.[104] "This cattle business is nothing but a mortgage on the Indians and it will do them no good in the long run. It looks very good but they are not in a position to pay for the 250 head of cattle."[105] Nevertheless, the Indian Bureau placed 250 cattle on the reservation (they were sold by the Bureau at a low price in 1921).[106] Over and over again, Montezuma passed on to the Indian Bureau letters from Fort McDowell, along with his restatement of the arguments. By making this issue a matter of public record, Montezuma prevented unilateral Indian Bureau activation of its plan to move the Fort McDowell Yavapai.

The situation simmered on and on, but Montezuma never wavered. In 1918, Latimer "secured a letter from Sec. Lane with approval of the Commissioner to allot McDowell for pasture land and give the acres of irrigation land to each Indian at Salt River. But the Indians will not accept it, because to have McDowell as pasture land means forfeit of the rights of the Verde River."[107]

In the spring of 1920, an executive order from President Wilson authorized the five-acre Salt River Reservation allotments and the establishment of the Fort McDowell reservation as grazing land. Commissioner Sells had concluded that there was not enough irrigable land at Fort McDowell and that it was too expensive to build a dam. Arrangements were made, without informing the Yavapai, Montezuma, or Latimer, to transfer the water rights of the Fort McDowell Indians to land at Salt River.[108] Only Montezuma's persistent involvement prevented this from happening.

That fall, in 1920, Montezuma and his wife vacationed in Arizona on the way to a speaking engagement at an Indian conference in California. It proved to be a difficult trip.

> I visited McDowell. It looks very unfavorable for the Indians. Water pipe line is in preparation to be laid through the reservation without the consent of the Indians. The Indian Department has specialized McDowell as pasture land for the Indians. This year

irrigation has been neglected. A herder is in charge and not a farmer. Fence wires are torn down and planting is not protected. Indians are suppressed in cutting wood, and they get low pay per cord. I discovered a large plant on the reservation for crush stones for cement pipe through McDowell without consulting the Indians. About a mile below the reservation line on Pima reservation the Water Users Association is sounding for a dam site. They tell me that they touch bottom rock at 40 feet. A new automobile road is being constructed along the side of the river and will pass through the reservation.

The Indians do not know how many cattle there are on reservation. They do not know how much they are indebted to the government nor do they know how much money has been received in sale of some of their cattle. The Indians complain of medical aid and the way things are carried on without their consent or knowledge.

A day school is in preparation and I was told that arrangement was made to allot the Indians by Oct 1st, but the allotting agent did not appear while I was there.

If the Indians are allotted, it will be for pasture and not with the rights of the Verde River. The Indians will protest if that will be the case. But what is the use of the Indians protesting? They have no rights to say anything. It is an awful thing to think of, but it is the truth.

Seven of us were in the mountains where we were surprised by a game warden and an Indian police. They informed us that Supt Sharp had ordered us to return. We obeyed. It meant forty miles of hard ride. At McDowell just before dusk an automobile took us to Salt River Agency by the officers. My wife and I were wanted only but I took Nellie Davis as interpreter and Chief Geo. Dickens with me. We arrived at the Agency way after dark without supper. After waiting outside awhile, Mr Sharp (Supt) took us to his office and seated us.

He began by saying, "Dr. Montezuma, you may not [be] aware that you are doing a great harm to the McDowell Indians. While you are here and after you leave the Indians maintain many wrong things. You are an undesirable person to these Indians. Legally McDowell does not belong to the Indians. You agitate these Indians contrary to the Indian Bureau. You have brought parties to violate state laws and that has given us a great deal of trouble."

Well, you can believe it was my turn to say something to him. For good two hours, I landed into him: "Mr. Sharp, since you are so candid with me, now I am going to speak candid with you."

I spoke of my blood relation to these Indians and the interest I have taken in all Indians before he was born. I went on with the spirit to guide my words. "I do not believe you that I am an undesirable man for these Indians. But I will leave that matter with Chief George Dickens. He being a Chief, he ought to know."

So I asked Nellie Davis to ask George Dickens what Mr. Sharp said. Mr. George Dickens replied that he being one of us, he has always help us and he never did any wrong but always good things for us.

I went on and contradicted everything he said and gave him a good lecture what to do to help the McDowell Indians & answered his questions where in he has failed to help the Indians. I pointed out a dozen of them and closed that he had more interest in the Phoenix people than for the Indians on McDowell. He asked me to go back providing that I will not say anything about the Indian Bureau or stay out of the reservation. I replied quickly, "I stay out of the reservation for no man can stop me from doing what is right & just."

I said, "It was a shame to bring us so far without any cause and without a bite to eat. Now take us back to the camp." & so he did. We agreed to disagree.

But here is another. Having four days to spare, I concluded to go to San Carlos. At Mesa, I made arrangement with the Pimas that I would listen to them on the evening of my return from San Carlos. I visited San Carlos and was treated nicely. On Thursday evening I returned to Mesa where the Pimas were waiting to take me to the Church (Mormon). We arrived at the dim lighted church. My wife & I walked in with our luggage.

There were no Indians in the church but were squatted outside by the [?]. A rough looking man approached me and asked what I wanted. I said, "that I was Dr. Montezuma and I understand there was to be a Pima meeting in this church."

He replied, "that by order of the Bishop (Mormon) if Dr. Montezuma is to speak, he cannot have this church."

"Who are you?" I asked.

"Mr Sorenson," He replied.

Having heard of him before I knew he was the Indian farmer. He lost self control and mentioned something about my paper *Wassaja*. I asked for the Bishop's name and where he lived. The Bishop lived at Scottsdale near the Agency. That gave me a clue that Mr. Sharp had words with the Bishop.

My wife and I walked out & the Indians took us to an Indian house, some distance from the church. It was a disagreeable night. About 25 of us were proceeding with our meeting nicely when I was called out of the house. I went out. Who did I face but Sorenson and Indian policeman. He said, "by order of Mr. Sharp, you and your wife go with me."

I said, alright and I went into the house & informed the Indians not to make any trouble. We have done nothing wrong but the Agent must be obeyed. My wife in excitement was left [with] the Indians and was carried in automobile to Mesa where we procured a bed for the night. My wife never experienced such thing in her life, she was greatly agitated.

I took things calmly for I know I did not do anything wrong. Next day we missed our train & had to lay over until next day. During the day at Mesa, I saw the Pimas and had a meeting that we were debarred from night before.

This shows one man's power on a reservation without a redress.[109]

Several months later, in February 1921, Montezuma learned from his Fort McDowell relatives that an allotting agent had visited the reservation to divide up the land as grazing land and to direct the Indians to their five-acre allotments on the Salt River Reservation. The Indian Bureau had taken advantage of the change in administration to secure an executive order from outgoing President Wilson to proceed with the plan it had been attempting to accomplish for over five years.[110] Montezuma requested Thomas Sloan, a lawyer living in Washington and now president of the Society of American Indians (Chapter 13), to secure an explanation from the Indian Bureau. The explanation, in a long letter from Assistant Commissioner Meritt to Sloan (with a copy to Montezuma), made it clear that the Bureau of Indian Affairs did not intend to abide by the decision made by Secretary of the Interior Walter Fisher in 1911 and that Montezuma was viewed as an opponent.

> Unfortunately, for some time past influences have been at work among these Indians, greatly to their detriment, advising them not to accept allotments of irrigable land at Salt River, which to my mind presents an opportunity of obtaining the highest possible benefit from their water rights. The McDowell Indians have been repeatedly advised where their best interests lay, but have been met with this counter-influence which has misled them into the belief that the Government has some ulterior motive in allotting them at Salt River.
>
> The letter referred to by you from former Secretary Fisher, under date of June 21, 1911, did contemplate the irrigation of a part of the lands at McDowell and the allotment of such lands to these Indians, but subsequently a more thorough investigation from an engineering standpoint was made of the situation which disclosed that the turbulent nature of the Verde River, being subject to violent and unexpected floods, is such that a diversion dam across this stream would cost upwards of $70,000.00, under the prices of labor and

material then prevailing. Adding to this the cost of the necessary canals and distributing system, and dividing the resultant cost by the limited number of acres susceptible of irrigation, made the cost of the project prohibitive.

…Accordingly, after a thorough consideration of the entire situation, it was concluded that the interests of these Indians could best be protected by prorating the entire area of the McDowell Reservation among the members of this band as "grazing lands" and in addition thereto allotting to each Indian five acres of irrigable land on the Salt River Reservation, Arizona, where a more permanent delivery of water can be assured, and where there is no danger of loss to the Indians of their irrigable land by erosion.

Arrangements have since been made for a transfer of the water rights of the McDowell Indians to the lands to be given them at Salt River, and instructions have recently been issued to an allotting agent to prorate and allot the entire Camp McDowell Reservation as grazing lands to the members of this tribe. There is no objection of course, to the McDowell Indians' diverting such water as may be available from the Verde River and utilizing such water for irrigation purposes on their grazing allotments on the McDowell Reservation, the only limitation being that those Indians who so use water at McDowell cannot also receive water for their irrigable lands at Salt River.[111]

MONTEZUMA DECIDED to go to the top. He wrote directly to the new president, Warren G. Harding. Just before the election in the previous fall, Montezuma was a member of a delegation of Indians that traveled to Marion, Ohio, to visit with Harding in his home. The group was entertained "like kings and queens;" Montezuma renewed an acquaintance with Harding's personal physician, and he obviously hoped that Harding would remember this visit.[112]

As a great friend of the Indians, I am going to ask a great favor of you. This may be a small matter to you, but it is everything to those Indians whose land was given to them for service rendered to the United States Government and the fulfillment of promises made to General Crook.

It is in behalf of the Mohave-Apaches of the Fort McDowell Indian reservation, Arizona. I am one of them. These Indians wish to be allotted on McDowell reservation pro rata as their home, with the rights of the Verde river water to irrigate, and that they will not accept five acres of irrigation land on the Salt River reservation. It is well to inform you that these same Indians had hearings, in 1911, before the Investigating Committee of the Expenditures in the Interior Department, very much on the same contention; and the result of the hearing was that these Indians shall have the McDowell reservation as their home, and that no one will cause them to move without their free will and accord; and that a small diversion dam would be considered and other help be extended to them. But since that time, weak averse opinions of the succeeding administration frustrated the order given by ex-Secretary Fisher in favor of the McDowell Indians.

The order of Secretary Fisher was not carried out, and the Indians have been hounded to move to Salt River reservation. The Indian Bureau has tried in every way to smoke out the Indians off the McDowell reservation, and has done everything to discourage these

Indians in the improvement of their lands. The Garden spot of Arizona was left unkept. Year in and year out, the Indians were told McDowell was not their land; McDowell was not good, and that they should move down to Salt River reservation. The agents, farmers and employees of the Indian office have persistently harped to these Indians to move to Salt River Reservation.

Now, it has taken on a serious aspect against the rights of the Indians on the McDowell reservation. It has taken on a shade, as though, against their will, they are going to be forced to move down to the Salt River reservation, to the effect and as a last resort, last May or June, the Indian Bureau induced President Wilson to give his authority to allot the McDowell Indians on the Fort McDowell reservation (pro rata) for grazing land only, and five acres of irrigation land on the Salt River reservation, transferring the water rights of the Verde river, which runs through the reservation, to that of the Roosevelt dam on the Salt River reservation.

This appears to be a generous offer to the Indians on the Fort McDowell reservation, on the part of the Indian Bureau; but to anyone who is acquainted with the whole situation, it is a dark plot, a decoy, and a bait to get the Indians off the McDowell Indian reservation. It is simply another case where someone wants the Indians' land, and the Indians must move. This is an intrigue, or insidious undercurrent of outside interests that have induced the Indian office to move the Mohave-Apaches off the McDowell reservation to the Salt River reservation, and not for the best interests of the Indians, as the Indian Bureau claims.

To be on the square, the order for the allotment of the Ft. McDowell Indians on the Ft. McDowell reservation should not be done without a careful consideration of all phases of the matter; nor without giving the persons directly affected an opportunity to be heard.

I therefore make this request of you, that since it was done without a chance for the Indians to be heard, that you revoke the order for the allotment of the Mohave-Apaches of Ft. McDowell, Arizona, until their side be heard, and a thorough investigation be made to ascertain the combined relation of the Indian Office and outside interests to force these Indians off the McDowell reservation.[113]

President Harding referred the letter to the new secretary of the interior, Albert B. Fall. Fall, previously senator from New Mexico, had a hidden agenda, the exploitation of minerals and oil on public land. In 1921 and 1922, Fall functioned as his own commissioner of Indian affairs.[114] He attempted to acquire land from the Pueblo Indians of New Mexico; he tried to establish a national park on Apache reservation land that bordered his own ranch. When oil was discovered on Navajo land in 1922 in western New Mexico, Fall issued his famous ruling that reservations created by presidential executive order (as was Fort McDowell) were open to oil leasing. Fall further attempted to open tribal funds and assets, including timber, coal, and minerals. Teapot Dome is a rock near Casper, Wyoming, that sits on top of oil-bearing land. The oil in public land such as Teapot Dome was kept in reserve for the navy by leasing the land to private companies. Secretary Fall attempted to open these reserves to private exploitation, the Teapot Dome scandal. Senate hearings revealed that Fall had received gifts and "loans" totalling around $400,000.[115] Fall resigned as secretary of the interior in 1923 and in 1929 was fined and sentenced to one year in prison for bribery. The Indian Oil Leasing Act in 1927 ensured that henceforth treaty and executive order reservations would be considered equal. This act prevented executive changes in reservation boundaries and extended mineral and oil development according to the same regulations affecting treaty reservations. This act firmly established Yavapai tribal ownership of the Fort McDowell reservation land.

At this critical point, early 1921, in this long controversy, Montezuma received renewed support from the Fort McDowell Yavapai Indians. A formal notice of reappointment as legal representative with full power to act on behalf of the tribe was signed by thirty-two Fort McDowell men and women.[116] But at the same time, Montezuma was discouraged by the response from Secretary Fall.

> I note your statement to the effect that the McDowell Indians do not wish to be allotted lands on the Camp McDowell Reservation unless they can receive water to irrigate said lands and that they will not accept irrigable allotments of five acres on the Salt River Reservation. I also note your suggestion that it is the intention of this Department to remove the McDowell Indians to the Salt River Reservation and that there is some ulterior motive behind the whole scheme of allotment.
>
> I have examined the facts in the case and I find that on May 25, 1920, the President authorized allotments to the camp McDowell Indians on the basis of a prorata distribution of their entire reservation, and in addition an allotment of five acres of irrigable land on the Salt River Reservation where a suitable area had been reserved for that purpose. Subsequently appropriate instructions were issued to the allotting agent who is now engaged in the work of allotment under the authority given by the President and instructions approved by this department. I do not find that any thought has been given by this Department to the proposition of removing the Camp McDowell Indians to the Salt River Reservation, nor have any instructions been issued to that effect. Moreover, I may say that no such action is being considered.
>
> The facts leading up to the plan of allotment may be summed up briefly as follows:
>
> In 1912 during former Secretary Fisher's regime, it was contemplated to irrigate a part of the Camp McDowell lands and to allot such lands to the Indians together with a reasonable amount of grazing lands. Subsequently a more thorough investigation from an engineering standpoint was made of the situation, which disclosed that the turbulent nature of the Verde River being subject to violent and unexpected floods, is such as to make the cost of the project prohibitive. Naturally these conditions indicated the advisability of pursuing some other course, and it was concluded that the interests of the Indians could best be protected by prorating the entire area of the Camp McDowell Reservation among the Indians entitled as "grazing lands" and in addition thereto allotting to each Indian five acres of irrigable land on the Salt River Reservation, with no danger of loss to the Indians by erosion. By this arrangement it will be seen that in addition to receiving a prorata division of their own reservation, the members of this band will also be given allotments of five acres each of irrigable land on the Salt River Reservation, which may be considered in the nature of a gratuity.
>
> From the examination I have made of the facts in the case, and after giving careful consideration to the several statements made by you, I am satisfied that the plan adopted by this department with respect to the allotment of the Camp McDowell Indians is in the best interests of those Indians and the best possible course that could be taken in their behalf in the circumstances. For these reasons I do not deem it advisable to take any action with a view to discontinuing the work of allotment, nor do I believe that any good purpose can be served by a series of hearings with the Indians for the purpose of obtaining their individual views. I will, however, consider it a kindness to the Indians if you will use such influence as you may have with them to persuade them to accept the allotments now being made to them, and at the same time assure them that this Department has no intention of removing them from the Camp McDowell Reservation or of taking any action adverse to their best interests.[117]

Montezuma responded with a short letter to Secretary Fall requesting a "hearing,"[118] but he again wrote at length directly to President Harding.

> I wish to thank you for transferring my letter to Secretary Fall. I received a reply from the same dated April 30, 1921, unfavorable in every way. He clinches Ex-Commissioner Cato Sells' views and ignores Ex-Secretary Fisher's claims as to be "a mistake" after a careful congressional hearing.
>
> I wish to refute the Engineer's report by ex-Commissioner Cato Sells. I saw personally the same engineer at San Carlos, Arizona. He stated to me that he did not expect the commissioner would publish his off-handed statement without actual testing for want of time. He was there only a few hours.
>
> I have known the Verde River for fifty years at McDowell agency, and know that "the turbulent nature of the Verde River" is absurd and it has no foundation. "The interest of the Indians is best protected by allotting them as grazing land" is another false and deceptive statement. If I am entitled to the rights of the Verde River for irrigation, the land for grazing my cattle, and where I can make my home, surrounded with the harvest of nature, and where no one can starve me out, would you, Mr. President, be allowed to be trapped to give up the Verde River water rights and go where I know not how long I can use the water of the Roosevelt Dam without paying for it. In a few years I would be crying for "water," as the Pimas are crying today.
>
> Mr. President, to be hounded in your rights, and behold the interwoven schemes to move these Mohave Apache Indians away from their homes, contrary to their wish, it makes one grow mad. I have seen these Indians deprived and discouraged in everything so that they may see the hopelessness of staying on the McDowell Reservation.
>
> Being their appointed representative, the Indian Bureau has kept everything from me relative to McDowell matters. I was out there last fall with my wife, and I was mistreated by Supt. Sharp. I was innocent of the cause, but now my eyes are opened. Supt. Sharp has been transferred.
>
> Mr President, I realize there are strong interested forces upholding and eagerly seeking the removal of the Mohave Apaches to Salt River Reservation. This chronic cold blooded scheme has been carried to the limit. The Indians are helpless; they have no voice in anything that belongs to them. The Indians are men, but they are treated like dogs. The Mohave Apache Indians were not consulted. They are kept ignorant and taken advantage of. They are cowed, even though they are brave men, and dare not say a word, and if they did, it would not carry any weight.
>
> Mr. President, it is not that these Indians do not want to be allotted and become self supporting citizens. They are human; they understand what is right and wrong; they understand human nature. They can see and feel that there is something wrong to persistently insist on their moving to Salt River Reservation when they do not want to.
>
> They ask to be allotted on McDowell as it now stands, with all the rights as they exist (pro rata). There are two thousand (2,000) acres of irrigable land on McDowell, immense timber, springs, and dryless Verde River, plenty of pasture land for their cattle and native foods. They do not want the rights of the Verde River "continual flow" transferred to the Roosevelt Dam water (class C). They do not want five acres of irrigable land on Salt River reservation that would legally deprive them of cultivating and using the Verde River for irrigation. What is the use of land in Arizona without water? The Indian Bureau says that it is "to the best interests of these Indians." It sounds good, but any one, who has a heart and unselfish interest in the welfare of the Mohave Apaches, and knows the strings being pulled to get the McDowell Indians to move to Salt River reservation, they are only words and no more.

Mr. President, this needs your personal interest and attention. On what is just and right, other men may jeer and say "there is nothing in it," but as President of the United States, right and justice must prevail and God his guide.

In behalf of your friends, the Mohave Apache Indians, I ask you to listen to me, with my attorney, Mr. Joseph W. Latimer, who acted as attorney for the McDowell Indians on the hearing before the Committee on expenditures in the Interior department of the House in 1911, and Mr. Gilbert Davis, a representative from the Mohave Apache Indians of McDowell, Arizona.[119]

This second letter to President Harding has a note handwritten at the top by someone in the president's office saying "Personal Attention, Comm. Burke."[120] However, the response was disappointing. Once again, Montezuma was informed that further discussion of the matter was not necessary.[121] Nellie Davis had assumed the role of Fort McDowell's English interpreter for Montezuma. She informed him that her husband, Gilbert Davis, was going to Washington, that none of the Yavapai had signed papers of any kind, and that Montezuma was "safe to go ahead with your big task."[122] Montezuma decided to go to Washington to seek an audience with the president, if possible, and especially with Secretary Fall and the new commissioner of Indian affairs, Charles H. Burke.

Charles H. Burke moved into the Dakota Territory at age twenty-one.[123] After serving as a Republican in the South Dakota House of Representatives, he was elected for three terms to the House of Representatives beginning in 1898, where he served on the House Committee on Indian Affairs. He was the author of the Burke Act of 1906 that withheld citizenship and maintained federal protection until the trust period of allotted land expired, but introduced the issue of "competency," allowing earlier termination (removal of allotted land from federal trust protection) by the secretary of the interior (in effect, reservation superintendents) for those deemed competent to manage their own property. This was something that Cato Sells vigorously pursued.[124] The Burke Act enabled an acceleration of the loss of Indian land in the years just before and during World War I.[125]

Burke was defeated in 1906, re-elected in 1908 and served until 1915 when he failed in his bid to win a seat in the Senate. He returned to Pierre, South Dakota, and his real estate business, until Harding appointed him commissioner of Indian affairs on May 7, 1921.

Upon taking office, Burke immediately revoked Cato Sell's policy of actively allotting land to "competent" Indians, and the loss of land was slowed. Burke attacked the previous administration for abusing the competency clause of his 1906 act. Nevertheless, Burke was as dedicated to assimilation as his predecessor. Burke regarded Indian religion as superstitious and backwards, and firmly directed reservation superintendents to limit ceremonies and dances. In 1923, Burke, in another example of the Indian Bureau's absolute rule, forbade any individual under the age of fifty to attend Indian dances!

Joseph W. Latimer, Montezuma's attorney, published a pamphlet in 1921, a collection of his correspondence with Bureau of Indian Affairs officials in the Yavapai dispute, entitled *The Rape of McDowell Reservation, Arizona, by the Indian Bureau.*[126] The legalese and stilted language of the letters make the pamphlet difficult to read, but the anger and frustration are easily discerned. The charges articulated at length by Latimer writing from his San Francisco office as Montezuma's lawyer are unceasingly repetitive and the bureaucratic replies are likewise recurring, failing to answer pointed questions, denying accusations and allegations, and reasserting the government's official position in short, terse sentences. A message and a lesson emerge from these pages: resisting the Bureau's position and plans required unrelenting stubbornness and aggressiveness. Fighting the Bureau of Indian Affairs was like trying to pick up mercury; each application of pressure yields multiple escaping silver beads.

Taking Latimer and copies of Latimer's pamphlet with him, Montezuma made the rounds in Washington, visiting senators, congressmen, and staff members of the Indian committees, leaving the pamphlet with each encounter. But he could not gain a personal meeting with Secretary Fall or Commissioner Burke.

SOMETIMES SMALL, UNPLANNED EVENTS AND INCIDENTS open the door for an important accomplishment. This was the case with Montezuma's final and decisive intervention on behalf of the Fort McDowell Yavapai Indians.

Montezuma went to Washington early in June 1921 and established himself in an inexpensive hotel, the Harrington, at 234 Third Street NW. This trip was a considerable sacrifice for Montezuma. His income depended upon being home and seeing patients. By 1921, the size of his practice had dwindled, and he was seeing patients only in his home office. At this point in time, he was earning only $200 per month and had only $500 in available cash.[127] He could ill afford to spend a month in Washington, and the fact that he did is a measure of his dedication and devotion for the Fort McDowell Yavapai. Montezuma's dedication was further challenged by the weather. It was exceptionally hot and humid that June in Washington. His small room was oppressive and thick with heat, and he found little relief by opening his window. Montezuma endured by sleeping and writing letters naked.[128]

After two weeks of multiple visits with government officials in Washington, Montezuma left for a trip to Rochester, Minnesota. Charles H. Mayo had invited his fellow classmates in the Chicago Medical College Class of 1888 to visit the Mayo Clinic to watch surgery and clinical demonstrations, to attend a formal meeting with medical presentations, and to have a class dinner—a program very much like those we have today. Although Montezuma graduated in 1889, remember that his graduation was delayed, and he was actually one of the thirty-two men in the Class of 1888. What motivated Montezuma to make this trip when he could not afford it, and it seemed so illogical? With his sense of honor and loyalty, Montezuma would have felt obligated to respond to Mayo's invitation. But more importantly, Montezuma, nattily dressed in his blue serge suit, cuffs, collar, and white bow tie, could mingle, an Indian, as an equal among his Anglo-Saxon classmates. This would have been an opportunity Montezuma could not resist.

Montezuma told Richard Pratt that the Mayo Clinic was "one of the wonders of the world."[129] There are two pages of scribbled notes suggesting that Montezuma stood up at the class dinner to praise his host.

One may stand in awe and wonder at the miraculous stride of progress of the world in every avenue of its make up.

Medical science has not stood still. Within a span of thirty years the town of Rochester, Minnesota, away from the whirr of city thoroughfare, a shark of medical activity took place.

Medical men who have gone around the world, admit that nothing equal to the greatness of the painstaking thoroughness of the work being done by the Mayo brothers in the world of medical science.

A visit to the place, we may say, "half has not been told." The system cannot be surpassed. Every nick and corner is permeated, has the atmosphere of system, pertaining to the human body. Nothing is spared to gain result for best and greatest interest of mankind. It is a case, where it has gone far beyond, the expectation of the founders.

Patients flock to the clinics from all over the world!

The best special workers are there and much research is being carried on. Skillful operators are daily operating. If there is a place where troubled souls are seeking for help in their body activity there is no place equal to that of Mayo brothers.

Great things in world, it must have many aids. So the great system upon which it runs, has army of workers. Buildings after buildings & new buildings are created to carry on the machinery of the system.[130]

When Dr. Charles Mayo learned of Montezuma's mission in Washington, and his frustration in gaining an audience with those at the top, Mayo provided Montezuma with a letter of introduction to Harding's personal physician, Dr. Sawyer.

Returning directly to Washington, Montezuma visited Dr. Carl E. Sawyer, but Sawyer pointed out that the letter of introduction from Mayo was unnecessary because Sawyer was already an acquaintance. When Montezuma had visited Harding the previous fall in Marion, Ohio, Sawyer had entertained him with a tour of the city and Sawyer's sanatorium.[131] "I asked a favor from him that I want to meet the President. He gave me a very fine letter to Mr. Christian, the President's secretary. I took the letter to Mr. Christian and I explained to him my mission. He asked me if I had seen the Commissioner. 'No,' I said. 'He and Secretary Fall have refused us a hearing on the matter.' 'Doctor, I will telephone to the Commissioner to give you a hearing.'"[132] And Commissioner Burke saw Montezuma the very next day. Montezuma described this pivotal meeting in a letter to his wife, a meeting that took place because Montezuma chose to go to his class meeting at the Mayo Clinic (even though he had little money), Charles Mayo reminded Montezuma to see the president's physician, Dr. Sawyer provided an entrée to the president's office, and the president's secretary, George B. Christian, Jr., felt obliged to make something happen.

I was ushered in the Commissioner's room, who received me cordially & introduced me to one of the secretaries of Secretary Fall. Mr. Bishop [secretary of the Society of American Indians, Chapter 13] accompanied me. A young lady acted as a stenographer, to take down what we had to say. Do you see, there were four of us in the room. Well, you can imagine myself talking to the Commissioner on the McDowell situation. Mr. Latimer was not present nor Gilbert Davis. I had to shoulder the whole thing. I stated my relation in the case and that I wanted him to understand that I am there to help him and not to make any disturbance. I traced the history of the McDowell Indians from the time they asked me to help them from being forced from McDowell and the Congressional hearings, the decision of ex Secretary Fisher's order to have these Indians allotted on McDowell & small dam be constructed for water to irrigate their land, but it was ignored by Cato Sells to force the order & the weak reasons given & I related them with great force. Then I mentioned outside interests cause the delay of the Fisher order.

I wish to mention that he asked me, why I did not come direct to him. Then, I said, that we had corresponded with your office and Secretary of the Interior, and at last, you have made us to understand that it was no use of writing on the matter. You have "my office?" I said, "Yes" & then I showed in the pamphlet the words of the letter received from his office and he said, "he did not know it." He was caught right there.

Again he [?] at me, when he forced me to answer his questions about the Indian Bureau. He squirmed & spoke of "sedition." Then that stirred my ire up. I could see a flag out of the window. I pointed to the flag & said, that I am only upholding that flag that speaks of freedom, equality, democracy, humanity, & justice; if that is sedition then I am guilty. Well then I landed into him as I did at Mr. Sharp at Salt River reservation. I had him spellbound for fifteen minutes. Then went back to the main subject of McDowell. I gave it to him in every way to inform him why the Indians do not want to move and the working of the outside interests with the Indian Bureau to move these Indians to Salt River.

Then he asked, "The letters from the Indian Office do not mention moving these Indians?" I said, "Yes, if you go through your letter file, you will see the word *removal* in them." We were together over one hour and we did have it. At length, we sobered down to business & he wished to understand that the Indians will not be moved & that he wanted to hear more about the matter. About the dam he said that $35,000.00 could be given towards the dam but for $90,000.00 we must get Congress to appropriate the rest & he will back the bill. That was what we got out of the Commissioner on the talk, but no telling what influence may come up to change his stand given to us.

Mr. Latimer will have a hearing with him in the morning. We want to act while the iron is hot. He saw Christian, the President's secretary, yesterday with favorable result. So you see, we are stirring up things. The President seems to be with [us]. It was the President who arranged our hearing with Burke. We are progressing slowly in our favor.[133]

The official transcript of Montezuma's meeting with Burke on June 24, 1921, fills sixteen pages with single-spaced typing.[134] The language is blunt and tense; Burke was not as spellbound as Montezuma implied in the letter to his wife. Burke argued that Fort McDowell had been allotted. Montezuma pointed out that that was for grazing purposes, and that without water, this was useless. Burke abruptly said: "But, Doctor, don't discuss it in an unfriendly spirit."[135] Montezuma replied: "It is so serious to me and I am giving you what is in my heart."[136] The verbatim interchange over flag and sedition went like this:

Montezuma: I want the Indian Bureau abolished.
Burke: That isn't going to happen in this immediate time—you think it is, but you and I will not live to see it happen.
Montezuma: I would be ashamed of the flag that floats over there, where it tells of freedom, where it tells of justice, and democracy. You are violating the freedom of that flag and what it expresses just as long as you uphold that view and the Indian Bureau.
Burke: And when you preach that doctrine to Indians you are preaching sedition.
Montezuma: If American is going in the wrong direction, I would not be a citizen should I encourage it to go on in the same direction, that is not sedition.
Burke: We differ in our opinion of sedition. When a man preaches a doctrine contrary to what the courts of the country have decided he is preaching sedition.[137]

Burke concluded the meeting by saying, "If it is to be reopened and reconsidered I am willing to do the best I can. I would like to have Mr. Latimer come up here; I want to be informed."[138] Latimer had his visit the next day, and Commissioner Burke was very upset by the Latimer pamphlet and did not hesitate in expressing his feelings to Latimer. Latimer complained directly to President Harding: "The Commissioner spent much of the three-quarters of the hour while there, adversely criticizing the language used by me in my booklet on above matter with the only position statement that: 'I really do not know anything about this matter and desire to look into the entire situation to ascertain for myself whether or not this present plan is for the good of these Indians.'"[139]

Montezuma was in Washington for two weeks prior to his visit to the Mayo Clinic and for two weeks after, a long time without income. He continued to visit, along with Thomas Bishop and Gilbert Davis, the Indian committees, senators, and representatives. He believed Secretary Fall was trying to oppose what had been accomplished with Burke. "Another day has passed away and I am not any near home. ...I am finding every day that these senators and congressmen and the Indian Bureau take the Indians as lower in the human scale than the Negro people. They do not want to tell you that, but they believe the Indian is not ready to protect and do for himself. They need the government's strong arm around them. When the Indians can dodge the crooks, keep the white rascals from robbing them and when they can support themselves, then & only then, will it be safe to abolish the Indian Bureau. That will be many years to come. We will not live to see that day. Well, someone must stand firm against these thoughts. What the attitude against the Indians may be in Washington that does not move me at all. My claim for my people is that much stronger and the Indians are with me."[140]

Montezuma and Latimer were very anxious and apprehensive during the late summer and autumn of 1921, awaiting news of the government's decision. Montezuma received many pessimistic letters from Latimer, complaining about specific individuals and pleading for funds to expand their campaign.[141] This reaction by Latimer was stimulated by a letter written by Commissioner Burke to Gilbert Davis:

> I have directed Col. Dorrington, one of the Inspectors of the Indian Bureau to go to the Camp McDowell Reservation, confer with the Indians and make a thorough investigation of the situation there and report to me the conditions as he finds them. Immediately upon receipt of this report, I will give the case my personal attention, with a view of submitting to the President a definite policy that will be for the best interests of the Camp McDowell Indians.[142]

Latimer's letters to Montezuma project a sense of being left out of the process because Burke communicated directly with the Yavapai through Davis. This prompted Montezuma to draft a letter from Davis to Burke (with a copy to President Harding) requesting that all communications flow through Montezuma.[143]

At this point, Burke favored retaining Verde River water rights for the Yavapai, but still proceeding with the five-acre allotments on the Salt River Reservation. To his credit, Commissioner Burke responded to Montezuma and Latimer by reopening the Fort McDowell case. Colonel L. A. Dorrington concluded on July 23, 1921: "They [the Yavapai] are not receiving enough water on Salt River to irrigate 5 acres. They should be given preference on their own reservation."[144] Fortified by Dorrington's report, Burke decided that irrigable land at Fort McDowell should remain tribal land. The rest of the reservation would be subject to individual allotment. This decision was passed up to the Secretary of the Interior, Albert Fall, who wrote to President Harding:

The Commissioner of Indian Affairs has had the Camp McDowell situation under active consideration for some months, and has reached the conclusion, as reported by him in his recent letter to me, that the present schedules of allotments should not be approved; that instead the lands susceptible of irrigation should be identified and segregated on the ground, and that such lands should continue to be held in tribal or communal ownership so that they may be utilized by the Indians, as now, and that the remainder of the reservation should be allotted pro rata so that each Indian will share equally. Further, that the allotment selections on the Salt River Reservations should remain intact as a gratuity to these Indians.

I have carefully considered the commissioner's suggestions for a settlement of the major difficulties complained of by these Indians, and recommend your approval of this letter, which will be considered as a modification of the former Executive Order authorizing allotments to the Camp McDowell Indians.[145]

Fall's letter was signed and approved by President Warren G. Harding on February 8, 1922.[146] Through perseverance, an unwavering commitment to his goal, and a little luck, Montezuma finally accomplished his mission and prevented the loss of Fort McDowell land and water rights, practically single-handedly obstructing the plans of the Federal Government.

IT IS IRONIC that Montezuma, an assimilated Indian who had been campaigning for years against the preservation of Indian culture and heritage, was identified in this Arizona conflict as representing the "old ones," those who wanted to "get back the ways of their ancestors."[147] First and foremost in Montezuma's mind was the need to preserve the tribal land, and there is no doubt that his strongest allies were the older tribal members, those not regarded as the younger progressive Indians. For this reason, Montezuma found himself as being portrayed by government officials as "non-progressive." His government testimony in 1911 gave him the opportunity to tell his life story, to demonstrate that indeed he was a progressive, and yet he urged the preservation of tribal land.

Montezuma was consistently and adamantly committed to the elimination of Indian reservations. Why, then, was he energetically fighting to preserve the Fort McDowell land? There are at least two good explanations. First, Montezuma must have been unable to resist joining his relatives in their fight against his long-standing enemy, the Bureau of Indian Affairs. But more importantly, this was the time of allotment; the agenda throughout this conflict between the Fort McDowell Yavapai and the Indian Bureau was ultimately the assignment of a plot of land to each Indian. This was the purpose of H.R. 6294, the bill introduced in Congress at Montezuma's urging. Montezuma told his cousin, Charles Dickens, "All of you Indians go to work and do all you can to raise a big crop."[148] And on another occasion: "The best thing for you all to do is to work hard and raise much bigger crop this year than last year. Show Washington that you all can work to make your living and earn enough to buy farming tools, etc."[149] The Fort McDowell men would become farmers, each owning his own plot of land, and preserving the Verde River water rights was an essential component in obtaining land of optimal quality. This was entirely consistent with the Indian reform policy of assimilation and allotment (Chapter 3), a policy totally supported by Montezuma.

Montezuma also had an eye to the future. "Railroads will come through McDowell very soon. Automobile road will be developed through McDowell. Electric road will run through McDowell. The *best water* is on McDowell. There will be a town at McDowell. There may be minerals on McDowell. ...*To look ahead*, they will be baptized in the *flood* of civilian environment in a few years, not more than 60 years. I believe if the Indians hold on to McDowell reservation, 28,000 acres, they will make more than accepting 1000 acres in the Salt River Valley."[150]

The government's dedication to relocating the Fort McDowell Yavapai meant that the Indian Bureau over many years refused to provide any expenditures for services and development on the reservation. However, the Indian Bureau's belief that time and time again the Fort McDowell Yavapai Indians were on the verge of moving had one positive and valuable consequence. The Fort McDowell Reservation land never completed the formal process of allotment. The land remains in tribal possession. In contrast, over half of the Salt River Reservation and over a fourth of the Gila River Reservation are allotted (after several generations, few tribal members control more than one acre).[151] Thus, Fort McDowell land was also never lost to leasing. The Fort McDowell Yavapai were fortunate to emerge from these difficult years with their land intact and with tribal ownership.

## TRIBAL LAND THREATENED AGAIN

The fight for water rights continued after Montezuma's death in 1923, with the on-going help of Joseph Latimer. In 1930, the Verde River Irrigation Company tried to get Verde water. Once again, federal investigation into the dispute took place, this time with a House Subcommittee on Indian Affairs, and once again the Fort McDowell Yavapai retained their Verde River water. A plea was again made to build a dam, but no appropriations were ever made.

The population of the Fort McDowell Reservation dropped from about 300 to 200 after the 1918–1920 flu epidemic, and, therefore, the amount of water allotted under the Kent Decree was not being used.[152] It was not until the 1930s that the tribe was able to resume farming, and finally the Bartlett Dam (Bartlett Lake) on the Verde River twenty miles above the confluence with the Salt River and eighteen miles above the Fort McDowell Reservation was completed in 1939 to control flooding and to maintain irrigation on reservation land. The Horseshoe Dam (Horseshoe Lake), thirteen miles upriver from the Bartlett Dam, was completed in the 1940s.

For a period of about fifty years (1920–1970), there was little change on the Fort McDowell Reservation. The population was slow to increase, and the Federal Government did little to improve the land or living conditions. It was a hard and impoverished life for the Yavapai.[153] But the Yavapai occupied a key geographical position on the Verde River, and this small tribe could not avoid a continuing conflict with the surrounding community and interests. The western border of the reservation abuts an affluent, house-next-to-house development with the reservation line, as sharp as a knife slice, giving way to desert reservation land with widely scattered houses. This suburb of Phoenix, Fountain Hills, makes a mockery of the critical importance of the water supply by shooting a fountain straight up into the desert dryness and heat.

## Arizona Reservations

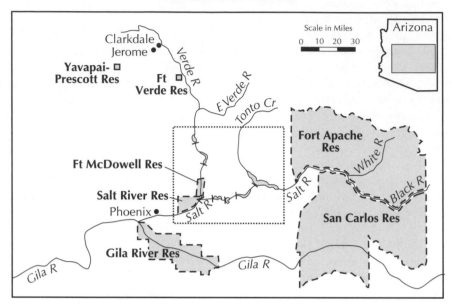

## Arizona Lakes and Dams

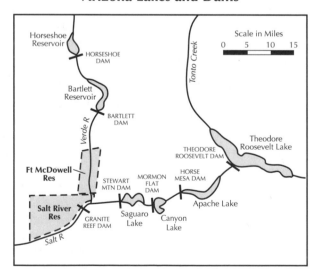

In 1931, the secretary of the interior allowed the city of Phoenix to establish a pumping station on 126 acres of reservation land, drawing water from wells.[154] This facility has provided employment for some of the reservation Indians, as well as annual rental income for the tribe, but the demand for water was still not appeased. The city of Phoenix receives seven inches or less of rain per year, and there is absolutely no doubt that its existence depends on obtaining and delivering water.

The Central Arizona Project was designed by the Bureau of Reclamation in the Department of the Interior to deliver water and hydroelectric power to Arizona and surrounding states by means of a system of aqueducts and four multipurpose dams. The Orme Dam was an integral part of this project. The fight over this dam was the final step in solidifying the Yavapai community.

The Central Arizona Project planned to build the Orme Dam, a mile long and about 190 feet high, at the confluence of the Salt River and the Verde River in the 1970s. The dam was named in honor of John P. Orme, a prominent landowner and participant in the early days of the Salt River Valley Water Users' Association.[155] The Orme Dam would have created a lake out of two-thirds of the Fort McDowell Reservation, flooding the valuable riverside land, the historic fort, and the tribal cemetery where Montezuma is buried. Once again the Yavapai chose to fight rather than accept an alternative reservation, and once again they prevailed.

The Central Arizona Project (introduced in Congress in 1947 and passed in 1968 as public law 90-537[156]) was planned to bring water 300 miles from the Colorado River to Phoenix and Tucson.[157] The long gestation of this law was due to the time it took for Arizona and California to adjudicate each state's rights to Colorado River water. The saga of the Central Arizona Project is one filled with mistrust, special interests, political bickering, and confusion. Significantly, the original legislation contained language that allowed a "suitable alternative" to the Orme Dam, an option that eventually would allow another solution.

The Orme Dam would have inundated portions of both the Salt River Reservation and the Fort McDowell Reservation. The Central Arizona Project law provided for relocation of affected Indians and payment for lands and changes required for the project. If an offer by the Secretary of the Interior was rejected, the Federal Government was empowered to acquire the land through eminent domain proceedings. Each Indian community was granted the right to develop and operate recreational facilities along the shoreline of the reservoir, and Fort McDowell was to be given an additional 2,500 acres from the townships bordering the reservation (although 12,000 to 15,000 acres would have been lost).[158] Involvement of the Fort McDowell Yavapai Indians was largely ignored in the early planning of the project. The Pima and the Maricopa of the Salt River Reservation were the ones who pointed out that the fluctuation of the water level in the reservoir (about sixty-five feet) would make recreational use of the shoreline totally impractical. By 1965, the objections of both the Fort McDowell and Salt River Indians were sufficiently apparent that Congressman Morris Udall of Arizona (the brother of Interior Secretary Stewart Udall) began to favor the elimination of the Orme Dam from the project.[159]

On December 25, 1972, the 100-year anniversary of the Skeleton Cave massacre (Chapter 1), the Yavapai sent a telegram to the secretary of the interior indicating their unwillingness to give up their land for the project.[160] From 1973 to 1975, the Yavapai struggled to stall construction of the Orme Dam. They asked for more land than was promised and proposed that old Camp McDowell and the Indians' cemetery be placed on the National Register of Historic Places.[161] In October 1975, five Yavapai (Dixie Davis, Andrew Johnson, Virginia Mott, Kimberley Williams, and John Williams) traveled to Washington with the results of a tribal poll that reflected nearly unanimous opposition to the project.[162] The group was supported by the Environmental Policy Center and the Friends Committee on National Legislation. The poll was presented to Senator Henry M. Jackson and other members of the Senate Interior and Insular Affairs Committee. The senators said that this was the first they knew that the tribe was opposed to the dam. "One Senator said that he had been told there were no Indians living at Fort McDowell."[163]

The Yavapai had significant help in their fight against the Orme Dam. In 1972, the Yavapai tribal chairman, Robert Doka, enlisted the involvement of Carolina Castillo Butler, a Scottsdale community activist.[164] Butler formed the Committee to Save Fort McDowell Reservation, and soon others joined the fight, including the Maricopa Audubon Society and the Citizens Concerned About the Project. The Audubon Society emphasized the detrimental effect on the streamside habitat along the rivers, a threat to the cottonwood tree nests of the endangered southern bald eagle. The Yavapai and these organizations of concerned citizens were opposed by strong forces, including two of the valley's most read newspapers, the *Arizona Republic* and the *Phoenix Gazette*. On August 24, 1975, the *Arizona Republic* wrote that "the 465 members of the McDowell Apache Indian tribe are going to be in clover" when the dam was completed.[165]

In the spring of 1976, the Federal Government repeated its offer of a compensation of $33.5 million for the loss of tribal land. Hiawatha Hood, a tribal elder and later tribal chairman, said: "You could fill this whole room with money and I'd still want land."[166] On September 26, 1976, members of the Yavapai tribe voted 144 to fifty-seven, rejecting sale of their land for the Orme Dam site. Finally, in 1977, the safety of the earthen dam was questioned, federal appropriations for the project were halted, and the governor of Arizona recommended that an alternative site be pursued.[167] Heavy storms and floods resurrected the fight in 1978 and 1980. The flow in what was usually a dry Salt River crossed by roads without bridges was especially fierce in the 1980 flood. Cars ill advisedly attempting to ford the river were easily thrown downstream. President Carter, with the support of Morris Udall, had previously refused to approve the Orme Dam, but eventually bowing to political pressure, he signed the bill in 1980 to begin construction, stirring up even more opposition.

Now the Yavapai and the citizen groups were joined by major religious groups in Arizona, as well as the American Civil Liberties Union and even the World Council of Churches, headquartered in Geneva, Switzerland.[168] In the summer of 1980, twenty-two individual groups joined together to form the Orme Alternatives Coalition to oppose the dam:[169]

> American Civil Liberties Union
> Arizona Democratic Party
> Arizona Ecumenical Council
> Arizona Libertarian Party
> Catholic Diocese of Phoenix
> Citizens Concerned About the Project
> Committee to Save Fort McDowell Indian Community
> Construction, Production & Maintenance Labors Union, Local 383

Friends Committee on National Legislation
Friends Meeting of Phoenix/Tempe
Friends of the Earth
Inter-tribal Councils of Arizona and New Mexico
Maricopa Audubon Society
National Indian Lutheran Board
National Wildlife Federation
Phoenix Gray Panthers
Presbytery of the Grand Canyon
Salt River Pima-Maricopa Indian Community
Sierra Club
Tempe Democrats
Valley Republicans
World Council of Churches

It was argued that flood control could be achieved with better bridges over the Salt River and with improvements to existing dams. On September 26, 1981, a band of Yavapai Indians marched thirty miles over three days to Phoenix where they were joined by others making a group of about 500 people who converged on the state capital where tribal chairman Norman Austin presented a letter affirming Indian opposition to the dam. A few days later, a governor's advisory committee voted nineteen to one to recommend an Arizona water policy that did not include Orme Dam.[170]

Carlos Montezuma, many years after his death, made a contribution to the Yavapai campaign against the Orme Dam. John W. Larner, Jr., the editor of the microfilm edition of the Carlos Montezuma Papers, met Dixie Davis, the Yavapai activist, in Washington, D.C., in the summer of 1978.[171] Larner offered the copy services of the National Archives being used for his Montezuma project, and Davis "grinned and said copy everything that might have Fort McDowell on or in it."[172] The Yavapai knew their land and water history, but lacked supporting documentation. Larner and his assistant, Tom Huppert, copied everything and hand-carried the documents to Fort McDowell via coach luggage racks on a train trip to Arizona for field research. Montezuma would have been pleased to know that these documents were of great assistance for the Yavapai and their support groups.

The successful fight against the Orme Dam was significantly aided by the change in attitude towards American Indians stimulated by the militant Indian activities in the 1970s (reviewed in Chapter 13). Fortunately for the Yavapai, they were able to stall dam construction until growing concerns for the environment and American Indians made it impossible. Today, the Fort McDowell Yavapai celebrate their victory every November with a festival, Orme Dam Recognition Days, a tribal fair and rodeo that commemorate this vital chapter in Yavapai history.

The repeated threats to the Yavapai land and the prolonged battle to retain the Fort McDowell Reservation with an uncertain outcome resulted in a federal reluctance to provide funds for housing, sanitary improvements, and any development.[173] For example, the first telephone was not installed until 1967, and five years later there was still only one phone on the reservation.[174] Not until recently, with funds from the Yavapai gaming operation, has the reservation been able to move forward. In 1990, the Fort McDowell Indian Water Settlement Act became law, settling all water rights and pending lawsuits with the

*Verde River and Four Peaks*

Salt River Project, the Roosevelt Water Conservation District and the neighboring communities of Chandler, Mesa, Phoenix, Scottsdale, and Tempe.[175] Not until this act was law were appropriations provided to allow the Federal Government to fulfill its legal and trust obligations to the Yavapai. The act established an amount of water for the Fort McDowell Indian Community, the ability to lease water to neighboring communities, and the establishment of a minimum stream flow on the Lower Verde River.

But there was yet one more important confrontation between the Yavapai and the government. The Fort McDowell Yavapai opened the first bingo hall in Arizona in 1983. The Fort McDowell Gaming Center, the first casino in Arizona, opened in 1991, operating under the Federal Indian Gaming Regulatory Act of 1988.[176] However, Indian gambling operations are further regulated according to an agreement with the state government, an agreement called a "compact." Arizona, under the direction of its governor, Fife Symington, had refused to negotiate compacts, and several tribes had proceeded to open gaming centers anyway.[177] On the morning of May 12, 1992, a surprise federal raid on Fort McDowell resulted in 349 gambling machines being loaded into eight moving vans. The tribal community was rapidly mobilized and soon all entrances and exits to the reservation were blocked with automobiles, trucks, and pieces of heavy machinery. The blockade lasted three weeks and attracted national attention. Eventually the gambling equipment was removed, but returned when a compact was established. The gaming center is now a booming success, having created a solid economic foundation for the tribe. The Fort McDowell Yavapai celebrate Sovereignty Day each May to commemorate their opposition to the federal raid.

THE FORT McDOWELL Mohave-Apache Community re-organized as the Fort McDowell Yavapai Nation (about 1,000 members with 600 living on the reservation) under a new constitution approved by the secretary of the interior on November 17, 1999.[178] After 130 years of confusion, the Yavapai finally set the record straight, officially eliminating "Apache" from the tribe's official designation. The Fort McDowell Tribal Council now consists of a president, vice-president, treasurer, secretary, and two council members, all elected by popular vote. No member can hold other employment while serving on the Tribal Council. There is both a Trial Court and a Supreme Court, with judges appointed by the Tribal Council.

The Fort McDowell Yavapai land and water rights battle was a story of one of the smallest Indian communities in the United States pitted against the Federal Government and overwhelmingly greater numbers in the surrounding White communities. It would have been relatively easy for the few Yavapai to become amalgamated into the Salt River Reservation and the nearby urban areas. Instead, a desire for their own land prevailed and made it possible to maintain an impressively high degree of tribal identity. The Fort McDowell Yavapai are proud of the role played by Montezuma from 1910 to 1922, and Montezuma would be proud today to see his band of the Yavapai on their own land, and doing well.

## CHAPTER THIRTEEN

# National Indian Organizations: I Am Not Here to Fight

Montezuma was an individualist, combative, and a fiery speaker with simple, unchanging, strongly held views. Hazel W. Hertzberg, in her seminal study of the first pan-Indian movement, commented: "Montezuma was by temperament and conviction, a factionalist. He helped to found the Society of American Indians and then spent most of his life attacking it."[1] Actually that statement was an exaggeration. Montezuma attacked the Society of American Indians for six years, but when the Society joined Montezuma's fight to abolish the Indian Bureau, he was a consistent and enthusiastic supporter during the last five years of his life.

Until 1900, the Indians of America consisted of a diverse collection of tribes with no common language. Nevertheless, a network of communication developed over centuries of time, based upon trade and conflict that produced rivalries, alliances, and commercial exchanges. There was no need for a uniform political organization, a pan-Indian movement, because there was no common rival or enemy until after 1492. Even an identity as an Indian is a relatively recent phenomenon, as prior to contact with Whites, the Native-American was identified by the language, religion, and customs of his tribe. Rapid transportation by train, the availability of mail service, and the use of English as a common language created greater contact and communication, gradually allowing the development of a broader, common identity forged out of shared needs and problems that were a consequence of the interactions with the rapidly growing White population.

Many, if not most, of the Indians educated in the Indian schools were devout Christians. The schools at this time were administered and staffed by individuals who believed that adopting Christianity was an essential part of "civilizing" Indians. The assimilation philosophy and process were reflections of the White Christian concepts of work, private property, and social and personal behavior. The failure of the assimilation effort can be attributed to an inability to appreciate any value or benefit in Indian culture. The all or nothing approach of the assimilation movement was uniquely applied only to Indians. Immigrant ethnic groups were allowed to maintain their cultural traditions and customs, probably because their notions of family, work, and property were not in conflict with prevailing White concepts, in contrast to the Indian way of life. Thus even Indian efforts to blend White and Indian beliefs, such as the Ghost Dance Religion and the peyote cult, were unacceptable. This conflict was reflected among the Indians themselves. Some wished to retain their Indian culture and to adopt what they viewed as the best aspects of White society and religion. Others, like Montezuma, agreed with the missionaries and White leaders that Indian society should vanish. This conflict was articulated by the opposing forces in the pan-Indian organizations.

## THE BEGINNING OF THE SOCIETY OF AMERICAN INDIANS

Fayette A. McKenzie was a Christian idealist and a supporter of assimilation philosophy although a critic of its implementation.[2] He became president of Fisk University and participated in the preparation of the Meriam Report in 1926–1928. Born in Pennsylvania in 1872, the year after Montezuma was captured by the Pima warriors, McKenzie graduated from Lehigh University, and prior to becoming a professor of economics and sociology at Ohio State University in 1905, he spent a year teaching at the Wind River Government Indian School in Wyoming. He received his Ph.D. from the University of Pennsylvania in 1906, and published his thesis as a book in 1908, *The American Indian in Relation to the White Population in the United States*.[3] The thesis expressed his belief that the civilization acquired over hundreds of years by the White population could be transferred to the Indians rapidly within a few generations. He believed wholeheartedly that tribal organization and culture must be eliminated, and it was that forceful, imposed elimination that would allow rapid assimilation. The methods included White education, an effective allotment policy with the establishment of vocational opportunities on the reservations, and ultimately, citizenship. Basically, McKenzie agreed with the assimilationists in advocating the purging of tribal control and influence, and he wished to replace government dependence by creating an industrial and religious White society on the reservations. He shared the common failure of that time to recognize any value in Indian society and culture. Appropriately he sought leaders for this effort among the "progressive" Indians. In the early twentieth century, "progressive" Indians were those who believed in adopting and adapting to White attitudes, values, and lifestyle. They were heavily influenced by the reformers of the 1890s, such as Richard Pratt and those who attended the Mohonk Conferences (Chapter 3).

Montezuma had been thinking of an all-Indian organization for a long time. He shared his thoughts with Zitkala-Ša in their correspondence in 1901 (Chapter 9). Undoubtedly, these thoughts surfaced in November 1908 when he joined Charles Eastman and Sherman Coolidge as guest lecturers in McKenzie's course on the Indian at Ohio State University.[4] In September 1909, McKenzie visited with Montezuma in his Chicago home; the two men hatched "our scheme" and created a list of potential participants in a national association of Indians.[5] McKenzie and Montezuma embarked on a national letter writing campaign in 1909 to promote support among Indians for an all-Indian organization.[6] Several months later, however, only nineteen Indians had communicated a positive reaction to McKenzie, and the idea fizzled.[7]

Undaunted, McKenzie and Montezuma continued to work toward an organizational meeting. McKenzie was very careful and emphatic in describing the nature of the meeting and his own role: "What we want is a solemn, at least a serious, conclave (not a spectacular festival) of men anxious to inaugurate a strong movement, which by its dignity, will possess and exert a great power in the interests of the natives of America. Power comes without parade through careful knowledge and quiet persistence. A Conference intimately associated with old time Indians & Wild West features & big crowds would lose half its value in importance. Trusting that wisdom may come out of counsel & that personal ambitions may not rule."[8]

A meeting planned for 1910 had to be postponed because an Indian Bureau convention in Muskogee, Oklahoma, that stressed Indian art and customs attracted many of the individuals being targeted. Finally, McKenzie, with the support of Montezuma and Charles Eastman, invited six educated Indians to a meeting in Columbus, Ohio, in April 1911. The six were: Carlos Montezuma, Charles A. Eastman, Thomas L. Sloan, Charles E. Dagenett, Laura M. Cornelius, and Henry Standing Bear (the same Henry Standing Bear pictured at Carlisle in Chapter 3). This group functioning as the Temporary Executive Committee formed an organization, the American Indian Association later to become the Society of American Indians, with the goals of bringing Indians into White society and developing Indian consciousness and leadership. The Executive Committee was enlarged to twenty members, and listed on the new stationery:

> Chas. H. Dagenett, Chairman
> Miss Laura M. Cornelius, Secretary
> Mrs. Rosa B. LaFlesche, Corresponding Secretary and Treasurer
> Dr. Chas. A. Eastman
> William Hazlett
> C. Parker
> Harry Kohpay
> Dr. Carlos Montezuma
> Thos. L. Sloan
> John M. Oskison
> Hon. Chas. D. Carter
> Miss Emma D. Johnson
> Henry Standing Bear
> Howard H. Gansworth
> Henry Roe Cloud
> Mrs. Marie L. Baldwin
> Robt. R. DePoe
> Charles Doxon
> Benjamin Caswell
> Prof. F. A. McKenzie (Local Representative) [9]

The leaders were well-established, well-educated, and well-recognized in their own communities and professional activities. At least eleven had attended the eastern boarding schools, most were professional people, and eleven had been or were currently employed by the Indian Service. A call was issued for a national conference to be held in Columbus in October 1911. At a second meeting in June 1911, letters of invitation were formulated, emphasizing that membership would be limited to Indians only.

## THE EARLY LEADERS

**Arthur C. Parker.**[10] Arthur Parker, a Seneca, served as editor of the organization's magazine, secretary-treasurer, and eventually president despite the fact that he was considerably younger than the other prominent members, sixteen years younger than Montezuma. Arthur Parker was a scholar with a prodigious output of articles and books. He tried to influence the Society to become an organized, academic group like White societies. His scholarship gave him a quiet, dignified air, but some thought him to be withdrawn and secretive. Parker was born in 1881 on the Cattaraugus Reservation at Iroquois, New York. His Christian family was influential and important on the reservation; the family name was adopted during the French and Indian War, not acquired by mixed marriage. His great-uncle was Ely S. Parker, General Grant's military secretary during the Civil War, and President Grant's commissioner of Indian affairs, until 1966, the only Indian to hold that office.

Parker's mother was White, a teacher on the Cattaraugus and Alleghany Reservations, and therefore Parker could not automatically be designated a Seneca because this had to be acquired by descent through the female line. He had to be officially adopted during his boyhood when he was given the name, *Gáwasowannah* (Big Snowsnake). Parker often used his Seneca name in his correspondence, and even as a pen name. Parker left the reservation with an interest in Iroquois history and nature. Living in White Plains, New York, he began to visit the Museum of Natural History in New York City where he stimulated the interest and support of anthropologists and educated people. He formed friendships with several individuals who later became prominent anthropologists, Mark R. Harrington (who also became Parker's brother-in-law), Frank G. Speck, and Alanson Skinner. He entered Dickinson Seminary in Williamsport, Pennsylvania, (now Lycoming College) to prepare for the ministry, but he was appointed as archaeological assistant at the Museum of Natural History in 1900, and he left Dickinson in 1903 without graduating. Parker became a self-taught anthropologist with informal study at the museum. In 1904, he was appointed as ethnologist with the New York State Library in Albany, and in that same year, he married Beatrice Tahamont, an Abnaki.

At the age of twenty-five, Parker won the competitive exam for the new post of archaeologist of the New York State Museum. The museum already housed a great Iroquois collection, under the direction of Lewis Henry Morgan, and under Parker, it became the leading institution for Iroquois studies, with several monographs of distinction published by Parker. Unfortunately, Parker took to calling himself Dr. Parker, but it wasn't until 1940 that he received an honorary doctorate in science from Union College. Nevertheless, he had a long and distinguished career. He became director of the Rochester Museum in 1925, and his book, *A Manual for History Museums*, published in 1935, became a bible in the museum profession. During the time Parker was involved with the Society of American Indians, he was building the collection of the New York State Museum. The still-life displays of Iroquois life that he created can still be viewed today. In 1919, he published his

*Arthur C. Parker*

biography of Ely S. Parker, his great-uncle. He went on to publish extensively, achieving international renown and being recognized by his own city and state for a lifetime of worthwhile contributions. He died in his home in Naples, New York, in 1955 at the age of seventy-three.

Parker was a statesman and a peacemaker, a perfect example of the Iroquois personality that permitted no outward display of emotions, especially anger. He worked toward a consensus, but once reached, he believed it was binding. He was a scholar and looked like one, a pipe-smoking short man (five-feet, six-inches) who was always impeccably dressed, topped with his trademark gray fedora.[11] Being an academic in White society, Parker influenced the Society of American Indians to publish a journal, to meet at academic institutions, and to conduct conferences with published papers and proceedings. Committed to the cause, he worked with great energy and enthusiasm. Parker was opposed to the peyote religion and was a devout Mason.

**Henry Roe Cloud.**[12] Roe Cloud joined the founders of the Society at age twenty-five soon after becoming in 1910 the first Indian to graduate from Yale. He was an even tempered Winnebago who was good at conciliation. Born on the Winnebago Reservation in Nebraska, he was influenced by the missionaries Dr. and Mrs. Walter Roe. Roe Cloud attended the Indian School at Genoa, Nebraska. After Yale, he attended the Auburn School of Theology, as well as Oberlin, becoming a Presbyterian minister, a Mason, an Elk, and a Rotarian. Although personally against the use of peyote, he was tolerant of the peyote religion, partly because of his personality and partly because the educated and ablest men in his tribe were devotees.

In 1914, Roe Cloud was a member of a federal commission that surveyed Indian schools, and in 1915, he founded a college preparatory school for Indian boys, the Roe Institute, which in 1920 became the American Indian Institute in Wichita, Kansas, that operated until 1939. Roe Cloud's wife assisted him in administering the school. Elizabeth Bender Roe Cloud, from a prominent Chippewa family, was also a member of the Society of American Indians. (Chippewa and Ojibwe are the same people; Chippewa is the name recognized by the U.S. Government and Ojibwe is the familiar name used by Indians.) She attended Hampton Institute, the University of Wichita, and the University of Kansas. Her pan-Indian career included important positions in the General Federation of Women's Clubs, and after 1945, the National Congress of American Indians. Henry Roe Cloud was the only Indian member of the staff of the Brookings Institution that produced the Meriam Report. In 1933, he became the superintendent of Haskell Institute in Lawrence, Kansas.

**Thomas L. Sloan.**[13] Sloan was a lawyer. Born in 1863 and raised on the Omaha Reservation by his grandmother, he graduated from Hampton in 1889. Sloan, like Montezuma, was a staunch admirer of Richard Pratt. Sloan's boyhood Omaha friend, Hiram Chase, graduated from Cincinnati Law School and was practicing law on the reservation. Sloan returned to the reservation and became a lawyer by working and studying with Chase. The two formed a partnership. Sloan's private practice specialized in Indian cases. He even served as county judge and county attorney in Thuston County, Nebraska. Sloan and Chase were believers in the peyote religion. Although originally opposed to it, Sloan came to see the peyote religion as a means to bring together Indian culture and Christianity. This belief earned him the hostility of those who were passionately opposed to peyotism, especially Zitkala-Ša. Nevertheless, Sloan was an active force for Indian causes in Washington and served as president of the Society.

**Sherman Coolidge.**[14] Born in 1863 in the Arapahoe tribe, Coolidge was captured by the army at age seven, and adopted by Lieutenant C. A. Coolidge and his family. Given the name, Sherman Coolidge, he seldom used his Indian name, "Runs Mysteriously on Ice." When the Coolidge family went East, Coolidge went to public schools in New York City. He attended the Shattuck Military School and received his divinity degree in 1884 from Bishop Whipple's Seabury Divinity School. As an Episcopal priest, he worked in Wyoming among the Shoshone and Arapahoe; he assisted James Mooney when Mooney researched the Ghost Dance Religion for the Bureau of American Ethnology. When the Society of American Indians was founded, Coolidge was in charge of the Indian Protestant Episcopal Missionary Service in western Oklahoma.

**Charles E. Dagenett.**[15] Dagenett, in 1911, was supervisor of employment in the Indian Bureau, the highest position held by an Indian. Dagenett was a Peoria from Oklahoma, born about 1872, who attended Carlisle in 1887 at the age of fifteen. At Carlisle, he learned to be a printer and worked on the *Red Man*, the school paper. He graduated in 1891, attended Dickinson College, and eventually graduated from Eastman College in Poughkeepsie, New York. He married a Carlisle graduate who was a Miami Indian.

Dagenett joined the Indian Service in 1894 and worked his way up to his position of supervisor of employment by 1907. Like Montezuma, Eastman, and Parker, Dagenett was a Mason. Dagenett was a trained bureaucrat, an organization man. As a highly placed Indian in the Bureau, he looked forward with hope for Indian advocacy but at the same time, with concern that he supported Bureau policies that could be regarded as obstructions to Indian progress.

**Charles A. Eastman.**[16] Eastman's mother, who died when Eastman was young, was the granddaughter of a Sioux chief and the daughter of a White man. Eastman's father, Many Lightnings, was captured during the Sioux Minnesota uprising of 1862. The family believed he was executed, and Eastman was raised by his uncle and grandmother to have an angry disposition against the Whites. First named Hakadah (The Pitiful Last—his mother died after his birth), he was renamed Ohiyesa (The Winner—earned by playing lacrosse) at age four. When Eastman was fifteen, his father was pardoned by President Lincoln and released from prison where he had become an ardent Christian. He even changed his name to Jacob Eastman, taking his deceased wife's maiden name. Leaving the reservation, he became a successful farmer on his own homestead. Seeking and finding his son, he named him Charles and guided him into a White man's way of life. Eastman attended the Santee Indian School where he was strongly influenced by the school supervisor, Reverend Alfred L. Riggs.

While at Santee, Eastman learned of his father's death, and shortly after went to Knox College and then to Dartmouth and Boston University Medical School. He was respected and liked by his colleagues and teachers, and made many friends wherever he was. His experience produced a blend of Sioux culture, New England conservatism, and Christianity. After graduation from medical school, he joined the Indian Service and was assigned as the agency physician at the Sioux Agency at Pine Ridge, South Dakota, arriving in time to care for the wounded after the Wounded Knee Massacre (Chapter 2).

Eastman met and married Elaine Goodale, a White woman from Massachusetts who was working for the Indian Service at the Sioux Agency as a school supervisor. Their experience with the deplorable conditions and grievances at the agency led to disillusionment and they resigned. Eastman established a private practice of medicine in Minneapolis and began writing the books that would bring him considerable recognition and a growing reputation as an educated, progressive Indian. Eastman became a field secretary for the YMCA, and traveled widely among Indian tribes, representing the interests of the Sioux and others in Washington. Working later again for the Indian Service, Eastman spent seven years on the special assignment of creating appropriate family names for the allotment process of the Sioux.

Eastman was a man of both worlds, treasuring his Indian culture in a mystic, romantic way but wanting the benefits of White society (he was a Mason). He spent his last years in New England, writing and lecturing. His wife published a biography of Richard Pratt in 1935 that was not highly regarded.[17] It emotionally and uncritically embraced Pratt's philosophy of total and abrupt assimilation of Indians. Although Eastman was one of the founders of the Society of American Indians, he was not an active force in the organization, being ambivalent about its usefulness.

## THE SOCIETY OF AMERICAN INDIANS

The founding conference of the Society of American Indians was, ironically and deliberately, on Columbus Day, October 12, 1911.[18] This time the Indians discovered Columbus, the city in Ohio. McKenzie had worked hard to develop support from the city government and from Ohio State University. Lodging was at the Hotel Hartmann, $1.25 per day for a room with two people, $1.50 for a single (without bath).[19]

The approximately fifty men and women who attended the conference were by dress and manner thoroughly middle-class Americans. It was clear from the onset that a primary goal was to develop a pan-Indian organization, a goal that challenged the participants to overcome historical Indian factionalism. The various presentations at the conference agreed in their emphasis on the importance of education and the need to adapt to White society. Disagreement focused on the differences of opinion regarding Indian individuality and the value of Indian cultures, art, and tradition. In general, more prominent speakers, such as Arthur Parker and Charles Eastman, spoke against the Pratt (and Montezuma) goal to make the Indian a White man, even though Carlisle graduates were a major influence on the conference. Simply put, most of the participants embraced an approach that would have Indians adjust to a new environment, not to make "new Indians." Native art, for example, was something to be preserved. The delegates expressed confusion regarding the legal state of individual Indians and tribes, in particular individual citizenship and tribal sovereignty. The conference called for a federal review and clarification of the legal status of Indians. At the business meeting, Thomas Sloan was named chairman of the Executive Committee, Charles Dagenett as secretary-treasurer, joining Sherman Coolidge, Hiram Chase, Arthur Parker, Laura Cornelius, and Henry Standing Bear on the Executive Committee. The name of the organization was changed from the American Indian Association to the Society of American Indians to emphasize that this was a movement run by Indians. Individuals of "non-Indian blood" could be non-voting associate members.

Where was Montezuma? It is not surprising that he was not a member of the Executive Committee because he did not even attend the meeting. On October 11, 1911, Montezuma received a telegram that read:

FIVE OF ORIGINAL COMMITTEE OF SIX ARE HERE AND DESIRE YOUR PRESENCE WITH US IN OUR FIRST ANNUAL CONFERENCE OTHERS PRESENT ALSO DESIRE YOU BE HERE SIGNED SLOAN EASTMAN CORNELIUS DAGENETT STANDING BEAR[20]

Angered because he believed the Indian Bureau was influencing the organization, Montezuma resigned and went to Arizona instead. Montezuma's concern regarding Indian Bureau influence on the organization had been long in building. Two years earlier, he had expressed his negative opinion of Charles Dagenett to Richard Pratt, and Pratt reinforced it with these words: "In speaking of Charlie Dagenett, I have been afraid for a long time that Charlie was managing a scheme for the enrichment of Charlie. I happen to know of investments of his, and inquiries for investments that have made me fear that he was making money pretty fast, and yet I have never had sufficient and direct proof to throw him off."[21] And just four months before the scheduled conference, Montezuma wrote to Pratt: "If he [McKenzie] is going to be guided by Charlie (who is a mouth piece of the Indian Department) he will receive cold water. I hope such will be the case then the conference at Columbus will be an *independent one*. I believe no one should rule but invite all prominent Indians to let them express themselves with freedom. Of course, then if Charley wishes to take part all right let him come but I have no fear of that because he is bound foot and hand by the Bureau. ...As you say, we shall do all we can if that convention at Columbus is independent. Though Prof McK. is little known I truly believe he is unselfish and sincere and wishes to do the most good for the Indians."[22]

Pratt counseled Montezuma to move ahead in supporting the new organization, and Montezuma seemed resigned to waiting for the right moment to work against the Indian Bureau. "Of course, you know my feeling against the 'bureau' is not too friendly. Yet I can afford to hold back for wisdom sake."[23] However, McKenzie accepted a government position to edit the Indian census, and despite his emphasis that he would have no connection with the administrative part of the government, Montezuma feared McKenzie would lose his independence of action.[24] Montezuma missed the Executive Committee meeting in June because of his testimony before Congress (he was in the midst of his fight to save the Fort McDowell land and water rights), and when the program for the upcoming meeting appeared, both Montezuma and Pratt objected to it. Pratt wrote to Montezuma: "You are dead right in your estimate of your Indian Association program. ...it essentially says that the program is a skillful suppression of the vital needs of the Indians and a dilettante dancing attendance upon the Bureau's methods and supervision. Where are your real Indians who are not bought by Bureau employment? I know of only one, Dr. Carlos Montezuma."[25]

Montezuma was incredibly busy in the summer of 1911. He was constantly writing letters regarding both the Society of American Indians and the Fort McDowell Yavapai fight over land and water rights. His anger towards the Bureau of Indian Affairs was at a high level. His attitude was cemented in September 1911, when an article in the *Los Angeles Times Sunday Magazine* portrayed the upcoming Indian conference in a way that supported Montezuma's complaints against Bureau interference. He wrote to Charles Dagenett, chairman of the temporary Executive Committee, feeling "compelled to withdraw entirely from any possibility of contact with, or seeming approval of, those officials such as their presence and speech in our coming meeting will carry."[26] This was supported by his experience that summer in the Congressional hearings and the Fort McDowell land fight: "By the evidence of official documents from the Indian Office files, which include letters from the commissioner himself and his immediate subordinates to their officials in the field and letters from them to the Indian Office there is presented a persistent and wicked duplicity of management to rob the Mohaves. I therefore resign from and regret I had any responsibility for the organizing of the Association of Educated Indians. I shall not be present at the coming meeting."[27] Montezuma then sent a circular letter to everyone on his lengthy mailing list, explaining his action: "The program of the meeting of the American Indian Association to be held at Columbus, Ohio, in October 1911 when considered in connection with the article appearing in the Los Angeles Sunday Times magazine conclusively confirms my past utterances in speeches and letters to my associates, regarding the attempted usurpation of control of our movement by the present Bureau of Indian Affairs of the Department of the Interior."[28] The letter was carefully typed, filling an entire page, single-spaced; surely he must have hired a typist in those days without copy machines (although carbon paper was available, patented in 1869).

Many of the leaders of the Society of American Indians looked to the organization for help in resolving their own personal ambiguities, living in two worlds, treasuring the old and wanting the new. Although aware of tribal life and occasionally involved with tribal affairs, they were not tribal leaders; they were on the margin, not in the heart, of tribal life. Although successful middle-class Americans, they were not political leaders in White society, and here, too, they were on the margin of the dominant circles. However, they were in a unique position, offering a means of communication and influence that went back and forth between the tribes and White government and society. For this, they were recognized, respected, and valued, a process that offered reward and satisfaction for these individuals who were trying to bridge two worlds.

The Society of American Indians was an organization of the Indian middle class that faced the challenge of connecting American society with the Indians on reservations. The delegates to this first conference reflected their own experiences in White society. They rejected tribalism and sought to become valued members of American society. Most had little knowledge or experience of reservation life and assumed (and believed) that all Indians could, by self-reliance and initiative, follow the same paths they had followed. Thus there was clear agreement that education was the means of success, and not surprising, the delegates, with a high prevalence of graduates from eastern boarding schools, had warm praise for Carlisle and Hampton. No one advocated the immediate abolition of the Indian Bureau (a statistic that surely would have been different had Montezuma been present); the fundamental policy of allotment was supported, and non-Christian religious issues (specifically the use of peyote) were not discussed. The organization and movement were received very favorably by the press and by White organizations dedicated to Indians.

## THE HALCYON DAYS OF THE SOCIETY

The Society opened its Washington, D. C., office in 1912, providing a site for the Executive Committee to draft the organization's constitution. Charles Dagenett promptly resigned as secretary-treasurer, apparently to defuse debate over the question (which would become divisive) whether Indian Bureau employees should hold office. Parker, regarded as a friendly critic of the Bureau, replaced Dagenett. J.N.B. Hewitte, a Tuscarora who spoke several Iroquois dialects and was a prominent anthropologist with the Smithsonian's Bureau of

American Ethnology, was added to the Executive Committee. The provisional constitution formalized the discussions at the founding conference, allowing active participation only by Indians and outlining a commitment to education, involvement with legislation on Indian affairs, and the preservation of Indian history, art and literature. Sloan then resigned as chairman, probably because of his controversial support of the peyote religion, to be replaced by Sherman Coolidge.

By 1912, the Society had approximately 100 active members and 100 associate members.[29] The proceedings of the first conference, about a 200-page pamphlet, were published, and once again the Society was warmly welcomed by Columbus, Ohio, for its second meeting. Montezuma was there, renewing his membership with his annual dues of $2, in response to the urging of Arthur Parker and perhaps appeased by Dagenett's resignation.

Parker had written to Montezuma: "I was very much disappointed in not seeing you at Columbus but I am hoping that our second conference will be honored by your presence. We need the true Indian spirit and I think the distinguished Apache has it."[30] Parker further persuaded Montezuma by addressing his concern regarding the influence of the Indian Bureau: "…I know, however, that the Indians have just cause for criticizing the Bureau, for I know something of its policy. Our report, soon to be ready for distribution, will show that our membership is about solid in its opinion that the Bureau is not all that it should be. Our criticism of its actions is pronounced and I believe will quell any rumor that as a body we are in any way in sympathy with it. The sooner it is abolished the better my ideas will be suited."[31]

The reservation system became the chief topic of discussion at the 1912 meeting of the Society. Most of the delegates, being educated members of the American middle class, believed the reservations and the Indian Bureau should be abolished. But there was no agreement about how this should be accomplished. Certainly, most favored the process of assimilation. Some argued for a gradual evolutionary change, whereas Montezuma, in one of the principal evening speeches, called for immediate destruction of the reservations, calling them Indian "prisons."[32] Montezuma viewed the reservation as involuntary segregation that branded the Indian as inferior, sapping the manhood of Indians and cutting them off from opportunities available to other Americans. Isolation made the individual Indian subject to the tyranny and conservatism of the tribe.

"To draw the lesson from this recital of my life, I wish you to note that I am not a Reservation Indian. I never was a Reservation Indian. The world was my sphere of action and not the limitations, nearly as binding as a prison, of a strictly Bureau-ruled reservation. It may have been cruel to have been forced away from paternal love, care and protection, but after all these years, to me it has proven the greatest blessing. I studied in public schools. I did not spend a few hours in a Reservation schoolroom and the rest of the time in Indian camps. At an early age I was compelled to earn my own way in life. The government never paid one cent for my education. I have no trouble with the Indian Bureau about my money, my property or my rights as a citizen. Indian Bureau care and restrictions are unknown to me. I obey the laws of the State and Nation under whose protection I live and so have the widest freedom."[33]

"I firmly believe that the only true solution of the so-called 'Indian problem' is the entire wiping out of the reservation system; of the absolute free association of the Indian race with the paleface."[34] Montezuma and Pratt objected to tribal influence and were totally against the reservation system; hence, they bitterly opposed the existence of the Bureau of Indian Affairs, the government agency dedicated to the support of the reservations.

Provoked by a plea for educated Indians to return to the reservations, Montezuma expressed the philosophy forged by his own life in the opening address on Saturday evening: "I am a practicing physician. ...Not that I do not revere my race, but I think if I had remained there on the reservation and not have been captured years and years ago, I would not be standing here today defending my race. I will not go back there. ...In these forty years absence from my people I have not forgotten them. They have been in my heart day and night. For them my pen and tongue have not been idle. ...I find that the only, the best thing for the good of the Indian is to be thrown on the world and so I would impress upon the Indian race to go out into the world. Better send every Indian away. Get hold and send them to Germany, France, China, Alaska, Cuba, if you please, and then when they come back 15 or 20 years from now you will find them strong, a credit to their country, a help and an ornament to this race."[35]

Richard Pratt was present in 1912, along with 150 voting members, at the second meeting of the Society. Pratt claimed that the very existence of the Society was evidence that his methods were successful, recognizing that the delegates were largely composed of graduates of the eastern boarding schools. He denounced the movement away from non-reservation schools, the Indian Bureau's support of Indian participation in wild west shows, and anything that supported Indian tribalism, especially reservation day schools. He was his characteristic unwavering bombastic self, but Pratt and Montezuma represented the radical point of view. The moderates in favor of gradual changes and efforts directed to specific problems of education, health, and sanitation were the dominant force in the organization.

Despite lively debate filled with differing views, the delegates approved the constitution, a constitution that failed to provide for tribal involvement. Although tribal involvement would have been difficult to achieve because of differences in languages, culture, and experiences, nevertheless, the constitution made it official that this was an organization of educated, Americanized Indians. The delegates were evenly divided, however, over whether employees of the Indian Bureau could hold office. Why did Indians work for the Indian Service? Often these were the only jobs educated Indians could get, but in addition, this was an obvious opportunity to serve the Indian people. However, this meant that Indian Service Indians were frequently in a position of administering a policy with which they disagreed. Working within a pan-Indian organization provided a means to voice this disagreement and work against the policy. The 1912 conference, after a lively debate, supported greater involvement and employment of Indians by the Bureau.

Afterwards, Montezuma wrote a moving letter to Fayette McKenzie: "...We [Montezuma and Pratt] were there for a cause that was near to our hearts. Professor McKenzie, I thank you with all of my heart for the unselfish sacrifice which you have taken to help all the Indians throughout the country. From me you have no criticism but my deepest appreciation. You acted wisely and deservingly. My brother, I want you to know that I am like yourself. I want to do the best thing for the Indians. I do not wish to be understood that I am speaking for myself. ...Now about yourself dropping out never think one moment of such thing. That would be knocking the bottom out of the whole thing. You have directed and started the ball rolling. You must stick to us and do the same as you have been doing. I don't think you can drop out any way. Wherever we go you must go with us. Do not let your interest lag one moment in the Society. Be a help to Parker and all of us. I know we overlook those who have been the greatest help to us but I do not think we can ever forget you. Again I say, do not entertain in the slightest degree of let go your hands in our behalf."[36]

The proceedings of the 1912 conference were published in the first issue of the *Quarterly Journal* on April 15, 1913, edited by Arthur Parker (forty cents per copy, $1 per year for members, and $1.50 per year for non-members).[37] The Society was organized and operating, and it was similar to other reform organizations. The Society would hold an annual conference, develop principles and goals to be presented to both Indians and Whites, maintain a Washington headquarters to monitor and lobby the Federal Government, publish a journal, and provide services such as legal aid and general advice. Each issue opened with the well-written thoughts of Arthur Parker, which over the years ranged over an incredible variety of topics and issues. Montezuma agreed to be a "contributing editor" of the journal.

By September 1913, there were 357 active members and 419 associate members.[38] The third annual conference met in Denver in October, with delegates representing (not officially) twenty-nine tribes. As membership in the Society increased, dominance shifted westward. More reservation Indians attended the meeting, and fewer from the East. Governmental appropriations for Hampton had been discontinued, and this was the time of the Congressional investigation of financial affairs at Carlisle. There were no Indians from Carlisle or Hampton at the conference.

No. 4

*Barrister Building,*
*Washington, D. C.,* May 3rd 1913

Dr. Carlos Montezuma,
7 W. Madison, Chicago. Ill

To **The Society of American Indians,** Dr.
1913

| | |
|---|---|
| Annual dues for the year | $2.00 |
| Subscription to the Quarterly Journal | Pro. 8.00 |
| Donation for the Year | |
| Total | $10.00 |

Received payment,

Date May 6/13. Arthur C. Parker
*Secretary-Treasurer.*

The City of Denver provided $2,000 for the meeting, motivated by a desire to enlist the Indian leaders in the planning of the "Council and Pageant of 1915," intended to be the greatest wild west show ever. Parker emphatically denied to Montezuma that the Society had agreed to participate in the 1915 show, and Montezuma in anticipation of attending the conference paid his annual dues and subscription fee to the *Quarterly Journal*, plus a $7 donation. Unfortunately the Denver newspapers quoted Dagenett as saying that the Indians would enter enthusiastically into the 1915 Council.[39] Despite disclaimers from Parker and Dagenett, Montezuma and Richard Pratt refused to attend the conference because they were convinced that the Society was being used by the Colorado Publicity League to stimulate interest in the 1915 big show.[40] Parker pulled no punches in letting Montezuma know what he thought of Montezuma's defection: "...I think the just way to help the army in its fight is to fight with it against the enemy and not desert its ranks, and that the proper way to steer a ship is not to abandon it in time of danger by putting off in a little boat alone, but by staying on and by cheering the pilot and captain to steer for a safe shore. If there are rats in the ship, let us kill the rats that gnaw the holes and not ignite the powder magazine and blow up the whole craft, because we think it is going to sink any way."[41] A month later, Parker again was pleading for Montezuma to attend: "When it comes to solidity some how I always think of you."[42]

The Denver meeting focused on the development of pan-Indian consciousness and unity, overcoming tribal limitations. There was no debate over the Bureau of Indian Affairs; Montezuma was not at the meeting, partly a protest against what he perceived as cooperation with Denver's hosting Buffalo Bill's Wild West show in 1915, and partly because he chose to participate in a week long hunting and camping trip in Arizona, leaving Chicago by train *the day after he was married.* The speakers looked toward a future in American society, but not without incorporating what they viewed as desirable and good aspects of Indian life. These included ethical and moral teachings, a reverence for nature, and Indian art. The meeting was an expression of idealism, asking that the legal process be totally open to Indians, calling for a reorganization of the Indian school system, and once again emphasizing the need to clearly establish the laws affecting Indians. It would be another fifteen to thirty years before these things were accomplished.

This was a high point for the Society. Flushed with optimism and a sense of success, the Executive Committee organized a black tie banquet at the Hotel Walton in Philadelphia the following winter. "The ladies were tastefully gowned in evening dress, and the gentlemen carefully groomed in full accord with polite society."[43] Although Montezuma had not attended the Denver conference, he was given the honor of presenting the major speech to the collection of prominent Indians and Whites (including Commissioner Cato Sells) at the banquet, apparently not a tribute to his speaking ability, but an attempt by the Executive Committee to give him an open forum in hopes that his position would be balanced, if not overcome.[44] His subject was no surprise to anyone, an attack on reservations and Indian education. "America stands pre-eminent for the unity of races and freedom of the individual. The first great barrier to be removed in all work of assimilating and unifying our diverse population is the barrier of difference in languages."[45] Montezuma compared the Indian to the immigrant who learned English by association. "We organize and force upon the Indian through our sustaining of the tribal relation by the congesting system of Indian reservations a condition calculated to not only discourage but to entirely prevent his acquiring the American language except in the impractical, homeopathic way we choose to dispense it to him by expensive, theoretical schools established in his communities."[46] Indian schools were "lacking in the essential elements of practical experience."[47] Indian basketry, Indian blanketry, Indian pottery, Indian art, Indian music, and other general Indian industries of a past generation were foolish activities. "Where does this help the Indian children into the ways of civilization?"[48]

"Purely Indian schools say to the Indian: 'You are Indians, you must remain Indians; you are not of the nation, and cannot become of the nation.'"[49] Indian schools should prepare the young Indian to enter the other schools of the nation, as fast as possible. "What a farce it would be to attempt to teach citizenship to the Negroes in Africa. They could not understand it, and if they did, in the midst of such contrary influences, they could make very little use of it. Neither can the Indians understand or use American citizenship theoretically taught to them on reservations. *They must get into the swim of American citizenship.*"[50] The Indian was not born "an inevitable savage. He is born a blank, like the rest of us. What happens to him depends on his environment."[51] Pratt wrote to Chauncey Yellow Robe and told him: "Montezuma made a red hot speech and was more fully quoted by the newspapers than any other speaker."[52]

Frank G. Speck, the University of Pennsylvania anthropologist, was scheduled to present a counterpoint to Montezuma.[53] Through a misunderstanding it was not delivered (although one account claims that Speck refused to give his speech).[54] Speck expressed to Arthur Parker the outrage and anger that he experienced listening to Montezuma's speech,[55] and Parker subsequently printed Speck's talk in the *Quarterly Journal*, immediately before Montezuma's speech.[56] It was only four pages long, a beautiful piece of thinking that captured the essence of an ideal anthropologist. Speck expressed admiration for Indian cultures and enumerated Indian virtues, among them being honesty, respect for women, knowledge of nature, bravery, and a rich social and ceremonial life. "A man who knows only one side of a subject involving the destiny of a race and who wants to speak, chiefly because he is the exponent of a certain policy, and who does not really understand what this policy will ultimately lead to, had better remain silent until he has lived with and studied the people with whom he desires to experiment."[57] He urged the preservation of Indian languages and knowledge of tribal customs. "Education is not deculturation—education should be constructive, using as a basis the spirit of tribal life which every race possesses for its own strengthening."[58] Speck declared that an "ethnologist never takes his stand against native cultures in which he sees so much good." And even more strongly: "Anybody who advocates total tribal disintegration is manifestly advocating race murder."[59]

It is easy to see today the values expressed by Speck. But it is important to understand the emotional and historical basis for Montezuma's urgings. Montezuma was influenced by the assimilation philosophy and allotment process underway from 1870 to 1930, affected by the many forces and events described in the chapters of this book. Speck was a man of foresight, expressing a point of view for which the times were not ready, a viewpoint that would not become a dominant one until the last decades of the twentieth century. It is ironical that in 1914, it was an Indian asking for instant assimilation and a White man supporting preservation of fundamental Indian culture.

## DAYS OF CONFLICT

By the time of the Society's annual conference in the fall of 1914 in Madison, Wisconsin, the mood had changed. Attendance was down, interest in the future of the Indian had waned, and most of the time was spent discussing details of organization and money, successfully resolving a financial crisis. Indeed, the organization could have disappeared at this time as Parker explained to Montezuma: "The job of Secy is one of considerable responsibility. The hundreds of letters that come in asking for help, information, giving complaints, requesting rulings, laws, etc. has kept me on the *qui vive* for months. But it has not been the work, even though it required social skills but the worry that has been hardest. Personally my debts are always met but with the Society in deep financial water and creditors buzzing around I get some feelings of apprehension—especially when nobody hustles except perhaps Mr. Dagenett. The consuming of my time has just about bankrupted me as it would perhaps you if you abandoned your profession. The Society of course never paid me $2,000 a year. I believe I drew $195 last year for 7 months of actual time put in. ...If our finances warrant it I shall keep on with the Quarterly. It has only 300 subscribers (about), nearly enough to pay for one issue. Yet it is the strongest paper published on the Indian question."[60] In the preceding year, the Society had paid Parker only $100; he was working on Society affairs about four hours per day with amazingly little complaint.[61] Financial reports of the Society indicate a balance of available funds that ranged from only $15 to no more than $100, a high that was reached only occasionally.[62]

Despite Montezuma's presence, the Indian Bureau and Commissioner Cato Sells were not attacked during the 1914 conference. Montezuma was surely tempered by his correspondence with Richard Pratt, in which Sells was touted as "the best Commissioner of Indian Affairs we have had within my knowledge, now running over 46 years."[63] Sells was a vigorous proponent of the allotment process, energetically supporting the leasing of allotted lands. He was undeterred by those who sold their land, focusing instead on his belief that many would survive the challenge.[64] Later, Sells was especially pleased that 10,000 Indians served in the military during World War I, side by side with White men (Chapter 16).

A few days after the end of the annual Society meeting, several prominent members attended the Lake Mohonk Conference, which for the first time highlighted what was called the "peyote menace." Presumably, the Society members (including Marie L. Baldwin, Henry Roe Cloud, Charles Dagenett, and Arthur Parker) agreed to the conference resolution that "the Federal prohibition of intoxicating liquors be extended to include this dangerous drug."[65]

A delegation of the Society, not including Montezuma and Eastman, met with President Wilson on December 10, 1914, to present a resolution that asked for a commission to clarify and codify Indian laws and to allow Indians access to the Court of Claims.[66] Montezuma was asked to be a member of the delegation, but decided he could not afford the cost of the trip. The meeting was heralded by the Society in its journal and at its winter banquet, but it had no effect on actual government policy. There was a rising current of opposition to the Society, voiced by Charles Eastman among others, that called for more attention to the Indians themselves and less to governmental affairs. For example, the Society had not aided at all the great need for legal services among reservation Indians. The inability to reform the problems it identified and the failure to address the needs and complaints of reservation Indians made the Society vulnerable to the factionalism that soon followed.

The Society of American Indians struggled with three major divisive issues: (1) its relationship with the Bureau of Indian Affairs, (2) the peyote religion, and (3) its responses to specific complaints and problems originating with a tribe or a faction within a tribe.[67] These issues began to be manifested by conflicts at the 1915 annual conference at Lawrence, Kansas. The sessions took place at the University of Kansas and the Haskell Institute, which was beginning to replace Carlisle as the leading off-reservation boarding school. The location encouraged a greater attendance from the western reservations, and this was achieved, bringing to the conference a significant number of practitioners of the peyote religion. In addition to the peyotists, many delegates in the total attendance of ninety-five came specifically to present tribal problems and complaints. The 1915 conference embraced the growing national movement of prohibition by calling for the suppression of alcohol sales to Indians.

In the spring of 1915, Montezuma enlisted the Society in his effort to obtain permission to visit various reservations in Arizona. Commissioner Sells in the midst of battling Montezuma over tribal land and water rights in Arizona (Chapter 12) refused to cooperate. This interaction with the Indian Bureau provided even more motivation for one of Montezuma's most successful and dramatic speeches, "Let My People Go," presented at the 1915 meeting of the Society, advocating immediate elimination of the Indian Bureau and attacking the Society for its inactivity. Montezuma worked hard on this speech. He told Pratt: "It took me over two weeks to arrange what I had already written and today a friend is going to type-write the manuscript then I will correct and boil it down to forty minutes."[68]

## LET MY PEOPLE GO

From Time immemorial, in the beginning of man's history, there come echoes and re-echoes of pleas that are deeper than life.

This is an age of abusiveness, "man's inhumanity to man," where man experiments with man; it is an age where money (the idol) is dominant; it is an age of tyranny, where might is right; yet producing such material achievements and advancement as the world has never seen. It is an age where we hide and ask God, "Am I my brother's keeper?" It is an age where man's noblest character that reaches to God must not waver but must be strong and see the right.

The Society of American Indians has met and met. This coming together every year has been the mere routine of shaking hands, appointing committees, listening to papers, hearing discussions, passing a few resolutions, electing officers, then reorganizing—and that has been the extent of our outlook and usefulness for our race. Our placing too much faith and confidence in the Indian Bureau has caused us to evade the vital, the most important and fundamental object of our Society. Mohonk Conferences, Indian Rights Association, Indian Friends, and other similar organizations have also evaded the vital, paramount issue; if they did touch on it, they did it in the form of a whisper.

In the bloody and gloomy days of Indian history, public sentiment was against the Indians—that they could not be civilized; they could not be educated; they were somewhat like human beings, but not quite within the line of human rights; the only hope was to let the bullets do the work, cover up the bloody deeds and say no more—God and humanity were forgotten.

At that hour, when Indians were made "good Indians," as a lightning from the clear sky, out from the frontier, among Indian-fighting soldiers, a voice came: "Stay the sword, the Indian is a man." That voice was no less than Lieut. R. H. Pratt, now our most beloved and honored benefactor, Brig. General, the founder of Indian education and the foremost student on Indian matters.

Patient, silent and distant the Indian race has been these many years.

There comes a time in human events when abandonment of racial responsibilities becomes very oppressive, unbearable, intolerable, and there seems to be no hope—then man must exert himself, speak and act.

The status of our people is not on the square, for that reason, Brothers, that time has come to our race. The Society of American Indians is not free. We are wards, we are not free! Wake up, Indians, all over America! We are hoodwinked, duped more and more every year; we are made to feel that we are free when we are not. We are chained hand and foot, we stand helpless, innocently waiting for the fulfillment of promises, that will never be fulfilled, in the overwhelming great ocean of civilization.

Civilization is our monarch. As a race, we are at a crisis. Our position as a race and our rights must not be questioned. Looking from all points of the compass, there is only one object for this Society of Indians to work for, namely— "Freedom for our people."

It seems so strange that some members of the Society cannot understand the object of this paper, and these are their questions:—"We are ready to abolish the Indian Bureau, but how?" "Wait, let us settle this and that first." Another one says, "Doctor, I stand pat with you on doing away with the Indian Bureau, but let us get an understanding of this and that first." "Do not stir up a revolution until we are ready." "Evolution and not revolution."

Some well-meaning people feel very bad over this matter of taking away the support of the Indians. They pass their hands over their foreheads, take a long sigh, sadly look into space and wonder how we are going to free the Indians. And what will become of the poor Indians then? This going here and there seeking to find a solution to the Indian problem is all nonsense. It has been a problem so long that it has become a problem.

Gen. Pratt's words are true, that "the Indian is no problem." It is all in our mind. To free the Indian is to free the Indian. There is nothing complicated about that. It is so simple that we cannot believe it.

Common sense teaches us that when you free the Indian in civilization the Indian will civilize himself—it is automatic and involuntary—and that to free the Indian from Bureauism is to free him from Bureauism.

My co-workers, if we disagree as a Society of Indians in this matter, those who do not think as we do will just chuckle and gloat over our factions. It is just what they want. It favors them and weakens us as an Indian organization. If we cannot attend to our own affairs as a Society of American Indians, they will point to us and say, "I thought so. They are Indians, they can't do anything." Now we must do something and show that the Indians CAN DO.

The question of abolishing the Indian Bureau is not a new idea. Eleven years ago the progress of the Indian race had reached that stage of preparation that enabled them to be independent of Government supervision and to be told to go their own way and be their own self-supporters.

Gen. Pratt sounded the keynote when he said: "I believe that nothing better could have happened to the Indians than the complete destruction of the Bureau which keeps them so carefully laid away in the dark of its numerous drawers, together with all its varied influences, which only serve to bolster and maintain tribal conditions. The early death of the 'Freedom's Bureau' was an infinite blessing to the Negro himself and to the country as well. If you say the turning loose of this large number of ignorant and unprepared people would threaten the peace of our communities, I say that not a year within the last thirty but we have imported from foreign countries and turned loose in the United States a much greater number of no less unprepared and ignorant people. One thing is certain, this Bureau will never lift its finger to end its own life, and we can rely on it that its emotions are most pleasurable when Congress adds to it increased responsibilities in the distribution of money, etc. It is a barnacle to be knocked off some time. Better, far better for the Indians had there never been a Bureau. Then self-preservation would have led the individual Indian to find his true place, and his real emancipation would have been speedily consummated."

When Gen. Pratt uttered these words, he thought that the country and the President were with him in heart and soul for the betterment of the Indians, as in the past. Not so—humiliatingly he was made to realize that there was some one higher than he, some one to be considered, some one to be reckoned with. He found himself relieved from the great institution he founded and cherished, and where he had hoped to see his last days. He had said too much. He was in the Indian service under the Bureau and his head was cut off—1904.

With regret the writer must mention the fact that the Mohonk Conference, Indian Rights Association, and National Indian Association were silent and dumb. Not a word of protest was heard from them. Shame upon them! If they were true and loyal friends of the Indians, such would not have occurred.

Government:—"Say, Sitting Bull, I know you are a good fellow, but you are as a child in looking after your business, you are easily cheated and robbed. I know it because I have done it myself. Now, my good friend Sitting Bull, I will tell you what to do. You give everything over to me and I will do everything for you."

That is about how we came to be wards of the government. They and we as their children, have paid dearly in every way to have the United States Government in charge of us as wards.

It is a psychological fact that by everlastingly hearing and pointing that "you are an Indian," that "you are a ward," that "you are a child and must be protected," that "you have property and we must be your real estate agent," that "you must not do anything without your superintendent's approval," that "you are not ready to live as a free man," it is a scientific fact that after awhile you will actually believe that it is all true, that you are different from other races, that you have "Washington" for your father, that he feels your weakness as a child, and that the government is so good as to protect you, that the superintendent and "Washington" will attend to your rights, and that if they want you to sign your thumb-mark or name to their papers, you have to. The Indian knows nothing else. Alas, everything is taken from him without his consent and without his being consulted. The jail is close by if the Indian does not obey.

Today the Indian Bureau is founded on a wrong basis. It is un-American. It is pursuing unnatural methods to reap natural results. Being unnatural, it has come to be a heavy burden instead of a help to the Indians. It is dominated by the Indian Service Regulations, thus dominating the Indians and perpetuating itself. It has swerved from its noble course. It has derailed the Indians from the main road that other races travel. It has gone into commercial business; it is methods and methods and promotions.

The original grand, noble and ideal object of the Indian Bureau was to aid and protect the Indian and prepare him to emerge from his wigwam into civilization, and it has been a total failure.

Within my period of years there have been ten or twelve commissioners of Indian affairs. Most of them are dead, and the machine still exists to be greased and tinkered with. It is a political machine, where one goes out and another comes in, taking turns greasing and adjusting the Indian machine.

The gradual process of civilizing the Indians seems well enough, but experience teaches us, and as we study the case, it seems more and more like the good Saint's method of shortening his dog's long tail. He was a very sympathetic and humane man. He concluded to shorten it by the gradual process. To do it nicely he cut off a little piece of the tail one day and another piece off at another time, and so he continued to sever the dog's tail by installments, so as not to hurt the dear dog too much.

This humane and sentimental process has not been practical and has done the Indian a great deal of harm before the world. It has been a blind; a pretension that you are doing something. It is never ceasing, never ending.

There is a wrong feeling, a wrong thought, and a wrong judgment that we must fight. It is an individual battle! It is called "prejudice."

Keep in mind that Indian Bureau, Indian Reservations, Indian Schools, Indian College, Indian Art, Indian Novels, Indian Music, Indian Shows, Indian Movies, and Indian Everything create prejudice and do not help our race. To tackle prejudice it is better to do it face to face in the busy world. To play the same card as the other fellow we must know him.

Before leaving the Indian Service I wrote to a good friend asking him what he thought of my leaving the government service and hanging out my shingle in Chicago. He replied, "Well, doctor, I would advise you to stick to the government job where the pay is sure. If you come to Chicago I am afraid you will not make a success here because there will be a prejudice against you, even though you may be the best physician—you are an Indian."

When I read these words, my Apache blood rushed into my head and I said, "God helping me, I will resign the government service and go back to Chicago and fight prejudice." I was willing to sacrifice everything for my race, so I took the choice of coming in contact with prejudice and going against the current of life and defying the world for the rights with which God has endowed the Indian, as one of His creatures, and I assure you I am not discouraged or dismayed.

To fight is to forget ourselves as Indians in the world. To think of oneself as different from the mass is not healthy. Push forward as one of them, be congenial and be in harmony with your environments and make yourselves feel at home as one of the units in the big family of America. Make good, deliver the goods, and convince the world by your character that the Indians are not as they have been misrepresented to be.

Members of this Society, we have been drilling in our uniforms, but not fighting. Now we must fight or go out of existence. When Gen. Pratt was unjustly dismissed from the Indian service, the bar that debarred special interest people was let down. The Indians were no longer protected by a wise father. These would-be friends of the Indians discovered the Indian to be an ideal and fit subject to be exploited by the Indian Bureau, by the missionaries, by the philanthropists, by the anthropologists, by the sociologists, by the psychologists, by the archaeologists, by the artists, by the novelists, and O Lord, no telling how many can use the Indian. Scientifically, the native child of the forest is so useful. They rushed in pell-mell, tumbling over one another, and the Indian was used as an Indian—as a man he was lost sight of. Our race fell back in its advancement fifty years, and where is our General Pratt?

The reservation is a hot-house, the wrong "melting pot," a demoralizing prison of idleness, beggary, gambling, pauperism, and ruin—where the Indians remain as Indians, a barrier against enlightenment and knowledge. There is not one redeeming feature on the Indian reservations for the Indians. The Indians condemn it; anyone who knows the reservation, condemns it, and those who have thought seriously to ascertain its redeeming qualities have condemned it; even the Indian department condemns it but does not dare to say so, or it would be without a job. The one feeds the other.

The reservation system is a ruinous phantom for the Indians, a deceptive dream of hope that has rainbow spectrum, it is like that mirage upon the burning sands of the desert; now you see it, now you don't see it, and you die dreaming of it. It is a decoy that leads us to our doom.

The pale-face boys and girls are kept at home and sent to public schools and sent away to colleges. When they finish school, these same boys and girls go away from home and make their own way in the busy active life of the country—to succeed or fail; survive or perish. They know not what may befall them, they only take their chance away from home. For in this journey of life God's decree is that we cannot see the path all the way—only from day to day; nor the hereafter, only by faith. The start is hard, we know it is hard and killing, but it fits us to compete with the world.

The Indian boys and girls are schooled on reservations near their Indian homes. By promotion they go into non-reservation Indian boarding schools. To go higher, they enter Carlisle, Haskell or other government Indian boarding schools, and when these same boys and girls finish the eighth grade, they are carefully sent back to their homes on the reservations. That ends his or her school chapter, and what has been the outcome of such method of Indian schooling? Back, back in everything, of course.

But thanks, be to God, names can be mentioned whose owners did not get all their education on reservations: Senator Owens, Congressman Carter, Ex-Senator Curtis, Dr. Eastman, the late Dr. Oronhyatekha, Mr. Parker—formerly of the Treasury—Rev. Wright, Dr. Favill, and many others.—Now, where are the names of those Indians who have been educated on reservations? It is not surprising that no name can be mentioned.

Somehow or other the idea prevails that the Indian's sphere of action in this life and in America should be limited within the wigwam. And when an Indian boy or girl goes away to school you hear the hounding voices saying, "Go back, go back to your home and people!" These good people and many others seem to convey the ideas that Indians are strangers in America. And strange to say, these people have the whole world for their action, and they are far away from their place of birth, and when they came the Indian was here; and, of course, the Indians, too, must have the whole world for their sphere of action.

There are hundreds of Indian employees in the Indian Service. To a casual observer this may appear as though the United States Government is magnanimous, considerate of its wards by giving employment to the schooled Indian boys and girls and to others who can fill positions and pass civil-service examinations. Man is the outcome of his environment. If employed in the Indian Service of the Government, that person will carry with him the atmosphere of that service, be he from any race. Anyone who conscientiously and unselfishly starts in the Indian Service to sacrifice his ambition in behalf of the Indian in time will fall into the rut, get tired, disgusted, and lose interest, and finally see no use, and he will fall into the level of his surroundings and stick to his job. He has lost sight of the grand object that he had at first, but he sticks to his job.

Just so with the Indian employees in the Indian Service; their personality is destroyed. To keep their positions, to be in the swim, they must not express themselves; they have nothing to say. They stick to the Indian Service and hate to lose their jobs.

Indian employees in the Indian Service are working against the freedom of their race.

What is the Society of American Indians good for? Dare we shy? Dare we run? Dare we cower? And dare we hide when our duty is so plainly written before us? As a Society with the greatest object for our people, it should be no longer possible to evade the issue—the responsibility rests with us to be message runners to every camp and to let every Indian know that it remains with every individual Indian to be free.

It is appalling and inexplicable that the pale-faces have taken all of the Indian's property—the continent of America—which was all he had in the world. The Indian asks for public school, college and university education for his children. To refuse such a noble request would be as cruel as to give a stone when he asks for bread. Will the Department defray the expenses of any college or university Indian students? The Indian Bureau's motto seems to be, "Eighth grade and no more." And therefore we may assume that the Indian department does not want the Indians educated. It may be wise, and is afraid that they will make too many lawyers who will fight it to a finish. It may be that the Indian Bureau fears something may happen from the Indian's knowledge of doing something.

To dominate a race you do not want to educate them. All one needs to do is to make them believe black is white, and get them to believe everything you do is all right. Let them live Indian life. Let them fear you. Let them quibble among themselves. Give them plenty of sweets and tell them things will come out all right; for them not to worry, but leave it all to their "Washington Father," he is "Good Medicine," and all will be well. Blessed is the Superintendent who has this executive ability.

The life of the Indian Bureau is supported by plausibilities and by civil service. No discredit to the principles of civil service, but when it comes to clinch and hold the lid down and keep the Indians from their liberty by its good name—than it is time that a loud protest should come from the Society of American Indians. The merit system has a limit when it stands in the way of human rights.

The Indian Bureau is willing and anxious to do everything for the Indians, but—! It says: "If there is anything wrong, we can remedy it ourselves because we are in a position to know the needs of the Indians, and do not believe, But—!

"Thou good and faithful servant" cannot be applied to the Indian Bureau; from a lamb it has grown to be a strong monster. It looks with furious glare at every movement we make, lest we take away the Indians from its blood-stained paws, because it pays to continue the same old policy, to keep us within due bonds.

The Indian Bureau could dissolve itself and go out of business, but what is the use? Just think, 8000 employees would be jobless, and there would be no eleven-million dollar appropriation! By dissolving, it would be killing its hen that lays the golden egg. Having nursed the Indians for so long, they might be lonesome living without Indians. There is no other race to draw upon to keep the wolf from the door. The last thing it thinks of is to let go of the Indians. It will fight to the last ditch because they are its bread and butter—they are its money and have sacrificed their service to the cause.

Therefore, it is useless to look within the Indian Department for relief. It must come from the outside—from Congress and the people.

Some may ask, can we not adjust or reform the Indian Bureau so that it will accomplish something for the Indians? The Indian Bureau system is wrong. The only way to adjust wrong is to abolish it, and the only reform is to let my people go. After freeing the Indian from the shackles of government supervision, what is the Indian going to do? Leave that with the Indian, and it is none of your business. Leave an Indian and a Yankee on a desert to live or die—I will vouch on an Indian every time, that he will make a living. This idea that the Indian will starve to death when the Indian Bureau is abolished is all talk, and there is nothing to it. He has to settle everything for himself. He has to do the same as you and I—and that is freedom.

The Indian Bureau has not left the Indians, but is awfully busy with a third party. The third party wants this and wants that, backed by Congressmen and by Senators, and by a long list of petitioners. The Indian Bureau jibes in with the third party, and they both agree that the Indian has too much land. "He has no use for so much. Let us open up a part of it to the public, sell the land and deposit the money to his credit—in the Treasury, and have the interest money paid to him quarterly." If the Indians want 50 cents and the tribe has $200.00 in the Treasury, the department takes the 50 cents from the $200.00 and the Indian believes it comes from Washington by taxing the public. That honest (if you can call it honest) method is called the reimbursement fund.

Reimbursement charity is the most damnable charity conceivable, and it takes away as much burden from the Indians as that good and kindhearted old lady did when she held her heavy market basket out of the wagon, on scaling the steep hill, so that the poor horses would not have such a heavy load to pull up the hill. The Indians have to pull the heavy load up the hill of the Indian Bureau System, while the Indian Bureau rides and thinks it is helping us by holding its heavy basket out of the wagon.

What did the Indians get for their land that is flooded? How much did the Indians get for the land that irrigation ditches pass through? How much did the Indians get from the forest reserve, and the natural park reserve? These are the questions yet to be settled, if the government has not protected us as its wards.

Is the Indians' reimbursement fund government appropriation, or is it the Indian paying himself?

Has the Indian no right to express himself or to be consulted and give his approval of the construction of a dam on his domain?

Has he no right to say what part of his reservation may be sold?

Coming down to the fine point, has the Indian any right to open his mouth, to think for himself, or to do for himself, or even to lie and breathe for himself?

Not at all—not at all! The Indian Bureau—the Indian Bureau does it all. If there is such a place as hell, O, It's like Hell! O, it's like Hell to me.

Fairly speaking, the "Century of Dishonor," by Helen Hunt Jackson, bears a tale that is mild in comparison to the present Indian administration.

The iron hand of the Indian Bureau has us in charge. The slimy clutches of horrid greed and selfish interests are gripping the Indian's property. Little by little the Indians' land and everything else is fading into a dim and unknown realm.

The Indian's prognosis is bad—unfavorable, no hope. The foreboding prodromic signs are visible here and there now—and when all the Indian's money in the United States Treasury is disposed of—when the Indian's property is all taken from him—when the Indians have nothing in this wide, wide world—when the Indians will have no rights, no place to lay their heads—and when the Indians will be permitted to exist only on the outskirts of the towns—when they must go to the garbage boxes in alleys, to keep them from starving—when the Indians will be driven into the streets, and finally the streets will be no place for them.—THEN what will the Indian Bureau do for them? NOTHING, BUT DROP THEM: The Indian Department will go out of business.

In other words, when the Indians will need the most help in this world, that philanthropic department of the government that we call the Indian Bureau, will cease to exist; bankrupt with liabilities—billions and billions—no assets, O Lord, my God, what a fate has the Indian Bureau for my people.

If we depend upon the employees of the Indian Bureau for our life, liberty and pursuit of happiness, we wait a long while. They are too busy looking after the machinery of Indian Affairs; they have no time to look ahead; they have no time to feel the pulse of the Indian; they have no time to think of outside matters; they have no time to adjust matters. "Well, what time have they?" you ask. All of their time is devoted to the pleasure and will of their master at Washington, that we call the Indian Bureau.

Blindly they think they are helping and uplifting, when in reality they are a hindrance, a draw-back and a blockade on the road that would lead the Indian to freedom, that he may find his true place in the realms of mortal beings.

The reservation Indians are prisoners; they cannot do anything for themselves. We are on the outside, and it is the outsiders that must work to free the Indians from Bureauism. There is no fear of the general public; they are our friends. When they find out that we are not free they will free us. We have a running chance with the public, but no chance with the Indian Bureau.

The abolishment of the Indian Bureau will not only benefit the Indians, but the country will derive more money annually from the Indians than the Government has appropriated to them. Why? Because by doing away with the Indian Bureau you stop making paupers and useless beings and start the making of producers and workers.

Does this seem like a dream to you? Is your position a foreign attitude? From aloft, do you look down? Have you gone so far as to forget your race? Have you quenched the spirit of our fathers? As their children, dare we stay back, hide ourselves and be dumb at this hour, when we see our race abused, misused and driven to its doom? If this be not so, then let whatever loyalty and racial pride be in you awaken and manifest itself in this greatest movement of "Let My People Go!"

The highest duty and greatest object, of the Society of American Indians, is to have a bill introduced in our next Congress to have the Indian Bureau abolished and to let the Indians go. We cannot be disinterested in this matter, we cannot be jealous or hate one another, we cannot quibble or be personal in this matter. There must be no suspicion.

We must act as one. Our hearts must throb with love—our souls must reach to God to guide us—and our bodies and souls must be used to gain our peoples' freedom.

In behalf of our people, with the spirit of Moses, I ask this—THE UNITED STATES OF AMERICA—"LET MY PEOPLE GO."[69]

Montezuma's speech generated a mixed response. Some, like Thomas Sloan, were pleased and considered it a righteous punch against the Indian Bureau. Others focused on Montezuma's failure to propose an alternative. Parker said: "The fiery Apache wields a scalping knife in the sure hand of an experienced physician, …[to] fail to provide adequate laws and regulations for the conservation of his heritage would be poor wisdom. …Let the Indian go. Surely, let him go as soon as he can go. Abolish the Bureau? Surely, abolish it and provide a sane commission for this human task. …just as soon as the Indian is actually able to compete on an equal footing with other men he has made himself free. Such a man needs no Bureau to concern itself with his Indianness. …But the Indian race is not yet competent, the Indian civilization is imperfect, the Indian commercial instincts are predatory, the ideal democracy has not yet been attained."[70]

Parker wrote to Montezuma right after the conference: "I believe that the only thing that prevented the majority from understanding the situation was the term 'abolish,' without a tentative plan at least for holding the various legal matters and property rights now pending settlement."[71] Although there were many who regarded the reservations as an evil to be eliminated, there were more who were committed to maintaining the formal treaty rights of Indians, knowing especially that this was essential in order to retain Indian lands. Montezuma publicized the problems of the reservation and the Bureau of Indian Affairs, but offered no plan to maintain Indian lands other than allotment. As a result of the assimilation and allotment philosophy, the Bureau of Indian Affairs dominated every aspect of life on the reservations. The cost of an abrupt end would be enormous. August Breuninger, a politically active Menominee Indian, wrote to Montezuma: "You, as well as myself, know that there is need of an organization among us. Yet, on the other hand, you adhere to a theory that is 'division' in itself. You preach separation. How can we unite, when we always shall be separated? Your theory is alright if the Indian did not have any physical property to look after and protect. Shall he let this go and jump in and say, 'let me sink or swim?' I don't believe in it. I don't care to throw away my property simply just because I can go out into the world and mingle with the masses, forget my home and folks and other things, but I believe in taking care of what I've got."[72]

Montezuma's emotional answers to these criticisms were adequate in his own mind, but they failed to provide a substantial plan:

> Those who advocate the continuance of the Indian Bureau have this to offer: first—If the Indians are freed from the Indian Bureau the pale face rascals will cheat them out of their property; second—If we do not have the Indian Bureau to look out for them the old people will starve because they cannot work; third—The Indian Bureau knows how to take care of the Indians and if they are freed from under their care in a short time a great many of them will be inmates of the poor houses.
>
> To answer the first argument: The other day the writer asked one of the best real estate men in the country—"How can one learn to keep and appreciate his property?" His reply was, "Lose it." In order to compete with the world we have to meet the rascals—the sooner the better. To help the Indians to escape that stage in life is a mere subterfuge. To answer the second—scare-crow: It is a real fact that among Indians everybody had a home; my home is your home and your home is mine. What is yours is mine and what is mine is yours. When the Indian Bureau goes out of existence, the aged, the orphans and the sick will always find a home among the Indians, as they did before the Indian Bureau ever existed, and they will find their pale face neighbors more helpful than the Indian Bureau.
>
> The third question: Several years ago when some Indians in the state of Washington were let loose from the supervision of the government, that argument was used before the Indians were freed, by the state against the government. The state did not want any more paupers to support. The state of Washington thought that Uncle Sam was better able to support Indian paupers than they were. Several months ago a prominent citizen thought he would go to the poor house and see whether there were any Indians there. He was shocked and dumbfounded to find no Indians in the poor house. That is the Indian of it, and you need not fear about the poor house for the emancipated Indians. Their affinity is somewhere else.[73]

Montezuma's description of the 1915 Society meeting, found as usual in a letter to Richard Pratt, conveys the excitement of the meeting and his own personal reaction to the reception of his speech.

Tonight a week ago I left Chicago for Lawrence, Kansas with John Oskison and arrived at our destination the next morning about eleven o'clock, where we found the receiving delegation and [were] escorted to the Eldrige Hotel. Mr. Parker, Mrs. Baldwin, Coolidge, Mrs Bonnin (Zitkala Za) [*sic*] Mrs Brown of Denver, Henry Roe Cloud, Mrs Roe, Miss De Pelt …I should say about 75 in all. We were lively greeting each other. For several days some one arrived for the Conference, delegation of three from Crow Agency, four from Pawnee, six or seven from Oklahoma, one from Wyoming, four from Wisconsin and as many from Minnesota. I should say in all there were 150 at the Conference. It was a fair showing.

The first evening we had the city Mayor and other prominent men to speak for us and several of our delegates responded. It was a very pleasant gathering. I enclose you the whole programme of each day. I assure you we did ourselves justice for the cause. But— But—when the crucial test came *they were not there*. You will understand what I mean after you read my "Let My People Go" which I enclose a copy.

Between 150 & 200 heard my voice as I stood there proclaiming the message of freedom. Over one hour I held them on the paper. God was with me but those missionaries, Indian Service employees, Indian Societies, and scientists were touched. They thought I was crazy and out of place to read such a foolish paper. I did not know what I was talking about. I was doing more harm than good. I was awful and ought to have staid [*sic*] away. The Secretary did not ask for my paper as he did with others. That paper marked me as "undesirable." General, in my heart I know I hit the mark and that was all I wanted for my people. That afternoon after the meeting I went right out and leave (hotel) alone. I had a long walk on the beautiful campus of the University. I did this in order that they may "boil over" to themselves and get "cool to themselves." The arrow of my words still hurts and the healing will leave a mark that they will never forget. No one but the real Indians and Sloan and Father Gordon complimented me for the paper. I gave the Apache shot and it landed in the right spot.

I will tell you another episode. Friday evening our meeting was held at the Haskell Institute. Folks from the city, University, pupils and employees of the Institute were there. The chapel was crowded. Several months ago I wrote an article on "Indian Day" and I brought it with me but did not expect to use it. I looked at the program that morning I saw for the first "Proclamation of Indian Day." So I took "the gun" with me thinking I might see a "big game." Sure enough after several speeches and music, Parker read his proclamation and Coolidge backed it up. Parker said that the honor of this movement must be shared by the Haskell students and he wished the vote of the students on the proclamation. That was decided upon but there I was. Quick as a flash after he finished I was on my feet and said, if the pupils are going to vote on this proclamation they ought to hear both sides before taking a vote. So I asked to be heard and the President consented. I took my manuscript and read my paper. You never saw such enthusiasm as manifested by the pupils. They were with me from the beginning to the end. I cannot begin to describe it. You must ask some one else. After I finished Coolidge tried to explain but he was drowned with noise, he was so embarrassed that he had to stop and drop the proclamation and hear the next paper. But that was not all. Unexpectedly a student from the audience got up and said that he thought the pupils were ready to take a vote in courtesy to the Society of American Indians. That made another commotion. In the roar another pupil arose and opposed any voting without discussing the whole situation. That same boy stood his ground and expressed what he had to say. Then I got up and said that it is not right to bring any questionable subject before this school. The pupils are in a peculiar position and it is not right to embarrass our good Superintendent and besides the Society has not voted on this matter. We better attend to our own business. There was such uneasyness, it was dropped. And that ended "Indian Day" craze. No telling what was done on Sunday on the matter. I left Sunday afternoon for Chicago.

The Society voted a special committee to form a resolution on my paper of doing away with the Indian Bureau. Sloan was the chairman. It was brought up but it was killed with a substitute resolution that had no words of doing away with Indian Bureau.

...Mrs. Goullette and Mrs. Bonnin opposed me strongly. You may be surprised as I was to know that Father Gordon stood firmly with Sloan and I. Missionaries and Indian Service employees carried the election, but what do you think, they elected Sloan as legal man for the Society. That is better than being President of the Society.

To tell you the truth I was disgusted to the highest degree to think that the Society ignored my plea for freedom, when it is to their interest as well as to the poor Indians.

Another thing I want you to know. I never saw Parker so weak. I guess I commended him in my paper as I did with many of the members. The past rolled in with missionaries and Indian employees. In one of my talks I said, "I did not come in the interest of the missionaries and Indian employees in the Indian Service." I feel as though the Society is protecting itself more than the Indians.

...I do not know what to think of the Society. Many times I have thought of leaving them alone and again I brighten up and take things philosophically that it is natural and the only thing for me to do is to stick and let others drop out. In the long run the Society will come out and travel in the right road.

General, yet with all mistakes I think I am on the top. They know where I stand and I have given something for them to think about.[74]

The Society had a different version, publishing in the *Quarterly Journal* that "American Indian Day, the second Saturday in May, was proclaimed tonight before an audience of 1,200 wildly cheering Indians, representing the majority of the tribes."[75]

Montezuma, with Pratt's prodding and a $10 contribution, decided to publish and distribute his speech. He had 5,000 copies of "Let My People Go" printed by the Hawthorne Press (adding his picture and some original cartoons, for example, an Indian with the weight of the Indian Bureau on his shoulders), addressed and mailed them himself, and sent them to many congressmen, newspaper editors, magazines, libraries, college presidents, city school superintendents, workers in the Indian Service, all the associate members of the Society, and everyone on his mailing list. What a mailing list he must have had! Indeed, he had to order 5,000 more copies and requested ten cents per copy from those who could pay (it cost Montezuma $60 for printing and $40 for stamps for each batch of 5,000).[76] This activity motivated Montezuma to begin thinking and planning for the publication of a monthly pamphlet, with only one objective: "Have the Indian Bureau abolished for the best interest of the Indians."[77]

GERTRUDE BONNIN (Zitkala-Ša) joined the advisory board of the Society of American Indians in 1914. At the 1915 annual conference, the Society called for the establishment of social and educational community centers on Indian reservations patterned after Zitkala-Ša's women's classes in Utah. Zitkala-Ša established the first center later in 1915 on the Uintah Ouray Ute reservation, and even successfully recruited agency funds. However, even this center had limited success, and without Society funds (and committed individuals such as Zitkala-Ša), the social service mission was never accomplished.

The Society changed the name of its journal in 1916, from *The Quarterly Journal* to *The American Indian Magazine, the Quarterly Journal of the Society of American Indians*. Arthur Parker, still the editor, wished to have the journal be less restrictive, to be more representative of all Indians. Parker addressed the divisive issues facing the Society in an editorial in the first issue of the new journal.[78] He reinforced the philosophy of assimilation, proclaiming that the Indian's future was with the White race in a civilization derived from the old world. The divisive issues, he claimed, paled when measured against the basic need to provide guidance to all Indians. Voicing specific complaints and political positions was not the primary purpose of the Society. "The Society must think of more and greater things than a defective bureau, ridden with inherited diseases, corrupt with politics and deformed with a crooked pedigree. *The political function of the Society is only one of its activities and not the greatest.*"[79] This same issue, in a spirit of openness, published an extract of Montezuma's speech, "Let My People Go," but it was only ten paragraphs and two pages long, not enough to please Montezuma. This issue also published Zitkala-Ša's poem that poignantly and publicly revealed her awakening and return to the Indians' cause (Chapter 9).

Parker countered the plea in Montezuma's speech with a carefully crafted clever statement. "The Indian Bureau has an amazing task. It is the laboratory for manmaking. Here are brewed the theories, here are concocted the elixirs, here are compounded the panaceas. In the middle of one experiment the chemist is shifted. His crucible is drenched with a land grabber's chloroform, a clever politician throws in pork hook, a mining interest casts in some steel shavings and the stockman mixes in a lump of cyanide. A new Commissioner steps to the task, tries to clear the table and serves the compound, mixed with his own healing balm. The red man swallows the dose. Alas, too many chemists have spoiled the elixir and Poor Lo is put in the cauldron and boiled over again. Little wonder in his misery he is like Frankenstein's creation. And so the Indian will become exactly what his laboratory manufactured environment makes him."[80] Parker favored reorganization of the Bureau in some way that would make it independent of politics. "With a definite purpose, with scientific method, with logical application we shall have genuine results, and our laboratory may view its finished product, a vigorous American Indian citizen."[81]

The Society had been promoting for several years the idea strongly supported by Arthur Parker of an American Indian Day, as presented to the Haskell students in the fall of 1915. This day, as suggested in *The American Indian Magazine*, was to emphasize the Indians, not only as a race, but also as Americans featuring the "Star Spangled Banner" and a salute to the American flag. American Indian Day was celebrated in many schools in America in 1916, but April 1916 also saw the appearance of the first issue of *Wassaja*, Montezuma's monthly newsletter.

In his first issue, Montezuma described American Indian Day as "a farce," an exercise that denied the importance of gaining freedom from the Indian Bureau. *The American Indian Magazine* became a recipient of his scorn: "Now it can straddle any old thing that comes along. Like all magazines, it cannot have any definite object, but to tickle its readers at the expense of the Indians. Buffalo Bill and P.T. Barnum used the Indians. Now it is the American Indian Magazine's turn."[82]

*Wassaja* called for equal treatment of Indians with the full privileges and responsibilities of citizenship. Montezuma's constant theme was to be reiterated again and again: the reservation system is an obstacle. Let the Indian stand on his own to be educated in the public school system; abolish the Indian Bureau and the Indian will be free. He went so far as to say that the Indian does not desire to preserve his distinctiveness, a personal statement that conflicted with Montezuma's own frequent flaunting of his "Apache" character and background. Montezuma's constant attacks on the Society only served to increase the divisiveness within the organization. His own position was weakened by a failure to offer any proposals to bring about a transition from before to after the Bureau. He steadfastly held to a sink or swim, Darwinian plan to abruptly drop all Indians into White society. He admitted to Pratt: "Many of the Indians do not understand the stand I take when I say abolish the Indian Bureau. They have an idea 'cut them off' at once without giving them what belongs to them. I know you understand me. It will take several years to close up books, see that the Indians are given what belongs to them before they are set free to do for themselves."[83] Nevertheless, Montezuma failed to spell out a plan for transition, and a workable plan would have had to be considered and accepted before American Indians would follow his lead.

Montezuma sarcastically criticized in *Wassaja* the 1915 annual meeting of the Society.

> *The sky is clear and we meet only to discuss.*
> *There is nothing wrong, only we meet to discuss.*
> *It is so nice to meet and discuss.*
> *We can meet and discuss as well as the Mohonk Conference, Indian Rights Association,*
> *Indian Service Teachers' Association, and the Missionaries.*
> *We will show them we can meet and discuss.*
> *What is the use of worrying? We are only going to meet and discuss.*
> *There is nothing like meeting and discussing.*
> *Meeting and discussing is so soothing and smoothing.*
> *Sh—! Sh—! Don't whisper about the Indian Bureau. We are here only to meet and discuss.*[84]

Parker replied in the next issue of *The American Indian Magazine*. "The Apache doctor is very earnest. He has at heart the real uplift and freedom of his people, and every one may admire him for this. He believes the Indian Bureau an agency of tyranny, by means of which, the Indians are kept in the dark, and the block to freedom. His statements are worthy of a detailed psychological examination. There are reasons why he thinks as he does and writes in his vigorous style. These reasons should be known in weighing the evidence and in estimating the value of his statements."[85] "Dr. Montezuma has a splendid sense of humor and luckily for the rest of us we have also. Dr. Montezuma and all the rest of us at Lawrence said all the things in our systems about the Indian Bureau and nobody stopped us. The only limit anybody had was the time we spent 'showing up the Bureau.' As to the Magazine, if we are using the Indian like a Barnum or a Buffalo Bill, dear readers, please show us how and where. And American Day—why we quoted Montezuma on that day until everybody wanted to 'let that Indian go.' We were glad to give publicity to his views just as we have done in these pages more than once. Montezuma is a vigorous fighter—no one will accuse him of lack of purpose or of intentionally trying to hurt his people. His heart is all the other way. We wish him every success in every noble purpose he undertakes. We wish him power to present without rancor, prejudice or unkindness, in a manner that will appeal to all for its logic and justness, the great truths that will make for efficient, loyal citizenship for the American Indian."[86] Zitkala-Ša commended Parker for not striking back in anger.[87]

The abolition of the Indian Bureau and the peyote religion became the hot topics at the 1916 annual conference of the Society in Cedar Rapids, Iowa. Montezuma continued to attack the *American Indian Magazine*, American Indian Day, and of course the Bureau, always the Bureau. "We cannot work side by side with the Indian Bureau and do any good for the Indians." The Society was going nowhere because Indians knew it was working with the Bureau. "I am not here to fight. I would like to see the Society grow, last year when I came I hoped, it is best of the Indians and friends of the Indians and they do wonderful for the Indians that cannot help themselves but they must go right. When it comes to doing anything radical, when it comes to the point of whether it is right or wrong they craw-fish, they duck. That is what the Society of American Indians do. Now if you want to get on the right side, get out of the talking business, get into the right road and do what you can for the Indian race and then you will succeed. Otherwise, you will die."[88] The Society incorporated a statement in its platform that agreed with the majority of its members, but it wasn't radical enough for Montezuma: "We believe the time has come when we ought to call upon the country and upon Congress to look to the closing of the Indian Bureau, so soon as trust funds, treaty rights and other just obligations can be individualized, fulfilled or paid."[89]

Debate over the Bureau resurrected the conflict that questioned the loyalty of Society members who were employees of the Indian Bureau. Montezuma found an ally in Father Philip Gordon, who became a friend despite the fact that he was a Catholic priest. Gordon claimed that it was not possible to be employed by the government and at the same time be loyal to the Society. Sherman Coolidge took exception, and argued that a Bureau employee could be loyal to his race and to his government. Montezuma said that he opposed the Bureau as a system, that he did not oppose the government or even the commissioner. Others, including Zitkala-Ša, argued that while it was good to have abolition of the Bureau as a goal, this was a goal that had to be achieved gradually, working to the point where the Bureau would no longer be needed. The argument grew heated.

Coolidge: I do not know how many times I must get up and say that I believe an Indian who is a Government employee can be loyal to his race and at the same time be loyal to his Government. Is the fact that I am a clergyman of an Episcopalian church to keep me at the same time from being loyal to the Government?

Montezuma: The Indian Bureau, not the Government.

Coolidge: The Government is represented by the Indian Bureau.

Montezuma: I think not.

Coolidge: I think it is.

Montezuma: It ought to be, but it is not. …As a hireling he is not himself, he cannot be.

> There are Indians in the service, and that is what I am trying to express—they are not supposed to do anything that will embarrass the Indian department, not only the whites but everybody. If I went into the Indian service I would shut my mouth on a good many things.

Coolidge: I think so. You would dare not say somethings. It is about time we are setting you right. You say you cannot mix with the Indian Bureau any more than oil with water. I think you can mix with the Indian Bureau. I have mixed with the Indian Bureau a good many times.[90]

Montezuma jumped to his feet, waving his arms wildly. "I am an Apache," he shouted to Coolidge, "and you are an Arapahoe, I can lick you. My tribe has licked your tribe before." Mr Coolidge replied, "I am from Missouri," a remark that created laughter and decreased the tension.[91] At least that was the version reported in the newspapers. The Indians in the audience, and apparently Montezuma and Coolidge, didn't take the interaction that seriously. "…the Doctor who has a saving sense of humor, humorously mentioned that the Apaches could whip the Araphahoes. 'I am an Apache,' said the doctor significantly. The joke was apparent to all except the reporters who evidently did not notice the towering physique of Sherman Coolidge, the athletic clergyman, president of the Society, and contrast it with the rather short stature of the Apache Doctor. The threat of getting a licking did not disturb the President who looking down at his adversary in the debate replied, 'Well, I'm from Missouri!' The papers from coast to coast, however, seized upon the incident to show that there was 'bad blood' between the two men."[92]

Upon his return to Chicago, Montezuma resigned one more time from the Society and wrote in his newsletter, "Ex-President Coolidge of the Society of American Indians says that he can be loyal to the Indian race and at the same time serve the Indian Bureau. WASSAJA wonders if he serves God and the Devil the same way."[93]

Montezuma explained his reasons to Pratt: "…when an organization of any kind considers itself greater than the object for which it was organized, that body is leaning in the wrong direction. That is about the conclusion I have come to about the Society of American Indians. You saw with your own eyes that missionaries, Indian Bureau and Indian employees in the Indian service were running the whole thing at Cedar Rapids. They may say they WERE NOT, but they did and that is all there is to it. They were forced to mention the abolishment of the Indian Bureau, but they left it in the shade by adding and adding nonsense to it. They seemed to oppose the Indian Bureau, but when it adjourned the Society was arm in arm with the Indian Bureau. You saw how I was downed again and again and I was much displeased to see the way you were treated. …I realize citizenship and freedom go hand in hand, but I am persuaded that the quickest way to make citizens out of the Indians is to free them first. If we go on and judge that this and that Indian is competent to be a citizen, I am afraid by this process we will always have incompetent Indians and, of course, the Indian Bureau must ever exist to look after the incompetent Indians."[94] "I believe more and more that the Indians ought to be freed at once and then adjust as natural laws will dictate. There will be more need of helping the Indians after they are freed than ever. The states and people will do that work. I trust the public more than I would with the Bureau."[95]

Gertrude Bonnin (Zitkala-Ša) wrote to Montezuma begging for conciliation: "My dear good friend, …Publicity is one of the necessary things; and you are right in trying to enlighten the public. So far, so good. I would like to beg you not to make reference to the

Society of American Indians in an unfriendly way. You yourself are not unfriendly. What if today, they seem to you, to do things wrong, be charitable, for we all must learn, day by day, how best to meet the problems of life. ...May I speak for the Society? We do value your membership in our society. We know and see the things you do; it is simply a difference in the method of working out a solution. ...If you could, if you would, Doctor, listen to the plea of one, heart and soul, in this work of Indian liberation, you would resolve, never more to print one word against your Society of American Indians. You would show them charity. I believe it would add strength to your paper, to confine your attack upon the main issue; and refrain from seeming to notice what may appear wrong to you, in the Indian Magazine. ...You are brave and strong. We want you to shield and help guide us, wayward though we appear; we do not want you to deal impatiently with us; or to emphasize our shortcomings to the world. So Doctor, I beg you, be kind to us."[96]

## THE SOCIETY OF AMERICAN INDIANS—DAYS OF DECLINE

The actions of the Society in 1916 began to cause a loss of members. The Society of American Indians at their 1916 conference adopted a resolution put forth by Richard Pratt supporting the passage of the Gandy Bill by Congress outlawing the trade and possession of peyote. The bill passed in the House, but failed in the Senate. The following year, Arizona Congressman Carl M. Hayden introduced a bill in the House to revise liquor traffic laws as they applied to Indians, and peyote was included. The bill passed the House in early 1918, but it failed again in the Senate.

The debate over the Bureau and the final gradualist position adopted by the Society along with the condemnation of peyote alienated important segments of the membership. A lack of Society funds prevented the establishment of effective legal and social services. The new officers faced a daunting challenge: Arthur Parker as president, John M. Oskison as vice president, Gertrude Bonnin (Zitkala-Ša) as secretary, and Marie Baldwin as treasurer. These individuals were moderates in regards to the Indian Bureau and very acceptable to the White associate members. Montezuma's notable and obvious failure to become an officer of the Society can easily be attributed to his radical views. Zitkala-Ša, the secretary of the Society, moved to Washington, established the office of the organization in her own apartment, and quickly became engaged in her conflict with the treasurer, Marie Baldwin (Chapter 9).

Parker, thirty-four years old, began his presidency of the Society at a time when America was threatened with involvement in World War I, and the organization was being weakened by its internal conflicts. He continued to champion assimilation and the dissolution of the tribes, and although he supported the moderate position of gradual change, he grew increasingly disappointed and frustrated with the lack of progress. Specifically, even though he was now the leader of the Society, he was losing confidence in the ability to achieve pan-Indian reform. At the same time, public attention to this domestic issue was diverted to the European war.

Parker, always a consensus builder, moved in 1917 to distance himself from the radical element in the Society. He no longer listed Montezuma and Dennison Wheelock as contributing editors to the *American Indian Magazine*, and he attempted to establish the magazine in a more independent direction. He believed that a magazine and organization, to be effective, had to be removed from the debate and conflict associated with an open, large association. To some degree, Parker's feelings and movements were a consequence of Montezuma's attacks in *Wassaja*.

Montezuma was zeroing in on Parker. As he told Richard Pratt: "General, I am perfectly disgusted with S.A.I. ...They know no more what to do for the Indians than a cat about astronomy. ...Parker likes to be President of the S.A.I. He likes to be at the Mohonk Conference. He likes to be at Universities. He likes the Indian Magazine. He likes Prof McKenzie because he is the father of S.A.I. He likes Gen Pratt because he is old and not for his views on Indian matters. Another reason that he likes Gen Pratt is that he may say, 'I am a personal friend of Gen Pratt's' and thus gain prestige for himself. Parker? I have no use for Parker."[97]

The 1917 annual conference of the Society, scheduled for Oklahoma City, was canceled, ostensibly because of the war, but Parker, and probably the other officers, were also leery of dissension and loss of control of the organization. Montezuma suspected that the Indian Bureau influenced the decision to avoid anti-war talk, and he objected: "Again we pounce upon the officials of the S.A.I. We think that there were not strong reasons to warrant the postponement of the Conference which should have taken place at Oklahoma City. ...If the officers think it has stopped breathing, and have taken the body away for burial, WASSAJA, too, would like to be there. At its birth we were there; so would we be at the grave. ...As an Indian, WASSAJA thinks that the meeting of Indians to discuss their welfare is more important than war (even though we are called savages)."[98]

As Parker grew distant, Zitkala-Ša grew bolder and pushed the organization to plan an annual conference in 1918, and succeeded in not only returning Montezuma to the fold, but maneuvering to provide him with considerable influence in planning the meeting. It was at this time that Zitkala-Ša testified before the House Subcommittee on Indian Affairs in favor of the Hayden Bill intended to suppress the use of liquor and peyote among the Indians, as detailed in Chapter 9.

Montezuma even urged the readers of *Wassaja* to attend the annual conference. The meeting in September 1918 in Pierre, South Dakota, was a success for Montezuma, but not for the organization. Only twenty-five active members were in attendance; even the president, Arthur Parker, was not there, short of funds and obligated by his military duties as a recruiting officer.[99] Many others were serving in the military. But the meeting represented the culmination of Montezuma's efforts, reaching an agreement that called for the immediate abolition of the Bureau of Indian Affairs, an agreement that would have been difficult to achieve if the attendance had been greater and included its usual wide diversity of opinions. Ironically, this was the same year that Carlisle officially closed, becoming U.S. Army Base Hospital No. 31 only three weeks before the Society's conference (Chapter 3). The new officers included Charles Eastman, president, Philip Gordon, vice-president, and Zitkala-Ša, secretary and treasurer. Montezuma, writing in *Wassaja*, was enthusiastic with his praise for the strong action against the Bureau and for the new officers. Montezuma had his presentation, "Abolish the Indian Bureau," printed in a twelve-page pamphlet.[100]

The annual conference re-elected Parker as editor of the *American Indian Magazine*, but he encouraged Zitkala-Ša to become the editor because he believed it was most efficient and practical to house the magazine in the same office as the secretary-treasurer.[101] Zitkala-Ša quickly appointed Montezuma and Gordon as members of the editorial board. The Society was now in the hands of Sioux leadership: Eastman as president and Zitkala-Ša as secretary-treasurer and editor of the magazine. Parker, truly a fine and accomplished man, left the Society, disillusioned and hurt, to concentrate on his own tribe and his own life.[102] The issues of *The American Indian Magazine* after Parker's departure noticeably lack the in depth writings of Parker, writings that flowed with an intelligent and colorful use of the English language.

When the 1918 conference passed a resolution calling for immediate abolition of the Indian Bureau, Montezuma was elated (he even paid for a membership for his wife).[103]

> Yes, I was at the Conference of the Society of Am. Indians. And, as usual, I scared up a hornet's nest by reading a paper on "Abolish the Indian Bureau." As in the past, the Indian Office had a representative on hand. When I finished reading, Mrs. Rhodes gave it to me hot and heavy. She lashed into me for about an hour. Once I saw myself behind the bars for twenty years. She claimed that my paper was seditious, and that I was doing injustice to the Government that has been so kind to the Indian race, and that I was poisoning the good work of the Indian department. My! She laid me out flatter than a pancake. Being a woman she knew how to do it. Roar of cannons and bursting of shells were no where. She pictured degradations and the need of the Indians and how much the Indians needed the Indian Bureau. In my heart I was glad to hear from her, and I knew very well she was doing her best. She finished with great excitement.
>
> Soon as Mrs. Rhodes gave up the floor, Mrs. Bonnin took the floor. She started in slowly and every word counted. She wanted Mrs. Rhodes to know that when I presented the paper, that I explained the matter fully, that the paper was not referring to Hon. Com. Of Indian Affairs nor to the employees in the Indian Service, but the paper was against the system; and that the paper had not one word that was seditious in character. Then she went on from strength to strength in arguments that I never heard from anyone's lips. She was eloquent and true to her race. She had us all in her power. I have heard her speak many times but her reply to Mrs. Rhodes was truly [?]. She went way ahead in arguments and in everything. I guess Mrs. Rhodes was not thinking very much. All she could do was to listen and wonder. All I can say is that it was a wonderful speech.
>
> ...I believe the Society is in the right road to do something. The platform for the abolishment of the Indian Bureau...we cannot any longer evade the vital issue. ...at last we did turn the Society of American Indians. It is now an Indian Society that the Indian Bureau has no voice in.[104]

"No one Indian has stood against the Society of American Indians and no one Indian has criticized it more than 'WASSAJA.' The criticism was not done to destroy the Society, but direct it aright for the best interest of the Indians. Once we withdrew our membership from the Society, because it was weak for the Indians and sought more for the aid of what appeared to be doing a great deal for the Indians. Impressed that the S.A.I can be power for the good of the Indian race, we renewed our membership with unselfish and zealous feeling for the cause which the Society was organized for. In our crude, and often, rude way, we tried to steer the Society in the right path that would lead the Indians into enlightenment, freedom and citizenship. A great many Indians throughout the country stood by us, because of our criticism of the Society, and hesitated to join the Society of American Indians. Also many of our Caucasian friends did not venture to join the Society for the same reason. At last we are in position to say to every one to join the Society of American Indians."[105]

The Society's strong position calling for the immediate abolition of the Indian Bureau left it with only a small band of ardent followers. Most Indians, both off-reservation, middle-class Indians and reservation Indians, could not support the abrupt elimination of the Bureau for two reasons. First, the Society offered no plan to protect those Indians who would abruptly lose government support and protection, and second, maintenance of the Bureau was the only visible method to preserve the Indian land base. Montezuma's position, strong and unswerving, was one of rigid opposition to the Bureau, but it was overly simplistic. Leaving Indians to abruptly fend for themselves was true to his philosophic ideas of assimilation, but it was inconsistent with his own inner generosity and compassion. He never succeeded in bridging his public policy with the subsequent plight of individuals. Like Richard Pratt, Montezuma did not accept and understand the need for the tribal educational preparation that would be necessary and essential before the Bureau could be eliminated. Montezuma, true to his acquired late nineteenth-century Anglo Protestant philosophy, focused on the individual, ignoring Indians as a group, a community. He failed to consider that preservation of tradition does not preclude evolution and change in response to contemporary political and economic problems and pressures, a process that would take over half a century and is still on going.

Montezuma, Eastman, and Gordon toured Wisconsin in May 1919 trying to raise funds and gather new members, promoting the call for citizenship and abolition of the Indian Bureau. At the height of his influence, Montezuma called for unity behind these two goals. "In the cause for freedom and citizenship by the abolishment of the Indian Bureau,

*Gordon and Montezuma in Wisconsin—1919*

we Indians must all unite and be of one mind on the matter; the churches of all denominations must help us. The same motive must prompt the Christian people as it did for the black race, to free the Indian race from the corrupt and enslaving system of the Indian Bureau."[106] Eastman joined in this cause, emphasizing the concept of self-determination, but it was not clear whether he meant individual rights or tribal government.

Montezuma and Gordon planned the 1919 annual conference of the Society. The ninth annual conference met in Minneapolis, Minnesota, in October 1919, with a focus on citizenship legislation. Attendance was better than the previous year, partly because the pro-peyote faction chose to participate. This led to a contest over the presidency between Eastman and Thomas Sloan, an advocate for the religious use of peyote. Despite Zitkala-Ša's efforts, Sloan was elected by an overwhelming margin. Stunned, Zitkala-Ša refused to be reelected as secretary-treasurer. The Society then nominated her husband, Raymond Bonnin, but he too refused the nomination, and Thomas G. Bishop became secretary-treasurer. Thus the Bonnins and Eastman withdrew from the Society. Despite the prominence and general acceptance of his views regarding the Indian Bureau, the best Montezuma could achieve was an appointment to the advisory board that served the elected officers. An inability to achieve consensus continued to plague the organization as the conference could not even agree on a resolution on citizenship. But Montezuma continued to be buoyed by the organization's opposition to the Indian Bureau.

> Many strangers were there that I had never seen. They were young and full of vim. It was noticeable that another generation of Indians are taking an interest in the affairs of their race. …when the meeting was called to order the room was filled. I should say there were about three hundred. More than we ever had at any other convention. The Indians were eager to be heard. Some had to be called down for some one else. I was called down several times. I was willing to give away because I want to hear what others had to say. …I read my paper, "Ye Shall Know the Truth and the Truth Shall Make You Free" on Thursday morning. It gave ginger to the great object of our gathering. …Right here I may say, I may be credited of having Tom Sloan elected President of the society. It is not so. I wanted the same officers to hold over another year.
>
> …The meeting was a great success. The resolution states that we believe in the abolishment of the Indian Bureau so that the Indians may enjoy freedom and effectual citizenship.[107]

Montezuma stayed out of the peyote argument. He did not want to antagonize the pro-peyote Indians; he wanted their participation in his battle against the Bureau of Indian Affairs. Montezuma believed that once the Bureau was abolished and Indians were citizens, peyote would fall under state laws and the issue would be resolved. Both Gordon and Montezuma had urged Gertrude Bonnin to cease fighting against peyote, recognizing that it was costing the Society membership, but Gertrude was not dissuaded.[108]

The new officers turned their attention to an attempt to have an Indian appointed as commissioner of Indian affairs. This was rather an awkward position, lobbying for an Indian leader of a government department while at the same time calling for abolition of the department. The Society of American Indians, under its new leadership, became another Washington lobbying group. The *American Indian Magazine* appeared in August 1920, in a new form, a magazine written by Whites about Indians in the past. This proved to be not only the first issue in this new form, but also the last issue of *American Indian Magazine* ever published.

Little was accomplished at the 1920 annual conference in St. Louis except to recognize that the Society had lost its direction and any effectiveness it once had. However, the meeting did provide an opportunity for Indians from the Southwest to report on their land and water disputes. Gilbert Davis was there from Fort McDowell and described in detail the Yavapai dispute with the Indian Bureau (Chapter 12).

The following year, the annual meeting was in Detroit. "I should say at the beginning of the conference there were no more than six or seven delegates at the conference, but delegates dropped in everyday until Friday. ...our sessions were poorly attended, but we held a small meeting to ourselves and derived much help & instructions. I read my paper and so did Mrs Springs. Those were the only papers read at the conference. ...Several were there to see the Society die. There was a time during the conference it looked as though the Society was going to pieces. It was hanging on a thread. One suggested to close the meeting and all of us go home. Not so, the ones who had their hearts for the Society stood firm & decided that we will stick to the Society for the best interest of the Indian people. ...There not being a quorum (20 members) we postpone the election of officers and other important business until some future date when we can get 20 together."[109]

Montezuma was only three and one-half months from death's door when he attended the 1922 annual conference in Kansas City. "I do not know what to say. I have been to S.A.I. Conference. Sloan & Bishop hold the reins of the S.A.I. Not of my will but the new Indian faces carried everything for Sloan & Bishop. I might have had a change in the officers had I gone around and explained the ups and downs of the organization. ...I told Sloan & Bishop they were way off. They are side tracking the Society of American Indians. They are going after fads. ...No Carlisle boys or girls were there. All were strange Indians."[110] Montezuma actively campaigned for new officers, but failed, partly because he had no one to propose.

Montezuma invited the Society to meet in Chicago in 1923, but even before it was time to plan the meeting, he was arranging his last trip to the Fort McDowell Reservation. Miss M. Austine Stanley was a grade school teacher, interested in American Indians, and active in women's volunteer groups. Beginning in 1919, Miss Stanley frequently communicated with Montezuma by phone and mail and had visited the Montezuma household becoming acquainted with Marie and Billy Moore.[111] A year after Montezuma died, she wrote to Arthur Parker: "Before Dr. Montezuma went away to the southwest, where he died about a month later, he sent for me and begged me with tears in his eyes to see this convention through. 'Miss Stanley you are the one woman in Chicago who is a true friend to the Indians. Promise me that you will see this convention through. They'll fight you, and try to tear down every time you build up, but don't give up. See the convention through. Promise me that. I am going away and may not be well enough to come back, but I leave everything in your hands.'"[112]

The annual conference was held in Chicago in September 1923, arranged and run by White sponsors. The Indians were relegated to being honored guests and staging pow wows. Meaningful pan-Indian political actions or programs no longer provided life to the society. Abolition of the Bureau was a hopeless, unwanted cause. The Society managed to eke out an existence, under the presidency of Philip Gordon, for only a few more years. Ultimately the leaders of the Society of American Indians did not sufficiently recognize that all Indians belong to the same family, and they allowed political and spiritual factionalism to disrupt the strength of the family. The greatest failure was the absence of any effort to reach out to the traditional people, to forge an effective alliance that would represent all Indians. Instead, the Society was a dissonant symphony conducted by competing maestros.

## The Annual Conferences of the Society of American Indians

1. October 12–15, 1911
Ohio State University & Hotel Hartman
Columbus, Ohio

2. October 2–6, 1912
Ohio State University & Hotel Hartman
Columbus, Ohio

3. October 14–20, 1913
Albany Hotel
Denver, Colorado

4. October 6–11, 1914
University of Wisconsin
State Historical Society of Wisconsin
New Park Hotel
Madison, Wisconsin

5. September 2–October 6, 1915
University of Kansas
The Haskell Institute
Lawrence, Kansas

6. September 26–October 1, 1916
Coe College
Majestic Theatre
Hotel Montrose
Cedar Rapids, Iowa

7. October 9–13, 1917
Oklahoma City, Oklahoma
(Cancelled)

8. September 25–28, 1918
St. Charles Hotel
Pierre, South Dakota

9. October 2–4, 1919
St. James Hotel
Minneapolis, Minnesota

10. November 15–19, 1920
Missouri Historical Society
Planters Hotel
St. Louis, Missouri

11. October 25–29, 1921
YMCA Auditorium
Lincoln Hotel
Detroit, Michigan

12. October 17–20, 1922
The Coates House
Kansas City, Missouri

13. September 27–30, 1923
Chicago Historical Society
Hotel Sherman
Chicago, Illinois

MONTEZUMA SHOULD NOT be judged by his inability to make an impact other than the preservation of the land and water rights for his own tribe (Chapter 12). The prevalent forces in American society and politics during Montezuma's life were too big for one man or even a minority group to battle. It was easy for Indian affairs to demand attention and priority when the country was agricultural and still expanding its frontiers. But in the process of rapid growth with industrialization and urbanization, Indians and their problems dropped lower and lower on the list of American interests and issues from which politicians derived reputations and power.

Industrialists and entrepreneurs lobbied for land, favorable taxes, higher tariffs, and political influence. The leading businessmen in banking, oil, railroads, mining, steel, and all forms of commerce became true barons. Indian leaders were overwhelmed as politics became more and more intertwined with business and not the fundamental issues of public welfare and justice. The attention, favors, and advantages went to the corporate world, not the disenfranchised, the unorganized, and the powerless. Even when reform came in earnest during the years of President Woodrow Wilson, it was exclusively directed to the majority of the population and its problems, not to any minorities in the United States. If you doubt the accuracy of this observation, review an acclaimed presidential biography of the times (for example, *Theodore Rex* by Edmund Morris or *Woodrow Wilson: American Prophet* by Arthur Walworth[113]) and look in vain for a significant, however brief, mention of American Indians, including the Bureau of Indian Affairs or one of the commissioners of Indian affairs.

## INDIAN ORGANIZATIONS IN THE 1920s

The assimilationist policy continued to be the official position of the government in the 1920s, and therefore allotment and assimilation were dominant forces throughout Montezuma's adult life.[114] The Bureau of Indian Affairs, now a large and complex bureaucracy, was the target of widespread and angry criticism. The allotment process had slowed, but the leasing and selling of allotted lands continued. Attacks on Indian culture and the loss of Indian lands drew the attention of the defenders of Indians' rights.

In the 1920s, the reform movement focused on tribal affairs. In 1922, the Secretary of the Interior, Albert Fall, ruled that "Executive Order Reservations," like the Fort McDowell Reservation, were public lands that under the General Leasing Act of 1920 dealing with oil and gas deposits could be retrieved. This stirred renewed activity on behalf of Indian rights, leading to the organization of the American Indian Defense Association in 1923 by John Collier. The members were writers, artists, social scientists, and concerned individuals who were devoted to the preservation of tribal culture. A change was taking place, significantly due to the collapse of the Protestant hegemony. Society was being secularized, fueled by new advances in science and technology. The belief that progress depended upon religion was being replaced by the belief that progress depended upon science. The old philanthropic approach of the Christian reformers was being replaced by cultural understanding derived from social science.

In response to pressure from the American Indian Defense Association as well as other groups, the new Secretary of the Interior, Hubert Work, created the Committee of One Hundred to convene in Washington and advise on Indian policy.[115] Many prominent Americans, such as Bernard M. Baruch, General John J. Pershing, and William Jennings Bryan, were involved, including many of the previous leaders of the Society of American Indians (Henry Roe Cloud, Sherman Coolidge, Charles Eastman, Philip Gordon, Arthur Parker, Thomas Sloan, Dennison Wheelock). Arthur Parker was elected to preside over the committee.

The committee's resolutions, which appeared in early 1924, contained both familiar and new recommendations. The committee advocated Indian admissions to public schools, better health and sanitation, and opening of the Court of Claims to the tribes. Native arts, crafts, dances, and ceremonies, as long as lawful, should not be curtailed. Most importantly, the committee recommended the suspension of all court proceedings under the "Executive Reservation Order." Later, the attorney general ruled that the original position taken by Albert Fall was illegal.

Although the Committee of One Hundred accomplished very little, the recommendations were instrumental in a request from the secretary of the interior to the Brookings Institution for a large and authoritative study of Indian Affairs. The study, financed by John D. Rockefeller, Jr., was issued in 1928 popularly known as the Meriam Report, named after its director Lewis Meriam, an anthropologist.[116] Henry Roe Cloud and Fayette McKenzie were members of the research group. The report offered no radical insights and plans, but once again highlighted the deplorable health, educational, and living conditions among the Indians. It emphasized what commissioners of Indian affairs had recognized for years, the inadequate financial support provided for the job that needed to be done. The Meriam Report and other government reports focused on the poor salaries that made it difficult, if not impossible, to attract competent teachers and other personnel.

This was a time of transition. The period of reform associated with assimilation had faded as the allotment process (Chapter 3) was perceived to be a failure. Government policy was giving way to the recommendations in the Meriam Report, to become manifest in the Indian New Deal. The first period of reform and the policy of assimilation as well as the Society of American Indians were a response to the reservation system. The next period of reform awaited stimulation by the emergence of a new policy. Carlisle was gone; Haskell was yet to produce new leaders.

Rather than reform, the 1920s saw the emergence of organizations that were of a fraternal and social nature.[117] Red Fox St. James founded the Tepee Order of America, and its first "head chief" was Charles Eastman. Eastman viewed the organization as a means to retrieve and maintain Indian ceremonies. At first, it was a secret organization for young Protestants directed by Indians and assisted by White men. St. James was an active member of the Society of American Indians who was raised in White society but whose grandmother was a Northern Blackfoot. St. James operated camps for White boys, and he originally intended that his organization would be an Indian alternative to the Boy Scouts. By 1920, the organization had become an adult secret fraternal order, combining ideas and rituals from the Masons with Indian ceremony. *The American Indian Tepee* was the order's official publication. In the early years of this secret organization, Montezuma served on its advisory board, until he came to the conclusion that Red Fox was a fraud.[118] With the demise of the Society of American Indians, the Tepee Order attempted to fill the breech, recruiting ex-Society members and promoting its publication as a national Indian journal. Its political expression was similar to the old Society, with the exception of not calling for the abolition of the Indian Bureau, but instead advocating a greater voice for Indians in the administration of Indian affairs. A branch of the Tepee Order, the American Indian Association, was established in 1922 with less ritual as a deliberate move to provide a home for previous members of the Society. The magazine and the Order became very chauvinistic pro-American, with blatant opposition to foreign-born and Black people, even appealing to the Ku Klux Klan to support the Indian.[119] Later, these extreme views were toned down and the American Indian Association concentrated on promoting positive and romantic images of Indians, both currently and historically. There was little interest in having a political impact.

The local chapters became clubs for Indians living in America's cities. By 1928, the magazine and the Order had faded away.

In the 1920s and early 1930s, the cities of America saw many club-like organizations arise and disappear, emphasizing Indian history, arts, and ceremonies. Alumni of Carlisle and Haskell were commonly the leaders of these organizations. The Grand Council Fire of the American Indians was founded in Chicago in 1923.[120] This organization of Indians and Whites raised money for scholarships for Indian students, extensively supported and promoted American Indian Day in the Chicago area, sponsored social and educational activities, and donated money and gifts to reservations. In 1932, the organization changed its name to Indian Council Fire. In the mid 1930s, it presented annual Indian Achievement Awards, three of which went to former members of the Society of American Indians, Charles Eastman, Henry Roe Cloud, and Arthur Parker. The organization published *Indians of Today*, a Who's Who of American Indians.

WHEREAS THE INDIAN CLUBS in the cities became the low-key fraternal and social expression of pan-Indianism for Indians working and living in the cities, the peyote religion became the unifying call for Indians living on reservations.[121] Spreading from Mexico to the Comanche and the Kiowa during the time of the Ghost Dance religion (Chapter 2), peyotism rapidly became a pan-Indian religion, enduring the opposition both of traditional tribal religions and Christian churches. Its spread and survival can be significantly attributed to its success in combating alcoholism. From 1900 to 1910, the peyote religion rapidly spread throughout the Midwest and the West, predominantly becoming the Christianized version. The common pattern featured an all night vigil during which eating peyote combined with prayer and meditation produced guidance in the form of a revelation. The service usually began on Saturday night and ended with a breakfast at dawn on Sunday, sometimes every week, sometimes several times a month. The ceremony included singing, drumming, and rattling with gourds. Although there was no central organization, the religion spread by travel and correspondence from tribe to tribe.

"Peyote" is derived from the Náhuatl (Mexican-Spanish) name, *peyotl*, which means silk cocoon. The peyote cactus is a flowering, blue-green plant of the family Cactaceae, which is distinguished by its numerous tufts of white "wool" or hair, hence the name that refers to a silk cocoon. Spines are present only in young seedlings. The peyote cactus can have a single head or a dense clump of multiple heads. Pink to white flowers arise from within the center at the top of each head. When the top of the peyote dries, the fleshy tissue is greatly reduced in volume, but the center does not change in size. The center is known as the "button." It contains mescaline, a hallucinogenic that is structurally similar to epinephrine, as well as smaller amounts of many other alkaloids. Growth is slow; it takes up to five years to progress from a seed to a plant a half-inch in diameter. Only the tops are harvested, allowing new buds and heads to develop. Although there has been considerable confusion and debate among botanists, the plants used as peyote are now grouped under the genus *Lophophora*, and consist mainly of two species, *Lophophora williamsii* (the peyote cactus found from northern Mexico to southern Texas) and *Lophophora diffus* (found in the dry central area of Mexico).[122] It takes six to ten dried or fresh buttons, chewed or swallowed, to produce a psychotropic reaction that can last six to twelve hours.

As the peyote religion grew from 1910 to 1920, it drew opposition from the Indian Bureau, missionary groups, and as we have seen, the Society of American Indians. Nevertheless, the peyote religion can be viewed as a powerful unifier of Indians, extending beyond tribal boundaries more effectively than the pan-Indian reform organizations. Bureau opposition can be partly explained by Christian churches that viewed peyotism as an unwelcome rival and alternative, and partly because this appeal to the brotherhood of the Indian race overcame the confinement of the reservation. Opposition can also be traced to the difficulty in accepting the use of a drug during the time of the prohibition movement, despite the publicized success against alcoholism. All of these factors solidified the growing opposition to peyotism in the Society of American Indians, which at first openly accepted peyotists.

In 1918, Congressman Carl M. Hayden of Arizona introduced bill HR 2614 that outlawed the use of peyote by Indians. The hearings during which Zitkala-Ša played a feature role (Chapter 9) were held before a subcommittee of the Committee of Indian Affairs of the Senate in February and March 1918. Richard Pratt testified in favor of the bill, but used his time mostly to present his usual tirade against the Indian Bureau and the Bureau of Ethnology. Most of the Indians who testified, both for and against, were or had been members of the Society of American Indians and were former students at Carlisle. The committee recommended passage of the anti-peyote bill, but it failed in the full Senate vote.

The hearings did have an important effect. Alerted now to the strength of the opposition, the peyotists sought the legal status that would provide them the protection of religious liberty provided by the Constitution. The Native American Church was incorporated in October 1918, and in 1944, the organization became the Native American Church of North America, which today is the largest Indian religious organization. James Mooney, the famed Smithsonian ethnohistorian, traveled throughout Oklahoma in 1891 participating in peyote ceremonies. Seeing an opportunity to unite Indians in the peyote religion, he wrote the charter for the initial incorporation in 1918 in Oklahoma of the Native American Church.

## THE INDIAN NEW DEAL

The Indian Reorganization Act of 1934 was a fundamental change in Indian policy, largely influenced by John Collier, appointed as commissioner of Indian affairs by Franklin D. Roosevelt.[123] This act was a response to the Meriam Report that documented the effects of government neglect and mismanagement, reflected by illiteracy, ill health, joblessness, substandard housing, and poverty. Actually, many changes stimulated by the Meriam Report were underway during the Hoover administration, but the enthusiasm and excitement of the New Deal provided the impetus for new legislation, prepared by John Collier and introduced by Senator Burton K. Wheeler of Montana and Representative Edgar Howard of Nebraska.[124] The major provisions of the act, passed in June 1934, included:

- The prohibition of allotment. The granting of full citizenship to Indians in 1924 signaled the end of the philosophy and policy of assimilation and allotment; land ownership was not necessary for citizenship nor was conformity to Anglo customs a requirement. This reversal of federal policy was formalized by the Indian Reorganization Act of 1934.

- Affirmation of the right of Indian self-determination and governance.
- The revival of tribal government and traditions with encouragement of Indian arts and crafts.
- Voluntary adoption of a tribal council system of representative, constitutional government and for the organization of tribes as business corporations to manage tribal resources.
- Authorization of the restoration of land to tribal ownership and provisions for the purchase of new land.
- Protection of religious freedom.
- Support of reservation day schools.
- Qualified Indians would henceforth be preferred for appointments to vacancies in the Indian office.

Indian and White reformers poured their energies into implementing the Indian New Deal, but not all Indians were supportive. The American Indian Federation, which included Thomas Sloan, the former president of the Society of American Indians, represented a right wing point of view allied with German-American groups, claiming that the New Deal was nothing but an effort to prevent Indians from becoming civilized. The Indian Rights Association, committed to allotment and assimilation, could not bring itself to change. By the time a new national pan-Indian organization supporting the New Deal emerged in 1944, it had to fight for attention against the war effort.

Not all the tribes voted to accept the Indian Reorganization Act, and some voted for acceptance but refused to organize. The Fort McDowell Yavapai organized as the Fort McDowell Mohave-Apache Community under a constitution approved by the secretary of the interior on November 24, 1936.[125] A problem for many tribes was that the system of elected organization was an Anglo system, and this was often viewed as another imposition of a White program, an alien system of governance compared with the traditional informal method of consensus. Nevertheless, the position and role of tribal councils were established, to become important in future years. Progress was severely affected by World War II, depleting all domestic budgets. After the war, all domestic programs were re-evaluated in a move away from federal expenditures and involvement.

The most significant change in the 1930s was the increasing interaction of Indians with multiple government agencies. The monopoly over Indian affairs held by the Bureau was broken. This was not a deliberate action aimed at the Bureau of Indian Affairs. It was the result of numerous activities that required the attention of specialized agencies, such as health, soil conservation, road building, agriculture, and power. Today, the majority of the funds appropriated by Congress for the Indians is not controlled by the Bureau of Indian Affairs.

Every phase in American Indian history has had a new direction (policy) followed by a reaction. The policy of removal to reservations was followed by assimilation and allotment. Assimilation and allotment were followed by citizenship and the Indian Reorganization Act. The "New Deal" Indian policy was followed by a determination to "terminate" relationships between the Indians and the Federal Government, although the Federal Government would still retain unilateral power over Indian policy. Some have argued that the Cold War period and its anti-communist scare re-awakened negative attitudes towards a tribal, communal lifestyle, setting the stage for the period of Termination.

## American Indian History

| Removal and Reservations | Assimilation and Allotment | Reorganization | Termination | Restoration and Recognition |
|---|---|---|---|---|
| | 1880 | 1934 | 1954 | 1970 |

### TERMINATION IN THE 1940s AND 1950s

World War II produced a massive shortage of personnel and services for Indians. About 22,000 Indians served in the military and more than 40,000 Indians obtained work off the reservations. The effect of the war was to result in a surge of assimilation, but this time with an emphasis on the preservation of Indian heritage and culture. This new drive to assimilate the Indians was branded "termination," the ending of federal responsibility and federal programs. Specifically, termination would abolish the tribal government and end the Federal Government's trust responsibility with a tribe.

A review of Indian conditions that called for a reduction in federal involvement was first formulated in 1949 by the Indian Bureau and emphasized in House Report 2503, issued in December 1952. Five years later government officials were actively seeking to withdraw the Federal Government from Indian affairs, as expressed in House Concurrent Resolution 108, passed in 1953.[126] This resolution provided for the states to assume responsibility for law and order on the reservations, and to end federal involvement with those tribes who voted for termination. Immediately, Congress passed legislation that removed federal services from sixty-one small tribes and communities.

The large tribes, although severely frightened, escaped termination. Although termination was cloaked in the attractive idea of freedom from federal intervention in Indian affairs, it was often (if not always) based upon an underlying motive of economic gain for private interests (for example, the acquisition of timber from the Klamath Indians in Oregon). Faced with new state tax obligations and the loss of federally sponsored social, educational, and health services, many tribes became even more impoverished. Mounting opposition, led by the National Congress of American Indians, and an appreciation for the major problems associated with termination eventually led to a movement to restore the trust and reservation status. Congress responded to this pressure, restoring tribes mostly on an individual basis, and shifting its focus to economic development for the reservations. Although the termination policy was short-lived and affected only 3 percent of the Indian population and lands, its psychologic impact on Indians was enormous. Fear of termination became a unifying force for Indians and a new reason to distrust federal policies.

In 1946, Congress created the Indians Claims Commission to provide financial compensation for treaty violations.[127] It lasted until 1978, granting awards of $800 million covering 60 percent of the cases brought before it (the Yavapai received $5.1 million in 1965). The Indian Claims Commission was in reality another act of termination. It was meant to produce finality to long-standing conflicts, and to prevent the future procurement of former lands by compensated tribes. Subsequently only a few tribes were successful in having lands returned, but at least the existence of the commission was an admission of injustice toward the Indians in the past. The main positive effect of this process was the increase in legal consciousness among the tribes, aiding the next round of pan-Indian movements. The legal battles made it obvious that the old grievances could not be settled by monetary compensation. Another benefit of the Claims Commission is the summary of the massive collection of original documents on the history and anthropology of American Indian tribes and groups, reports that were written to be used as evidence in the legal proceedings and that filled more than 600 file drawers, published as the Garland American Indian Ethnohistory series of 118 volumes.[128]

The United States Public Health Service took over Indian health and medical services in 1955, creating the Indian Health Service. It can be and is argued that the Indians purchased a prepaid health care plan by their cession of lands.[129] Indeed, many Indians believed and still do that federal appropriations and programs are their just due in return for the loss of their lands. Termination as a policy ended in 1970; for the more than 100 tribes that went through the process, the effects were devastating, with loss of more land, services, and independence.

## RESTORATION AND RECOGNITION AFTER 1960

The change in federal direction after 1960 was marked by key pieces of legislation. The Indian Civil Rights Act in 1968 required tribal consent before states could assume jurisdiction on Indian land. The Indian Education Act of 1972 formally recognized new programs and directions in Indian education that had begun operating in the 1960s. The Indian Self-Determination and Education Assistance Act of 1975 directed the secretary of the interior to respond to requests from Indian tribes to plan and administer various programs (actually a restatement of the Indian Reorganization Act of 1934). Multiple government task forces and reports in the 1960s and 1970s called attention to Indian education and health conditions, and called for greater tribal involvement and self-government. Growing Indian militancy in the 1960s contributed to the increased public awareness of Indian problems. This resulted in a series of Congressional acts, providing assistance in housing improvement, economic development, vocational training, and funding assistance through many pathways as opposed to the single previous resource, the Bureau of Indian Affairs. The federal trust relationship has been maintained providing for the protection of tribal assets, as well as economic and social programs, but since 1975, there has been a gradual shift to more and more self-determination. Today, for example, many tribes operate their own hospitals and health centers; most tribes provide at least some of their own health services.[130] Although self-government is a concept imposed by the non-Indian society, it provides an opportunity for modern Indians to interweave their own spiritual and cultural ideas into the White system of organization.

There are more than 550 federally recognized tribes in the United States speaking more than 250 basic languages.[131] Other tribes exist without federal charters or trust status, but are recognized by states. Because treaty making ended in 1871, federal recognition of tribes now requires an act of Congress or an executive order (many tribes are still in the process of petitioning for recognition). There are about 315 federal reservations, totalling approximately 56 million acres held in trust by the Federal Government.[132] Some reservations are solid blocks of land, others are interrupted by non-reservation lands. Some reservation land is owned or rented by non-Indians. Reservation sizes range from the 14-million-acre Navajo reservation to some that are only a few acres. Some reservations in the

East are state-recognized only. On federally recognized reservations, the Bureau of Indian Affairs operates elementary and secondary schools. The federal and state reservations today have taken on more meaning than just a geographic site for the segregation of Indians.[133] Reservations are now important home bases for cultural identity, with sacred sites and traditional ceremonies. The reservations today, despite the many well-recognized problems, are now special places for most Indians, including those living off the reservations (only about 21 percent of the Indian population today lives on reservations).

Individual Indians have the same rights as all other individual American citizens. The Indian Citizenship Act of 1924 gives all Indians born within the United States full citizenship, but this does not infringe upon the rights associated with tribal membership.[134] Indian tribal members have a special relationship with the Federal Government. They cannot sell trust lands without both tribal and Bureau approval. Tribal reservation laws must be observed (for example, some reservations have non-drinking laws). The fundamental underlying problem is unchanged and unsolved. Accomplishing self-determination and maintaining political sovereignty of the tribes while at the same time having Indian programs dependent upon federal appropriations and support is a challenging task. The trust responsibility of the Federal Government for Indian land and property continues and is desired, and tension is inevitable from the fact that sovereignty and tribal authority exist only at the sufferance of Congress. A long track record of court rulings has established that Indian tribes are subject to the legislative and plenary power of the United States Government. Indians themselves expand the concept of trust responsibility to include education, health, and other services.[135] Some degree of paternalism is inherent in the provision of these services. The evolution of this relationship remains for the future, but at least unilateral federal action is unlikely, given the present day sophistication of tribal governments.

It is unlikely that current Indian policy will stimulate a new round of assimilation and repression. The termination policy after World War II was a temporary setback in the steady progress toward Indian self-determination and cultural freedom. Indian awareness and self-determination have reached a position of established power, making it extremely difficult, if not impossible, for a re-emergence of unilateral federal policy. This progress is testimony to successful evolution and change, without sacrifice of tribal and group identity and uniqueness, a process that will continue. An adaptation to modern life that is rooted in tribal heritage and community allows the maintenance of Indian pride, a process that was vigorously opposed by the proponents of assimilation for nearly 100 years.

Previous unilateral actions by the Federal Government changed the concept of sovereignty that was implied in the making of treaties. Nevertheless, tribes today still possess a degree of sovereignty, although it is limited by federally imposed regulations. Tribal governments have the right to regulate tribal membership, make laws, establish courts and tribal police, enforce laws and administer justice (except for major crimes that since 1885 continue to be under the jurisdiction of federal courts),[136] levy taxes on tribal members, regulate land and resource use and development. Some tribes have written constitutions and codes; some operate by traditional unwritten systems. Most govern by some form of representative council with an elected chief or president.

SINCE 1950, the Indian population has been increasing faster than the non-Indian population of the United States (on a percentage basis).[137] This represents major growth in the Indian population since the low point of a little under 250,000 in 1900; the number more than doubled from 1970 to 1990. This growth cannot be totally explained by demographic parameters (birthrates, death rates, and immigration); therefore, some of this growth is attributed to the fact that Indians in recent decades are more willing and motivated to identify themselves as American Indian to census takers. There was a total of 1,967,367 American Indians in the 1990 census, and 65 percent lived in cities.[138] Of the total population in all fifty states, two and one-half million people (0.9 percent) reported in the 2000 census that they were only American Indians, and an additional 1.6 million people reported that they were partially American Indian.[139] About 43 percent live west of the Mississippi River, with 25 percent in California and Oklahoma. The majority of American Indians now live in cities, especially New York, Los Angeles, Phoenix, San Diego, Anchorage, and Albuquerque. This is partly a result of an active effort by the Bureau of Indian Affairs to "relocate" Indians off the reservations during the termination period in the 1950s and partly because of many individual Indians seeking better economic opportunities. The urbanization of American Indians

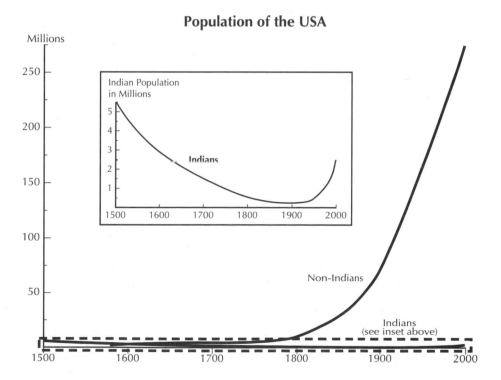

**Population of the USA**

was an instrumental factor in the activism that arose after 1960. Indians living in cities became adapted to off-reservation lifestyles (including education and an appreciation for the importance of the media and the courts), and at the same time these urban Indians yearned for their roots in tribal heritage and culture. This was the mix that prompted confrontational activities that garnered publicity and stimulated legal and legislative steps towards the modern era of Indian self-determination.

The National Congress of American Indians, founded in 1944, had a strong tribal emphasis, consistent with the goals of the Indian New Deal. Like the leaders of the Society of American Indians, the new leadership consisted of successful Indians in professions and businesses, as well as Indian Bureau employees. Many had attended Carlisle and Haskell, and the first officers were all college graduates. The organization successfully fought the termination policy of the 1940s and 1950s and worked for the anti-poverty programs of the 1960s. A more militant organization, the National Indian Youth Council was established in 1961, an expression of vocal and angry young Indians.

A wave of confrontational activism appeared in the 1960s and 1970s, sparked by younger Indians. This period of activity involved many national and regional organizations, and often centered on occupying federal land or property and claiming it for educational and cultural uses.[140] The occupation of Alcatraz in 1969, initially by seventy-eight Indians from many tribes who were students in California colleges and universities, attracted recruits from all over the country.[141] It was a symbolic act that served as a rallying cry and turning point in Indian protest.

The Trail of Broken Treaties caravan, composed of Indians from many organizations, marched on Washington in 1972, occupied the Indian Bureau offices, and destroyed files and property.[142] The most publicized group was the American Indian Movement, founded by Chippewa Indians in Minneapolis in 1968, that rapidly became a national focal group for urban Indians. The initial purpose of the march on Washington was to present a document, The Twenty Points, summarizing the reforms needed to re-establish a treaty making relationship between Indians and the Federal Government.[143] They never intended to occupy the Bureau of Indian Affairs building, but a lack of food and accommodations due to poor logistical planning stirred an angry spontaneous movement of over 1,000 Indians into the building. A forceful entry by police that was repelled led to a week-long occupation that produced a vandalism spawned by decades of hatred and frustration towards the records and offices of the Indian Bureau. Eventually the government negotiated and paid for an exit from the city, and at the same time rejected the proposal to reopen the treaty process.

In 1973, American Indian Movement members and supporters occupied the site of the Wounded Knee Massacre of 1890, a village of about 100 people, and proclaimed the Independent Oglala Nation.[144] The occupation was precipitated by a conflict between traditional and militant Indians and the established tribal government. It reflected the ongoing problems of all Indians struggling with the new forms of tribal government, the lack of resolution for Indian claims against the Federal Government, and continuing unhappiness with Indian education. Federal agents besieged the occupants for seventy-one days, at the end of which two Indians had been killed and a federal marshal wounded. These confrontational activities served notice to both Whites and Indians that Indians were still fighting for their rights.

A second shooting on the Pine Ridge Reservation, in 1975, caused the deaths of two FBI agents, and eventually Leonard Peltier was arrested, tried in Fargo, North Dakota, and sentenced to two life sentences. His guilt is still challenged. In the last decades, violence has diminished. Indeed, the last major event in the 1970s was "The Longest Walk," a march into Washington, D.C., by several hundred Indians that was a peaceful event. However, political and legal activism continued to define Indian uniqueness and to identify issues. An important outcome of this activism was the establishment of centers for American Indian studies in many universities in the country.

POOR SOCIAL CONDITIONS are still prevalent among Indians, manifested in a shorter lifespan, low income, high unemployment, and a high rate of alcoholism. The individual tribes continue their struggles fighting for water rights and lands taken for dams and parks, to gain a fair share of revenues, and to prevent land pollution because resources have had to be leased to powerful corporations. The causes are the same today, but the tactics have changed from military confrontations to political and legal action. Indians continue to work for a redress of past wrongs, for awareness in the American public of their presence and problems, and for official and public recognition of tribal sovereignty and self-sufficiency.

At one point in our history, it was assumed that Indians would disappear. Today, it is believed, with good reason, that Indians will always constitute an American subgroup in a pluralistic twenty-first century that is a striking contrast to the one dominant culture of the late nineteenth century. The special relationship between the Federal Government and Indians will continue, and Indians will continue to have a moral and legal claim against the United States. Today, the U.S. Congress is the trustee for protection of Indian property, for protection of the Indian right to self-government with recognition of tribal sovereignty, and for the provision of social, medical, and educational services for support and advancement.[145] This relationship, often called trust responsibility, is at the tribal level, and therefore individual Indians are not regarded as wards of the government. The major responsibility continues to be in the Bureau of Indian Affairs in the Department of the Interior, along with the Indian Health Service in the Public Health Service. This arrangement is the result of treaties, executive orders, Congressional legislation, and judiciary decisions. The result is a dual status, dependence under the trust relationship but political independence; individuals are citizens both of their Indian nation and the United States.[146] Avoiding conflicts in this arrangement has been very difficult, and the relationships between tribes and the Federal Government continue to be uneasy and uncertain.

In recent years, Indian gaming has provided the money to solve problems and acquire political clout. It started with bingo parlors and developed into immensely profitable casinos. One of the most effective and powerful pan-Indian groups is the National Indian Gaming Association, founded in 1985. Basically this has been possible because the Supreme Court ruled that state laws regulating gambling cannot be enforced on reservations. In 1988, Congress passed the Indian Gambling Regulatory Act, allowing tribes to enter into "compacts" with states for high-stakes gaming (slot machines, blackjack, lotteries, and sports betting).[147] The act allowed tribes to purchase additional lands for business purposes, and created another strong pan-Indian organization, the National Indian Gaming

Commission. The commission is responsible for the regulation of Indian gaming and for vigilance against organized crime. Most Indians are not associated with tribes that have successful casinos, and spreading the gains and benefits represents a serious challenge for Indian leadership. For some tribes, the impact has been enormous.

The Fort McDowell Yavapai people are benefitting from their gaming center with solid income, new houses, better and free education, and better healthcare with specialized counseling. Houses and people are scattered on the reservation, but the land is packed with the stories in this book. The Yavapai language is being taught in the new school on the reservation. On December 12, 1996, the Fort McDowell Yavapai community dedicated its new health center, the Dr. Carlos Montezuma, Wassaja, Memorial Health Center.

Financial assistance is now available at Arizona universities in the Wassaja Scholarship program for any students who are committed to serve the Indian community. In addition to the gaming center, the Fort McDowell tribe operates a sand and gravel business that includes the Yavapai Sports Surfaces unit providing material for baseball fields and golf courses, the We-Ko-Pa Golf Club, Fort McDowell Adventures (a catering and western experience center) and the Ba 'Ja gas station and store on the highway that passes through the lowest part of the reservation. The Fort McDowell Yavapai tribal headquarters are housed in an impressive modern facility, and farming now encompasses more than 2,000 irrigated acres, including 600 acres of alfalfa and 1,325 acres of citrus and pecan orchards. As Robin Russell said to me when he was vice-president of the Yavapai Nation: "Things happen when you have money."

## CHAPTER FOURTEEN

# *WASSAJA*, Montezuma's Newsletter

*W*ASSAJA, MONTEZUMA'S NEWSLETTER, was published monthly from April 1916 to November 1922. The last issue appeared only two months before Montezuma died. *Wassaja* could be purchased for five cents a copy or fifty cents for a year's subscription. Montezuma encouraged local distribution by providing 100 copies of an issue for $2. In 1920, Montezuma doubled the rates, citing an increase in printing costs. Eighty years later, the New York University Department of Journalism nominated *Wassaja* for consideration as one of the top 100 works of journalism in the United States in the twentieth century.[1] *Wassaja* didn't make the final 100,[2] but how gratified Montezuma would have been to know the distinguished names among which he had been placed. In another statement of recognition, the Native American Journalists Association provides the Wassaja Award, granted to individuals who make extraordinary contributions to Indian journalism.

Father Philip B. Gordon, a Catholic priest and a Chippewa, was teaching at the Haskell Institute when he started a monthly four-leaf newsletter that he called *The War Whoop*.[3] The publication was promptly forbidden by his Catholic superiors, and when Montezuma spoke at Haskell in February 1916, Gordon urged Montezuma to take over the newsletter. Encouraged by a large volume of mail in response to his *Let My People Go* pamphlet, Montezuma decided this would be worth doing, a means to reach a broad audience. He told Pratt: "I expect to get out a pamphlet called 'Wassaja' *Freedom's Signal to the Indians*. The object is to down the Indian Bureau and will cease when that is accomplished. It will take much of my time [?] of my professional work, but since I cannot rely on the Society's Magazine, I can have a small paper of my own to scatter throughout the country. It will come out monthly. I do not expect [to] attack any one but I will use solid materials to show that the Indians are men and they should be free as any other native born Americans."[4]

*Wassaja* was "to be published only so long as the Indian Bureau exists."[5] Montezuma's mailing list at times numbered 1,000, but usually a little less, including selected representatives and senators, and all members of the Indian committees of the House and the Senate.[6] The newsletter was four pages long in double columns. The format varied over time but *Wassaja* frequently featured a main article, four to six columns long, focusing on a theme, with emotional language that was often eloquent. By the time Montezuma published *Wassaja*, he was an experienced writer. Hardly a month went by after 1900, that didn't see the appearance of one of his articles in a magazine or a column in a newspaper. His titles covered many of the issues that were to be featured in *Wassaja*, including "Justice to the Indian,"

"Indians are Men, not Freaks," "The Government, the Public, and the American Indian," and, of course, many articles aimed at the elimination of the Bureau of Indian Affairs.

"WASSAJA is an Apache word for beckoning or signaling, and was the name given to Dr. Montezuma by his mother and father. The illustration above shows the rays of signal from the realm of freedom to the handicapped Indian under the log of Bureauism. The poor Indian looks up from his present condition and sees the signal that some one is coming to his aid. Will you aid us to gain freedom for the Indian? Let all who read this little pamphlet be touched, that it may be so very soon. You may ask what you can do to help the coming of that day. You can read the leaflet and send us your subscription and pass it on for others to read and subscribe, and in that way circulate the cause from one end of the country to the other. It is your work as well as ours."[7]

The first issue appealed to economics. In an article entitled, "Indian Bureau Economy," Montezuma argued that elimination of the Bureau would save money. "The word money is a term to conjure with, and often secures attention when other things fail."[8]

> If the thing to be done with the Indian was to coerce him, limit him, nurse him, coddle him, deceive him, belittle him, and to a certain extent feed and clothe him, all the time eliminating the thought of him as a man with no future as such, either for him or his decendents, then all these institutions, things and persons connected therewith, for which the said vast expenditures are made, must be maintained regardless of the fact that the government by pursuing the proper, and therefore a different course, could have avoided such a burden.[9]

Montezuma talked about what he called "The Repression of the Indian." "All that is necessary to do is to accept the fact that the Indian is a man, a citizen of the United States and that there is nothing about him now that requires the special attention of the government. Let him assume the place to which he is entitled as a member of the national household and his affairs will be managed and his rights maintained by the same laws and regulations that control in the case of other persons. ...Crutches for the lame have no curative properties; and so long as nothing is done to cure the man's lameness he will cling to them. ...It has become a formidable branch of the government and it is going to be a difficult thing to get it out of the way. It furnishes a living to such a large number of persons that it would be useless to attempt to legislate it out of existence. We realize that it would be about as easy to remove a mountain as it would be to get a bill through Congress abolishing the Indian Bureau. It therefore becomes absolutely necessary to terminate its existence by getting the Indians out of its control; and like a mill with out grist to grind, it would soon be out of business. ...A human being cannot be stationary. By virtue of his construction he is either going forward or backward. This is the situation of the Indian on the reservation."[10] Montezuma constantly urged his fellow Indians to work. "To inspire others, you must perspire."[11]

"Arrow Points" was a short column, ten or less paragraphs in length, often with only one or two sentences per paragraph. As the title connoted, the column aimed barbed comments, usually at the Bureau of Indian Affairs. "What ye sow ye also reap. The Indian Bureau has sown, and it has brought forth nothing but pangs of sorrow and ruination to the Indian race."[12] "What is there in the freedom for the Indians that will be harmful for the Indians? Did it ever hurt you? Has freedom got to be like a rattle-snake? Is it too much of a dose for the Indians? Do you think freedom is good enough for you and not for the Indians?"[13]

Many issues of *Wassaja* shared with the readers Montezuma's correspondence, mostly letters from Indians all over the country, many thanking Montezuma for his efforts. Another method of his was a Socratic dialogue, entitled "Heap Big Pow-Wow," between "Wassaja" and "Anxious Inquirer." Montezuma also reprinted portions of articles from newspapers, magazines, and Indian school publications. He even provided an occasional obituary:

> Col. Wm. F. Cody—"Buffalo Bill"—is dead. —wild life of the West is hushed! He was a friend of the Indians, and again in a higher sense, he was not; just as there are friends and friends of the Indians, so was "Buffalo Bill" one of them.
>
> He has been a great character. As a man he acted well as a representative of the real "Buffalo Bill." He won fame.
>
> Mr. Cody and WASSAJA started out from Chicago with "Texas Jack" and Ned Bunton in the winter of 1872. So you see we are old friends, but WASSAJA never approved his friend's method of showing off the Indian race, off-setting the progress the Indians have made and implanting the wrong idea in the minds of the public that an Indian was a savage and that was all.
>
> As an old friend, WASSAJA mourns and extends sympathy to the bereaved.[14]

Montezuma sometimes expressed his thoughts in free verse, usually serious, but occasionally tongue-in-cheek:

> *It is so because Washington (Indian Bureau) **SAYS SO**.*
> *It is so because the Agent **SAYS SO**.*
> *It is so because the superintendent **SAYS SO**.*
> *It is so because the police **SAY SO**.*
> *It is so but not what the law **SAYS SO**.*
> *Such is **SO, SO** with the Indians.*
> *Would you like to be governed **SO, SO**?*[15]

## CHANGING IS NOT VANISHING

*Who says the Indian race is vanishing?*
*The Indians will not vanish.*
*The feathers, paint and moccasin will vanish, but the Indians—never!*
*Just as long as there is a drop of human blood in America, the Indians will not vanish.*
*His spirit is everywhere; the American Indian will not vanish.*
*He has changed externally but he has not vanished.*
*He is an industrial and commercial man, competing with the world; he has not vanished.*
*Wherever you see an Indian upholding the standard of his race, there you see the Indian man—*
*he has not vanished.*
*The man part of the Indian is here, there and everywhere.*
*The Indian race vanishing? No, never! The race will live on and prosper forever.*[16]

Montezuma took the churches of America to task. "There is something radically wrong and we do not dare to dwell upon it. Look you around! You see no papooses in the rooms of the public schools with the children of other races; no Indians worshipping with you under the same church roof; no Indians working in your stores and factories and taking part in your body politic and social life. Extinct! Do you say? In plain English, it is day-light robbery; it is kidnapping for the almighty dollar, and jailing them from all that other races enjoy in the world. …condition is most damnable: where you expected the most help and the most good, you are aghast to find them heading in a wrong direction and unwilling to listen to right teaching. …Therefore, the churches have not done their duty toward the Indian race. They blindly thought that by sending missionaries to them they were fulfilling their mission. They believed in saving their souls and neglecting their rights and enslaving their faculties. …Churches, you fought against slavery and yet you tolerate this monstrous conscienceless devil-fish—the Indian bureau—which squeezes and sucks the life-blood out of the Indians."[17]

### INDIAN THIS AND INDIAN THAT

Indian Schools, Indian Hospitals, Indian Churches, Indian Missions, Indian Music, Indian Shows, Indian Reservations, Indian Day, Indian this and Indian that, or anything Indian, creates prejudice and does the Indian more harm than good.

What is WASSAJA driving at? It is this: Columbus made a mistake by calling us Indians. By being branded and constantly reminded that we are Indians, the Indian race has suffered untold harm as a race. What if we received Englishmen by calling them Johnny Bulls, Germans as Sauerkrauts, Irishmen as Pats and Mikes, and Italians as Dagoes, continually hounding them with incorrect and offensive appellations. Do you think that they would thank you?

Yet that has been exactly the position that Indians have endured these many years. It does not help the Indian to belittle him and make him a laughing stock before the world. It is related that Fred Douglas said that Abraham Lincoln was the only white man who ever talked to him who did not remind him, by direct statement or by inference, that he was a negro, and Douglas added that Lincoln, by his conduct, demonstrated that he "was a great man, stooping, not wishing to let his fellows know that they were mean and small," and "WASSAJA" expresses the hope that the public will, in dealing with the Indian, follow the example of the immortal Lincoln.

Forget the Indians, and by kindness, generosity and helpfulness lift up the man to your own stature, and God will reward you for this work of benevolence and the Indian and his posterity will bless you forever.[18]

Starting in January 1917, a column appeared entitled "Sledge Hammer Taps," with a byline of "Junius." Appearing irregularly, the column was a collection of aphorisms, sarcastic comments, and pithy observations.

> If the Indian Bureau is doing harm to Indians, those working with the Bureau are doing harm to Indians.[19]

> Did anybody ever hear the likes of the faint squeak of some Indians in the Bureau: "We do want the Bureau abolished, but not this instant." Oh my, pat my wrist!![20]

> "Friends" of Indians feel that if the Indians are let loose they will forthwith become the prey of scamps. Well, better for us to be a prey to unlegalized crooks than a prey to legal rascals—Indian Bureau people![21]

> The Indian Rights Association: "This organization is not for the liberation of the Indians, but is openly supporting the atrocious Indian Office. Fie on you, shameless white men from the City of Brotherly Love."[22]

> The Board of Indian Commissioners: " ...a useless and entirely unnecessary body of men of dotage. Besides, the commissioners are for the Indian Bureau, heart and soul. There's a reason. A little salary here and a little trip there. Indians are useful!"[23]

> Indians in the army: "5,000 loyal redman. Fighting for real democracy and the eternal rights of humanity. Mr. President, cast one look on Poor Lo. Where are his rights and where is his liberty? Mr. President, give us FREEDOM. Tell the Indian Office to be human at least even it has to be unjust and arbitrary and un-American."[24]

> The general consensus of opinion among all Indian tribes is that Cato Sells is a great specimen of the 100 per cent four-flusher and hypocrite. The man ought to be arrested for criminal negligence in his handling of Indians, defrauding the United States tax-payers by drawing a salary, and collecting money under false pretenses.[25]

> Talk of hearing pigs squeal! Listen to the grunts of agony from the "bunch" in the Indian Office when Wassaja takes a fling at the inhumanity of the whole business.[26]

> It is a good bet that 50 per cent of our Indians have more real merit and ability to fulfill the responsibilities of American citizenship than the hungry horde of Government employees now engaged in taking care of Poor Lo.[27]

> The best education the Indians ever gained was that given by Army Service. A few months in Uncle Sam's army was worth more than a dozen years in any Government School. And this to boot: U.S. taxpayers didn't have to dig down and pay a lot of cheap, under-grade old maids and derelict subnormal male disciplinarians, industrial teachers, dishonest superintendents and special disbursing agents to give this great life to Indian youths. The present Indian system of education is an additional crime perpetrated on the helpless remnants of America's first inhabitants.[28]

Junius is an amazingly common name today as revealed by a search on the internet, and it is an old name in history. Lucius Junius Brutus conquered the last Roman king and was the leader of the first Roman republic in 509 B.C. Marcus Brutus is well known as one of the conspirators against Julius Caesar, but how many know that Junius was his middle name? What prompted Montezuma to choose this byline? Perhaps he was familiar with an anonymous anti-war pamphlet circulated in Germany in 1916, under the byline of Junius.

There is also the anonymous political writer in England who signed his anti-government letters to a London newspaper from 1769 to 1772 with the signature, Junius. Montezuma must have perceived this common theme associated with "Junius," opposition to the establishment. How fitting that he chose this byline.

A verse from Alexander Pope's "Essay on Man" starts with "Lo, the poor Indian:"

> *Lo!, the poor Indian, whose untutor'd mind*
> *Sees God in clouds, or hears him in the wind;*
> *His soul proud Science never taught to stray*
> *Far as the solar walk, or milky way;*
> *Yet simple Nature to his hope has giv'n,*
> *Behind the cloud-topt hill, an humbler heaven.*

Montezuma's "Poor Lo" makes a play on the fact that nineteenth-century readers interpreted "Lo" as the proper name of an Indian.[29] "Lo, the Poor Indian" was also the title of a popular painting by William Holbrook Beard in 1876. It was a common practice for educated Indians around 1920 to use "Poor Lo" as a sarcastic reference to Indians.

Richard Pratt was pleased with Montezuma's effort. "Your last 'Wassaja' is a good deal of a rip-snorter. I do not especially disagree nor do I intend to take hold of your coat-tails and pull you back, but, my dear Monte, your imagination has played havoc with your memory, when you assert that I at any time intended to commit arson, and that I felt so strongly that I cried about it. Undoubtedly I used strong language, for I have always felt strongly on the subject. ...I do not ask you to correct your statement; let it go. What I think I ought to say is this, that such extreme statements too often nullify the object of the stater. ...War, thunder and lightening, earthquakes, pestilence, hurricanes, etc. make people think, and clear the atmosphere. You must bear this fact in mind as we go forward."[30] But he obviously was a little worried about the polemic nature of the newsletter. "[Allow] me to suggest that you will be stronger if you avoid language that borders on the profane. I am sure you will allow an old friend to say that much."[31]

The last half of 1916 was a high point in Montezuma's life. A wave of publicity was initiated by his speech, "Let My People Go," given at the annual meeting of the Society of American Indians in 1915 (Chapter 13). Newspaper accounts of the speech and its publication in the *Congressional Record* started the ball rolling, and Montezuma maintained the momentum by mailing out 10,000 copies of the speech.[32] This was followed by the newsletter in April 1916, and almost suddenly Montezuma was receiving letter after letter, from every corner of the United States, from young and old, congratulating him on his speech, requesting subscriptions to the newsletter, inviting him to lecture, and urging him on.[33]

This success inspired Marianna Burgess, now working with a Quaker organization in Los Angeles, to propose that she become the business manager of *Wassaja*, drawing on her experience with the printing office at Carlisle.[34] She suggested a goal of publishing 10,000 copies each month, working up to 100,000 copies with a worldwide distribution. She even suggested the possibility of a movie. Montezuma was more realistic and did not follow through on her proposal.

In the middle of 1917, Montezuma used a new masthead, but his message was the same, unrelenting attack on the Indian Bureau. "The Indian Office force is composed largely of antiquated clerks, a number of old dames, withered and forlorn, a few bright business men and a swarm of third-rate teachers with a following of uncouth, ignorant hangers-on. Just think of this selection of incompetent Whites set aside by law to impart competencys [*sic*] to Poor Lo!"[35]

### INDIAN OFFICE ATTITUDE

He is a ward and I am his guardian. God appointed me his guardian—(in the horn).
Your home is on a reservation. Mine is on land, sea and air—the whole d—d world.
He can stay there and I will stay here.
He is a child and I am a man.
He is a savage and I am civilized.
He is a heathen and I am a Christian.
Those red-skin devils are good for something, but they are not good enough for freedom and citizenship.
Our democracy is not good for the Indian.
Our rights are not good for the Indian, either.
He is competent to fight Germans, but he is not competent to be a citizen.
"Stay down there, you savage! Don't dare to come higher in the scale of life!"
"I belong up here and you belong down there."
"You are an Indian and I am the whole thing."[36]

Copies of *Wassaja* were passed on to reservation superintendents who made sure that the officials in the Indian Bureau saw them, including the commissioner of Indian affairs. Montezuma knew this and seized the opportunity to express his opinions.

As usual, Cato Sells is a great "get up" man. His position is a reward for one of those "get ups." He is not behind the times. He believes in change of hobbies on his "Merry-go-round," to captivate the public. To make himself famous, first it was "farming and fairs for the Indians;" second, "stock raising for the Indians;" third "Tepee Industries for the Indian women;" fourth, "reorganization of Indian Schools;" fifth, liquor; sixth, tracoma [*sic*];

seven, tuberculosis; eight, babies; ninth, "Indians are no Longer Wards." He says the Indians are not wards of the government and yet right on top of that he sways the reservation as a little Czar of America, and says to the Indians, "Use your lands for War Emergency"—not by their approval, but— He strikes the iron while it is hot to exploit his Indian Office and show the public that everything is well and that his subjects are at the disposal of the War department. Does this show the Indians are free and not wards of the United States Government as Cato Sells tried to make the public believe a few weeks ago? Regardless of what Cato Sells may say, we ARE WARDS OF THE GOVERNMENT. The Indian Bureau may see freedom, but the Indians can not. The Indian Bureau stands between the Indians and freedom. To free the Indians, we must do away with the Indian Bureau or any supervision whatever.[37]

## CATO SELLS SEES MONTEZUMA'S GHOST

Hon. Cato Sells, the present Commissioner of Indian Affairs, still believes that Dr. Carlos Montezuma of Chicago is publishing WASSAJA as a personal revenge upon him and not for the best interest of the Indians. We wish to say that the Hon. Cato Sells does not understand us. WASSAJA will continue long after he retires from the Commissionership of Indian Affairs, and long after he is dead, if the Indian Office is not abolished by that time. WASSAJA speaks of him often because he is the main engineer that greases the Indian machine. He need not credit himself that WASSAJA is sneaking behind him to take his scalp. Mr. Cato Sells, sleep and sweet dreams to you. The danger you think is not real. The Apache is far away and his footprints are leading to freedom and citizenship for his race. That pathway is unknown to you. Cheer up Cato Sells, Montezuma's ghost is harmless. Hold up, Cato Sells, did not this savage Apache Indian write to you for an explanation of a certain conversation you had with a certain senator right after the appearance of my "Let My People Go" in the Congressional Record? This savage Apache has several times reminded him for an answer, but regret to say that not a sign of courtesy has come from this Cato Sells to date, and therefore we publish Dr. Montezuma's first letter to the Hon. Cato Sells. …Not a word has come from Cato Sells. "HE HEAP AFRAID!"[38]

### Dedicated to Cato Sells

In the beginning of his administration he started in as an actor on a plot of intrigue. When he wished to please and to demonstrate his heart interest in the Indians he shed tears; but the tears were crocodile tears, they were false as false could be. He tells you—and pats you on the back as a four-flusher. He stands up and yells at you as a bluffer. He goes around and tells of his self sacrifice to the Indian cause and preaches false doctrines about the Indians. …Cato Sells paints Indians black who are working for the best interest of their race. He poisons characters of those Indians who know about Indians better than he does. He causes the arrest of those Indians who are protecting and safeguarding the rights of their people; instead of seeing the right and standing firm in the right, he says: "Take them, take them!" …He acts as a traitor to the country that he is a servant of, to the country that fought for liberty, equality, democracy, justice and humanity. …When Cato sells took charge of the Indian Bureau, little did we think he was so weak. He slanders the Indian who is getting the best of him; he threatens to those who try to enlighten the Indians in self government and he mums his Indian employees. Hon. Cato Sells is the Commissioner of Indian Affairs. It appears, what does he care? He came in with his party and he is going out with his party. That is glory enough for him.[39]

Occasionally, but not often, Montezuma displayed his sense of humor. "'A dead Indian' went to heaven. He was at liberty, strolling around in the Happy Hunting Grounds. The heavenly host plead with Peter to throw the Indian out. There was a great uproar in heaven because of the Indian. Finally the Indian spoke: 'Go, find Indian Agent to put me out.' The heavenly host searched high and low, in every nook and corner of that far-off land and they could not find a United States Indian Agent. 'That being the case,' Peter said, 'Surely this is Indian heaven; let him stay.' The Indian stayed and was ever thereafter everlastingly happy because there were no Indian agents to put him out."[40]

Montezuma introduced a new masthead in January 1919, holding up his favorite speech and essay, "Let My People Go," subtitled, "An Indian Classic." His good friend, Joe Scheuerle, drew the mastheads. Scheuerle, born in Austria, trained as an artist at the Art Academy of Cincinnati. He came to Chicago in 1905 and worked as an illustrator, producing cartoons, posters, and art for calendars. For twenty years, Scheuerle traveled each summer to the West and accumulated a portfolio of 200 paintings of Indians.[41] But he struggled during his lifetime to become established as a political cartoonist, never succeeding as a freelance artist or as a newspaper cartoonist. After Scheuerle left Chicago to live near New York in Orange, New Jersey, and then back to Cincinnati, he maintained a warm correspondence with Montezuma.

Montezuma now addressed the returning Indian veterans. "Brave warriors, you left your humble homes; whether it was a grass hut, tepee or log hut, to fight and die under the flag of your country for the principles that throbbed in your hearts, namely, FREEDOM, EQUALITY, DEMOCRACY, HUMANITY AND JUSTICE. …My dear boys, do you know that you *have demonstrated to the world by taking up arms for your country and standing shoulder to shoulder with your pale face comrades that the Indian race is not helpless and incompetent for freedom and citizenship?* …Now what is your duty? Carry on the fight—not as you experienced in the front, but for the FREEDOM AND CITIZENSHIP OF YOUR RACE. …A crown of glory is not only won by scars on the battle fields. It may be had by standing firm to a purpose true to your race. No soldier was ever braver, no statesman ever so great and no man ever truer to his race than Moses when he stood before Pharoh [*sic*] and asked, 'LET MY PEOPLE GO.'"[42]

There was some talk after World War I about restoring Carlisle as an Indian school. In August 1919, Montezuma let his readers know that was not an acceptable idea.

> The writer has followed the Carlisle Indian School from its birth and understands the feeling among Indians on the matter. The object of the Carlisle school has been killed and the INDIAN PEOPLE DO NOT WANT ANY MORE INDIAN SCHOOLS. What they do want is PUBLIC SCHOOLS. There is no more need of Indian schools when public schools are all around them. It is to these schools the Indians want to send their children. They are right. Indian schools should be whipped off the earth and the Indian children should be taken into the public schools. What children have better right to the public schools than the Indian children? But here comes the Indian Bureau. It is this monster that keeps the Indian children from the public schools. The Indian Bureau creates prejudice feelings against Indian children going into the public schools. You see the reason why. Their Indian schools would be empty and the Indian school employees would be out of easy jobs. INDIAN SCHOOLS ARE UN-AMERICAN INSTITUTIONS and should not be tolerated to exist. The Indians do not want Carlisle Indian School any more nor any other Indian school for their children. ...As much as we loved the first Carlisle Indian School, the Indians do not want it back. It would only be a sham and mockery to the first Carlisle Indian School. General Pratt will not be there. The Indian Bureau and sentimentalists cannot replace him. If your patriotism is to take away that which is most highly prized by the Indian race. KEEP IT! It is the same old story and the American history is as black as ever with the aboriginal Americans. "Bring back, bring back Carlisle to me!" IS NOT THE CRY OF THE INDIAN RACE.[43]

*Wassaja* produced a marked increase in Montezuma's already large volume of correspondence. On one occasion, Montezuma told Richard Pratt that he had a hundred letters before him and he intended to answer every one of them.[44] Zitkala-Ša wrote to tell Montezuma, "Was glad to refresh myself in reading the Wassaja."[45] Even the Chicago Historical Society was a subscriber.[46]

Buffalo Ben in White Swan, Washington, wrote: "...I hadn't heard of such a man as Carlos Montezuma or Red Fox, Eastman, Coolidge or any of the others that I have read about since I have had your little paper. My ideas ran the same way yours but couldn't express myself in language and after I had read the message from you to your people, I soon forgot on account of my own troubles and the only time I would kindle up the fire is when I would read the next issue of Wassaja. Now I am a convert, body and soul. I know my duty we must forget our selves while working for a great cause or rather count our selves in the same boat. They will never sink our boat, no they can't do it. I am talking and showing Let My People Go. I have 2 boys Indian full working for me, that I am convincing your ideas too. I let them read them then I bring up many things that they know to be the fact and compare them. They are enthusiastic now, and if I can do my work thoroughly with a few more good boys they will be more your apostles in preaching Indian rights and freedom. ...I like to write you these letters, hart to hart [*sic*] talks. It does my brain lots of good. I have been sleep so long, now I want you to know I am not."[47]

By 1920, Montezuma was receiving letters daily with complaints from different reservations. He funneled the letters to Sloan and Bishop of the Society of American Indians. Montezuma was at his desk answering letters into the "midnight hours."[48]

If we go on limping and scarred; it shows that we have been in the battle. The reservation agents and white employees do not love "Wassaja." The loyal reservation Indians read "Wassaja" as a boy would read a dime novel. They dare not be seen with it; if they read it they must seek a secluded place. If they are discovered, they are spotted or branded, and made to feel uneasy with the agent and reservation employees. It takes a great courage to read "Wassaja." And let it be known on a reservation.

"Wassaja" is a small paper, but when the editor goes on a reservation, he is called an intruder, agitator, and undesirable person. He is watched as a lion let loose. Anything and everything is being thought of to catch him in a trap, that he may be kept from holding any meetings with the Indians, or either get him out of the reservation.[49]

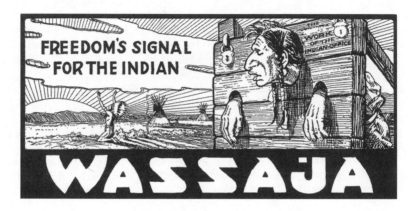

Montezuma introduced his fourth and final masthead in January 1921, symbolizing Indians in bondage. In his last issues, the message never changed.

The Indians' primitive arts have captivated the interest of the public and surplanted what should have been devoted to the man part of the Indian. Studying the Indian has not contributed to his progress, but rather places him as an odd creature, to be kept distinctive for the benefit of future generations. The Indian relics have been made of greater importance than the man part of the Indian. His paint, feathers and moccasins attract the attention of the public more than the man part of the Indian. They have not benefited the Indians. Too much attention to the Indian songs, music, legends, customs, and habits have derailed the noblest and highest ideals we entertained for the Indian people. The Indians, while starving for want of development as men, as a race, have been handicapped by the Indian Bureau. To do the most good for the Indian people and to do a most godly act, is to have Congress pass a bill to abolish the Indian Bureau, and thus give freedom and citizenship to the Indian people.[50]

Supporting *Wassaja* financially became increasingly difficult, costing Montezuma at least $20 per month (his total income was only $200 per month).[51] Part of the problem was due to the fact that once a name was on the subscription list, it stayed on, regardless of payment. Montezuma was having trouble getting people to renew subscriptions. "They are willing the first year, but their sympathy for the cause soon dies out."[52] Even Zitkala-Ša canceled her subscription, with a cold postcard that read:

Editor of Wassaja,
Kindly drop my name from the subscription list as I AM NOT ABLE TO CONTINUE
TAKING YOUR PUBLICATION
                            Respectfully[53]


Four months before his death, Montezuma complained to Richard Pratt: "This September issue was killing on me. I had to foot the bills. I do not stop to think about it. All I can do is to go right on. I have to forego many things in order to get out the Wassaja. I want to take a rest in Arizona a month, but now I can see no way to do it. If I were wealthy I do not think I would think very much about my people, but being poor, my heart yearns for them."[54]

BY MEANS OF *WASSAJA*, newspaper columns, magazine articles, and lectures, Montezuma took his message to the public. But the public wasn't interested. This was a time in history when American society was in the midst of a prolonged and intense battle between progressives and conservatives, between big capital and big labor. The years of *Wassaja*, mainly the years of Woodrow Wilson's presidency, were a time when America first tried to avoid war, then fought in a world war, and then turned victory in the war into an international defeat. The Republicans and Democrats were focused on gaining power over each other, and at the same time, keeping the radical element out of the fabric of our nation. The conflict between capitalists and labor was marred by strikes affecting essential components of our society, such as mining, the railroads, and the police. American Indians were not even on the priority list.

Montezuma wrote a piece in *Wassaja* that seemed to justify the tremendous energy and time that he poured into his newsletter. More than that, it articulated the reward gained by Montezuma in this effort.


### I HAVE STOOD UP FOR YOU

*Being of your blood,*
*Through thick and thin,*
        *I have stood up for you.*
*When the world's most devilish*
*Intrigue of humanity was set*
*And was coiling around you tighter and tighter—*
        *I have stood up for you.*
*When public sentiment was against you*
*And sent you to oblivion.*
        *I have stood up for you.*

*When the country was hysterically enraged*
*For defending your loved ones*
*And your birthright of priority—*
    *I have stood up for you.*
*When you were tagged as "Indians"*
*And outlawed creatures—*
    *I have stood up for you.*
*Haunted and hunted on thy domain,*
*With no chance of redress*
*But doomed, as though thy fate—*
    *I have stood up for you.*
*When you were described and pictured*
*And cartooned as cruel and savage—*
    *I have stood up for you.*
*When prejudice, hate and scorn*
*Sounded the keynote against you—*
    *I have stood up for you.*
*When starving and naked,*
*At the verge of your annihilation*
*By swords in the hands of criminals—*
    *I have stood up for you.*
*When the palefaces said*
*There was no hope for you—*
    *I have stood up for you.*
*When you were condemned and relegated*
*To the reservation system of hell—*
    *I have stood up for you.*
*When in prison and in bondage,*
*When you could neither speak nor see—*
    *I have stood up for you.*
*When decreed by the people across the sea*
*That you could neither learn nor be taught.*
    *I have stood up for you.*
*When it was put down black and white*
*That you could neither work nor support yourselves,*
*And that you were lazy and worthless—*
    *I have stood up for you.*
*When politics and greed were working you*
*For all that you were worth—*
    *I have stood up for you.*
*When everything you possessed was disappearing,*
*And your personal rights ignored—*
    *I have stood up for you.*
*As the Indian Bureau, like an octopus,*
*Sucked your very life blood.*
    *I have stood up for you.*

*For your freedom and citizenship,*
*By the abolishment of the Indian Bureau,*
    *I have stood up for you.*
*When the Indian Bureau says, "Were you freed*
*You would starve and be cheated"—*
*Only to feed its 7000 employees—*
    *I have stood up for you.*
*When you were judged "incompetent"*
*For freedom and citizenship by the Indian Bureau—*
    *I have stood up for you.*
*God knows that I am with thee day and night;*
*That is why I have stood up for you.*
*It might have been self-sacrifice,*
*It might have been the hand of God leading me,*
*Whatever it was, you have proven yourselves to be*
*What I have stood up for you to be.*[55]

## CHAPTER FIFTEEN

# Marriage to My Dovie

MONTEZUMA HAD COUNTLESS OPPORTUNITIES to meet young women. He gave his Indian talks to community clubs, ladies' organizations, church groups, libraries, and schools throughout greater Chicago and its nearby towns. His correspondence was voluminous. At the end of a draft of a letter to Richard Pratt he lists twenty names, indicating letters to be written. His correspondence reached out to many young women.[1] In all the letters, the greetings and salutations are always formal and respectful, but it is tempting to read between the lines.

A year after Montezuma and Zitkala-Ša parted ways, there was a lively correspondence with Laura W. Ronaldson who lived in Effingham, Illinois. She was a young woman known to Montezuma, who supported his views on the evils of Indian reservations. On June 21, 1903, she wrote: "Your jolly letter gave me a good laugh. I wished to reply sooner but waited to find out something of my own plans. Men always say that a woman can make up everything else except her mind. But at last I see my way quite clearly. I will go to Chicago on Friday, June 26—and stay over until Sunday evening. I know of a nice boarding house near the depot—where *visitors are admitted*. It is very, very good of you to spare me 'several afternoons' as I want to talk about traveling, Champaign, and—best of all—Indians. You are quite right about the 'old chief'—I will certainly *not* bring home an *old* one if there are any available *young* ones in sight. You are a base flatterer, Doctor! How do you know the chief would be the gainer? I am making slow progress in photography—I came to Effingham solely to study it. I hate the town & the people in it! I will tell you my plans when I see you. While in Chicago I did not mention them particularly as I dislike to push myself, notions, hobbies etc on my friends. As you are not easy to scare I will confess my doings. Also, bring my paper on the Apaches. I wish I could go to Arizona but fear that pleasure must be postponed as I do not see a legacy staring me in the face. My train gets into Chicago about 11 o'clock and I will go to your office at noon and we can talk. I repeat that you brought all this on yourself, Cordially, Laura W. Ronaldson."[2]

Only four days later, Laura wrote again. "My Dear Doctor— I am so glad to know that my letter did not startle or frighten you but you spoiled the effect of your compliment about 'angels' when you assured me that letters from them were *every day occurrences*! I agree with you perfectly about innocent jokes and fun and I am sure this world would be very dull without them. I haven't any very wicked sins to 'confess' but right here I must really confess something in earnest. It is very very kind of you to invite me to stop with you and I thank you sincerely but I must decline. You and I are good friends, true Bohemians and innocently inclined, but the world is so quick—anxious to criticize a woman alone in the world—as I am, and I am afraid the people in your house—not knowing me—would question my action. When we meet we can talk over this matter. The old chief and travels. I do not know when my train gets into Chicago so you had better not try to meet me. I will go to your office—100 State at noon and I am sure we will have a fine time. Please do not think that I decline the invitation because I do not want to go (nothing would give me greater pleasure) but you see the reason. ...Cordially, Laura W. Ronaldson."[3]

Laura Ronaldson addressed Montezuma as "My dear Bohemian," and signed her letters as "Bohemia." Two years later in 1905, she was traveling in Europe and wrote Montezuma from a hotel in Athens, Greece: "I thought of you many times & intended to write, but could not—I was wretched. Why is it that men can inflict so much suffering on women & never for one instant realize it?"[4]

Laura Ronaldson was preceded by Teena Knox who spurned Montezuma in 1898, and in 1901, Montezuma failed to resolve his differences with Zitkala-Ša (Chapter 9). A letter with no date or address indicates one more relationship with no fruition:

When we first met, you were so candid and free but suddenly that changed.

Intruding is far from my noblest and sublimest self. [I would rather] sacrifice than to make others unhappy.

If I am right, do not expect me Tuesday evening. Let this note be my final farewell. There is no regret of my ever meeting you. The world will not know of the cherished memory in the sacred chambers of my heart. May God bless and [keep] you—Again Farewell!

C. Monte[5]

In 1904 at the age of thirty-eight, he is frustrated once again in an effort to marry. Reading Montezuma's correspondence, it is apparent that he would write drafts of his letters (which he often saved) and then meticulously copy the final version with no additions, corrections, or marks. The drafts, however, contain alterations, scratched out words, and the handwriting is hurried and less precise. Such a draft of a letter to William H. Underwood at 40 Exchange Place, New York City, written in May 1904 reveals another love:

By the prompting of my ablest manhood and with the loving assurance of your precious daughter Lillian's love, I pray you for that sacred sanction to take her as my helpmate through life.

Our union of love has not been spontaneous nor is it a mere infatuation. We have been true friends going on two years. Her likes and dislikes have been mine. Our noble ambitions and ideals are as one, and finally we have considered everything which would involve our marriage with our matured age of discretion.

If you feel any hesitation because of my nativity I do not blame you one bit. Even though I am an Indian, had I a loving daughter who was thinking of marrying an Indian, before knowing the man I would emphatically rebel against such an outrageous idea.

Remember today there are Indians and Indians. In my case it is so different, it is an unusual exception—one out of the noble race or I would not allow myself this greatest request for my life happiness.

On the Indian question I am known all over the United States. My home life has been in the best of Christian families. Against all odds I worked my own way through the public school, the University of Illinois and Medical Department of the Northwestern University. During my fourteen years of practice I served seven years in the Government service as Physician and Surgeon. My acquaintance is among the best and most influential. I'm a member of the First Baptist Church. In the literary line I am personally enumerated with the Press Club. In my medical work (specialist) I am highly recognized by the medical profession.

If such is your feeling; if you ever sacrificed before in your life—leave criticism aside (anything can be criticized) and allow God to guide your words to say, "Yes, you may have my precious daughter, all my blessings go with you both."

Both of us await with loving suspense for your fatherly answer.[6]

Alas, there is no answer to be found in Montezuma's correspondence and no further reference to Lillian Underwood.

Montezuma certainly fell in love easily. There was *at least* one more episode of unrequited love. Helena Warner, a resident of Chicago, became ill while traveling in Texas in the summer of 1911. Rather than her parents, she asked Montezuma to send her money. Montezuma sent $15 and a letter. Warren answered from Dallas: "I know tho' there really is only one way of repaying you—that which you ask, but which I cannot give—myself. Monte, I am absolutely without imagination since receiving your letter. I cannot realize that you should care for me as you say you do. Really when I think of it my mind is blank and my poor little half human heart feels like a ball of lead. I had always thought I had one real true friend in this whole wide world and just beginning to believe there was true friendship, but not now, never. I know I have many admirers but now, no friends. I don't believe I can ever love any man. I may marry, but that is all, and now I couldn't dream of any serious propositions. I am sorry, Monte, very sorry, but why worry about it. There is too much sorrow for us all... ."[7]

Montezuma also received letters that could have been the consequence of misunderstandings or unintended comments and behavior, or perhaps there was more to it.

Friend:
Having just come to my senses and realizing what happened yesterday by your heartless act toward me, thought it best to take this means of settling the matter as I dislike the publicity that a court proceedings would make and I know you wouldn't like it either. I have not said anything to any person and you will see from the above that I am writing this little note from a friends [sic]. So why not keep this scandalous act a secret while I know if (mama) knew it would be taken into court without any hesitation so I feel that it is only right that you should settle with me for a reasonable sum as you know I need it and know you will send check.
I remain Your former patient,
Frances O'Leary[8]

Sir,
I received a bill from you the amount was $25.00 which bill you claim is due you for medical attendance to my wife Mrs. I. Den Ouden or as you spell it Neouden and you have your nerve to send a bill. You treated my wife shamefully and if it wasn't for the scandal I would have had the law after you at the time but I warn you if you try and collect this bill after the way you insulted my wife I will put the case in the hands of an attorney and I won't be slow about it.
Mr. I. M. Den Ouden[9]

MONTEZUMA MARRIED MARIE KELLER on September 19, 1913; she was twenty-five years old and Montezuma was forty-seven (the marriage certificate incorrectly gives his age as forty-five). Marie was a German-speaking native of Romania, blue-eyed and fair skinned.[10] We know that her father was not alive and that her mother lived in Aurora, a nearby rural area.[11] She was able to correspond with friends in the German language,[12] and perhaps Montezuma was able to retrieve some German from his two-year exposure thirty years earlier at the University of Illinois. In her later years, she often preferred to be addressed as "Mary," and even the marriage certificate records her as "Maria." A friend of the Montezumas described her as quiet with a traditional immigrant view of a husband's partner as a housewife whose role was to remain in the background.[13]

Little is known about the circumstances of their meeting and relationship before marriage. An intriguing letter is that from Charles Dickens sixteen months before the marriage that asked: "How is Mrs. Montezuma getting along?"[14] A close friend of Montezuma's reported that Marie was the daughter of Montezuma's housekeeper.[15] In an interview in 1934, Marie stated that she first met Montezuma in 1910 when she came to him as a patient (she lived nearby).[16] She said he drove a good car and took her for long rides, most likely in a borrowed automobile, given Montezuma's financial circumstances.

Reverend William Stedman, the Baptist minister from Urbana, Illinois, who welcomed eleven-year-old Montezuma into his home in 1878, married the Montezumas in Chicago on the evening of the nineteenth. Remarkably, Montezuma left the very next day for his annual trip to Arizona. Only three days after the marriage, Montezuma wrote a strange letter to his new wife from Sante Fe, en route to Phoenix.

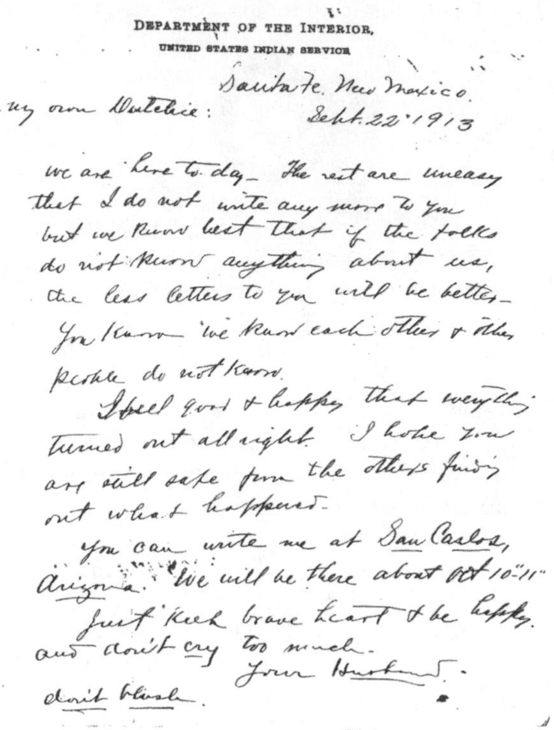

DEPARTMENT OF THE INTERIOR,
UNITED STATES INDIAN SERVICE

*[handwritten letter reproduced below in print]*

My own Dutchie,

We are here today– The rest are uneasy that I do not write any more to you but we know best that if the folks do not know anything about us, the less letters to you will be better– You know we know each other & other people do not know.

I feel good and happy that everything turned out all right. I hope you are still safe from the others finding out what happened.

You can write me at *San Carlos, Arizona*. We will be there about Oct 10-11.

Just keep brave heart & be happy. And don't *cry* too much.

Your *husband*

*don't blush*[17]

What did this letter mean? What happened? Was the marriage a secret one, without permission of Marie's mother? Who are the "others?" Relatives? Friends? People of German background who would not take kindly to a marriage with an Indian? Something unusual surrounded this marriage. However, subsequently, there is never a hint that the marriage was anything but loving, supportive, and solid.

Richard Pratt learned of the marriage from a paragraph in the Chilocco School Journal a month later.[18] "As you have said nothing to me about it and have failed to ask my permission, I am not a little surprised. If it is true, of course, I congratulate you. At your years, I should be entirely willing to believe that you have been wise in your selection and that great happiness was in store for you in consequence. However, I refuse to entirely believe it until I hear from you."[19]

Pratt was mollified when a letter caught up to him, and he learned that Montezuma wrote to him *the very same* evening he was married. "Your letter of September 19th was forwarded to me at the Shoreham in this city, and only reached me yesterday. I note that you say in it 'I was married by Dr. Steadman [*sic*] this evening.' This, of course exonerates you in every way from any previous criticism I made in regard to your getting married without my knowledge and consent."[20] Pratt joins with Mrs. Pratt in their warmest congratulations. "The fact that you have such a practical, homemaking companion is a source of the greatest possible gratification to us. We shall hope to see you and Mrs. Montezuma some time in the future, and you can both feel assured of our continued fatherhood and motherhood."[21]

In the months that followed, Montezuma was obviously happy. Pratt told him, "I am glad to find that your wife responds so promptly to her tutelage. That, however, was naturally to be expected, for every body that falls within the atmosphere of your enthusiasm inevitably succumbs."[22] Guests in their home offered their appreciation: "I would like to have others have the same great pleasure of meeting Mrs. Montezuma as I had, even if they do not have the benefit of her good cooking as I had and that I remember so well."[23] Marie specialized in German meals featuring chicken and dumplings, sauerkraut, and spareribs.[24] And some guests were received in fancy style. A year after the marriage, Richard Pratt and his wife stayed at the Montezuma house after being met at the train station by Montezuma with a limousine.[25]

In the only picture we have of the Montezumas together (sometime around 1920), Marie appears to be about five-feet two-inches tall, thick-waisted with a stocky body, not unlike that of her husband. Montezuma has a warm, relaxed smile that is inviting. His hands are sturdy, suggesting strength not delicacy. Montezuma is wearing his white dress shirt, albeit sloppily, with the tiny white bow tie that he favored.

Montezuma addressed Marie as "Dutchie," or "Dovie" in his letters to her, and he signed them "Wassaja." He settled mainly on "Dovie" after experimenting in the first year of their marriage with "My own Snooky, Snooky," "My own Cubby, Cubby," and "My dear Pee Wee."[26] Her hospitality matched that of Montezuma's. On one occasion, when Montezuma was in Arizona, Richard Pratt stopped in Chicago and stayed in the Montezuma home with Marie.[27] Zitkala-Ša wrote: "Wishing you and your wife all happiness for the kind way in which you treat all Indians going through Chicago, believe me."[28]

June 1921 was the month Montezuma spent in Washington, D.C., when he successfully brought the Fort McDowell land and water rights

*Marie & Carlos Montezuma—around 1920*

controversy to a conclusion (Chapter 12). His letters to Marie provide some insight into their relationship. He was writing from his room in an inexpensive hotel, where he endured sweltering heat, as Washington in June was more like a steaming August.

My dear Dovey Dovie:

In my room it so hot that I feel comfortable with nothing on me. I have come in earlier than usual.[29]

Another day has passed away and I am not any near home. ...I am finding every day that these senators and congressmen and the Indian Bureau take the Indians as lower in the human scale than the Negro people. They do not want to tell you that, but they believe the Indian is not ready to protect and do for himself They need the government's strong arm around them. When the Indians can dodge the crooks, keep the white rascals from robbing them and when they can support themselves, then & only then, will it be safe to abolish the Indian bureau. That will be many years to come. We will not live to see that day.

Well, someone must stand firm against these thoughts. What the attitude against the Indians may be in Washington that does not move me at all. My claim for my people is that much stronger and the Indians are with me.

Good night with many kisses

Your Wassaja[30]

...I received your good letter. I am glad to know that you are not lonesome. Keep up a brave heart and do the best you know how until I get back. ...Do my business while I am away. Tell people that I am in Washington on business & that you will take their names for me.[31]

Immediately after Montezuma's return from Washington, Marie left by automobile for a trip to Fort McDowell. Montezuma was to join her later, but it became apparent that he could not afford to leave Chicago, and even her expenses became a strain. It is moving to observe Marie's affection for Montezuma, and how Montezuma's family accepted Marie and how she felt towards them. Her letters are difficult to read, with little punctuation, tiring detail, rambling thoughts, and no paragraphs.

Dear Wassaja

We are have tire trouble so I have time to write again. Having tire trouble now very close to colorado and will be in Denver Sunday. ...Write me to Santa Fe and send me the money there as we will stay a little while. I hope every thing is allright at home. I shall write more about the trip.

With lots of love, Marie[32]

"Hope you have send me some letters. Have been dreaming of you spending about 2 to 4 dollars per day[33]

Received your letter August the first and was very glad to get the money I had only $10 left I expect an answer from the letter I wrote you about my expenses I am not getting along with the Pimos as I expected the only thing is that they are always talking about not having any money and will have to stay in Santa Fe to work no telling how long because they had not expected that it would cost so much to run a car we had lots of tire trouble because too much of a load or because of no experience I thought Mr. Pimo said that Gilbert could go along for nothing or for helping to drive but not so as Mrs Pimo said she did not understand it

...I am longing for you with love[34]

Montezuma's responses are endearing, revealing the domestic side of his life as well as his affection for his wife.

Dear Dovie
...The black cat is on the table before me as I am writing with sad heart because I drowned her kittens today. She is crying for them. They were such beautiful kittens. I hated to kill them. I feel as bad as the black cat.
...Again Miss Kate & Mrs Brier were together & I made supper for them. I do not like this idea of cooking for them. In the morning I get up & cook for Mrs Brier. That does not suit me. I do not know what to do. Something must be done, but I will bear it as long as I can.
Today I had three patients that is doing pretty good. Tomorrow I will have just as many.
Everything is very quiet. I do not hear from Washington. No one knows where the Society's Conference will be held.
...My love, I am keeping up my own. So I expect to hear from you that you want more money. I know the way you are traveling it will require money. No one can travel without money, but I do not know where to send it. ...
your loving husband[35]

...You and Zi know the work for the Indians is discouraging. There is no great work that is not discouraging. That is the time we need to forget ourselves and go right on. If we think before the dark side too much, we will give up and our efforts have been wasted and disappear. It is by going on under difficulties and discouragement that wins in the long run.
...I guess your mother is working for her husband brought the clothes yesterday. I paid $25 on that mortgage. The man said there was $31 more to pay. So I think I will pay it all the next time.
Dovie, have a good time but be careful of yourself,
your loving husband,<br>Wassaja[36]

In September 1921, Marie was short of money. "Send me some money if you have not already sent it I am out of money and I will come home as soon as I get it will go to see Mrs. Roberts for two days after I get money I am out of money to a dollar it is very warm here but cool at night I am feeling fine here now the water is good the best since I left home the Indian boys are not all working to some of them is to hot to work and there is not much do to until later they have taken a lot of Mexican in the reservation work some Indians think it is not right that they should come in the Reservation to work when there is a lot of Indian men here not working I met a Maricopa Indian he told me that the agent let some people come in to get work when the Pimas have not any themself he say there is trouble over there The Agent is the one that took Sharp's place Gilbert has gone back to his wife and the other man is trying hard to have his wife take him back which she will do as the womens have no way to make a living are glad if there Husband ask them to come back he will have to talk to a little while as she is mad Gilbert went to his wife the very evening he arrived I thing he could not wait any longer and did not care as long she have him so everything be allright Nellie come over to see me after I told some of them how she has been to me as if I remember told you all about in the last letter and we had a good talk about everything and will tell you what she said when I see her I would call her a she Apache I know all I shall say nothing to anybody it is not my business what she will do she wants to play the big bug in the battle and pull Gilbert a long thats why he has a big head all time I was thinking of taking a girl along if you write right away if its allright I will ask George his girl wants to come if not Richard has a girl if you remember she went to day school last year and is good look and then there is a girl Nellie and she was then in Phoenix this spring and ready for high school so tell me what you want me to do will close with Love and kisses, Yours forever, Marie"[37]

My dear Dovie

I am waiting for my grape juice to boil down to a consistency for jam. I bought for 5 cents spilt grapes and I am going to make jam out of them. I will get four glasses.

...I am glad that you have Gilbert along with you, because he feels at home and he can make you feel safe and he knows what to do, in order to get to McDowell. I know the Indians will be glad to see you both. You can tell them so many things that they do not know. How strange and restful you will feel to be at home. You do not have to get up and get ready to travel. You can now take a long rest and do as you please. The Indians will be kind to you and you can [?] and be at rest.

...Tonight I can imagine you are asleep and maybe dreaming of Chicago & when you awake, you are at McDowell, many miles from home. But you must think you are at home with those blood relations of mine.

You can believe I am relieved. Mr. And Mrs. Brier and Miss Leta Meyers left on the first. I am alone & feel like myself.

Your mother was here yesterday and will be back tomorrow night and on Monday we will do a little cleaning. ...I am everlastingly killing cockroaches. I take one hour every night. Good exercise. I do not think my jam is successful.

Business is better. Do not leave until I am sure that I cannot come. If I come it will be the last of this month. I can get reduced rate then. Now have a good time. I am getting long nicely. I know your mother will help me. She did not like me to those other people here.[38]

Again I am writing to you. Had a busy day. Was up at half past eight. Had patient at 9:30 & another between 10 & 11 o'clock.

Tried to can tomatoes but could not. Had lodge man come at 1–2 o'clock. Boiled meat. Had to make a call. When I returned at 6 o'clock had a telephone from Joe Latimer to meet him at 8 o'clock at La Salle Hotel. I returned at 9:30. Your mother is here to help me. Tomorrow at 10 o'clock who should ring my bell but Leta & her husband Mr. Smart. They ordered Yellow cab & went home after being here an hour.[39]

I am a goose to allow everybody to sponge off me. I brace up & told them that I want the rooms after the 1st of September.

The other day I put up twelve glasses of black berries. Your mother's husband was here today & brought the washed clothes.

...My Dovie, you ask me if I am coming out to Arizona. How I want to come & be with you & bring you home, but the way I look at is now I hate to spend so much money when we need the money for home. If I come I will spend about $200.00 or more, and just think what we could do with that money. I have on hand now about $350.00. You can see for yourself that it would be foolish for me to spend nearly all of that & get no return. If I remain at home I can make that much & be easy after you get home.

The way I look at things you stay out there as long as you think best & then come home. Find out everything about McDowell matters & tell those Indians that I have not enough money to come out there. I want to but how can I when I have so little money. They will understand. Let them tell you everything. Have meetings & listen to them. Have Gilbert write down what they say & bring that with you.[40]

"Dear Wassaja, Received your money did not want you to send me so much I shall take good care of it and not spent more than I have to will not be able to get it till Richard comes back from San Carlos as they are not back yet I think she [Nellie Davis] is the trouble maker around this place [Marie says Nellie always complains of starving, but Marie cannot understand how she could be starving and so fat.] I do not say to anybody that I am starving like Nellie what I had to eat was quash and Indian Bread or just beans with bread no meat sometime some Rabbitt one Jack Rabbitt John shot one day I could count just how many time I had meat today Pauline ask me to cook a chicken they don't know how so they never eat one. I could tell you lots more but I wish I could write better I will tell you when I see you or later in writing I do not like to write about trouble all time here is everything quiet now from what I hear Mike Burns is gone in the mountains getting some nuts but I think Nellie is working against you not against McDowell but only against you and it is because she don't understand and wants to work for Glory for her self her own relative are against her something must be wrong she don't like me because she can't say things to me like she can to the Indians and she tells me she only stays here because she want to help her people and it is hard for her to live among them because they drink and gamble and lie about her."[41]

"...I think if you have $500.00 and have or do not owe anything for rent or paper we would have plenty of money left to pay for Insurance. $200.00 would be plenty to cover all when we come back and $300.00 is plenty for you to come and both to go back as $200.00 for you and $100.00 for me to come back on will be plenty your Railroad ticket will 115.00 or 125 with sleeper All the Indians like to have you come I do not care what Gilbert or his wife say about you as long the other Indians are with you if you can get some one to trust our home to that is. ...The other day I was counting how many there is of us and what do you think there is just 12 of us with 6 dogs and one cat but there are all Happy People no matter what there is to eat. ...the Indian here think you are rich and I think you are to but not in money as much as in the way you keep busy here they can't see nor hear or do something or understand anything they need to get in with other people. ...they come to me as if I was Christ and could help and know everything in the world they have no confidence in them self to do anything one minute they are mad at each other the next minute they are sorry because they feel as so they are all one there is a lot to look after here some one to see after to make them do things."[42]

When Marie went to the Verde River to wash her clothes, the young Yavapai girls secretly watched her. Mrs. Montezuma's undergarments fascinated them.[43] Marie's stay at Fort McDowell lasted three months as she and Montezuma kept thinking he could join her. But eventually, Montezuma admitted he could not afford a vacation.

My dear lonely Dovie,

I know you and the Indians want me out there, but I see no way to get off long enough to come out to the home of my birth. I know you will all be disappointed for you all thought I would come.

I was at the Santa Fe office and they told me it would cost $140.00 and some odd dollars for a ticket to Phoenix and return in October. One fare cost $82.50 Yesterday I paid for my yearly accident insurance $30.00. This evening I counted my cash on hand $473.00 Tomorrow I will send you $50.00 money order at Mesa. You may need more to pay your fare back. If you do, you can telegraph me and I will send how you say by telegram.

...On October 8th, 15th & 25th I have appointments to keep. The 15th I get $15.00 and on the 25th I go to Detroit to the Society of American Indians Conference. With my practice, you see I will be busy in the month of October. I may make $200.00 in October. When you get back we will be comfortably situated and can save for next year to take the trip together.

It would be a risk for me to leave and when I get back I would feel the weight of starting on nothing & then to take that trip to Detroit would not be the same without money.

Just received your letter about Gilbert's arrest. Will send $100.00 instead of $50.00 as I see you will be needed longer at McDowell.[44]

My dear Dovie

I paid $50.00 to the Masonic Building and accident Insurance $30.00.

Those Indians are always poor. They want some one to do for them all the time. That is a bad habit the Indian Bureau has taught the Indians. You can see for yourself that a reservation life is degrading. What you see there is the same on all reservations. Some are worse.

Well, my dear, you have had a good vacation. When you get home you will dream of Arizona. You will be talking to the Indians in your sleep.

I hope you have enough money to get a tourist sleeper or regular sleeper. Get your meals in Harvey meal stations. IT COST $82.50 FOR ONE FARE

The cats will be glad to see you.[45]

Marie made it home by herself, and Montezuma was unable to travel to Arizona until fourteen months later when he made the last trip of his life.

WILLIAM THOMAS MOORE, a Pima Indian, lived with Carlos and Marie Montezuma. This was a friendship that began in 1916 when Billy Moore, age eighteen, wrote to Montezuma, asking him to take an interest in a young musician, educated in the Phoenix public schools. Moore maintained the correspondence, also receiving Montezuma's monthly newsletter, during World War I when he was in the company band of the 158th Infantry of the Fortieth Division, stationed at Fort Kearny in California.[46] When the war ended, Moore moved to Chicago to room in the Montezuma household.

A year after Montezuma's death, Moore married Marie. She was thirty-five years old and he was twenty-five.[47] The couple moved in 1924 to a new house at 2219 Prairie Street in Blue Island, a suburb of Chicago. A trained musician, Billy Moore played and taught music (his specialties were the cornet and the violin) in addition to his job as a cabinet-maker for the Illinois Bell Telephone Company.[48] After their father died in Arizona in 1924, Billy's nephews, Everett and Russell Moore, came to live with Billy and Marie. Everett became an accomplished pianist, and Russell graduated from the Sherman Institute in Riverside, California, and became a well-known jazz musician, playing with Lionel Hampton, and then the trombone with Louis Armstrong.

Gladys Brown, a friend living in Ohio, wrote to Marie on July 29, 1924:

It certainly was news to hear you were married again but I don't blame you in the least for when one has their own home once there is nothing like it. Another Indian! How could it be otherwise? You had such a wonderful Indian in Montezuma. How could you marry a plain White Man, of course not. (I hope my father never sees that line).[49]

Marie never conceived. There is no mention of pregnancy or an infertility problem in any of the available documents. A friend of Montezuma's said that there were no children because Montezuma was opposed to mixed racial offspring.[50] Marie herself told an interviewer that Montezuma's marriage proposal had one condition, that there would be no children because he didn't believe in mixing races.[51] However, there is not a single hint in Montezuma's extensive writings that he believed such a thing.

Did the Montezumas use contraception? In the last decades of the 1800s, condoms, diaphragms, pessaries, and douching syringes were widely advertised; however, their use for contraception was limited.[52] The knowledge and application of contraception began slowly around 1900, but Margaret Sanger did not open the first family planning clinic until 1916. Contraception teaching did not become part of medical education until the 1960s, and the last state laws prohibiting the distribution of contraceptives were not overthrown until 1972 and 1973. In the early 1900s, contraception and its methods were considered to fall under the Comstock Law of 1873, named after Anthony Comstock, a self-appointed crusader against anything he regarded as obscene, prohibiting the use of the U.S. Mail to send obscene literature. The Comstock Law was used to prosecute those who distributed birth control information or devices, including Margaret Sanger in 1916. It was not until 1936 that a federal court ruled in a case involving Margaret Sanger that doctors could prescribe contraceptives to save a life or promote the well-being of patients. Therefore, contraception was not actively encouraged or promoted during Montezuma's lifetime; however, barrier methods of contraception were available, and most physicians, if motivated, could find a resource and obtain the materials and devices.

Many Americans at this time in history, especially religious Americans, believed contraception was morally wrong. Montezuma's Baptist affiliation may have made it difficult for him to support the use of these methods. However, even if the Montezumas utilized these barrier methods of contraception, a 10 to 15 percent failure rate per year makes it unlikely that Marie could have avoided pregnancy for twenty years. The fact that Marie did not become pregnant with either of her two husbands makes it more likely that there was a problem on her side. There is no way to know the real reason for the lack of children.

Billy Moore died in 1951, and Marie Keller Montezuma Moore died in 1956 when she was sixty-eight years old.

## CHAPTER SIXTEEN

# World War I:
# Is This Justice?

T HE FEDERAL GOVERNMENT accused Montezuma of sedition during the tense
days of World War I. Montezuma seized upon military participation in the war as a
visible and prominent example of the unjust and inequitable treatment of American Indians.
His blunt and loud proclamations on this subject easily attracted the attention of government officials.

There are many military veterans buried alongside of Montezuma in the Fort McDowell
Cemetery. The cemetery is reached by Wassaja and Ba-Hon-Nah (Good Man, Bill Doka)
Roads. Located near the ruins of the old military post, it has been at this site since 1865.
The entrance is marked by a white metal archway over the road holding the words, "Ba Dah
Mod Jo," (Yavapai for cemetery, literally meaning "people buried here"). Here lie Charles
Dickens who died in 1963 at the age of ninety-eight and Mike Burns who died in 1934 at
the estimated age of seventy-four. The graves of military veterans are easily distinguished.

They are neatly manicured, decorated with flags and flowers. The warrior tradition among American Indians is preserved even today by their volunteer participation in the military forces. Veterans, carrying flags and in uniforms adorned with medals, are always a feature in Indian parades and celebrations. It has been argued, very convincingly, that this military participation by American Indians does not reflect a desire for adventure and fighting, but a sense of responsibility and duty.[1]

Throughout the many Euro-American conflicts in early American history, various bands of American Indians fought individually and as tribes against each other and as allies of opposing sides. Participation in American war experiences continued in the Civil War and the Spanish-American War. In the late nineteenth century, Indians could be found on both sides in the many western Indian campaigns. This was never more evident than in the use of Apache and Yavapai scouts against each other in Arizona. Fighting was not new for Indians, but fighting in an organized, Euro-American military war was a different experience. Indian fighting was usually a raid for revenge or to gain prestige. It was a hit and run affair with few casualties.[2]

The successful use of Indian scouts in the western Indian battles eventually led the U.S. Army, under the direction of John M. Schofield, commanding general of the army, and Redfield Proctor, secretary of war, to establish two all-Indian units in 1891.[3] Recruiting was slow, but eventually the economic benefits and the appeal to those with warrior traditions accumulated over 400 regular soldiers. Within six years, the plan was a failure. The problems were too difficult to overcome.[4] The biggest obstacle was communication because few of the recruits were capable in English. Added to that was the difficulty in abruptly adjusting to Anglo-Saxon culture combined with a harsh military discipline (especially uniforms and haircuts), separation from family and home, and blatant racism. This experience was instrumental in the subsequent insistence of military officials that Indian soldiers would not be segregated in all-Indian units, but distributed (integrated) into White units.

The effort in 1890 to develop all-Indian units in the army was directed by the assimilationist policy, but in World War I the motivation was more mixed. Some favored all-Indian units as a means of preserving Indian identity. The motivation to produce all-Indian combat units for World War I was partly the thinking of philanthropists that this would be one way to solve the problem of unemployment on the reservations. In addition, it was argued that educated Indians would find a place to exercise their skills. Others, like Montezuma and Pratt, viewed all-Indian units as nothing more than segregation, contrary to their lifetime goal of mixing individual Indians in White "civilization." All, especially the Society of American Indians and Zitkala-Ša, believed that Indian participation in World War I would provide ammunition in the campaign to gain citizenship for all Indians.

Joseph Kossuth Dixon, a subscriber to Montezuma's newsletter, *Wassaja*, was a very loud advocate of all-Indian units. Dixon was chosen by Rodman Wanamaker to be the director of the Philadelphia-based Wanamaker Department Store's "Educational Bureau," and specifically the leader of three photographic expeditions to the West that recorded Indian life and culture.[5] Dixon was dedicated to preserving Indian history and culture, but at the same time building patriotism and loyalty among Indians for the United States. Dixon was joined by Edward E. Ayer and the Board of Indian Commissioners in pressuring the government to organize all-Indian units. Bills were introduced in both branches of Congress to create Indian units, including the granting of citizenship upon enlistment. The failure of these bills was partially due to the negative impact of Dixon's eccentric testimony that liberally manipulated and interpreted history.[6] Arthur C. Parker pulled no punches with J. K. Dixon: "We believe that his speeches would be highly illuminating to the investigator and reveal the astounding egotism of the man. …If the [Wanamaker] expedition has resulted in confusion to the Indian, in embarrassment to Mr. Wanamaker, in astonishment to the intelligent man of Indian affairs, it has to a greater degree injured the unfortunate leader of the expedition [Dixon], and we are sorry."[7] Virtually every Indian organization of significance voiced consistent and powerful opposition to the idea of segregation (viewed as an obstacle to assimilation), and this opposition could not be overcome in Congress.

There were some successful experiences with segregated all-Indian military units. Prior to World War I, Arizona maintained an all-Indian unit in the National Guard, Company F, composed of graduates of the Phoenix Indian School.[8] The Phoenix School, like all off-reservation schools, stressed patriotism and treated its students with military discipline, and undoubtedly the graduates included some Yavapai from nearby Fort McDowell. During World War I, Company F remained stateside, fighting with striking miners.[9] This Arizona tradition can be traced back to an even earlier time. Two companies of Indians, 100 Pima in one and 100 Maricopa in the other, assisted the California Volunteers when they established Fort McDowell in 1865 (Chapter 12).

In addition to the Indian organizations, the idea of segregated all-Indian units was opposed by the considerable weight of the Bureau of Indian Affairs and even the army. Of course, the idea was also totally inconsistent with Richard Pratt's long-held views, and he wrote extensively to Secretary of War Newton Baker championing dispersal and integration.[10] One of Pratt's enduring attributes was his consistent opposition to segregation of any race. The army remembered the failure of the effort in the 1890s and did not want to duplicate that experience. The rest, including Commissioner of Indian Affairs Cato Sells, continued to believe in rapid assimilation and citizenship of Indians and that this would be best accomplished by the distribution of individual Indians among White soldiers. Indeed, Sells pushed the allotment process to a new level of activity during World War I. Despite his difficulties with Sells, Montezuma shared a dedication with Sells to the policy of assimilation.

IN APRIL 1917, Cato Sells, with the approval of the Secretary of the Interior Franklin Lane, proclaimed a new declaration of policy, an "emancipation of American Indians," that revealed the intensity of his commitment to assimilation.[11] "Broadly speaking, a policy of greater liberalism will henceforth prevail in Indian administration to the end that every Indian, as soon as he has been determined to be as competent to transact his own business as the average white man, shall be given full control of his property and have all his lands and moneys turned over to him, after which he will no longer be a ward of the Government."[12] It was heralded as the dawn of a new era that would allow reduced appropriations by the government and create more self-respect and independence for the Indian, with ultimate absorption of the Indian race into the nation.

### A Declaration of Policy by Cato Sells

1. *Patents in fee.*—To all able-bodied adult Indians of less than one-half Indian blood, there will be given as far as may be under the law full and complete control of all their property. Patents in fee shall be issued to all adult Indians of one-half or more Indian blood who may, after careful investigation, be found competent, provided, that where deemed advisable patents in fee shall be withheld for not to exceed 40 acres as a home. Indian students, when they are 21 years of age, or over, who complete the full course of instruction in the Government schools, receive diplomas and have demonstrated competency will be so declared.

2. *Sale of lands.*—A liberal ruling will be adopted in the matter of passing upon applicants for the sale of inherited Indian lands where the applicants retain other lands and the proceeds are to be used to improve homesteads or for other equally good purposes. A more liberal ruling than has hitherto prevailed will hereafter be followed with regard to the applications of non-competent Indians for the sale of their lands where they are old and feeble and need the proceeds for their support.

3. *Certificates of competency.*—The rules which are made to apply in the granting of patents in fee and the sale of lands will be made equally applicable in the matter of issuing certificates of competency.

4. *Individual Indian moneys.*—Indians will be given unrestricted control of all their individual Indian moneys upon issuance of patents in fee or certificates of competency. Strict limitations will not be placed upon the use of funds of the old, the indigent, and the invalid.

5. *Pro-rata shares–trust funds.*—As speedily as possible their pro rata shares in tribal trust or other funds shall be paid to all Indians who have been declared competent, unless the legal status of such funds prevents. Where practicable the pro rata shares of incompetent Indians will be withdrawn from the treasury and placed in banks to their individual credit.

6. *Elimination of ineligible pupils from the government Indian schools.*—In many boarding schools Indian children are being educated at government expense whose parents are amply able to pay for their eduction and have public school facilities at or near their homes. Such children will not hereafter be enrolled in government Indian schools supported by gratuity appropriations, except on payment of actual per capita cost and transportation.[13]

This "new policy" was the rationale for an acceleration in the allotment of Indian lands. The allotment and loss of Indian land reached a peak level during Cato Sells' tenure as commissioner of Indian affairs. Sells was moved not only by his dedication to the assimilation philosophy, but also by the general war-motivated desire to increase the agricultural and stock-raising productivity of western Indian lands. One cannot ignore the racist assumption that mixed-bloods (less than one-half Indian blood) were automatically deemed competent because of their White blood component. Of course land was lost because many Indians sold or leased their allotted land. Montezuma published in his newsletter, *Wassaja*, a copy of a circular from the Indian Bureau listing land in South Dakota to be opened for bids. There were 331 parcels of land, almost all were the 160 acres provided in the allotment process, with prices ranging from $480 to $1,600.[14] Montezuma said, "...this selling business by the Indian Office is an outrage and not helpful to the Indians. Let the Indians do their own business and farm the land themselves, which they would do if freedom was theirs."[15] Sells' policy was not slowed until the new secretary of the interior, John B. Payne, called a halt in 1920 to allotments based on competency.

Montezuma replied to Commissioner Sells' "new policy" in *Wassaja*. "Permit me to say that what the commissioner of Indian affairs refers to has been going on more than forty years.

It is nothing new, but Commissioner Sells would have the people believe that he is doing a great deal for the Indians. He is going to 'give closer attention to the incompetent' Indians hereafter. The Indians as a race were the most competent people to get along in America. Who made the Indians incompetent? The Indian Office. And now the Commissioner wants to use the Indian Office to make competent Indians. That is something like using the devil to prepare one for heaven. …This business of judging is radically wrong. What is the Indian Office, that the Indians should be judged by it? It is un-American. If the Indians who were here before Columbus are not competent to be citizens of America, who is competent?"[16]

"…no one likes to die. Just so, the Indian Bureau does not want to go out of existence. It has been as poisonous as a rattle snake to the Indians, and it will die hard like a rattle snake. Its life is fed by sucking the blood from incompetent Indians, which it has manufactured from the most competent human beings on the face of the earth, and now, the Indian Office is assorting the Indians—separating the chaff from the seed. Just hear their pious voices: This is a perfect one, this is a rotten one; this one is an exception, this one we must leave for evolution; this one is competent, this one is incompetent; put that one over there and this Indian over here. That Indian is no good and this one is; this one is a goat and that one is a lamb; this one you can let loose outside of the fence of the Indian Reservation, that one over there must be kept in, he is not a 'fit creature to associate with our children.' If this is not autocracy, what is autocracy? …Indians, what are we, anyway? Are we freaks? Have we no souls? Are we possessed with venomous fang? Is there no living with us until the Indian Office makes us fit subjects? Must we live muzzled and dominated by the hellishness of the human government? Are we so low that we cannot thrive within human justice? It is all wrong. …Every bill that comes before Congress has not one ring of freedom for the Indians, nor has it one word of abolishing the Indian Office. It is full of 'approvals of the Secretary of the Interior, Indian Office or Superintendent'—NEVER 'with consent of the Indian tribe.' …Indians, wake up! If you have money in the treasury, you have a voice in the matter; if you have land, you have a voice in the matter; if you are not free, you have a voice in the matter; if you have a string tied to your citizenship, you have a voice in the matter. You are a man and as such you are entitled to the rights of a man. NOW IS THE TIME TO EXERT YOUR RIGHTS. No one can do it for you. You must do it yourself. You have been asleep long enough. Stir yourself to your manhood and look after your own interest. The future is just as bright for you as for any man in the world."[17]

THE DECISION to integrate Indian military personnel was finally made by the secretary of war, Newton D. Baker, who sided with the army and concluded that the failed effort of all-Indian units in the 1890s was a valuable lesson and could not be ignored.[18] Some units from states with a large Indian population were by logistics ultimately nearly all-Indian units (for example, some companies from Oklahoma and Dakota). But nearly all American Indians in World War I served side by side with White men.

## INDIANS IN WORLD WAR I

World War I started for the United States on April 6, 1917, and this was rapidly followed by legislation for a draft. Congress passed the Selective Service Act on May 18, 1917. The law required all men between the ages of twenty-one and thirty-one to register with their local draft boards. In 1918, the age limits were extended to eighteen and forty-five. By the end of the war, 24 million men had been registered and 2,758,542 were drafted into the armed forces.[19]

Indians were required to register, but only citizens were eligible for the draft. The director of the Selective Service, Enoch Herbert Crowder, and the commissioner of Indian affairs, Cato Sells, agreed to the need for a special system to manage the draft of American Indians. Sells established draft stations, in effect local draft boards for Indians, on selected Indian reservations. The boards consisted of the superintendent of the reservation, the reservation physician, and the chief clerk.[20] The commissioner of Indian affairs was granted the authority and power held by each state governor over the draft boards. The major problem confronting the boards was the fact that not every American Indian was a citizen in 1917.[21] The official instruction was to consider anyone with a doubtful status as a non-citizen.[22] Nevertheless in actual practice, many Indians were accepted who were non-citizens or were otherwise exempt (for example, failed medical examinations). In many cases, individual Indians did not know whether they were citizens. However, there was little Indian resistance to the draft; most problems were due to misunderstandings and lack of information.[23]

Sells provided the boards with the following criteria in order to determine if an individual was a citizen:[24]

- Citizenship gained before May 8, 1906, by means of the Dawes Act through ownership of land.
- Citizenship gained after May 8, 1906, according to the Burke Act (that allowed issuing of deeds and citizenship before the expiration of the trust period).
- Indians who had lived apart from their tribes in White society.
- Children who had gained citizenship by having citizen parents.

This was not a smooth process. It has been estimated that two-thirds of American Indians were citizens before the Citizenship Act of 1924, but probably only 50 percent at the time of the Selective Service Act of 1917.[25] There were citizens who didn't want to go to war; there were non-citizens who wanted to participate. And the biggest problem of all, many Indians did not understand the regulations and requirements, and communication efforts solely in English were not adequate. Finally, it was decided that even non-citizens could volunteer for duty.

The motivations among American Indians to participate in World War I were to a large extent the same desires and conditions that prevailed twenty to twenty-five years earlier, when Indians volunteered to serve in the West. Some wished to escape the poverty of the reservations. Others were attracted to the possibilities of income, new skills, and adventure. In 1916, the average salary of an employed Indian was about $92 per year.[26] The average pay for an enlisted man was $528 per year. In some tribes, the warrior tradition continued to be a force, seeking an outlet. The Federal Government and especially the Bureau of Indian Affairs strongly supported Indian participation, and this active campaign was surely directed to the various Indian emotions and motivations. There is no doubt that the Bureau of Indian Affairs from its highest level (the commissioner) to its field level (the reservation superintendents) vigorously promoted military service, believing that this would be a powerful method of assimilation.

Whatever the reasons, for the first time in U. S. history, along with a resurgence in Indian pride, participation in the war fostered a pride in being American, a part of the country.[27] There was a very high level of participation among students and graduates of Indian schools, except in isolated southwestern schools, and there was a strong sense of patriotism among these Indians.[28] Indians on remote southwestern reservations scarcely participated (less than 1 percent of the adult men), compared with 10 to 15 percent of the Sioux and 40 to 50 percent of Oklahoma tribes.[29] The Indian off-reservation boarding schools compiled an amazing record; virtually every male volunteered for duty. This degree of patriotism must have reflected the teaching and military routines experienced in these schools dedicated to assimilation.

Opposition to the draft on a reservation provided an opportunity to express dissatisfaction with reservation life. These episodes were publicized as being unpatriotic, even suggesting that they were inspired by German agents.[30] However, overall there was little opposition. The Onondaga Nation even declared war in 1918 against the Axis in a statement written by Arthur C. Parker, who was at that time president of the Society of American Indians. They were shortly followed by the Oneida. Parker conceived of this action as a symbol to emphasize the sovereignty of the Iroquois.[31]

Prior to September 1918, 11,803 American Indians registered for the draft. Of these, 6,509 were inducted, amounting to 55 percent of registrants and 13 percent of Indian adult males.[32] After September 1918, another 5,500 registered, but how many were drafted is unknown. A negligible number, only 228 of the total registered, requested deferment. The number of volunteers is not known exactly, confused by exaggerated numbers proclaimed by Commissioner Cato Sells.[33] The Bureau of Indian Affairs estimated that slightly over 10,000 Indians were soldiers, almost 20 percent of the Indian adult male population. This would indicate that about 3,500 Indians volunteered for service. The consensus estimate is that 12,000 to 13,000 American Indians served in World War I, which would have been about 25 percent of the Indian adult males, compared with 15 percent of all other adult American men. About half were drafted and half were volunteers.[34] No matter the exact number, in terms of percentage of the adult male population, American Indians participated in World War I at a level greater than other segments of the population.

Indian participation was at a high level, but so were the morbidity and mortality rates. A total of 53,000 men were killed in combat in World War I, and 204,000 wounded.[35] Another 63,000 died, but not in combat—many in the influenza epidemic. The morbidity and mortality rates among American Indians were proportionately higher compared with the overall figures.

American Indians were more often assigned to duties that carried higher risks. One reason was the practice instituted in World War I to perform intelligence tests on all recruits. The instrument was an army version of the relatively new Stanford-Binet tests.[36] The test was better suited to assess the educated, middle class, and it is not surprising that poorly educated soldiers from impoverished backgrounds, as well as those from new immigrant families, would perform poorly and end up in higher percentages in the infantry.

In one survey of American Indians serving in World War I, about 62 percent served in the infantry, 16 percent in the artillery, 8 percent with ammunition supplies, and 14 percent served in the other branches of the military.[37]

American Indians reached France in June 1917, and for the next four months, fought in every major engagement. About 5 percent of Indian military personnel died in combat compared with the 1 percent overall mortality rate in the American military.[38] Along with heroism and exposure in battle, the increased mortality rate was also due to a greater susceptibility to disease.

Some tribes had mortality rates of 10 to 14 percent that reflected the high exposure to risk experienced by certain groups (mainly those from isolated reservations) that were assigned to duties as scouts, snipers, and messengers. This selection was significantly influenced by the stereotypic images of Indians (their martial reputation) held by White officers. There is good reason to believe that the German military carried a high regard and concern for their Indian opponents because of their own stereotypic images. The Buffalo Bill Wild West show had been enormously popular in Germany, and many of the German soldiers grew up reading the American western novels that were the imaginary products of the German writer, Karl May.[39] Charles Eastman's autobiographical story of his boyhood went through four printings within one year of the release of the German translation.[40] German soldiers knew they were fighting their childhood heroes.

The use of native languages by American Indians to foil eavesdropping and tapping of radio lines in order to keep orders and movements secret occurred first in World War I. The precedent for the Navajo "code-talkers" in World War II was established by the Choctaw telephone squad in October 1918, in the 142nd Infantry Regiment of the Thirty-sixth Division.[41] In the last two months of World War I, messages were transmitted by Comanche, Osage, Cheyenne, and Sioux Indians.

During and after the war, there was a certain amount of "over-glorification" of the Indian soldiers.[42] This was gratifying for many, and enhanced Indian identity, but at the same time, it has been argued that this only served to reinforce racial stereotypes.[43] The patriotism of the American Indians, real or exaggerated, was held up as evidence that the Indian Bureau was succeeding in the process of assimilation. The war did allow some escape from Indian Bureau suppression of Indian culture. Dances, giveaways, and feasts were organized to recognize returning veterans. For many young Indians, this was their first experience with some of the old ways. The Indian Bureau found it difficult to oppose these tribal expressions of patriotism and regard for the veterans.

## ESPIONAGE, SEDITION, AND PROPAGANDA

There was a reason why Montezuma attracted attention. In the early years of World War I in Europe, a pacifistic and isolationist mood prevailed in the United States. Indeed, Woodrow Wilson's victory in the presidential election of 1916 followed a campaign that featured the slogan, "He kept us out of the war."[44] This promise was shattered by the resumption of unrestricted German submarine warfare beginning in January 1917 that caused the loss of American ships and lives, and the United States entered the war in April 1917. Leadership in the Federal Government faced a major challenge. They believed they had to change antagonism and apathy towards the war into enthusiastic public support, and they had to accomplish this rapidly. The method chosen for this purpose was official propaganda.

A presidential executive order established the Committee on Public Information only seven days after entering the war.[45] The Committee was charged with building patriotism and unification in a battle against the Germans, to be cast as absolute and archetypical villains. The wide spectrum of its activities to stir the emotions of the country included press releases, war stories, essays and pamphlets by academic writers and thinkers, posters, cartoons, advertisements, and movies featuring the villainous Germans.[46]

The Committee was successful, and rapidly the country was united in the war to save democracy. However, the propaganda was rooted in the nineteenth-century desire for an American way of life with a single set of values, and this was now being challenged by immigrants and an organized working class. Therefore, the propaganda effort fueled a vicious wave of intolerance, taking to new heights the suppression of "radicals" that had been part of American life for the previous thirty years. Anything German was vilified. Towns with German-sounding names changed their names. German measles were renamed liberty measles! An angry mob near St. Louis hanged a German accused of collecting explosives; none were found.[47] The American people during the war years were very sensitive about the enemy, seeing plots and spies behind practically every unusual experience, truly a wartime hysteria with a patriotism rooted in fear. Those in the political fringe, especially those struggling against corporate capitalism, were easily branded with an "antiwar" label. The activities of the Committee came to a close at the end of 1918, but the accomplishments were noted by many, and a lasting impact was made on advertising and politics. The anti-radical attitude towards immigrants culminated in the imposition of a quota system by Congress in 1921 that discriminated against southern and eastern European immigrants.

The Committee was instrumental in gaining passage of The Espionage Act of June 15, 1917, and its amendment, The Sedition Act in May 1918.[48] These acts provided for the obvious, fines and jail terms for spying and sabotage, but they also were directed to not only those who refused military service, but to anyone who even said anything that obstructed recruitment or enlistment or that could be considered disloyal or abusive of the government, the military, or the flag. The Act covered any statements that would obstruct the sale of war bonds. The postmaster general, Albert S. Burleson, was allowed by The Sedition Act to deny mailing privileges to any publication that *in his judgment* was disloyal or supported the enemy. Punishment was set as a fine not more than $10,000 or imprisonment for not more than twenty years, or both.

The American Protective League was a quasi-vigilante organization that had the approval and cooperation of the attorney general, Thomas W. Gregory. Its stationery featured the words: "Organized With the Approval and Operating Under the Direction of the United States Department of Justice, Bureau of Investigation."[49] It was a citizen's auxiliary under the Bureau of Investigation that enlisted 250,000 badge-wearing members by war's end. "Its 'agents' bugged, burglarized, slandered, and illegally arrested other Americans. They opened mail, intercepted telegrams, served as *agent provocateurs*, and were the chief commandos in a series of extralegal and often violent 'slacker raids' against supposed draft evaders in 1918."[50]

Eugene V. Debs ran as the Socialist Party candidate for president of the United States in five consecutive elections, 1900–1920. After a campaign conducted while in the Atlanta federal prison, he collected nearly a million votes in 1920. He was in prison for making an anti-war speech on June 16, 1918, in Canton, Ohio.[51] Debs was convicted in a federal court in Cleveland, Ohio, according to the wartime Espionage and Sedition Acts. The conviction was upheld in the U.S. Supreme Court when Oliver Wendell Holmes ruled, to his later regret, that there may have been an intent to encourage the obstruction of military recruitment.[52] Sentenced to ten years in prison and loss of his citizenship, Debs was pardoned after two years and eight months by President Harding on Christmas Day, 1921.

This federal program stimulated and approved of suppression and persecution of dissenters and nonconformists. All forms of dissent were suppressed, not only by the government, but by the private vigilante groups as well. Citizens with German names were hounded and abused. Criticism of the war was not tolerated. These abuses of civil rights led to the founding of the American Civil Liberties Union in 1920.

The Federal Bureau of Investigation (the FBI) originated in a small force of Special Agents created by the Attorney General in 1908.[53] This investigative arm of the Department of Justice was named the Bureau of Investigation in March 1909. World War I accounted for a major expansion as the Bureau of Investigation became responsible for the Selective Service Act and the Espionage and Sedition Acts. In 1919, criminals who crossed state lines were classified as having committed federal crimes and came under the jurisdiction of the Bureau. J. Edgar Hoover worked for the Justice Department during the war years, in charge of enemy alien operations and assisting in the investigation of suspected anarchists and communists. Hoover, at the age of twenty-six, was named assistant director of the Bureau in 1919, and in 1924, he became director. The Bureau of Investigation was renamed the United States Bureau of Investigation in 1932, and finally, the Federal Bureau of Investigation in 1935. It was the Bureau of Investigation that scrutinized Montezuma in 1917 and 1918.

## MONTEZUMA AND SEDITION

During World War I, the Federal Government regarded Montezuma's statements and writing as unpatriotic. The Justice Department even considered treason and asked its Bureau of Investigation to probe Montezuma.

Montezuma was concerned that his writings in his newsletter would antagonize the government, a concern that was apparent in his editorial: "WASSAJA appears in its tone as though it is very disloyal to the United States Government and very unappreciative for turning on the Indian Bureau when the Indian Bureau 'has done everything for the Indians.' For forty years the writer has been silent. He is a man and a citizen. He would be unworthy of his country were he to remain dumb and do nothing when he sees his country is going wrong by keeping up the Indian Bureau that is crushing the very life out of his race."[54] "The Editor wishes to say that 'Steady, Indians, Steady,' and 'Civilization' in this issue are not written for the purpose of antagonizing the war sentiment, but WASSAJA sees the opportune moment to throw the same limelight that has placed the Indian before the world as cruel and savage. And to imprint on the minds of the public, the real and unjust status of the Indians in the United States."[55]

# CIVILIZATION
—April, 1917

*Savagery! Oh, say!*
*Indians? You say?*
*High up in the air you see,*
*Almost reach to God—civilization!*
*To the heathen they carried God.*
*They say God no fight, God is peace.*
*Civilization called Indians Savages;*
*Indians love to scalp and fight.*
*Talk about Indians behind trees,*
*They did not dig trenches and live there.*
*Indians used bows and arrows, spears and stones,*
*Play-toys to modern weapons for fighting brother against brother.*
*Now, where is the worst savagery?*
*Blush! No blush in civilization today.*
*Civilization, thou art great, thou canst raise millions to slaughter.*
*Tear to pieces thy brother in the air;*
*Blow up cargoes to feed whales and little fishes,*
*And if need be kill and call it square.*
*Civilization, thou are using God as front.*
*Behind, thou are playing the cunningness of human nature.*
*You furled your flag and call it patriotism.*
*You say that you are fighting for this and that.*
*You do not know what you are fighting for.*
*You think it is for righteousness.*
*In the crucible, you will find it to be greed.*
*Pretension is the worst kind of patriotism.*
*Patriotic jealousy lurks in every move you make.*
*It has you bound hand and foot.*
*In your greatness you are acting like a child,*
*Peevish and snarling at everybody.*
*You may talk about honor, Kings, Kaisers and Czars*
*(as though they were the cause of your patriotism).*
*Ah! They are nothing;*
*It is the Almighty dollar*
*That is might and not right.*
*Age has made civilization gruesome, hard as stone.*
*"Business is business,"*
*And growlingly he says,*
*"What have I to do with thee?"*
*And hurries on to war.*
*Civilization! Civilization!*
*Thou hast been a light on a hill,*
*Spreading thy rays far and wide.*

*God has permitted thee to reign.*
*What is thy stewardship?*
*Thy knowledge and wisdom thou hast turned into greed.*
*Thou wantest the land, thou wantest the sea;*
*Thou forgettest God, thou forgettest thy brother.*
*Civilization, thou hast lost thy soul,*
*While carrying the cross to the heathen.*
*The temptations to satisfy thy greed have been too great.*
*Thy greed has blinded thy vision for the right.*

*Your soul is stupid, goaded with greed.*
*You are intoxicated for more and more.*
*You are not fighting for righteousness,*
*You are fighting on high seas,*
*To see who can outdo trading here and there.*
*It is but commercialism, and nothing more.*

*O God of Righteousness, stay the tide*
*That is rushing madly into the abyss of war.*
*Help us to see the right.*
*O Lord God Almighty, teach us to know,*
*Names we may have, but we are the same.*
*Teach us to look up to Thee and learn of Thee*
*What is right, justice and peace.*[56]

## STEADY, INDIANS, STEADY!
### —April, 1917

*The Ghost Craze has come and gone,*
*The War Craze is on.*
*If you want to fight—fight—*
*But let no one force you in.*
     *Steady, Indians, Steady!*

*In the excitement of war fury,*
*It requires a level head*
*Not to get dizzy.*
     *Steady, Indians, Steady!*

*"Fight for your country and flag" is noble and grand,*
*But have you a country? Is that your flag?*
*With a sober mind, think on it, and do the right.*
     *Steady, Indians, Steady!*

*Pause, with calm mind, think on it.*
*But let no one push you in it.*
*If you do not know what you are fighting for, stay at home.*
     *Steady, Indians, Steady!*

*They have taken your country,*
*They have taken your manhood,*
*They have imprisoned you,*
*They have made you wards,*
*They have stunted your faculties.*
         *Steady, Indians, Steady!*

*You are not entitled to the rights of man,*
*You are not an American citizen—*
*You are an Indian;*
*You are nothing and that is all.*
         *Steady, Indians, Steady!*

*Redskins, true Americans, you have a fight with those whom*
*you wish to fight for;*
*It is your birthright—Freedom;*
*Let them make good;*
*With better heart you will fight,*
*Side by side under the same flag.*
         *Steady, Indians, Steady!*[57]

## INDIANS ARE FIGHTING FOR THEIR FREEDOM, LIBERTY AND RIGHTS
—June, 1917

We hear on all sides that America must maintain her true spirit of democracy, we must see that all men are treated on an equal footing, equality and human rights must be upheld. …Indian Bureauism is the Kaiserism of America toward the Indians. It enslaves and dominates the Indians without giving them their rights. It is praise-worthy for a nation to hold up to the world such a high standard of justice. But the question may well be asked, "Why does this liberty-loving country discern injustices across the sea, and close its eyes to the same thing at home?" Does this not show that America has failed at home?[58]

"WASSSAJA—the son of the blood-thirsty Apache CO-LU-YE-VAH—smiles and laughs audibly (those cruel Apaches, devilish creatures, seekers of blood do not smile and laugh, you know) to see, hear, and read about the cultured, refined and God-like war of the civilized Christian pale-faced nations. …Well, can you beat it? Just think, Christian nations killing each other by millions. And sending missionaries to teach 'Thou shalt not kill.'"[59]

"Indians have peculiar, creeping feelings about this war of humanity, freedom, democracy, equal rights and justice. If Sitting Bull could come to life and hear the voices rend the air, and read of patriotism, and see his people in a worse condition than that in which he left them, he, too, would have chills and between the shakes he would grunt: 'White man! Ugh—white man!'"[60]

Montezuma was surely affected by the reaction of his own relatives to the draft, and more specifically, to the Indian Bureau enforcement of the draft. His cousin, George Dickens, wrote to Montezuma only eleven days after Congress passed the Selective Service Act: "Last I write to you, told you about our Supt Coggshall. He said President of United States want us to be soldiers, and get fifteen of our men already. He just get them before they want to go. And he also told them if they don't go he is going to put them jail. But some of these men are not quite size to be soldiers, some were bad bodies, some were lame fellows."[61]

Simon Kahquados, an Indian from Wausaukee, Wisconsin, wrote to Montezuma in 1918 asking whether Indians could be drafted. Montezuma replied: "Indians must register. Indians as wards cannot be drafted into war; they can volunteer to go into the army. If you do not pay taxes and do not vote you are not a citizen. If you depend on the United States Government you are not a citizen, and cannot be forced to go into war. If the young men who are Indians and are cared for by the Indian department, those young Indian men cannot be forced or drafted in the army, unless they volunteer. I do not think it is just for the super-intendents of the Indian service to get Indian young men to go to war. Why, because the United States Government has not given freedom to these young men. The Indian young men would be fighting for the United States government that is keeping them as slaves and not citizens of their own country. It does not look right to me or to those who love justice. The Indian is competent to be a soldier but not a citizen. *That does not look right* either. Indians that do not vote and live from the Government they cannot be drafted or forced into the war."[62] Montezuma believed that Indians who wanted to participate should be allowed to do so, but the government had no right to force Indians to serve. In some tribes, elders argued that the draft was an imposition on tribal rights and sovereignty.

Three months later, Montezuma wrote again to Simon Kahquados: "I believe this is the conclusion about the Indians: No Indian that is ward of the Government can be drafted into war. Indian that is a ward of the Government can volunteer into the war. An Indian that is a ward of the Government *cannot be forced into this war*. A citizen Indian is one that is not under care of the Government, pays taxes, votes and lives under the laws that other races live, such Indian can be drafted, if he is in the draft age (21 to 31 years old). The law is all men who are within drafted age must register whether citizens or *aliens* (not citizens but belong to another country). So you see all Indian men between 21 & 31 years old must register and answer greetings that are given to them on paper. On paper the Indians can say *they are Government wards* that will keep them from going to war, unless they want to go on their own free will and accord, then they must express that on the question papers. If the Indian that wants to go to war for United States cannot speak much English that does not matter, if he is qualified & is taken, he did it upon his own free will & accord, but if he is forced against his will he can get a lawyer & go to law & prove that he cannot be forced into the army."[63]

Montezuma wrote similar letters to other Indians who were stimulated to write Montezuma by reading *Wassaja*. James Charging Crow was in prison for not registering with his draft board. Montezuma told him: "Indians are not free and have not the rights of citizenship, even if they vote, because Indian money and property are kept by the United States Government. No citizen that votes would allow such thing. Technically speaking, even though you did vote, you are not a true citizen."[64]

Montezuma complained to Richard Pratt:

> The Indians on reservations are filled with patriotism and loyalty to Washington and work for the war. It is the [?] thing for the employees of the Indian service to work upon the minds of the reservation Indians. They (Indians) forget they are in bondage to a degree they are tickled that Washington (Indian Bureau) is after all a very kind father regardless what "Wassaja" may say to the contrary.

There is the Society of American Indians head over heels in the work for the war and so are the rest of like Societies. Mind you, General, this is not criticizing the war. That is far from my heart, but if these same organizations are sincere about Freedom, Equal Rights, Democracy, Humanity and Justice, why in the name of God, are not they hitting the metal while it is hot for the Indians? There can be no better time to pass a bill through Congress to free the Indians than at this very hour. This country would disgrace itself were it to hesitate upon the very thing they are fighting for. It is a greater disgrace for us who claim to be friends of the Indians to sit down, fold our hands, and piously wait until the war of freedom rolls over.[65]

"The way the Indian Bureau uses the word 'Competency' exasperates 'Wassaja.' What right has the Indian Bureau to judge whether we Indians are competent or incompetent? 'Judge not that ye be not judged.' It is wrong and nothing else can be made out of this being equal with God. What are you gong to do with the 'incompetent' Indians? Help them to be competent by giving them freedom from Bureauism, which has caused them to be incompetent."[66]

*Wassaja* featured an article in October 1917, entitled, "Drafting Indians and Justice:"

WASSAJA is not against the war nor against Indians going into the army if they so wish, of their own free will. But is it just to force them to be soldiers?

…Can we not see that the Indians are wards in their dispossessed country, and they are not aliens?

…We Indians are ready to defend the country of our forefathers as we have been doing these five hundred years against all odds, but what have we and what are we? We are nothing but wards; we are not citizens and we are without a country in this wide world. It is a sad picture that haunts America's conscience, and now worse than ever we are forced into the army as though we were citizens or at least aliens. The wards are called upon to protect their Protectors! Has God given us Indians to the world to be used as tools, without justice? It is damnable to be an Indian!

WASSAJA believes that this drafting of the Indians into the army is another wrong perpetuated upon the Indian without FIRST bestowing his just title—THE FIRST AMERICAN CITIZEN. Why not? He was here before Columbus, he was here before Washington, he was here before Lincoln and he was here and you came. There is Justice. Is this Justice?

…WASSAJA hopes that these words will stir up the patriotic feelings throughout these United States of America, so that his race will be freed from the bondage of the Indian Office and so that the Indians will be made citizens. Then, and only then, can this country proudly draft them so that they will march side by side under the same flag with the brave patriots to victory truly then, in behalf of THEIR COUNTRY.[67]

## INCONSISTENT
### —February, 1918

WASSAJA was at a meeting the other night where the lecture was on "Patriotism." The speaker spoke forcibly on the Constitution of the United States and plainly showed that we are fighting for the principle of our Constitution under which we live. WASSAJA kept in his mind the following: "Of the people, for the people and by the people; consent of the people. Life without liberty is not worth living. There is not liberty where the consent of people is not recognized. Justice cannot exist where domination takes place without the voice of the people, etc." The strain was high, lofty and unselfish in every way. If there is an American the Indian people are. There is no getting around that. Has the United States of America given freedom and liberty to the real Americans of America? WASSAJA can say the United States has not. Is that justice? Is that following the Constitution of the United States? ...That is worse than plunging through Belgium without getting consent from the Belgians.[68]

MONTEZUMA'S VIEWS of the Indian Bureau and the reservations were not softened by patriotism. On the contrary, his attitude was probably hardened during the war years because reservation conditions were palpably worse. Public expenditures during the war were redirected to meet the cost of the war. Appropriations for health, education, personnel, and supplies on the reservations were drastically reduced. The Indian mortality rate during the 1918 influenza epidemic was four times greater than that of Whites in large cities.[69]

The Bureau of Indian Affairs made the situation worse by waging a successful campaign to attract Indian resources into the war effort. American Indians purchased over $25 million worth of Liberty bonds during the war.[70] Many of these bonds were purchased by the secretary of the interior, Franklin K. Lane, in the names of individual Indians, and the government often denied individual access to or control of these funds. Lane even engineered Congressional legislation to allow the secretary of the interior to invest tribal funds in government bonds. Fortunately, the legislation was not passed until May 25, 1918, only six months before the end of the war.

During World War I, the Bureau of Indian Affairs actively campaigned to increase agriculture on reservation lands.[71] This same message to support the war effort was promoted by the government to all landowners and farmers. Non-Indian ranchers and farmers were motivated to move on to reservation land, and the Bureau of Indian Affairs cooperated in this movement.[72] The amount of reservation land leased or sold during World War I increased dramatically.[73] It is likely that the renewed effort to move the Yavapai off the Fort McDowell land, resulting in the executive order in 1920 (Chapter 12), began with the intense focus on land and agriculture during World War I.

In 1916, Montezuma learned from his cousins that the Indian Bureau had agreed to rent four acres of reservation land that contained a spring to a Phoenix cattleman, Howard Hughes, without consulting the Fort McDowell Yavapai.[74] Montezuma was told by the commissioner's office that a five-year permit had been granted for an annual rental of $40, "which will be expended for the benefit of the Indians."[75] Montezuma further learned that the Indian Bureau already had a plan in effect to place 250 head of cattle on the Fort McDowell land.

Montezuma repeatedly urged the Fort McDowell Yavapai to not rent their spring or any of their land to cattlemen, to not accept the Indian Bureau plan to place cattle upon their land, and of course, to not move off of their land.[76] Montezuma asked the Indian Bureau: "May I inquire whether the cattle which the department is in process of purchasing will be the property of the McDowell Indians, or will the said cattle be the property of others, merely pastured on McDowell reservation? In order to protect the Indians' grain from outside cattle, the Department caused the McDowell reservation to be fenced. Is it now the intention of the Department to install cattle on this property which was understood by the Indians to have been fenced to encourage them to raise grain thereon?"[77] The Bureau advised Montezuma that 250 cattle were to be placed on Fort McDowell, and they would be the property of the Indians, but of course the Indians would first have to repay the funds used for the purchase, until then the cattle belonged to the government.[78] In 1917, Montezuma composed an appropriate letter that refused the cattle and asked for an end of the rental agreement. The letter was signed by thirty-three Yavapai men and forwarded by Montezuma to the commissioner's office.[79] Montezuma believed that if the Indians did not pay for the cattle, the McDowell land would be taken in payment.[80] Nevertheless, the Indian Bureau placed 250 cattle on the reservation (they were sold by the Bureau at a low price in 1921).[81] It is not hard to see how Indian Bureau officials viewed Montezuma's actions as unpatriotic.

Montezuma was also concerned about the paychecks earned by the Indians in the armed services. "It is common knowledge that when an Indian has any money coming to him it is sent to the superintendent in charge of the agency where he resides by the Indian Office."[82] Montezuma had an impressive data base for this thought in the many letters he received (stimulated by his newsletter, *Wassaja*) recounting personal experiences by reservation Indians.

In 1918, near the end of World War I, Commissioner Cato Sells asked the secretary of the interior that reservation officials be allowed to endorse checks and warrants from Indian soldiers who had gone abroad without delegating someone at home to collect the money.[83] Walter W. Warwick, comptroller, well-advisedly informed Secretary Lane that such a practice would not be possible without the previous consent of the individuals involved. Another opportunity for fraud and abuse could be found in the fact that the same officials who controlled individual bank accounts were responsible for selling government war stamps and bonds.[84]

Did not Montezuma's emotional but logical demands and questions deserve an answer? There was no letter from the president's office. There was no letter from a congressman. There was no letter from the commissioner of Indian affairs. There was no letter from anyone in the Bureau of Indian Affairs, or any other government official. One cannot help but believe that this disregard was deliberate, a lack of response that must have reflected the priority given to this "problem" during a time when the focus was on the war effort itself.

MONTEZUMA WAS VERY AWARE of the government's attitude towards him during the war years. He informed Richard Pratt: "…I am the worst creature to the Indian Office. They think my place is in jail. It is humble to grant what I want, of course. Just think of commissioner of Indian affairs altering such horror! The attention of the country is taken up by the war, we Indians are not going to sleep. In the atmosphere there is a talk of a meeting in Washington this Winter by the Indians. We are stirring up to request our personal rights, using the same material for our fight as the United States against Germany.

The people are ignorant of our status. They do not know that we are not citizens; they do not know that we are in bondage; that we are real Americans and still have not the rights of American citizenship. ...It looks very strange to have hundreds of Indian soldiers fighting for the country that is keeping them in bondage."[85] Montezuma had proposed a "League for the Extension of Democracy to the American Indians," a league with no regular organization or dues, just a plan to urge members to write the press, influential friends, and congressmen. But the league never came into existence.[86]

The very same month Montezuma heard from the Department of Justice, he made a careful statement in his newsletter, *Wassaja*: "...Keep in mind that the Indian Office is not the Government. It is a department of the United States Government. The Indian Office may be wrong, but that does not mean that the Government is wrong. The United States Government and the Indian Office are two different entities. Speaking against the system of the Indian Office or working to abolish the Indian Office is not necessarily betraying your loyalty to the United States Government. It may appear so, but in the case of the Indian Office, it is not. We all agree that the Indian department is a temporary appendage to the United States Government. Why? Because the Constitution of the United States is against slavery; its slogan is freedom; the people rule; equal rights on equal footing; man is a man, high or low, rich or poor, from every clime on earth; to vote the ballot at the polls and to the rights and privileges of citizenship."[87]

Montezuma came to the attention of the Department of Justice when "Operative Hiram Nichols of the American Protective League, Badge #763" made this complaint on October 31, 1917:

> The above subject In the past has been a very loyal and highly useful citizen. Was at one time a Government Physician on various Indian reservations and was for some time Attendant Physician at the Carlisle Industrious [*sic*] School, Carlisle, Pa. Under the regime of Colonel R. H. Pratt, now retired as brigadier.
>
> Dr. Montezuma has for years acted as a [*sic*] intermediary between the San Carlos Apache Indians and the Government, and the Pima Apache Indians and the Government. He has within the last two years been very active at Washington with reference to the Fort McDowell Land allotments. He is very well known in official circles in Washington, but some three years ago he married a German woman with a very strong minded mother from the Strassburg Region of Germany. She has succeeded in convincing him that Germany is alright and that Uncle Sam is all wrong. He now denounces in no uncertain language the President, His Cabinet, the Army, Navy and Secret Service in particular, and the war in general. Express the opinion that the German system of espionage is perfectly legitimate and it is right to operate in this country is as justifying as that of our own investigators. So strong are his opinions that he has effectually divorced himself from his former associates. His opinions and beliefs would perhaps be of very little danger were it not for the fact that he is in a position to disaffect a very large number of Indians in the South West.[88]

Two weeks later, Lieutenant Colonel R. H. Van Deman, the chief of the Military Intelligence Section of the General Staff, wrote to A. Bruce Bielski, the chief of the Bureau of Investigation: "With reference to Dr. Carlos Montezuma—no doubt the matter has been called to the attention of Cato Sells, Commissioner, Indian Affairs. He would be interested to know that he has a pro-German wolf among the Apache sheep."[89]

The Chicago office of the American Protective League became involved, forwarding copies of *Wassaja*, labeled as a "Seditious Publication," to Washington, with the comment that "it is published with a view to inciting insurrection and disloyalty among the Indian tribes."[90] About three months later, Eban R. Minahan of the Green Bay Division of the American Protective League sent to Washington a copy of the first letter to Simon Kahquados, even a copy of the envelope in which it was received, along with notes that said, "the above written with blue ink. Envelope much crumpled up, as though crushed in hand."[91] League headquarters again passed the material to the chief of the Bureau of Investigation, A. Bruce Bielski.

In January 1918, Montezuma received a telephone message from the Department of Justice "to appear before Mr. Groh and bring down copies of the Wassaja. I did so but did not see the man."[92] Pratt tried to reassure Montezuma and bolster his resolve. "You can't now stand still. You must either advance or retreat. If you advance it shows your confidence in all you have done and undertaken and compels action or retreat of the force that joins issue with you which is of course the Cause. ...If Wassaja was suppressed what would be the effect? You brought the challenge are you going to withdraw it? Your experience in not finding the representative of the department of Justice after two visits shows triviality and bluff. You have invited martyrdom. Why evade it. Keep right on—don't stop until you are stopped by a force you can't overcome and you then keep on."[93]

Finally in August 1919, the Bureau of Justice sent an investigator, Peter P. Mindak, to Montezuma's home. It is evident from Mr. Mindak's report that the interview was lengthy, and the investigator was the recipient of a good lecture by Montezuma. Mindak was obviously an objective, reasonable man, and for that, Montezuma was truly fortunate.

> Pursuant to instructions agent went to the home of the subject who lives at 3135 South Park Avenue Chicago Ill. Dr. *Carlos Montezuma* is the name that subject has adopted many years ago. He stated to employee he is the owner and publisher of the publication in question, which he has been publishing for the last three years. He stated that it's [*sic*] circulation at present amounts to about 600 each month, of this amount about two thirds is among the various Indian reservations, the other third is among philanthropists and sympathizers. He gave employee a brief sketch of his life. He stated that he was born in Arizona, that his parents were full blooded Apaches. While he was four years old he was captured by other Indians, who later sold him to white man named C. Gentile. He lived with this man until he was about 12 or 13 years old and came to Ill. Where he began to shift for himself. He was educated in the public schools, later he graduated from the University of Ill as a pharmacist, and still later graduated from the medical department of the Northwestern Univ. in 1888. He has been a licensed physician ever since then. For a period of about seven years he was connected with the Indian Bureau and was resident physician of the Carlisle University.
>
> Employee had a long interview with subject in which the question of Indian segregation was discussed. From this interview employee feels satisfied that Dr. Montezuma is not connected with any radical societies, and that he is sincere in his work of advocating the abolishment of the Indian Bureau. Among various points that he raised in support of his contention that the Indians would be better off were allowed to shift for himself, were that the policy of the Government in segregating the Indian on a reservation tended to cause a mental stagnation in the average Indian, that it was responsible for the lack of initiative in the Indian, that this policy has caused the Indian to become inactive, lazy, and to rely

entirely on the government for support. Subject is a well educated man, and in his home there is a very large collection of books which subject has accumulated and evidently read. He stated that he has made a long study of the Indian both on and off the reservation, and feels deeply the lack of progress and development of his race. When employee called his attention to the strong language that he used in the articles, he stated that in order to get some action he must use strong language. Subject dwelled at length on the subject of the Indian's ability to earn a lifelyhood [*sic*] and develop.

Summarizing the chief points raised by the Subject in support of his agitation, for the freeing of all Indians, they can be stated as follows. First that the majority of the Indians are sufficiently civilized, and conversant with the ways of the white man to be able to shift for himself. Second that the continued segregation of the Indian, will tend only to set the race still further back and work irreparable injury. That the younger element is educated enough to not only look after their own interests, but also to protect the interests and welfare of the old folks. That the educational facilities on the reservation are too narrow and do not offer the Indian opportunity enough to educate himself, most of them being wards, and not permitted to leave the reservations. That if the Indian was given his freedom and his just allotment he would develop rapidly and would soon became amalgamated with the white race. The strongest point raised by subject in support of his contention, was the fact that the Indian was here before the white man, and that he has a just right to demand his freedom, and his share of the lands, particularly at this time after so many years of bondage and segregation, and his gradual civilization.

Employee questioned Subject whether or not any one else is connected with the publication in question and whether anyone else is aiding him financially. He stated that no one else is in any way connected with this paper. That he is the sole owner and publisher.

Subject is a man of short stocky built [*sic*], dark skin (except for the sharp piercing brown eyes) might be easily taken for a negro.

He has in his flat a very large collection of Indian curios, relics, and statistics on Indian warfare.

Subject has been and still is, as he states, a very active member of the Society of American Indians, which will hold it's [*sic*] convention at Minneapolis Minn. From Oct 1st to the 4th 1919.

Subject is also the author of a lecture which he read at the convention of the Society of the American Indians at Lawrence Kansas In September 1915, entitled "Let My People Go."[94]

A reaction to the Justice Department appeared in Montezuma's newsletter, *Wassaja*: "The Bureau of Justice says: 'But you are using strong words.' My dear friend, we have to use strong words to get justice and justice requires strong words. To the hearts of the Indians this matter of freedom is just as precious to them as to those who fought at Bunker Hill or at Gettysburg. ...Do you know you fought for your freedom and the INDIANS HELPED YOU? Do you know you have given freedom to the black man and the INDIANS HELPED YOU? Do you know you fought for the freedom of the Philippines and the INDIANS HELPED YOU? Do you know you fought for the freedom of the world and the INDIANS HELPED YOU?"[95]

Montezuma heard no more from the Department of Justice, the Bureau of Investigation, or the American Protective League. Postmaster General Burleson did not revoke the mailing privileges for *Wassaja*. The government decided to ignore Montezuma.

COMPARE HOW THE GOVERNMENT ignored Montezuma with the response (imprisonment) given to Eugene V. Debs. The presentation given by Debs to 1,200 wildly cheering and applauding members of the Ohio Socialist Party in Canton, Ohio, was a typical socialist rally speech that blamed the war on capitalists and the ruling class.[96] There was no call to avoid the draft. There was no plea to refuse military service. There was no mention of Liberty bonds. Indeed, some of the sentences voiced by Debs could have been lifted out of Montezuma's newsletter, *Wassaja*:

> You are their wards; they are your guardians and they know what is best for you to read and hear and know.
>
> It is the minorities who have made the history of this world. It is the few who have had the courage to take their places at the front; who have been true enough to themselves to speak the truth that was in them; who have dared oppose the established order of things; who have espoused the cause of the suffering, struggling poor; who have upheld without regard to personal consequences the cause of freedom and righteousness.
>
> You need at this time especially to know that you are fit for something better than slavery and cannon fodder. You need to know that you were not created to work and produce and impoverish yourself to enrich an idle exploiter. You need to know that you have a mind to improve, a soul to develop, and a manhood to sustain.
>
> You need to know that as long as you are ignorant, as long as you are indifferent, as long as you are apathetic, unorganized and content, you will remain exactly where you are.
>
> If you would be respected you have got to begin by respecting yourself.[97]

But, of course, Eugene V. Debs and the Socialist Party represented a major political threat to those running the Federal Government. On the other hand, Montezuma was a single man making a lonely noise about 300,000 people who were not organized, not meeting in rallies, and of the 150,000 eligible, few bothered to vote. Otherwise, Montezuma would have died of his tuberculosis in prison.

## CHAPTER SEVENTEEN

# Tuberculosis and Death
# on the Reservation

TUBERCULOSIS WAS THE MAJOR CAUSE of death among young adults until the 1940s.[1] Ordinary people, political figures, royalty, and well-known artists and writers were struck down in the midst of the productive period of their lives. Tuberculosis killed Carlos Montezuma at the relatively young age of fifty-six, two months short of his fifty-seventh birthday.

The major events in the story of tuberculosis occurred during Montezuma's lifetime. Scientific discoveries caused a shift to an emphasis on public health, a shift that must have had an impact, not only on Montezuma's practice of medicine, but on his personal philosophy as well. It is logical to conclude that the rising consciousness for public welfare influenced a change in the direction of Montezuma's efforts, from a focus on individual Indians to the collective health and status of all American Indians and the tribal interests of the Yavapai. An understanding of the historical course of tuberculosis, therefore, provides further insight into the life of Montezuma.

Tuberculosis is caused by bacteria called *Mycobacterium tuberculosis* (the tubercle bacillus), or by two closely related species, *Mycobacterium bovis* and *Mycobacterium africanum*. The tuberculosis bacillus is a very small slender rod, stained by a method developed by Robert Koch's pupil, Paul Ehrlich. First stained by fuchsin, then washed by a strong acid, the method accounted for another name, the acid-fast bacillus. Although hardy—surviving in dark corners and cracks in floor boards for years—it grows and multiplies much more slowly than other organisms.

Only people who are sick with pulmonary or laryngeal tuberculosis are infectious because spread is through the air from coughing, sneezing, spitting, singing, or even talking.[2] The particles of infection (tiny droplets of water containing bacilli) are very small and can be kept airborne for prolonged periods of time by normal air currents. They spread throughout rooms and buildings, and the bacillus can lie dormant but infectious for long periods of time. When the infected droplets are inhaled, infection with tuberculosis occurs when the droplets reach the alveoli (the terminal air spaces) of the lungs. In the alveoli, the bacilli are ingested by the first barrier of the immune system, the macrophages (phagocytosing cells that originate in the bone marrow). Within the first two to ten weeks, the immune response limits further multiplication and spread. However, the tuberculosis bacilli can remain dormant and viable for many years. In addition, a small number multiply in the macrophages and when the macrophages die, the bacilli can be distributed throughout the body by the lymphatic system and then through the bloodstream. Wherever the immune response kills the bacilli, a characteristic lesion is formed, the tubercle granuloma. This condition is known as latent tuberculosis infection, and although asymptomatic and non-infectious, people with latent infections and a normal immune system will test positively with the tuberculin skin test and have about a 10 percent risk of developing active disease during their lifetimes.[3] In the United States, about 5 percent develop active disease in the first two years after infection and another 5 percent later in life.[4] Individuals with latent infections who are at high risk for active disease are significantly protected by a course of drug treatment.

The probability of getting infected after exposure depends on the concentration of the infectious droplets in the air, the duration of exposure, and the virulence of the organism. The association of tuberculosis with crowded living conditions reflects the increased probability of infection due to exposure in relatively small enclosed spaces, inadequate ventilation that allows concentration of the infectious droplets, and recirculation of infected air. Individuals at the highest risk of becoming infected are those with close contacts (family, friends, coworkers) with a person with active disease. It wasn't until the middle of the twentieth century that studies established the fact that only airborne transmission of tubercle bacilli causes infection.[5]

Although the majority (about 80 percent) of active tuberculosis cases are lung infections, tuberculosis can occur in almost any site in the body. The symptoms of pulmonary tuberculosis are productive and prolonged coughing, chest pain, and hemoptysis (coughing up of blood). Tuberculosis disease at any site produces fever (usually late in the day or at night), chills, night sweats, loss of appetite, weight loss, and loss of stamina and strength. Ultimately the body wastes away, literally consumed by the disease, earning the appropriate appellation, "consumption." Physicians, too, used the term consumption, impressed with the disease process that consumed the lungs.

When tuberculous lesions grow in size, the coalescence of tissue and infected white cells produces an amorphous mass resembling cheese (it is solid pus); hence it was called "caseation." Located in lymph nodes or bones, these lesions had the appearance of "cold abscesses." The body's attempt to heal these lesions produces thick bands of scar tissue, adhering adjoining tissues, such as the lungs and the lining of the pulmonary cavity, and producing pain.

In the lungs, tuberculous lesions exert pressure on the air passages, eventually causing their destruction and the entry of the caseous material into the passageway. This material is coughed up, leaving behind a cavity lined with infected tissue. Breathing now brings oxygen to the tuberculous bacilli; the bacillus is a strict aerobe (it will not grow and multiply without oxygen). Cavitation then was not only a sign of advanced disease but also an indication of an inexorable fatal course. Cavitation was associated with erosion of large blood vessels, and the coughing of blood could turn into a massive bleed. In addition, individuals with cavitated lungs were extremely infectious, there being easy access to the air for a large number of vigorous organisms. The coughing up of an effluvium of dead tissue and pus produced a foul smelling breath that was not an inconsequential burden.

Virtually every body organ, joint, or space could be the site of active infection. Tuberculosis of the small intestine and the lymph nodes of the abdomen produced matted loops of bowel with painful vomiting, colicky pain, and diarrhea due to obstruction.

The abdomen acquires a "doughy" characteristic that can be appreciated by palpation. Tuberculosis of the spine was named Pott's disease, after Percival Pott, an English surgeon of the 1700s. Those who survived the infection became elderly hunchbacks (like Victor Hugo's famous bell-ringing Quasimodo) because the destroyed vertebral bodies collapse forward. One of the mysteries is the rarity, if not total absence, of testicular involvement throughout the centuries of this disease.

With tuberculosis so prevalent in European life, it became for a time fashionable to portray infected individuals in the arts. The disease became romanticized, and the thin, frail appearance of the infected was considered beautiful. Violetta in Verdi's *La Traviata* and Mimi in Puccini's *La Bohéme* were models of the infatuation with this imagery. In reality, however, tuberculosis is not a pleasant mode of death. In its late stages, tuberculosis causes severe pain. Coughing with scarred lungs and pleural cavities can be excruciating. Pleural adhesions make every breath difficult. The lodgment of infected material in the throat produces a laryngitis that reduces speaking to a hoarse, agonizing whisper. The swallowing of infected material irritates the stomach, causing nausea, vomiting, and the pain of ulceration. Eventually, not even narcotics can grant a night's sleep.

## THE HISTORY OF TUBERCULOSIS

There has never been a time in history when the disease of tuberculosis has not been recognized in all parts of the world. For many years, physicians referred to tuberculosis infection as phthisis, from the Greek, meaning, "wasting." "Tuberculosis" supplanted phthisis around 1850. Scrofula, now an obsolete term, referred to the tuberculous infection of the lymph glands in the neck. Many individuals in the pre-antibiotic past were marked by puckered scars on their necks, the sites of infected lymph nodes that either drained spontaneously or were punctured by physicians. The very slow healing process almost always left a nasty scar. When Montezuma was the school physician at the Carlisle Indian School, he opened and drained scrofulous glands in the neck of Gilmore Hawk.[6]

Pulmonary tuberculosis has also been called graveyard cough. While the course could be acute, it was usually chronic, even intermittent with startling remissions, often erroneously attributed to some coincident life event, but usually fatal in five to fifteen years. In the years when tuberculosis was in everyone's minds, lassitude, inability to work, loss of weight, and cough raised the fear of infection. For hundreds of years, physicians struggled to make an accurate diagnosis.

Percussion of the lungs (thumping the chest), to detect solid masses or cavities, began with Leopold Aunebrugger, a physician in Vienna who was said to have been inspired by his innkeeper father who tapped the wine kegs in the cellar to assess their contents.[7] But it was Jean Nicolas Corvisart, Napolean's personal physician, who established percussion of the chest as an essential part of physical diagnosis in the early 1800s. Prior to percussion, physical examination did not require disrobing. Until then, physicians limited themselves to palpation of the pulse, and perhaps a study of the tongue.

Use of the stethoscope was added by the mid 1800s, an innovation of the Frenchman, René Théophile Hyacinthe Laënnec.[8] Laënnec was a preeminent expert on the diseases of the lung, and it was in 1818, while examining a plump woman, he realized that percussion and direct auscultation would be impossible; he used a rolled up paper notebook as a simple tube to listen to her heart. His first stethoscope was a foot long hollow wooden tube, two inches in diameter, with a funnel-like opening at one end and a narrow opening at the other end for the physician's ear. Laënnec's treatise presented his accurate interpretations of what he heard, especially the sounds of infected lungs. His accuracy was enhanced by the many post-mortem examinations of tuberculous lungs he performed, an exposure that was also probably instrumental in Laënnec's eventual demise from pulmonary tuberculosis.

The Dutchman, Antony Leeuwenhoek, invented the microscope and was the first to see microbes, probably in 1660. But it wasn't until the scientific triumphs of Louis Pasteur in the late 1800s that the role of microbes in disease came to be appreciated. Inspired by Pasteur's work, Robert Koch, a German general practitioner turned scientist, working out of his home that housed both his practice office and his laboratory, confirmed that a specific bacillus caused anthrax.[9] He then discovered the cause of tuberculosis. The tubercular bacillus was hard to demonstrate. It was small, difficult to stain, and slow-growing, taking weeks instead of days to appear in culture, and Koch's success was in major part due to his perseverance and patience. One of his assistants, R. J. Petri, created a standard tool still used today, the Petri dish. Using guinea pigs and rabbits and now working in a new laboratory at the Imperial Health Office in Berlin, Koch established his famous postulates:

- The organism must be found in every lesion.
- The organism should be capable of being cultivated outside the body for several generations.
- After pure culture over several generations, the organism should be able to reproduce the original illness in laboratory animals.

In March 1882, Koch summarized his findings to the Berlin Physiological Society, reporting that he had fulfilled his postulates with bacilli obtained from a patient with tuberculosis. The reaction was amazing. Seventeen days later, Koch's scientific paper was published; twenty-nine days later it was summarized in *The Times* of London, and within days in the *New York Times*. Within a year, the results were verified, and within a few years, preventive health measures, such as the prohibition of spitting, were being instituted. Koch instantly became famous; he received the Nobel Prize in 1905, and died in 1910 of a heart attack at the age of sixty-seven. Unfortunately, Koch's discovery did not immediately yield a practical and effective cure.

Robert Koch announced a "vaccine" in 1900. However, Koch's vaccine, called Old Tuberculin and filtered from culture media with heat-killed bacteria, did not work. It took almost thirty years to realize this, but Koch did recognize that this material could be used for diagnosis. Tuberculin is what remains after boiling culture media with tubercle bacilli and then concentrating it by evaporation. It contains proteins that stimulate a reaction in an infected person. Tuberculin skin testing was first used by veterinarians, and it soon became the standard method to identify infected cattle. An Austrian pediatrician, Clemens von Pirquet, developed the specialty of allergy and was the first to use the tuberculin skin test in humans.[10] He presented his results in children using a technique that scratched the skin to the Chicago Medical Society on October 14, 1908 (was Montezuma present?). That same year, Charles Mantoux described the method still used, injection of a small amount into the skin. It was not until 1930–1940 that tuberculin was purified into the product used today, the tuberculin purified protein derivative skin test, the PPD. Widespread testing revealed that exposure to other mycobacteria that are similar to the tubercle bacillus, but harmless, was responsible for false positive reactions. The prevalence of false positive reactions makes it no longer worthwhile to perform routine skin testing in populations at low risk of tuberculosis (for example, American school children).

In 1921, a French bacteriologist, Albert Calmette, and a French veterinarian, Camille Guérin, after twenty years of work, reported the production of a vaccine using attenuated bacteria, the Bacilli Calmette-Guérin (known as BCG).[11] Progressive attenuation of virulence was achieved by repeated cultures in a medium that impaired growth of the bacillus. Development was slow, impaired by some studies with very poor results, probably the result of virulent, not attenuated, bacilli. Finally after World War II, skin administration of BCG was demonstrated to increase resistance to disease, decreasing the risk of progressing from infection to active disease. An outbreak of tuberculosis in Europe after World War II led to the massive vaccination of babies and children. Erratic and unpredictable response rates have limited the popularity of BCG; it is little used in the United States, but it remains part of the World Health Organization's effort against tuberculosis.

Wilhem Conrad Röntgen discovered X-rays in November 1895. This discovery also was rapidly publicized, and Röntgen, who refused to patent his discovery, received the Nobel Prize in 1901. Despite rapid advances, it took a long time before widespread application of X-ray screening for tuberculosis was established, partly because of World War I.

The most important consequence that followed the recognition of the infectious, communicable nature of tuberculosis was the public health emphasis on prevention. As early as 1890, campaigns were mounted for the isolation of infected individuals, disinfection of rooms exposed to tuberculosis, especially hospital rooms, and inspection of dairy and meat cattle. Spitting became the target of posters and policemen. It rapidly became common practice in the first two decades of the 1900s to isolate infected patients in hospitals and special institutions called sanatoria.

SANATORIUM CARE, LAUNCHED after 1850, became the unchallenged mainstay of tuberculosis treatment for nearly 100 years.[12] Before the mid 1800s, an inherited predisposition was believed to be a primary factor in the disease, coupled with exposure to foul air. The association of tuberculosis with poverty, overcrowding, and poor hygiene was not recognized until late in the 1800s. The impact of these conditions on contagion and the strength of the immune system made tuberculosis a major killer of the poor. The breathing of foul air was an obvious conclusion when tuberculosis was observed in crowded conditions like army barracks and poorly ventilated work sites. In the late 1800s, most prisoners sentenced to life imprisonment died of tuberculosis.[13] These observations led to the recommendations that fresh air and a better climate would be regenerative. And indeed, fresh air could have a beneficial effect; the ultraviolet light in ordinary daylight easily kills the tubercle bacilli, but, of course, daylight does not reach the cavities and organs of the body.

The sanatorium started in Germany in 1859, but soon, the mountain resorts of Switzerland became the fashionable model. Starting in Davos, sanatorium resorts sprouted in the late 1800s throughout Swiss valleys and villages. Davos was the setting for Thomas Mann's 1980 classic novel, *The Magic Mountain*, that described daily life in a sanatorium. By 1946, there were 325 registered sanatoria in Switzerland, many of which became ski resorts in the post-antibiotic era. By 1900, most countries had specialized hospitals taking care of tuberculosis patients. The lay public had learned that tuberculous bacilli could be spread by sputum, and survive for months in dust particles, but be killed by ultraviolet light. The notion quickly spread that sunlight would kill the bacillus rapidly. Open air and sunlight would limit contagion and healthy living would fight infection, the sanatorium prescription.

Edward Livingston Trudeau was a Louisianan Cajun who was born into a wealthy family, grew up in Paris, and graduated from the College of Physicians and Surgeons of Columbia University, eventually establishing a medical practice in New York City. Stricken with tuberculosis, he seemed to improve in 1882 living in Saranac Lake in New York. Raising money from the wealthy, Trudeau established in Saranac Lake in 1884 the first and foremost sanatorium in the United States, caring for hundreds of patients and becoming a center for research. Trudeau was the first American to grow the tubercle bacillus, and his experiments demonstrated the immune response to tuberculosis. The Saranac Lake prescription of isolation, fresh air combined with rest (lying out in the open air became a common feature), and good diet soon spread throughout the United States. In 1900, the United States had thirty-four sanatoria, by 1925, there were 536 sanatoria, and staff physicians now regulated care.[14] Trudeau eventually died in November 1915, at Saranac Lake, a victim of tuberculosis. Trudeau's sanatorium became the Trudeau Institute in 1954, a research laboratory.

The sanatorium approach was doomed from the start. It wasn't until around 1925 that skin testing and X-ray screening allowed the detection of tuberculosis at an early stage of the disease. The sanatorium then was a resting place for the incurable. At best, the patient was made comfortable in a compassionate environment. The outcome of sanatorium patients was not assessed until 1960.[15] The inactive rates and mortality rates were those to be expected with tuberculosis in any general setting; only 22 percent recovered and remained free of active disease.

The second major therapeutic intervention for tuberculosis in the pre-antibiotic era began a little after the sanatoria, thoracoplasty (any procedure that increases the space in the chest) for collapse of the lungs. The prevalent philosophy was that resting the body (in sanatoria) allowed a maximal attack on the infection. It was a logical progression to extend that philosophy to the idea that the infected lungs themselves should be put at rest. Allowing the lungs to collapse and rest not only provided an opportunity for the body to direct its resources to the infected tissue, but the harmful effects of expectorated material could be prevented, and the infected tissue would be deprived of the oxygen required for growth and multiplication of the bacilli.

Artificial pneumothorax, the introduction of a gas into the pleural cavity to cause collapse of the lungs, became a prevalent intervention in the 1920s.[16] Its popularity in the United States (even in the world) is attributed to John Benjamin Murphy of Wisconsin, who became chief of surgery at the Mercy Hospital in Chicago, the hospital used by Montezuma.[17] The huge amphitheater at Mercy was Murphy's stage for visiting physicians from all over the world. By the early 1900s, Murphy was promoting the removal of ribs and the infusion of large volumes of nitrogen gas. Despite the impressive pain associated with the procedure and the need for repeated procedures, by the mid 1920s, thoracoplasty (rib removal) and pneumothorax were administered to most patients in sanatoria. The procedure was very difficult due to adhesions with scarred lungs, and often yielded poor results. Paralysis of the diaphragm to further rest the lungs was added to the surgical treatment, using the "phrenic crush," crushing the nerves in the neck that controlled the diaphragm, producing a partial paralysis that lasted about six months. John Alexander, stricken with spinal tuberculosis and a patient at Saranac Lake, recovered to become the major mentor (at the University of Michigan) for thoracic surgeons in the English-speaking world.[18] Thoracoplasty peaked in the mid 1940s and gave way to antibiotic treatment. Thoracic surgeons then learned to operate on the heart.

TUBERCULOSIS COULD BE DEMONSTRATED to be present in the majority of autopsies performed in the major big city hospitals in the early 1900s. The clinical problem for physicians who had little in the way of laboratory diagnosis to help them was that until the late stages of the disease, the early symptoms were very non-specific. The most common early sign, slightly bloody sputum (along with a cough and fluctuating fever), was not severe enough to send a patient to a physician. The picture of early infection with tuberculosis could be due to any number of conditions, including the common cold. Physicians, too, most often did not consider tuberculosis as the cause of these early symptoms, even, as was the case with Montezuma, in themselves. Early diagnosis was also made essentially impossible by the fact that incipient infection could be asymptomatic. Even after a bacteriologic understanding of the disease became prevalent, demonstration of tubercle bacilli in the sputum was frequently not possible.

Besides the chest X-ray, the only other method to detect tuberculosis in its early stages is the skin test. The injection of minute doses of proteins from the tuberculin bacillus stimulates an immune response in infected individuals that produces a local reaction. The body's immune system can not only recognize and attempt to reject foreign material, but it can remember the event, and when the same or similar foreign material is encountered again, a renewed (and often stronger) effort is made for rejection. The immune system is thus primed by the primary tuberculosis infection; it recognizes the same proteins in the skin test and even this small amount of material produces a reaction that is visible and palpable.

It is estimated that tuberculosis due to *Mycobacterium bovis* accounted for about 15 percent of tuberculous deaths.[19] The bovine strain usually entered by oral ingestion and was a major cause of intestinal and peritoneal tuberculosis in children. It was also a common cause of non-pulmonary infections. Meat products can be infectious, but cooking destroys the organisms. Thus, infected milk was the problem. The United States virtually eliminated bovine tuberculosis before the antibiotic era (before 1940) by performing tuberculin tests on cattle and destroying infected animals. Most of the world had strict tuberculin testing rules for cattle by 1915. The heating of milk for about twenty minutes, followed by quick cooling, is called pasteurization, a process that kills organisms discovered by Louis Pasteur in the 1890s. Pasteurization of milk is an important preventive measure, but it was vigorously opposed by the dairy industry. Eventually the combination of tuberculin testing and pasteurization controlled bovine tuberculosis, but this was not accomplished worldwide until after World War II. The city of Chicago tried to order that all milk be either pasteurized or from cows tested for tuberculosis as early as 1908.[20] However, state legislators resisted this effort, and it wasn't until 1916 that pasteurization was required in Chicago and 1926 that tuberculin testing of cows was mandatory.

The antibiotic era began in the Department of Soil Microbiology of the Agricultural Experimental Station of Rutgers College, New Jersey, with Selman Abraham Waksman.[21] Waksman coined the word antibiotic to designate substances produced by one microorganism that kill or inhibit the growth of another. In 1944, Waksman and his assistant Alfred Shatz reported the isolation of streptomycin, and within a year proved that streptomycin suppressed tuberculosis in guinea pigs. By 1950, PAS (para-aminosalicylic acid) was added to the armamentarium, and by 1955, the therapeutic combination of streptomycin, PAS, and isoniazid was available. The ability of a person to infect another diminishes rapidly once drug therapy is started, and resistant organisms are attacked by simultaneously treating with more than one drug. Treatment with two drugs for two years cured most patients, and treatment no longer required hospitalization. Today, the standard length of treatment is nine months, and more than 85 percent of cases can be cured.[22]

By 1950, sanatoria and tuberculosis hospitals were closing down or converting to other uses. The tuberculosis villages in Switzerland were frantically building ski lifts. If ever visiting one of the Swiss ski resorts, notice the balconies on the older hotels, once used to air tuberculosis patients.

## TUBERCULOSIS TODAY

Tuberculosis slowly began to disappear from the United States after effective drug treatment began in the 1940s. This success led to elimination of federal public health funding targeted for tuberculosis in 1983, and in the late 1980s, a new outbreak appeared. Effective public health measures were restored, and the decline of tuberculosis resumed in 1993, producing a new all time low in tuberculosis in the United States. Death from tuberculosis in the United States is now rare. Nevertheless, 10 to 15 million people in the United States carry the infection, requiring the persistence of appropriate public health measures.[23] Tuberculosis in the United States is now mainly a problem in the large cities, in foreign-born individuals from countries where tuberculosis is common, and in the homeless, HIV-infected, and prison populations. The number of cases of tuberculosis in the United States in foreign-born persons has remained constant for over a decade due to the reactivation of latent infections acquired in the native countries.[24] Montezuma almost certainly died because of the reactivation of a dormant infection, and even now this is the reason why it is urged that immigrants from countries with a high prevalence of tuberculosis should be tested for a latent infection, and a positive response should be treated with nine months of isoniazid.[25]

In the world, tuberculosis continues to be a leading infectious cause of death, now second to HIV infection. And in the United States, Indians are five times more likely to have tuberculosis compared with Whites, largely reflecting the difference in socioeconomic status and the consequences of poverty and malnourishment.[26] Although American Indians had and still have a higher susceptibility to tuberculosis, it has been established by studies of burial remains that tuberculosis existed in America before contact with Whites.[27]

Because HIV weakens the immune system, tuberculosis is a leading cause of death among people who are HIV-positive (about 15 percent of AIDS deaths worldwide).[28] The risk of active tuberculosis disease is more than 100 times greater with HIV infection. Impaired immune function and a greater risk of active tuberculosis are not limited to HIV infection. Weak immune systems can be found in babies and young children, people with serious illnesses, substance abuse, and with certain medical treatments such as corticosteroid medications. Malnourishment associated with poverty must also be a contributing factor by weakening the immune system.

Today, tuberculosis still kills over two million people in the world per year, and one-third of the world's population is currently infected (95 percent of them in developing countries). In recent years, tuberculosis infection has increased in certain areas and populations, most notably pockets of poverty (homeless people) and infection with HIV (human immunodeficiency virus), especially in Eastern Europe, Africa, and Southeastern Asia. The emergence of tuberculosis bacilli that are multi-drug resistant has added to the new global problem. One of the most important causes of drug resistance is inconsistent or partial treatment, emphasizing the importance of a renewed and effective public health program. However, many cases of drug-resistant tuberculosis are due to a resistant strain of the bacillus, especially causing infections in immuno-compromised individuals. In most of the world, effective tuberculosis control programs have kept the prevalence of multidrug-resistant tuberculosis from increasing, but resistance is a major public health problem in countries with inadequate programs (Eastern Europe, China, Pakistan, Iran).[29] Drug-resistant tuberculosis is treatable, but it requires up to two years of treatment with multiple drugs. In the presence of drug resistance, modern initial treatment utilizes a combination of three or four drugs for two months, followed by a long course with two drugs. The most common drugs currently used are isoniazid, rifampin, pyrazinamide, ethambutol, and streptomycin. Effective public health programs incorporate direct observation of therapy (referred to as DOT) by trained health care workers to ensure treatment is taken and completed.

Tuberculin skin testing is recommended for all who are at high risk of infection (including health care professionals), and isoniazid treatment is offered as prophylaxis to tuberculin skin test-positive individuals. Isoniazid treatment must be done with care according to proper guidelines to avoid liver toxicity. The entire genetic code of the tuberculosis bacterium has been mapped, and new and better treatments are sure to follow, especially effective methods to combat multi-drug resistant infections.

## MONTEZUMA'S LAST DAYS

Tuberculosis was an occupational disease for health care workers.[30] Montezuma could easily have been infected with tuberculosis either during his student days, his work on the Indian reservations or at the Carlisle Indian School, or even from his private patients. At the beginning of the twentieth century, 40 percent of medical and nursing students became infected with tuberculosis during their training.[31] Although the world learned that bacteria caused tuberculosis in 1882, it took decades to bring about the proper procedures that minimize infection. The first city sanatorium in Chicago opened in 1909, one year after tuberculosis was required to be reported to the city health department, the same year that saw an anti-spitting campaign. Even now, the medical care of individuals who unknowingly are infected with tuberculosis carries a risk of infection for physicians and nurses.

It was well-recognized that medical students in the pre-antibiotic era developed tuberculosis at a rate that was three to ten times greater than that in the general population.[32] However, the death rate from tuberculosis among physicians and surgeons prior to the age of antibiotics was relatively low; presumably because medical personnel were frequently exposed to infected patients (and cadavers) and developed primary infections that conferred some degree of immunity.[33] It was common to use patients with advanced tuberculosis for teaching purposes, and many patients and cadavers had undiagnosed disease. By graduation, nearly 100 percent of medical students in the pre-antibiotic era had positive tuberculin skin tests.[34] Today, antibiotic treatment is recommended when health care workers convert from a negative tuberculin skin test to positive, a treatment that virtually eliminates subsequent active disease.

Remember that the body's immune system can hold the tubercle bacilli in check and protect against active disease. The early, primary infection even confers protective immunity against another infection. This protection is a major benefit of a healed infection. Unfortunately, healed infections are at risk for reactivation.[35] Years later the immune system may fail or be overcome, and the disease begins its relentless and inexorable progression. Active disease appearing in an older adult most certainly is due to reactivation of old tuberculosis previously held under control. Once reactivated, the disease usually progresses rapidly, within weeks or months. What was the cause with Montezuma? Did he have diabetes?

Diabetes mellitus is one of the most common diseases among American Indians.[36] Diabetes mellitus is a metabolic disorder arising from a primary defect in insulin secretion and activity. The consequence is an inability to utilize glucose as a fuel, eventually over time causing impaired kidney function, impairment of vision, and a high rate of heart and vascular disease. The most common form, especially in Indians, has its onset after age thirty, is often but not always associated with obesity, and can in many cases be managed by lifestyle changes (diet and exercise). Adequate control of sugar metabolism to avoid the secondary complications often requires insulin administration. Individuals with diabetes are more susceptible to infections. A study among the Sioux Indians concluded that adults with diabetes mellitus were four times more likely to develop tuberculosis.[37] The general metabolic dysfunction associated with diabetes mellitus suppresses the immune system, and tuberculosis can be reactivated. The high incidence of diabetes mellitus in Indians in modern times is believed to be a result of a White style of life, specifically decreased physical activity and an increase in body weight. This conclusion is supported by a failure to find specific genetic causes for diabetes in Indians. The Pima Indians have had an especially striking increase in diabetes mellitus since World War II. Intensive studies of the Pima Indians indicate that the primary factor is a change in diet coupled with a decrease in physical activity.[38] However, one cannot discount the impact of years of confinement on reservations that would make the genetic pool more homogenous and allow an inherited trait like diabetes to increase in prevalence.

MONTEZUMA WAS IN BED with the "flu" for two weeks in May 1922.[39] He told Richard Pratt that "For a doctor to get sick does sound strange, but they do get sick and die."[40]

In the summer of 1922, Carlos and Marie Montezuma moved to 2720 South Michigan Avenue. "We have not finished our arranging. We had more old things than I ever thought of. I have many Indian periodicals and car load of books and pictures. Not many would appreciate them but I would not feel at home without them. Living on Michigan Ave. is not so pleasant after all. There is too much noise from the continual whirr of the automobiles. Still my wife and I are making the best of it."[41] A month later Montezuma was in bed again, this time for ten days.[42] He never did regain his strength, and complained of feeling wobbly.

Despite feeling weak, Montezuma went to Kansas City to attend the annual conference of the Society of American Indians. When Montezuma returned home in October 1922, there was no longer any doubt in his mind that he was struggling with a chronic illness; however, he had no diagnosis.

> I thank you [Joseph Latimer] very much for being patient with me. I am going through a change of life, I believe. If not that I may have Bright's Disease. At any rate since my sickness last Spring and this Summer I have lost about 30–40 pounds. As I look at myself when I go to bed I am all bones. I coughed considerable 3 or 4 months ago, but not very much now. I was weak when I left the bed and not very strong when I went to Kansas City to the SAI Conference. I am growing stronger and have more faith in myself.[43]

In that same month, October 1922, Montezuma announced his ill health in his newsletter. He was too weak to address and mail the last two issues of *Wassaja*; the task fell to his wife.

### Dr. Montezuma Is Not Well

No time in the history of Wassaja had he to slow down upon his work. For many years he thought he was made of cast iron physically, but for a year, he found that he was a mere flesh, bone and blood.

Since publishing "Wassaja" he did his work between 12 and 2 a.m. while Chicago was asleep. He devoted all day to his profession. But for two months Wassaja was down and out. He just gathered enough strength to attend the S.A.I. Conference at Kansas City. On return to Chicago, he is slowly improving. He hopes in time that he will regain his health, providing that he takes care of himself—from exposure and overwork.

Wassaja, as long as he breathes, will work for the citizenship of his people.

My friends, now is the time to pay for your dues on your subscriptions, and donate to the publication of the "Wassaja." For want of funds, for two years Wassaja had to forego his annual vacation with his primitive people in Arizona. Camp life would regain him his health, but he is poor and helpless. The only thing for him to do is to stay in Chicago, do his best and see what the Lord will do.[44]

*Montezuma in SAI Conference Group Picture—October, 1922*

On a cold Sunday at midday, in the middle of December 1922, Carlos Montezuma, a man who had been to almost all parts of the United States, boarded The Navajo in Chicago for the last journey of his life, on the Santa Fe Railroad direct to Phoenix. The fare was $70 for a travel time of fifty-six hours. Father Philip Gordon accompanied Marie to help Montezuma board the train.[45]

William (Billy) Thomas Moore, a Pima Indian who lived with Carlos and Marie Montezuma,[46] sent a telegram to his sister Anna, asking her to meet Montezuma, "a very sick man," at the railroad station on Tuesday at 9:00 P.M.[47] Her husband, Ross Shaw, rode the trolley to the station, and when the train pulled in, he noticed a distinguished Indian sitting in a Pullman car. After introductions, Montezuma wondered why the Dickens family was not there to greet him. Ross took him home by taxicab, where Anna met him for the first time. Montezuma kept repeating: "You so much resemble your brother Bill. He is a fine boy. My Billy! My Billy!"[48] Montezuma stayed with the Shaws and their two children for five days. He would sit and talk, and Anna personally heard many of the lines from his numerous speeches. Finally the Dickens arrived in an open Ford to take Montezuma over the rough desert track to Fort McDowell. Anna was surprised to find that Montezuma left five silver dollars on the table next to his bed.

Marie Montezuma indicated in letters to friends that the two of them intended to live in Arizona for the rest of Montezuma's life.[49] The decision to go to Arizona was made almost impulsively and quickly carried out.[50] The plan was for Marie to stay in Chicago to "sell out everything we have. His Indian curios is an old collection of fifty years back. Any of our things will be no use to us on reservation and we will need all the money we can get to keep us alive. …It is a pity that he should end up in such a way at his age."[51]

Sam Dickens and Jim Keill recalled in 1966 that: "He didn't look like a famous doctor during his last days on earth but was dressed in old pants and shirt and had tuberculosis real bad."[52] The Dickens family constructed an *oo-wah* in a secluded spot about two miles down river from the cemetery and old fort, among the mesquite and cottonwood trees lining the river bank, and there Montezuma awaited his final day. His relatives stoked the fire, and he had a steady stream of company. John Smith, son-in-law of Mike Burns, was one who kept the fire going and the water supply refreshed. He remembered Montezuma saying: "I'm cold! I'm going to die of cold in here!"[53]

Sometime a few weeks before he died, Montezuma wrote to his wife in Chicago, in a scrawling handwriting that is difficult to read, "I am still fighting to keep above water. It is hard work to keep warm. Arizona is change to get warmer but it get pretty cold for George to keep up the fire. If you were here I know it would be different. Now I am writing on a box. I have been inside every [sic] since I came. What I am fed is not the best, but I take it like a cat. I am sitting up on my spring bed. The [?] not sanitary, but that be Indian sanitary. If I should think If I should plan, it would hurt me. All I can do is resign everything & take may come, be brave & God's will. You must keep your cool. Do everything the best what you see to do. Do not pay freight for books to Arizona. Keep everything arrange all right. Be a brave girl & get up for the best."[54]

The Fort McDowell Indians notified a medical missionary, C. H. Ellis, of Montezuma's condition. Ellis was a physician at the Presbyterian Indian Mission in Scottsdale, one of the missionaries who had years ago strenuously objected to the Yavapai dances. Ellis and a government physician, R. J. Stroud of Tempe, visited him, but they were ordered by

Montezuma to leave him alone.[55] Stroud, the physician under contract for services to the Fort McDowell, Salt River, and Lehi Reservations, ignored Montezuma's orders. At his first visit on January 3, four weeks before Montezuma died, Stroud found Montezuma in a Yavapai *oo-wah* with an entrance extended by a canvas entryway that was six-feet long.[56] A fire was burning, with the smoke inefficiently leaving by the opening in the center of the top so that the smell of mesquite permeated everything inside and constantly irritated the eyes of visitors, although not bothering Montezuma. He seemed to have no desire to expose himself to sunshine and fresh air, the standard of prescribed treatment for tuberculosis at that time.

Stroud encountered Montezuma sitting on the floor, disdaining a mattress and springs that had been sent by a friend in a Phoenix Masonic Lodge. He was dressed only in a loin-cloth with a bathrobe over his shoulders. Two cowhide suitcases were scattered to the sides. He was partially bald with bright eyes, emaciated with labored breathing, and talked with great agitation in a disjointed manner. A diagnosis of pulmonary tuberculosis was easily made upon Stroud's examination. Montezuma mentioned the *possibility* of diabetes, but he refused to provide a specimen of urine for testing.

Nineteen days before he died, Montezuma wrote his last letter. It was to his wife, still in Chicago. The handwriting is weak, and there are many words and meanings that cannot be deciphered. But even with these gaps, his last words still have some power, even a sense of humor, and poignantly convey his loss of vitality, especially when he signed it, "Your sick and useless husband, Wassaja."[57]

My dearest in hand:

 this is the first period I taken—I have been [?] & dazed. I know what was [?] happening but I took little interest. Don't tell you cannot my two weeks experience since left Chicago. Zero weather, left Kansas City, zero, left Trinidad, and zero weather. Albuquerque, left there zero weather. It was zero weather at [?]. Road to Phoenix was awful. I bang from hurting chair. I was might glad to get into Phoenix. You gave me small load of food. I was so weak that I had no appetite for them. Moore's brother-in-law on there on time. In an automobile he took me his home. It was cold! The [?] you had me to take enough came handy.

 …At Phoenix I bought 6 woolen blankets & 6 comforters. When I moved in zero, they came handy. I guess I did make use of the blankets & comforters myself. We have had plenty of Mohave Indians to see me & outside.

 Indians are doing nicely & working on roads near Roosevelt dam, in mines, …

 George will do everything. At first I was so much better that I had all the Indians[?]. I had singing all night over me. …Well after a while I had to stop [?] I guess so they have stopped everything.

 I have not given my face a cleaning washing. I'm on the ground ever since I arrived. What you think one Indian friend sent me a good spring bed.

 …I never felt such a change in my life. I am comfortable. The weather is little warm. Have not been able to go out doors.

 I feel so out of place. This morning I little meat and gravy, that I was [?] & coffee; some tried get corn meal & coffee, soup with meat, bread, & coffee. They feed me so funny. It may be the best thing. …

 Pack books to send to your mother. It cost too much. Keep away from Dr. Butterfield. I told you that before I went away. Pay him $15.00 is too much.

 When you sell out get out the house—go to mother.

 Lodge people been out? Let them pay on mother's rent.

 I write as though I were well—far from it.

 Faithful George has come in from cutting wood.

 Your sick and useless husband, Wassaja.[58]

George Webb, a Pima Indian born about 1893, published in 1959 his memories of Pima history and traditions. He reported a visit to Fort McDowell when he was told Dr. Montezuma was dying on the reservation.[59] He entered the *oo-wah* with such a small entrance that he had to crawl in on hands and knees. Montezuma lay on a blanket spread on the dirt floor, and to the side was his suitcase still filled with clothes. The room was filled with people; he lived only a few more days.

Ellis had obtained from Montezuma the name of his Masonic Lodge and the address of the Master. It was a special delivery letter from Ellis to the Master that notified Marie of Montezuma's deteriorating condition.[60] Marie Montezuma left Chicago on January 22 and upon her arrival in Phoenix, a telegram from Dr. Stroud found her at Anna Shaw's house.[61] She immediately went to Fort McDowell and was astounded by Montezuma's living conditions.[62]

The next time Stroud visited Montezuma, he was subdued and the light had left his eyes.[63] His fiery spirit was sapped, consumed by a classical course of tuberculosis. A few days later he died, on Wednesday, January 31, 1923, at 3 P.M.[64] Stroud incorrectly recorded Montezuma's age as fifty-four instead of fifty-six on the death certificate. It was a breezy, cloudy day, but dry until evening when a light rain began to fall.[65] The Yavapai burned the *oo-wah* and all of its contents. A visit to the site eleven years later indicated that it had been undisturbed; the frame of an iron cot and some utensils were still lying in a small hole.[66]

Vernon Evans, a mortician with Merryman's Funeral Home in Phoenix, in response to a phone call from Marie Montezuma, left immediately for Fort McDowell.[67] The rain was now steady, and the muddy road made for slow progress; he arrived at 4 A.M. He immediately returned to Phoenix with Montezuma's body, followed slowly by Marie in another car. Learning from Marie that Montezuma was a Baptist, Evans called his friend, Reverend W. B. Percival at the First Baptist Church in Phoenix. Reverend Percival led services on Saturday afternoon, February 3, 1923. The pallbearers were students from the Phoenix Indian School.[68] Evans also informed the Master of a Phoenix Masonic Lodge who arranged for a friend of Montezuma's, James McClintock (the Arizona State Historian), to recount his history at the funeral. Anna Moore Shaw wrote to her brother Billy: "I had the pleasure of attending Dr. Montezuma's funeral. …Dr. had a very pretty coffin and he looked natural as if he were only asleep. [The casket cost $425, and the bill from the George Merryman Company totaled $655.[69]] I bo't some flowers for him as we sure think a lot of him. Yes, the Indians have lost a good friend and helper. P.S. Mrs. Montezuma will be here tomorrow and will go to Los Angeles for a week before returning to Chicago. She is sure a nice woman. She is the kind I want you to get when you think of settling down."[70] Marie, however, looked gaunt and drawn in her dark funeral outfit, the effect of an obvious loss of weight.

*Marie at the Funeral*

*First Baptist Church, Phoenix—1923*

### "Sunday Sermon," *The Arizona Republican*, February 5, 1923

In the passing away of Dr. Carlos Montezuma, a wife has lost her husband and our first thought is of the one bereft of her companion. Whatever helpfulness there may be in human sympathy, and whatever consolation there may be in divine comfort is hers today.

But we are not here simply to comfort her or to lament the passing away of her husband. We are here to do honor to the memory of one whose life and death touch a wider circle than that of a few intimate friends.

The life of Dr. Montezuma symbolized for us the wonderful relationship between two peoples, the red and white, the Indian and the American, the first American and the last American. His life links together in a marvelous way the past and the present of our country—its oldest savagery with its newest civilization. He was not an old man, and yet within the half century of his life he has run all the gamut of primitive tribal life, of savage warfare and massacre, of capture and slavery, of travel across the great plains to the cities of the east, where he grew up with the metropolis of the middle west, studying in our schools, learning the lessons of the streets of the big city, fighting the battle for higher education, that he might go back into the slums of the city and the reservations of the west and help heal and uplift his own people and the newer immigrants to these shores. He has seen the worst of our civilization, but he has chosen the best.

His life becomes a two-fold lesson to us today. To the Indians he is an example of what any Indian may become who will avoid the worst and seek the best in our civilization.

To the American (the newer American) he is a reminder of what capacity the Indian possesses.

His life says to us, "Give to my brothers the same opportunity which came to me and they too can become useful servants of humanity."

A few months ago I camped one night with 30 boy scouts in Fish creek canyon. We got there after night and pitched our camp. In the morning we found that 30 Apache Indians had been sleeping about 100 yards from us. Had we known it we would have slept as peacefully as we did in our ignorance. For these were our friends, and in the morning they took up their work of making the roads smooth and safe. It was probably in the same canyon that 50 years ago the raid took place in which the little Apache Indian boy was carried away captive by the Pimas. Today this canyon is part of the great Apache trail, over which our tourists travel with more safety than they can walk the streets of Chicago at night.

The road to friendship and cooperation between the Indian and the white man has been a long one and a hard one. There have been many rough spots and many accidents along the way, but it is a road that has become smoother and better with the passing years. It has been lives like Dr. Montezuma's that have helped to make the road a better and safer one to travel.

There is another element in the doctor's life of which I would speak. It has to do with his religion. He was no doubt brought up in the nature religion of his people, and he has always kept that natural love for the out-of-doors. He was out here a few years ago hunting in the mountains of our state. The man who first adopted him was an Italian and a Roman Catholic, and when a boy of four years Carlos was baptized in the Catholic church at or near Florence. Later he was taken under the care of a Baptist minister in Illinois, and he then came to have a Christian experience and faith of his own. This experience has stayed with him through life. As a man in Chicago he was a member of the First Baptist church and, in spite of a busy practice, he had time to do missionary work among the foreign elements of that city. He taught a Sunday school class in the Bohemian mission, conducted by the Baptists—the same one in which my own wife taught when she was attending our Baptist missionary training school in Chicago.

Truly his has been a life of service, a life of conquest over difficulties, a life of attainment. He has at last won the final victory and is ready to receive a crown of reward.[71]

After the funeral in Phoenix, Montezuma's body was taken to Fort McDowell. Marie was concerned over the impression the usual black hearse would have on the reservation, and, therefore, the body was wrapped in canvas and roped to the body of a truck.[72] The next day, a second funeral attended by the Yavapai and led by the Masons, was held at the Fort McDowell Presbyterian Church, the same one that was constructed by the Indians under Reverend Gill's direction in 1906. According to the mortician, Vernon Evans, a telegram was received by the funeral home from a Knights Templar Commandery in Chicago, indicating that Montezuma was a Knight Templar and

*Presbyterian Church, Fort McDowell*

asking the Phoenix Knights Templars to participate in his burial, and about a dozen came to Fort McDowell in full dress and conducted the services.[73] However, a search of the York Rite, Knights Templar records failed to find any evidence that Montezuma was a Knight Templar.[74] The Masons participating in the funeral were regular members of a Phoenix Lodge, who responded to a request received from Montezuma's Dearborn Lodge in Chicago.[75]

The church is small, and most of the large crowd must have stood outside.[76] The rain had stopped, and Montezuma was buried Sunday, February 4, 1923, on a pleasant afternoon with a clear desert sky, fifty-five-degree temperature, and a slight breeze from the east.[77] The casket was carried after the service in the Presbyterian Church to the old military cemetery at Fort McDowell. The pallbearers were the Masons, and then first one team and then a second team of Fort McDowell Indians. The procession was led by the Masons (wearing the aprons of Master Masons). Montezuma was buried in a barren, empty section of the cemetery; today his grave is surrounded by many graves with white crosses.

*Montezuma's Funeral Procession at Fort McDowell*

Montezuma's grave is marked by a large stone that features the Masonic square and the compass, symbols of living on earth with honor and integrity, and spiritual life, respectively, enclosing a "G," the Masonic symbol for geometry and God. The first time I visited Montezuma's grave, I stood before it with Robin Russell when he was vice-president of the Yavapai Tribal Council. After a moment of silence, Russell said, in a voice that was soft but strong with pride, especially when he emphasized the last two letters: "Carlos Montezuma, M.D.!"

After the funeral, Marie lived with Ross and Anna Shaw for several months. In November 1923, the Masonic Dearborn Lodge reported in its monthly bulletin that Mrs. Carlos Montezuma was back in Chicago.[78] In 1924, after marrying Billy Moore, the couple moved to a new house at 2219 Prairie Street in Blue Island, a suburb of Chicago. Marie Montezuma returned periodically to Fort McDowell to paint the iron fence around the grave.[79]

The Society of American Indians published two pieces (by unknown authors, perhaps it was Zitkala-Ša) to honor Montezuma after his death, a poem and a eulogy in a two-page pamphlet issued from the Washington, D.C., office.

### To the Memory of Dr. Carlos Montezuma

*Montezuma!*
*Montezuma!*
*Spirit potent and immortal,*
*From this land of crowding shadows.*
*We, as brothers, praise and bless you,*
*As we trail through many sorrows.*

*We have called you Brave Was-sa-ja,*
*Mighty signal—for the people.*
*As you stood a flashing beacon,*
*Lifted from a lofty steeple.*

*Sad the days, O! Montezuma,*
*Greatly do we mourn your passing.*
*We shall miss your honest counsel,*
*Magic voice with wisdom ringing.*

*Rest Was-sa-ja—"It is finished."*
*Tribe to tribe shall tell your story.*
*Hoary braves to youth relate it,*
*Mon-te-zu-ma's fame and glory!*[80]

### To An Indian Leader
### (Was-sa-ja)

The Society of American Indians mourns the loss of one of its greatest leaders, in the death of Doctor Carlos Montezuma, of Chicago, Ill. Born in Arizona, 1858 [*sic*].

Doctor Montezuma was one of the outstanding figures of this country, so far as Indians are concerned. He was present at the inception of this Society, and ever afterward took a keen interest in the complicated affairs of the Society. There probably has never lived a full-blooded Indian who so effectively demonstrated the capabilities of the Indian race to high culture, and a life of real usefulness than Doctor Montezuma. With a most remarkable personal history that reads more like fiction, than actual occurrence, his life was one of unique success. He became a most competent physician and successfully practiced in the midst of fiercest competition in Chicago, winning for himself fame and distinction.

There probably never has been an Indian that burned with patriotism, with greater ardor than Doctor Montezuma. Like many great historical figures, he was often misunderstood, and sometimes almost persecuted, because of honest political and economic opinions. All were not expected to be in accord, it is true. With the Doctor's conclusions, nevertheless, none can be found who doubt the utmost sincerity of the great and good man now in eternity. Doctor Montezuma was a great and good man, an intense patriot, a lover of freedom, a hater of deceit and hypocrisy, and natural-born orator. His voice was ever raised in defense of oppressed peoples of any race or color.

Many think of Doctor Montezuma as a ruthless opponent, but a kinder man never lived. He loved the little ones, and nothing so pleased him, than a romp with children.

The Society of American Indians has lost one of its greatest leaders, and the Indian race, its greatest lover and greatest benefactor. He died on Wednesday, January 31, 1923, at Fort McDowell, Arizona.[81]

Joe Scheuerle, Montezuma's cartoonist friend, wrote Marie: "Now he is sleeping with his people, and his life's work will go on, by others, but very few know what the doctor did, and I hope his footsteps will be filled by one as serious, or at least as honest, as dear doc."[82]

## CLOSURE WITH PRATT

Where was Richard Pratt in Montezuma's last days? This was a friendship that lasted over thirty years, based on a mutual philosophical and political commitment. The two men had similar personalities: honest, dedicated, energetic, dynamic, combative, and unwavering in their beliefs, goals, and personal integrity. They developed and maintained respect, admiration, and a deep affection for each other. Just three and one-half years before his death, Montezuma wrote these emotional words to Pratt:

> …How glad I am that you are living and that you are able to give aid to the S.A.I. We need your help more than any one in the world. No progress can exist without the power. Gen, you are the power that can move the Society of American Indians. Dr. Eastman & Mrs. Bonnin have worked with you at Carlisle and all the Indians idealize you as the man who can lead them in the right trail. It is glorious to think that we can have you as a father to advise in all things for our own good. …Even though we have been separate from each other we have always been of one mind on Indian matters. To know this to be a fact has been a great encouragement in my work. It is a great thing to know you have a great backer. General, you are backer for all Indians. That is why the Indian Bureau has a strange idea about you. They can take away Carlisle but they cannot take you away from the Indians. We Indians look up to you as never before.[83]

Pratt replied, "Yours of the 17th came this morning and quite touched my heart."[84] But there is no communication to be found between the two men in the last months of Montezuma's life. On the occasion of Pratt's eightieth birthday, only two years before Montezuma's death, Montezuma again opened his heart to Pratt when he wrote:

> My dear good & father General,
>
> It gives my wife and I the greatest pleasure of sending you our hearty congratulations on your eightieth birthday.
>
> How we wish that we were there to greet you by the hand and express from the fullness of our hearts, the great goodness you have bestowed on mankind within the time God has blessed you.
>
> In behalf of the Indian race, you have sacrificed the best part of your life. To no man living or ever will live, can the Indians say, "we owe everything to you—our greatest benefactor."
>
> On your eightieth birthday there is no heart that throbs with greater thankfulness than my own, because I have been with you in person and spirit in the noblest work that man can do for man. You have been my greatest inspiration and helper.
>
> On Dec 5th you can truly say, "I have fought a good fight." Our happiness in life consists in being conscious of the good deeds we have done.

> ...Gen. Pratt, our father, fear not. We Indians are struggling bravely and faithfully bearing the standard banner of which you have ceaselessly voiced in our behalf. The Indian race will never forget you.[85]

Pratt learned of Montezuma's death from Thomas Sloan who had received a telegram from Marie Montezuma.[86] Pratt wrote to Marie: "He seemed so strong and well and was with it all such a heroic figure in trying to get righteousness for the Indians into our people. Now we are interested in your welfare. Faithfully yours."[87] Pratt died fifteen months later, a month before Congress passed the Indian Citizenship Act.

Montezuma would have been disappointed to know that Pratt's memoirs contain only two sentences about Montezuma, an idle observation that Montezuma served as the Carlisle school physician. "On one occasion, having received a large number of new pupils from the agencies, my school physician reported that there were twenty-three who ought to go to Dr. Fox (an eye specialist in Phil) for special treatment. Carlisle sent Dr. Carlos Montezuma, a full-blood Apache Indian then the school physician, in charge of these to Philadelphia, and Dr. Fox gave each of them his personal attention and also instructions to the school physician how to proceed with those returned to school, keeping seven of them in his hospital for special treatment."[88] Montezuma's story, however, cannot be told without repeated and relevant references to Pratt, his "good and father General."

## WHY DID MONTEZUMA RETURN TO HIS TRIBE AND THE RESERVATION?

Many incorrect statements regarding Montezuma appeared in the years following his death. For example, it was claimed that Montezuma was offered the position of commissioner of Indian affairs, not once, but twice, first by President Theodore Roosevelt, and then by President Woodrow Wilson.[89] There is not even a hint of any evidence to support those assertions. He was said to be wealthy and a high society doctor, but as we have seen, Montezuma's patients were not rich, and he often struggled financially. It has even been alleged that Montezuma was jailed; however, no record of such an occurrence can be found. And finally, writers have tried to explain why Montezuma returned to his tribe to die.

Montezuma was an educated, assimilated, Protestant American Indian, who for decades wanted to eliminate the reservations and make Anglo-Saxons out of Indians, leaving no vestiges of tribal culture and heritage. He never wavered in his support of Richard H. Pratt, and he refused to join Zitkala-Ša to live and work on a reservation. Yet he chose to die as a reservation Indian, and in the last years of his life, to fight for his tribe's land and water rights. Why the change? Historians have repeatedly concluded that Montezuma's return to the Yavapai was a simple, emotional return to his roots.[90] But Montezuma was a very intelligent, orderly, and rational man. I believe there is a logical and understandable explanation for this major shift in his life. Montezuma lived in a time of acute and profound change, and his behavior reflected the changing times.

Montezuma's formative years (1872–1900) spanned the decades of Protestant dominance, with its focus on the individual: individual property ownership, individual accumulation of wealth, and survival of the most rugged, fittest individual (the policy of assimilation and allotment described in Chapter 3). In the last decades of Montezuma's life, the political and social philosophy of America changed to a greater consideration of the public good. The shift away from Protestant dominance had its roots in the rapid acceleration of scientific and technologic knowledge and the social unrest that was a consequence of industrialization. The emphasis moved from the individual to social reform, with an effort to establish political and economic controls. Montezuma experienced this change firsthand in his life and medical practice in Chicago.

In the last twenty years of the nineteenth century, Chicago grew dramatically, engineered by the accomplishments of individual entrepreneurs (Chapter 7). Consistent with the Protestant concept of wealth defined by Andrew Carnegie,[91] the wealthy Chicago capitalists were active philanthropists, founding museums and universities. The success of Chicago was an admired example of the dominant Protestant ethic described in Chapter 3 that supported the policy of assimilation and allotment for American Indians. Montezuma, influenced by the Baptist household of Reverend William Stedman and the outspoken but dedicated Richard H. Pratt, wholeheartedly endorsed this ethic and philosophy. But social unrest, marked in Chicago by the Haymarket Affair in 1886, the Pullman Company strike in 1894, and the Race Riot of 1919, challenged Protestant domination. The makeup of American society changed with massive waves of immigration from Eastern and Southern Europe, the movement of people from the country into urban areas, and migration of Black people to northern cities.

For years Montezuma hammered on the importance of environment (nurture) over nature. The Indian was not born "an inevitable savage: He is born a blank, like the rest of us. What happens to him depends on his environment."[92] "We earnestly advocated that in a change of environment we have the key to the solution of the Indian problem."[93] Having intellectually and repeatedly articulated this theme, I would expect Montezuma to have been very sensitive to his environment. If he didn't perceive social changes simply by reading the Chicago newspapers, he certainly could view social forces through the lives of his patients. His patients came mainly from the lower levels of society and this experience along with his time in the Free Clinic gave him first hand opportunities, patient by patient, to see the impact of social change on individuals.

The nature of Montezuma's medical practice changed substantially in the early 1900s (Chapters 5 and 8). Montezuma belonged to the Chicago Medical Society, and he was on the faculty of the University of Illinois and the Postgraduate School. This provided him with multiple opportunities to learn and assess the new advances in medicine. Here again Montezuma must have gained an appreciation for a shift in focus from the individual to public welfare. The story of tuberculosis is a good illustration of the change in thinking in that initially it was believed the disease was due to an inherited predisposition and individual circumstances, and later because of the knowledge gained by the science of bacteriology, the emphasis was on public health measures.

As Montezuma reconnected with his tribal roots, it is only logical that his interaction with the Yavapai reflected the growing public awareness that philanthropic kindness and generosity were not sufficient to solve social problems, and that *laissez-faire* individualism was not working for everyone, especially those oppressed by difficult political and social conditions. In the last decade of his life, it surely must have been apparent to Montezuma that the country and American life were not the same as it was in the last two decades of the nineteenth century. Scientific progress and the changes it brought in medicine and industry had challenged the simple notion of Puritan rugged individualism.

The philosophic shift in Montezuma from assimilation of individual Indians to concern for his tribe was testimony to his ability to respond to the intellectual and social world around him. This was one of his strengths, an ability to adapt and remain influential and effective. Montezuma was caught up in a new social philosophy that emphasized the public good rather than the individual. Just as state and federal governments took on the collective interests of the people, Montezuma began to think collectively of his tribe. He knew from his own experience that the problems of American Indians were low on the priority list of the Federal Government, and that the Bureau of Indian Affairs would do little to change conditions without prodding and agitation. It was appropriate in the new social environment of America for Montezuma to fight for the rights and welfare of his tribe. And thus it became appropriate for him to choose to die as a Yavapai in his tribal home.

## CHAPTER EIGHTEEN

# Citizenship:
# You Must Free All the Indians

MONTEZUMA COVETED U.S. CITIZENSHIP, a subject for editorial comment in nearly every issue of his newsletter, *Wassaja*. "WASSAJA contends that in order to place the Indian on a just basis as a man, the country must first make him a free man, and then give him his citizenship. But to give him citizenship with conditions attached to it, is not citizenship that is enjoyed by true American citizens. That is a false freedom!"[1]

The problem of citizenship for Indians was complicated by the changing and uncertain nature of the relationship between the Federal Government and Indian tribes.[2] The European colonial powers established the tradition of treating Indian tribes as independent nations, the basis for treaty making. The United States continued this tradition, but it was not until 1831 that the U. S. Supreme Court defined the tribes as separate nations, although at the same time not foreign states. Chief Justice Marshall further defined the tribes as "domestic dependent nations."[3] This fundamental ruling established the process by which Indians would have to seek changes in their relationships with the Federal Government, specifically a political process working through Congress. Because the Indian tribes were no longer considered as independent, foreign nations, citizenship now had to be achieved through the U. S. political system. Placing American Indians under the political sphere of the United States was formalized when treaty making was banned in 1871.[4]

In the last decades of the nineteenth century, individual Indians were regarded as citizens *of their tribes* as long as they maintained their tribal relationships. This was recognized legally when the U.S. courts concluded that federal and state governments had no jurisdiction over crimes committed upon reservations and involving only Indians. The legal rulings of the U.S. courts were the motivation for the efforts to develop a uniform system of laws and courts for the reservations. This state of affairs reached a climax with the famous case of Crow Dog. Crow Dog, a Brulé Sioux chief, murdered Chief Spotted Tail on the reservation. The territorial court of Dakota sentenced Crow Dog to death; however, the U.S. Supreme Court released Crow Dog to his tribe on the grounds that the United States had no jurisdiction over crimes committed by one Indian against another.[5] Crow Dog returned to his tribe, and was allowed to be free when the matter was resolved according to traditional Sioux customs. As a result of the public protest that followed, Congress passed the Major Crimes Act in 1885, listing the seven major crimes (murder, manslaughter, rape, assault with intent to kill, arson, burglary, and larceny) that would fall under the jurisdiction of the U. S. courts.[6] The constitutionality of the law was upheld a year later,[7] further emphasizing that reservation Indians were under federal control, not state, and at the same time, further reducing tribal control. The legal emphasis was to extend to the individual Indian the laws of the republic, ignoring the tribe, but in truth, this was totally consistent with the desire during the period of assimilation and allotment to eliminate tribal allegiance. From this point on, it was absolutely clear that changes to affect Indians had to be accomplished in Congress.

The citizenship status of individuals who voluntarily disassociated from their tribes was not resolved until 1884 when an Indian, named John Elk, living in Omaha, Nebraska, tried to register to vote and was refused. The Supreme Court upheld the refusal, establishing that an Indian could not become a citizen by abandoning tribal allegiance without the consent and cooperation of the U.S. Government.[8] It would take an act of Congress to give Indians the rights of citizenship.

The work of the Indian humanitarian reformers reviewed in Chapter 3 highlighted the needs of Indians, and most importantly, the ability of individual Indians to be educated in White society. The Indian reform organizations campaigned for Indian citizenship, believing strongly that only citizenship would grant the legal protection that is such an essential component of Anglo-Saxon civilization. Richard H. Pratt, of course, supported a program of education to prepare individuals for citizenship. Others, with the passage of the Land-In-Severalty Act (the Dawes Act) in 1887, believed land ownership and citizenship should come immediately, and education could follow (Chapter 3). Indeed, the Dawes Act granted citizenship, including state jurisdiction, to those who voluntarily separated themselves from the tribe and took up life on their private property. The problem was that life on the reservation did not change, and it was practically impossible to live independently from the tribe. This was not only true in terms of culture and heritage, but also economically as the conditions on the reservations continued to ensure that the Indians depended upon federal support for their survival. Furthermore, most Indians involved in the allotment process were not eligible for citizenship until they received titles to their lands after the twenty-five-year trust period. Citizenship actually came to fruition for only a few.

## CITIZENSHIP LEGISLATION

Citizenship came by steps aimed at individuals. In 1888, a Congressional act declared that an Indian woman would become an American citizen by marrying a citizen.[9] In 1901, all Indians in the Indian Territory were granted citizenship.[10] A major problem in granting individual Indians citizenship was the effect on a tribe's ability to hold on to its land. It wasn't until 1916 that a landmark Supreme Court case finally established that U.S. citizenship was compatible with tribal existence and maintenance of the Federal Government relationships with the tribes.[11] This removed the final obstacle to the granting of citizenship, allowing those Indians who remained on the reservations on tribal lands to be eligible. About half of American Indians had acquired citizenship prior to World War I. In 1919, about 125,000 were still not citizens.

The end of the war brought a round of recognition for Indians in the military and renewed urging for citizenship. Carl Hayden, Senator from Arizona, introduced a bill in 1917 conferring citizenship on all American Indians, but it also called for the elimination of tribes and the disbursal of tribal funds. Montezuma, in the midst of loudly clamoring for Indian citizenship, strongly opposed the Hayden Bill, arguing that giving citizenship to the

Indians in four or five years and then keeping them bound up for ten years longer before complete freedom "is a pervertive good-will bill for the Indians."[12]

Other bills were introduced that coupled citizenship with the elimination of the Bureau of Indian Affairs. This certainly met with the approval of the long-standing Indian Bureau antagonists, like Montezuma and Pratt, but as within the debates at the meetings of the Society of American Indians (Chapter 13), others feared the abrupt elimination of the Bureau without proper resolution of its trust responsibilities.

Richard Pratt seized on the military service of American Indians as a powerful argument to grant citizenship:

> If through perilous army service they have proven they are after all not so unequal to us in ability and patriotism and are ready to die for the country, it demonstrated the highest attributes of citizenship. If shoulder to shoulder and comrades in war, why not shoulder to shoulder and comrades in peace?[13]

Homer P. Snyder of New York, the chairman of the House Committee on Indian Affairs, introduced HR 5007 on June 5, 1919. The bill granted citizenship to every Indian who served in the military during World War I and did not require the forfeiture of tribal rights and property. The bill passed the Senate on October 22, 1919, and became law on November 6, 1919.

### Citizenship for World War I Veterans

> Be it enacted…that every American Indian who served in the Military or Naval Establishments of the United States during the war against the Imperial German Government, and who has received or who shall hereafter receive an honorable discharge, if not now a citizen and if he so desires, shall, on proof of such discharge and after proper identification before a court of competent jurisdiction, and without other examination except as prescribed by said court, be granted full citizenship with all the privileges pertaining thereto, without in any manner impairing or otherwise affecting the property rights, individual or tribal, of any such Indian or his interest in tribal or other Indian property.[14]

Unfortunately, Indians seeking citizenship according to this law were required to accomplish a complicated process. An application had to be completed before an official (usually a reservation superintendent), and the application was then mailed to the Bureau of Naturalization, which selected a date for a court hearing of the individual's qualifications; following this, the individual made formal application with the clerk of the court to obtain a certificate of citizenship.[15] Many Indians were unwilling to pursue the process, and many feared that loss of tribal benefits and property might still occur. It should be emphasized that citizenship was not automatic for veterans with an honorable discharge, they had to apply for it, and apparently few did. Citizenship was not something that was coveted by all. Many Indians viewed it simply as another imperialistic maneuver on the part of White society.

Homer P. Snyder introduced the final piece of legislation (HR 6355) in January 1924, conveying blanket citizenship to all remaining non-citizen Indians. As originally introduced, the bill allowed the secretary of the interior to issue citizenship at his "discretion." The bill was drastically altered by the Senate Committee on Indian Affairs providing citizenship to all non-citizen Indians born within the United States. This final piece of citizenship legislation has been attributed to the social philosophies of "progressives" in the post-war government.[16] Members of the Senate Committee on Indian Affairs included Robert M. LaFollette of Wisconsin, Burton K. Wheeler of Montana, Lynn J. Frazier of North Dakota, Charles L. McNary of Oregon, Henry F. Ashurst of Arizona, C. C. Dill of Washington, and Robert L. Owen of Oklahoma—all participants in the progressive movement of the early 1920s.[17] Granting blanket citizenship appealed to the progressive senators because it prevented abuse of citizenship regulations by the Interior Department or the Bureau of Indian Affairs.

### Indian Citizenship Act

Be it enacted…that all non-citizen Indians born within the territorial limits of the United States be, and they are hereby, declared to be citizens of the United States: *Provided*, That the granting of such citizenship shall not in any manner impair or otherwise affect the right of any Indian to tribal or other property.[18]

The Indian Citizenship Act was supported by all major Indian organizations (by this time the Society of American Indians was essentially inactive) and passed smoothly through Congress. The bill passed the Senate on May 15, 1924 and the House on May 23; it was presented to the president on May 26, 1924. Calvin Coolidge signed it into law on June 2, 1924.[19] The bill granted all native-born Indians citizenship without affecting any rights to tribal or individual property. The only requisite is that individuals have to meet state suffrage requirements. Thus an Indian tribal member has dual citizenship, a fact that is evident when you visit reservations and see both tribal and American flags flying.

Charles H. Burke, commissioner of Indian affairs from 1921 to 1929, defined the extent of the 1924 citizenship act. The Indian Bureau made it clear that federal authority would continue over unallotted lands or allotted Indians still in the trust period. At the same time, all Indians were encouraged to register to vote; however, Arizona and New Mexico did not allow Indians to vote until 1948 when federal suits successfully challenged state laws.

Frank Harrison and Harry Austin, Fort McDowell Yavapai World War II veterans, tried to vote in Maricopa County in 1947, but their registration was refused by the County Recorder who cited a 1928 ruling by the Arizona Supreme Court that the federal trust relationship was a guardianship, and this implied an inability to carry out the functions of citizens.[20] Harrison, supported by the National Congress of American Indians and the federal Justice and Interior Departments, appealed to the Arizona Supreme Court. The court ruled on July 15, 1948, that the Indians were not under a judicially established guardianship but in a relationship designed to protect Indians, and, therefore, the right to vote was ensured by the Fifteenth Amendment, another story with a Yavapai victory.[21]

# Epilogue

**An Evening's Reverie**
by
Carlos Montezuma
(date unknown)

*I sit in thought at my window
And I look far over the town,
To the distant sky in the westward
Where the sun has just gone down.*

*I see its tinted reflections
On the clouds in the far off west,
That it left in its downward progress
As it silently sank to rest.*

*Though tired and weary from labor,
Yet the thoughts come fluttering by
That resemble the brilliant reflections
That are left on the far off sky.*

*And like the sun before me
Who has gone its sunny way,
So I leave behind in the darkness
The cares and thoughts of the day.*

*I turn like him in his progress
To another inviting clime,
To another field of labor
To the field of the muse and rhyme.*

*But this thought crowds upon me,
Oh! How like life is a day
With its first sweet glow of the morning
Then it silently steals away.*

*The hopes, the longings, the fancies,*
*They come and they go so fast,*
*That a life's work is scarcely founded*
*Til the man of life is past.*

*Then help me Oh! Our Father*
*For the work that we are to do,*
*To be both earnest and faithful*
*To work for the good and true.*[1]

EVERY PERSON has a story. Within that story, a major force can often be identified that proves to be a deciding factor in the direction of a life. The influence is frequently a parent, either acting as a caring guide or sometimes with behavior that evokes an antithetical response. Some individuals are fortunate to follow the path of a wise and considerate mentor. Or there is an experience that becomes an epiphany, a revelation of inner strengths and purpose or a motivation to pursue a life dedication. Montezuma had no parent during his formative years. His friendships were many, but only Carlo Gentile and Reverend Stedman were in place at a critical time to exert an influence. However, they were limited by a relatively short duration of interaction. Montezuma was an energetic man of honor. He lived a life of decency, responsibility, and honesty that deserved admiration; he was a man who kept his word. The force within Montezuma that formed his life was his identity as an American Indian. In 1912, he took the floor during a discussion period at the meeting of the Society of American Indians and said: "If I should do anything disgraceful in my life or practice, it would reflect as a wrong to my people, and I have lived within the law's limit to this date."[2] It was not a simple commitment; it was total and passionate dedication that empowered Montezuma to make others of his race proud of him, to direct his abilities to helping the American Indian, to never deny who he was, to behave in a way that made him worthy as a hero.

What is a hero? It seems to me that a hero is someone who elevates one's inner self. It is someone with a sincere goodness, with substantial accomplishments without sacrifice of generosity or compassion. A hero is almost never, if ever, disappointing; there is a consistency of behavior that can be relied upon to triumph over wrongs. This requires physical presence and mental strength because there is always physical and mental risk in being this brave. These qualities carry others to a higher level, inspiring others to persevere, to live a better life. No one seeks to be a hero, nor does one decide to be a hero; it just happens. Carlos Montezuma was a Yavapai and is a genuine American hero. He was a hero to his many friends and patients, even Zitkala-Ša. He was a hero, an inspiration to countless young Indians who met him, read about him, or heard him speak. He even had children named after him.[3] He received a huge number of unsolicited letters from Indians and Whites who were encouraged or inspired by his words printed in various newspapers in the country. He was a hero to the Fort McDowell Yavapai; their allegiance and affection are his lasting tributes. He was a hero in American history, playing a pivotal role in shaping events. He is the hero of this book, not to be forgotten.

# Chapter References

**CHAPTER ONE**

1. **Corbusier WT,** *Verde to San Carlos. Recollections of a Famous Army Surgeon and His Observant Family on the Western Frontier 1869-1886,* Six Shooter Gulch, Tucson, Arizona, 1968.

2. **Larner JW, Jr.,** The Papers of Carlos Montezuma, Microfilm Edition, *Scholarly Resources, Inc., Wilmington, Delaware,* 1984, Reel 2, October 7, 1905.

3. **Russell F,** (The Bureau of American Ethnology), The Pima Indians, Report No. 26th Annual, 1908, **Schroeder AH,** A Study of Yavapai History. Commission Findings, In: Horr DA, ed. *Yavapai Indians,* Garland Publishing Inc., New York, 1974, p. 193.

4. **Larner JW, Jr.,** The Papers of Carlos Montezuma, Microfilm Edition, *Scholarly Resources, Inc., Wilmington, Delaware,* 1984, Reel 2, October 7, 1905.

5. Ibid., Reel 2, October 7, 1905, **Montezuma C,** Letter to William H. Holmes, The Smithsonian Institution, *National Anthropological Archives,* 1905, **Davis C,** (National Archives and Record Services Record Group 75, Bureau of Indian Affairs, San Carlos Central Classified Files, 1907-1939), Testimony Regarding Montezuma's Family, March 20, 1922, Report No. 45642-20-053, **Arnold O,** *Savage Son,* University of New Mexico Press, Albuquerque, 1951, **Montezuma Collection, Arizona State University.** *MSS-60, CMC, Box 2, Folder 5,* Davis interview with Hiram Ward.

6. **Larner JW, Jr.,** The Papers of Carlos Montezuma, Microfilm Edition, *Scholarly Resources, Inc., Wilmington, Delaware,* 1984, Reel 7, Hearings Before the Committee on Expenditures in the Interior Department, June 5-17, 1911, **Maher RC,** Carlos Montezuma M.D. The Saga of Wassaja, *Arizona Highways* 16:18-19, 35-36, 1940, **Robinson B,** The Great Yavapai, *Arizona Highways* 28:14-17, 1952.

7. **Montezuma C,** *The Indian of Yesterday. The Early Life of Dr. Carlos Montezuma,* The National Woman's Christian Temperance Union, 1888, Available in Larner JW, Jr., The Papers of Carlos Montezuma, Microfilm Edition, *Scholarly Resources, Inc., Wilmington, Delaware,* 1984.

8. **Clark NM,** Dr. Montezuma, Apache: Warrior in Two Worlds, Based on an Interview in 1921, *Montana: The Magazine of Western History* 23:56-65, 1973.

9. **Epple AO,** *A Field Guide to the Plants of Arizona,* Falcon Publishing, Inc., Helena, Montana, 1995.

10. **Schroeder AH,** A Study of Yavapai History. Commission Findings, In: Horr DA, ed. *Yavapai Indians,* Garland Publishing Inc., New York, 1974, p. 33.

11. **Hodge FW,** ed. *Handbook of American Indians North of Mexico, Smithsonian Institution Bureau of American Ethnology, Bulletin 30, 2 Volumes,* Government Printing Office, 1912, reprinted by Scholarly Press, Gross Pointe, Michigan, 1968.

12. **Schroeder AH,** A Study of Yavapai History. Commission Findings, In: Horr DA, ed. *Yavapai Indians,* Garland Publishing Inc., New York, 1974, pp. 23-354.

13. **Ruland-Thorne K,** *Yavapai, The People of the Red Rocks, The People of the Sun,* Thorne Enterprises Publications, Inc., Sedona, Arizona, 1993, **Harrison M, Williams J,** How Everything Began and How We Learned to Live Right, In: Chaudhuri JO, ed. *The Yavapai of Fort McDowell,* Mead Publishing, Mesa, Arizona, 1995, pp. 40-46.

14. **Hodge FW,** ed. *Handbook of American Indians North of Mexico, Smithsonian Institution Bureau of American Ethnology, Bulletin 30, 2 Volumes,* Government Printing Office, 1912, reprinted by Scholarly Press, Gross Pointe, Michigan, 1968.

15. **Kelly WH,** *Indians of the Southwest. A Survey of Indian Tribes and Indian Administration in Arizona,* University of Arizona, Tucson, 1953, p. 2.

16. **Khera S,** The Yavapai: Who They Are and From Where They Come, In: Chaudhuri JO, ed. *The Yavapai of Fort McDowell,* Mead Publishing, Mesa, Arizona, 1995, pp. 1-16.

17. **Schroeder AH,** A Study of Yavapai History. Commission Findings, In: Horr DA, ed. *Yavapai Indians,* Garland Publishing Inc., New York, 1974, p. 50.

18. **Schroeder AH,** *Apache Indians. A Study of the Apache Indians, Parts I, II, and III,* Garland Publishing Inc., New York, 1974, pp. 21-25. **Schroeder AH,** A Study of Yavapai History. Commission Findings, In: Horr DA, ed. *Yavapai Indians,* Garland Publishing Inc., New York, 1974, p. 256, Ibid., pp. 23-354.

19. **Schroeder AH,** *Apache Indians. A Study of the Apache Indians, Parts I, II, and III,* Garland Publishing Inc., New York, 1974, pp. 40-41.

20. **Schroeder AH,** A Study of Yavapai History. Commission Findings, In: Horr DA, ed. *Yavapai Indians,* Garland Publishing Inc., New York, 1974, pp. 23-354, **Schroeder AH,** *A Study of Yavapai History. Part I,* Original Copy, Occidental College Library, Los Angeles, Santa Fe, New Mexico, 1959, **Schroeder AH,** *A Study of Yavapai History, Part II,* Original Copy, Occidental College Library, Los Angeles, Sante Fe, New Mexico, 1959, **Schroeder AH,** *A Study of Yavapai History, Part III, Appendices & Bibliography,* Original Copy, Occidental College Library, Los Angeles, Sante Fe, New Mexico, 1959, pp. 57-59

21. **Schroeder AH,** *A Study of Yavapai History. Part I,* Original Copy, Occidental College Library, Los Angeles, Santa Fe, New Mexico, 1959.

22. **Hodge FW,** ed. *Handbook of American Indians North of Mexico, Smithsonian Institution Bureau of American Ethnology, Bulletin 30, 2 Volumes,* Government Printing Office, 1912, reprinted by Scholarly Press, Gross Pointe, Michigan, 1968.

23. **Schroeder AH,** *Apache Indians. A Study of the Apache Indians, Parts I, II, and III,* Garland Publishing Inc., New York, 1974, p. 31.

24. **Gifford EW,** The Southeastern Yavapai, *University of California Publications in American Archaeology* 29:177-252, 1932, p. 180.

25. **Corbusier WT,** *Verde to San Carlos. Recollections of a Famous Army Surgeon and His Observant Family on the Western Frontier 1869-1886,* Six Shooter Gulch, Tucson, Arizona, 1968, **Corbusier WH,** The Apache-Yumas and Apache-Mojaves, *American Antiquarian* 8:276-284, 325-339, 1886.

26. **Gifford EW,** The Southeastern Yavapai, *University of California Publications in American Archaeology* 29:177-252, 1932.

27. **Schroeder AH,** A Study of Yavapai History. Commission Findings, In: Horr DA, ed. *Yavapai Indians,* Garland Publishing Inc., New York, 1974, pp. 23-354, **Schroeder AH,** *A Study of Yavapai History. Part I,* Original Copy, Occidental College Library, Los Angeles, Santa Fe, New Mexico, 1959, **Schroeder AH,** *A Study of Yavapai History, Part II,* Original Copy, Occidental College Library, Los Angeles, Sante Fe, New Mexico, 1959, **Schroeder AH,** *A Study of Yavapai History, Part III, Appendices & Bibliography,* Original Copy, Occidental College Library, Los Angeles, Sante Fe, New Mexico, 1959.

28. **Corbusier WT,** *Verde to San Carlos. Recollections of a Famous Army Surgeon and His Observant Family on the Western Frontier 1869-1886,* Six Shooter Gulch, Tucson, Arizona, 1968, **Khera S,** The Yavapai: Who They Are and From Where They Come, In: Chaudhuri JO, ed. *The Yavapai of Fort McDowell,* Mead Publishing, Mesa, Arizona, 1995, pp. 1-16, **Corbusier WH,** The Apache-Yumas and Apache-Mojaves, *American Antiquarian* 8:276-284, 325-339, 1886.

29. **Corbusier WT,** *Verde to San Carlos. Recollections of a Famous Army Surgeon and His Observant Family on the Western Frontier 1869-1886*, Six Shooter Gulch, Tucson, Arizona, 1968, p. 35, **Corbusier WH,** The Apache-Yumas and Apache-Mojaves, *American Antiquarian* 8:276-284, 325-339, 1886.

30. **Corbusier WH,** The Apache-Yumas and Apache-Mojaves, *American Antiquarian* 8:276-284, 325-339, 1886.

31. **Gifford EW,** The Southeastern Yavapai, *University of California Publications in American Archaeology* 29:177-252, 1932, p. 222.

32. **Corbusier WH,** The Apache-Yumas and Apache-Mojaves, *American Antiquarian* 8:276-284, 325-339, 1886.

33. **Gifford EW,** The Southeastern Yavapai, *University of California Publications in American Archaeology* 29:177-252, 1932, p. 232, **Corbusier WH,** The Apache-Yumas and Apache-Mojaves, *American Antiquarian* 8:276-284, 325-339, 1886.

34. **Mariella PS,** The Political Economy of Federal Resettlement Policies Affecting Native American Communities: the Fort McDowell Yavapai Case, Dissertation for Doctor of Philosophy, Arizona State University, 1983, **Mariella P,** Yavapai Farming, In: Chaudhuri JO, ed. *The Yavapai of Fort McDowell*, Mead Publishing, Mesa, Arizona, 1995, pp. 28-35.

35. **Schroeder AH,** A Study of Yavapai History. Commission Findings, In: Horr DA, ed. *Yavapai Indians*, Garland Publishing Inc., New York, 1974, pp. 23-354, **Schroeder AH,** *A Study of Yavapai History. Part I*, Original Copy, Occidental College Library, Los Angeles, Santa Fe, New Mexico, 1959.

36. **Gifford EW,** The Southeastern Yavapai, *University of California Publications in American Archaeology* 29:177-252, 1932, pp. 206-207, **Corbusier WH,** The Apache-Yumas and Apache-Mojaves, *American Antiquarian* 8:276-284, 325-339, 1886.

37. **Gifford EW,** The Southeastern Yavapai, *University of California Publications in American Archaeology* 29:177-252, 1932, p. 205.

38. Ibid., p. 182.

39. **McCarty T**, Yavapai Weapons and Games, In: Chaudhuri JO, ed. *The Yavapai of Fort McDowell*, Mead Publishing, Mesa, Arizona, 1995, pp. 52-62.

40. **Schroeder AH,** *Apache Indians. A Study of the Apache Indians, Parts I, II, and III*, Garland Publishing Inc., New York, 1974, p. 4, **Schroeder AH,** A Study of Yavapai History. Commission Findings, In: Horr DA, ed. *Yavapai Indians*, Garland Publishing Inc., New York, 1974, p. 30.

41. **Weir JA,** Army Medicine on the Western Frontier, *U.S. Army Military History Institute, Carlisle Barracks, Pennsylvania*, 1973.

42. **Corbusier WT,** *Verde to San Carlos. Recollections of a Famous Army Surgeon and His Observant Family on the Western Frontier 1869-1886*, Six Shooter Gulch, Tucson, Arizona, 1968.

43. **Waterstrat E,** *Hoomothya's Long Journey 1865-1897*, Mount McDowell Press, Fountain Hills, Arizona, 1998, p. 76.

44. Ibid.

45. **Bourke JG,** *On the Border With Crook*, University of Nebraska Press, Lincoln, 1891, reprinted 1971, p. 188, **Waterstrat E,** *Hoomothya's Long Journey 1865-1897*, Mount McDowell Press, Fountain Hills, Arizona, 1998, pp. 53-59.

46. **Bourke JG,** *On the Border With Crook*, University of Nebraska Press, Lincoln, 1891, reprinted 1971, pp. 190-201, **Waterstrat E,** *Commanders and Chiefs. A Brief History of Fort McDowell, Arizona (1865-1890), Its Officers and Men and the Indians They Were Ordered To Subdue*, Mount McDowell Press, Fountain Hills, Arizona, 1992, pp. 58-59.

47. **Britten TA,** *American Indians in World War I. At Home and at War,* University of New Mexico Press, Albuquerque, 1997, p. 12.

48. **Corbusier WH,** The Apache-Yumas and Apache-Mojaves, *American Antiquarian* 8:276-284, 325-339, 1886.

49. Ibid.

50. **Corbusier WT,** *Verde to San Carlos. Recollections of a Famous Army Surgeon and His Observant Family on the Western Frontier 1869-1886,* Six Shooter Gulch, Tucson, Arizona, 1968.

51. **Prucha FP,** *The Great Father. The United States Government and the American Indians, Abridged Edition,* University of Nebraska Press, Lincoln, 1986, pp. 72-77, 85-87.

52. **Indian Removal Act, U. S. Statutes at Large 4:411-412, May 28, 1830,** In: Prucha FP, ed. *Documents of United States Indian Policy, 2nd Edition,* University of Nebraska Press, Lincoln, 1990, pp. 52-53.

53. **Cherokee Nation v. Georgia, Peters 5:15-20, 1831,** Ibid., pp. 58-59, **Worcester v. Georgia, Peters 6:534-536, 558-563, 1832,** Ibid., pp. 58-60.

54. **Waldman C,** *Atlas of the North American Indian,* Facts On File, Inc., New York, 2000.

55. **Thornton R,** *American Indian Holocaust and Survival. A Population History Since 1492,* University of Oklahoma Press, Norman, 1987, pp. 114-118.

56. Ibid.

57. **Stuart P,** *Nations Within a Nation. Historical Statistics of American Indians,* Greenwood Press, New York, 1987.

58. **Curtis Act, U. S. Statutes at Large 30:497-498, 502, 504-505, June 28, 1898,** In: Prucha FP, ed. *Documents of United States Indian Policy, 2nd Edition,* University of Nebraska Press, Lincoln, 1990, pp. 197-198.

59. **Seymour FW,** *Indian Agents of the Old Frontier,* Octagon Books, New York, 1941, reprinted 1975.

60. **Collier J,** *From Every Zenith. A Memoir and Some Essays on Life and Thought,* Sage Books, Denver, 1963, p. 130.

61. **Spicer EH,** *A Short History of the Indians of the United States,* D. Van Nostrand Company, reprinted by Robert E. Krieger Publishing Company, Inc., Malabar, Florida, 1983.

62. **Hagan WT,** *American Indians,* Third Edition, The University of Chicago Press, Chicago, 1993, p. 135.

63. **Gallaher RA,** The Indian Agent in the United States Since 1850, *Iowa Journal of History and Politics* April:173-238, 1916.

64. Ibid.

65. Ibid.

66. **Schroeder AH,** *A Study of Yavapai History. Part I,* Original Copy, Occidental College Library, Los Angeles, Santa Fe, New Mexico, 1959.

67. **Ruland-Thorne K,** *Yavapai, The People of the Red Rocks, The People of the Sun,* Thorne Enterprises Publications, Inc., Sedona, Arizona, 1993.

68. **Mariella PS,** The Political Economy of Federal Resettlement Policies Affecting Native American Communities: the Fort McDowell Yavapai Case, Dissertation for Doctor of Philosophy, Arizona State University, 1983.

69. **Schroeder AH,** A Study of Yavapai History. Commission Findings, In: Horr DA, ed. *Yavapai Indians,* Garland Publishing Inc., New York, 1974, p. 118.

70. **Ruland-Thorne K,** *Yavapai, The People of the Red Rocks, The People of the Sun,* Thorne Enterprises Publications, Inc., Sedona, Arizona, 1993, p. 27, **Waterstrat E,** *Hoomothya's Long Journey 1865-1897,* Mount McDowell Press, Fountain Hills, Arizona, 1998, p. 21.

71. **Ruland-Thorne K,** *Yavapai, The People of the Red Rocks, The People of the Sun,* Thorne Enterprises Publications, Inc., Sedona, Arizona, 1993, p. 27.

72. **Goff JS,** *King S. Woolsey,* Black Mountain Press, Cave Creek, Arizona, 1981.

73. **Ruland-Thorne K,** *Yavapai, The People of the Red Rocks, The People of the Sun,* Thorne Enterprises Publications, Inc., Sedona, Arizona, 1993, p. 28.

74. **Schroeder AH,** A Study of Yavapai History. Commission Findings, In: Horr DA, ed. *Yavapai Indians,* Garland Publishing Inc., New York, 1974, p. 40.

75. Ibid., p. 43.

76. **Ruland-Thorne K,** *Yavapai, The People of the Red Rocks, The People of the Sun,* Thorne Enterprises Publications, Inc., Sedona, Arizona, 1993, p. 31.

77. **Corbusier WT,** *Verde to San Carlos. Recollections of a Famous Army Surgeon and His Observant Family on the Western Frontier 1869-1886,* Six Shooter Gulch, Tucson, Arizona, 1968, pp. 265-281, **Bronson L,** The Long Walk of the Yavapai, *Wassaja, The Indian Historian* 13:37-43, 1980.

78. **Schroeder AH,** A Study of Yavapai History. Commission Findings, In: Horr DA, ed. *Yavapai Indians,* Garland Publishing Inc., New York, 1974, p. 124.

79. **Hagan WT,** *Indian Police and Judges. Experiments in Acculturation and Control,* Yale University Press, New Haven, 1966, pp. 25-34.

80. **Schroeder AH,** A Study of Yavapai History. Commission Findings, In: Horr DA, ed. *Yavapai Indians,* Garland Publishing Inc., New York, 1974, pp. 23-354, p. 126.

81. **Corbusier WH,** The Apache-Yumas and Apache-Mojaves, *American Antiquarian* 8:276-284, 325-339, 1886.

82. **Schmitt MF,** ed. *General George Crook. His Autobiography,* University of Oklahoma Norman, 1946, reprinted 1960, pp. 243-244.

83. Ibid., p. 255.

84. **Mariella PS,** The Political Economy of Federal Resettlement Policies Affecting Native American Communities: the Fort McDowell Yavapai Case, Dissertation for Doctor of Philosophy, Arizona State University, 1983.

## CHAPTER TWO

1. **Montezuma C,** *The Indian of Yesterday. The Early Life of Dr. Carlos Montezuma,* The National Woman's Christian Temperance Union, 1888, Available in Larner JW, Jr., The Papers of Carlos Montezuma, Microfilm Edition, *Scholarly Resources, Inc., Wilmington, Delaware,* 1984, **Montezuma C,** Letter to William H. Holmes, the Smithsonian Institution, *National Anthropological Archives,* 1905, **Clark NM,** Dr. Montezuma, Apache: Warrior in Two Worlds, Based on an Interview in 1921, *Montana: The Magazine of Western History* 23:56-65, 1973, **Larner JW, Jr.,** The Papers of Carlos Montezuma, Microfilm Edition, *Scholarly Resources, Inc., Wilmington, Delaware,* 1984, Reel 2, October 7, 1905.

2. **Dunn JP, Jr.,** *Massacres of the Mountains: A History of the Indian Wars of the Far West,* 1815-1875, Harper & Brothers, New York, 1886, reprinted 1958, Archer House, Inc., New York.

3. **Montezuma C,** *The Indian of Yesterday. The Early Life of Dr. Carlos Montezuma,* The National Woman's Christian Temperance Union, 1888, Available in Larner JW, Jr., The Papers of Carlos Montezuma, Microfilm Edition, *Scholarly Resources, Inc., Wilmington, Delaware,* 1984, **Arnold O,** *Savage Son,* University of New Mexico Press, Albuquerque, 1951, **Brown OH,** Carlos Montezuma, M.D., *Southwestern Medicine* November:400-404, 1937.

4. **Montezuma C,** *The Indian of Yesterday. The Early Life of Dr. Carlos Montezuma,* The National Woman's Christian Temperance Union, 1888, Available in Larner JW, Jr., The Papers of Carlos Montezuma, Microfilm Edition, *Scholarly Resources, Inc., Wilmington, Delaware,* 1984.

5. **Clark NM,** Dr. Montezuma, Apache: Warrior in Two Worlds, Based on an Interview in 1921, *Montana: The Magazine of Western History* 23:56-65, 1973, **Larner JW, Jr.,** The Papers of Carlos Montezuma, Microfilm Edition, *Scholarly Resources, Inc., Wilmington, Delaware,* 1984, Reel 2, October 7, 1905.

6. **Montezmua. Gentile's Little Indian Protegé,** *The Chicago Tribune,* March 21, 1875.

7. Ibid.

8. **Montezuma C,** *The Indian of Yesterday. The Early Life of Dr. Carlos Montezuma,* The National Woman's Christian Temperance Union, 1888, Available in Larner JW, Jr., The Papers of Carlos Montezuma, Microfilm Edition, *Scholarly Resources, Inc., Wilmington, Delaware,* 1984, **Larner JW, Jr.,** The Papers of Carlos Montezuma, Microfilm Edition, *Scholarly Resources, Inc., Wilmington, Delaware,* 1984, Reel 2, October 7, 1905, Reel 5, November 13, 1920, **Dr. Carlos Montezuma. A Bright and Well Educated Apache With an Interesting History,** *Arizona Republican,* October 11, 1901.

9. **Montezuma C,** *The Indian of Yesterday. The Early Life of Dr. Carlos Montezuma,* The National Woman's Christian Temperance Union, 1888, Available in Larner JW, Jr., The Papers of Carlos Montezuma, Microfilm Edition, *Scholarly Resources, Inc., Wilmington, Delaware,* 1984.

10. **Montezmua. Gentile's Little Indian Protegé,** *The Chicago Tribune,* March 21, 1875.

11. **Larner JW, Jr.,** The Papers of Carlos Montezuma, Microfilm Edition, *Scholarly Resources, Inc., Wilmington, Delaware,* 1984, Reel 1.

12. **Clark NM,** Dr. Montezuma, Apache: Warrior in Two Worlds, Based on an Interview in 1921, *Montana: The Magazine of Western History* 23:56-65, 1973.

13. **Larner JW, Jr.,** Supplement to the Papers of Carlos Montezuma, Microfilm Edition, *Scholarly Resources, Inc., Wilmington, Delaware,* 2002, Reel 1, June, 1898.

14. **Marino C,** *The Remarkable Carlo Gentile,* Carl Mautz Publishing, Nevada City, California, 1998.

15. **King Freezy,** *Daily British Colonist,* February 2, 1864.

16. **Mattison D,** The Victoria Theatre Photographic Gallery (and the Gallery Next Door), *British Columbia Historical News* 14:1-14, 1980.

17. *Daily British Colonist,* October 27, 1866.

18. **Montezmua. Gentile's Little Indian Protegé,** *The Chicago Tribune,* March 21, 1875.

19. **Lockwood FC,** *Pioneer Portraits: Selected Vignettes,* University of Arizona Press, Tucson, 1968.

20. **Marino C,** *The Remarkable Carlo Gentile,* Carl Mautz Publishing, Nevada City, California, 1998.

21. **Larner JW, Jr.,** The Papers of Carlos Montezuma, Microfilm Edition, *Scholarly Resources, Inc., Wilmington, Delaware,* 1984, Reel 2, October 7, 1905.

22. **Arnold O,** *Savage Son,* University of New Mexico Press, Albuquerque, 1951.

23. **Barnes WC,** *Life of Carlos Montezuma (Unpublished Manuscript),* Will C. Barnes Collection, Arizona Historical Foundation, Arizona State University, 1934.

24. **Arnold AR,** *Red Son Rising,* Dillon Press, Inc., Minneapolis, Minnesota, 1974.

25. **Montezuma C,** *The Indian of Yesterday. The Early Life of Dr. Carlos Montezuma,* The National Woman's Christian Temperance Union, 1888, Available in Larner JW, Jr., The Papers of Carlos Montezuma, Microfilm Edition, *Scholarly Resources, Inc., Wilmington, Delaware,* 1984.

26. **Larner JW, Jr.,** Supplement to the Papers of Carlos Montezuma, Microfilm Edition, *Scholarly Resources, Inc., Wilmington, Delaware,* 2002, Reel 1.

27. Ibid.

28. Ibid., Reel 1, March 12, 1901.

29. Ibid., Reel 8, April 8, 1901.

30. **Larner JW, Jr.,** The Papers of Carlos Montezuma, Microfilm Edition, *Scholarly Resources, Inc., Wilmington, Delaware,* 1984, Reel 2, October 7, 1905.

31. **Church of the Assumption, Florence, Arizona,** Baptism Register No. 1, p. 14, 1871, Donald P. Brosnan, Archivist/Historian, Diocese of Tucson, 2002.

32. Ibid.

33. **Montezuma C,** *The Indian of Yesterday. The Early Life of Dr. Carlos Montezuma,* The National Woman's Christian Temperance Union, 1888, Available in Larner JW, Jr., The Papers of Carlos Montezuma, Microfilm Edition, *Scholarly Resources, Inc., Wilmington, Delaware,* 1984, **Montezuma C,** From an Apache Camp to a Chicago Medical College: The Story of Carlos Montezuma's Life as Told by Himself, *The Red Man* 8:3, 6, 1888.

34. **Montezuma C,** From an Apache Camp to a Chicago Medical College: The Story of Carlos Montezuma's Life as Told by Himself, *The Red Man* 8:3, 6, 1888.

35. **Montezuma C,** *The Indian of Yesterday. The Early Life of Dr. Carlos Montezuma,* The National Woman's Christian Temperance Union, 1888, Available in Larner JW, Jr., The Papers of Carlos Montezuma, Microfilm Edition, *Scholarly Resources, Inc., Wilmington, Delaware,* 1984.

36. **Russell D,** *The Wild West. A History of the Wild West Shows,* Amon Carter Museum of Western Art, Fort Worth, Texas, 1970, **Burke J,** *Buffalo Bill. The Noblest Whiteskin,* G. P. Putnam's Sons, New York, 1973, **Carter RA,** *Buffalo Bill Cody. The Man Behind the Legend,* John Wiley & Sons, Inc., New York, 2000.

37. **Carter RA,** *Buffalo Bill Cody. The Man Behind the Legend,* John Wiley & Sons, Inc., New York, 2000, p. 93.

38. Ibid., p. 110.

39. Ibid., p. 174.

40. Ibid., p. 143.

41. **Marino C,** *The Remarkable Carlo Gentile,* Carl Mautz Publishing, Nevada City, California, 1998, p. 45.

42. **Larner JW, Jr.,** The Papers of Carlos Montezuma, Microfilm Edition, *Scholarly Resources, Inc., Wilmington, Delaware,* 1984, Reel 6, Autobiographical notes.

43. **Marino C,** *The Remarkable Carlo Gentile,* Carl Mautz Publishing, Nevada City, California, 1998.

44. **Carter RA,** *Buffalo Bill Cody. The Man Behind the Legend,* John Wiley & Sons, Inc., New York, 2000, p. 177.

45. Ibid., p. 200.

46. **Moses LG,** *Wild West Shows and the Images of American Indians, 1883-1933,* University of New Mexico Press, Albuquerque, 1996, p. 182.

47. **Ninety-Two Horses Killed. Col. Cody's Show Train Wrecked. Engineer Misread His Orders,** *Charlotte Daily Observer,* October 30, 1901.

48. **Deloria V, Jr.,** The Indians, *Buffalo Bill and the Wild West,* Falcon Press, Philadelphia, 1981, pp. 45-56.

49. **Moses LG,** *Wild West Shows and the Images of American Indians, 1883-1933,* University of New Mexico Press, Albuquerque, 1996, pp. 92-103, 108, 118, 122-124.

50. **Fritz HE,** *The Movement for Indian Assimilation, 1860–1890,* Greenwood Press, Publishers, Westport, Connecticut, 1963, reprinted 1981, pp. 56-183, **Prucha FP,** *The Great Father. The United States Government and the American Indians, Abridged Edition,* University of Nebraska Press, Lincoln, 1986, pp. 152-166.

51. **Treaty of Fort Laramie, April 29, 1868,** In: Prucha FP, ed. *Documents of United States Indian Policy, 2nd Edition,* University of Nebraska Press, Lincoln, 1990, pp. 110-114.

52. **Hoxie FE,** *A Final Promise: The Campaign to Assimilate the Indians, 1880-1920,* University of Nebraska Press, Lincoln, 1984, p. 45.

53. **Prucha FP,** *The Great Father. The United States Government and the American Indians, Abridged Edition,* University of Nebraska Press, Lincoln, 1986, pp. 78-93.

54. Ibid., pp. 213-214.

55. **Hyde GE,** *A Sioux Chronicle,* University of Oklahoma Press, Norman, 1956.

56. **Thornton R,** *American Indian Holocaust and Survival. A Population History Since 1492,* University of Oklahoma Press, Norman, 1987, **Stuart P,** *Nations Within a Nation. Historical Statistics of American Indians,* Greenwood Press, New York, 1987, **U.S. Census Bureau,** The American Indian and Alaska Native Population: 2000, *www.census.gov/prod/2002pubs/c2kbr01-15.pdf,* 2002.

57. **U.S. Census Bureau,** The American Indian and Alaska Native Population: 2000, *www.census.gov/prod/2002pubs/c2kbr01-15.pdf,* 2002.

58. **Martin DL, Goodman AH,** Health Conditions Before Columbus. The Paleopathology of Native North Americans, In: Rhoades ER, ed. *American Indian Health. Innovations in Health Care, Promotion, and Policy,* The Johns Hopkins University Press, Baltimore, 2000, p. 24.

59. **Daniel TM,** *Captain of Death. The Story of Tuberculosis,* University of Rochester Press, Rochester, 1997, p. 14, **Martin DL, Goodman AH,** Health Conditions Before Columbus. The Paleopathology of Native North Americans, In: Rhoades ER, ed. *American Indian Health. Innovations in Health Care, Promotion, and Policy,* The Johns Hopkins University Press, Baltimore, 2000, pp. 19-40, p. 30.

60. **Martin DL, Goodman AH,** Health Conditions Before Columbus. The Paleopathology of Native North Americans, In: Rhoades ER, ed. *American Indian Health. Innovations in Health Care, Promotion, and Policy,* The Johns Hopkins University Press, Baltimore, 2000, p. 34.

61. **Dobyns HE,** *Their Number Become Thinned. Native American Population Dynamics in Eastern North America,* The University of Tennessee Press, Knoxville, 1983, p. 343.

62. **Utley RM,** *The Last Days of the Sioux Nation,* Yale University Press, New Haven, 1963, pp. 60-83.

63. **Bailey P,** *Wovoka, The Indian Messiah,* Westernlore Press, Los Angeles, 1957.

64. **Utley RM,** *The Last Days of the Sioux Nation,* Yale University Press, New Haven, 1963, p. 73.

65. Ibid., **Mooney J,** *The Ghost-Dance Religion and the Sioux Outbreak of 1890, Fourteenth Annual Report of the Bureau of American Ethnology,* Government Printing Office, Washington, D.C., 1896, **Mooney J,** *The Ghost-Dance Religion and the Sioux Outbreak of 1890, Abridged Edition,* University of Chicago Press, Chicago, 1965, pp. 84-112.

66. **Feraca SE, Howard JH,** The Identity and Demography of the Dakota or Sioux Tribe, *Plains Anthropologist* 8:80-84, 1963.

67. **Utley RM,** *The Last Days of the Sioux Nation,* Yale University Press, New Haven, 1963, p. 6

68. Ibid., pp. 84-112.

69. Ibid., pp. 339-360.

70. Ibid., p. 20.

71. Ibid., p. 114.

72. Ibid., p. 125. **Carter RA,** *Buffalo Bill Cody. The Man Behind the Legend,* John Wiley & Sons, Inc., New York, 2000, p. 347.

73. **Carter RA,** *Buffalo Bill Cody. The Man Behind the Legend,* John Wiley & Sons, Inc., New York, 2000, p. 350.

74. **Utley RM,** *The Last Days of the Sioux Nation,* Yale University Press, New Haven, 1963, pp. 227-228.

75. **Wilson R,** *Ohiyesa. Charles Eastman, Santee Sioux,* University of Illinois Press, Urbana, 1983.

76. **Moses LG,** *Wild West Shows and the Images of American Indians, 1883-1933,* University of New Mexico Press, Albuquerque, 1996, p. 122.

## CHAPTER THREE

1. **Pratt RH,** *Battlefield and Classroom: Four Decades with the American Indian, 1867–1904,* Yale University Press, New Haven, 1964, p. 251.

2. **The Buffalo Soldier Project,** http://www.femalebuffalosoldier.org/, 2001.

3. **Hagan WT,** *American Indians,* Third Edition, The University of Chicago Press, Chicago, 1993.

4. **Pratt RH,** *Battlefield and Classroom: Four Decades with the American Indian, 1867–1904,* Yale University Press, New Haven, 1964, pp. 107-108, **Tousey TG,** *Military History of Carlisle and Carlisle Barracks,* The Dietz Press, Richmond, Virginia, 1939, pp. 278-280.

5. **Morton L,** How the Indians Came to Carlisle, *Pennsylvania History* 29:53-63, 1962.

6. Ibid.

7. **Pratt RH,** *Battlefield and Classroom: Four Decades with the American Indian, 1867–1904,* Yale University Press, New Haven, 1964, p. 219.

8. **House Report,** No. 29, p. 2: HR 1735.

9. **Tousey TG,** *Military History of Carlisle and Carlisle Barracks,* The Dietz Press, Richmond, Virginia, 1939.

10. **Pratt RH,** *Battlefield and Classroom: Four Decades with the American Indian, 1867–1904,* Yale University Press, New Haven, 1964, p. 230.

11. **Brunhouse RL,** The Founding of the Carlisle Indian School, *Pennsylvania History* 6:72-85, 1969.

12. **Bell G,** Telling Stories Out of School: Remembering the Carlisle Indian Industrial School, 1879-1918, Dissertation for the Degree of Doctor of Philosophy in Anthropology, Stanford, 1998, pp. 105-107.

13. **Larner JW, Jr.,** Supplement to the Papers of Carlos Montezuma, Microfilm Edition, *Scholarly Resources, Inc., Wilmington, Delaware,* 2002, Reel 1, February 26, 1902.

14. **Bell G,** Telling Stories Out of School: Remembering the Carlisle Indian Industrial School, 1879-1918, Dissertation for the Degree of Doctor of Philosophy in Anthropology, Stanford, 1998, p. 122.

15. Ibid., p. 77.

16. **Waterstrat E,** *Hoomothya's Long Journey 1865-1897*, Mount McDowell Press, Fountain Hills, Arizona, 1998, p. 169.

17. **Walker-McNeil PL,** The Carlisle Indian School. A Study of Acculturation, Dissertation for the Degree of Doctor of Philosophy in Anthropology, The American University, 1979.

18. **Standing Bear L,** *My People the Sioux*, University of Nebraska Press, Lincoln, 1928, reprinted 1975, pp. 137-138.

19. **Walker-McNeil PL,** The Carlisle Indian School. A Study of Acculturation. Dissertation for the Degree of Doctor of Philosophy in Anthropology, The American University, 1979.

20. **Adams DW,** *Education for Extinction. American Indians and the Boarding School Experience, 1875–1928*, University Press of Kansas, Lawrence, 1995, pp. 209-238.

21. **Trennert RA, Jr.,** *The Phoenix Indian School. Forced Assimilation in Arizona, 1891-1935*, University of Oklahoma Press, Norman, 1988, p. 126.

22. **Bell G,** Telling Stories Out of School: Remembering the Carlisle Indian Industrial School, 1879-1918, Dissertation for the Degree of Doctor of Philosophy in Anthropology, Stanford, 1998, pp. 209-248.

23. Ibid., p. 286.

24. **Adams DW,** *Education for Extinction. American Indians and the Boarding School Experience, 1875–1928*, University Press of Kansas, Lawrence, 1995, pp. 121-122.

25. **Walker-McNeil PL,** The Carlisle Indian School. A Study of Acculturation, Dissertation for the Degree of Doctor of Philosophy in Anthropology, The American University, 1979, p. 179.

26. Ibid., pp. 197-199.

27. **Bell G,** Telling Stories Out of School: Remembering the Carlisle Indian Industrial School, 1879-1918, Dissertation for the Degree of Doctor of Philosophy in Anthropology, Stanford, 1998, p. 128.

28. **Pratt RH,** *Battlefield and Classroom: Four Decades with the American Indian, 1867–1904*, Yale University Press, New Haven, 1964.

29. Ibid., p. 294.

30. Ibid., pp. 294-310.

31. **Rose JK,** World's Columbian Exposition: The Legacy of the Fair, *http://xroads.virginia.edu/*, 2001.

32. **Pratt RH,** *Battlefield and Classroom: Four Decades with the American Indian, 1867–1904*, Yale University Press, New Haven, 1964.

33. **Hyde GE,** *A Sioux Chronicle*, University of Oklahoma Press, Norman, 1956, pp. 51-57.

34. **Gilcreast EA,** Richard Henry Pratt and American Indian Policy, 1877-1906: A Study of the Assimilation Movement, Dissertation for the Degree of Doctor of Philosophy in History, Yale University, New Haven, Connecticut, 1967, p. 64.

35. **Pratt RH,** *Battlefield and Classroom: Four Decades with the American Indian, 1867–1904*, Yale University Press, New Haven, 1964, p. 239.

36. **Prucha FP,** *The Great Father. The United States Government and the American Indians, Abridged Edition*, University of Nebraska Press, Lincoln, 1986, p. 222.

37. **Gilcreast EA,** Richard Henry Pratt and American Indian Policy, 1877-1906: A Study of the Assimilation Movement, Dissertation for the Degree of Doctor of Philosophy in History, Yale University, New Haven, Connecticut, 1967, p. 109, **Adams DW,** *Education for Extinction. American Indians and the Boarding School Experience, 1875–1928*, University Press of Kansas, Lawrence, 1995, p. 58.

38. **Adams DW,** *Education for Extinction. American Indians and the Boarding School Experience, 1875–1928,* University Press of Kansas, Lawrence, 1995, p. 58.

39. **Gilcreast EA,** Richard Henry Pratt and American Indian Policy, 1877-1906: A Study of the Assimilation Movement, Dissertation for the Degree of Doctor of Philosophy in History, Yale University, New Haven, Connecticut, 1967.

40. **Adams DW,** *Education for Extinction. American Indians and the Boarding School Experience, 1875–1928,* University Press of Kansas, Lawrence, 1995, pp. 124-135, **Bell G,** Telling Stories Out of School: Remembering the Carlisle Indian Industrial School, 1879-1918. Dissertation for the Degree of Doctor of Philosophy in Anthropology, Stanford, 1998, p. 387.

41. **Hagan WT,** *Indian Police and Judges. Experiments in Acculturation and Control,* Yale University Press, New Haven, 1966, pp. 74-79.

42. **Adams DW,** *Education for Extinction. American Indians and the Boarding School Experience, 1875–1928,* University Press of Kansas, Lawrence, 1995, pp. 82-94.

43. **Vest GG,** *Congressional Record:*4067, May 12, 1984.

44. **Richard H. Pratt to Charles L. Hall,** Richard H. Pratt Papers, Beinecke Library, Yale University, September 17, 1895.

45. **Adams DW,** *Education for Extinction. American Indians and the Boarding School Experience, 1875–1928,* University Press of Kansas, Lawrence, 1995, p. 113.

46. Ibid., p. 300.

47. **Gilcreast EA,** Richard Henry Pratt and American Indian Policy, 1877-1906: A Study of the Assimilation Movement, Dissertation for the Degree of Doctor of Philosophy in History, Yale University, New Haven, Connecticut, 1967, pp. 135-135.

48. **Congressional Record,** March 10, 1886, pp. 2265 ff.

49. **Larner JW, Jr.,** The Papers of Carlos Montezuma, Microfilm Edition, *Scholarly Resources, Inc., Wilmington, Delaware,* 1984, Reel 1, March 3, 1892.

50. **Jackson H,** *A Century of Dishonor: A Sketch of the United States Government's Dealings with Some of the Indian Tribes,* Harper and Brothers, New York, 1881, reprinted by the University of Oklahoma Press, 1995.

51. **Prucha FP,** *The Great Father. The United States Government and the American Indians, Abridged Edition,* University of Nebraska Press, Lincoln, 1986, p. 208.

52. **Jackson H,** *A Century of Dishonor: A Sketch of the United States Government's Dealings with Some of the Indian Tribes,* Harper and Brothers, New York, 1881, reprinted by the University of Oklahoma Press, 1995, pp. 2-3

53. **Fritz HE,** *The Movement for Indian Assimilation, 1860–1890,* Greenwood Press, Publishers, Westport, Connecticut, 1963, reprinted 1981, pp. 186-197, **Prucha FP,** *The Great Father. The United States Government and the American Indians, Abridged Edition,* University of Nebraska Press, Lincoln, 1986, pp. 183-185, **Hoxie FE,** *A Final Promise: The Campaign to Assimilate the Indians, 1880-1920,* University of Nebraska Press, Lincoln, 1984, pp. 6-11, **Prucha FP,** *American Indian Policy in Crisis: Christian Reformers and the Indian, 1865–1900,* University of Oklahoma Press, Norman, 1976, pp. 113-119.

54. **Standing Bear v. Crook, May 12, 1879,** In: Prucha FP, ed. *Documents of United States Indian Policy,* 2nd ed. University of Nebraska Press, Lincoln, 1990, pp. 151-153.

55. **Thornton R,** *American Indian Holocaust and Survival. A Population History Since 1492,* University of Oklahoma Press, Norman, 1987, p. 58.

56. **Prucha FP,** *American Indian Policy in Crisis: Christian Reformers and the Indian, 1865–1900,* University of Oklahoma Press, Norman, 1976, pp. 138-143, **Hagan WT,** *The Indian Rights Association. The Herbert Welsh Years 1882–1904,* The University of Arizona Press, Tucson, 1985.

57. **Hagan WT,** *The Indian Rights Association. The Herbert Welsh Years 1882–1904,* The University of Arizona Press, Tucson, 1985.

58. **Prucha FP,** *American Indian Policy in Crisis: Christian Reformers and the Indian, 1865–1900,* University of Oklahoma Press, Norman, 1976, pp. 143-168.

59. **Partington FE,** *The Story of Mohonk,* The Morrill Press, Fulton, New York, 1911.

60. **Richard H. Pratt to Charles L. Hall,** Richard H. Pratt Papers, Beinecke Library, Yale University, September 17, 1895.

61. **Elk v. Wilkins, U. S. Supreme Court Reports, 112:98-99, 109, November 3, 1884,** In: Prucha FP, ed. *Documents of United States Indian Policy, 2nd Edition,* University of Nebraska Press, Lincoln, 1990, pp. 166-167.

62. **United States v. Kagama, U.S. Supreme Court Reports, 118:375, 382-185, May 10, 1886,** Ibid., pp. 168-169.

63. **General Allotment Act (Dawes Act), U.S. Statutes at Large 24:388-391, February 8, 1887,** Ibid., pp. 171-174.

64. **Hagan WT,** *American Indians,* Third Edition, The University of Chicago Press, Chicago, 1993, p. 165.

65. **Burke Act, U.S. Statutes at Large 34:182-183, May 8, 1906,** In: Prucha FP, ed. *Documents of United States Indian Policy, 2nd Edition,* University of Nebraska Press, Lincoln, 1990, p. 207.

66. **Blauch Educational Service for Indians,** Washington, D. C., 1939.

67. **Mead SE,** *The Lively Experiment. The Shaping of Christianity in America,* Harper & Row Publishers, New York, 1963.

68. **Carnegie A,** Wealth, *North American Review* June:653-664, 1889.

69. **Harrod HL,** *Mission Among the Blackfeet,* University of Oklahoma Press, Norman, 1971. [A description of the Blackfeet experience with the Christian missions in Montana.]

70. **Amendment to the Dawes Act, U. S. Statutes at Large 26:794-796, February 28, 1891,** In: Prucha FP, ed. *Documents of United States Indian Policy, 2nd Edition,* University of Nebraska Press, Lincoln, 1990, pp. 184-185.

71. **U. S. Statutes at Large,** 28:305, August 15, 1894.

72. **Mohonk Conference Proceedings:** pp. 48-52, 1895.

73. **Richard H. Pratt to Reverend T. S. Childs,** Richard H. Pratt Papers, Beinecke Library, Yale University, September 1, 1892.

74. **Larner JW, Jr.,** The Papers of Carlos Montezuma, Microfilm Edition, *Scholarly Resources, Inc., Wilmington, Delaware,* 1984, Reel 1, March 15, 1892.

75. Ibid., Reel 1.

76. **Office of Indian Affairs,** *28 Stat. L.,* 904:p. 212, 1901.

77. **39 Stat. L.,** 988, March 2, 1917.

78. **Bell G,** Telling Stories Out of School: Remembering the Carlisle Indian Industrial School, 1879-1918, Dissertation for the Degree of Doctor of Philosophy in Anthropology, Stanford, 1998, p. 331.

79. **Standing Bear L,** *My People the Sioux,* University of Nebraska Press, Lincoln, 1928, reprinted 1975.

80. **Ryan CS,** The Carlisle Indian Industrial School. Dissertation for the Degree of Philosophy, Georgetown University, Washington, D. C., 1962.

81. **The Red Man & Helper,** Richard H. Pratt Papers, Beinecke Library, Yale University, June 24-July 1, 1904.

82. **Larner JW, Jr.,** The Papers of Carlos Montezuma, Microfilm Edition, *Scholarly Resources, Inc., Wilmington, Delaware,* 1984, Reel 4, April 13, 1915.

83. Ibid., Reel 2, June 29, 1904.

84. Ibid.

85. Ibid., Reel 2, August 2, 1904.

86. Ibid., Reel 2, October 7, 1908.

87. Ibid., Reel 2, October, 1904.

88. Ibid., Reel 2, March 17, 1905.

89. Ibid., Reel 2, July 22, 1907.

90. Ibid., Reel 2, 1907.

91. Ibid., Reel 6, November 24, 1907.

92. Ibid., Reel 2, December 18, 1909.

93. Ibid., Reel 2, December 18, 1909.

94. Ibid., Reel 7.

95. Ibid., Reel 2, May 29, 1909.

96. **Powers FJ,** *The Life Story of Glen S. (Pop) Warner. Gridiron's Greatest Strategist,* The Athletic Institute, Chicago, 1969.

97. **Steckbeck JS,** *The Fabulous Redmen: The Carlisle Indians and Their Famous Football Teams,* Jack Horace McFarland, Harrisburg, Pennsylvania, 1951.

98. **Warner GS,** The Indian Massacres, *Collier's,* 88:61, October 17, 1931.

99. **Returned Student Survey,** Records of the Board of Indian Commissioners, *National Archives,* Group 75, Bulletin No. 57.

100. **Bell G,** Telling Stories Out of School: Remembering the Carlisle Indian Industrial School, 1879-1918, Dissertation for the Degree of Doctor of Philosophy in Anthropology, Stanford, 1998, p. 77.

101. **Collins CC,** The Broken Crucible of Assimilation. Forest Grove Indian School and the Origins of Off-reservation Boarding-school Education in the West, *Oregon Hist Quarterly* 101:466-507, 2001.

102. **Institute for Government Research,** *The Problem of Indian Administration,* Johns Hopkins University Press, Baltimore, 1928.

## CHAPTER FOUR

1. **Larner JW, Jr.,** Supplement to the Papers of Carlos Montezuma, Microfilm Edition, *Scholarly Resources, Inc., Wilmington, Delaware,* 2002, Reel 8.

2. **Montezuma C,** From an Apache Camp to a Chicago Medical College: The Story of Carlos Montezuma's Life as Told by Himself, *The Red Man* 8:3, 6, 1888, **Larner JW, Jr.,** The Papers of Carlos Montezuma, Microfilm Edition, *Scholarly Resources, Inc., Wilmington, Delaware,* 1984, Reel 1, 1887, Ibid., Reel 6, Autobiographical notes.

3. **Montezmua. Gentile's Little Indian Protegé,** *The Chicago Tribune,* March 21, 1875.

4. Ibid.

5. **Montezuma C,** From an Apache Camp to a Chicago Medical College: The Story of Carlos Montezuma's Life as Told by Himself, *The Red Man* 8:3, 6, 1888, **Montezuma C,** *The Indian of Yesterday. The Early Life of Dr. Carlos Montezuma,* The National Woman's Christian Temperance Union, 1888, Available in Larner JW, Jr., The Papers of Carlos Montezuma, Microfilm Edition, *Scholarly Resources, Inc., Wilmington, Delaware,* 1984.

6. **Montezuma C,** *The Indian of Yesterday. The Early Life of Dr. Carlos Montezuma,* The National Woman's Christian Temperance Union, 1888, Available in Larner JW, Jr.,The Papers of Carlos Montezuma, Microfilm Edition, *Scholarly Resources, Inc., Wilmington, Delaware,* 1984.

7. **Marino C,** *The Remarkable Carlo Gentile,* Carl Mautz Publishing, Nevada City, California, 1998.

8. **Larner JW, Jr.,** The Papers of Carlos Montezuma, Microfilm Edition, *Scholarly Resources, Inc., Wilmington, Delaware,* 1984, Reel 1, 1887.

9. **Montezuma C,** *The Indian of Yesterday. The Early Life of Dr. Carlos Montezuma,* The National Woman's Christian Temperance Union, 1888, Available in Larner JW, Jr., The Papers of Carlos Montezuma, Microfilm Edition, *Scholarly Resources, Inc., Wilmington, Delaware,* 1984.

10. **Hohler JS,** ed. *The Papers of Carlos Montezuma 1892-1937 (Microfilm Edition),* The State Historical Society of Wisconsin, Madison, 1975, Reel 1.

11. **Marino C,** *The Remarkable Carlo Gentile,* Carl Mautz Publishing, Nevada City, California, 1998.

12. **Arnold O,** *Savage Son,* University of New Mexico Press, Albuquerque, 1951.

13. **Marino C,** *The Remarkable Carlo Gentile,* Carl Mautz Publishing, Nevada City, California, 1998.

14. **Larner JW, Jr.,** The Papers of Carlos Montezuma, Microfilm Edition, *Scholarly Resources, Inc., Wilmington, Delaware,* 1984, Reel 7, Autobiographical notes.

15. **Ingalls GW,** Letter to President of YMCA of the Ill. Industrial University, October 16, 1878, *Chicago Historical Society,* Carlos Montezuma file.

16. Ibid.

17. **Hopkins CH,** *History of the Y.M.C.A. in North America,* Association Press, New York, 1951.

18. **YMCA,** A Brief History of the YMCA Movement, *www.ymca.net/about/cont/history.htm,* 2002.

19. **Mjagkij N, Spratt M,** Introduction, In: Mjagkij N, Spratt M, eds. *Men and Women Adrift. The YMCA and the YWCA in the City,* New York University Press, New York, 1997, pp. 1-21.

20. **Larner JW, Jr.,** The Papers of Carlos Montezuma, Microfilm Edition, *Scholarly Resources, Inc., Wilmington, Delaware,* 1984, Reel 2.

21. **Montezuma C,** *The Indian of Yesterday. The Early Life of Dr. Carlos Montezuma,* The National Woman's Christian Temperance Union, 1888, Available in Larner JW, Jr., The Papers of Carlos Montezuma, Microfilm Edition, *Scholarly Resources, Inc., Wilmington, Delaware,* 1984.

22. Ibid.

23. **Clark NM,** Dr. Montezuma, Apache: Warrior in Two Worlds, Based on an Interview in 1921, *Montana: The Magazine of Western History* 23:56-65, 1973.

24. **Solberg WU,** *The University of Illinois, 1867–1894: An Intellectual and Cultural History,* University of Illinois Press, Urbana, 1968, p. 235.

25. **Larner JW, Jr.,** The Papers of Carlos Montezuma, Microfilm Edition, *Scholarly Resources, Inc., Wilmington, Delaware,* 1984, Reel 7, Hearings Before the Committee on Expenditures in the Interior Department, June 5-17, 1911.

26. **Solberg WU,** *The University of Illinois, 1867–1894: An Intellectual and Cultural History,* University of Illinois Press, Urbana, 1968, p. 100.

27. **Morrill Act,** 12 Stat 503, 1862.

28. **Solberg WU,** *The University of Illinois, 1867–1894: An Intellectual and Cultural History,* University of Illinois Press, Urbana, 1968, pp. 226-227.

29. Ibid., pp. 233-234.

30. Ibid., p. 235.

31. Ibid.

32. **Hopkins CH,** *History of the Y.M.C.A. in North America,* Association Press, New York, 1951, pp. 271-308, **Solberg WU,** *The University of Illinois, 1867–1894: An Intellectual and Cultural History,* University of Illinois Press, Urbana, 1968, p. 180.

33. **Solberg WU,** *The University of Illinois, 1867–1894: An Intellectual and Cultural History,* University of Illinois Press, Urbana, 1968, p. 243.

34. Ibid., p. 249.

35. Ibid., pp. 274-326.

36. Ibid., pp. 215, 273.

37. Ibid., p. 283.

38. *The Illini,* October 1, 1883.

39. **Solberg WU,** *The University of Illinois, 1867–1894: An Intellectual and Cultural History,* University of Illinois Press, Urbana, 1968, p. 277.

40. Ibid., p. 300.

41. Ibid., p. 279.

42. Ibid., p. 219.

43. Ibid., p. 302.

44. Ibid., p. 303.

45. **Larner JW, Jr.,** The Papers of Carlos Montezuma, Microfilm Edition, *Scholarly Resources, Inc., Wilmington, Delaware,* 1984, Reel 5.

46. Ibid., Reel 5, *The Illini,* March 10, 1884.

47. Ibid., Reel 5.

48. *The Illini,* October 1, 1883.

49. **Larner JW, Jr.,** The Papers of Carlos Montezuma, Microfilm Edition, *Scholarly Resources, Inc., Wilmington, Delaware,* 1984, Reel 7, *The Illini,* May 5, 1883.

50. **Clark NM,** Dr. Montezuma, Apache: Warrior in Two Worlds, Based on an Interview in 1921, *Montana: The Magazine of Western History* 23:56-65, 1973.

51. **Montezuma C,** Light on the Indian Situation, *Quarterly J Soc Am Indians* 1:50-55, 1913.

52. **Marino C,** *The Remarkable Carlo Gentile,* Carl Mautz Publishing, Nevada City, California, 1998.

53. Ibid., pp. 60-67.

54. Ibid., p. 62.

55. **Summit L,** Montezuma, M.D., *Spectrum* 14:70-71, 1966, **Summit L,** The Strange Story of Dr. Carlos Montezuma, *Westerners Brand Book* 11:84-87, 1967, **Peplow EH, Jr.,** WASSAJA: The True—But Incomplete—Story of Dr. Carlos Montezuma, Physician to the White Man, Known Variously as "That Damned Radical Indian" and "The Indian's Abraham Lincoln," *Outdoor Arizona* April:15-17, 30-33, 1974.

56. **Marino C,** *The Remarkable Carlo Gentile,* Carl Mautz Publishing, Nevada City, California, 1998, p. 65.

57. **Larner JW, Jr.,** Supplement to the Papers of Carlos Montezuma, Microfilm Edition, *Scholarly Resources, Inc., Wilmington, Delaware,* 2002, Reel 1, October 27, 1893.

58. Ibid., Reel 1, November 9, 1893.

59. **Larner JW, Jr.,** The Papers of Carlos Montezuma, Microfilm Edition, *Scholarly Resources, Inc., Wilmington, Delaware,* 1984, Reel 1.

60. Ibid., Reel 1. **Montezuma C,** Light on the Indian Situation, *Quarterly J Soc Am Indians* 1:50-55, 1913.


## CHAPTER FIVE

1. **Blumgart H,** Caring for the Patient, *New Engl J Med* 270:449-456, 1964.

2. **Rothstein WG,** *American Physicians in the Nineteenth Century. From Sects to Science,* The Johns Hopkins University Press, Baltimore, 1972, reprinted 1992, p. 31.

3. **Dormandy T,** *The White Death. A History of Tuberculosis,* New York University Press, New York, 2000, p. 8.

4. **Starr D,** *Blood. An Epic History of Medicine and Commerce,* Perennial, HarperCollins Publishers Inc., New York, 2002, pp. 17-30.

5. **Duffy J,** *From Humors to Medical Science. A History of American Medicine,* 2nd Edition, University of Illinois Press, Urbana, 1993, p. 74.

6. **Chuinard EG,** *Only One Man Died. The Medical Aspects of the Lewis and Clark Expedition,* The Arthur H. Clark Company, Glendale, California, 1979, pp. 121-144, **Duffy J,** *From Humors to Medical Science. A History of American Medicine,* 2nd Edition, University of Illinois Press, Urbana, 1993, pp. 62-68

7. **McCullough D,** *John Adams,* Simon & Schuster, New York, 2001, pp. 96-97.

8. Ibid., pp. 646-650.

9. **Goldsmith MF,** At Pennsylvania Hospital, 250 Years of Care, *JAMA* 285:2313-2316, 2001.

10. **Chuinard EG,** *Only One Man Died. The Medical Aspects of the Lewis and Clark Expedition,* The Arthur H. Clark Company, Glendale, California, 1979, pp. 146-152.

11. Ibid., p. 224.

12. Ibid., pp. 288-292.

13. **Wilson R,** *Ohiyesa. Charles Eastman, Santee Sioux,* University of Illinois Press, Urbana, 1983, pp. 177-179.

14. **Rothstein WG,** *American Physicians in the Nineteenth Century. From Sects to Science,* The Johns Hopkins University Press, Baltimore, 1972, reprinted 1992, pp. 89-95.

15. Ibid., pp. 118-119.

16. Ibid., p. 119.

17. Ibid., p. 188.

18. Ibid.

19. Ibid., p. 191.

20. Ibid., p. 196.

21. Ibid., pp. 317, 345.

22. Ibid., p. 324.

23. Ibid., p. 213.

24. Ibid., p. 291.

25. Ibid.

26. Ibid., p. 286.

27. **Flexner A,** *Medical Education in the United States and Canada*, Carnegie Foundation for the Advancement of Teaching, New York, 1910.

28. **Rothstein WG,** *American Physicians in the Nineteenth Century. From Sects to Science*, The Johns Hopkins University Press, Baltimore, 1972, reprinted 1992, p. 292.

29. **Arey LB,** *Northwestern University Medical School 1859-1979. A Pioneer in Educational Reform*, Northwestern University, Evanston, 1979, p. 117.

30. **Tong B,** *Susan La Flesche Picotte, M.D.: Omaha Indian Leader and Reformer*, University of Oklahoma Press, Norman, 1999.

31. **Arey LB,** *Northwestern University Medical School 1859-1979. A Pioneer in Educational Reform*, Northwestern University, Evanston, 1979, p. 29.

32. Ibid., p. 26.

33. Ibid., p. 49.

34. Ibid., p. 72.

35. Ibid., pp. 413-423.

36. Ibid.

37. Ibid., p. 91.

38. Ibid., p. 168.

39. **Larner JW, Jr.,** The Papers of Carlos Montezuma, Microfilm Edition, *Scholarly Resources, Inc., Wilmington, Delaware*, 1984, Reel 6.

40. **Arey LB,** *Northwestern University Medical School 1859-1979. A Pioneer in Educational Reform*, Northwestern University, Evanston, 1979, p. 97.

41. Ibid., pp. 125-126.

42. **Larner JW, Jr.,** The Papers of Carlos Montezuma, Microfilm Edition, *Scholarly Resources, Inc., Wilmington, Delaware*, 1984, Reel 8.

43. **Bonner TN,** *Medicine in Chicago 1850–1950*, American History Research Center, Madison, Wisconsin, 1957, pp. 85-87.

44. Ibid., p. 102.

45. Ibid., p. 210.

46. Ibid., pp. 210-212.

47. Ibid., p. 211.

48. **Arey LB,** *Northwestern University Medical School 1859-1979. A Pioneer in Educational Reform*, Northwestern University, Evanston, 1979, p. 125.

49. Ibid., p. 127.

50. **Walker N,** The Medical Profession in the United States, *Edinburgh Med J* 37:240-241, 1891.

51. **Montezuma C,** The Indian of Tomorrow, *Chicago Historical Society*, Carlos Montezuma file.

52. Ibid.

53. **Larner JW, Jr.,** The Papers of Carlos Montezuma, Microfilm Edition, *Scholarly Resources, Inc., Wilmington, Delaware*, 1984, Reel 5, Vol. 8, November, 1922.

54. Ibid., Reel 1, June 18, 1887.

55. Ibid., Reel 7, *New York Herald*, February 5, 1887.

56. **Arey LB,** *Northwestern University Medical School 1859-1979. A Pioneer in Educational Reform,* Northwestern University, Evanston, 1979.

57. **Larner JW, Jr.,** The Papers of Carlos Montezuma, Microfilm Edition, *Scholarly Resources, Inc., Wilmington, Delaware,* 1984, Reel 1, February 19, 1888.

58. Ibid., Reel 1, February 23, 1888.

59. Ibid., Reel 1, March 26, 1888.

60. **Clark NM,** Dr. Montezuma, Apache: Warrior in Two Worlds, Based on an Interview in 1921, *Montana: The Magazine of Western History* 23:56-65, 1973.

61. **Larner JW, Jr.,** The Papers of Carlos Montezuma, Microfilm Edition, *Scholarly Resources, Inc., Wilmington, Delaware,* 1984, Reel 1, March 26, 1888.

62. Ibid., Reel 1, March 28, 1888.

63. Ibid., Reel 1, April 1, 1889.

64. **Larner JW, Jr.,** Supplement to the Papers of Carlos Montezuma, Microfilm Edition, *Scholarly Resources, Inc., Wilmington, Delaware,* 2002, Reel 7.

65. **Larner JW, Jr.,** The Papers of Carlos Montezuma, Microfilm Edition, *Scholarly Resources, Inc., Wilmington, Delaware,* 1984, Reel 1, August 14, 1889.

66. **Prucha FP,** *The Great Father. The United States Government and the American Indians, Abridged Edition,* University of Nebraska Press, Lincoln, 1986, pp. 237-241.

67. **Larner JW, Jr.,** The Papers of Carlos Montezuma, Microfilm Edition, *Scholarly Resources, Inc., Wilmington, Delaware,* 1984, Reel 1, August 3, 1889.

68. Ibid., Reel 1, August 12, 1889.

69. Ibid., Reel 1, September 2, 1889.

## CHAPTER SIX

1. **Larner JW, Jr.,** The Papers of Carlos Montezuma, Microfilm Edition, *Scholarly Resources, Inc., Wilmington, Delaware,* 1984, Reel 1, June 21, 1892.

2. **Hodge FW,** ed. *Handbook of American Indians North of Mexico, Smithsonian Institution Bureau of American Ethnology, Bulletin 30, 2 Volumes,* Government Printing Office, 1912, reprinted by Scholarly Press, Gross Pointe, Michigan, 1968, pp. 21-24.

3. **Larner JW, Jr.,** The Papers of Carlos Montezuma, Microfilm Edition, *Scholarly Resources, Inc., Wilmington, Delaware,* 1984, Reel 1, November 6, 1889.

4. **Bird GG,** *The Indians of To-Day,* Herbert S. Stone and Company, Chicago, 1900, p. 90.

5. **Larner JW, Jr.,** The Papers of Carlos Montezuma, Microfilm Edition, *Scholarly Resources, Inc., Wilmington, Delaware,* 1984, Reel 1, November 6, 1889.

6. Ibid., Reel 5, January 24, 1890.

7. Ibid., Reel 1, December 14, 1889.

8. Ibid., Reel 1, May 14, 1890.

9. Ibid., Reel 1, June 17, 1890.

10. Ibid., Reel 1, June 27, 1890.

11. Ibid., Reel 1, July 1, 1890.

12. Ibid., Reel 1, July 31, 1890.

13. **Larner JW, Jr.,** Supplement to the Papers of Carlos Montezuma, Microfilm Edition, *Scholarly Resources, Inc., Wilmington, Delaware*, 2002, Reel 1, April 10, 1891.

14. **Bird GG,** *The Indians of To-Day*, Herbert S. Stone and Company, Chicago, 1900, p. 104.

15. **Larner JW, Jr.,** The Papers of Carlos Montezuma, Microfilm Edition, *Scholarly Resources, Inc., Wilmington, Delaware*, 1984, Reel 1, July 30, 1890.

16. Ibid., Reel 1, May 19, 1892.

17. Ibid., Reel 5.

18. Ibid.

19. Ibid., Reel 1, November 17, 1890.

20. Ibid., Reel 1, March 31, 1890.

21. Ibid., Reel 1, April 4, 1890.

22. Ibid., Reel 1.

23. **Prucha FP,** *American Indian Policy in Crisis: Christian Reformers and the Indian, 1865–1900*, University of Oklahoma Press, Norman, 1976, pp. 200-201.

24. **Larner JW, Jr.,** The Papers of Carlos Montezuma, Microfilm Edition, *Scholarly Resources, Inc., Wilmington, Delaware*, 1984, Reel 1, July 8, 1892.

25. Ibid., Reel 1, July 20, 1892.

26. Ibid., Reel 5.

27. **Larner JW, Jr.,** Supplement to the Papers of Carlos Montezuma, Microfilm Edition, *Scholarly Resources, Inc., Wilmington, Delaware*, 2002, Reel 1, April 21, 1891.

28. **Larner JW, Jr.,** The Papers of Carlos Montezuma, Microfilm Edition, *Scholarly Resources, Inc., Wilmington, Delaware*, 1984, Reel 1.

29. **Bird GG,** *The Indians of To-Day*, Herbert S. Stone and Company, Chicago, 1900, p. 81.

30. **Larner JW, Jr.,** The Papers of Carlos Montezuma, Microfilm Edition, *Scholarly Resources, Inc., Wilmington, Delaware*, 1984, Reel 1, January 11, 1893.

31. Ibid., Reel 1, January 27, 1893.

32. Ibid.

33. Ibid., Reel 1.

34. **Prucha FP,** *The Great Father. The United States Government and the American Indians, Abridged Edition*, University of Nebraska Press, Lincoln, 1986, pp. 288-290.

35. **Larner JW, Jr.,** Supplement to the Papers of Carlos Montezuma, Microfilm Edition, *Scholarly Resources, Inc., Wilmington, Delaware*, 2002, Reel 1.

36. **Larner JW, Jr.,** The Papers of Carlos Montezuma, Microfilm Edition, *Scholarly Resources, Inc., Wilmington, Delaware*, 1984, Reel 1.

37. Ibid., Reel 7, Hearings Before the Committee on Expenditures in the Interior Department, June 5–17, 1911.

38. Ibid., Reel 5.

39. Ibid.

40. **Larner JW, Jr.,** Supplement to the Papers of Carlos Montezuma, Microfilm Edition, *Scholarly Resources, Inc., Wilmington, Delaware*, 2002, Reel 1, August 26, 1895.

41. **Larner JW, Jr.,** The Papers of Carlos Montezuma, Microfilm Edition, *Scholarly Resources, Inc., Wilmington, Delaware,* 1984, Reel 5.

42. Ibid., Reel 1, November 22, 1895.

43. **Clark NM,** Dr. Montezuma, Apache: Warrior in Two Worlds, Based on an Interview in 1921, *Montana: The Magazine of Western History* 23:56-65, 1973.

44. **Larner JW, Jr.,** The Papers of Carlos Montezuma, Microfilm Edition, *Scholarly Resources, Inc., Wilmington, Delaware,* 1984, Reel 8.

45. Ibid., Reel 1.

46. Ibid., Reel 1, June 15, 1893.

47. Ibid., Reel 1, April 10, 1893.

48. Ibid., Reel 1.

49. Ibid.

## CHAPTER SEVEN

1. **Miller DL,** *City of the Century. The Epic of Chicago and the Making of America,* Simon & Schuster, New York, 1996, p. 42.

2. Ibid., p. 96.

3. **Standing Bear L,** *My People the Sioux,* University of Nebraska Press, Lincoln, 1928, reprinted 1975, p. 130.

4. **Duis PR,** *Challenging Chicago. Coping with Everyday Life, 1837-1920,* University of Illinois Press, Urbana, 1998, p. 5.

5. **Miller DL,** *City of the Century. The Epic of Chicago and the Making of America,* Simon & Schuster, New York, 1996, p. 135.

6. Ibid., pp. 124-127.

7. **Dreiser T,** The Smallest and Busiest River in the World, *Metropolitan Magazine* 7:355-363, 1898.

8. **Duis PR,** *Challenging Chicago. Coping with Everyday Life, 1837-1920,* University of Illinois Press, Urbana, 1998, p. 11.

9. **Miller DL,** *City of the Century. The Epic of Chicago and the Making of America,* Simon & Schuster, New York, 1996, pp. 138-142.

10. Ibid., p. 135.

11. **Cronon W,** *Nature's Metropolis. Chicago and the Great West,* W.W. Norton & Company, New York, 1991, pp. 207-259.

12. Ibid., pp. 313-318, **Miller DL,** *City of the Century. The Epic of Chicago and the Making of America,* Simon & Schuster, New York, 1996, pp. 104-105.

13. **Cronon W,** *Nature's Metropolis. Chicago and the Great West,* W.W. Norton & Company, New York, 1991, pp. 97-147.

14. Ibid., pp. 148-206.

15. **Miller DL,** *City of the Century. The Epic of Chicago and the Making of America,* Simon & Schuster, New York, 1996, p. 113.

16. Ibid.

17. Ibid., p. 133, **Dreiser T,** The Smallest and Busiest River in the World, *Metropolitan Magazine* 7:355-363, 1898.

18. **Chicago Public Library,** Chicago in 1900—A Millennium Bibliography, *www.chipublib.org/004chicago/1900/,* 2001.

19. **Miller DL,** *City of the Century. The Epic of Chicago and the Making of America,* Simon & Schuster, New York, 1996, p. 147.

20. Ibid., p. 165.

21. Ibid., p. 152.

22. Ibid., pp. 163-164.

23. Ibid., p. 177.

24. **Duis PR,** *Challenging Chicago. Coping with Everyday Life, 1837-1920,* University of Illinois Press, Urbana, 1998, p. 31.

25. Ibid., pp. 39-40.

26. **Dreiser T,** The Smallest and Busiest River in the World, *Metropolitan Magazine* 7:355-363, 1898.

27. **Chicago Public Library,** Chicago in 1900—A Millennium Bibliography, *www.chipublib.org/004chicago/1900/,* 2001.

28. **Chicago Tunnel Company Site Map,** The History of Chicago's Freight Tunnels, *www.ameritech.net/users/chicagotunnel/,* 2001.

29. **Duis PR,** *Challenging Chicago. Coping with Everyday Life, 1837-1920,* University of Illinois Press, Urbana, 1998, p. 45.

30. **Miller DL,** *City of the Century. The Epic of Chicago and the Making of America,* Simon & Schuster, New York, 1996, pp. 314-335.

31. Ibid., pp. 309-311.

32. Ibid., pp. 321-322.

33. Ibid., p. 348.

34. Ibid., p. 350.

35. **Dreiser T,** *Sister Carrie,* New American Library, Penguin Putnam Inc., New York, 1900, Signet Classic Printing (Lingeman Introduction), 2000.

36. **Miller DL,** *City of the Century. The Epic of Chicago and the Making of America,* Simon & Schuster, New York, 1996, p. 133.

37. Ibid., pp. 244-247, **Cronon W,** *Nature's Metropolis. Chicago and the Great West,* W.W. Norton & Company, New York, 1991, pp. 333-340

38. **Miller DL,** *City of the Century. The Epic of Chicago and the Making of America,* Simon & Schuster, New York, 1996, pp. 247-250.

39. **Cronon W,** *Nature's Metropolis. Chicago and the Great West,* W.W. Norton & Company, New York, 1991, pp. 74-81.

40. **Miller DL,** *City of the Century. The Epic of Chicago and the Making of America,* Simon & Schuster, New York, 1996, p. 381.

41. **Cronon W,** *Nature's Metropolis. Chicago and the Great West,* W.W. Norton & Company, New York, 1991, p. 343.

42. **Miller DL,** *City of the Century. The Epic of Chicago and the Making of America,* Simon & Schuster, New York, 1996, pp. 496-497.

43. **Duis PR,** *Challenging Chicago. Coping with Everyday Life, 1837-1920,* University of Illinois Press, Urbana, 1998, p. 215.

44. **Gilbert J,** *Perfect Cities. Chicago's Utopias of 1893,* The University of Chicago Press, Chicago, 1991, pp. 75-130.

45. Ibid., p. 121.

46. **Hoxie FE,** *A Final Promise: The Campaign to Assimilate the Indians, 1880-1920,* University of Nebraska Press, Lincoln, 1984, p. 85.

47. **Hoffman C,** *The Depression of the Nineties: An Economic History,* Greenwood Publishing, Westport, Connecticut, 1970.

48. **Chicago Public Library,** Chicago in 1900—A Millennium Bibliography, *www.chipublib.org/004chicago/1900/,* 2001.

49. Ibid.

50. Ibid.

51. Ibid.

52. **Miller DL,** *City of the Century. The Epic of Chicago and the Making of America,* Simon & Schuster, New York, 1996, p. 491.

53. **Chicago Public Library,** Chicago in 1900—A Millennium Bibliography, *www.chipublib.org/004chicago/1900/,* 2001.

54. **Miller DL,** *City of the Century. The Epic of Chicago and the Making of America,* Simon & Schuster, New York, 1996, p. 191.

55. Ibid., pp. 446-448.

56. **Barrett JR,** *Work and Community in the Jungle. Chicago's Packinghouse Workers, 1894-1922,* University of Illinois Press, Urbana, 1987, p. 82.

57. **Duis PR,** *Challenging Chicago. Coping with Everyday Life, 1837-1920,* University of Illinois Press, Urbana, 1998, p. 157.

58. **Encyclopaedia Britannica,** Chicago, *www.britannica.com/eb/,* 2001.

59. **Bonner TN,** *Medicine in Chicago 1850–1950,* American History Research Center, Madison, Wisconsin, 1957, p. 20.

60. **Chicago Public Library,** Chicago in 1900—A Millennium Bibliography, *www.chipublib.org/004chicago/1900/,* 2001.

61. Ibid.

62. **Duis PR,** *Challenging Chicago. Coping with Everyday Life, 1837-1920,* University of Illinois Press, Urbana, 1998, p. 276.

63. **Chicago Public Library,** Chicago in 1900—A Millennium Bibliography, *www.chipublib.org/004chicago/1900/,* 2001.

64. **Miller DL,** *City of the Century. The Epic of Chicago and the Making of America,* Simon & Schuster, New York, 1996, p. 529.

65. **Barrett JR,** *Work and Community in the Jungle. Chicago's Packinghouse Workers, 1894-1922,* University of Illinois Press, Urbana, 1987, pp. 76-80.

66. **Larner JW, Jr.,** The Papers of Carlos Montezuma, Microfilm Edition, *Scholarly Resources, Inc., Wilmington, Delaware,* 1984, Reel 2, November 22, 1906.

67. **Bonner TN,** *Medicine in Chicago 1850–1950,* American History Research Center, Madison, Wisconsin, 1957, p. 135.

68. Ibid., p. 23.

69. **Miller DL,** *City of the Century. The Epic of Chicago and the Making of America*, Simon & Schuster, New York, 1996, p. 457.

70. **Barrett JR,** *Work and Community in the Jungle. Chicago's Packinghouse Workers, 1894-1922*, University of Illinois Press, Urbana, 1987, p. 69.

71. **Miller DL,** *City of the Century. The Epic of Chicago and the Making of America*, Simon & Schuster, New York, 1996, p. 117.

72. **Barrett JR,** *Work and Community in the Jungle. Chicago's Packinghouse Workers, 1894-1922*, University of Illinois Press, Urbana, 1987, p. 69.

73. **Miller DL,** *City of the Century. The Epic of Chicago and the Making of America*, Simon & Schuster, New York, 1996, p. 199.

74. Ibid.

75. **Cronon W,** *Nature's Metropolis. Chicago and the Great West*, W.W. Norton & Company, New York, 1991, pp. 230-259, **Miller DL,** *City of the Century. The Epic of Chicago and the Making of America*, Simon & Schuster, New York, 1996, pp. 201-204.

76. **Barrett JR,** *Work and Community in the Jungle. Chicago's Packinghouse Workers, 1894-1922*, University of Illinois Press, Urbana, 1987, p. 44.

77. **Miller DL,** *City of the Century. The Epic of Chicago and the Making of America*, Simon & Schuster, New York, 1996, p. 215.

78. **Schlosser E,** American Slaughterhouses Are Grinding Out Meat Faster Than Ever—and the Production Line Keeps Moving, Even When Workers Are Maimed by the Machinery, *Mother Jones* July/August:39-47, 2001.

79. **Miller DL,** *City of the Century. The Epic of Chicago and the Making of America*, Simon & Schuster, New York, 1996, p. 241.

80. Ibid., pp. 468-482, **Ginger R,** *Altgeld's America. The Lincoln Ideal versus Changing Realities*, Quadrangle Books, Inc., Chicago, Funk & Wagnalls Company 1958, Quadrangle Paperback 1965, pp. 35-88.

81. **Gilbert J,** *Perfect Cities. Chicago's Utopias of 1893*, The University of Chicago Press, Chicago, 1991, pp. 131-168, **Miller DL,** *City of the Century. The Epic of Chicago and the Making of America*, Simon & Schuster, New York, 1996, pp. 224-240.

82. **Miller DL,** *City of the Century. The Epic of Chicago and the Making of America*, Simon & Schuster, New York, 1996, pp. 542-549.

83. Ibid., pp. 417-423.

84. **Sklar KK,** Hull House in the 1890s: A Community of Women Reformers, *Signs: Journal of Women in Culture and Society* 10:658-677, 1985.

85. **Lissak RS,** *Pluralism & Progressives. Hull House and the New Immigrants, 1890–1919*, University of Chicago Press, Chicago, 1989, p. 5.

86. **Sklar KK,** Hull House in the 1890s: A Community of Women Reformers, *Signs: Journal of Women in Culture and Society* 10:658-677, 1985.

87. **Lissak RS,** *Pluralism & Progressives. Hull House and the New Immigrants, 1890–1919*, University of Chicago Press, Chicago, 1989.

88. **Miller DL,** *City of the Century. The Epic of Chicago and the Making of America*, Simon & Schuster, New York, 1996, **Lissak RS,** *Pluralism & Progressives. Hull House and the New Immigrants, 1890–1919*, University of Chicago Press, Chicago, 1989, p. 460.

89. **Gunther J,** The High Cost of Hoodlums, In: Mowry GE, ed. *The Twenties. Fords, Flappers & Fanatics*, Prentice-Hall, Inc., Englewood Cliffs, New Jersey, 1963, pp. 114-120.

90. **Mowry GE,** ed. *The Twenties. Fords, Flappers & Fanatics,* Prentice-Hall, Inc., Englewood Cliffs, New Jersey, 1963, pp. 109-114.

91. **Holman CW,** Race Riots in Chicago, In: Mowry GE, ed. *The Twenties: Fords, Flappers & Fanatics,* Prentice-Hall, Inc., Englewood Cliffs, N.J., 1963, pp. 126-129.

92. **Barrett JR,** *Work and Community in the Jungle. Chicago's Packinghouse Workers, 1894-1922,* University of Illinois Press, Urbana, 1987, pp. 219-221.

93. **Automotive History,** *www.autoshop-online.com/auto101/histtext.html,* 2001.

94. **Duis PR,** *Challenging Chicago. Coping with Everyday Life, 1837-1920,* University of Illinois Press, Urbana, 1998, p. 50.

## CHAPTER EIGHT

1. **Duffy J,** *From Humors to Medical Science. A History of American Medicine,* 2nd Edition, University of Illinois Press, Urbana, 1993, p. 182.

2. **Starr P,** *The Social Transformation of American Medicine,* Basic Books, 1982, p. 85.

3. **Walker N,** The Medical Profession in the United States, *Edinburgh Med J* 37:240-241, 1891.

4. **Starr P,** *The Social Transformation of American Medicine,* Basic Books, 1982, p. 142.

5. **Larner JW, Jr.,** Supplement to the Papers of Carlos Montezuma, Microfilm Edition, *Scholarly Resources, Inc., Wilmington, Delaware,* 2002, Reel 8.

6. **Larner JW, Jr.,** The Papers of Carlos Montezuma, Microfilm Edition, *Scholarly Resources, Inc., Wilmington, Delaware,* 1984, Reel 4.

7. Ibid., Reel 5, May 27, 1899.

8. **Chicago Public Library,** Chicago in 1900—A Millennium Bibliography, *www.chipublib.org/004chicago/1900/,* 2001.

9. **Hohler JS,** ed. *The Papers of Carlos Montezuma 1892-1937 (Microfilm Edition),* The State Historical Society of Wisconsin, Madison, 1975, Reel 8.

10. **Larner JW, Jr.,** The Papers of Carlos Montezuma, Microfilm Edition, *Scholarly Resources, Inc., Wilmington, Delaware,* 1984, Reel 6.

11. **Bonner TN,** *Medicine in Chicago 1850–1950,* American History Research Center, Madison, Wisconsin, 1957, p. 75.

12. **Larner JW, Jr.,** The Papers of Carlos Montezuma, Microfilm Edition, *Scholarly Resources, Inc., Wilmington, Delaware,* 1984, Reel 4.

13. Ibid., Reel 4, November 27, 1917.

14. **Bonner TN,** *Medicine in Chicago 1850–1950,* American History Research Center, Madison, Wisconsin, 1957, p. 31.

15. **Larner JW, Jr.,** The Papers of Carlos Montezuma, Microfilm Edition, *Scholarly Resources, Inc., Wilmington, Delaware,* 1984, Reel 5.

16. **Minute Book,** Papers of the Medical Society of Cumberland County, *Cumberland Historical Society* MG-011:Box 1, 1895.

17. **Larner JW, Jr.,** The Papers of Carlos Montezuma, Microfilm Edition, *Scholarly Resources, Inc., Wilmington, Delaware,* 1984, Reel 5.

18. Ibid., Reel 8.

19. **Hohler JS,** ed. *The Papers of Carlos Montezuma 1892-1937 (Microfilm Edition),* The State Historical Society of Wisconsin, Madison, 1975, Reel 8.

20. **Larner JW, Jr.,** The Papers of Carlos Montezuma, Microfilm Edition, *Scholarly Resources, Inc., Wilmington, Delaware,* 1984, Reel 1, December 23, 1895.

21. **Clark NM,** Dr. Montezuma, Apache: Warrior in Two Worlds, Based on an Interview in 1921, *Montana: The Magazine of Western History* 23:56-65, 1973.

22. **Turck FB,** Treatment of the Abdominal Viscera Through the Colon, *JAMA*:881-886, October 7, 1899, **Turck FB,** Further Observation on the Treatment of the Abdominal Viscera Through the Colon, *JAMA,* May 5, 1900.

23. **Turck FB,** Further Observation on the Treatment of the Abdominal Viscera Through the Colon, *JAMA,* May 5, 1900.

24. **Turck FB,** Treatment of the Abdominal Viscera Through the Colon, *JAMA*:881-886, October 7, 1899.

25. **Larner JW, Jr.,** The Papers of Carlos Montezuma, Microfilm Edition, *Scholarly Resources, Inc., Wilmington, Delaware,* 1984, Reel 5, May 27, 1899.

26. Ibid., Reel 3, May 9, 1913.

27. **Turck FB,** *The Action of the Living Cell. Experimental Researches in Biology,* The MacMillian Company, New York, 1933.

28. **Larner JW, Jr.,** The Papers of Carlos Montezuma, Microfilm Edition, *Scholarly Resources, Inc., Wilmington, Delaware,* 1984, Reel 8.

29. **Hohler JS,** ed. *The Papers of Carlos Montezuma 1892-1937 (Microfilm Edition),* The State Historical Society of Wisconsin, Madison, 1975, Reel 7.

30. Ibid., Reel 5.

31. **Larner JW, Jr.,** The Papers of Carlos Montezuma, Microfilm Edition, *Scholarly Resources, Inc., Wilmington, Delaware,* 1984, Reel 3, February 13, 1913.

32. **Larner JW, Jr.,** Supplement to the Papers of Carlos Montezuma, Microfilm Edition, *Scholarly Resources, Inc., Wilmington, Delaware,* 2002, Reel 1.

33. **Larner JW, Jr.,** The Papers of Carlos Montezuma, Microfilm Edition, *Scholarly Resources, Inc., Wilmington, Delaware,* 1984, Reel 4, August 19, 1915.

34. **Voight TF,** Carlos Montezuma — American Indian Leader, Thesis for Master of History in American History, University of Wisconsin—Milwaukee, 1976, p. 62.

35. **Hohler JS,** ed. *The Papers of Carlos Montezuma 1892-1937 (Microfilm Edition),* The State Historical Society of Wisconsin, Madison, 1975, Reel 5, **Larner JW, Jr.,** Supplement to the Papers of Carlos Montezuma, Microfilm Edition, *Scholarly Resources, Inc., Wilmington, Delaware,* 2002, Reel 7.

36. **Larner JW, Jr.,** Supplement to the Papers of Carlos Montezuma, Microfilm Edition, *Scholarly Resources, Inc., Wilmington, Delaware,* 2002, Reel 8.

37. **Illinois Historic Preservation Agency,** Chicago Savings Bank Building, *http://www.state.il.us/HPA/ps/200789.htm,* 2002.

38. **Larner JW, Jr.,** The Papers of Carlos Montezuma, Microfilm Edition, *Scholarly Resources, Inc., Wilmington, Delaware,* 1984, Reel 5, May 29, 1922.

39. Ibid., Reel 1.

40. Ibid.

41. **Moses LG,** *Wild West Shows and the Images of American Indians, 1883-1933,* University of New Mexico Press, Albuquerque, 1996, pp. 168-184.

42. **Larner JW, Jr.,** The Papers of Carlos Montezuma, Microfilm Edition, *Scholarly Resources, Inc., Wilmington, Delaware,* 1984, Reel 2, April 27, 1911.

43. **Standing Bear L,** *My People the Sioux,* University of Nebraska Press, Lincoln, 1928, reprinted 1975, pp. 270-271.

44. **Russell D,** *The Wild West. A History of the Wild West Shows,* Amon Carter Museum of Western Art, Fort Worth, Texas, 1970, p. 95.

45. **Larner JW, Jr.,** The Papers of Carlos Montezuma, Microfilm Edition, *Scholarly Resources, Inc., Wilmington, Delaware,* 1984, Reels 1 & 2.

46. **Starr P,** *The Social Transformation of American Medicine,* Basic Books, 1982, p. 201.

47. **Larner JW, Jr.,** The Papers of Carlos Montezuma, Microfilm Edition, *Scholarly Resources, Inc., Wilmington, Delaware,* 1984, Reel 1, April 21, 1904.

48. Ibid.

49. Ibid., Reel 2, May 2, 1904.

50. Ibid., Reel 2, May 9, 1904.

51. Ibid., Reel 1, May 6, 1904.

52. Ibid., Reel 2, May 20, 1904.

53. Ibid.

54. Ibid., Reel 2, May 28, 1904.

55. **Chicago Public Library,** Chicago in 1900—A Millennium Bibliography, *www.chipublib.org/004chicago/1900/,* 2001.

56. **Clark NM,** Dr. Montezuma, Apache: Warrior in Two Worlds, Based on an Interview in 1921, *Montana: The Magazine of Western History* 23:56-65, 1973, Dr. Carlos Montezuma. A Bright and Well Educated Apache With an Interesting History, *Arizona Republican,* October 11, 1901.

57. **Bakeless J,** Letter to the Alumni Secretary, University of Illinois, *University Archives, University of Illinois at Urbana-Champaign,* August 22, 1955.

58. **Montezuma C,** Information for The National Cyclopedia of American Biography, *Chicago Historical Society, Carlos Montezuma file.*

59. **Larner JW, Jr.,** The Papers of Carlos Montezuma, Microfilm Edition, *Scholarly Resources, Inc., Wilmington, Delaware,* 1984, Reel 3, May 9, 1913.

60. **Clark NM,** Dr. Montezuma, Apache: Warrior in Two Worlds, Based on an Interview in 1921, *Montana: The Magazine of Western History* 23:56-65, 1973.

61. **Hohler JS,** ed. *The Papers of Carlos Montezuma 1892-1937 (Microfilm Edition),* The State Historical Society of Wisconsin, Madison, 1975, Reel 1.

62. **Larner JW, Jr.,** The Papers of Carlos Montezuma, Microfilm Edition, *Scholarly Resources, Inc., Wilmington, Delaware,* 1984, Reel 8, **Larner JW, Jr.,** Supplement to the Papers of Carlos Montezuma, Microfilm Edition, *Scholarly Resources, Inc., Wilmington, Delaware,* 2002, Reel 7, January 25, 1889.

63. **Larner JW, Jr.,** Supplement to the Papers of Carlos Montezuma, Microfilm Edition, *Scholarly Resources, Inc., Wilmington, Delaware,* 2002, Reel 7, Reel 8.

64. **Hohler JS,** ed. *The Papers of Carlos Montezuma 1892-1937 (Microfilm Edition),* The State Historical Society of Wisconsin, Madison, 1975, Reel 1, November 24, 1899.

65. **Larner JW, Jr.,** The Papers of Carlos Montezuma, Microfilm Edition, *Scholarly Resources, Inc., Wilmington, Delaware,* 1984, Reel 8.

66. Ibid., Reel 5, *Wassaja,* Vol. 3, No. 2, May, 1918.

67. Ibid., Reel 8.

68. Ibid., Reel 9, June 24, 1920.

69. **Larner JW, Jr.,** Supplement to the Papers of Carlos Montezuma, Microfilm Edition, *Scholarly Resources, Inc., Wilmington, Delaware*, 2002, Reel 1.

70. Ibid., Reel 8.

71. Ibid., Reel 1, August,1914.

72. **Larner JW, Jr.,** The Papers of Carlos Montezuma, Microfilm Edition, *Scholarly Resources, Inc., Wilmington, Delaware*, 1984, Reel 5, The Indian Problems From An Indian's Standpoint.

73. Ibid., Reel 5, An Indian's View of the Indian Question.

74. Ibid., Reel 5, The Indian Problem From An Indian's Standpoint.

75. Ibid., Reel 2, August 2, 1906.

76. Ibid., Reel 2, May 16, 1909.

77. Ibid., Reel 6.

78. Ibid., Reel 3, February 27, 1914.

79. Ibid., Reel 6.

80. Ibid., Reel 7, Lawrence Daily Journal-World, September 30, 1915.

81. **Larner JW, Jr.,** Supplement to the Papers of Carlos Montezuma, Microfilm Edition, *Scholarly Resources, Inc., Wilmington, Delaware*, 2002, Reel 6, July 7, 1916.

82. Ibid., Reel 2, February 1, 1916, May 19, 1916.

83. Ibid., Reel 2.

84. **Larner JW, Jr.,** The Papers of Carlos Montezuma, Microfilm Edition, *Scholarly Resources, Inc., Wilmington, Delaware*, 1984, Reel 5, September 28, 1921.

85. Ibid., Reel 5, October 3, 1921.

86. Ibid., Reel 5, August 22, 1921.

87. **Starr P,** *The Social Transformation of American Medicine*, Basic Books, 1982, p. 142.

88. **Larner JW, Jr.,** The Papers of Carlos Montezuma, Microfilm Edition, *Scholarly Resources, Inc., Wilmington, Delaware*, 1984, Reel 5, September 4, 1921.

89. Ibid., Reel 5, August 19, 1921.

90. **Bonner TN,** *Medicine in Chicago 1850–1950*, American History Research Center, Madison, Wisconsin, 1957, p. 217.

91. **Montezuma Collection, Arizona State University.** *MSS-60, CMC, Box 2, Folder 5.*

92. **Larner JW, Jr.,** The Papers of Carlos Montezuma, Microfilm Edition, *Scholarly Resources, Inc., Wilmington, Delaware*, 1984, Reel 8.

93. Ibid., Reel 7, Hearings Before the Committee on Expenditures in the Interior Department, June 5–17, 1911.

94. **Fitz RH,** Perforating Inflammation of the Vermiform Appendix: With Special Reference to its Early Diagnosis and Treatment, *Trans Assoc Am Physicians* 1:107-144, 1886.

95. **McBurney C,** Experience with Early Operative Interference in Cases of Disease of the Vermiform Appendix, *NY Med J* 50:676-684, 1889, **McBurney C,** The Incision Made in the Abdominal Wall in Cases of Appendicitis, with a Description of a New Method of Operating, *Ann Surg* 20:38-43, 1894.

96. **Larner JW, Jr.,** Supplement to the Papers of Carlos Montezuma, Microfilm Edition, *Scholarly Resources, Inc., Wilmington, Delaware*, 2002, Reel 9, February 12, 1923.

## CHAPTER NINE

1. **Welch DS,** Zitkala-Sa: An American Indian Leader, 1876-1938, Dissertation for Degree of Philosophy in History, University of Wyoming, Laramie, 1985.

2. **Rappaport D,** *The Flight of Red Bird. The Life of Zitkala-Sa*, Puffin Books, New York, 1997, **Hafen PJ,** ed. *Dreams and Thunder. Stories, Poems, and The Sun Dance Opera*, University of Nebraska Press, Lincoln, 2001.

3. **Welch DS,** Zitkala-Sa: An American Indian Leader, 1876-1938, Dissertation for Degree of Philosophy in History, University of Wyoming, Laramie, 1985, **Rappaport D,** *The Flight of Red Bird. The Life of Zitkala-Sa*, Puffin Books, New York, 1997, **Fisher D,** Zitkala-Sa: The Evolution of a Writer, *American Indian Quarterly* 5:229-238, 1979.

4. **Welch DS,** Zitkala-Sa: An American Indian Leader, 1876-1938, Dissertation for Degree of Philosophy in History, University of Wyoming, Laramie, 1985, p. viii.

5. **Zitkala-Sa,** *American Indian Stories*, reprinted from original published by Hayworth Publishing House, Washington, D. C, 1921, University of Nebraska Press, Lincoln, 1985.

6. Ibid.

7. Ibid.

8. **Rappaport D,** *The Flight of Red Bird. The Life of Zitkala-Sa*, Puffin Books, New York, 1997, pp. 61-64, **Simmons G,** Side by Side, *The Earlhamite,*1896, March 16:177-179.

9. **Simmons G,** Side by Side, *The Earlhamite,*1896, March 16:177-179.

10. Ibid.

11. **Welch DS,** Zitkala-Sa: An American Indian Leader, 1876-1938, Dissertation for Degree of Philosophy in History, University of Wyoming, Laramie, 1985, **Fisher AP,** The Transformation of Tradition: A Study of Zitkala-Sa and Mourning Dove, Two Transitional American Indian Writers, Thesis for Doctor of Philsophy in English, City University of New York, 1979.

12. **Welch DS,** Zitkala-Sa: An American Indian Leader, 1876-1938, Dissertation for Degree of Philosophy in History, University of Wyoming, Laramie, 1985.

13. **Zitkala-Sa,** *American Indian Stories*, reprinted from original published by Hayworth Publishing House, Washington, D. C, 1921, University of Nebraska Press, Lincoln, 1985.

14. Ibid., p. 97.

15. **Rappaport D,** *The Flight of Red Bird. The Life of Zitkala-Sa*, Puffin Books, New York, 1997.

16. **Welch DS,** Zitkala-Sa: An American Indian Leader, 1876-1938, Dissertation for Degree of Philosophy in History, University of Wyoming, Laramie, 1985.

17. **Hohler JS,** ed. *The Papers of Carlos Montezuma 1892-1937 (Microfilm Edition)*, The State Historical Society of Wisconsin, Madison, 1975, Reel 1.

18. **Zitkala-Sa,** *American Indian Stories*, reprinted from original published by Hayworth Publishing House, Washington, D. C, 1921, University of Nebraska Press, Lincoln, 1985.

19. **Welch DS,** Zitkala-Sa: An American Indian Leader, 1876-1938, Dissertation for Degree of Philosophy in History, University of Wyoming, Laramie, 1985, p. 28.

20. **Our Band on the Road,** *The Indian Helper,* March 30, 1900.

21. **Hohler JS,** ed. *The Papers of Carlos Montezuma 1892-1937 (Microfilm Edition)*, The State Historical Society of Wisconsin, Madison, 1975, Reel 1.

22. Ibid., Reel 1, March 9, 1901.

23. Ibid., Reel 1, October 7, 1898.

24. Ibid., Reel 1, October 10, 1898.

25. Ibid., Reel 1, February 20, 1901.

26. **Zitkala-Sa,** *Old Indian Legends,* Ginn & Co., Boston, 1901.

27. **Hohler JS,** ed. *The Papers of Carlos Montezuma 1892-1937 (Microfilm Edition),* The State Historical Society of Wisconsin, Madison, 1975, Reel 1, February 20, 1901.

28. Ibid., Reel 1, March 5, 1901.

29. **Zitkala-Sa,** *Old Indian Legends,* Ginn & Co., Boston, 1901.

30. **Zitkala-Sa,** *American Indian Stories,* reprinted from original published by Hayworth Publishing House, Washington, D. C, 1921, University of Nebraska Press, Lincoln, 1985.

31. **Hohler JS,** ed. *The Papers of Carlos Montezuma 1892-1937 (Microfilm Edition),* The State Historical Society of Wisconsin, Madison, 1975, Reel 1, March 17, 1901.

32. Ibid., Reel 1, March, 1901.

33. Ibid., Reel 1, March 17, 1901.

34. Ibid., Reel 1, April 3, 1901.

35. Ibid., Reel 1, April 12, 1901.

36. Ibid., Reel 1, April 18, 1901.

37. Ibid., Reel 1, April 19, 1901.

38. Ibid.

39. Ibid., Reel 1, April, 1901.

40. Ibid.

41. Ibid., Reel 1, May, 1901.

42. Ibid.

43. **Jazz Age Chicago, Passenger Rail Station Index,** *www.suba.com/~scottn/explore/sites/transpor/tran_idx.htm,* 2002.

44. **Hohler JS,** ed. *The Papers of Carlos Montezuma 1892-1937 (Microfilm Edition),* The State Historical Society of Wisconsin, Madison, 1975, Reel 1, May 13, 1901.

45. Ibid., Reel 1, May 28, 1901.

46. Ibid., Reel 1, May 29, 1901.

47. Ibid., Reel 1, May, 1901.

48. Ibid., Reel 1, June 1, 1901.

49. Ibid., Reel 1, June, 1901.

50. Ibid., Reel 1, June 6, 1901.

51. Ibid., Reel 1, June, 1901.

52. Ibid., Reel 1, June 17, 1901.

53. Ibid., Reel 1, June, 1901.

54. Ibid., Reel 1, July, 1901.

55. Ibid.

56. Ibid.

57. Ibid.

58. Ibid., Reel 1, August 11, 1901.

59. Ibid., Reel 1, August 21, 1901.

60. Ibid., Reel 1, August 31, 1901.

61. Ibid., Reel 1, September 4, 1901.

62. Ibid., Reel 1, October 18, 1901.

63. Ibid., Reel 1.

64. Ibid.

65. Ibid., Reel 1, January 1, 1902.

66. Ibid., Reel 1.

67. Ibid.

68. Ibid., Reel 1, July, 1902.

69. Ibid., Reel 1, July 26, 1902.

70. Ibid., Reel 1, July 29, 1902.

71. Ibid., Reel 1, June 11, 1902.

72. **Welch DS,** Zitkala-Sa: An American Indian Leader, 1876-1938, Dissertation for Degree of Philosophy in History, University of Wyoming, Laramie, 1985, **Rappaport D,** *The Flight of Red Bird. The Life of Zitkala-Sa*, Puffin Books, New York, 1997.

73. **Welch DS,** Zitkala-Sa: An American Indian Leader, 1876-1938, Dissertation for Degree of Philosophy in History, University of Wyoming, Laramie, 1985.

74. Ibid., p. 72.

75. **Hanson WF,** *Sun Dance Land*, J. Grant Stevenson, Provo, Utah, 1967.

76. Ibid., p. 69.

77. Ibid., pp. 116-117, **Hafen PJ,** ed. *Dreams and Thunder. Stories, Poems, and The Sun Dance Opera*, University of Nebraska Press, Lincoln, 2001, p. 128.

78. **Hafen PJ,** Zitkala-Ša: Sentimentality and Sovereignity, *Wicazo Sa Review* 12:31-41, 1997.

79. **Bureau of Catholic Indian Missions Records,** Letter from Gertrude Bonnin to Reverend William H. Ketcham, *Marquette University Libraries, Department of Special Collections and University Archives* Series 1-1 General Correspondence, Box 87, Folder 13, October 4, 1913.

80. **Larner JW, Jr.,** The Papers of Carlos Montezuma, Microfilm Edition, *Scholarly Resources, Inc., Wilmington, Delaware*, 1984, Reel 3, May 15, 1913.

81. Ibid., Reel 3, June 23, 1913.

82. Ibid., Reel 5, January 16, 1922.

83. **Hafen PJ,** ed. *Dreams and Thunder. Stories, Poems, and The Sun Dance Opera*, University of Nebraska Press, Lincoln, 2001.

84. **Zitkala-Ša,** The Indian's Awakening, *Am Indian Magazine, Quarterly J Soc Am Indians* IV:57-59, 1916.

85. **Clements KA,** *The Presidency of Woodrow Wilson*, University Press of Kansas, Lawrence, 1992, p. 133.

86. **Larner JW, Jr.,** The Papers of Carlos Montezuma, Microfilm Edition, *Scholarly Resources, Inc., Wilmington, Delaware*, 1984, Reel 4, December 10, 1916.

87. **Larner JW, Jr.,** ed. The Papers of the Society of American Indians, Microfilm Edition, *Scholarly Resources, Inc., Wilmington, Delaware*, 1987, Reel 1, Bonnin to Parker.

88. Ibid., Reel 2, Parker to Coolidge, February 6 & 20, 1916.

89. **Larner JW, Jr.,** The Papers of Carlos Montezuma, Microfilm Edition, *Scholarly Resources, Inc., Wilmington, Delaware,* 1984, Reel 4, October 16 & November, 1918.

90. **Willard W,** The First Amendment, Anglo-Conformity and American Indian Religious Freedom, *Wicazo Sa Review* 7:25-41, 1991.

91. **Stewart OC,** Gertrude Simmons Bonnin, *University of South Dakota Bulletin* 87:10-11, 1981.

92. **Willard W,** The First Amendment, Anglo-Conformity and American Indian Religious Freedom, *Wicazo Sa Review* 7:25-41, 1991.

93. **Indian Woman in Capital to Fight Growing Use of Peyote Drug by Indians,** *Washington Times,* February 17, 1918.

94. **Lisa LO,** The Life Story of Zitkala-Sa/Gertrude Simmons Bonnin: Writing and Creating a Public Image, Dissertation for the Degree of Doctor of Philosophy, Arizona State University, 1996, p. 157.

95. **Mooney J,** *The Ghost Dance-Religion and the Sioux Outbreak of 1890, Fourteenth Annual Report of the Bureau of American Ethnology,* Government Printing Office, Washington, D.C., 1896.

96. **Welch DS,** Zitkala-Sa: An American Indian Leader, 1876-1938, Dissertation for Degree of Philosophy in History, University of Wyoming, Laramie, 1985, p. 143, **Willard W,** The First Amendment, Anglo-Conformity and American Indian Religious Freedom, *Wicazo Sa Review* 7:25-41, 1991.

97. **Willard W,** The First Amendment, Anglo-Conformity and American Indian Religious Freedom, *Wicazo Sa Review* 7:25-41, 1991.

98. **American Indian Religious Freedom Act Amendments, October 6, 1994,** In: Josephy AMJ, Nagel J, Johnson T, eds. *Red Power. The American Indians' Fight for Freedom,* University of Nebraska Press, Lincoln, 1999, pp. 251-152.

99. **Larner JW, Jr.,** ed. The Papers of the Society of American Indians, Microfilm Edition, *Scholarly Resources, Inc., Wilmington, Delaware,* 1987, Reel 1, Parker to Bonnin, December 21, 1916.

100. Ibid., Reel 1, Parker to Bonnin, October 14, 1918.

101. **Larner JW, Jr.,** The Papers of Carlos Montezuma, Microfilm Edition, *Scholarly Resources, Inc., Wilmington, Delaware,* 1984, Reel 4, Nobember 22, 1918.

102. **Collier J,** *From Every Zenith. A Memoir and Some Essays on Life and Thought,* Sage Books, Denver, 1963.

103. **Willard W,** The First Amendment, Anglo-Conformity and American Indian Religious Freedom, *Wicazo Sa Review* 7:25-41, 1991.

104. **Kelly LC,** *The Assault on Assimilation. John Collier and the Origins of Indian Policy Reform,* University of New Mexico Press, Albuquerque, 1983.

## CHAPTER TEN

1. **Gibson CB,** *Doctor Carlos Montezuma,* University Archives, University of Illinois at Urbana-Champaign.

2. **Piatigorsky A,** *Freemasonry. The Study of a Phenomenon,* The Harvill Press, London, 1999, p. xiii.

3. Ibid., p. 106, **Ridley J,** *The Freemasons. A History of the World's Most Powerful Secret Society,* Arcade Publishing, New York, 2001, pp. 1-8.

4. **Piatigorsky A,** *Freemasonry. The Study of a Phenomenon,* The Harvill Press, London, 1999, p. 100, **Bullock SC,** *Revolutionary Brotherhood. Freemasonry and the Transformation of the American Social Order, 1730–1840,* University of North Carolina Press, Chapel Hill, 1996, p. 13.

5. **Piatigorsky A,** *Freemasonry. The Study of a Phenomenon,* The Harvill Press, London, 1999, p. 215, **Ridley J,** *The Freemasons. A History of the World's Most Powerful Secret Society,* Arcade Publishing, New York, 2001, p. 3.

6. **Robinson JJ,** *Born in Blood. The Lost Secrets of Freemasonry,* M. Evans & Company, New York, 1989, **Bruno ST,** *Templar Organization: The Management of Warrior Monasticism,* 1st Books Library, www.1stbooks.com, 2000.

7. **Robinson JJ,** *Born in Blood. The Lost Secrets of Freemasonry,* M. Evans & Company, New York, 1989, p. 184.

8. **Hohler JS,** ed. *The Papers of Carlos Montezuma 1892-1937 (Microfilm Edition),* The State Historical Society of Wisconsin, Madison, 1975, Reel 7.

9. **Piatigorsky A,** *Freemasonry. The Study of a Phenomenon,* The Harvill Press, London, 1999, pp. 37-97.

10. **Robinson JJ,** *Born in Blood. The Lost Secrets of Freemasonry,* M. Evans & Company, New York, 1989, p. 182.

11. **Piatigorsky A,** *Freemasonry. The Study of a Phenomenon,* The Harvill Press, London, 1999, **MacNulty WK,** *Freemasonry. A Journey Through Ritual and Symbol,* Thames and Hudson Ltd., London, 1991, **Dumenil L,** *Freemasonry and American Culture 1880–1930,* Princeton University Press, Princeton, New Jersey, 1984, pp. 31-71.

12. **Dumenil L,** *Freemasonry and American Culture 1880–1930,* Princeton University Press, Princeton, New Jersey, 1984, pp. 40-41.

13. **Bullock SC,** *Revolutionary Brotherhood. Freemasonry and the Transformation of the American Social Order, 1730–1840,* University of North Carolina Press, Chapel Hill, 1996, pp. 52-59.

14. **Piatigorsky A,** *Freemasonry. The Study of a Phenomenon,* The Harvill Press, London, 1999, pp. 163-197.

15. **Bullock SC,** *Revolutionary Brotherhood. Freemasonry and the Transformation of the American Social Order, 1730–1840,* University of North Carolina Press, Chapel Hill, 1996.

16. Ibid., p. 85.

17. **Cook County, Illinois,** Restoration of Inscription of the Chicago Water Tower Cornerstone, 1913, *Cook County, Illinois USGenWeb,* http://www.rootsweb.com/~ilcook/rdata/orgs/1913_msn_wtrtwr.htm.

18. **Piatigorsky A,** *Freemasonry. The Study of a Phenomenon,* The Harvill Press, London, 1999, p. 167.

19. **North Carolina Section of the Royal Arch Mason,** York Rite, *http://ncmason.org/yorkrite.htm,* 2001.

20. **Ridley J,** *The Freemasons. A History of the World's Most Powerful Secret Society,* Arcade Publishing, New York, 2001, p. 267.

21. **Bullock SC,** *Revolutionary Brotherhood. Freemasonry and the Transformation of the American Social Order, 1730–1840,* University of North Carolina Press, Chapel Hill, 1996, pp. 277-307, **Ridley J,** *The Freemasons. A History of the World's Most Powerful Secret Society,* Arcade Publishing, New York, 2001, pp. 176-190.

22. **Dumenil L,** *Freemasonry and American Culture 1880–1930,* Princeton University Press, Princeton, New Jersey, 1984, p. 225.

23. **Ridley J,** *The Freemasons. A History of the World's Most Powerful Secret Society,* Arcade Publishing, New York, 2001, p. 275 **Dumenil L,** *Freemasonry and American Culture 1880–1930,* Princeton University Press, Princeton, New Jersey, 1984, p. 218.

24. **Dumenil L,** *Freemasonry and American Culture 1880–1930,* Princeton University Press, Princeton, New Jersey, 1984, pp. 115-147.

25. Ibid. pp. 122-125.

26. **Parker AC,** *American Indian Freemasonry*, New York State Library, Native American Language and Culture Preservation Project, Reel 61, Item 364, 1919.

27. Ibid., p. 11.

28. Ibid., p. 16.

29. Ibid., p. 18.

30. Ibid., p. 33.

31. Ibid., pp. 35-36.

32. **Dumenil L,** *Freemasonry and American Culture 1880–1930*, Princeton University Press, Princeton, New Jersey, 1984, p. 13.

33. **Bullock SC,** *Revolutionary Brotherhood. Freemasonry and the Transformation of the American Social Order, 1730–1840*, University of North Carolina Press, Chapel Hill, 1996, p. 143.

34. **Kreider C,** Historian and Librarian, Grand Lodge of Oregon, *Personal Interview by Leon Speroff*, May 1, 2002.

35. **Will C. Barnes Collection,** Arizona Historical Foundation, Arizona State University, January 19, 1934, Letter from Charles B. Gibson.

36. **Kalb R,** Grand Secretary of the Grand Lodge of Illinois, *Personal Communication*, May 2, 2002.

37. **Passing of Bro. (Dr.) Carlos Montezuma,** *Dearborn Lodge Bulletin*, May, 1923.

38. **Larner JW, Jr.,** The Papers of Carlos Montezuma, Microfilm Edition, *Scholarly Resources, Inc.*, *Wilmington, Delaware*, 1984, Reel 1, March 3, 1892.

## CHAPTER ELEVEN

1. **Larner JW, Jr.,** The Papers of Carlos Montezuma, Microfilm Edition, *Scholarly Resources, Inc.*, *Wilmington, Delaware*, 1984, Reel 2, October 7, 1905.

2. Ibid., Reel 1, June 15, 1887.

3. Ibid., Reel 1, June 28, 1887.

4. Ibid., Reel 1, July 22, 1887.

5. Ibid., Reel 1, August 20, 1887.

6. Ibid., Reel 1.

7. Ibid.

8. Ibid.

9. Ibid.

10. Ibid., Reel 1, August 15, 1901.

11. Ibid., Reel 1.

12. **Hohler JS,** ed. *The Papers of Carlos Montezuma 1892-1937 (Microfilm Edition)*, The State Historical Society of Wisconsin, Madison, 1975, Reel 1.

13. **Maher RC,** Carlos Montezuma M.D. The Saga of Wassaja, *Arizona Highways* 16:18-19, 35-36, 1940, **Robinson B,** The Great Yavapai, *Arizona Highways* 28:14-17, 1952.

14. **Robinson B,** The Great Yavapai, *Arizona Highways* 28:14-17, 1952.

15. **Larner JW, Jr.,** The Papers of Carlos Montezuma, Microfilm Edition, *Scholarly Resources, Inc.*, *Wilmington, Delaware*, 1984, Reel 1.

16. **Larner JW, Jr.,** Supplement to the Papers of Carlos Montezuma, Microfilm Edition, *Scholarly Resources, Inc., Wilmington, Delaware*, 2002, Reel 1, June, 1898.

17. **Larner JW, Jr.,** The Papers of Carlos Montezuma, Microfilm Edition, *Scholarly Resources, Inc., Wilmington, Delaware*, 1984, Reel 1, October 1, 1901.

18. **Maher RC,** Carlos Montezuma M.D. The Saga of Wassaja, *Arizona Highways* 16:18-19, 35-36, 1940.

19. **Larner JW, Jr.,** The Papers of Carlos Montezuma, Microfilm Edition, *Scholarly Resources, Inc., Wilmington, Delaware*, 1984, Reel 8.

20. Ibid., Reel 1, October 10, 1901.

21. Ibid., Reel 2, June 20, 1906.

22. Ibid., Reel 1, October 10, 1901.

23. **Dr. Montezuma. A Bright and Well Educated Apache With an Interesting History,** *Arizona Republican*, October 11, 1901.

24. **Larner JW, Jr.,** The Papers of Carlos Montezuma, Microfilm Edition, *Scholarly Resources, Inc., Wilmington, Delaware*, 1984, Reel 1.

25. Ibid.

26. Ibid., Reel 2, July 14, 1910.

27. Ibid., Reel 2, July 18, 1910.

28. **Oskison J,** With Apache Deer-Hunters in Arizona, *Outing* April:65-78, 150-163, 1914.

29. Ibid., pp. 55-56.

30. Ibid., p. 76.

31. Ibid., p. 77.

32. Ibid., p. 153.

33. Ibid., p. 161.

34. **Larner JW, Jr.,** The Papers of Carlos Montezuma, Microfilm Edition, *Scholarly Resources, Inc., Wilmington, Delaware*, 1984, Reel 3, February 15, 1913.

35. Ibid., Reel 3, September 11, 1913.

36. **Oskison J,** With Apache Deer-Hunters in Arizona, *Outing* April:65-78, 150-163, 1914.

37. **Coe CE,** (National Archives and Record Services, Record Group 75, Bureau of Indian Affairs, San Carlos Classified Collection Files, 1907–1939, Box 1), Letter to Commissioner, September 15, 1914, Report No. 111718-1913-063.

38. **Gebby GH,** (National Archives and Record Services, Record Group 75, Bureau of Indian Affairs, San Carlos Classified Collection Files, 1907–1939, Box 1), Letter to the Commissioner, October 26, 1913, Report No. 111718-1913-063.

39. **Larner JW, Jr.,** The Papers of Carlos Montezuma, Microfilm Edition, *Scholarly Resources, Inc., Wilmington, Delaware*, 1984, Reel 3, June 20, 1914.

40. **Bourke JG,** *On the Border With Crook*, University of Nebraska Press, Lincoln, 1891, reprinted 1971, pp. 190-201, **Waterstrat E,** *Commanders and Chiefs. A Brief History of Fort McDowell, Arizona (1865-1890), Its Officers and Men and the Indians They Were Ordered To Subdue*, Mount McDowell Press, Fountain Hills, Arizona, 1992, pp. 58-59.

41. **Burial Place of Cave Victims Revealed.** *Arizona Days and Ways Sunday Magazine, Arizona Republic*, November 9, 1958, p. 52.

42. **Larner JW, Jr.,** The Papers of Carlos Montezuma, Microfilm Edition, *Scholarly Resources, Inc., Wilmington, Delaware,* 1984, Reel 4, December, 1913.

43. Ibid., Reel 3, January 5, 1914.

44. Ibid., Reel 4, August 2, 1915.

45. Ibid., Reel 4, January 25, 1916.

46. Ibid., Reel 4, May 24, 1920.

47. Ibid., Reel 4, June, 1920.

48. Ibid., Reel 5, November 13, 1920.

49. **Montezuma Collection, Arizona State University,** *MSS-60, CMC, Box 2, Folder 5.*

50. **Sharp BA,** (National Archives and Record Services, Record Group 75, Bureau of Indian Affairs, San Carlos Classified Collection Files, 1907–1939, 45642-20-053), Letter to A. H. Symonds, January 10, 1921, Report No. 45642-20-053.

51. **Symonds AH,** (National Archives and Record Services Record Group 75, Bureau of Indian Affairs, San Carlos Central Classified Files, 1907-1939), Report to Commissioner of Indian Affairs, Report No. 45642-20-053.

52. **Montezuma Collection, Arizona State University,** *MSS-60, CMC, Box 2, Folder 5.*

53. Ibid.

54. **Davis CL,** (National Archives and Record Services Record Group 75, Bureau of Indian Affairs, San Carlos Central Classified Files, 1907-1939), Testimony Regarding Montezuma's Family, March 20, 1922, Report No. 45642-20-053.

55. **Davis CL,** (National Archives and Record Services Record Group 75, Bureau of Indian Affairs, San Carlos Central Classified Files, 1907-1939), Final Report, Davis to Commissioner, April 15, 1922, Report No. 45642-20-053.

56. **Larner JW, Jr.,** The Papers of Carlos Montezuma, Microfilm Edition, *Scholarly Resources, Inc., Wilmington, Delaware,* 1984, Reel 5, June 17, 1922.

57. Ibid., Reel 5, June 12, 1922.

58. Ibid., Reel 5, June 24, 1922.

59. Ibid., Reel 5, July 8, 1922.

60. Ibid., Reel 5, July 11, 1922.

61. Ibid., Reel 5, July 7, 1922.

62. Ibid., Reel 5, July 10, 1922.

## CHAPTER TWELVE

1. **Pevar SL,** *The Rights of Indians and Tribes. The Basic ACLU Guide to Indian and Tribal Rights, 2nd Ed.* Southern Illinois University Press, Carbondale, Illinois, 1992, pp. 209-210, **Hundley N, Jr.,** The Dark and Bloody Ground of Indian Water Rights: Confusion Elevated to Principle, *Western Historical Quarterly* 9:455-482, 1978.

2. **Massie M,** The Cultural Roots of Indian Water Rights, Master's Thesis, University of Wyoming, 1980.

3. **Pevar SL,** *The Rights of Indians and Tribes. The Basic ACLU Guide to Indian and Tribal Rights, 2nd Ed.* Southern Illinois University Press, Carbondale, Illinois, 1992, pp. 211-212.

4. Ibid., pp. 213-223, **Hundley N, Jr.,** The Dark and Bloody Ground of Indian Water Rights: Confusion Elevated to Principle, *Western Historical Quarterly* 9:455-482, 1978.

5. **Pevar SL,** *The Rights of Indians and Tribes. The Basic ACLU Guide to Indian and Tribal Rights, 2nd Ed.* Southern Illinois University Press, Carbondale, Illinois, 1992, p. 219.

6. **Clum JP,** The San Carlos Apache Police, *New Mexico Historical Review* IV, July:203-219, 1929, **Hagan WT,** *Indian Police and Judges. Experiments in Acculturation and Control,* Yale University Press, New Haven, 1966, pp. 25-34.

7. **Reed B,** *The Last Bugle Call. A History of Fort McDowell, Arizona Territory, 1865-1890,* McClain Printing Company, Parsons, West Virginia, 1977, p. 103, **Waterstrat E,** *Commanders and Chiefs. A Brief History of Fort McDowell, Arizona (1865-1890), Its Officers and Men and the Indians They Were Ordered To Subdue,* Mount McDowell Press, Fountain Hills, Arizona, 1992, p. 87.

8. **Reed B,** *The Last Bugle Call. A History of Fort McDowell, Arizona Territory, 1865-1890,* McClain Printing Company, Parsons, West Virginia, 1977, **Waterstrat E,** *Commanders and Chiefs. A Brief History of Fort McDowell, Arizona (1865-1890), Its Officers and Men and the Indians They Were Ordered To Subdue,* Mount McDowell Press, Fountain Hills, Arizona, 1992.

9. **Irwin McDowell,** *www.civilwarhome.com/mcdowellbio.htm,* 2002.

10. **Reed B,** *The Last Bugle Call. A History of Fort McDowell, Arizona Territory, 1865-1890,* McClain Printing Company, Parsons, West Virginia, 1977.

11. Ibid.

12. Ibid., pp. 153-155, **Waterstrat E,** *Commanders and Chiefs. A Brief History of Fort McDowell, Arizona (1865-1890), Its Officers and Men and the Indians They Were Ordered To Subdue,* Mount McDowell Press, Fountain Hills, Arizona, 1992, p. 93.

13. **Reed B,** *The Last Bugle Call. A History of Fort McDowell, Arizona Territory, 1865-1890,* McClain Printing Company, Parsons, West Virginia, 1977, p. 153.

14. Ibid., pp. 121-122.

15. **Mariella PS,** The Political Economy of Federal Resettlement Policies Affecting Native American Communities: the Fort McDowell Yavapai Case, Dissertation for Doctor of Philosophy, Arizona State University, 1983.

16. **Jones WA,** Letter to Secretary of Interior, *Correspondence, Land Division, Office of Indian Affairs,* 312:330-341, September 12, 1903, **Commissioner of Indian Affairs,** *Annual Reports of the Department of the Interior for the fiscal year ended June 30, 1905, Indian Affairs, Part I, Camp McDowell Reservation, Arizona,* Vol. 19, Document No. 5, Government Printing Office, Washington, DC, 1906.

17. **Mariella PS,** The Political Economy of Federal Resettlement Policies Affecting Native American Communities: the Fort McDowell Yavapai Case, Dissertation for Doctor of Philosophy, Arizona State University, 1983, pp. 128-129.

18. **Khera S,** The Yavapai: Who They Are and From Where They Come, In: Chaudhuri JO, ed. *The Yavapai of Fort McDowell,* Mead Publishing, Mesa, Arizona, 1995, pp. 1-16.

19. **Jones WA,** Letter to Secretary of Interior, *Correspondence, Land Division, Office of Indian Affairs,* 312:330-341, September 12, 1903, **Commissioner of Indian Affairs,** *Annual Reports of the Department of the Interior for the fiscal year ended June 30, 1905, Indian Affairs, Part I, Camp McDowell Reservation, Arizona,* Vol. 19, Document No. 5, Government Printing Office, Washington, DC, 1906.

20. Ibid.

21. **28 Stat. 491,** August 23, 1904.

22. **Larner JW, Jr.,** The Papers of Carlos Montezuma, Microfilm Edition, *Scholarly Resources, Inc., Wilmington, Delaware,* 1984, Reel 1.

23. **Heider KG,** Fort McDowell Yavapai Acculturation: A Preliminary Study, B. A. Honors Thesis, Harvard College, 1956, p. 21.

24. **Prucha FP,** *The Great Father. The United States Government and the American Indians, Abridged Edition,* University of Nebraska Press, Lincoln, 1986, pp. 303-305.

25. **McDonnell JA,** *The Dispossession of the American Indian, 1887–1934,* Indiana University Press, Bloomington, 1991, p. 84.

26. **Massie M,** The Cultural Roots of Indian Water Rights, Master's Thesis, University of Wyoming, 1980.

27. **Chamberlain SA,** The Fort McDowell Indian Reservation. Water Rights and Indian Removal, 1910–1930, *J of the West* 14:27-34, 1975, **Lamb TJ,** Early Twentieth Century Efforts at Economic Development in Nigeria and Arizona, Dissertation for Doctor of Philosophy, Temple University, 1978, pp. 161-175, **Khera S,** The Yavapai: Who They Are and From Where They Come, In: Chaudhuri JO, ed. *The Yavapai of Fort McDowell,* Mead Publishing, Mesa, Arizona, 1995, pp. 1-16.

28. **Mariella P,** Yavapai Farming, In: Chaudhuri JO, ed. *The Yavapai of Fort McDowell,* Mead Publishing, Mesa, Arizona, 1995, pp. 28-35, **Coffeen WR,** The Effects of the Central Arizona Project on the Fort McDowell Indian Community, *Ethnohistory* 19:345-377, 1972.

29. **Coffeen WR,** The Effects of the Central Arizona Project on the Fort McDowell Indian Community, *Ethnohistory* 19:345-377, 1972, p. 352.

30. **Mariella P,** Yavapai Farming, In: Chaudhuri JO, ed. *The Yavapai of Fort McDowell,* Mead Publishing, Mesa, Arizona, 1995, pp. 28-35.

31. **Larner JW, Jr.,** The Papers of Carlos Montezuma, Microfilm Edition, *Scholarly Resources, Inc., Wilmington, Delaware,* 1984, Reel 2.

32. **Coffeen WR,** The Effects of the Central Arizona Project on the Fort McDowell Indian Community, *Ethnohistory* 19:345-377, 1972, p. 352, **Lamb TJ,** Early Twentieth Century Efforts at Economic Development in Nigeria and Arizona, Dissertation for Doctor of Philosophy, Temple University, 1978, p. 157, **Schilling RK,** Indians and Eagles. The Struggle Over Orme Dam, *J Arizona History* 41:57-82, 2000, p. 59.

33. **Petition from Fort McDowell Yavapais to Commissioner of Indian Affairs,** *National Archives, Salt River:*30858-30853-30810-30133, May 7, 1910.

34. **Larner JW, Jr.,** The Papers of Carlos Montezuma, Microfilm Edition, *Scholarly Resources, Inc., Wilmington, Delaware,* 1984, Reel 2, May 7, 1910.

35. Ibid., Reel 2, October 15, 1910.

36. Ibid., Reel 2, January 27, 1911.

37. Ibid., Reel 2, January 30, 1911.

38. Ibid., Reel 2.

39. Ibid., Reel 2, January 29, 1911.

40. **Valentine RG,** Office Circular No. 497, *National Archives, Record Group 75, Bureau of Indian Affairs,* December 23, 1910.

41. **Larner JW, Jr.,** The Papers of Carlos Montezuma, Microfilm Edition, *Scholarly Resources, Inc., Wilmington, Delaware,* 1984, Reel 2, February 9, 1911.

42. Ibid., Reel 2, March 13, 1911.

43. Ibid., Reel 2, March 11, 1911.

44. **Khera S,** The Yavapai: Who They Are and From Where They Come, In: Chaudhuri JO, ed. *The Yavapai of Fort McDowell,* Mead Publishing, Mesa, Arizona, 1995, pp. 1-16, **Coffeen WR,** The Effects of the Central Arizona Project on the Fort McDowell Indian Community, *Ethnohistory* 19:345-377, 1972, p. 352, **Larner JW, Jr.,** The Papers of Carlos Montezuma, Microfilm Edition, *Scholarly Resources, Inc., Wilmington, Delaware,* 1984, Reel 4, May 14, 1917.

45. **Larner JW, Jr.,** The Papers of Carlos Montezuma, Microfilm Edition, *Scholarly Resources, Inc., Wilmington, Delaware,* 1984, Reel 2, March 31, 1911.

46. Ibid., Reel 2, April 22, 1911.

47. Ibid., Reel 3.

48. Ibid., Reel 4, October, 1914.

49. **Larner JW, Jr.,** Supplement to the Papers of Carlos Montezuma, Microfilm Edition, *Scholarly Resources, Inc., Wilmington, Delaware,* 2002, Reel 4, July 4, 1919.

50. **Larner JW, Jr.,** The Papers of Carlos Montezuma, Microfilm Edition, *Scholarly Resources, Inc., Wilmington, Delaware,* 1984, Reel 3, October, 1911.

51. Ibid., Reel 3, May 1, 1912.

52. Ibid., Reel 3, July 20, 1912.

53. Ibid., Reel 3, March 12, 1912.

54. Ibid., Reel 7, Hearings Before the Committee on Expenditures in the Interior Department, June 5-17, 1911.

55. **Kelly WH,** *Indians of the Southwest. A Survey of Indian Tribes and Indian Administration in Arizona,* University of Arizona, Tucson, 1953, p. 2.

56. **Larner JW, Jr.,** The Papers of Carlos Montezuma, Microfilm Edition, *Scholarly Resources, Inc., Wilmington, Delaware,* 1984, Reel 7, Hearings Before the Committee on Expenditures in the Interior Department, **Leupp FE,** *The Indian and his Problem,* Charles Scribner's Sons, 1910, reprinted. Arno Press, New York, 1971.

57. **Larner JW, Jr.,** The Papers of Carlos Montezuma, Microfilm Edition, *Scholarly Resources, Inc., Wilmington, Delaware,* 1984, Reel 5, Vol. 5, No. 2, May, 1921.

58. Ibid., Reel 3, August 27, 1912.

59. Ibid., Reel 3, September 14, 1912.

60. **Thackery FA,** Dr. Montezuma and the Pima Indians, *The Indian School Journal—About Indians (Chilocco Indian School)* 14:504-506, 1914.

61. **Putney DT,** Robert Grosvenor Valentine, In: Kvasnicka RM, Viola HJ, eds. *The Commissioners of Indian Affairs, 1824-1977,* University of Nebraska Press, Lincoln, 1979, 233-242.

62. **Larner JW, Jr.,** The Papers of Carlos Montezuma, Microfilm Edition, *Scholarly Resources, Inc., Wilmington, Delaware,* 1984, Reel 3, November 11, 1912.

63. Ibid., Reel 3, January 5, 1913.

64. Ibid., Reel 3, February 3, 1913.

65. Ibid., Reel 3, April 16, 1912.

66. Ibid., Reel 3, March 19, 1913.

67. **Kelly LC,** Cato Sells, In: Kvasnicka RM, Viola HJ, eds. *The Commissioners of Indian Affairs, 1824-1977,* University of Nebraska Press, Lincoln, 1979, pp. 243-250.

68. **Larner JW, Jr.,** The Papers of Carlos Montezuma, Microfilm Edition, *Scholarly Resources, Inc., Wilmington, Delaware,* 1984, Reel 3, July 17, 1913.

69. Ibid., Reel 3, July 28, 1913.

70. Ibid., Reel 3, September 3, 1913.

71. **Thackery FA,** Dr. Montezuma and the Pima Indians, *The Indian School Journal—About Indians (Chilocco Indian School)* 14:504-506, 1914.

72. **Larner JW, Jr.,** The Papers of Carlos Montezuma, Microfilm Edition, *Scholarly Resources, Inc., Wilmington, Delaware,* 1984, Reel 3, October 28, 1913.

73. **Oskison J,** With Apache Deer-Hunters in Arizona, *Outing* April:65-78, 150-163, 1914.

74. **Larner JW, Jr.,** The Papers of Carlos Montezuma, Microfilm Edition, *Scholarly Resources, Inc., Wilmington, Delaware,* 1984, Reel 3, September 29, 1913.

75. Ibid., Reel 3, December 12, 1913.

76. Ibid., Reel 3, May 12, 1914.

77. **Larner JW, Jr.,** ed. The Papers of the Society of American Indians, Microfilm Edition, *Scholarly Resources, Inc., Wilmington, Delaware,* 1987, Reel 5, July 31, 1914.

78. **Larner JW, Jr.,** The Papers of Carlos Montezuma, Microfilm Edition, *Scholarly Resources, Inc., Wilmington, Delaware,* 1984, Reel 4, April 16, 1915.

79. Ibid., Reel 4, April 17, 1915.

80. Ibid., Reel 4, May 10, 1918.

81. Ibid., Reel 3, January 5, 1914.

82. Ibid., Reel 3, August 28, 1914.

83. Ibid., Reel 4, November 15, 1914.

84. Ibid., Reel 4, November 21, 1914.

85. Ibid., Reel 4, November 20, 1914.

86. Ibid., Reel 4, August 6, 1915.

87. Ibid., Reel 4, October 5 & 27, 1914.

88. Ibid., Reel 4, July 10, 1915.

89. Ibid., Reel 4, August 28, 1915.

90. Ibid., Reel 4, April 2, 1915.

91. Ibid., Reel 4, August 17, 1915.

92. Ibid., Reel 4, September 7, 1915.

93. **Chamberlain SA,** The Fort McDowell Indian Reservation. Water Rights and Indian Removal, 1910-1930, *J of the West* 14:27-34, 1975, **Larner JW, Jr.,** Supplement to the Papers of Carlos Montezuma, Microfilm Edition, *Scholarly Resources, Inc., Wilmington, Delaware,* 2002, Reel 5, June 8, 1922.

94. **Larner JW, Jr.,** The Papers of Carlos Montezuma, Microfilm Edition, *Scholarly Resources, Inc., Wilmington, Delaware,* 1984, Reel 3, May 1, 1912.

95. Ibid., Reel 4, January 15, 1916.

96. Ibid., Reel 4, April 28, 1916.

97. Ibid., Reel 4, April 3, 1918.

98. Ibid., Reel 4, September 9, 1915.

99. **Records of the Bureau of Indian Affairs,** (National Archives and Record Services, Record Group 75, Bureau of Indian Affairs, San Carlos Classified Collection Files, 1907–1939, Box 1), Report No. 10106-1917-061.

100. **Larner JW, Jr.,** Supplement to the Papers of Carlos Montezuma, Microfilm Edition, *Scholarly Resources, Inc., Wilmington, Delaware,* 2002, Reel 8.

101. **Larner JW, Jr.,** The Papers of Carlos Montezuma, Microfilm Edition, *Scholarly Resources, Inc., Wilmington, Delaware,* 1984, Reel 4, November 20, 1917.

102. **Lane H,** *Congressional Record,* Vol. 53, No. 123:pp. 8888-8891, May 12, 1916.

103. **Larner JW, Jr.,** The Papers of Carlos Montezuma, Microfilm Edition, *Scholarly Resources, Inc., Wilmington, Delaware,* 1984, Reel 4, July 12, 1916.

104. Ibid., Reel 4, March 22, 1917.

105. Ibid., Reel 4, March 30, 1917.

106. Ibid., Reel 5, June 13, 1922.

107. Ibid., Reel 4, November 22, 1918.

108. Ibid., Reel 9, October 22, 1918, December 16, 1920.

109. Ibid., Reel 5, November 3, 1920.

110. **Larner JW, Jr.,** Supplement to the Papers of Carlos Montezuma, Microfilm Edition, *Scholarly Resources, Inc., Wilmington, Delaware,* 2002, Reel 8, May 26, 1920.

111. **Larner JW, Jr.,** The Papers of Carlos Montezuma, Microfilm Edition, *Scholarly Resources, Inc., Wilmington, Delaware,* 1984, Reel 5, March 7, 1921.

112. Ibid., Reel 5, September 4, 1920.

113. Ibid., Reel 5, April 6, 1921.

114. **Kelly LC,** Charles Henry Burke, In: Kvasnicka RM, Viola HJ, eds. *The Commissioners of Indian Affairs, 1824-1977,* University of Nebraska Press, Lincoln, 1979, pp. 251-261.

115. **Bates JL,** Teapot Dome, *http://gi.grolier.com/presidents/ea/side/teapot.html,* 2002.

116. **Larner JW, Jr.,** The Papers of Carlos Montezuma, Microfilm Edition, *Scholarly Resources, Inc., Wilmington, Delaware,* 1984, Reel 5, April 11, 1921.

117. Ibid., Reel 5, April 30, 1921.

118. Ibid., Reel 5, May 2, 1921.

119. Ibid., Reel 5, May 23, 1921.

120. Ibid.

121. Ibid., Reel 5, June 8, 1921.

122. Ibid., Reel 5, June 1, 1921

123. **Kelly LC,** Charles Henry Burke, In: Kvasnicka RM, Viola HJ, eds. *The Commissioners of Indian Affairs, 1824-1977,* University of Nebraska Press, Lincoln, 1979, pp. 251-261.

124. **Burke Act, U.S. Statutes at Large 34:182-183, May 8, 1906,** In: Prucha FP, ed. *Documents of United States Indian Policy, 2nd Edition,* University of Nebraska Press, Lincoln, 1990, p. 207.

125. **Flynn S,** Western Assimilationist: Charles H. Burke and the Burke Act, Dissertation for Master of Arts, Texas Tech University, 1988.

126. **Latimer JW,** *The Rape of McDowell Reservation, Arizona by the Indian Bureau. Statement of Facts,* Hayworth Publishing House, Washington, D.C., 1921.

127. **Larner JW, Jr.,** The Papers of Carlos Montezuma, Microfilm Edition, *Scholarly Resources, Inc., Wilmington, Delaware,* 1984, Reel 5, September 28, 1921.

128. Ibid., Reel 5, June 24, 1921.

129. Ibid., Reel 5, June 26, 1921.

130. Ibid., Reel 5, June 17, 1921.

131. Ibid., Reel 5, September 4, 1920.

132. Ibid., Reel 5, June 26, 1921.

133. Ibid., Reel 5, June 24, 1921.

134. Ibid., Reel 7, Meeting with Charles H. Burke, June 24, 1921.

135. Ibid.

136. Ibid.

137. Ibid.

138. Ibid.

139. Ibid., Reel 9, June 25, 1921.

140. Ibid., Reel 5, June 28, 1921.

141. **Larner JW, Jr.,** Supplement to the Papers of Carlos Montezuma, Microfilm Edition, *Scholarly Resources, Inc., Wilmington, Delaware*, 2002, Reel 5.

142. Ibid., Reel 8, July 6, 1921.

143. Ibid.

144. **Montezuma Collection, Arizona State University.** *MSS-60, CMC, Box 2, Folder 5.*

145. **Larner JW, Jr.,** The Papers of Carlos Montezuma, Microfilm Edition, *Scholarly Resources, Inc., Wilmington, Delaware*, 1984, Reel 9, February 8, 1922.

146. Ibid.

147. **Thackery FA,** Dr. Montezuma and the Pima Indians, *The Indian School Journal—About Indians (Chilocco Indian School)* 14:504-506, 1914.

148. **Larner JW, Jr.,** The Papers of Carlos Montezuma, Microfilm Edition, *Scholarly Resources, Inc., Wilmington, Delaware*, 1984, Reel 2, January 29, 1911.

149. Ibid., Reel 3, February 16, 1912.

150. Ibid., Reel 4, February 25, 1918.

151. **Mariella PS,** The Political Economy of Federal Resettlement Policies Affecting Native American Communities: the Fort McDowell Yavapai Case, Dissertation for Doctor of Philosophy, Arizona State University, 1983, p. 185.

152. **Mariella P,** Yavapai Farming, In: Chaudhuri JO, ed. *The Yavapai of Fort McDowell*, Mead Publishing, Mesa, Arizona, 1995, pp. 28-35.

153. **Heider KG,** Fort McDowell Yavapai Acculturation: A Preliminary Study, B. A. Honors Thesis, Harvard College, 1956.

154. **Coffeen WR,** The Effects of the Central Arizona Project on the Fort McDowell Indian Community, *Ethnohistory* 19:345-377, 1972.

155. **Schilling RK,** Indians and Eagles. The Struggle Over Orme Dam, *J Arizona History* 41:57-82, 2000, p. 63.

156. **Colorado River Basin Act,** Public Law 90-357, September 30, 1968.

157. **Coffeen WR,** The Effects of the Central Arizona Project on the Fort McDowell Indian Community, *Ethnohistory* 19:345-377, 1972, **Butler C,** Fort McDowell and Orme Dam, In: Chaudhuri JO, ed. *The Yavapai of Fort McDowell*, Mead Publishing, Mesa, Arizona, 1995, pp. 17-23.

158. **Schilling RK,** Indians and Eagles. The Struggle Over Orme Dam, *J Arizona History* 41:57-82, 2000, p. 58, **Coffeen WR,** The Effects of the Central Arizona Project on the Fort McDowell Indian Community, *Ethnohistory* 19:345-377, 1972, p. 359.

159. **Coffeen WR,** The Effects of the Central Arizona Project on the Fort McDowell Indian Community, *Ethnohistory* 19:345-377, 1972, p. 361.

160. **Butler C,** Fort McDowell and Orme Dam, In: Chaudhuri JO, ed. *The Yavapai of Fort McDowell,* Mead Publishing, Mesa, Arizona, 1995, pp. 17-23.

161. **Coffeen WR,** The Effects of the Central Arizona Project on the Fort McDowell Indian Community, *Ethnohistory* 19:345-377, 1972, p. 365.

162. **Butler C,** Fort McDowell and Orme Dam, In: Chaudhuri JO, ed. *The Yavapai of Fort McDowell,* Mead Publishing, Mesa, Arizona, 1995, pp. 17-23.

163. Ibid.

164. **Schilling RK,** Indians and Eagles. The Struggle Over Orme Dam, *J Arizona History* 41:57-82, 2000, p. 65.

165. **Heap Big Offer,** *Arizona Republic,* August 24, 1975.

166. **Shuey C,** Hiawatha Hood Wants His Land, Not Money, *Scottsdale Daily Progress,* April 29, 1976.

167. **Schilling RK,** Indians and Eagles. The Struggle Over Orme Dam, *J Arizona History* 41:57-82, 2000, p. 72.

168. Ibid., p. 76.

169. **Welsh F,** *How To Create a Water Crisis,* Johnson Books, Boulder, 1985, p. 166.

170. **Schilling RK,** Indians and Eagles. The Struggle Over Orme Dam, *J Arizona History* 41:57-82, 2000, p. 78.

171. **Larner, JW, Jr.,** Personal communication, July, 2002.

172. Ibid.

173. **Coffeen WR,** The Effects of the Central Arizona Project on the Fort McDowell Indian Community, *Ethnohistory* 19:345-377, 1972, p. 365.

174. **Schilling RK,** Indians and Eagles. The Struggle Over Orme Dam, *J Arizona History* 41:57-82, 2000, p. 66.

175. **Fort McDowell Indian Water Settlement Act,** http://thomas.loc.gov/cgi-bin/query/D?r101:1:./temp/~r101kig3Bm:e0, *Congressional Record* October 27:S17732, 1990.

176. **Indian Gaming Regulatory Act, October 18, 1988,** In: Josephy AMJ, Nagel J, Johnson T, eds. *Red Power. The American Indians' Fight for Freedom,* University of Nebraska Press, Lincoln, 1999, pp. 168-171.

177. **Chaudhuri JO,** The Stand Off at Fort McDowell, In: Chaudhuri JO, ed. *The Yavapai of Fort McDowell,* Mead Publishing, Mesa, Arizona, 1995, pp. 87-89.

178. **Constitution of the Fort McDowell Yavapai Nation,** http://www.narf.org/nill/Constitutions/FtMcDowellConst/ftmcdowellconstit.htm, 1999.

## CHAPTER THIRTEEN

1. **Hertzberg HW,** *The Search for an American Indian Identity. Modern Pan-Indian Movements,* Syracuse University Press, Syracuse, 1971, p. 44.

2. Ibid., pp. 31-38.

3. **McKenzie FA,** *The Indian in Relation to the White Population of the United States,* Published by the Author, Columbus, Ohio, 1908.

4. **Larner JW, Jr.,** ed. The Papers of the Society of American Indians, Microfilm Edition, *Scholarly Resources, Inc., Wilmington, Delaware,* 1987, Reel 8, September 15, 1909.

5. **Larner JW, Jr.,** The Papers of Carlos Montezuma, Microfilm Edition, *Scholarly Resources, Inc., Wilmington, Delaware,* 1984, Reel 2, September 2 and 4, 1909.

6. **Larner JW, Jr.,** ed. The Papers of the Society of American Indians, Microfilm Edition, *Scholarly Resources, Inc., Wilmington, Delaware,* 1987, Reel 8, September 15, 1909.

7. **Larner JW, Jr.,** The Papers of Carlos Montezuma, Microfilm Edition, *Scholarly Resources, Inc., Wilmington, Delaware,* 1984, Reel 2, November 1, 1909.

8. Ibid., Reel 2, June 6, 1910.

9. Ibid., Reel 2.

10. **Hertzberg HW,** *The Search for an American Indian Identity. Modern Pan-Indian Movements,* Syracuse University Press, Syracuse, 1971, pp. 48-58, **Thomas WS,** Arthur Caswell Parker: 1881-1955. Anthropologist, Historian and Museum Pioneer, *Rochester History* 17:1-20, 1955, **Porter J,** *To Be Indian. The Life of Iroquois-Seneca Arthur Caswell Parker,* University of Oklahoma Press, Norman, 2001.

11. **Porter J,** *To Be Indian. The Life of Iroquois-Seneca Arthur Caswell Parker,* University of Oklahoma Press, Norman, 2001, p. xvii.

12. **Hertzberg HW,** *The Search for an American Indian Identity. Modern Pan-Indian Movements,* Syracuse University Press, Syracuse, 1971, pp. 47-48.

13. Ibid., pp. 46-47.

14. Ibid., pp. 45-46.

15. Ibid., pp. 42-43.

16. Ibid., pp. 38-42, **Wilson R,** *Ohiyesa. Charles Eastman, Santee Sioux,* University of Illinois Press, Urbana, 1983.

17. **Eastman EG,** *Pratt. The Red Man's Moses,* University of Oklahoma Press, Norman, 1935.

18. **Hertzberg HW,** *The Search for an American Indian Identity. Modern Pan-Indian Movements,* Syracuse University Press, Syracuse, 1971, pp. 59-78.

19. **Larner JW, Jr.,** The Papers of Carlos Montezuma, Microfilm Edition, *Scholarly Resources, Inc., Wilmington, Delaware,* 1984, Reel 2.

20. Ibid., Reel 3.

21. Ibid., Reel 2, November 15, 1909.

22. Ibid., Reel 2, June 2, 1910.

23. Ibid., Reel 2, April 18, 1911.

24. Ibid., Reel 2, May 13 & 17, 1911.

25. Ibid., Reel 2, July 4, 1911.

26. Ibid., Reel 2, September 25, 1911.

27. Ibid.

28. Ibid.

29. **Hertzberg HW,** *The Search for an American Indian Identity. Modern Pan-Indian Movements,* Syracuse University Press, Syracuse, 1971, p. 83.

30. **Larner JW, Jr.,** The Papers of Carlos Montezuma, Microfilm Edition, *Scholarly Resources, Inc., Wilmington, Delaware,* 1984, Reel 3, March 4, 1912.

31. Ibid., Reel 3, March 28, 1912.

32. **Montezuma C,** Light on the Indian Situation, *Quarterly J Soc Am Indians* 1:50-55, 1913.

33. Ibid.

34. Ibid.

35. Ibid.

36. **Larner JW, Jr.,** The Papers of Carlos Montezuma, Microfilm Edition, *Scholarly Resources, Inc., Wilmington, Delaware,* 1984, Reel 3, October 17, 1912.

37. **Society of American Indians,** *Quarterly J Soc Am Indians,* I, No. 1, 1913.

38. **Larner JW, Jr.,** The Papers of Carlos Montezuma, Microfilm Edition, *Scholarly Resources, Inc., Wilmington, Delaware,* 1984, Reel 3, September 4, 1913.

39. Ibid., Reel 3, May 7, 1913.

40. Ibid., Reel 3, May 25, 1913.

41. Ibid., Reel 3, August 5, 1913.

42. Ibid., Reel 3, September 16, 1913.

43. **Parker AC,** The Quaker City Meeting of the Society of American Indians, *Quarterly J Soc Am Indians* II:59, 1914.

44. **Hertzberg HW,** *The Search for an American Indian Identity. Modern Pan-Indian Movements,* Syracuse University Press, Syracuse, 1971, pp. 119-120, **Montezuma C,** The Reservation System Is Fatal to the Development of Good Citizenship, *Quarterly J Soc Am Indians* II:69-74, 1914, **Larner JW, Jr.,** ed. The Papers of the Society of American Indians, Microfilm Edition, *Scholarly Resources, Inc., Wilmington, Delaware,* 1987, Reel 6, Parker to Speck, February 25, 1914.

45. **Montezuma C,** The Reservation System Is Fatal to the Development of Good Citizenship, *Quarterly J Soc Am Indians* II:69-74, 1914.

46. Ibid.

47. Ibid.

48. Ibid.

49. Ibid.

50. Ibid.

51. Ibid.

52. **Larner JW, Jr.,** The Papers of Carlos Montezuma, Microfilm Edition, *Scholarly Resources, Inc., Wilmington, Delaware,* 1984, Reel 3, February 27, 1914.

53. **Hertzberg HW,** *The Search for an American Indian Identity. Modern Pan-Indian Movements,* Syracuse University Press, Syracuse, 1971, pp. 119-123.

54. **Porter J,** *To Be Indian. The Life of Iroquois-Seneca Arthur Caswell Parker,* University of Oklahoma Press, Norman, 2001, pp. 115-116.

55. **Larner JW, Jr.,** ed. The Papers of the Society of American Indians, Microfilm Edition, *Scholarly Resources, Inc., Wilmington, Delaware,* 1987, Reel 6, Parker to Speck, February 25, 1914.

56. **Speck FG,** Educating the White Man Up to the Indians, *Quarterly J Soc Am Indians* II:64-68, 1914.

57. Ibid.

58. Ibid.

59. Ibid.

60. **Larner JW, Jr.,** The Papers of Carlos Montezuma, Microfilm Edition, *Scholarly Resources, Inc., Wilmington, Delaware,* 1984, Reel 3, April 18, 1914.

61. Ibid., Reel 4, September 30, 1914.

62. **Larner JW, Jr.,** ed. The Papers of the Society of American Indians, Microfilm Edition, *Scholarly Resources, Inc., Wilmington, Delaware,* 1987, Reel 1.

63. **Larner JW, Jr.,** The Papers of Carlos Montezuma, Microfilm Edition, *Scholarly Resources, Inc., Wilmington, Delaware,* 1984, Reel 3, July 17 and 18, September 3, 1913.

64. **Prucha FP,** *The Great Father. The United States Government and the American Indians, Abridged Edition,* University of Nebraska Press, Lincoln, 1986, pp. 300-301.

65. **Hertzberg HW,** *The Search for an American Indian Identity. Modern Pan-Indian Movements,* Syracuse University Press, Syracuse, 1971, p. 127.

66. Ibid., p. 128.

67. Ibid., pp. 135-154.

68. **Larner JW, Jr.,** The Papers of Carlos Montezuma, Microfilm Edition, *Scholarly Resources, Inc., Wilmington, Delaware,* 1984, Reel 4, September 7, 1915.

69. Ibid., Reel 6, Let My People Go, 1915.

70. **Parker AC,** Certainly Abolish the Indian Bureau, *Quarterly J Soc Am Indians* 3:261-263, 1915.

71. **Larner JW, Jr.,** The Papers of Carlos Montezuma, Microfilm Edition, *Scholarly Resources, Inc., Wilmington, Delaware,* 1984, Reel 4, October 11, 1915.

72. Ibid., Reel 2, March 2, 1911.

73. Ibid., Reel 5, Vol. 1, No. 1, June, 1916.

74. Ibid., Reel 4, October 4, 1915.

75. *Quarterly J Soc Am Indians* III:316, 1915.

76. **Larner JW, Jr.,** The Papers of Carlos Montezuma, Microfilm Edition, *Scholarly Resources, Inc., Wilmington, Delaware,* 1984, Reel 4, February 19, 1916, Ibid., Reel 4, March 22, 1917.

77. Ibid., Reel 4, November 8, 1915.

78. **Parker AC,** The Function of the Society of American Indians, *Am Indian Magazine, Quarterly J Soc Am Indians* IV:8-20, 1916.

79. Ibid.

80. **Parker AC,** The Indian, the Country and the Government. A plea for an efficient Indian service., *Am Indian Magazine, Quarterly J Soc Am Indians* IV:38-49,

81. Ibid.

82. **Larner JW, Jr.,** The Papers of Carlos Montezuma, Microfilm Edition, *Scholarly Resources, Inc., Wilmington, Delaware,* 1984, Reel 5, Vol. 1, No. 1, May, 1916.

83. Ibid., Reel 4, June 19, 1916.

84. Ibid., Reel 5, Vol. 1, No. 1, May, 1916.

85. **Parker AC,** Editorial, *Am Indian Magazine, Quarterly J Soc Am Indians* IV:170-171, 1916.

86. Ibid.

87. **Larner JW, Jr.,** ed. The Papers of the Society of American Indians, Microfilm Edition, *Scholarly Resources, Inc., Wilmington, Delaware,* 1987, Reel 1, August 15, 1916.

88. **Montezuma C,** Address Before the Sixth Conference, *Quarterly J Soc Am Indians* IV:260-262, 1916.

89. **Society of American Indians,** Platform, *Am Indian Magazine, Quarterly J Soc Am Indians* IV:223, 1916.

90. **Society of American Indians,** Open Debate on the Loyalty of Indian Employees in the Indian Service, *Am Indian Magazine, Quarterly J Soc Am Indians* IV:252-256, 1916.

91. Ibid.

92. **Society of American Indians,** Reporters Took Indian Humor Seriously, *Am Indian Magazine, Quarterly J Soc Am Indians* IV:265-266, 1916.

93. **Larner JW, Jr.,** The Papers of Carlos Montezuma, Microfilm Edition, *Scholarly Resources, Inc., Wilmington, Delaware,* 1984, Reel 5, Vol. 1, No. 7, October, 1916.

94. Ibid., Reel 4, October 14, 1916.

95. Ibid., Reel 4, January 19, 1917.

96. Ibid., Reel 4, December 10, 1916.

97. Ibid., Reel 4, July 11, 1917.

98. Ibid., Reel 5, Vol. 2, No. 7, October, 1917.

99. **Larner JW, Jr.,** ed. The Papers of the Society of American Indians, Microfilm Edition, *Scholarly Resources, Inc., Wilmington, Delaware,* 1987, Reel 1, October 2, 1917.

100. **Montezuma C,** Abolish the Indian Bureau, *Am Indian Magazine, Quarterly J Soc Am Indians* VII:9-19, 1919., **Larner JW, Jr.,** The Papers of Carlos Montezuma, Microfilm Edition, *Scholarly Resources, Inc., Wilmington, Delaware,* 1984, Reel 6.

101. **Larner JW, Jr.,** ed. The Papers of the Society of American Indians, Microfilm Edition, *Scholarly Resources, Inc., Wilmington, Delaware,* 1987, Reel 1, October 14, 1918.

102. **Hertzberg HW,** *The Search for an American Indian Identity. Modern Pan-Indian Movements,* Syracuse University Press, Syracuse, 1971, p. 185, **Porter J,** *To Be Indian. The Life of Iroquois-Seneca Arthur Caswell Parker,* University of Oklahoma Press, Norman, 2001, p. 135.

103. **Larner JW, Jr.,** The Papers of Carlos Montezuma, Microfilm Edition, *Scholarly Resources, Inc., Wilmington, Delaware,* 1984, Reel 4, November 6, 1918.

104. Ibid., Reel 4, October 26, 1918.

105. Ibid., Reel 5, Vol. 3, No. 7, October, 1918.

106. Ibid., Reel 5.

107. Ibid., Reel 4, December 1, 1919.

108. **Larner JW, Jr.,** Supplement to the Papers of Carlos Montezuma, Microfilm Edition, *Scholarly Resources, Inc., Wilmington, Delaware,* 2002, Reel 4, June 27, 1919.

109. **Larner JW, Jr.,** The Papers of Carlos Montezuma, Microfilm Edition, *Scholarly Resources, Inc., Wilmington, Delaware,* 1984, Reel 5, November 6, 1921.

110. Ibid., Reel 5, October 27, 1922.

111. **Larner JW, Jr.,** Supplement to the Papers of Carlos Montezuma, Microfilm Edition, *Scholarly Resources, Inc., Wilmington, Delaware,* 2002, Reel 4, June, 1919.

112. **Larner JW, Jr.,** ed. The Papers of the Society of American Indians, Microfilm Edition, *Scholarly Resources, Inc., Wilmington, Delaware,* 1987, Reel 6, Stanley to Parker, August 2, 1923.

113. **Morris E,** *Theodore Rex,* Random House, New York, 2001, **Walworth A,** *Woodrow Wilson: American Prophet,* W. W. Norton & Company, New York, 1979.

114. **Prucha FP,** *The Great Father. The United States Government and the American Indians, Abridged Edition,* University of Nebraska Press, Lincoln, 1986, pp. 272-279.

115. **Hertzberg HW,** *The Search for an American Indian Identity. Modern Pan-Indian Movements,* Syracuse University Press, Syracuse, 1971, pp. 202-204.

116. **Meriam L,** *The Problem of Indian Administration,* Johns Hopkins Press, Baltimore, 1928.

117. **Hertzberg HW,** *The Search for an American Indian Identity. Modern Pan-Indian Movements,* Syracuse University Press, Syracuse, 1971, pp. 213-236.

118. **Larner JW, Jr.,** The Papers of Carlos Montezuma, Microfilm Edition, *Scholarly Resources, Inc., Wilmington, Delaware,* 1984, Reel 5, 1921.

119. **Hertzberg HW,** *The Search for an American Indian Identity. Modern Pan-Indian Movements,* Syracuse University Press, Syracuse, 1971, p. 222.

120. Ibid., pp. 231-234.

121. Ibid., pp. 239-258, **Willard W,** The First Amendment, Anglo-Conformity and American Indian Religious Freedom, *Wicazo Sa Review* 7:25-41, 1991.

122. **Erowid Peyote Vault,** *www.erowid.org/plants/peyote,* 2001.

123. **Hertzberg HW,** *The Search for an American Indian Identity. Modern Pan-Indian Movements,* Syracuse University Press, Syracuse, 1971, pp. 287-298, **Kelly LC,** *The Assault on Assimilation. John Collier and the Origins of Indian Policy Reform,* University of New Mexico Press, Albuquerque, 1983.

124. **Wheeler-Howard Act (Indian Reorganization Act), U. S. Statutes at Large 48:984-988, June 18, 1934,** In: Prucha FP, ed. *Documents of United States Indian Policy, 2nd Edition,* University of Nebraska Press, Lincoln, 1990, pp. 222-225.

125. **Constitution of the Fort McDowell Yavapai Nation,** http://www.narf.org/nill/Constitutions/FtMcDowellConst/ftmcdowellconstit.htm, 1999.

126. **House Concurrent Resolution 108, August 1, 1953,** In: Prucha FP, ed. *Documents of United States Indian Policy, 2nd Edition,* University of Nebraska Press, Lincoln, 1990, p. 233.

127. **Prucha FP,** *The Great Father. The United States Government and the American Indians, Abridged Edition,* University of Nebraska Press, Lincoln, 1986, pp. 341-344, **Indian Claims Commission Act, U. S. Statutes at Large, 60:1049-1056,** August 13, 1946, In: Prucha FP, ed. *Documents of United States Indian Policy, 2nd Edition,* University of Nebraska Press, Lincoln, 1990, pp. 231-233.

128. **Thomas AB,** The Yavapai Indians, 1582–1848, In: Horr DA, ed. *Yavapai Indians,* Garland Publishing Inc., New York, 1974, pp. 355-386, **Schroeder AH,** *Apache Indians. A Study of the Apache Indians, Parts I, II, and III,* Garland Publishing Inc., New York, 1974, **Schroeder AH,** A Study of Yavapai History. Commission Findings, In: Horr DA, ed. *Yavapai Indians,* Garland Publishing Inc., New York, 1974, pp. 23-354.

129. **Johnson EA, Rhoades ER,** The History and Organization of Indian Health Services and Systems, In: Rhoades ER, ed. *American Indian Health. Innovations in Health Care, Promotion, and Policy,* The Johns Hopkins University Press, Baltimore, 2000, pp. 74-92.

130. Ibid.

131. **Waldman C,** *Atlas of the North American Indian,* Facts On File, Inc., New York, 2000.

132. Ibid.

133. **Snipp CM,** Selected Demographic Characteristics of Indians, In: Rhoades ER, ed. *American Indian Health. Innovations in Health Care, Promotion, and Policy,* The Johns Hopkins University Press, Baltimore, 2000, pp. 49-51.

134. **Indian Citizenship Act, U. S. Statutes at Large 43:252, 1924,** In: Prucha FP, ed. *Documents of United States Indian Policy, 2nd Edition,* University of Nebraska Press, Lincoln, 1990, p. 218.

135. **Prucha FP,** *The Great Father. The United States Government and the American Indians, Abridged Edition,* University of Nebraska Press, Lincoln, 1986, pp. 399-402.

136. **Major Crimes Act, U.S. Statutes at Large 23:385, March 3, 1885,** In: Prucha FP, ed. *Documents of United States Indian Policy*, University of Nebraska Press, Lincoln, 1990, pp. 167-168.

137. **Thornton R,** *American Indian Holocaust and Survival. A Population History Since 1492*, University of Oklahoma Press, Norman, 1987, **U.S. Census Bureau,** The American Indian and Alaska Native Population: 2000, *www.census.gov/prod/2002pubs/c2kbr01-15.pdf*, 2002.

138. **Waldman C,** *Atlas of the North American Indian*, Facts On File, Inc., New York, 2000.

139. **U.S. Census Bureau,** The American Indian and Alaska Native Population: 2000, *www.census.gov/prod/2002pubs/c2kbr01-15.pdf*, 2002.

140. **Josephy AM, Jr., Nagel J, Johnson T,** ed. *Red Power. The American Indians' Fight for Freedom*, 2nd Ed., University of Nebraska Press Lincoln, 1999.

141. **Smith PC, Warrior RA,** *Like a Hurricane. The Indian Movement from Alcatraz to Wounded Knee*, The New Press, New York, 1996.

142. Ibid.

143. **The Twenty-Point Proposal of Native Americans on the Trail of Broken Treaties, Washington DC, October, 1972,** In: Josephy AMJ, Nagel J, Johnson T, eds. *Red Power. The American Indians' Fight for Freedom*, University of Nebraska Press, Lincoln, 1999, pp. 44-47.

144. **Smith PC, Warrior RA,** *Like a Hurricane. The Indian Movement from Alcatraz to Wounded Knee*, The New Press, New York, 1996.

145. **Kickingbird K, Rhoades ER,** The Relation of Indian Nations to the U.S. Government, In: Rhoades ER, ed. *American Indian Health. Innovations in Health Care, Promotion, and Policy*, The Johns Hopkins University Press, Baltimore, 2000, pp. 61-73.

146. Ibid. pp. 63-73.

147. **Indian Gaming Regulatory Act, October 18, 1988,** In: Josephy AMJ, Nagel J, Johnson T, eds. *Red Power. The American Indians' Fight for Freedom*, University of Nebraska Press, Lincoln, 1999, pp. 168-171.

## CHAPTER FOURTEEN

1. **Nominees for the Top 100 Works of Journalism,** *http://www.nyu.edu/gsas/dept/journal/Dept_news/News_stories/990301_nominees.htm*, 2002.

2. **The Top 100 Works of Journalism in the United States in the 20th Century,** *http://www.nyu.edu/gsas/dept/journal/Dept_news/News_stories/990301_topjourn.htm*, 2002.

3. **Larner JW, Jr.,** The Papers of Carlos Montezuma, Microfilm Edition, *Scholarly Resources, Inc., Wilmington, Delaware*, 1984, Reel 4, February 19, 1916.

4. Ibid., Reel 4, March 20, 1916.

5. Ibid., Reel 5, Vol. 1, No. 1, April, 1916.

6. Ibid., Reel 5, October 4, 1922.

7. Ibid., Reel 5, Vol. 1, No. 3, June, 1916.

8. Ibid., Reel 5, Vol. 1, No. 1, April, 1916.

9. Ibid.

10. Ibid., Reel 5, Vol. 1, No. 2, May, 1916.

11. Ibid., Reel 5, Vol. 1, No. 2, August, 1916.

12. Ibid., Reel 5, Vol. 1, No. 1, April, 1916.

13. Ibid., Reel 5, Vol. 1, No. 8, November, 1916.

14. Ibid., Reel 5, Vol. 1, No. 10, January, 1917.

15. Ibid., Reel 5, Vol 1., No. 1, April, 1916.

16. Ibid., Reel 5, Vol. 1, No. 3, June, 1916.

17. Ibid., Reel 5, Vol. 1, No. 4, July, 1916.

18. Ibid., Reel 5, Vol. 1, No. 11, February, 1917.

19. Ibid., Reel 5, Vol. 1, No. 10, January, 1917.

20. Ibid.

21. Ibid., Reel 5, Vol. 1, No. 11, February, 1917.

22. Ibid., Reel 5, Vol. 2, No. 11, February, 1918.

23. Ibid.

24. Ibid.

25. Ibid., Reel 5, Vol. 3, No. 12, March, 1919.

26. Ibid., Reel 4, Vol. 5, No. 4, July, 1919.

27. Ibid.

28. Ibid., Reel 5, Vol. 5, No. 4, July, 1920.

29. **Word For The Wise,** *http://www.m-w.com/wftw/00mar/032700.htm*, 2002.

30. **Larner JW, Jr.,** The Papers of Carlos Montezuma, Microfilm Edition, *Scholarly Resources, Inc., Wilmington, Delaware*, 1984, Reel 4, September 11, 1916.

31. Ibid., Reel 4, January 30, 1917.

32. Ibid., Reel 4, February 19, 1916; March 22, 1917.

33. **Larner JW, Jr.,** Supplement to the Papers of Carlos Montezuma, Microfilm Edition, *Scholarly Resources, Inc., Wilmington, Delaware*, 2002, Reel 2.

34. Ibid., Reel 2, August 28, 1917.

35. **Larner JW, Jr.,** The Papers of Carlos Montezuma, Microfilm Edition, *Scholarly Resources, Inc., Wilmington, Delaware*, 1984, Reel 5, Vol. 2, No. 3, June, 1917.

36. Ibid., Reel 5, Vol. 2, No. 5, August, 1917.

37. Ibid., Reel 5, Vol. 2, No. 2, May, 1917.

38. Ibid., Reel 5, Vol. 2, No. 10, January, 1918.

39. Ibid., Reel 5, Vol. 5, No. 1, April, 1920.

40. Ibid., Reel 5, Vol. 3, No. 2, May, 1918.

41. **Portraits Capture Lost Culture,** *http://enquirer.com/editions/2000/11/05/tem_portraits_capture.html*, 2002.

42. **Larner JW, Jr.,** The Papers of Carlos Montezuma, Microfilm Edition, *Scholarly Resources, Inc., Wilmington, Delaware*, 1984, Reel 5, Vol. 3, No. 11, February, 1919.

43. Ibid., Reel 5, Vol. 4, No. 5, August, 1919.

44. Ibid., Reel 4, February 9, 1919.

45. Ibid., Reel 4, January 24, 1919.

46. **Larner JW, Jr.,** Supplement to the Papers of Carlos Montezuma, Microfilm Edition, *Scholarly Resources, Inc., Wilmington, Delaware*, 2002, Reel 4, July 9, 1919.

47. **Larner JW, Jr.,** The Papers of Carlos Montezuma, Microfilm Edition, *Scholarly Resources, Inc., Wilmington, Delaware,* 1984, Reel 4, February 21, 1919.

48. Ibid., Reel 4, March 22, 1920.

49. Ibid., Reel 5, Vol. 5, No. 8, December, 1920.

50. Ibid., Reel 5, Vol. 8, No. 7, July, 1922.

51. Ibid., Reel 5, Vol. 2, No. 8, November, 1917.

52. Ibid., Reel 4, Spring, 1921.

53. Ibid., Reel 4, January 17, 1921.

54. Ibid., Reel 5, October 4, 1922.

55. Ibid., Reel 5, Vol. 4, No. 3, June, 1919.

## CHAPTER FIFTEEN

1. **Larner JW, Jr.,** The Papers of Carlos Montezuma, Microfilm Edition, *Scholarly Resources, Inc., Wilmington, Delaware,* 1984, Reel 2, August 2, 1904.

2. Ibid., Reel 2.

3. Ibid.

4. **Larner JW, Jr.,** Supplement to the Papers of Carlos Montezuma, Microfilm Edition, *Scholarly Resources, Inc., Wilmington, Delaware,* 2002, Reel 1, August 6, 1905.

5. **Hohler JS,** ed. *The Papers of Carlos Montezuma 1892-1937 (Microfilm Edition),* The State Historical Society of Wisconsin, Madison, 1975, Reel 10.

6. **Larner JW, Jr.,** The Papers of Carlos Montezuma, Microfilm Edition, *Scholarly Resources, Inc., Wilmington, Delaware,* 1984, Reel 1.

7. **Larner JW, Jr.,** Supplement to the Papers of Carlos Montezuma, Microfilm Edition, *Scholarly Resources, Inc., Wilmington, Delaware,* 2002, Reel 1, 1911.

8. **Larner JW, Jr.,** The Papers of Carlos Montezuma, Microfilm Edition, *Scholarly Resources, Inc., Wilmington, Delaware,* 1984, Reel 3, April 26, 1912.

9. Ibid., Reel 3, December 10, 1912.

10. **Barnes WC,** *Life of Carlos Montezuma (Unpublished Manuscript),* Will C. Barnes Collection, Arizona Historical Foundation, Arizona State University, 1934, pp. 122-129.

11. **Montezuma C,** Information for The National Cyclopedia of American Biography, *Chicago Historical Society, Carlos Montezuma file.*

12. **Larner JW, Jr.,** The Papers of Carlos Montezuma, Microfilm Edition, *Scholarly Resources, Inc., Wilmington, Delaware,* 1984, Reel 9, March 25, 1923.

13. **Severance EE,** Interview by Charles C. Colley, Archivist, Hayden Library, Arizona State University, 1976.

14. **Larner JW, Jr.,** The Papers of Carlos Montezuma, Microfilm Edition, *Scholarly Resources, Inc., Wilmington, Delaware,* 1984, Reel 3, March 29, 1912.

15. **Will C. Barnes Collection,** Arizona Historical Foundation, Arizona State University, February 11, 1934, Letter from Charles B. Gibson.

16. **Barnes WC,** *Life of Carlos Montezuma (Unpublished Manuscript),* Will C. Barnes Collection, Arizona Historical Foundation, Arizona State University, 1934, pp. 122-129.

17. **Larner JW, Jr.,** The Papers of Carlos Montezuma, Microfilm Edition, *Scholarly Resources, Inc., Wilmington, Delaware,* 1984, Reel 3, September 22, 1913.

18. Ibid., Reel 3, October 31, 1913.

19. Ibid.

20. Ibid., Reel 3, November 28, 1913.

21. Ibid., Reel 3, November 7, 1913.

22. Ibid., Reel 3, January 16, 1914.

23. Ibid., Reel 3, April 30, 1914.

24. **Shaw AM,** *A Pima Past,* The University of Arizona Press, Tucson, 1974, pp. 248-249.

25. **Larner JW, Jr.,** The Papers of Carlos Montezuma, Microfilm Edition, *Scholarly Resources, Inc., Wilmington, Delaware,* 1984, Reel 4.

26. **Larner JW, Jr.,** Supplement to the Papers of Carlos Montezuma, Microfilm Edition, *Scholarly Resources, Inc., Wilmington, Delaware,* 2002, Reel 1, 1914.

27. **Larner JW, Jr.,** The Papers of Carlos Montezuma, Microfilm Edition, *Scholarly Resources, Inc., Wilmington, Delaware,* 1984, Reel 4, November 20, 1917.

28. Ibid., Reel 4, October 14, 1918.

29. Ibid., Reel 5, June 24, 1921.

30. Ibid., Recl 5, June 28, 1921.

31. Ibid., Reel 5, June 29, 1921.

32. Ibid., Reel 5, July, 1921.

33. Ibid.

34. Ibid., Reel 5, August 1, 1921.

35. Ibid., Reel 5, August 19, 1921.

36. Ibid., Reel 5, August 22, 1921.

37. Ibid., Reel 5, September, 1921.

38. Ibid., Reel 5, September 3, 1921.

39. Ibid., Reel 5, September 4, 1921.

40. Ibid., Reel 5, September 5, 1921.

41. Ibid., Reel 5, September 13, 1921.

42. Ibid., Reel 5, September 19, 1921.

43. **Larner JW, Jr.,** Interview with Bessie Mike, 1979, Personal communication, 2002.

44. **Larner JW, Jr.,** The Papers of Carlos Montezuma, Microfilm Edition, *Scholarly Resources, Inc., Wilmington, Delaware,* 1984, Reel 5, September 28, 1921.

45. Ibid., Reel 5, October 3, 1921.

46. **Larner JW, Jr.,** Supplement to the Papers of Carlos Montezuma, Microfilm Edition, *Scholarly Resources, Inc., Wilmington, Delaware,* 2002, Reel 2, **Larner JW, Jr.,** The Papers of Carlos Montezuma, Microfilm Edition, *Scholarly Resources, Inc., Wilmington, Delaware,* 1984, Reel 9, October 24, 1934.

47. **Shaw AM,** *A Pima Past,* The University of Arizona Press, Tucson, 1974, p. 248.

48. Ibid., p. 249.

49. **Larner JW, Jr.,** The Papers of Carlos Montezuma, Microfilm Edition, *Scholarly Resources, Inc.,* *Wilmington, Delaware,* 1984, Reel 9, July 29, 1924.

50. **Will C. Barnes Collection,** Arizona Historical Foundation, Arizona State University, February 11, 1934 Letter from Charles B. Gibson.

51. **Barnes WC,** *Life of Carlos Montezuma (Unpublished Manuscript),* Will C. Barnes Collection, Arizona Historical Foundation, Arizona State University, 1934, pp. 122-129.

52. **Speroff L, Darney PD,** *A Clinical Guide for Contraception,* Lippincott Williams & Wilkins, Philadelphia, 2001, pp. 259-261.

## CHAPTER SIXTEEN

1. **Wise JC,** *The Red Man in the New World Drama. A Politico-Legal Study with a Pageantry of American Indian History,* The Macmillian Company, New York, 1931, revised in 1971, pp. 322-323.

2. **Britten TA,** *American Indians in World War I. At Home and at War,* University of New Mexico Press, Albuquerque, 1997, p. 25.

3. Ibid., pp. 18-21, **Barsh RL,** American Indians in the Great War, *Ethnohistory* 38:276-303, 1991.

4. **Britten TA,** *American Indians in World War I. At Home and at War,* University of New Mexico Press, Albuquerque, 1997, pp. 22-27, **Barsh RL,** American Indians in the Great War, *Ethnohistory* 38:276-303, 1991.

5. **Britten TA,** *American Indians in World War I. At Home and at War,* University of New Mexico Press, Albuquerque, 1997, pp. 32-34.

6. Ibid., p. 40.

7. **Parker AC,** Current comment, *Quarterly J Soc Am Indians* II:5, 1914.

8. **Barsh RL,** American Indians in the Great War, *Ethnohistory* 38:276-303, 1991.

9. **Tate ML,** From Scout to Doughboy: The National Debate Over Integrating American Indians into the Military, 1891–1918, *Western Historical Quarterly* 17:417-437, 1986.

10. **Larner JW, Jr.,** The Papers of Carlos Montezuma, Microfilm Edition, *Scholarly Resources, Inc.,* *Wilmington, Delaware,* 1984, Reel 4, February 25, 1918.

11. **Sells C,** *A Declaration of Policy,* Annual Report of the Commissioner of Indian Affairs, Washington, D.C., 1917, pp. 3-5.

12. Ibid.

13. Ibid.

14. **Larner JW, Jr.,** The Papers of Carlos Montezuma, Microfilm Edition, *Scholarly Resources, Inc.,* *Wilmington, Delaware,* 1984, Reel 5, Vol. 2, No. 1, April, 1917.

15. Ibid.

16. Ibid., Reel 5, Vol. 2, No. 2, May, 1917.

17. Ibid., Reel 5, Vol. 2, No. 12, March, 1918.

18. **Britten TA,** *American Indians in World War I. At Home and at War,* University of New Mexico Press, Albuquerque, 1997, p. 42, **Barsh RL,** American Indians in the Great War, *Ethnohistory* 38:276-303, 1991.

19. **Clements KA,** *The Presidency of Woodrow Wilson,* University Press of Kansas, Lawrence, 1992, p. 145.

20. **Britten TA,** *American Indians in World War I. At Home and at War,* University of New Mexico Press, Albuquerque, 1997, p. 52, **Barsh RL,** American Indians in the Great War, *Ethnohistory* 38:276-303, 1991, **Tate ML,** From Scout to Doughboy: The National Debate Over Integrating American Indians into the Military, 1891–1918, *Western Historical Quarterly* 17:417-437, 1986.

21. **Britten TA,** *American Indians in World War I. At Home and at War,* University of New Mexico Press, Albuquerque, 1997, p. 52.

22. **Camurat D,** The American Indian in the Great War: Real and Imagined. Master's Thesis, Institut Charles V of the University of Paris VII, 1993.

23. Ibid.

24. **Britten TA,** *American Indians in World War I. At Home and at War,* University of New Mexico Press, Albuquerque, 1997, p. 54.

25. **Barsh RL,** American Indians in the Great War, *Ethnohistory* 38:276-303, 1991, **Camurat D,** The American Indian in the Great War: Real and Imagined. Master's Thesis, Institut Charles V of the University of Paris VII, 1993.

26. **Britten TA,** *American Indians in World War I. At Home and at War,* University of New Mexico Press, Albuquerque, 1997, p. 62.

27. Ibid., p. 51.

28. Ibid., pp. 64-66.

29. **Tate ML,** From Scout to Doughboy: The National Debate Over Integrating American Indians into the Military, 1891–1918, *Western Historical Quarterly* 17:417-437, 1986.

30. **Camurat D,** The American Indian in the Great War: Real and Imagined. Master's Thesis, Institut Charles V of the University of Paris VII, 1993.

31. **Hertzberg HW,** *The Search for an American Indian Identity. Modern Pan-Indian Movements,* Syracuse University Press, Syracuse, 1971, p. 175.

32. **Britten TA,** *American Indians in World War I. At Home and at War,* University of New Mexico Press, Albuquerque, 1997, pp. 58-59.

33. Ibid., p. 59.

34. Ibid., p. 84, **Tate ML,** From Scout to Doughboy: The National Debate Over Integrating American Indians into the Military, 1891–1918, *Western Historical Quarterly* 17:417-437, 1986.

35. **Clements KA,** *The Presidency of Woodrow Wilson,* University Press of Kansas, Lawrence, 1992, p. 151.

36. **Britten TA,** *American Indians in World War I. At Home and at War,* University of New Mexico Press, Albuquerque, 1997, p. 73.

37. Ibid., p. 102.

38. **Barsh RL,** American Indians in the Great War, *Ethnohistory* 38:276-303, 1991, **Tate ML,** From Scout to Doughboy: The National Debate Over Integrating American Indians into the Military, 1891–1918, *Western Historical Quarterly* 17:417-437, 1986.

39. **Britten TA,** *American Indians in World War I. At Home and at War,* University of New Mexico Press, Albuquerque, 1997, p. 108.

40. Ibid.

41. Ibid., p. 106, **Barsh RL,** American Indians in the Great War, *Ethnohistory* 38:276-303, 1991.

42. **Tate ML,** From Scout to Doughboy: The National Debate Over Integrating American Indians into the Military, 1891–1918, *Western Historical Quarterly* 17:417-437, 1986.

43. **Wise JC,** *The Red Man in the New World Drama. A Politico-Legal Study with a Pageantry of American Indian History,* The Macmillian Company, New York, 1931, revised in 1971, pp. 325-326.

44. **Clements KA,** *The Presidency of Woodrow Wilson,* University Press of Kansas, Lawrence, 1992, p. 133.

45. Ibid., pp. 152-153, **Kennedy DM,** *Over Here. The First World War and American Society,* Oxford University Press, Oxford, 1980, pp. 45-92.

46. **Wartime Propaganda: World War I,** *http://carmen.artsci.washington.edu/propaganda/war2.htm,* 2002.

47. Ibid.

48. **The U.S. Sedition Act,** U.S. Statutes at Large 40:553-554, May 16, 1918.

49. **Larner JW, Jr.,** The Papers of Carlos Montezuma, Microfilm Edition, *Scholarly Resources, Inc., Wilmington, Delaware,* 1984, Reel 7, March 19, 1918.

50. **Kennedy DM,** *Over Here. The First World War and American Society,* Oxford University Press, Oxford, 1980, p. 82.

51. **Eugene V. Debs,** *http://www.eugenevdebs.com/pages/histry.html,* 2002.

52. **Debs v. United States,** *U.S. 249:211,* 1919.

53. **History of the Federal Bureau of Investigation,** *http://www.fbi.gov/fbinbrief/historic/history/text.htm,* 2002.

54. **Larner JW, Jr.,** The Papers of Carlos Montezuma, Microfilm Edition, *Scholarly Resources, Inc., Wilmington, Delaware,* 1984, Reel 5, Vol. 1, No. 3, June, 1916.

55. Ibid., Reel 5, Vol. 2, No. 1, April, 1917.

56. Ibid.

57. Ibid.

58. Ibid., Reel 5, Vol. 2, No. 3, June, 1917.

59. Ibid., Reel 5, Vol. 2, No. 5, August, 1917.

60. Ibid., Reel 5, Vol. 2, No. 6, September, 1917.

61. **Larner JW, Jr.,** Supplement to the Papers of Carlos Montezuma, Microfilm Edition, *Scholarly Resources, Inc., Wilmington, Delaware,* 2002, Reel 2, May 29, 1917.

62. **Larner JW, Jr.,** The Papers of Carlos Montezuma, Microfilm Edition, *Scholarly Resources, Inc., Wilmington, Delaware,* 1984, Reel 4, February 25, 1918.

63. Ibid., Reel 4, May 17, 1918.

64. Ibid., Reel 4, July 12, 1918.

65. Ibid., Reel 4, May 10, 1918.

66. Ibid., Reel 5, Vol. 1, No. 6, September, 1916.

67. Ibid., Reel 5, Vol. 2, No. 7, October, 1917.

68. Ibid., Reel 5, Vol. 2, No. 11, February, 1918.

69. **Britten TA,** *American Indians in World War I. At Home and at War,* University of New Mexico Press, Albuquerque, 1997, p. 154.

70. Ibid., p. 133.

71. **Barsh RL,** American Indians in the Great War, *Ethnohistory* 38:276-303, 1991.

72. **Barsh RL,** Plains Indians Agrarianism and Class Conflict, *Great Plains Quarterly* 7:83-90, 1987.

73. **Britten TA,** *American Indians in World War I. At Home and at War,* University of New Mexico Press, Albuquerque, 1997, pp. 144-145, 149.

74. **Larner JW, Jr.,** The Papers of Carlos Montezuma, Microfilm Edition, *Scholarly Resources, Inc., Wilmington, Delaware,* 1984, Reel 4, August 11, 1916.

75. Ibid., Reel 4, August 19, 1916.

76. Ibid., Reel 4, October 8, 1916.

77. Ibid., Reel 4, November 6, 1916.

78. Ibid., Reel 4, December 9, 1916.

79. Ibid., Reel 4, March 18, 1917.

80. Ibid., Reel 4, March 2, 1917.

82. Ibid., Reel 5, June 13, 1922.

83. Ibid., Reel 5, Vol. 2, No. 3, June, 1917.

84. **Office of the Secretary of the Interior,** *CCF 1907–1936; Box 1438, RDI, RG48, National Archives.*

85. **Tate ML,** From Scout to Doughboy: The National Debate Over Integrating American Indians into the Military, 1891–1918, *Western Historical Quarterly* 17:417-437, 1986.

86. **Larner JW, Jr.,** The Papers of Carlos Montezuma, Microfilm Edition, *Scholarly Resources, Inc., Wilmington, Delaware,* 1984. Reel 4, December 7, 1917.

87. Ibid., Reel 5, Vol. 2, No. 9, December, 1917.

88. Ibid., Reel 5, Vol. 2, No. 10, January, 1918.

89. Ibid., Reel 7.

90. Ibid., Reel 7, November 16, 1917.

91. Ibid., Reel 7, November 26, 1917.

92. Ibid., Reel 7, March 19, 1918.

93. Ibid., Reel 4, January 20, 1918.

94. Ibid., Reel 4, January 24, 1918.

95. Ibid., Reel 7, August 23, 1919.

96. Ibid., Reel 5, Vol. 4, No. 6, September, 1919.

97. **Eugene Debs,** "The Canton, Ohio Speech," *http://douglass.speech.nwu.edu/debs_a78.htm,* 2002.

98. Ibid.

## CHAPTER SEVENTEEN

1. **Rothstein WG,** *American Physicians in the Nineteenth Century. From Sects to Science,* The Johns Hopkins University Press, Baltimore, 1972, reprinted 1992, p. 267, **Dormandy T,** *The White Death. A History of Tuberculosis,* New York University Press, New York, 2000.

2. **Centers for Disease Control,** *www.cdc.gov,* 2002.

3. **World Health Organization,** *www.who.int/inf-fs,* 2002.

4. **Small PM, Fujiwara PI,** Management of Tuberculosis in the United States, *New Engl J Med* 345:189-200, 2001.

5. **Daniel TM,** *Captain of Death. The Story of Tuberculosis,* University of Rochester Press, Rochester, 1997, pp. 93-94.

6. **Hohler JS,** ed. *The Papers of Carlos Montezuma 1892-1937 (Microfilm Edition),* The State Historical Society of Wisconsin, Madison, 1975, Reel 1.

7. **Dormandy T,** *The White Death. A History of Tuberculosis,* New York University Press, New York, 2000, p. 27.

8. Ibid., pp. 32-39.

9. **Daniel TM,** *Captain of Death. The Story of Tuberculosis,* University of Rochester Press, Rochester, 1997, pp. 74-86.

10. **Lees HD,** Tuberculosis in Medical Students and Nurses, *JAMA* 147:1754-1757, 1951.

11. **Daniel TM,** *Captain of Death. The Story of Tuberculosis,* University of Rochester Press, Rochester, 1997, pp. 131-142, **Dormandy T,** *The White Death. A History of Tuberculosis,* New York University Press, New York, 2000, pp. 340-341.

12. **Daniel TM,** *Captain of Death. The Story of Tuberculosis,* University of Rochester Press, Rochester, 1997, pp. 178-194, **Dormandy T,** *The White Death. A History of Tuberculosis,* New York University Press, New York, 2000, pp. 147-159.

13. **Dormandy T,** *The White Death. A History of Tuberculosis,* New York University Press, New York, 2000, p. 79.

14. Ibid., p. 176.

15. **Alling DW, Bosworth ER,** The After History of Pulmonary Tuberculosis. VI. The First Fifteen Years Following Diagnosis, *Am Rev Respir Dis* 81:839-849, 1960.

16. **Daniel TM,** *Captain of Death. The Story of Tuberculosis,* University of Rochester Press, Rochester, 1997, pp. 195-202.

17. **Dormandy T,** *The White Death. A History of Tuberculosis,* New York University Press, New York, 2000, pp. 256-257.

18. Ibid., p. 357.

19. Ibid., pp. 329-330.

20. **Duis PR,** *Challenging Chicago. Coping with Everyday Life, 1837-1920,* University of Illinois Press, Urbana, 1998, pp. 138-139.

21. **Dormandy T,** *The White Death. A History of Tuberculosis,* New York University Press, New York, 2000, pp. 361-375.

22. **Small PM, Fujiwara PI,** Management of Tuberculosis in the United States, *New Engl J Med* 345:189-200, 2001, **Dye C, Williams BG, Espinal MA, Raviglione MC,** Erasing the World's Slow Stain: Strategies to Beat Multidrug-resistant Tuberculosis, *Science* 295:2042-2046, 2002.

23. **Small PM, Fujiwara PI,** Management of Tuberculosis in the United States, *New Engl J Med* 345:189-200, 2001.

24. **Geng E, Kreiswirth B, Driver C, Li J, Burzynski J, DellaLatta P, LaPaz A, Schluger NW,** Changes in the Transmission of Tuberculosis in New York City from 1990 to 1999, *New Engl J Med* 346:1453-1458, 2002.

25. Ibid.

26. **Centers for Disease Control,** *www.cdc.gov,* 2002.

27. **Daniel TM,** *Captain of Death. The Story of Tuberculosis,* University of Rochester Press, Rochester, 1997, p. 30, **Rieder HL,** Tuberculosis Among American Indians of the Contiguous United States, *Public Health Reports* 104:653-657, 1989, p. 35, **Martin DL, Goodman AH,** Health Conditions Before Columbus. The Paleopathology of Native North Americans, In: Rhoades ER, ed. *American Indian Health. Innovations in Health Care, Promotion, and Policy,* The Johns Hopkins University Press, Baltimore, 2000, pp. 19-40.

28. **World Health Organization,** *www.who.int/inf-fs*, 2002.

29. **Dye C, Williams BG, Espinal MA, Raviglione MC,** Erasing the World's Slow Stain: Strategies to Beat Multidrug-resistant Tuberculosis, *Science* 295:2042-2046, 2002, **Espinal MA, Laszlo A, Simonsen L, Boulahbal F, Kim SJ, Reiniero A, Hoffner S, Rieder HL, Binkin N, Dye C, Williams R, Raviglione MC, for the World Health Organization-International Union Against Tuberculosis and Lung Disease Working Group on Anti-tuberculosis Drug Resistance Surveillance,** Global Trends in Resistance to Antituberculosis Drugs, *New Engl J Med* 344:1294-1303, 2001.

30. **Barrett-Connor E,** The Epidemiology of Tuberculosis in Physicians, *JAMA* 241:33-38, 1979.

31. **Lees HD,** Tuberculosis in Medical Students and Nurses, *JAMA* 147:1754-1757, 1951.

32. **Hetherington HW, McPhedran FM, Landis HRM, Opie EL,** Further Study of Tuberculosis Among Medical and Other University Students, *Arch Intern Med* 55:709-734, 1935, **Abruzzi WA, Jr., Hummel RJ,** Tuberculosis: Incidence Among American Medical Students, Prevention and Control and the Use of BCG, *New Engl J Med* 248:722-729, 1953.

33. **Hetherington HW, McPhedran FM, Landis HRM, Opie EL,** Further Study of Tuberculosis Among Medical and Other University Students, *Arch Intern Med* 55:709-734, 1935, **Brahdy L,** Tuberculosis in Hospital Personnel, *JAMA* 114:102-106, 1940.

34. **Hetherington HW, McPhedran FM, Landis HRM, Opie EL,** Further Study of Tuberculosis Among Medical and Other University Students, *Arch Intern Med* 55:709-734, 1935.

35. **Stead WW,** Pathogenesis of a First Episode of Chronic Pulmonary Tuberculosis in Man: Recrudescence of Residuals of the Primary Infection or Exogenous Reinfection?, *Am Rev Resp Dis* 95:729-739, 1967.

36. **Gohdes DM, Acton K,** Diabetes Mellitus and its Complications, In: Rhoades ER, ed. *Amerian Indian Health. Innovations in Health Care, Promotion, and Policy,* The Johns Hopkins University Press, Baltimore, 2000, pp. 221-243.

37. **Mori MH, Leonard G, Welty TK,** The Benefits of Isoniazid Chemo-prophylaxis and Risk Factors for Tuberculosis Among Oglala Sioux Indians, *Arch Intern Med* 152:547-550, 1992.

38. **Gohdes DM, Acton K,** Diabetes Mellitus and its Complications, In: Rhoades ER, ed. *Amerian Indian Health. Innovations in Health Care, Promotion, and Policy,* The Johns Hopkins University Press, Baltimore, 2000, pp. 221-243.

39. **Larner JW, Jr.,** The Papers of Carlos Montezuma, Microfilm Edition, *Scholarly Resources, Inc., Wilmington, Delaware,* 1984, Reel 5, May 29, 1922.

40. Ibid., Reel 5, June 13, 1922.

41. Ibid.

42. Ibid., Reel 5, October 4, 1922.

43. Ibid., Reel 5, October 27, 1922.

44. Ibid., Vol. 8, No. 20, October, 1922.

45. **Larner JW, Jr.,** Supplement to the Papers of Carlos Montezuma, Microfilm Edition, *Scholarly Resources, Inc., Wilmington, Delaware,* 2002, Reel 9, February 6, 1923.

46. **Shaw AM,** *A Pima Past,* The University of Arizona Press, Tucson, 1974, p. 248.

47. Ibid., p. 156.

48. Ibid., p. 158.

49. **Larner JW, Jr.,** The Papers of Carlos Montezuma, Microfilm Edition, *Scholarly Resources, Inc., Wilmington, Delaware,* 1984, Reel 9.

50. **Barnes WC,** *Life of Carlos Montezuma (Unpublished Manuscript),* Will C. Barnes Collection, Arizona Historical Foundation, Arizona State University, 1934, pp. 122-129.

51. **Larner JW, Jr.,** The Papers of Carlos Montezuma, Microfilm Edition, *Scholarly Resources, Inc., Wilmington, Delaware,* 1984, Reel 9, December 10, 1922.

52. **Unger HF,** The Remarkable Dr. Montezuma, *Arizona Days and Ways, Arizona Republic:*17-18, April 17, 1966.

53. **Iverson P,** *Carlos Montezuma and the Changing World of American Indians,* University of New Mexico Press, Albuquerque, 1982, p. 184.

54. **Larner JW, Jr.,** The Papers of Carlos Montezuma, Microfilm Edition, *Scholarly Resources, Inc., Wilmington, Delaware,* 1984, Reel 5, December-January, 1922.

55. **Unger HF,** The Remarkable Dr. Montezuma, *Arizona Days and Ways, Arizona Republic:*17-18, April 17, 1966.

56. **Stroud RJ,** The "Last Days" of Carlos Montezuma, M.D., *Southwestern Medicine* November:404-405, 1937.

57. **Larner JW, Jr.,** The Papers of Carlos Montezuma, Microfilm Edition, *Scholarly Resources, Inc., Wilmington, Delaware,* 1984, Reel 5, January 4, 1922.

58. Ibid.

59. **Webb G,** *A Pima Remembers,* University of Arizona Press, Tuscon, 1959, p. 31.

60. **Barnes WC,** *Life of Carlos Montezuma (Unpublished Manuscript),* Will C. Barnes Collection, Arizona Historical Foundation, Arizona State University, 1934, pp. 150-155.

61. **Shaw AM,** *A Pima Past,* The University of Arizona Press, Tucson, 1974, p. 162.

62. **Barnes WC,** *Life of Carlos Montezuma (Unpublished Manuscript),* Will C. Barnes Collection, Arizona Historical Foundation, Arizona State University, 1934, pp. 122-129.

63. **Stroud RJ,** The "Last Days" of Carlos Montezuma, M.D., *Southwestern Medicine* November:404-405, 1937.

64. **Larner JW, Jr.,** The Papers of Carlos Montezuma, Microfilm Edition, *Scholarly Resources, Inc., Wilmington, Delaware,* 1984, Reel 9, February, 1923.

65. **Weather Report,** *The Arizona Republican,* February 1, 1923.

66. **Barnes WC,** *Life of Carlos Montezuma (Unpublished Manuscript),* Will C. Barnes Collection, Arizona Historical Foundation, Arizona State University, 1934, p. 158.

67. Ibid., pp. 133-136.

68. **Shaw AM,** *A Pima Past,* The University of Arizona Press, Tucson, 1974, p. 163.

69. **Larner JW, Jr.,** Supplement to the Papers of Carlos Montezuma, Microfilm Edition, *Scholarly Resources, Inc., Wilmington, Delaware,* 2002, Reel 9.

70. Ibid., Reel 8, February, 1923.

71. **Hohler JS,** ed. *The Papers of Carlos Montezuma 1892-1937 (Microfilm Edition),* The State Historical Society of Wisconsin, Madison, 1975, Reel 5, "Sunday Sermon," *The Arizona Republican,* February 5, 1923.

72. **Barnes WC,** *Life of Carlos Montezuma (Unpublished Manuscript),* Will C. Barnes Collection, Arizona Historical Foundation, Arizona State University, 1934, pp. 133-136.

73. Ibid.

74. **Kalb R,** Personal communication, *Grand Secretary of the Grand Lodge of Illinois,* June 6, 2002.

75. **Passing of Bro. (Dr.) Carlos Montezuma,** *Dearborn Lodge Bulletin,* May, 1923.

76. **Final Tribute Paid To Dr. Montezuma,** *The Arizona Republican*, February 5, 1923.

77. **Weather Report,** *The Arizona Republican*, February 5,1923.

78. **Hohler JS,** ed. *The Papers of Carlos Montezuma 1892-1937 (Microfilm Edition),* The State Historical Society of Wisconsin, Madison, 1975, Reel 7.

79. **Maher RC,** Carlos Montezuma M.D. The Saga of Wassaja, *Arizona Highways* 16:18-19, 35-36, 1940.

80. **Larner JW, Jr.,** The Papers of Carlos Montezuma, Microfilm Edition, *Scholarly Resources, Inc., Wilmington, Delaware,* 1984, Reel 8, February 6, 1923.

81. Ibid.

82. **Larner JW, Jr.,** Supplement to the Papers of Carlos Montezuma, Microfilm Edition, *Scholarly Resources, Inc., Wilmington, Delaware,* 2002, Reel 9, February 4, 1923.

83. **Larner JW, Jr.,** The Papers of Carlos Montezuma, Microfilm Edition, *Scholarly Resources, Inc., Wilmington, Delaware,* 1984, Reel 4, March 17, 1919.

84. Ibid., Reel 4, March 21, 1919.

85. Ibid., Reel 5, December 1, 1920.

86. Ibid., Reel 9, February 9, 1923.

87. Ibid.

88. **Pratt RH,** *Battlefield and Classroom: Four Decades with the American Indian, 1867–1904,* Yale University Press, New Haven, 1964, p. 329.

89. **Summit L,** The Strange Story of Dr. Carlos Montezuma, *Westerners Brand Book* 11:84-87, 1967, **Unger HF,** Out of the Wilds—A Medical Genius, *The West* 12 (May):20-21, 59-62, 1970, Carlos Montezuma, *Arizona Highways*:p.5, June, 2002.

90. **Iverson P,** *Carlos Montezuma and the Changing World of American Indians,* University of New Mexico Press, Albuquerque, 1982, **Unger HF,** Out of the Wilds—A Medical Genius, *The West* 12 (May):20-21, 59-62, 1970, **Marino C,** *The Remarkable Carlo Gentile,* Carl Mautz Publishing, Nevada City, California, 1998.

91. **Carnegie A,** Wealth, *North American Review* June:653-664, 1889.

92. **Montezuma C,** The Reservation System Is Fatal to the Development of Good Citizenship, *Quarterly J Soc Am Indians* II:69-74, 1914.

93. **Larner JW, Jr.,** The Papers of Carlos Montezuma, Microfilm Edition, *Scholarly Resources, Inc., Wilmington, Delaware,* 1984, Reel 5, Vol. 1, No. 7, October, 1916.

## CHAPTER EIGHTEEN

1. **Larner JW, Jr.,** The Papers of Carlos Montezuma, Microfilm Edition, *Scholarly Resources, Inc., Wilmington, Delaware,* 1984, Reel 5, Vol. 2, No. 12, March, 1918.

2. **Smith MT,** The History of Indian Citizenship, *Great Plains Journal* 10:25-35, 1970.

3. **Cherokee Nation v. Georgia, Peters 5:15-20, 1831,** In: Prucha FP, ed. *Documents of United States Indian Policy, 2nd Edition,* University of Nebraska Press, Lincoln, 1990, pp. 58-59.

4. **Abolition of Treaty Making, U.S. Statutes at Large 16:566, 1871,** In: Prucha FP, ed. *Documents of United States Indian Policy, 2nd Edition,* University of Nebraska Press, Lincoln, 1990, p. 136.

5. **Ex Parte Crow Dog, U.S. Reports 109:557, 571-572,** In: Prucha FP, ed. *Documents of United States Indian Policy, 2nd Edition,* University of Nebraska Press, Lincoln, 1990, 162-163.

6. **Major Crimes Act, U.S. Statutes at Large 23:385, March 3, 1885,** In: Prucha FP, ed. *Documents of United States Indian Policy*, University of Nebraska Press, Lincoln, 1990, pp. 167-168.

7. **United States v. Kagama, U.S. Supreme Court Reports, 118:375, 382-185, May 10, 1886,** In: Prucha FP, ed. *Documents of United States Indian Policy, 2nd Edition*, University of Nebraska Press, Lincoln, 1990, pp. 168-169.

8. **Elk v. Wilkins, U. S. Supreme Court Reports, 112: 98-99, 109, November 3, 1884,** In: Prucha FP, ed. *Documents of United States Indian Policy, 2nd Edition*, University of Nebraska Press, Lincoln, 1990, pp. 166-167.

9. **Marriage Between White Men and Indian Women, U. S. Statutes at Large 25:392, 1888,** In: Prucha FP, ed. *Documents of United States Indian Policy, 2nd Edition*, University of Nebraska Press, Lincoln, 1990, pp. 176-177.

10. **Citizenship for Indians in the Indian Territory, U. S. Statutes at Large 31:1447, 1901,** In: Prucha FP, ed. *Documents of United States Indian Policy, 2nd Edition*, University of Nebraska Press, Lincoln, 1990, p. 199.

11. **United States v. Nice,** *United States Reports* 241:591, 1916.

12. **Larner JW, Jr.,** The Papers of Carlos Montezuma, Microfilm Edition, *Scholarly Resources, Inc.,* *Wilmington, Delaware*, 1984, Reel 5, Vol. 2, No. 8, December, 1917.

13. Ibid., Reel 4, December 17, 1918.

14. **Citizenship for World War I Veterans, U. S. Statutes at Large 41:350, 1919,** In: Prucha FP, ed. *Documents of United States Indian Policy, 2nd Edition*, University of Nebraska Press, Lincoln, 1990, p. 215.

15. **Britten TA,** *American Indians in World War I. At Home and at War,* University of New Mexico Press, Albuquerque, 1997, p. 179.

16. **Stein GC,** The Indian Citizenship Act of 1924, *New Mexico Historical Review* 47:257-274, 1972.

17. Ibid.

18. **Indian Citizenship Act, U. S. Statutes at Large 43:252, 1924,** In: Prucha FP, ed. *Documents of United States Indian Policy, 2nd Edition*, University of Nebraska Press, Lincoln, 1990, p. 218.

19. **Hertzberg HW,** *The Search for an American Indian Identity. Modern Pan-Indian Movements,* Syracuse University Press, Syracuse, 1971, pp. 205-207, **Stein GC,** The Indian Citizenship Act of 1924, *New Mexico Historical Review* 47:257-274, 1972.

20. **Porter v. Hall,** *34 Arizona 308* 271:411, 1928, **Deloria V, Jr., Lytle CM,** *American Indians, American Justice*, University of Texas Press, Austin, 1983, p. 222.

21. **Harrison v. Laveen,** *67 Arizona* 337 196:2d, 456, 1948.

## EPILOGUE

1. **Larner JW, Jr.,** The Papers of Carlos Montezuma, Microfilm Edition, *Scholarly Resources, Inc.,* *Wilmington, Delaware*, 1984, Reel 7.

2. **Montezuma C,** Discussion, *Quarterly J Soc Am Indians* 1:171, 1913.

3. **Larner JW, Jr.,** The Papers of Carlos Montezuma, Microfilm Edition, *Scholarly Resources, Inc.,* *Wilmington, Delaware*, 1984, Reel 4, June 11, 1918.

# Illustration Acknowledgments

Photographs not acknowledged below are by the author. Maps and chapter icons are by Becky Slemmons, Portland, Oregon.

| | |
|---|---|
| **COVER and**<br>**TITLE PAGE PHOTOGRAPH** | University Archives, University of Illinois at Urbana-Champaign. |

**CHAPTER ONE**

| | |
|---|---|
| Agave parryi | George H. H. Huey Photography, Inc., Prescott, Arizona. |
| William H. Corbusier | H-20-8, Fort Verde State Historic Park, Camp Verde, Arizona, with permission of Nancy Knox, Santa Fe, New Mexico. |

**CHAPTER TWO**

| | |
|---|---|
| Adamsville | Doris Collester Collection of Hand Colored Lantern Slides, Photo Lot 73, Negative No. NAA 53525, Smithsonian Institution National Anthropological Archives. |
| Queen and King of the Songhish | Negative No. PN 6198, Courtesy of the Royal British Columbia Museum, Victoria, British Columbia. |
| Carlo Gentile | ICHI-33202, Chicago Historical Society. |
| Wassaja and Sisters | Doris Collester Collection of Hand Colored Lantern Slides, Photo Lot 73, Negative No. NAA 53529, Smithsonian Institution National Anthropological Archives. |
| Church of the Assumption Register | Donald P. Brosnan, Archivist/Historian, the Archives, Diocese of Tucson, Arizona. |
| Montezuma—Age Six | Doris Collester Collection of Hand Colored Lantern Slides, Photo Lot 73, Negative No. NAA 53530, Smithsonian Institution National Anthropological Archives. |

Newspaper Advertisement — MS6.S9.B1, Buffalo Bill Historical Center, Cody, Wyoming.

Sitting Bull and Buffalo Bill — Vincent Mercaldo Collection, P.71,454, Buffalo Bill Historical Center, Cody, Wyoming.

## CHAPTER THREE

Richard Henry Pratt — Cumberland County Historical Society, Carlisle, Pennsylvania.

Marianna Burgess and Annie Ely — U.S. Army Military History Institute, United States Army War College and Carlisle Barracks.

Pratt and Faculty — John Choate Photo Lot 81-12, 06913000, Smithsonian Institution National Anthropological Archives.

Mike Burns at Carlisle — Cumberland County Historical Society, Carlisle, Pennsylvania.

Before and Three Months Later — Negatives NAA-57489, NAA-57490, Smithsonian Institution National Anthropological Archives.

Richard Henry Pratt on Horse — Cumberland County Historical Society, Carlisle, Pennsylvania.

The Carlisle Band — Cumberland County Historical Society, Carlisle, Pennsylvania.

Luther Standing Bear — John Choate Photo Lot 81-12, 06819200, Smithsonian Institution National Anthropological Archives.

Pratt at His Desk — Cumberland County Historical Society, Carlisle, Pennsylvania.

Anna Laura Mason Pratt and Richard Henry Pratt — U.S. Army Military History Institute, United States Army War College and Carlisle Barracks.

Carlisle Football Team — Cumberland County Historical Society, Carlisle, Pennsylvania.

**CHAPTER FOUR**

Montezuma—Age Eight

NAA 53531, Smithsonian Institution, National Anthropological Archives.

Montezuma at the University of Illinois

University Archives, University of Illinois at Urbana-Champaign.

Student Chemistry Laboratory

University Archives, University of Illinois at Urbana-Champaign.

Montezuma Near Graduation

University Archives, University of Illinois at Urbana-Champaign.

Transcript

University of Illinois at Urbana-Champaign.

**CHAPTER FIVE**

Chicago Medical College

Courtesy Northwestern University Archives.

Chicago Medical College Lecture Hall

Courtesy Northwestern University Archives.

**CHAPTER SIX**

At Fort Stevenson

Mont–48, CP Mont 1–70, National Archives and Record Administration, Carlos Montezuma Collection, Arizona Collection, Arizona State University Libraries.

Carlisle Hospital

Cumberland County Historical Society, Carlisle, Pennsylvania.

Montezuma and Carlisle Students

Negative No. NAA 53533, Smithsonian Institution National Anthropological Archives.

Montezuma and Nurses

Cumberland County Historical Society, Carlisle, Pennsylvania.

**CHAPTER SEVEN**

Ferris Wheel

ICHI–27807, Chicago Historical Society.

**CHAPTER EIGHT**

Montezuma—Age Thirty

Cumberland County Historical Society, Carlisle, Pennsylvania.

| | |
|---|---|
| Turck's Special Table | *JAMA*, May 5, 1900, Copyrighted 1900, American Medical Association. |
| Montezuma—Age Thirty-seven | ICHI–33201, Chicago Historical Society. |
| The Reliance Building—1900 | ICHI–01065–B, Chicago Historical Society. |
| Montezuma—Age Thirty-nine | WHi-4337, Wisconsin Historical Society. |
| Montezuma—Age Forty-nine | University Archives, University of Illinois at Urbana-Champaign. |

**CHAPTER NINE**

| | |
|---|---|
| Zitkala-Ša—Age Twenty-four | Negative No. 83-904, Photographic History Collection, National Museum of American History, Smithsonian Institution. |
| Zitkala-Ša—Age Thirty-seven | LC-USZ62-119349 cph 3c19349, Library of Congress, Washington, D.C. |
| Gertrude Bonnin—Age Forty-five | WHi-4343, Wisconsin Historical Society. |
| Gertrude Bonnin—Age Fifty-four | Department of Special Collections and University Archives, Marquette University Libraries. |

**CHAPTER TWELVE**

| | |
|---|---|
| Yuma Frank | Negative No. NAA 53590, Smithsonian Institution National Anthropological Archives. |
| Charles, Richard, and Sam Dickens | Mont–18 C.1, CP Mont 1–70, Carlos Montezuma Collection, Arizona Collection, Arizona State University Libraries. |

**CHAPTER THIRTEEN**

| | |
|---|---|
| Arthur C. Parker | RM 1545, Rochester Museum and Science Center. |
| Gordon and Montezuma in Wisconsin | Department of Special Collections and University Archives, Marquette University Libraries. |

**CHAPTER FOURTEEN**

Mastheads — Larner JW, Jr., The Papers of Carlos Montezuma, Microfilm Edition, *Scholarly Resources, Inc., Wilmington, Delaware*, 1984, Reels 4 and 5.

**CHAPTER FIFTEEN**

Marriage License — Clerk's Office, Cook County, Illinois.

Marie and Carlos Montezuma — Mont–47, CP Mont 1–70, Carlos Montezuma Collection, Arizona Collection, Arizona State University Libraries.

**CHAPTER SEVENTEEN**

Montezuma—October, 1922 — WHi-4344, Wisconsin Historical Society.

Death Certificate — Bureau of Vital Statistics, Arizona State Board of Health.

Marie at the Funeral — WHi-4335, Wisconsin Historical Society.

First Baptist Church, Phoenix, 1923 — *100 Year History*, First Baptist Church, Phoenix, Arizona, 1983.

Montezuma's Funeral Procession — University Archives, University of Illinois at Urbana-Champaign.

# Bibliography

## MICROFILM COLLECTIONS

The most valuable resources for a biography of Carlos Montezuma are the microfilm collections. Bringing together this broadly distributed information into accessible collections certainly made the task of research easier. Scholars forever owe a debt of gratitude to those who invested so much time and energy to make this material readily available. Nevertheless, the frame-by-frame review of these microfilm reels is a tedious, slow process, even though it is occasionally punctuated by the joy of discovery.

1. Hohler, Joanne Stranberg, Editor, *The Papers of Carlos Montezuma 1892–1937*, Microfilm Edition, Ten Reels, The State Historical Society of Wisconsin, Madison, 1975.

This part of the Montezuma collection was held by Marie Montezuma Moore until her death in 1956. It subsequently appeared at an auction house near Huntsville, Alabama. According to the *Huntsville Times*, September 15, 1966, an old trunk containing Indian papers and artifacts was purchased by Richard Dahlman, of Franklin, Wisconsin, who sold it in 1971 to his friends, John and Carol Fryer, owners of the Memorabilia Antique Co. of Denver.[1] Bids for the collection were nationally advertised, and it was purchased in 1972 by the University of Wisconsin and the Wisconsin History Foundation, and then donated to the State Historical Society of Wisconsin (now the Wisconsin Historical Society). There are 112 items of Montezuma's artifact collection in the Wisconsin Historical Society Museum. Each item has a note written by Montezuma with a short description of how he obtained it. Included are shell casings and knife blades from Skeleton Cave and pottery fragments from Iron Mountain. The Wisconsin Historical Society also has 269 items from the Montezuma personal library, including novels, medical textbooks, music for the piano, books of American, French, and English history, and many classics of literature.

2. Larner, John William, Jr., Editor, *The Papers of Carlos Montezuma*, Microfilm Edition, Nine Reels, Scholarly Resources Inc., Wilmington, Delaware, 1984.

"Jack" Larner, now a retired professor of history, initiated this project in 1977, and the work began in earnest when it was partially supported by a grant from the National Historical Publications and Records Commission in June 1978. The grant was administered by the University of Wisconsin-LaCrosse, which provided matching funds from its Minorities Studies Center. Larner then returned to his high school teaching, and the project was relocated to the Klein Independent School District in Klein, Texas. The huge effort of collecting material from seventy-two collections and sixty-three newspapers and periodicals took five years, and the final year of support was from the American Historical Association.

Marie Montezuma Moore reported in 1934 to Will C. Barnes that Montezuma's papers were packed and placed in storage after his death. When she moved to Blue Island she took the collection with her. Will Barnes intended to write a biography and reviewed the collection. His notes were provided to Owen Arnold who wrote the historical novel about Montezuma, *Savage Son*.[2] In January 1935, the Arizona Historical Society appealed to Mrs. Moore to donate the papers or to provide for a donation in her will. She did neither. The papers that Will Barnes borrowed ended up at the Arizona Historical Society in the Will C. Barnes Collection.

After Marie Montezuma Moore died in 1956, her house was raided by looters. Three trunks containing the disrupted collection were put at the street curb, perhaps by neighbors, to be taken by the trash man. From there the story is foggy.

The University of Arizona received its Montezuma collection in 1967 as a gift from James G. Lotter of Chicago. The Arizona State University Hayden Library collection was purchased in 1973 from Frank D. Novak, Sr., of Calument Park, Illinois. Newspaper stories report that Novak found the collection in an old trunk that he purchased in 1962, but didn't open for many years.

> 3. Larner, John William, Jr., Editor, *Supplement to the Papers of Carlos Montezuma*, Microfilm Edition, Nine Reels, Scholarly Resources Inc., Wilmington, Delaware, 2002.

Leon Summit was writing a story about the Great Chicago Fire and kept encountering Montezuma's name in old newspaper articles. Intrigued, Summit pursued Montezuma's history and discovered that the story ended with the trash man in 1956. Summit told me that he learned, with the help of the Chicago Historical Society, that at least a portion of the collection had been saved by the trash man and stored in an old barn that was about to be demolished for a construction project. Summit purchased what was in the barn for $3,000 and rescued the collection within an hour of the barn's destruction. Leon Summit acquired his Montezuma collection in late 1966. The *Chicago Tribune*, November 30, 1966, and the *Tucson Daily Citizen*, January 5, 1967, reported that his holdings were expanded by items given freely by people from all parts of the country, and that Summit intended to donate the documents to the University of Arizona after completing a biography. Photocopies of the Summit collection were made in 1980 by Jack Larner and Roger Bruns in Summit's basement using a rented copier. These copies were indexed with *The Papers of Carlos Montezuma*, Microfilm Edition, but the copies were held until 2001 when they were put on microfilm at the National Archives.

> 4. Larner, John William, Jr., Editor, *The Papers of the Society of American Indians*, Microfilm Edition, Ten Reels, Scholarly Resources, Inc., Wilmington, Delaware, 1987.

When Arthur C. Parker left the New York State Museum in Albany for the Rochester Museum and Science Center, he left behind a large collection of material, the accumulation of Parker's years as an officer of the Society of American Indians. This collection was the primary resource for the seminal work of Hazel Hertzberg from Columbia University, *The Search for an American Indian Identity*, published in 1971.[3] The collection on microfilm, another effort by Jack Larner, covered an additional forty-two resources, with nearly 6,000 items, and reports from seventy-five newspapers. This project was supported by Juniata College in Huntingdon, Pennsylvania, and the National Historical Publications and Records Commission.

---

[1] **Kelly B**, The Strange Story of Dr. Montezuma, *Empire Magazine* 23, Feburary:26-31, 1972.
[2] **Arnold O**, *Savage Son*, University of New Mexico Press, Albuquerque, 1951.
[3] **Hertzberg HW**, *The Search for an American Indian Identity. Modern Pan-Indian Movements*, Syracuse University Press, Syracuse, 1971.

## BOOKS

**Adams DW,** *Education for Extinction. American Indians and the Boarding School Experience, 1875–1928,* University Press of Kansas, Lawrence, 1995.

**Arey LB,** *Northwestern University Medical School 1859-1979. A Pioneer in Educational Reform,* Northwestern University, Evanston, 1979.

**Arnold O,** *Savage Son,* University of New Mexico Press, Albuquerque, 1951.

**Arnold AR,** *Red Son Rising,* Dillon Press, Inc., Minneapolis, Minnesota, 1974.

**Bailey P,** *Wovoka, The Indian Messiah,* Westernlore Press, Los Angeles, 1957.

**Barnes WC,** *Life of Carlos Montezuma (Unpublished Manuscript),* Will C. Barnes Collection, Arizona Historical Foundation, Arizona State University, 1934.

**Barrett JR,** *Work and Community in the Jungle. Chicago's Packinghouse Workers, 1894-1922,* University of Illinois Press, Urbana, 1987.

**Berger T,** *Little Big Man,* Dell Publishing, New York, 1964, reprinted 1989.

**Bird GG,** *The Indians of To-Day,* Herbert S. Stone and Company, Chicago, 1900.

**Bonner TN,** *Medicine in Chicago 1850–1950,* American History Research Center, Madison, Wisconsin, 1957.

**Borland H,** *When Legends Die,* Dell Laurel-Leaf, New York, 1963, Laurel-Leaf, 2001.

**Bourke JG,** *On the Border With Crook,* University of Nebraska Press, Lincoln, 1891, reprinted 1971.

**Britten TA,** *American Indians in World War I. At Home and at War,* University of New Mexico Press, Albuquerque, 1997.

**Brown L,** *The Story of Clinical Pulmonary Tuberculosis,* Williams & Wilkins, Baltimore, 1941.

**Brown D,** *Bury My Heart at Wounded Knee. An Indian History of the American West,* Henry Holt and Company, New York, 2001, first published 1971.

**Browne JR,** *Adventures in the Apache Country: A Tour Through Arizona and Sonora, with Notes on the Silver Regions of Nevada,* Harper & Brothers, New York, 1871, reprinted 1974, Promontory Press, New York.

**Bullock SC,** *Revolutionary Brotherhood. Freemasonry and the Transformation of the American Social Order, 1730–1840,* University of North Carolina Press, Chapel Hill, 1996.

**Burke J,** *Buffalo Bill. The Noblest Whiteskin,* G. P. Putnam's Sons, New York, 1973.

**Calloway CG,** *First Peoples. A Documentary Survey of American Indian History,* Bedford/St. Martin's, Boston, 1999.

**Carter RA,** *Buffalo Bill Cody. The Man Behind the Legend,* John Wiley & Sons, Inc., New York, 2000.

**Churchill W,** *A Little Matter of Genocide. Holocaust and Denial in the Americas. 1492 to the Present,* City Lights Books, San Francisco, 1997.

**Chuinard EG,** *Only One Man Died. The Medical Aspects of the Lewis and Clark Expedition,* The Arthur H. Clark Company, Glendale, California, 1979.

**Clements KA,** *The Presidency of Woodrow Wilson,* University Press of Kansas, Lawrence, 1992.

**Collier J,** *From Every Zenith. A Memoir and Some Essays on Life and Thought,* Sage Books, Denver, 1963.

**Corbusier WT,** *Verde to San Carlos. Recollections of a Famous Army Surgeon and His Observant Family on the Western Frontier 1869-1886,* Six Shooter Gulch, Tucson, Arizona, 1968.

**Cronon W,** *Nature's Metropolis. Chicago and the Great West,* W.W. Norton & Company, New York, 1991.

**Cushman D,** *Stay Away, Joe,* Dan Cushman, 1953.

**Daniel TM,** *Captain of Death. The Story of Tuberculosis,* University of Rochester Press, Rochester, 1997.

**Deloria V, Jr., Lytle CM,** *American Indians, American Justice,* University of Texas Press, Austin, 1983.

**Deloria V, Jr.,** *Custer Died For Your Sins,* University of Oklahoma Press, Norman, 1988, originally published in 1969.

**Deloria V, Jr., Lytle CM,** *The Nations Within. The Past and Future of American Indian Sovereignty,* 2nd Edition, University of Texas Press, Austin, 1998.

**Dobyns HE,** *Their Number Become Thinned. Native American Population Dynamics in Eastern North America,* The University of Tennessee Press, Knoxville, 1983.

**Dreiser T,** *Sister Carrie,* New American Library, Penguin Putnam Inc., New York, 1900, Signet Classic Printing (Lingeman Introduction), 2000.

**Duffy J,** *From Humors to Medical Science. A History of American Medicine,* 2nd Edition, University of Illinois Press, Urbana, 1993.

**Duis PR,** *Challenging Chicago. Coping with Everyday Life, 1837-1920,* University of Illinois Press, Urbana, 1998.

**Dumenil L,** *Freemasonry and American Culture 1880–1930,* Princeton University Press, Princeton, New Jersey, 1984.

**Dunn JP, Jr.,** *Massacres of the Mountains: A History of the Indian Wars of the Far West, 1815–1875,* Harper & Brothers, New York, 1886, reprinted 1958, Archer House, Inc., New York.

**Eastman EG,** *Pratt. The Red Man's Moses,* University of Oklahoma Press, Norman, 1935.

**Epple AO,** *A Field Guide to the Plants of Arizona,* Falcon Publishing, Inc., Helena, Montana, 1995.

**Feraca SE,** *Why Don't They Give Them Guns?,* University Press of America, Inc., Lanham, Maryland, 1990.

**Flexner A,** *Medical Education in the United States and Canada,* Carnegie Foundation for the Advancement of Teaching, New York, 1910.

**Frazier I,** *On the Rez,* Picador USA, Farrar, Straus and Giroux, New York, 2001.

**Fritz HE,** *The Movement for Indian Assimilation, 1860–1890,* Greenwood Press, Publishers, Westport, Connecticut, 1963, reprinted 1981.

**Gibson AM,** *The American Indian. Prehistory to the Present,* D. C. Heath and Company, Lexington, Massachusetts, 1980.

**Gilbert J,** *Perfect Cities. Chicago's Utopias of 1893,* The University of Chicago Press, Chicago, 1991.

**Ginger R,** *Altgeld's America. The Lincoln Ideal versus Changing Realities,* Quadrangle Books, Inc., Chicago, Funk & Wagnalls Company, 1958, Quadrangle Paperback, 1965.

**Goff JS,** *King S. Woolsey,* Black Mountain Press, Cave Creek, Arizona, 1981.

**Hagan WT,** *Indian Police and Judges. Experiments in Acculturation and Control,* Yale University Press, New Haven, 1966.

**Hagan WT,** *The Indian Rights Association. The Herbert Welsh Years 1882–1904,* The University of Arizona Press, Tucson, 1985.

**Hagan WT,** *American Indians,* Third Edition, The University of Chicago Press, Chicago, 1993.

**Hanson WF,** *Sun Dance Land,* J. Grant Stevenson, Provo, Utah, 1967.

**Harrod HL,** *Mission Among the Blackfeet,* University of Oklahoma Press, Norman, 1971.

**Hertzberg HW,** *The Search for an American Indian Identity. Modern Pan-Indian Movements,* Syracuse University Press, Syracuse, 1971.

**Hodge FW,** ed. *Handbook of American Indians North of Mexico, Smithsonian Institution Bureau of American Ethnology, Bulletin 30, 2 Volumes,* Government Printing Office, 1912, reprinted by Scholarly Press, Gross Pointe, Michigan, reprinted 1968.

**Hoffman C,** *The Depression of the Nineties: An Economic History,* Greenwood Publishing, Westport, Connecticut, 1970.

**Hopkins CH,** *History of the Y.M.C.A. in North America,* Association Press, New York, 1951.

**Hoxie FE,** *A Final Promise: The Campaign to Assimilate the Indians, 1880-1920,* University of Nebraska Press, Lincoln, 1984.

**Hyde GE,** *A Sioux Chronicle,* University of Oklahoma Press, Norman, 1956.

**Institute for Government Research,** *The Problem of Indian Administration,* Johns Hopkins University Press, Baltimore, 1928.

**Iverson P,** *Carlos Montezuma and the Changing World of American Indians,* University of New Mexico Press, Albuquerque, 1982.

**Jackson H,** *A Century of Dishonor: A Sketch of the United States Government's Dealings with Some of the Indian Tribes,* Harper and Brothers, New York, 1881, reprinted by the University of Oklahoma Press, 1995.

**Josephy AM, Jr., Nagel J, Johnson T,** ed. *Red Power. The American Indians' Fight for Freedom,* 2nd Edition, University of Nebraska Press, Lincoln, 1999.

**Kelly WH,** *Indians of the Southwest. A Survey of Indian Tribes and Indian Administration in Arizona,* University of Arizona, Tucson, 1953.

**Kelly LC,** *The Assault on Assimilation. John Collier and the Origins of Indian Policy Reform,* University of New Mexico Press, Albuquerque, 1983.

**Kennedy DM,** *Over Here. The First World War and American Society,* Oxford University Press, Oxford, 1980.

**Kvasnicka RM, Viola HJ,** ed. *The Commissioners of Indian Affairs, 1824-1977,* University of Nebraska Press, Lincoln, 1979.

**Latimer JW,** *The Rape of McDowell Reservation, Arizona, by the Indian Bureau. Statement of Facts,* Hayworth Publishing House, Washington, D.C., 1921.

**Lazarus E,** *Black Hills White Justice. The Sioux Nation Versus The United States, 1775 To The Present,* University of Nebraska Press, Lincoln, 1991, reprinted 1999.

**Leupp FE,** *The Indian and his Problem,* Charles Scribner's Sons, 1910, reprinted, Arno Press, New York, 1971.

**Lissak RS,** *Pluralism & Progressives. Hull House and the New Immigrants, 1890–1919,* University of Chicago Press, Chicago, 1989.

**Lockwood FC,** *Pioneer Portraits: Selected Vignettes,* University of Arizona Press, Tucson, 1968.

**MacNulty WK,** *Freemasonry. A Journey Through Ritual and Symbol,* Thames and Hudson Ltd., London, 1991.

**Magner LN,** *A History of Medicine,* Marcel Dekker, Inc., New York, 1992.

**Marino C,** *The Remarkable Carlo Gentile,* Carl Mautz Publishing, Nevada City, California, 1998.

**McCullough D,** *John Adams,* Simon & Schuster, New York, 2001.

**McDonnell JA,** *The Dispossession of the American Indian, 1887–1934,* Indiana University Press, Bloomington, 1991.

**McKenzie FA,** *The Indian in Relation to the White Population of the United States,* published by the author, Columbus, Ohio, 1908.

**Mead SE,** *The Lively Experiment. The Shaping of Christianity in America,* Harper & Row Publishers, New York, 1963.

**Meriam L,** *The Problem of Indian Administration,* Johns Hopkins Press, Baltimore, 1928.

**Miller DL,** *City of the Century. The Epic of Chicago and the Making of America,* Simon & Schuster, New York, 1996.

**Mooney J,** *The Ghost-Dance Religion and the Sioux Outbreak of 1890; Fourteenth Annual Report of the Bureau of American Ethnology,* Government Printing Office, Washington, D.C., 1896.

**Mooney J,** *The Ghost-Dance Religion and the Sioux Outbreak of 1890,* Abridged Edition, University of Chicago Press, Chicago, 1965.

**Moses LG,** *Wild West Shows and the Images of American Indians, 1883-1933,* University of New Mexico Press, Albuquerque, 1996.

**Mowry GE,** ed. *The Twenties. Fords, Flappers & Fanatics,* Prentice-Hall, Inc., Englewood Cliffs, New Jersey, 1963.

**O'Gara G,** *What You See In Clear Water,* Vintage Departures, Vintage Books, New York, 2000.

**Partington FE,** *The Story of Mohonk,* The Morrill Press, Fulton, New York, 1911.

**Pevar SL,** *The Rights of Indians and Tribes. The Basic ACLU Guide to Indian and Tribal Rights,* 2nd Edition, Southern Illinois University Press, Carbondale, Illinois, 1992.

**Piatigorsky A,** *Freemasonry. The Study of a Phenomenon,* The Harvill Press, London, 1999.

**Porter J,** *To Be Indian. The Life of Iroquois-Seneca Arthur Caswell Parker,* University of Oklahoma Press, Norman, 2001.

**Powers FJ,** *The Life Story of Glen S. (Pop) Warner. Gridiron's Greatest Strategist,* The Athletic Institute, Chicago, 1969.

**Pratt RH,** *Battlefield and Classroom: Four Decades with the American Indian, 1867–1904,* Yale University Press, New Haven, 1964.

**Prucha FP,** *American Indian Policy in Crisis: Christian Reformers and the Indian, 1865–1900,* University of Oklahoma Press, Norman, 1976.

**Prucha FP,** *The Indians in American Society. From the Revolutionary War to the Present,* University of California Press, Berkeley, 1985.

**Prucha FP,** *The Great Father. The United States Government and the American Indians,* Abridged Edition, University of Nebraska Press, Lincoln, 1986.

**Prucha FP,** ed. *Documents of United States Indian Policy, 2nd Edition,* University of Nebraska Press, Lincoln, 1990.

**Rappaport D,** *The Flight of Red Bird. The Life of Zitkala-Sa,* Puffin Books, New York, 1997.

**Reed B,** *The Last Bugle Call. A History of Fort McDowell, Arizona Territory, 1865-1890,* McClain Printing Company, Parsons, West Virginia, 1977.

**Reisner M,** *Cadillac Desert. The American West and Its Disappearing Water, Revised and Updated,* Penguin Books, New York, 1993.

**Ridley J,** *The Freemasons. A History of the World's Most Powerful Secret Society,* Arcade Publishing, New York, 2001.

**Robinson JJ,** *Born in Blood. The Lost Secrets of Freemasonry,* M. Evans & Company, New York, 1989.

**Rothstein WG,** *American Physicians in the Nineteenth Century. From Sects to Science*, The Johns Hopkins University Press, Baltimore, 1972, reprinted 1992.

**Ruland-Thorne K,** *Yavapai, The People of the Red Rocks, The People of the Sun*, Thorne Enterprises Publications, Inc., Sedona, Arizona, 1993.

**Russell D,** *The Wild West. A History of the Wild West Shows*, Amon Carter Museum of Western Art, Fort Worth, Texas, 1970.

**Schmitt MF,** ed. *General George Crook. His Autobiography*, University of Oklahoma, Norman, 1946, reprinted 1960.

**Schroeder AH,** *A Study of Yavapai History. Part I*, Original Copy, Occidental College Library, Los Angeles, Santa Fe, New Mexico, 1959.

**Schroeder AH,** *A Study of Yavapai History, Part II*, Original Copy, Occidental College Library, Los Angeles, Sante Fe, New Mexico, 1959.

**Schroeder AH,** *A Study of Yavapai History, Part III, Appendices & Bibliography*, Original Copy, Occidental College Library, Los Angeles, Sante Fe, New Mexico, 1959.

**Schroeder AH,** *Apache Indians. A Study of the Apache Indians, Parts I, II, and III*, Garland Publishing Inc., New York, 1974.

**Seymour FW,** *Indian Agents of the Old Frontier*, Octagon Books, New York, 1941, reprinted 1975.

**Shaw AM,** *A Pima Past*, The University of Arizona Press, Tucson, 1974.

**Smith PC, Warrior RA,** *Like a Hurricane. The Indian Movement from Alcatraz to Wounded Knee*, The New Press, New York, 1996.

**Solberg WU,** *The University of Illinois, 1867–1894: An Intellectual and Cultural History*, University of Illinois Press, Urbana, 1968.

**Standing Bear L,** *My People the Sioux*, University of Nebraska Press, Lincoln, 1928, reprinted 1975.

**Starr D,** *Blood. An Epic History of Medicine and Commerce*, Perennial, HarperCollins Publishers Inc., New York, 2002.

**Starr P,** *The Social Transformation of American Medicine*, Basic Books, 1982.

**Steckbeck JS,** *The Fabulous Redmen: The Carlisle Indians and Their Famous Football Teams*, Jack Horace McFarland, Harrisburg, Pennsylvania, 1951.

**Stuart P,** *Nations Within a Nation. Historical Statistics of American Indians*, Greenwood Press, New York, 1987.

**The Brooklyn Museum,** *Buffalo Bill and the Wild West*, Falcon Press, Philadelphia, 1981.

**Thornton R,** *American Indian Holocaust and Survival. A Population History Since 1492*, University of Oklahoma Press, Norman, 1987.

**Tong B,** *Susan La Flesche Picotte, M.D.: Omaha Indian Leader and Reformer*, University of Oklahoma Press, Norman, 1999.

**Tousey TG,** *Military History of Carlisle and Carlisle Barracks*, The Dietz Press, Richmond, Virginia, 1939.

**Trennert RA, Jr.,** *The Phoenix Indian School. Forced Assimilation in Arizona, 1891-1935*, University of Oklahoma Press, Norman, 1988.

**Turck FB,** *The Action of the Living Cell. Experimental Researches in Biology*, The MacMillian Company, New York, 1933.

**Utley RM,** *The Last Days of the Sioux Nation*, Yale University Press, New Haven, 1963.

**Vizenor G,** *Crossbloods. Bone Courts, Bingo, and Other Reports*, University of Minnesota Press, Minneapolis, 1990.

**Waldman C,** *Atlas of the North American Indian,* Facts On File, Inc., New York, 2000.

**Warrior RA,** *Tribal Secrets. Recovering American Indian Intellectual Traditions,* University of Minnesota Press, Minneapolis, 1995.

**Waterstrat E,** *Commanders and Chiefs. A Brief History of Fort McDowell, Arizona (1865-1890), Its Officers and Men and the Indians They Were Ordered To Subdue,* Mount McDowell Press, Fountain Hills, Arizona, 1992.

**Waterstrat E,** *Hoomothya's Long Journey 1865-1897,* Mount McDowell Press, Fountain Hills, Arizona, 1998.

**Webb G,** *A Pima Remembers,* University of Arizona Press, Tuscon, 1959.

**Welsh F,** *How To Create a Water Crisis,* Johnson Books, Boulder, 1985.

**Wilson R,** *Ohiyesa. Charles Eastman, Santee Sioux,* University of Illinois Press, Urbana, 1983.

**Wise JC,** *The Red Man in the New World Drama. A Politico-Legal Study with a Pageantry of American Indian History,* The Macmillian Company, New York, 1931, revised in 1971.

**Wissler C,** *Indian Cavalcade or Life on the Old-Time Indian Reservations,* Sheridan House, New York, 1938.

**Zitkala-Sa,** *Old Indian Legends,* Ginn & Co., Boston, 1901.

**Zitkala-Sa,** *American Indian Stories,* reprinted from original published by Hayworth Publishing House, Washington, D. C., 1921, University of Nebraska Press, Lincoln, 1985.

## BOOK CHAPTERS

**American Indian Religious Freedom Act Amendments, October 6, 1994,** In: Josephy AMJ, Nagel J, Johnson T, eds. *Red Power. The American Indians' Fight for Freedom,* University of Nebraska Press, Lincoln, 1999, pp. 251-152.

**Burns M,** From the Manuscript of Mike Burns, In: Chaudhuri JO, ed. *The Yavapai of Fort McDowell,* Mead Publishing, Mesa, Arizona, 1995, pp. 36-39.

**Butler C,** Fort McDowell and Orme Dam, In: Chaudhuri JO, ed. *The Yavapai of Fort McDowell,* Mead Publishing, Mesa, Arizona, 1995, pp. 17-23.

**Corbusier WH,** Yavapai Clothing and Adornment, In: Chaudhuri JO, ed. *The Yavapai of Fort McDowell,* Mead Publishing, Mesa, Arizona, 1995, pp. 47-51.

**Deloria V, Jr.,** The Indians. *Buffalo Bill and the Wild West,* Falcon Press, Philadelphia, 1981, pp. 45-56.

**Gohdes DM, Acton K,** Diabetes Mellitus and Its Complications, In: Rhoades ER, ed. *American Indian Health. Innovations in Health Care, Promotion, and Policy,* the Johns Hopkins University Press, Baltimore, 2000, pp. 221–243.

**Harrison M, Williams J,** How Everything Began and How We Learned to Live Right, In: Chaudhuri JO, ed. *The Yavapai of Fort McDowell,* Mead Publishing, Mesa, Arizona, 1995, pp. 40-46.

**Holman CW,** Race Riots in Chicago, In: Mowry GE, ed. *The Twenties: Fords, Flappers & Fanatics,* Prentice-Hall, Inc., Englewood Cliffs, N.J., 1963, pp. 126-129.

**Indian Gaming Regulatory Act, October 18, 1988,** In: Josephy AMJ, Nagel J, Johnson T, eds. *Red Power. The American Indians' Fight for Freedom,* University of Nebraska Press, Lincoln, 1999, pp. 168-171.

**Johnson EA, Rhoades ER,** The History and Organization of Indian Health Services and Systems, In: Rhoades ER, ed. *American Indian Health. Innovations in Health Care, Promotion, and Policy,* the Johns Hopkins University Press, Baltimore, 2000, pp. 74–92.

**Khera S,** The Yavapai: Who They Are and From Where They Come, In: Chaudhuri JO, ed. *The Yavapai of Fort McDowell*, Mead Publishing, Mesa, Arizona, 1995, pp. 1-16.

**Kickinbird K, Rhoades ER,** The Relation of Indian Nations to the U. S. Government, In: Rhoades ER, ed. *American Indian Health. Innovations in Health Care, Promotion, and Policy*, the Johns Hopkins University Press, Baltimore, 2000, pp. 61–73.

**Mariella P,** Yavapai Farming, In: Chaudhuri JO, ed. *The Yavapai of Fort McDowell*, Mead Publishing, Mesa, Arizona, 1995, pp. 28-35.

**Martin DL, Goodman AH,** Health Conditions Before Columbus. The Paleopathology of Native North Americans, In: Rhoades ER, ed. *American Indian Health. Innovations in Health Care, Promotion, and Policy*, the Johns Hopkins University Press, Baltimore, 2000, pp. 19–40.

**Mjagkij N, Spratt M,** Introduction, In: Mjagkij N, Spratt M, eds. *Men and Women Adrift. The YMCA and the YWCA in the City*, New York University Press, New York, 1997, pp. 1-21.

**McCarty T,** Yavapai Weapons and Games, In: Chaudhuri JO, ed. *The Yavapai of Fort McDowell*, Mead Publishing, Mesa, Arizona, 1995, pp. 52-62.

**Schroeder AH,** A Study of Yavapai History. Commission Findings, In: Horr DA, ed. *Yavapai Indians*, Garland Publishing Inc., New York, 1974, pp. 23-354.

**Schneider G,** Historical Documents on the Fort McDowell Reservation, In: Chaudhuri JO, ed. *The Yavapai of Fort McDowell*, Mead Publishing, Mesa, Arizona, 1995, pp. 24-27.

**Snipp CM,** Selected Demographic Characteristics of Indians, In: Rhoades ER, ed. *American Indian Health. Innovations in Health Care, Promotion, and Policy*, the Johns Hopkins University Press, Baltimore, 2000, pp. 41–57.

**The Twenty-Point Proposal of Native Americans on the Trail of Broken Treaties, Washington DC, October, 1972,** In: Josephy AMJ, Nagel J, Johnson T, eds. *Red Power. The American Indians' Fight for Freedom*, University of Nebraska Press, Lincoln, 1999, pp. 44-47.

**Thomas AB,** The Yavapai Indians, 1582–1848, In: Horr DA, ed. *Yavapai Indians*, Garland Publishing Inc., New York, 1974, pp. 355-386.

## DISSERTATIONS

**Bell G,** Telling Stories Out of School: Remembering the Carlisle Indian Industrial School, 1879-1918, Dissertation for the Degree of Doctor of Philosophy in Anthropology, Stanford; 1998.

**Camurat D,** The American Indian in the Great War: Real and Imagined, Master's Thesis, Institut Charles V of the University of Paris VII; 1993.

**Fisher AP,** The Transformation of Tradition: A Study of Zitkala-Sa and Mourning Dove, Two Transitional American Indian Writers, Thesis for Doctor of Philosophy in English, City University of New York; 1979.

**Flynn S,** Western Assimilationist: Charles H. Burke and the Burke Act, Dissertation for Master of Arts, Texas Tech University, Lubbock, 1988.

**Gilcreast EA,** Richard Henry Pratt and American Indian Policy, 1877-1906: A Study of the Assimilation Movement, Dissertation for the Degree of Doctor of Philosophy in History, Yale University, New Haven, Connecticut; 1967.

**Heider KG,** Fort McDowell Yavapai Acculturation: A Preliminary Study, B. A. Honors Thesis, Harvard College; 1956.

**Lamb TJ,** Early Twentieth Century Efforts at Economic Development in Nigeria and Arizona, Dissertation for Doctor of Philosophy, Temple University; 1978.

**Lisa LO,** The Life Story of Zitkala-Sa/Gertrude Simmons Bonnin: Writing and Creating a Public Image, Dissertation for the Degree of Doctor of Philosophy, Arizona State University; 1996.

**Mariella PS,** The Political Economy of Federal Resettlement Policies Affecting Native American Communities: the Fort McDowell Yavapai Case, Dissertation for Doctor of Philosophy, Arizona State University; 1983.

**Massie M,** The Cultural Roots of Indian Water Rights, Master's Thesis, University of Wyoming; 1980.

**Putney DT,** Fighting the Scourge: American Indian Morbidity and Federal Policy, 1897-1928, Dissertation for Doctor of Philosophy, Graduate School, Marquette University; 1980.

**Ryan CS,** The Carlisle Indian Industrial School, Dissertation for the Degree of Philosophy, Georgetown University, Washington, D. C.; 1962.

**Voight TF,** Carlos Montezuma — American Indian Leader, Thesis for Master of History in American History, University of Wisconsin—Milwaukee; 1976.

**Walker-McNeil PL,** The Carlisle Indian School. A Study of Acculturation, Dissertation for the Degree of Doctor of Philosophy in Anthropology, The American University; 1979.

**Welch DS,** Zitkala-Sa: An American Indian leader, 1876-1938, Dissertation for Degree of Philosophy in History, University of Wyoming, Laramie; 1985.


## JOURNAL ARTICLES

**Abruzzi WA, Jr., Hummel RJ,** Tuberculosis: Incidence Among American Medical Students, Prevention and Control and the Use of BCG, *New Engl J Med* 248:722-729, 1953.

**Alling DW, Bosworth ER,** The After History of Pulmonary Tuberculosis. VI. The First Fifteen Years Following Diagnosis, *Am Rev Respir Dis* 81:839-849, 1960.

**Barrett-Connor E,** The Epidemiology of Tuberculosis in Physicians, *JAMA* 241:33-38, 1979.

**Barsh RL,** Plains Indians Agrarianism and Class Conflict, *Great Plains Quarterly* 7:83-90, 1987.

**Barsh RL,** American Indians in the Great War, *Ethnohistory* 38:276-303, 1991.

**Blumgart H,** Caring for the Patient, *New Engl J Med* 270:449-456, 1964.

**Brahdy L,** Tuberculosis in Hospital Personnel, *JAMA* 114:102-106, 1940.

**Bronson L,** The Long Walk of the Yavapai, *Wassaja, The Indian Historian* 13:37-43, 1980.

**Brown OH,** Carlos Montezuma, M.D., *Southwestern Medicine* November:400-404, 1937.

**Brunhouse RL,** The Founding of the Carlisle Indian School, *Pennsylvania History* 6:72-85, 1969.

**Carnegie A,** Wealth, *North American Review* June:653-664, 1889.

**Chamberlain SA,** The Fort McDowell Indian Reservation. Water Rights and Indian Removal, 1910–1930, *J of the West* 14:27-34, 1975.

**Clum JP,** The San Carlos Apache Police, *New Mexico Historical Review* IV, July:203-219, 1929.

**Coffeen WR,** The Effects of the Central Arizona Project on the Fort McDowell Indian Community, *Ethnohistory* 19:345-377, 1972.

**Collins CC,** The Broken Crucible of Assimilation. Forest Grove Indian School and the Origins of Off-reservation Boarding-school Education in the West, *Oregon Hist Quarterly* 101:466-507, 2001.

**Corbusier WH,** The Apache-Yumas and Apache-Mojaves, *American Antiquarian* 8:276-284, 325-339, 1886.

**Deloria V, Jr.,** Alcatraz, Activism, and Accomodation, *Am Indian Culture Research J* 18:25-32, 1994.

**Dye C, Williams BG, Espinal MA, Raviglione MC,** Erasing the World's Slow Stain: Strategies to Beat Multidrug-resistant Tuberculosis, *Science* 295:2042-2046, 2002.

**Espinal MA, Laszlo A, Simonsen L, Boulahbal F, Kim SJ, Reiniero A, Hoffner S, Rieder HL, Binkin N, Dye C, Williams R, Raviglione MC, for the World Health Organization-International Union Against Tuberculosis and Lung Disease Working Group on Anti-tuberculosis Drug Resistance Surveillance,** Global Trends in Resistance to Antituberculosis Drugs, *New Engl J Med* 344:1294-1303, 2001.

**Feraca SE, Howard JH,** The Identity and Demography of the Dakota or Sioux Tribe, *Plains Anthropologist* 8:80-84, 1963.

**Fisher D,** Zitkala-Sa: The Evolution of a Writer, *American Indian Quarterly* 5:229-238, 1979.

**Fitz RH,** Perforating Inflammation of the Vermiform Appendix: With Special Reference to Its Early Diagnosis and Treatment, *Trans Assoc Am Physicians* 1:107-144, 1886.

**Gallaher RA,** The Indian Agent in the United States Since 1850, *Iowa Journal of History and Politics* April:173-238, 1916.

**Geng E, Kreiswirth B, Driver C, Li J, Burzynski J, DellaLatta P, LaPaz A, Schluger NW,** Changes in the Transmission of Tuberculosis in New York City from 1990 to 1999, *New Engl J Med* 346:1453-1458, 2002.

**Gifford EW,** The Southeastern Yavapai, *University of California Publications in American Archaeology* 29:177-252, 1932.

**Goldsmith MF,** At Pennsylvania Hospital, 250 Years of Care, *JAMA* 285:2313-2316, 2001.

**Hafen PJ,** Zitkala Ša: Sentimentality and Sovereignity, *Wicazo Sa Review* 12:31-41, 1997.

**Hetherington HW, McPhedran FM, Landis HRM, Opie EL,** Further Study of Tuberculosis Among Medical and Other University Students, *Arch Intern Med* 55:709-734, 1935.

**Hundley N, Jr.,** The Dark and Bloody Ground of Indian Water Rights: Confusion Elevated to Principle, *Western Historical Quarterly* 9:455-482, 1978.

**Johnson DL, Wilson R,** Gertrude Simmons Bonnin, 1876-1938: "Americanize the First American", *Am Indian Quarterly* 12:27-40, 1988.

**Lees HD,** Tuberculosis in Medical Students and Nurses, *JAMA* 147:1754-1757, 1951.

**McBurney C,** Experience with Early Operative Interference in Cases of Disease of the Vermiform Appendix, *NY Med J* 50:676-684, 1889.

**McBurney C,** The Incision Made in the Abdominal Wall in Cases of Appendicitis, with a Description of a New Method of Operating, *Ann Surg* 20:38-43, 1894.

**McDonnell J,** Carlos Montezuma's Crusade Against the Indian Bureau, *J Arizona History* 22:429-444, 1981.

**Montezuma C,** Light on the Indian Situation, *Quarterly J Soc Am Indians* 1:50-55, 1913.

**Montezuma C,** The Reservation System is Fatal to the Development of Good Citizenship, *Quarterly J Soc Am Indians* 2:69-74, 1914.

**Montezuma C,** Address Before the Sixth Conference, *Quarterly J Soc Am Indians* 4:260-262, 1916.

**Montezuma C,** Abolish the Indian Bureau, *Am Indian Magazine, Quarterly J Soc Am Indians* 7:9-19, 1919.

**Mori MH, Leonard G, Welty TK,** The Benefits of Isoniazid Chemo-prophylaxis and Risk Factors for Tuberculosis Among Oglala Sioux Indians, *Arch Intern Med* 152:547-550, 1992.

**Morton L,** How the Indians Came to Carlisle, *Pennsylvania History* 29:53-63, 1962.

**Parker AC,** Certainly Abolish the Indian Bureau, *Quarterly J Soc Am Indians* 3:261-263, 1915.

**Parker AC,** The Function of the Society of American Indians, *Am Indian Magazine, Quarterly J Soc Am Indians* 4:8-20, 1916.

**Parker AC,** The Indian, the Country and the Government. A Plea for an Efficient Indian Service, *Am Indian Magazine, Quarterly J Soc Am Indians* 4:38-49, 1916.

**Parker AC,** American Indian Freemasonry, New York State Library, Native American Language and Culture Preservation Project, Reel 61, Item 364, 1919.

**Reider HL,** Tuberculosis Among American Indians of the Contiguous United States, *Public Health Reports* 104:653-657, 1989.

**Schilling RK,** Indians and Eagles. The Struggle Over Orme Dam, *J Arizona History* 41:57-82, 2000.

**Sklar KK,** Hull House in the 1890s: A Community of Women Reformers, *Signs: Journal of Women in Culture and Society* 10:658-677, 1985.

**Small PM, Fujiwara PI,** Management of Tuberculosis in the United States, *New Engl J Med* 345:189-200, 2001.

**Smith MT,** The History of Indian Citizenship, *Great Plains Journal* 10:25-35, 1970.

**Society of American Indians,** Open Debate on the Loyalty of Indian Employees in the Indian Service, *Am Indian Magazine, Quarterly J Soc Am Indians* 4:252-256, 1916.

**Society of American Indians,** Reporters Took Indian Humor Seriously, *Am Indian Magazine, Quarterly J Soc Am Indians* 4:265-266, 1916.

**Speck FG,** Educating the White Man Up to the Indians, *Quarterly J Soc Am Indians* 2:64-68, 1914.

**Stead WW,** Pathogenesis of a First Episode of Chronic Pulmonary Tuberculosis in Man: Recrudescence of Residuals of the Pimary Infection or Exogenous Reinfection?, *Am Rev Respir Dis* 95:7629-739, 1967.

**Stein GC,** The Indian Citizenship Act of 1924, *New Mexico Historical Review* 47:257-274, 1972.

**Stewart OC,** Gertrude Simmons Bonnin, *University of South Dakota Bulletin* 87:10-11, 1981.

**Stroud RJ,** The "Last Days" of Carlos Montezuma, M.D., *Southwestern Medicine* November:404-405, 1937.

**Tate ML,** From Scout to Doughboy: The National Debate Over Integrating American Indians into the Military, 1891–1918, *Western Historical Quarterly* 17:417-437, 1986.

**Thackery FA,** Dr. Montezuma and the Pima Indians, *The Indian School Journal—About Indians (Chilocco Indian School)* 14:504-506, 1914.

**Thomas WS,** Arthur Caswell Parker: 1881-1955. Anthropologist, Historian and Museum Pioneer, *Rochester History* 17:1-20, 1955.

**Trolander JA,** Hull-House and the Settlement House Movement. A Centennial Reassessment, *J Urban History* 17:410-420, 1991.

**Turck FB,** Further observation on the treatment of the abdominal viscera through the colon, *JAMA*, May 5, 1900.

**Turck FB,** Treatment of the abdominal viscera through the colon, *JAMA*:881-886, October 7, 1899.

**Unrau WE,** The Civilian as Indian Agent: Villain or Victim?, *Western Historical Quarterly* October:405-420, 1972.

**Willard W,** The First Amendment, Anglo-Conformity and American Indian Religious Freedom, *Wicazo Sa Review* 7:25-41, 1991.

**Willard W,** Zitkala Sa: A Women Who Would Be Heard, *Wicazo Sa Review* 1:11-15, 1985.

## MAGAZINE ARTICLES

**Arnold O,** Dr. Tom-Tom Beating the Wind, *Phoenix Point West* 5 (February):29-32, 1963.

**Burial Place of Cave Victims Revealed,** *Arizona Days and Ways Sunday Magazine, Arizona Republic,* November 9, 1958; p. 52.

**Kelly B,** The Strange Story of Dr. Montezuma, *Empire Magazine* 23, Feburary:26-31, 1972.

**Clark NM,** Dr. Montezuma, Apache: Warrior in Two Worlds, Based on an Interview in 1921, *Montana: The Magazine of Western History* 23:56-65, 1973.

**Deloria V, Jr.,** This Country Was a Lot Better Off When the Indians Were Running It, *The New York Times Magazine,* March 8, 1970.

**Dreiser T,** The Smallest and Busiest River in the World, *Metropolitan Magazine* 7:355-363, 1898.

**Maher RC,** Carlos Montezuma M.D. The Saga of Wassaja, *Arizona Highways* 16:18-19, 35-36, 1940.

**Mattison D,** The Victoria Theatre Photographic Gallery (and the Gallery Next Door), *British Columbia Historical News* 14:1-14, 1980.

**Oskison JM,** Arizona and Forty Thousand Indians, *The Southern Workman* March:148-156, 1914.

**Parker AC,** Problems of Race Assimilation in America. With Special Reference to the American Indians, *American Indian Magazine* IV:285-304, 1916.

**Peplow EH, Jr.,** WASSAJA: The True—But Incomplete—Story of Dr. Carlos Montezuma, Physician to the White Man, Known Variously as "That Damned Radical Indian" and "The Indian's Abraham Lincoln," *Outdoor Arizona* April:15-17, 30-33, 1974.

**Robinson B,** The Great Yavapai, *Arizona Highways* 28:14-17, 1952.

**Schlosser E,** American Slaughterhouses Are Grinding Out Meat Faster Than Ever—and the Production Line Keeps Moving, Even When Workers Are Maimed by the Machinery, *Mother Jones* July/August:39-47, 2001.

**Summit L,** Montezuma, M.D., *Spectrum* 14:70-71, 1966.

**Summit L,** Carlos Montezuma, Apache M.D., *Westerns Brand Book* 23:81-83, 85-88, 1967.

**Unger HF,** Out of the Wilds—A Medical Genius, *The West* 12 (May):20-21, 59-62, 1970.

**Unger HF,** The Remarkable Dr. Montezuma, *Arizona Days and Ways, Arizona Republic*:17-18, April 17, 1966.

**Warner GS,** The Indian Massacres, *Collier's,* 88:61, October 17, 1931.


## NEWSPAPER ARTICLES

**Dr. Carlos Montezuma. A Bright and Well Educated Apache With an Interesting History,** *The Arizona Republican,* October 11, 1901.

**Final Tribute Paid To Dr. Montezuma,** *The Arizona Republican,* February 5, 1923.

**Montezuma C,** From an Apache Camp to a Chicago Medical College: The Story of Carlos Montezuma's Life as Told by Himself, *The Red Man* 8:3, 6, 1888.

**Montezmua. Gentile's Little Indian Protegé,** *The Chicago Tribune,* March 21, 1875.

**Ninety-Two Horses Killed, Col. Cody's Show Train Wrecked, Engineer Misread His Orders,** *Charlotte Daily Observer,* October 30, 1901.

**Shuey C,** Hiawatha Hood Wants His Land, Not Money, *Scottsdale Daily Progress,* April 29, 1976.

**Simmons G,** Side by Side, *The Earlhamite,* March 16:177–179,1896.

**Warrior RA,** Dances with Ghosts. Pain and Suffering on the Big Foot Trail, *The Village Voice,* January 15:33–37, 1991.

## U.S. GOVERNMENT DOCUMENTS

**Records of the Bureau of Indian Affairs,** Record Group 75, National Archives and Record Services.

**Records of the Department of the Interior,** Record Group 48, National Archives and Record Services.

# Index

Page numbers in **bold** denote photographs, graphics and charts.

# About the Type

The body text of this book was set in Janson Text, a font based on the original matrices created by Nicholas Kis in 1690. Kis was a theologian, type designer, and printer; his full Hungarian name was Miklós Tótfalusi Kis. He was devoted to elevating the culture of the people of Hungary by providing access to the written word. Because printing was not yet well-established in Hungary, he traveled to Amsterdam to learn engraving and punch-cutting from the Dutch master, Dirk Voskens. Returning to Hungary, Kis completed the Hungarian Bible project, and printed law and math texts, cookbooks, and children's books.

By the 1920s, Kis's font was no longer used in printing. It was revived in 1937 for modern Linotype and Monotype machines, but incorrectly presumed to be designed by the Dutch printer Anton Janson. The font's accurate history was discovered in the 1950s, but the misnomer remains.

Janson is a typeface that carries a rich history, designed by a man motivated by a desire to improve the social and cultural status of his people. For these reasons, it is an especially appropriate choice for the content of this book.

The charts, graphs, and maps of this book are set in Optima, a font originally designed by Herman Zapf in 1958. Despite the clarity of its modern look, its design influences can be traced to the stone inlay alphabets of Roman antiquity.